P9-DFF-247

Acknowledgments

The 2016 edition of *AHA Hospital Statistics* is published by Health Forum, an affiliate of the American Hospital Association, Rick Pollack, President and CEO.

Advisements

The data published here should be used with the following advisements: The data are based on replies to an annual survey that seeks a variety of information, not all of which is published in this book. The information gathered by the survey includes specific services, but not all of each hospital's services. Therefore, the data do not reflect an exhaustive list of all services offered by all hospitals. For information on the availability of additional data, please contact Health Forum, (800) 821-2039.

Health Forum does not assume responsibility for the accuracy of information voluntarily reported by the individual institutions surveyed. The purpose of this publication is to provide basic data reflecting the delivery of health care in the United States and associated areas, and is not to serve an official and all-inclusive list of services offered by individual hospitals.

AHA Hospital Statistics™

2016 Edition

AHA Institutional Members $215
Nonmembers $275
AHA Catalog NUMBER 082016
Telephone ORDERS 1-800-AHA-2626

ISSN 0090-6662
ISBN-13: 978-0-87258-964-3

Contents

Update on Hospital Experience with New Delivery Models, Payment Programs, Care Coordination, and Physician Employment

Government payors and increasingly more commercial payors are using payment methodologies to strongly encourage hospitals to reduce the costs of services provided and improve the quality of those services in order to maximize the payment received. The new way that care is being paid for is often referred to as value based payment. The objective of the new payment models is to more closely align payment with the efficient delivery and quality of the care rendered. Results from the 2014 AHA Annual Survey and the 2014 Survey of Care Systems and Payment can be used to describe how the nation's hospitals are responding to the new payment pressures.

Delivery Models

Accountable Care Organizations (ACO)

An ACO is a network of physicians and hospitals that shares financial and medical responsibility for providing care to patients in the hopes of limiting unnecessary spending. ACO's have the broader goal of coordinating care across the entire continuum of health care from physicians to hospitals to other clinicians. The idea is that, by improving care coordination within an ACO and reducing fragmented care, costs can be reduced and outcomes improved. ACO participants can then keep some of the money that they helped save or receive bonuses relating to performance on quality measures. Growth in ACO's established by hospitals and systems has been continual since 2011, the first year data were collected, moving from 6 percent to 25 percent in 2014 (Figure 1).

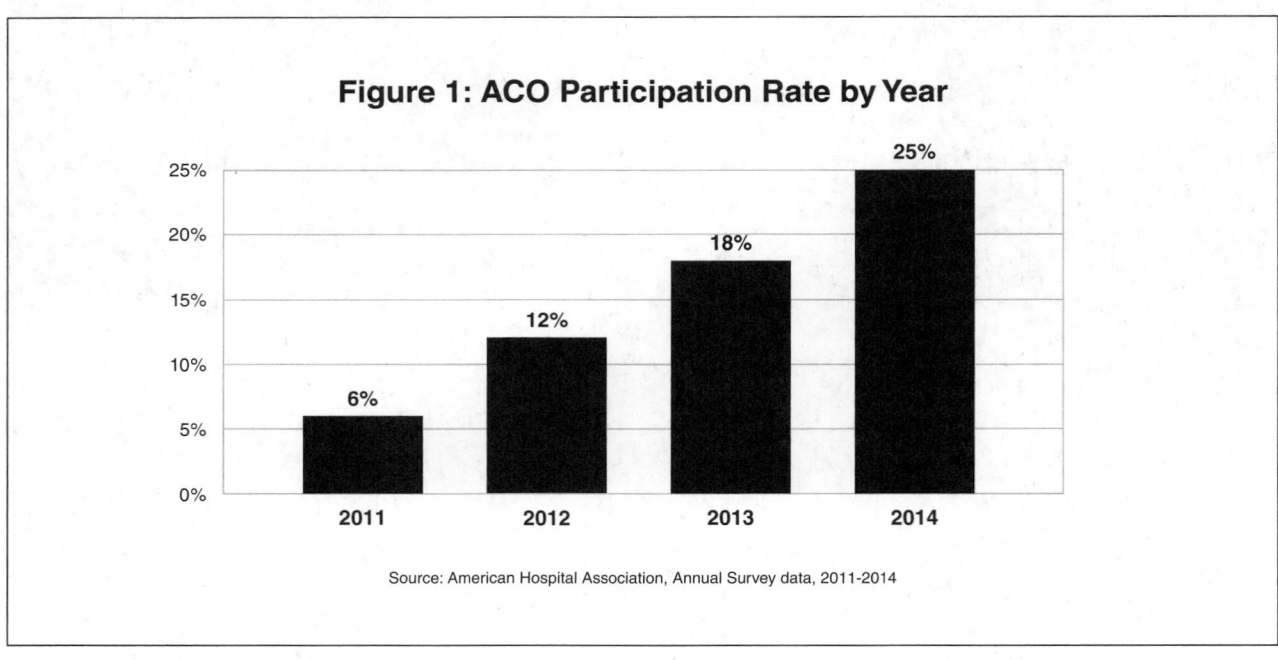

Figure 1: ACO Participation Rate by Year

Source: American Hospital Association, Annual Survey data, 2011-2014

Clinically Integrated Networks

A clinically integrated network is defined as a network of providers including physicians that establishes and operates on an ongoing and active basis: mechanisms to monitor and control utilization of healthcare services that are designed to control costs and ensure quality; selectively chooses network providers who are likely to further these efficiency objectives; and, utilizes investment of significant monetary and human capital in the necessary infrastructure and capability to realize the cost and quality objectives. According to the 2014 Survey of Care Systems and Payment approximately 43 percent of hospitals have established such networks (Figure 2).

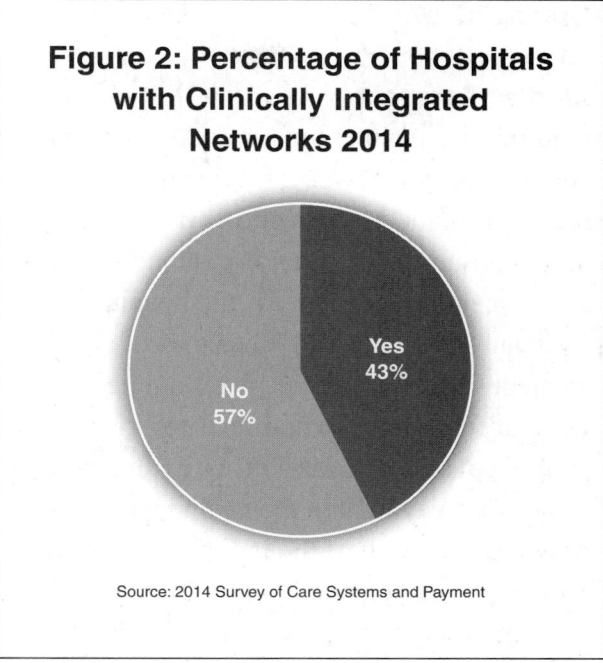

Figure 2: Percentage of Hospitals with Clinically Integrated Networks 2014

Source: 2014 Survey of Care Systems and Payment

Medical Homes

The patient centered medical home is a model of care in which patients have a direct relationship with a provider who coordinates a cooperative team of healthcare professionals, takes collective responsibility for the care provided to the patient, and arranges for appropriate care with other qualified providers as needed. In 2014, a quarter of all hospitals had a medical home up from approximately 14 percent in 2011 (Figure 3).

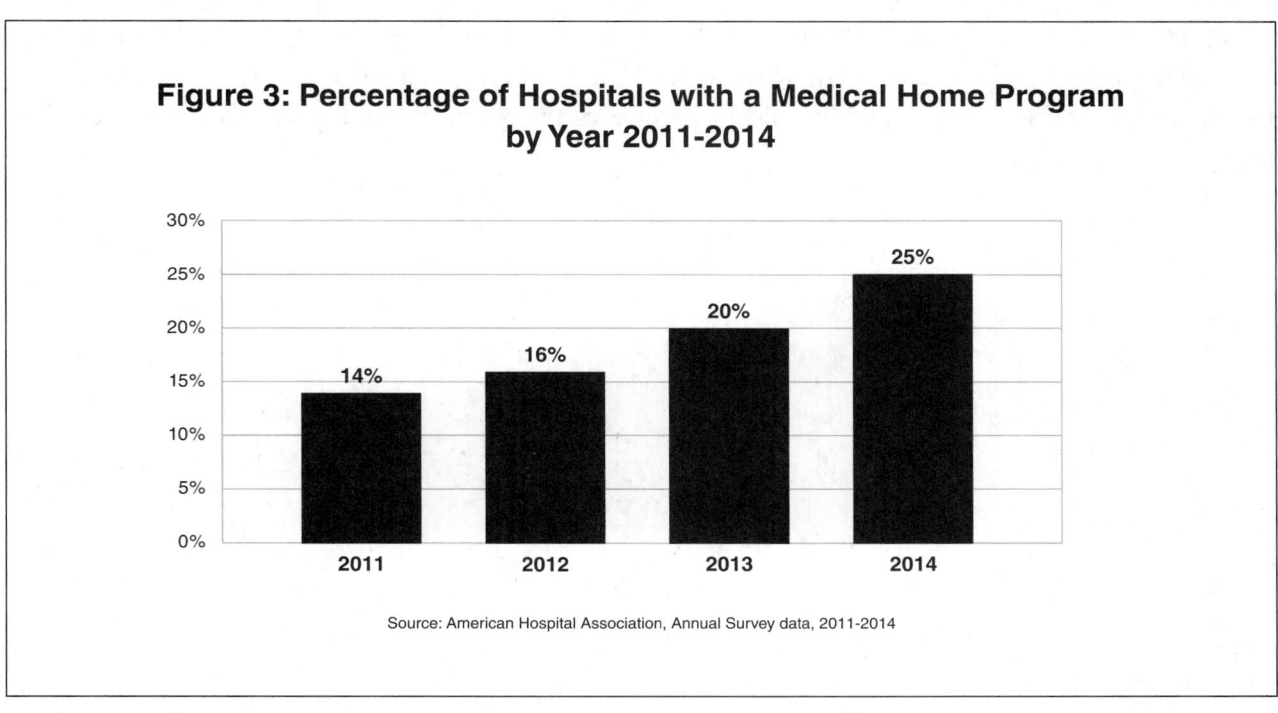

Figure 3: Percentage of Hospitals with a Medical Home Program by Year 2011-2014

Source: American Hospital Association, Annual Survey data, 2011-2014

Payment Models

Bundled Payment

Bundling is a payment mechanism whereby a provider entity receives a single payment for services provided across one or parts of the care continuum. For example, an entity might receive a single payment for the hospital and physician services provided as part of an inpatient stay, or might receive a single payment for the post-acute services involved in a single episode of care. The entity that receives the bundled payment is then responsible for compensating each of the individual providers involved in the episode of care. Bundled payment models assign a fixed fee to cover a set of treatment services. If the provider's cost of services is less than the fee amount, they keep the difference. However, if the costs are greater than the fixed payment, providers are not compensated for the difference. In 2014, just 11 percent of hospitals participated in a bundled payment program, which is slightly up

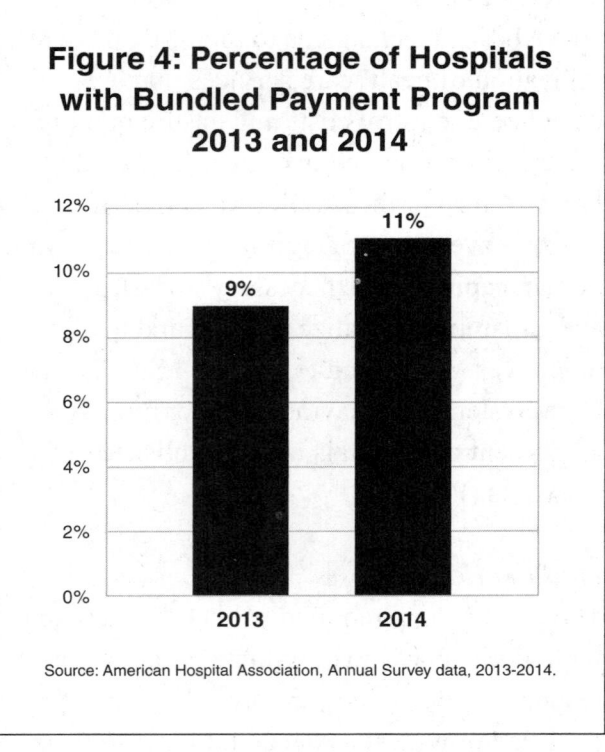

Figure 4: Percentage of Hospitals with Bundled Payment Program 2013 and 2014

Source: American Hospital Association, Annual Survey data, 2013-2014.

from the 9 percent participation rate in 2013 (Figure 4). It is expected that participation in bundled payment programs will continue to rise. According to the 2014 Survey of Care Systems and Payment, 7 percent of the respondents are currently negotiating with a private payor about a bundled payment program. An additional 17 percent of the respondents are seriously considering applying for a program.

Capitation

Capitation is an at-risk payment arrangement in which a provider receives a fixed prearranged payment and in turn guarantees to deliver or arrange all medically necessary care required by enrollees in the capitated plan. The fixed amount is specified within contractual agreements between the payor and the involved organization. Providers profit when their costs are less than the fixed amount paid but are at a loss if their costs exceed the fixed payment. Capitation is probably the most difficult of the at-risk payment programs to successfully operate. Therefore, as expected, a very low and static percentage of hospitals participate in this type of program. In 2014, 8 percent of hospitals received capitated related patient revenue unchanged from the rate in 2013 (Figure 5).

Shared Risk/Savings

Shared Risk is a payment arrangement in which the hospital and the payor share the risk of adverse claims experience. There are a couple versions of shared risk. One is where the provider receives a share of savings when their actual spending for the delivery of required care is below the expected or target cost of the same care. In this type of arrangement, the hospital is not at risk if their spending exceeds the total cost of care target. In the second more complicated type of shared risk, the hospital receives a portion of the shared savings if their costs of the care is less than the targeted costs. However, the hospital is at risk if their costs exceed the targeted costs. Because hospitals take on more risk under this type of arrangement, the upside for financial gain is greater if they are entitled to a share of any savings. As with capitation, the percentage of hospitals participating in shared risk/savings programs is low at 11 percent. However the rate was up over the 8 percent in 2013 (Figure 6).

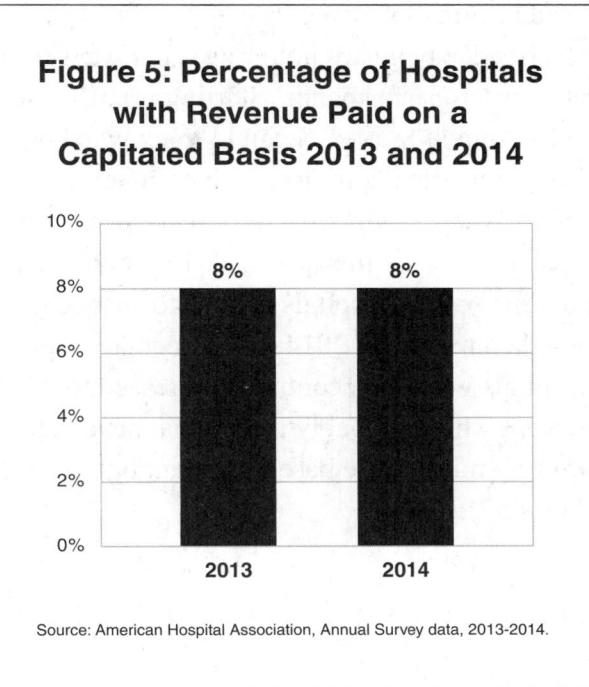

Figure 5: Percentage of Hospitals with Revenue Paid on a Capitated Basis 2013 and 2014

Source: American Hospital Association, Annual Survey data, 2013-2014.

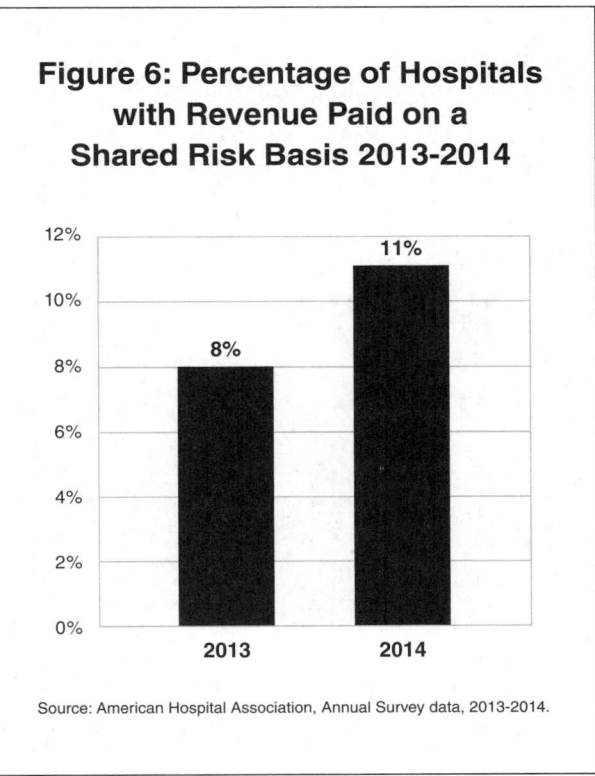

Figure 6: Percentage of Hospitals with Revenue Paid on a Shared Risk Basis 2013-2014

Source: American Hospital Association, Annual Survey data, 2013-2014.

Other Payment Programs

In addition to the more formal programs just described, payors are initiating other ways to tie payment to performance. Starting in 2013, the AHA Annual Survey began to track whether the hospital had contracts with commercial payors where payment is tied to performance on quality/safety metrics. In 2013, almost one-third of all hospitals had performance based contracts. In 2014, the percentage of hospitals with such contracts increased to 42 percent which probably means that payors are offering more value based payment options (Figure 7).

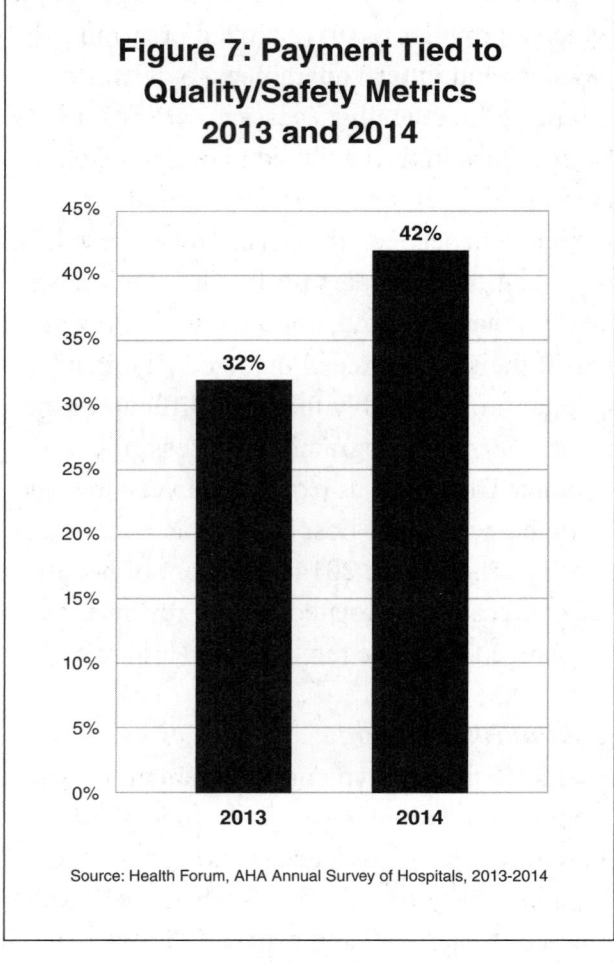

Figure 7: Payment Tied to Quality/Safety Metrics 2013 and 2014

Source: Health Forum, AHA Annual Survey of Hospitals, 2013-2014

Physician Relationships

Critically important in successfully moving into a value based payment model is tighter alignment between hospitals and their physicians. As a result, hospitals have been employing more physicians. Since 2000, physician employment has grown by 58 percent from 158,000 to 249,000 (Figure 8). From 2010 alone, employed physicians increased by 17 percent. For hospitals, greater physician integration, which employment provides, makes it easier to engage physicians in efforts to reduce costs and improve quality which the new payment arrangements demand. For physicians, employment represents an opportunity to shield themselves from financial economic risk and work more predictable hours.

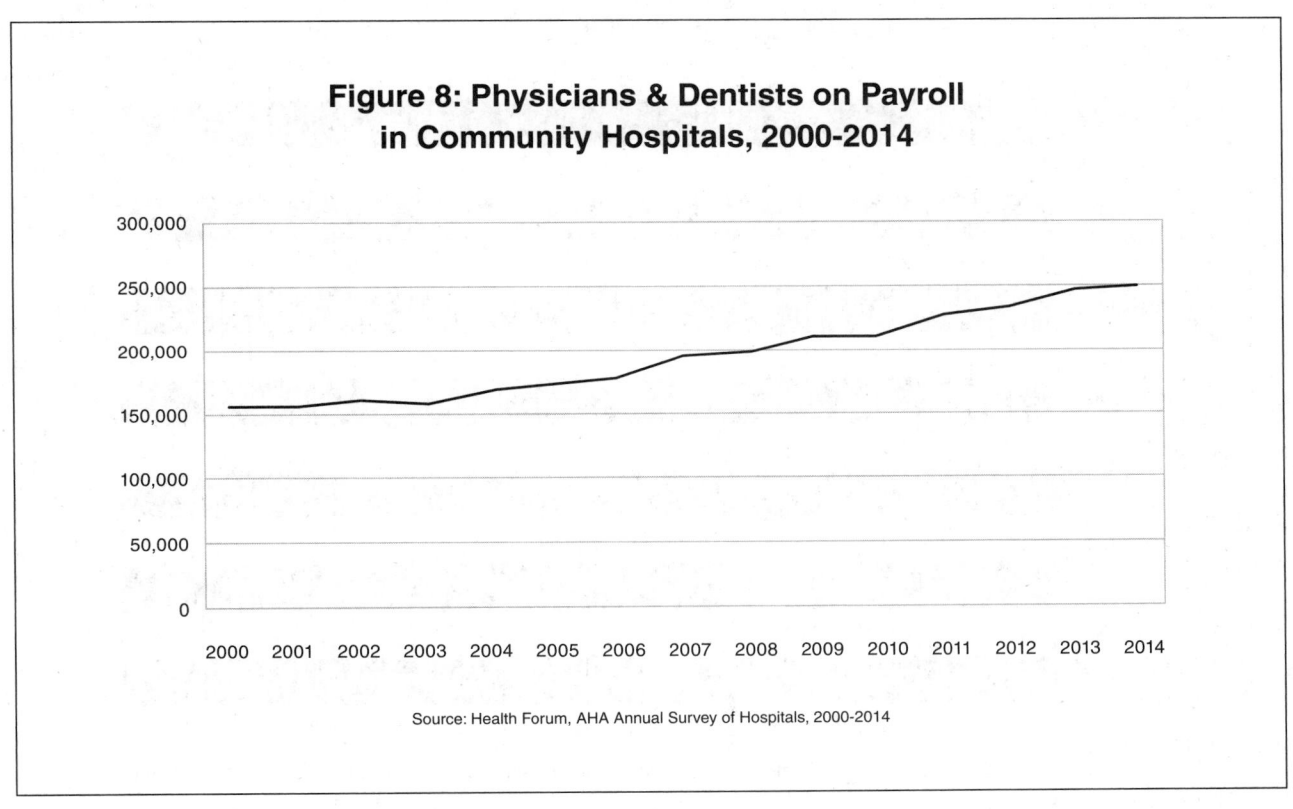

Figure 8: Physicians & Dentists on Payroll in Community Hospitals, 2000-2014

Source: Health Forum, AHA Annual Survey of Hospitals, 2000-2014

Employment is not the only way that hospitals engage their physicians although it is certainly a growing way. Hospitals have always contracted with a physician group or individual physicians as an alternative to employment. When looking at physicians by specialty, emergency physicians are the most likely to be under group contract followed by radiologists/pathologists/anesthesiologists (Figure 9). Hospitalists are the most likely to be employed followed by intensivists. Primary care physicians and other specialists are highly likely to be either not employed or under contract.

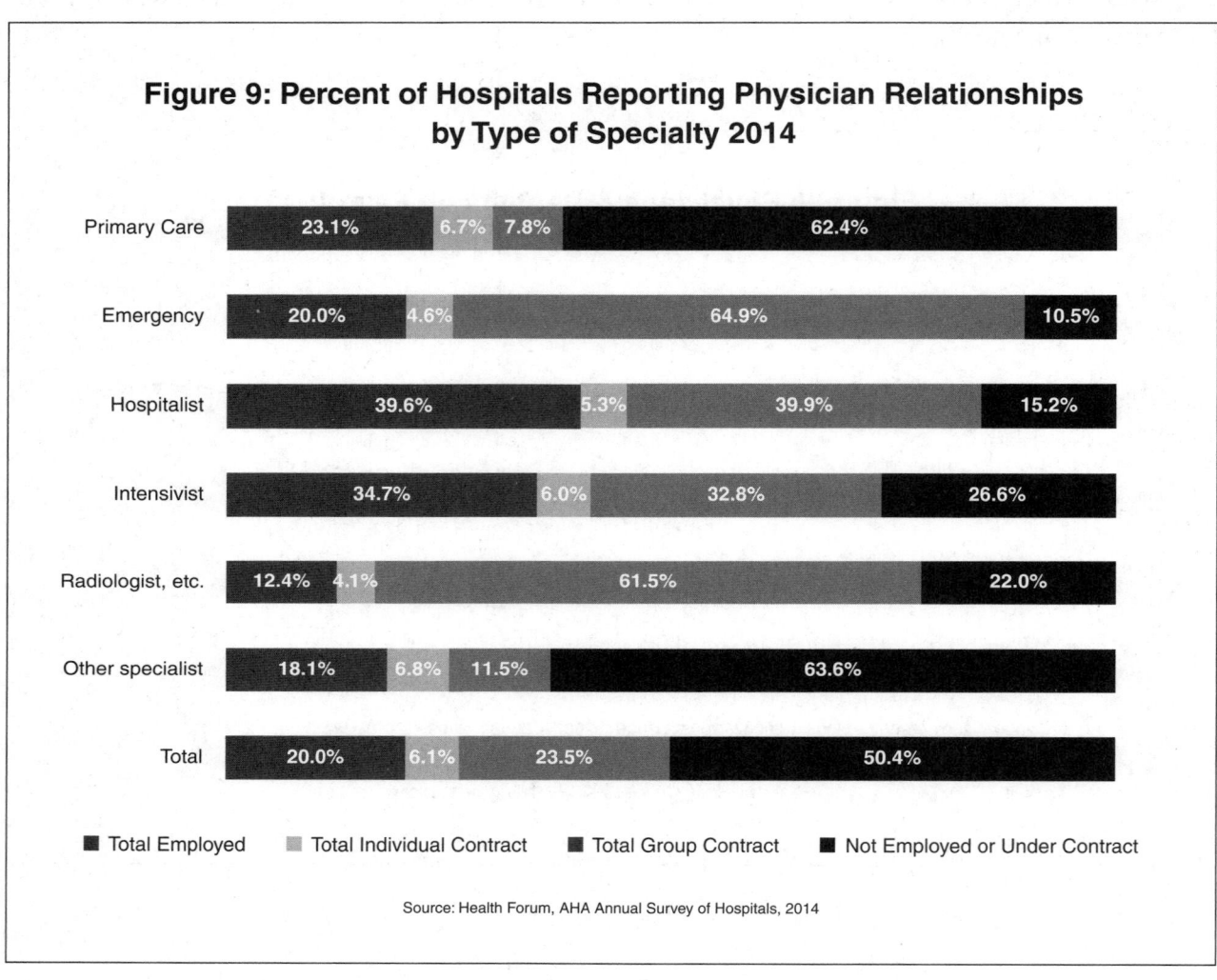

Figure 9: Percent of Hospitals Reporting Physician Relationships by Type of Specialty 2014

Specialty	Total Employed	Total Individual Contract	Total Group Contract	Not Employed or Under Contract
Primary Care	23.1%	6.7%	7.8%	62.4%
Emergency	20.0%	4.6%	64.9%	10.5%
Hospitalist	39.6%	5.3%	39.9%	15.2%
Intensivist	34.7%	6.0%	32.8%	26.6%
Radiologist, etc.	12.4%	4.1%	61.5%	22.0%
Other specialist	18.1%	6.8%	11.5%	63.6%
Total	20.0%	6.1%	23.5%	50.4%

Source: Health Forum, AHA Annual Survey of Hospitals, 2014

Care Coordination

In order to be successful with the new risk or performance related payment programs, it is imperative that there is tight alignment between hospitals and physicians. In addition, there must be very effective programs in place to ensure that care is highly coordinated across the care continuum. Proper care coordination is essential in preventing avoidable and costly re-admissions.

Based on results from the 2014 Survey of Care Systems and Payment, hospitals are engaged in various coordination of care activities that are either widely used or used hospital wide (Figure 10). Among them are medication reconciliation (88%), provision of visit summaries to outpatients and scheduling follow-up visits/referrals (52%), and disease management programs for chronic care conditions (37%).

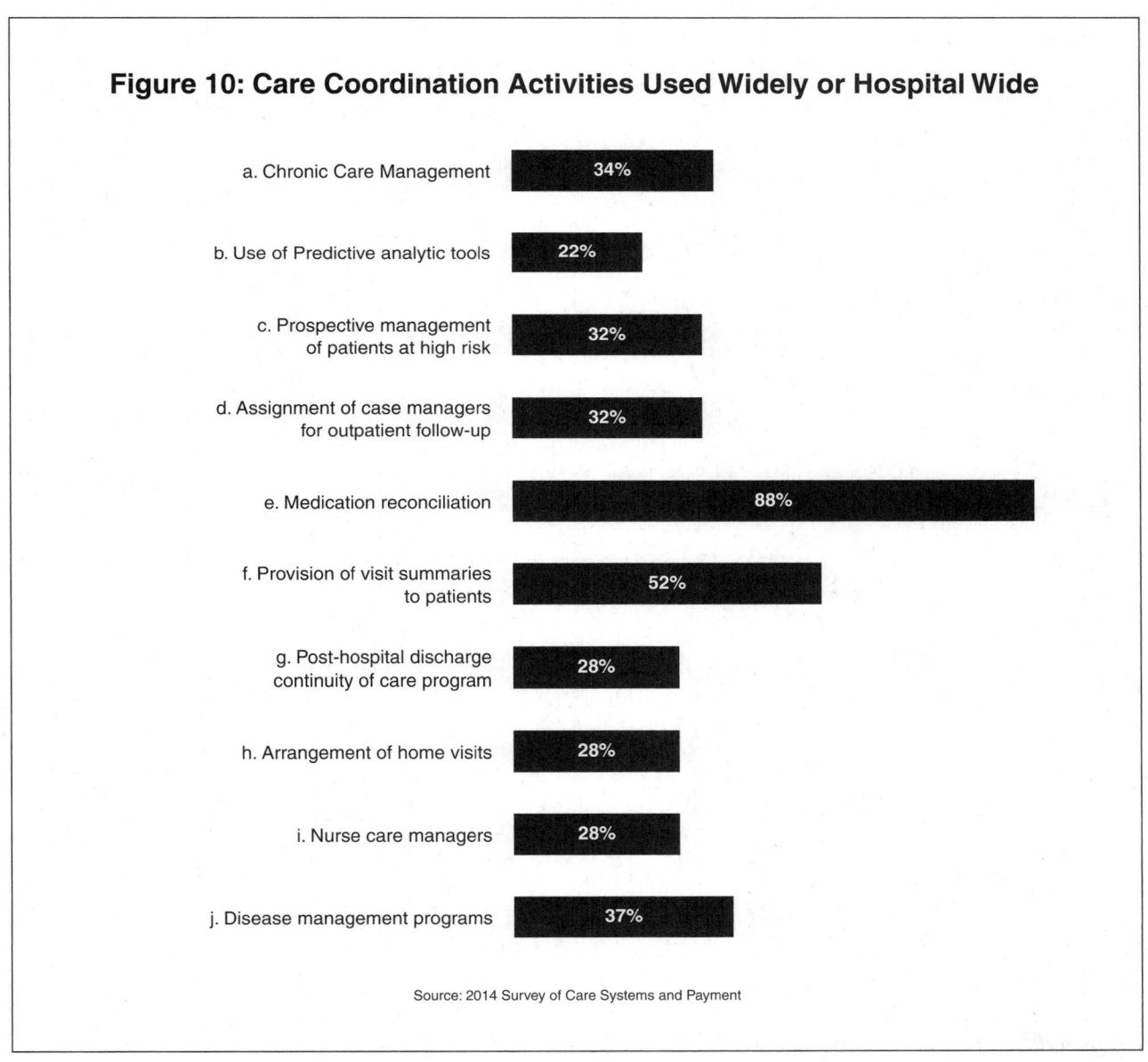

Figure 10: Care Coordination Activities Used Widely or Hospital Wide

Activity	Percentage
a. Chronic Care Management	34%
b. Use of Predictive analytic tools	22%
c. Prospective management of patients at high risk	32%
d. Assignment of case managers for outpatient follow-up	32%
e. Medication reconciliation	88%
f. Provision of visit summaries to patients	52%
g. Post-hospital discharge continuity of care program	28%
h. Arrangement of home visits	28%
i. Nurse care managers	28%
j. Disease management programs	37%

Source: 2014 Survey of Care Systems and Payment

Conclusion

Results show that hospital experience with payment models other than traditional volume based fee-for-service is slowly but steadily progressing. It is clear that the pressure to transform to an accountable care orientation will intensify. Both public and private payors are increasingly demanding that providers share the financial risk and deliver both improved outcomes and lower costs. In order to be successful with accountable care payment approaches, hospitals and physicians must establish relationships that allow for the systematic monitoring of both cost and quality with sufficient opportunity to take corrective actions as warranted. It is important that the AHA continue to monitor how hospitals are responding to the current set of very influential transformative pressures.

Prepared by the Health Forum's Health Care Data Center

How to Use this Book

For more than seven decades, *AHA Hospital Statistics*™ has reported aggregate hospital data derived from the AHA Annual Survey and is the definitive source when doing trend analysis with data by bed size category, U.S. Census Divisions, States, and Metropolitan Statistical Areas (MSAs). As the health care delivery system changes, so have the data tracked by the survey and presented in this report. Recent additions include:

- **Community health indicators** that offer readers a connection to the community for their analysis and planning: the data are broken down into beds, admissions, inpatient days, ER outpatient visits, and other indicators per 1000 population, as well as expense per capita.

- **Utilization, personnel and finance** by all MSAs in the United States.

- **Five-year trend data** on physician models, insurance products, and managed care contracts enable you to identify changes in relationships between hospitals and other health care systems and providers.

- **Tables 3 through 6 have been organized** to show breakdowns between inpatient and outpatient care to better reflect market shifts toward outpatient-centered care. Additional clarity is gained by the breakdown between total facility data (which includes nursing home type units under the control of the hospital) and hospital units (which exclude the nursing home data).

TABLE 6	Sample State

U.S. Registered Community Hospitals
(Nonfederal, short-term general and other special hospitals)

Overview 2010-2014

	2014	2013	2012	2011	2010
Physician Models					
Independent Practice Association	14	17	17	17	14
Group Practice without Walls	4	5	5	8	4
Open Physician-Hospital Organization	20	21	24	23	18
Closed Physician-Hospital Organization . . .	21	17	18	17	11
Management Service Organization	14	18	20	14	9
Integrated Salary Model	35	29	30	26	24
Equity Model	4	3	4	6	3
Foundation	9	8	23	21	19
Insurance Products					
Health Maintenance Organization	20	22	23	24	19
Preferred Provider Organization	39	47	52	53	37
Indemnity Fee for Service.	7	12	14	12	6
Managed Care Contracts					
Health Maintenance Organization.	64	67	62	49	42
Preferred Provider Organization	97	93	92	87	72

Example of five-year trend data

- **Facilities and Services information** on more than 100 categories of hospital facilities and services in Table 7. At a glance, you can determine the number and percentage of hospitals offering a specific service such as Oncology, Palliative Care Program, Complementary Medicine, Women's Health Services and Tobacco Cessation.

- **Plus, System and Network involvement along with Group Purchasing Organizations** that demonstrate ways in which organizations are linked.

The survey instrument and the glossary

A good place to begin your analysis is the AHA Annual Survey instrument. Found on page 217, it includes the instructions, questions, and terms that were used to gather the data for fiscal year 2014. This can be extremely valuable for a clearer understanding of the data we collect and the tables presented in *AHA Hospital Statistics*.

Please also review the glossary in the back of the book. The glossary contains complete definitions for specific terms used in the tables and text of *AHA Hospital Statistics*. These definitions will clarify how terminology is being used.

As mentioned above, it is important to note that the primary focus of the most detailed data contained in *AHA Hospital Statistics* is community hospitals. As defined, community hospitals are all non-federal, short-term general and special hospitals whose facilities and services are available to the public. If the majority of a hospital's patients are admitted to units where the average length of stay is 30 days or less, a hospital may still be classified as short-term even if it includes a nursing- home-type unit. (For a more complete definition of community hospitals, please see the glossary definition, located on page 207.)

Getting the most out of
AHA Hospital Statistics
This section of the book provides an introduction for getting the most out of your *AHA Hospital Statistics* 2016 edition. Here, you'll find a guide to the book, with insights into each table.

Equity model: An arrangement that allows established practitioners to become shareholders in a professional corporation in exchange for tangible and intangible assets of their existing practices.

Expenses: Includes all expenses for the reporting period including payroll, non-payroll, and all nonoperating expenses. *Payroll expenses* include all salaries and wages. *Non-payroll expenses* are all professional fees and those salary expenditures excluded from payroll. *Labor related expenses* are defined as payroll expenses plus employee benefits. *Non-labor related expenses* are all other non-payroll expenses. *Bad debt* has been reclassified from a "reduction in revenue" to an expense in accordance with the revised AICPA Audit Guide. However, for purposes of historical consistency, the expense total that appears throughout *AHA Hospital Statistics does not include "bad debt" as an expense item.* Note: Financial data may not add due to rounding.

Extracorporeal shock wave lithotripter (ESWL): A medical device used for treating stones in the kidney or urethra. The device disintegrates kidney stones noninvasively through the transmission of acoustic shock waves directed at the stones.

Fitness center: Provides exercise, testing, or evaluation programs and fitness activities to the community and hospital employees.

Example of Glossary definitions.

Table	Historical Trends in Utilization, Personnel, and Finances for Selected Years from 1946 through 2014
1	

Example of Table 1

CLASSIFICATION	YEAR	HOSPITALS	BEDS (in thousands)	ADMISSIONS (in thousands)	AVERAGE DAILY CENSUS (in thousands)	ADJUSTED AVERAGE DAILY CENSUS (in thousands)
Total United States	1946	6,125	1,436	15,675	1,142	—
	1950	6,788	1,456	18,483	1,253	—
	1955	6,956	1,604	21,073	1,363	—
	1960	6,876	1,658	25,027	1,402	—
	1965	7,123	1,704	28,812	1,403	—
	1970	7,123	1,616	31,759	1,298	—
	1971	7,097	1,556	32,664	1,237	—
	1972	7,061	1,550	33,265	1,209	—
	1973	7,123	1,535	34,352	1,189	—
	1974	7,174	1,513	35,506	1,167	—
	1975	7,156	1,466	36,157	1,125	—
	1976	7,082	1,434	36,776	1,090	—
	1977	7,099	1,407	37,060	1,066	—
	1978	7,015	1,381	37,243	1,042	—
	1979	6,988	1,372	37,802	1,043	—
	1980	6,965	1,365	38,892	1,060	—
	1981	6,933	1,362	39,169	1,061	—
	1982	6,915	1,360	39,095	1,053	—
	1983	6,888	1,350	38,887	1,028	—
	1984	6,872	1,339	37,938	970	—
	1985	6,872	1,318	36,304	910	—
	1986	6,841	1,290	35,219	883	—
	1987	6,821	1,267	34,439	873	—
	1988	6,780	1,248	34,107	863	—
	1989	6,720	1,226	33,742	853	—
	1990	6,649	1,213	33,774	844	—
	1991	6,634	1,202	33,567	827	—
	1992	6,539	1,178	33,536	807	—
	1993	6,467	1,163	33,201	783	—
	1994	6,374	1,128	33,125	745	—
	1995	6,291	1,081	33,282	710	—
	1996	6,201	1,062	33,307	685	—
	1997	6,097	1,035	33,624	673	—
	1998	6,021	1,013	33,766	662	—
	1999	5,890	994	34,181	657	—
	2000	5,810	984	34,891	650	—
	2001	5,801	987	35,644	658	—
	2002	5,794	976	36,326	662	—
	2003	5,764	965	36,611	657	—
	2004	5,759	956	36,942	658	—
	2005	5,756	947	37,006	656	—

Table 1 — Historical Trends in Utilization, Personnel and Finances for Selected Years from 1946 through 2014

Table 1 at a Glance

This table is used to evaluate historical data and allows you to examine long-term trends in health care with data dating back more than sixty years. Table 1 reports on all AHA registered hospitals in the United States. One important note: To be considered an AHA-registered hospital, a hospital does not need to be an AHA member. Rather, the hospital must meet particular certification or satisfy a number of requirements. These Registration Requirements immediately follow this section and begin on page xxviii.

This table segments the data into various organizational structure categories. Here's a brief look at these different classifications:

- Total United States Hospitals
- Total Non-Federal Short-term and other special hospitals
- Community hospitals
- Non-government not-for-profit community hospitals
- Investor-owned (for-profit) community hospitals
- State and local government community hospitals

Table 1 also provides input on nationwide utilization, personnel and finance trends. You'll find answers to questions such as: *Over the past 25 years, what trends do I see comparing the average length of stay at government and non-government not-for-profit community hospitals and investor-owned for-profit community hospitals?* or *What has been the trend in outpatient visits?*

Table 2 — 2014 U.S. Registered Hospitals: Utilization, Personnel and Finances

Table 2 at a Glance

This table takes a closer look at U.S. Registered Hospitals for 2014. It offers a snapshot of utilization, personnel and finance statistics, and breaks down this information for specialty hospitals. In addition, this is the only table that outlines data on federal hospitals. You'll be able to use this table to better understand the number of beds set-up and staffed, how many personnel and trainees are on the payroll, and what the financial implications of these may be.

TABLE 3

TOTAL UNITED STATES

U.S. Registered Community Hospitals
(Nonfederal, short-term general and other special hospitals)

Utilization, Personnel, Revenue and Expenses, Community Health Indicators 2010-2014

	2014	2013	2012	2011	2010
TOTAL FACILITY (Includes Hospital and Nursing Home Units)					
Utilization - Inpatient					
Beds	839,988	853,287	862,352	872,736	902,061
Admissions	31,811,673	31,576,960	31,098,959	30,945,357	30,718,136
Inpatient Days	191,430,450	192,504,015	193,747,004	199,876,367	207,180,278
Average Length of Stay	6.0	6.1	6.2	6.5	6.7
Inpatient Surgeries	9,735,705	9,509,081	9,545,612	9,700,613	9,833,938
Births	3,726,233	3,742,191	3,723,871	3,764,698	3,809,367
HOSPITAL UNIT (Excludes Separate Nursing Home Units)					
Utilization - Inpatient					
Beds	758,186	769,505	782,504	794,502	824,969
Admissions	31,265,867	31,047,930	30,652,820	30,577,564	30,403,766
Inpatient Days	165,644,176	165,605,620	168,189,130	174,898,504	182,702,882
Average Length of Stay	5.3	5.3	5.5	5.7	6.0
Personnel					
Total Full Time	3,235,153	3,183,730	3,154,603	3,166,729	3,147,922
Total Part Time	1,213,426	1,214,232	1,153,790	1,146,082	1,122,957
Revenue and Expenses - Totals					
(Includes Inpatient and Outpatient)					
Total Net Revenue	$333,054,828,642	$322,459,942,930	$310,513,291,998	$298,519,717,355	$285,858,018,951
Total Expenses	314,709,758,455	301,905,101,393	290,128,641,153	282,372,557,487	272,840,121,437

Example of Table 3. Helps contrast acute and long-term care

Table 3 — Total United States

Table 3 at a Glance

This table provides a look at all U.S. Registered Community Hospitals, in terms of general overview with utilization by inpatient and outpatient, personnel, revenue, expenses and community health indicators. It provides a snapshot of the past five years, allowing you to track emerging trends.

This national information can be compared to local or regional trends, for benchmarking:

- Both inpatient and outpatient information is included, for better evaluation of data.

- Reporting by total facility *Includes hospital and Nursing Home Units* and hospital unit only *Excludes Separate Nursing Home Units* helps contrast acute and long-term care.

- Community health indicators can help uncover trends and help determine future facility needs.

TABLE **4**   BED SIZE CATEGORY 25-49

	2014	2013	2012	2011	2010
Total U.S. Community Hospitals in Bed Size Category 25-49	900	890	906	922	900

Location
Hospitals Urban . . . . . .
Hospitals Rural . . . .

Control
State and Local Gove
Not for Profit . . . .
Investor owned . . . . . .

Physician Models
Independent Practice A
Group Practice without
Open Physician-Hospi
Closed Physician-Hos
Management Service
Integrated Salary Mod
Equity Model . . . . .
Foundation . . . .

Insurance Products
Health Maintenance O
Preferred Provider Org
Indemnity Fee for Ser

Managed Care Contract
Health Maintenance O
Preferred Provider Org

Bed Size Categories

TABLE **4**   BED SIZE CATEGORY 100-199

	2014	2013	2012	2011	2010
Total U.S. Community Hospitals in Bed Size Category 100-199	1,304	1,289	1,338	1,324	1,331

Location
Hospitals Urban . . . .
Hospitals Rural . . . . . .

Control
State and Local Governm
Not for Profit . . . .
Investor owned . . . .

Physician Models
Independent Practice Asse
Group Practice without W
Open Physician-Hospital O
Closed Physician-Hospital
Management Service Org
Integrated Salary Model
Equity Model . . . .
Foundation . . . .

Insurance Products
Health Maintenance Orga
Preferred Provider Organi
Indemnity Fee for Service

Managed Care Contracts
Health Maintenance Orga
Preferred Provider Organi

Bed Size Categories

TABLE **4**   BED SIZE CATEGORY 500 +

	2014	2013	2012	2011	2010
Total U.S. Community Hospitals in Bed Size Category 500 + ...	254	255	251	264	273
Location					
Hospitals Urban	251	251	247	260	270
Hospitals Rural	3	4	4	4	3
Control					
State and Local Government	42	43	48	53	56
Not for Profit	198	197	186	197	208
Investor owned	14	15	17	14	9
Physician Models					
Independent Practice Association	85	86	93	93	93
Group Practice without Walls	25	28	38	34	35
Open Physician-Hospital Organization	79	87	79	83	82
Closed Physician-Hospital Organization . . .	53	50	61	68	53
Management Service Organization	80	93	108	90	90
Integrated Salary Model	103	97	96	97	94
Equity Model	17	17	18	17	16
Foundation	35	41	52	53	49
Insurance Products					
Health Maintenance Organization	138	130	121	115	116
Preferred Provider Organization	122	127	119	121	122
Indemnity Fee for Service	34	37	35	35	35
Managed Care Contracts					
Health Maintenance Organization	197	206	199	213	217
Preferred Provider Organization	193	202	199	215	211

Example of Table 4. Compares facilities with peers.

Table 4 — Bed Size Categories

Table 4 at a Glance

This table provides a look at all U.S. Registered Community Hospitals, broken down by bed size. The table includes general overview, utilization, personnel, and revenue and expense information. These categories of bed sizes were developed by the AHA, and have become an industry standard. By categorizing each facility into a peer group, this table provides a snapshot of the past five years allowing you to compare facilities with their peers.

TABLE 5

U.S. Registered Community Hospitals
(Nonfederal, short-term general and other special hospitals)

Utilization, Personnel, Revenue and Expenses, Community Health Indicators 2010-2014

	2014	2013	2012	2011	2010
COMMUNITY HEALTH INDICATORS PER 1000 POPULATION					
Total Population (in thousands)...	38,292	38,216	38,184	38,147	38,108
Inpatient					
Beds.........................	3.6	3.8	3.9	4.0	4.1
Admissions....................	135.8	136.7	136.2	138.3	137.4
Inpatient Days.................	963.5	988.8	1,019.0	1,093.8	1,145.0
Inpatient Surgeries.............	42.2	41.4	41.2	42.7	43.6
Births........................	13.0	13.2	13.6	13.7	14.3
Outpatient					
Emergency Outpatient Visits......	367.7	362.0	363.4	379.5	360.1
Other Outpatient Visits...........	1,970.9	1,802.3	1,767.7	1,680.3	1,573.9
Total Outpatient Visits...........	2,338.6	2,164.3	2,131.1	2,059.8	1,934.0
Outpatient Surgeries............	67.8	62.4	59.9	55.4	53.5
Expense per Capita (per person)....	$1,494.9	$1,462.7	$1,428.6	$1,429.8	$1,369.2

Example of Table 5. Uncovers trends to determine future facility needs.

Table 5 — U.S. Census Divisions

Table 5 at a Glance

This table provides a look at all U.S. Registered Community Hospitals, broken down by Census Division. The table includes general overview, utilization, personnel, and expenses, and community health indicator information. It provides a snapshot of the past five years, allowing you to track trends on a regional level. In addition, this allows you to compare this data to other population based health indicators, offering a more comprehensive look than the survey data alone. Community health indicators can help uncover trends and help determine future facility needs.

Table 6 — States

Table 6 at a Glance

This table provides a look at all U.S. Registered Community Hospitals, broken down by State. The table includes general overview, utilization, personnel, revenue and expenses, and community health indicator information. It provides a snapshot of the past five years, allowing you to track trends on a state level.

Note:

You can use the information in tables 3, 4, 5 and 6 to make accurate comparisons across Total U.S., Bed Size Category, Census Division and State.

Table 7 — 2014 Facilities and Services in the U.S. Census Divisions and States

Table 7 at a Glance

This table examines facilities and services by both Census Division and State. A comprehensive alphabetical guide helps make each facility or service easy to find. This table will allow you to better understand what service lines are emerging and how many facilities offer a particular service in a discrete state or region.

This collection of facilities and services information data is unique to *AHA Hospital Statistics* and the list is continually growing. Recent additions include:

- Pediatric Emergency Department
- Psychiatric Residential Treatment
- Magneotoencephalography (MEG)

These new categories reflect the trends as hospitals expand their service lines to mirror the needs of their patients. For example, services such as acupuncture or massage therapy are now accounted for in the Complementary Medicine service item.

This table can answer questions such as: *What percentage of hospitals in the United States offer complementary medicine or wound management?* or *How are these new services distributed by state?*

Table 7 (Continued)

CLASSIFICATION	HOSPITALS REPORTING	CASE MANAGEMENT		CHILDREN WELLNESS PROGRAM		CHIROPRACTIC SERVICES		COMMUNITY OUTREACH	
		Number	Percent	Number	Percent	Number	Percent	Number	Percent
UNITED STATES	4,707	2,990	62.1	789	16.3	61	1.3	2,725	56.6
COMMUNITY HOSPITALS	4,113	2,620	63.7	742	18.0	53	1.3	2,491	60.6
CENSUS DIVISION 1, NEW ENGLAND	230	157	68.3	63	27.4	6	2.6	169	73.5
Connecticut	42	32	76.2	15	35.7	3	7.1	32	76.2
Maine	39	20	51.3	9	23.1	0	0.0	30	76.9
Massachusetts	85	64	75.3	21	24.7	2	2.4	62	72.9
New Hampshire	31	20	64.5	10	32.3	0	0.0	23	74.2
Rhode Island	16	12	75.0	4	25.0	1	6.3	11	68.8
Vermont	17	9	52.9	4	23.5	0	0.0	11	64.7
CENSUS DIVISION 2, MIDDLE ATLANTIC	461	344	74.6	143	31.0	7	1.5	345	74.8
New Jersey	71	66	93.0	29	40.8	2	2.8	60	84.5
New York	194	146	75.3	61	31.4	2	1.0	140	72.2
Pennsylvania	196	132	67.3	53	27.0	3	1.5	145	74.0
CENSUS DIVISION 3, SOUTH ATLANTIC	724	484	66.9	123	17.0	8	1.1	450	62.2
Delaware	9	5	55.6	4	44.4	0	0.0	5	55.6
District of Columbia	17	13	76.5	3	17.6	2	11.8	10	58.8
Florida	138	117	84.8	23	16.7	3	2.2	89	64.5
Georgia	144	87	60.4	19	13.2	0	0.0	75	52.1
Maryland	64	47	73.4	10	15.6	1	1.6	46	71.9
North Carolina	119	84	70.6	20	16.8	1	0.8	71	59.7
South Carolina	71	25	35.2	25	35.2	0	0.0	64	90.1
Virginia	98	72	73.5	9	9.2	0	0.0	55	56.1
West Virginia	64	34	53.1	10	15.6	1	1.6	35	54.7
CENSUS DIVISION 4, EAST NORTH CENTRAL	741	429	64.5	140	18.9	15	2.0	464	62.6
Illinois	190	128	66.3	45	23.3	5	2.6	132	69.4
Indiana	110	68	61.8	20	18.2	1	0.9	76	69.1
Michigan	148	92	62.2	32	21.6	0	0.0	101	68.2
Ohio	156	108	69.2	34	21.8	5	5.8	109	69.9
Wisconsin	134	82	61.2	9	6.7	0	0.0	46	34.3
CENSUS DIVISION 5, EAST SOUTH CENTRAL	403	229	56.8	26	6.5	3	0.7	198	49.1
Alabama	94	60	63.8	5	5.3	1	1.1	52	55.3
Kentucky	104	64	61.5	12	11.5	0	0.0	49	47.1
Mississippi	106	45	42.5	0	0.0	0	0.0	56	52.8
Tennessee	99	60	60.6	9	9.1	2	2.0	41	41.4
CENSUS DIVISION 6, WEST NORTH CENTRAL	703	308	43.8	85	12.1	11	1.6	370	52.6
Iowa	126	68	54.0	25	19.8	2	1.6	68	54.0
Kansas	139	48	34.5	12	8.6	3	2.2	46	33.1
Minnesota	115	33	28.7	9	7.8	1	0.9	74	64.3
Missouri	151	106	70.2	23	15.2	4	2.6	97	64.2
Nebraska	81	28	34.6	5	6.2	0	0.0	45	55.6
North Dakota	35	7	20.0	5	14.3	1	2.9	16	45.7
South Dakota	56	18	32.1	6	10.7	0	0.0	24	42.9
CENSUS DIVISION 7, WEST SOUTH CENTRAL	777	492	63.3	76	9.8	4	0.5	316	40.7
Arkansas	65	44	67.7	5	7.7	0	0.0	27	41.5
Louisiana	111	70	63.1	18	16.2	1	0.9	44	39.6
Oklahoma	115	63	52.2	9	7.8	1	0.9	49	42.6
Texas	486	318	65.4	44	9.1	2	0.4	196	40.3
CENSUS DIVISION 8, MOUNTAIN	333	194	58.3	47	14.1	2	0.6	162	48.6
Arizona	64	44	81.5	8	14.8	0	0.0	25	46.3
Colorado	59	40	67.8	10	16.9	1	1.7	41	69.5
Idaho	35	17	48.6	5	14.3	0	0.0	19	54.3
Montana	54	12	22.2	7	13.0	0	0.0	14	25.9
Nevada	20	15	75.0	3	15.0	0	0.0	10	50.0
New Mexico	40	22	55.0	7	17.5	0	0.0	18	45.0
Utah	44	25	59.1	6	13.6	1	2.3	20	45.5
Wyoming	27	18	66.7	1	3.7	0	0.0	15	55.6
CENSUS DIVISION 9, PACIFIC	425	294	69.2	80	18.8	5	1.2	251	59.1
Alaska	15	9	60.0	1	6.7	0	0.0	6	40.0
California	280	209	74.6	55	19.6	3	1.1	173	61.8
Hawaii	16	10	62.5	3	18.8	0	0.0	8	50.0
Oregon	52	28	53.8	11	21.2	0	0.0	31	59.6
Washington	62	38	61.3	10	16.1	2	3.2	33	53.2

Example of Table 7.

Table 8 — Utilization, Personnel and Finances in Community Hospitals by MSAs for 2014

Table 8 at a Glance

This table provides a look at all U.S. Registered Community Hospitals, broken down by Metropolitan Statistical Area (MSA). The table includes general overview, utilization, personnel, and finance information. It provides a snapshot of the past year.

Additional Resources

Again, in the back of the book you will find the comprehensive glossary and the 2014 annual survey questionnaire. The survey itself can be a valuable resource to understanding what was asked in order to gather the data in the book. This survey is also used to produce the *AHA Guide®* and AHA Annual Survey Database™.

AHA-Registered Hospitals

Any institution that can be classified as a hospital according to the requirements may be registered if it so desires. Membership in the American Hospital Association is not a prerequisite.

The American Hospital Association may, at the sole discretion of the Executive Committee of the Board of Trustees, grant, deny, or withdraw the registration of an institution.

An institution may be registered by the American Hospital Association as a hospital if it is accredited as a hospital by The Joint Commission or is certified as a provider of acute services under Title 18 of the Social Security Act and has provided the Association with documents verifying the accreditation or certification.

In lieu of the preceding accreditation or certification, an institution licensed as a hospital by the appropriate state agency may be registered by AHA as a hospital by meeting the following alternative requirements:

Function: The primary function of the institution is to provide patient services, diagnostic and therapeutic, for particular or general medical conditions.

1. The institution shall maintain at least six inpatient beds, which shall be continuously available for the care of patients who are nonrelated and who stay on the average in excess of 24 hours per admission.

2. The institution shall be constructed, equipped, and maintained to ensure the health and safety of patients and to provide uncrowded, sanitary facilities for the treatment of patients.

3. There shall be an identifiable governing authority legally and morally responsible for the conduct of the hospital.

4. There shall be a chief executive to whom the governing authority delegates the continuous responsibility for the operation of the hospital in accordance with established policy.

5. There shall be an organized medical staff of fully licensed physicians* that may include other licensed individuals permitted by law and by the hospital to provide patient care services independently in the hospital. The medical staff shall be accountable to the governing authority for maintaining proper standards of medical care, and it shall be governed by bylaws adopted by said staff and approved by the governing authority.

6. Each patient shall be admitted on the authority of a member of the medical staff who has been granted the privilege to admit patients to inpatient services in accordance with state law and criteria for standards of medical care established by the individual medical staff. Each patient's general medical condition is the responsibility of a qualified physician member of the medical staff. When nonphysician members of the medical staff are granted privileges to admit patients, provision is made for prompt medical evaluation of these patients by a qualified physician. Any graduate of a foreign medical school who is permitted to assume responsibilities for patient care shall possess a valid license to practice medicine, or shall be certified by the Educational Commission for Foreign Medical Graduates, or shall have qualified for and have successfully completed an academic year of supervised clinical training under the direction of a medical school approved by the Liaison Committee on GAT Medical Education.

7. Registered nurse supervision and other nursing services are continuous.

8. A current and complete‡ medical record shall be maintained by the institution for each patient and shall be available for reference.

9. Pharmacy service shall be maintained in the institution and shall be supervised by a registered pharmacist.

10. The institution shall provide patients with food service that meets their nutritional and therapeutic requirements; special diets shall also be available.

Types of Hospitals

In addition to meeting these 10 general registration requirements, hospitals are registered as one of four types of hospitals: general, special, rehabilitation and chronic disease, or psychiatric. The following type of hospital and special requirements for registration are employed:

General

The primary function of the institution is to provide patient services, diagnostic and therapeutic, for a variety of medical conditions. A general hospital also shall provide:

- diagnostic x-ray services with facilities and staff for a variety of procedures
- clinical laboratory service with facilities and staff for a variety of procedures and with anatomical pathology services regularly and conveniently available
- operating room service with facilities and staff.

Special

The primary function of the institution is to provide diagnostic and treatment services for patients who have specified medical conditions, both surgical and nonsurgical. A special hospital also shall provide:

- such diagnostic and treatment services as may be determined by the Executive Committee of the Board of Trustees of the American Hospital Association to be appropriate for the specified medical conditions for which medical services are provided shall be maintained in the institution with suitable facilities and staff. If such conditions do not normally require diagnostic x-ray service, laboratory service, or operating room service, and if any such services are therefore not maintained in the institution, there shall be written arrangements to make them available to patients requiring them.
- clinical laboratory services capable of providing tissue diagnosis when offering pregnancy termination services.

Rehabilitation and Chronic Disease

The primary function of the institution is to provide diagnostic and treatment services to handicapped or disabled individuals requiring restorative and adjustive services. A rehabilitation and chronic disease hospital also shall provide:

- arrangements for diagnostic x-ray services, as required, on a regular and conveniently available basis
- arrangements for clinical laboratory service, as required on a regular and conveniently available basis
- arrangements for operating room service, as required, on a regular and conveniently available basis
- a physical therapy service with suitable facilities and staff in the institution
- an occupational therapy service with suitable facilities and staff in the institution
- arrangements for psychological and social work services on a regular and conveniently available basis

---

* Physician—Term used to describe an individual with an M.D. or D.O. degree who is fully licensed to practice medicine in all its phases.

‡ The completed records in general shall contain at least the following: the patient's identifying data and consent forms, medical history, record of physical examination, physicians' progress notes, operative notes, nurses' notes, routine x-ray and laboratory reports, doctors' orders, and final diagnosis.

- arrangements for educational and vocational services on a regular and conveniently available basis
- written arrangements with a general hospital for the transfer of patients who require medical, obstetrical, or surgical services not available in the institution.

Psychiatric

The primary function of the institution is to provide diagnostic and treatment services for patients who have psychiatric-related illnesses. A psychiatric hospital also shall provide:

- arrangements for clinical laboratory service, as required, on a regular and conveniently available basis
- arrangements for diagnostic x-ray services, as required on a regular and conveniently available basis
- psychiatric, psychological, and social work service with facilities and staff in the institution
- arrangements for electroencephalograph services, as required, on a regular and conveniently available basis.
- written arrangements with a general hospital for the transfer of patients who require medical, obstetrical, or surgical services not available in the institution.

The American Hospital Association may, at the sole discretion of the Executive Committee of the Board of Trustees, grant, deny, or withdraw the registration of an institution.

Data Comparability

The economic climate, demographic characteristics, personnel issues, and health care financing and payment policies differ by region, state, and city across the country. *Differences in these factors must be taken into account when using the data.* In addition, the profiles of hospitals across comparison groups vary. For example, states will differ in terms of the number and percentage of hospitals by size, ownership, services provided, types of patients treated, and so forth. *Differences in these variables also must be taken into consideration when doing a comparative analysis.*

Notes on the Survey

The 2016 edition of *AHA Hospital Statistics*™ draws its data from the 2014 AHA Annual Survey of Hospitals. It is the statistical complement to the 2016 edition of the *AHA Guide*®, which contains selected data about individual hospitals.

The AHA Survey was mailed to all hospitals, both AHA-registered and nonregistered, in the U.S. and its associated areas: American Samoa, Guam, the Marshall Islands, Puerto Rico, and the Virgin Islands. U.S. government hospitals located outside the U.S. were not included. Overall, the average response rate over the past five years has been approximately 83 percent.

Reporting Period

In completing the survey, hospitals were requested to report data for a full year, in accord with their fiscal year, ending in 2014. The statistical table present data reported or estimated for a 12-month period, except for data on personnel, which represent situations as they existed at the end of the reporting period.

Respondents

Data for Tables 1 and 2 include 5,627 AHA-registered hospitals in the U.S. Data on community hospitals (nonfederal, short-term general and other special hospitals) only are presented in Tables 3-6, and Table 8.

It is important to note that the AHA-registered hospitals included in *AHA Hospital Statistics* are not necessarily identical to those included in *AHA Guide*. The institutions listed in the 2016 edition of *AHA Guide* include all of those institutions CMS certified, Joint Commission accredited, or AHA registered as of August 2015. Tables 1-6 in *AHA Hospital Statistics* present data for AHA-registered hospitals that were in operation during the 12-month reporting period ending 2014.

Estimates

Estimates were made of data for nonreporting hospitals and for reporting hospitals that submitted incomplete AHA Annual Survey questionnaires. Estimates were not made for beds, bassinets and facilities and services. Data for beds and bassinets of nonreporting hospitals were based on the most recent information from those hospitals. (Note that in all statistical tables, whenever bed-size categories are listed, all eight categories appear, whether or not there are hospitals in every category.)

Missing revenue, expenses, admissions, births, inpatient days, surgical operations, outpatient visits, and full-time-equivalent personnel values are estimates from regression models. For all other variables the estimates were based on ratios such as per bed averages derived from data reported by hospitals similar in size, control, major service provided, length of stay, and geographical characteristics to the hospitals that did not report this information.

Tables 1–2

Table

1

Historical Trends in Utilization, Personnel, and Finances for Selected Years from 1946 through 2014

Data are for all AHA-registered hospitals in the United States. Data are estimated for nonreporting hospitals with the exception of newborn and outpatient data before 1972. Personnel data exclude residents, interns, and students from 1952 on; personnel data include full-time personnel and full-time equivalents for part-time personnel from 1954 on. As a result of the AHA Annual Survey validation process, the New York state expense data from 1976 were revised after the 1977 edition was published. The revised figures are included below. In order to provide trend data on a consistent basis, the 1970 and 1971 psychiatric and long-term data have been slightly modified. The 1982 FTE figures have been updated to provide the most accurate data possible.

Classification: Total United States

YEAR	HOSPITALS	BEDS (in thousands)	ADMISSIONS (in thousands)	AVERAGE DAILY CENSUS (in thousands)	ADJUSTED AVERAGE DAILY CENSUS (in thousands)	AVERAGE STAY (days)	OUTPATIENT VISITS (in thousands)	NEWBORNS Bassinets	NEWBORNS Births	FTE PERSONNEL Number (in thousands)	FTE PERSONNEL Per 100 Adjusted Census	TOTAL EXPENSES Amount (In Millions of dollars)	TOTAL EXPENSES Adjusted per Inpatient Stay (dollars)	TOTAL EXPENSES Adjusted per Inpatient Day (dollars)
1946	6,125	1,436	15,675	1,142	—	—	—	85,585	2,135,327	830	—	$1,963	—	—
1950	6,788	1,456	18,483	1,253	—	—	—	90,101	2,742,780	1,058	—	$3,651	—	—
1955	6,956	1,604	21,073	1,363	—	—	—	98,823	3,476,753	1,301	—	$5,594	—	—
1960	6,876	1,658	25,027	1,402	—	—	—	102,764	3,835,735	1,598	—	$8,421	—	—
1965	7,123	1,704	28,812	1,403	—	—	125,793	101,287	3,565,344	1,952	—	$12,948	—	—
1970	7,123	1,616	31,759	1,298	—	—	181,370	97,128	3,537,000	2,537	—	$25,556	—	—
1971	7,097	1,556	32,664	1,237	—	—	199,725	94,344	3,464,513	2,589	—	$28,812	—	—
1972	7,061	1,550	33,265	1,209	—	—	219,182	92,960	3,231,875	2,671	—	$32,667	—	—
1973	7,123	1,535	34,352	1,189	—	—	233,555	90,071	3,087,210	2,769	—	$36,290	—	—
1974	7,174	1,513	35,506	1,167	—	—	250,481	88,269	3,043,386	2,919	—	$41,406	—	—
1975	7,156	1,466	36,157	1,125	—	—	254,844	86,875	3,091,629	3,023	—	$48,706	—	—
1976	7,082	1,434	36,776	1,090	—	—	270,951	85,284	3,067,063	3,108	—	$56,005	—	—
1977	7,099	1,407	37,060	1,066	—	—	263,775	83,193	3,223,699	3,213	—	$63,630	—	—
1978	7,015	1,381	37,243	1,042	—	—	263,606	80,650	3,250,373	3,280	—	$70,927	—	—
1979	6,988	1,372	37,802	1,043	—	—	262,009	79,720	3,376,467	3,382	—	$79,796	—	—
1980	6,965	1,365	38,892	1,060	—	—	262,951	79,842	3,500,043	3,492	—	$91,886	—	—
1981	6,933	1,362	39,169	1,061	—	—	265,332	78,823	3,558,274	3,661	—	$107,146	—	—
1982	6,915	1,360	39,095	1,053	—	—	313,667	77,998	3,615,751	3,746	—	$123,219	—	—
1983	6,888	1,350	38,887	1,028	—	—	273,168	77,837	3,596,146	3,707	—	$136,315	—	—
1984	6,872	1,339	37,938	970	—	—	276,566	77,845	3,563,106	3,630	—	$144,114	—	—
1985	6,872	1,318	36,304	910	—	—	282,140	77,202	3,630,961	3,625	—	$153,327	—	—
1986	6,841	1,290	35,219	883	—	—	294,634	76,002	3,680,178	3,647	—	$165,194	—	—
1987	6,821	1,267	34,439	873	—	—	310,707	74,770	3,698,294	3,742	—	$178,662	—	—
1988	6,780	1,248	34,107	863	—	—	336,208	72,568	3,794,369	3,839	—	$196,704	—	—
1989	6,720	1,226	33,742	853	—	—	352,248	71,491	3,920,384	3,937	—	$214,886	—	—
1990	6,649	1,213	33,774	844	—	—	368,184	70,539	4,046,704	4,063	—	$234,870	—	—
1991	6,634	1,202	33,567	827	—	—	387,675	69,464	4,047,504	4,165	—	$258,508	—	—
1992	6,539	1,178	33,536	807	—	—	417,874	69,052	4,007,179	4,236	—	$282,531	—	—
1993	6,467	1,163	33,201	783	—	—	435,619	67,911	3,949,788	4,289	—	$301,538	—	—
1994	6,374	1,128	33,125	745	—	—	453,584	67,311	3,886,667	4,270	—	$310,834	—	—
1995	6,291	1,081	33,282	710	—	—	483,195	66,256	3,833,132	4,273	—	$320,252	—	—
1996	6,201	1,062	33,307	685	—	—	505,455	65,138	3,790,678	4,276	—	$330,531	—	—
1997	6,097	1,035	33,624	673	—	—	520,600	64,649	3,811,522	4,333	—	$342,334	—	—
1998	6,021	1,013	33,766	662	—	—	545,481	63,485	3,795,212	4,407	—	$355,450	—	—
1999	5,890	994	34,181	657	—	—	573,461	62,714	3,829,881	4,369	—	$372,933	—	—
2000	5,810	984	34,891	650	—	—	592,673	61,915	3,940,017	4,454	—	$395,391	—	—
2001	5,801	987	35,644	658	—	—	612,276	61,527	3,929,733	4,535	—	$426,849	—	—
2002	5,794	976	36,326	662	—	—	640,515	62,151	3,934,421	4,610	—	$462,222	—	—
2003	5,764	965	36,611	657	—	—	648,560	60,699	3,976,886	4,651	—	$498,104	—	—
2004	5,759	956	36,942	658	—	—	662,131	59,660	3,965,906	4,696	—	$533,853	—	—
2005	5,756	947	37,006	656	—	—	673,689	59,073	4,048,442	4,791	—	$570,534	—	—
2006	5,747	947	37,189	653	—	—	690,425	58,670	4,126,598	4,907	—	$607,355	—	—
2007	5,708	945	37,120	645	—	—	693,510	58,429	4,128,796	5,024	—	$641,124	—	—
2008	5,815	951	37,529	649	—	—	709,960	58,133	4,109,081	5,116	—	$690,074	—	—
2009	5,795	944	37,480	641	—	—	741,551	58,078	4,001,748	5,178	—	$726,671	—	—
2010	5,754	942	36,915	627	—	—	750,408	57,396	3,871,751	5,184	—	$750,602	—	—
2011	5,724	924	36,565	615	—	—	754,454	57,022	3,767,697	5,196	—	$773,547	—	—
2012	5,723	921	36,156	600	—	—	777,961	56,693	3,754,085	5,258	—	$829,665	—	—
2013	5,686	915	35,416	592	—	—	787,422	57,037	3,749,696	5,342	—	$859,419	—	—
2014	5,627	902	34,879	584	—	—	802,680	56,481	3,787,573	5,314	—	$892,701	—	—

Table 1 (Continued)

CLASSIFICATION: Total nonfederal short-term general and other special

YEAR	HOSPITALS	BEDS (in thousands)	ADMISSIONS (in thousands)	AVERAGE DAILY CENSUS (in thousands)	ADJUSTED AVERAGE DAILY CENSUS (in thousands)	AVERAGE STAY (days)	OUTPATIENT VISITS (in thousands)	NEWBORNS Bassinets	NEWBORNS Births	FTE PERSONNEL Number (in thousands)	FTE PERSONNEL Per 100 Adjusted Census	TOTAL EXPENSES Amount (In Millions of dollars)	TOTAL EXPENSES Adjusted per Inpatient Stay (dollars)	TOTAL EXPENSES Adjusted per Inpatient Day (dollars)
1946	4,444	473	13,655	341	—	9.1	—	80,987	2,087,503	505	—	$1,169	—	—
1950	5,031	505	16,663	372	—	8.1	—	86,019	2,660,982	662	—	$2,120	—	—
1955	5,237	568	19,100	407	—	7.8	—	93,868	3,304,451	826	—	$3,434	—	—
1960	5,407	639	22,970	477	—	7.6	—	98,127	3,678,051	1,080	—	$5,617	—	—
1965	5,736	741	26,463	563	620	7.8	92,631	96,782	3,413,370	1,386	224	$9,147	$316.37	$40.56
1970	5,859	848	29,252	662	727	8.2	133,545	93,079	3,403,064	1,929	265	$19,560	$604.59	$73.73
1971	5,865	867	30,142	665	736	8.0	148,423	90,444	3,337,605	1,999	272	$22,400	$667.44	$83.43
1972	5,843	884	30,777	664	739	7.9	166,983	89,315	3,119,446	2,056	278	$25,549	$747.42	$94.61
1973	5,891	903	31,761	681	768	7.8	178,939	86,851	2,987,089	2,149	280	$28,496	$793.88	$101.78
1974	5,977	931	32,943	701	793	7.8	194,838	85,208	2,947,342	2,289	289	$32,751	$883.04	$113.21
1975	5,979	947	33,519	708	806	7.7	196,311	83,834	2,998,590	2,399	298	$39,110	$1,024.72	$133.08
1976	5,956	961	34,068	715	816	7.7	207,725	82,307	2,962,305	2,483	304	$45,402	$1,172.25	$152.24
1977	5,973	974	34,353	717	820	7.6	204,238	80,228	3,117,756	2,581	315	$51,832	$1,316.70	$173.25
1978	5,935	980	34,575	720	841	7.6	204,461	78,090	3,156,570	2,662	323	$58,348	$1,470.13	$193.81
1979	5,923	988	35,160	729	841	7.6	203,873	77,277	3,287,157	2,762	328	$66,184	$1,631.16	$215.75
1980	5,904	992	36,198	748	861	7.6	206,752	77,539	3,408,699	2,879	334	$76,970	$1,844.19	$244.44
1981	5,879	1,007	36,494	764	876	7.6	206,729	76,567	3,465,683	3,039	347	$90,739	$2,167.70	$283.94
1982	5,863	1,015	36,429	763	882	7.6	250,888	75,739	3,514,761	3,110	353	$105,094	$2,493.09	$326.68
1983	5,843	1,021	36,201	750	869	7.6	213,995	75,471	3,490,629	3,102	357	$116,632	$2,775.55	$368.01
1984	5,814	1,020	35,202	703	824	7.3	216,474	75,587	3,456,467	3,023	367	$123,550	$2,984.00	$409.85
1985	5,784	1,003	33,501	650	780	7.1	222,773	74,899	3,521,296	3,003	385	$130,700	$3,238.94	$459.57
1986	5,728	982	32,410	631	774	7.1	234,270	73,688	3,584,530	3,032	392	$140,907	$3,529.60	$499.57
1987	5,659	961	31,633	624	780	7.2	247,704	72,516	3,602,416	3,120	400	$152,909	$3,848.79	$536.96
1988	5,579	949	31,480	622	795	7.2	271,436	70,361	3,706,748	3,209	404	$168,941	$4,194.39	$581.08
1989	5,497	936	31,141	619	805	7.3	287,909	69,436	3,831,051	3,307	411	$185,204	$4,572.23	$630.59
1990	5,420	929	31,203	620	820	7.3	302,691	68,443	3,958,646	3,423	417	$203,927	$4,929.93	$681.52
1991	5,370	926	31,084	612	828	7.2	323,202	67,440	3,965,489	3,539	427	$225,230	$5,345.63	$745.37
1992	5,321	923	31,053	606	832	7.1	349,397	67,095	3,925,024	3,624	436	$248,318	$5,788.52	$815.99
1993	5,289	921	30,770	593	834	7.0	368,358	66,060	3,870,392	3,681	441	$266,382	$6,120.94	$874.98
1994	5,256	904	30,739	569	814	6.8	384,880	65,728	3,809,367	3,697	454	$276,148	$6,230.33	$929.65
1995	5,220	874	30,966	549	811	6.5	415,710	64,742	3,764,756	3,718	458	$286,073	$6,220.54	$966.79
1996	5,160	864	31,116	531	800	6.2	440,845	63,646	3,723,907	3,728	466	$293,920	$6,225.95	$1,005.45
1997	5,082	855	31,595	529	813	6.1	450,907	63,247	3,742,240	3,794	467	$306,088	$6,266.24	$1,031.68
1998	5,039	842	31,830	527	821	6.0	474,366	62,162	3,726,234	3,835	467	$319,035	$6,387.53	$1,064.93
1999	4,977	831	32,377	527	835	5.9	495,850	61,534	3,760,295	3,840	460	$335,405	$6,512.44	$1,101.47
2000	4,934	825	33,089	527	850	5.8	522,970	60,845	3,880,166	3,916	461	$356,757	$6,650.68	$1,147.99
2001	4,927	828	33,834	534	866	5.8	539,316	60,454	3,873,395	3,990	461	$383,911	$6,979.29	$1,216.04
2002	4,949	823	34,501	541	887	5.7	557,336	59,974	3,870,191	4,072	459	$416,791	$7,353.17	$1,288.63
2003	4,918	815	34,800	540	895	5.7	563,804	59,662	3,915,842	4,112	459	$450,403	$7,798.19	$1,378.78
2004	4,942	810	35,098	542	910	5.6	573,126	58,710	3,931,508	4,151	456	$481,517	$8,168.06	$1,449.90
2005	4,956	804	35,265	542	930	5.6	587,296	58,195	3,987,766	4,260	458	$516,172	$8,538.30	$1,521.58
2006	4,947	805	35,403	540	940	5.6	599,597	57,832	4,075,193	4,347	462	$552,276	$8,972.85	$1,610.76
2007	4,915	803	35,370	535	944	5.5	603,411	57,546	4,077,962	4,468	473	$583,550	$9,377.82	$1,694.38
2008	5,026	810	35,776	538	963	5.5	624,185	57,301	4,073,724	4,552	473	$626,823	$9,789.69	$1,780.45
2009	5,023	807	35,603	529	973	5.4	643,420	57,302	3,960,432	4,594	472	$657,242	$10,042.56	$1,851.44
2010	4,995	806	35,160	520	974	5.4	651,617	56,610	3,818,399	4,603	473	$678,254	$10,316.07	$1,908.59
2011	4,983	799	34,852	514	983	5.4	657,071	56,290	3,730,342	4,654	473	$702,822	$10,542.09	$1,959.69
2012	5,010	802	34,438	508	992	5.4	675,223	55,987	3,715,479	4,732	477	$757,213	$11,222.23	$2,089.07
2013	4,986	797	33,625	501	963	5.4	678,203	56,342	3,699,411	4,788	497	$782,360	$11,653.75	$2,155.63
2014	4945	789	33,093	496	1,004	5.5	693,346	55,824	3,735,593	4,758	474	$809,361	$12,016.89	$2,210.78

Table 1 (Continued)

CLASSIFICATION	YEAR	HOSPITALS	BEDS (in thousands)	ADMISSIONS (in thousands)	AVERAGE DAILY CENSUS (in thousands)	ADJUSTED AVERAGE DAILY CENSUS (in thousands)	AVERAGE STAY (days)	OUTPATIENT VISITS (in thousands)	NEWBORNS Bassinets	NEWBORNS Births	FTE PERSONNEL Number (in thousands)	FTE PERSONNEL Per 100 Adjusted Census	EXPENSES Amount (In Millions of dollars)	EXPENSES Adjusted per Inpatient Stay (dollars)	EXPENSES Adjusted per Inpatient Day (dollars)
Total community hospitals	1975	5,875	942	33,435	706	798	7.7	190,672	83,829	2,998,552	2,392	300	$38,962	$1,030.34	$133.81
	1976	5,857	956	33,979	713	810	7.7	201,247	82,296	2,962,216	2,475	306	$45,240	$1,176.25	$152.76
	1979	5,842	984	35,099	727	833	7.6	198,778	77,266	3,287,012	2,756	331	$66,004	$1,641.67	$217.34
	1980	5,830	988	36,143	747	857	7.6	202,310	77,522	3,408,482	2,873	335	$76,851	$1,851.04	$245.12
	1981	5,813	1,003	36,438	763	873	7.6	202,768	76,561	3,465,401	3,033	347	$90,572	$2,171.20	$284.33
	1982	5,801	1,012	36,379	762	878	7.6	248,124	75,733	3,514,457	3,103	353	$104,876	$2,500.52	$327.37
	1983	5,783	1,018	36,152	749	864	7.6	210,044	75,465	3,490,254	3,096	358	$116,438	$2,789.18	$369.49
	1984	5,759	1,017	35,155	702	820	7.3	211,961	75,581	3,456,308	3,017	368	$123,336	$2,995.38	$411.10
	1985	5,732	1,001	33,449	649	777	7.1	218,716	74,893	3,521,135	2,997	386	$130,499	$3,244.74	$460.19
	1986	5,678	978	32,379	629	770	7.1	231,912	73,682	3,584,408	3,025	393	$140,654	$3,532.51	$500.81
	1987	5,611	958	31,601	622	776	7.2	245,524	72,510	3,602,296	3,114	401	$152,585	$3,850.16	$538.96
	1988	5,533	947	31,453	620	787	7.2	269,129	70,325	3,706,402	3,205	407	$168,722	$4,206.73	$586.33
	1989	5,455	933	31,116	618	796	7.2	285,712	69,405	3,830,615	3,303	415	$184,898	$4,587.87	$636.96
	1990	5,384	927	31,181	619	813	7.2	301,329	68,412	3,958,263	3,420	421	$203,693	$4,946.68	$686.83
	1991	5,342	924	31,064	611	820	7.2	322,048	67,434	3,965,396	3,535	431	$225,023	$5,359.56	$752.10
	1992	5,292	921	31,034	604	827	7.1	348,522	67,089	3,924,944	3,620	437	$248,095	$5,794.43	$819.83
	1993	5,261	919	30,748	592	828	7.0	366,885	66,054	3,870,376	3,677	444	$266,089	$6,132.06	$880.52
	1994	5,229	902	30,718	568	812	6.7	382,924	65,722	3,809,367	3,692	455	$275,779	$6,229.83	$930.71
	1995	5,194	873	30,945	548	809	6.5	414,345	64,736	3,764,698	3,714	459	$285,588	$6,215.51	$967.69
	1996	5,134	862	31,099	531	799	6.2	439,863	63,640	3,723,871	3,725	466	$293,755	$6,224.94	$1,006.14
	1997	5,057	853	31,577	528	811	6.1	450,140	63,241	3,742,191	3,790	467	$305,763	$6,261.93	$1,032.70
	1998	5,015	840	31,812	525	819	6.0	474,190	62,156	3,726,233	3,831	468	$318,834	$6,385.99	$1,066.96
	1999	4,956	830	32,359	526	833	5.9	495,346	61,528	3,760,295	3,838	461	$335,246	$6,511.72	$1,102.61
	2000	4,915	824	33,089	526	849	5.8	521,404	60,839	3,880,166	3,911	461	$356,564	$6,648.82	$1,149.40
	2001	4,908	826	33,814	533	865	5.7	538,480	60,448	3,873,395	3,987	461	$383,735	$6,979.53	$1,217.27
	2002	4,927	821	34,478	540	886	5.7	556,404	59,974	3,870,191	4,069	459	$416,591	$7,354.60	$1,289.87
	2003	4,895	813	34,783	539	894	5.7	563,186	59,662	3,915,842	4,109	460	$450,124	$7,796.41	$1,379.48
	2004	4,919	808	35,086	541	909	5.6	571,569	58,710	3,931,508	4,148	456	$481,247	$8,165.55	$1,450.35
	2005	4,936	802	35,239	540	929	5.6	584,429	58,195	3,987,766	4,257	458	$515,740	$8,534.90	$1,522.42
	2006	4,927	803	35,378	538	939	5.6	599,553	57,832	4,075,193	4,343	463	$551,835	$8,970.31	$1,612.23
	2007	4,897	801	35,346	533	943	5.5	603,300	57,546	4,077,962	4,465	474	$583,252	$9,377.17	$1,696.10
	2008	5,010	808	35,761	536	962	5.5	624,098	57,301	4,073,724	4,550	473	$626,577	$9,788.25	$1,782.28
	2009	5,008	806	35,527	528	970	5.4	641,953	57,282	3,959,605	4,585	472	$656,156	$10,045.15	$1,852.59
	2010	4,985	805	35,149	520	973	5.4	651,424	56,610	3,818,399	4,600	473	$677,968	$10,313.44	$1,909.64
	2011	4,973	797	34,843	513	982	5.4	656,079	56,290	3,730,342	4,650	473	$702,091	$10,532.52	$1,959.58
	2012	4,999	801	34,422	507	991	5.4	674,971	55,987	3,715,479	4,731	477	$756,917	$11,220.70	$2,090.01
	2013	4,974	796	33,609	500	962	5.4	677,951	56,342	3,699,411	4,786	497	$782,035	$11,650.90	$2,156.94
	2014	4,926	787	33,067	494	1,002	5.5	693,107	55,824	3,735,593	4,755	474	$808,869	$12,015.42	$2,212.22

Table 1 (Continued)

CLASSIFICATION: Nongovernment not-for-profit community hospitals

YEAR	HOSPITALS	BEDS (in thousands)	ADMISSIONS (in thousands)	AVERAGE DAILY CENSUS (in thousands)	ADJUSTED AVERAGE DAILY CENSUS (in thousands)	AVERAGE STAY (days)	OUTPATIENT VISITS (in thousands)	NEWBORNS Bassinets	NEWBORNS Births	FTE PERSONNEL Number (in thousands)	FTE PERSONNEL Per 100 Adjusted Census	EXPENSES Amount (In Millions of dollars)	EXPENSES Adjusted per Inpatient Stay (dollars)	EXPENSES Adjusted per Inpatient Day (dollars)
1975	3,339	658	23,722	510	574	7.8	131,435	57,496	2,131,057	1,712	298	$27,938	$1,040.21	$133.36
1976	3,345	670	24,082	517	586	7.9	140,914	56,442	2,100,917	1,791	306	$32,764	$1,208.23	$152.94
1979	3,330	690	24,874	528	603	7.7	139,565	52,859	2,308,548	1,999	332	$47,937	$1,684.40	$218.06
1980	3,322	692	25,566	542	621	7.7	142,156	52,659	2,389,478	2,086	336	$55,780	$1,901.64	$245.74
1981	3,340	706	25,945	555	636	7.8	143,380	52,302	2,455,033	2,213	399	$66,267	$2,225.17	$285.64
1982	3,338	712	25,898	553	637	7.8	176,245	51,566	2,483,345	2,265	355	$76,806	$2,572.93	$330.41
1983	3,347	718	25,827	544	629	7.7	150,839	51,649	2,465,604	2,270	362	$85,637	$2,868.80	$373.78
1984	3,351	716	25,236	512	598	7.4	153,281	51,491	2,446,540	2,222	372	$90,814	$3,072.51	$415.04
1985	3,349	707	24,179	476	569	7.2	158,953	51,424	2,507,288	2,216	389	$96,150	$3,307.41	$462.69
1986	3,323	689	23,483	460	563	7.2	167,633	50,885	2,547,170	2,241	398	$103,524	$3,589.64	$503.64
1987	3,274	673	22,937	455	566	7.2	177,413	50,133	2,557,294	2,298	406	$112,325	$3,914.23	$543.67
1988	3,242	668	22,939	456	577	7.3	195,363	48,828	2,653,794	2,373	412	$124,703	$4,272.95	$591.13
1989	3,220	661	22,792	455	584	7.3	209,191	48,305	2,751,426	2,454	420	$136,889	$4,649.22	$642.45
1990	3,191	657	22,878	455	596	7.3	221,073	47,441	2,833,204	2,533	424	$150,673	$5,001.24	$692.36
1991	3,175	656	22,964	451	603	7.2	238,204	47,229	2,845,995	2,624	435	$166,806	$5,393.30	$758.21
1992	3,173	656	23,056	445	606	7.1	257,887	47,185	2,846,386	2,692	443	$183,793	$5,808.80	$828.44
1993	3,154	651	22,749	432	602	6.9	270,138	46,214	2,802,164	2,711	451	$197,187	$6,177.69	$897.70
1994	3,139	637	22,704	413	589	6.6	282,653	46,381	2,792,116	2,719	462	$204,219	$6,256.72	$950.31
1995	3,092	610	22,557	393	578	6.4	303,851	45,198	2,725,641	2,702	468	$209,614	$6,279.17	$994.39
1996	3,045	598	22,542	379	567	6.1	320,746	44,650	2,683,750	2,711	478	$215,950	$6,344.05	$1,042.04
1997	3,000	591	22,905	376	575	6.0	330,215	44,484	2,698,086	2,765	481	$225,287	$6,392.74	$1,074.26
1998	3,026	588	23,282	377	587	5.9	352,114	44,087	2,715,958	2,834	483	$237,978	$6,525.68	$1,110.50
1999	3,012	587	23,871	381	605	5.8	370,784	44,172	2,746,453	2,862	473	$251,534	$6,607.51	$1,139.89
2000	3,003	583	24,452	382	618	5.7	393,168	43,655	2,833,615	2,919	472	$267,051	$6,717.48	$1,182.32
2001	2,998	585	24,983	385	628	5.6	404,901	43,640	2,829,691	2,971	473	$287,250	$7,051.76	$1,255.25
2002	3,025	582	25,425	391	646	5.6	416,910	43,241	2,820,159	3,039	471	$312,726	$7,457.84	$1,328.81
2003	2,984	575	25,668	389	647	5.5	424,215	42,965	2,854,764	3,059	473	$337,696	$7,904.93	$1,429.62
2004	2,967	568	25,757	388	655	5.5	430,262	41,968	2,844,617	3,077	470	$359,414	$8,266.64	$1,501.09
2005	2,958	561	25,881	388	667	5.5	441,653	41,585	2,876,677	3,155	473	$385,993	$8,670.83	$1,585.34
2006	2,919	559	25,798	385	671	5.4	453,501	40,888	2,905,275	3,207	478	$412,868	$9,189.58	$1,685.62
2007	2,913	554	25,752	380	673	5.4	455,825	40,681	2,907,002	3,286	488	$436,319	$9,592.93	$1,776.06
2008	2,923	557	25,899	380	683	5.4	469,804	40,567	2,901,854	3,340	489	$468,080	$10,080.50	$1,875.78
2009	2,918	556	25,783	375	690	5.3	485,935	40,467	2,822,527	3,369	488	$492,853	$10,379.09	$1,956.71
2010	2,904	556	25,532	368	691	5.3	494,178	39,946	2,750,163	3,388	490	$510,744	$10,651.81	$2,025.05
2011	2,903	548	25,185	362	694	5.2	496,643	39,651	2,692,577	3,427	494	$528,303	$10,932.55	$2,088.05
2012	2,894	545	24,751	354	697	5.2	512,237	39,778	2,684,600	3,477	499	$563,960	$11,563.17	$2,214.26
2013	2,904	544	24,319	350	683	5.3	516,162	40,180	2,687,441	3,500	513	$585,470	$12,000.35	$2,288.77
2014	2,870	535	23,742	344	704	5.3	525,424	39,497	2,707,766	3,494	496	$602,571	$12,384.99	$2,345.55

Table 1 (Continued)

CLASSIFICATION	YEAR	HOSPITALS	BEDS (in thousands)	ADMISSIONS (in thousands)	AVERAGE DAILY CENSUS (in thousands)	ADJUSTED AVERAGE DAILY CENSUS (in thousands)	AVERAGE STAY (days)	OUTPATIENT VISITS (in thousands)	NEWBORNS Bassinets	NEWBORNS Births	FTE PERSONNEL Number (in thousands)	FTE PERSONNEL Per 100 Adjusted Census	EXPENSES Amount (in Millions of dollars)	EXPENSES Adjusted per Inpatient Stay (dollars)	EXPENSES Adjusted per Inpatient Day (dollars)
Investor-owned (for-profit) community hospitals	1975	775	73	2,646	48	53	6.6	7,713	4,062	141,392	139	263	$2,561	$876.48	$132.80
	1976	752	76	2,734	50	54	6.6	8,048	4,044	144,751	147	272	$3,085	$1,031.91	$156.35
	1979	727	83	2,963	53	59	6.6	9,289	4,110	174,843	174	300	$4,820	$1,476.42	$225.87
	1980	730	87	3,165	57	62	6.5	9,696	4,439	199,722	189	304	$5,847	$1,675.85	$257.12
	1981	729	88	3,239	58	63	6.5	9,961	4,523	207,405	203	322	$6,856	$1,952.56	$299.02
	1982	748	91	3,316	60	66	6.6	13,193	4,736	219,675	212	320	$8,177	$2,224.75	$340.03
	1983	757	94	3,299	59	66	6.5	10,389	5,039	228,883	213	323	$9,208	$2,517.53	$385.42
	1984	786	100	3,314	57	64	6.3	11,090	5,807	242,088	214	335	$10,251	$2,748.51	$438.30
	1985	805	104	3,242	54	63	6.1	12,378	6,117	266,839	221	350	$11,486	$3,033.06	$500.48
	1986	834	107	3,231	54	65	6.1	14,896	6,305	291,112	229	354	$12,987	$3,341.79	$552.40
	1987	828	106	3,157	54	66	6.2	16,566	6,391	306,492	242	367	$14,067	$3,617.19	$585.01
	1988	790	104	3,090	53	66	6.2	17,926	6,254	308,828	249	379	$15,545	$4,022.77	$649.33
	1989	769	102	3,071	53	67	6.3	19,341	6,354	325,711	261	390	$17,240	$4,406.20	$707.90
	1990	749	101	3,066	54	69	6.4	20,110	6,261	340,555	273	396	$18,822	$4,727.27	$751.55
	1991	738	100	3,016	52	69	6.3	21,174	6,358	359,115	281	409	$20,516	$5,133.53	$820.19
	1992	723	99	2,969	51	69	6.3	22,900	6,519	357,776	285	412	$22,496	$5,548.24	$888.73
	1993	717	99	2,946	51	69	6.2	24,936	6,395	363,358	289	417	$23,077	$5,643.21	$914.39
	1994	719	101	3,035	50	70	6.1	26,443	6,329	354,477	302	434	$23,445	$5,528.91	$923.90
	1995	752	106	3,428	55	77	5.8	31,940	7,164	408,339	343	443	$26,653	$5,425.20	$946.99
	1996	759	109	3,684	56	82	5.6	37,347	7,441	444,697	359	437	$28,385	$5,207.44	$945.49
	1997	797	115	3,953	60	89	5.5	40,919	8,026	465,919	385	433	$31,179	$5,218.69	$961.96
	1998	771	113	3,971	60	90	5.5	42,072	7,895	466,025	383	425	$31,732	$5,262.44	$968.00
	1999	747	107	3,905	58	86	5.5	39,896	7,486	467,585	362	422	$31,179	$5,350.07	$999.03
	2000	749	110	4,141	61	90	5.4	43,378	7,792	503,497	378	418	$34,969	$5,642.18	$1,057.32
	2001	754	109	4,197	63	92	5.4	44,706	7,413	494,669	379	413	$37,348	$5,971.81	$1,121.31
	2002	766	108	4,365	64	93	5.3	45,215	7,467	496,988	380	407	$40,082	$6,161.44	$1,180.83
	2003	790	110	4,481	65	95	5.3	44,246	7,491	515,693	391	411	$43,953	$6,589.91	$1,264.50
	2004	835	113	4,599	68	100	5.4	44,962	7,763	534,503	406	406	$48,971	$7,139.13	$1,362.42
	2005	868	114	4,618	68	101	5.3	46,016	7,714	546,307	421	418	$51,833	$7,351.96	$1,412.74
	2006	890	115	4,735	68	103	5.2	44,237	8,012	574,113	423	413	$55,030	$7,422.08	$1,471.53
	2007	873	116	4,626	66	101	5.2	43,943	7,760	555,670	432	429	$56,405	$7,823.44	$1,535.98
	2008	982	121	4,839	70	109	5.3	44,897	7,791	562,711	450	414	$61,762	$7,984.62	$1,555.55
	2009	998	122	4,887	70	112	5.3	47,281	7,965	553,233	464	414	$64,367	$8,037.18	$1,573.64
	2010	1,013	125	4,925	71	113	5.3	48,201	7,968	525,427	474	420	$67,168	$8,336.16	$1,628.90
	2011	1,025	128	5,060	73	119	5.3	50,013	8,137	508,330	485	409	$70,340	$8,262.74	$1,627.65
	2012	1,068	135	5,224	77	124	5.3	53,854	8,192	530,941	515	414	$79,114	$8,860.94	$1,746.85
	2013	1,060	135	5,052	77	118	5.5	53,191	8,228	522,864	553	469	$81,552	$9,296.42	$1,791.20
	2014	1,053	136	5,119	77	130	5.5	56,299	8,478	537,273	522	401	$85,398	$9,413.69	$1,797.74

Table 1 (Continued)

State and local government community hospitals

YEAR	HOSPITALS	BEDS (in thousands)	ADMISSIONS (in thousands)	AVERAGE DAILY CENSUS (in thousands)	ADJUSTED AVERAGE DAILY CENSUS (in thousands)	AVERAGE STAY (days)	OUTPATIENT VISITS (in thousands)	NEWBORNS		FTE PERSONNEL		EXPENSES		
								Bassinets	Births	Number (in thousands)	Per 100 Adjusted Census	Amount (In Millions of dollars)	Adjusted per Inpatient Stay (dollars)	Adjusted per Inpatient Day (dollars)
1975	1,761	210	7,067	148	171	7.6	51,525	22,271	726,103	540	316	$8,463	$1,030.86	$135.64
1976	1,760	210	7,163	146	170	7.5	52,286	21,810	716,548	537	315	$9,391	$1,132.50	$151.00
1979	1,785	211	7,262	146	171	7.4	49,924	20,297	803,621	583	341	$13,247	$1,561.04	$211.89
1980	1,778	209	7,413	149	174	7.3	50,459	20,424	819,282	598	343	$15,204	$1,750.13	$238.63
1981	1,744	210	7,255	150	174	7.6	49,427	19,736	802,963	618	354	$17,449	$2,071.57	$274.25
1982	1,715	210	7,165	149	175	7.6	58,685	19,431	811,437	627	320	$19,893	$2,364.09	$311.56
1983	1,679	207	7,025	145	170	7.6	48,816	18,777	795,767	613	360	$21,593	$2,621.28	$347.56
1984	1,622	201	6,606	133	158	7.3	47,590	18,283	767,680	581	368	$22,271	$2,823.13	$385.17
1985	1,578	189	6,028	119	145	7.2	47,386	17,352	747,008	561	387	$22,863	$3,106.14	$432.84
1986	1,521	182	5,665	114	142	7.4	49,383	16,492	746,126	555	391	$24,143	$3,404.69	$466.17
1987	1,509	180	5,507	113	144	7.5	51,544	15,986	738,510	573	399	$26,192	$3,717.77	$499.33
1988	1,501	175	5,424	112	145	7.6	55,840	15,243	743,780	583	403	$28,474	$4,033.67	$538.63
1989	1,466	170	5,253	110	145	7.7	57,179	14,746	753,478	589	406	$30,769	$4,430.12	$582.15
1990	1,444	169	5,236	111	148	7.7	60,146	14,710	784,504	614	415	$34,198	$4,837.76	$634.45
1991	1,429	168	5,084	108	148	7.8	62,670	13,847	760,286	630	424	$37,701	$5,339.75	$695.89
1992	1,396	166	5,008	108	152	7.9	67,734	13,385	720,782	643	424	$41,806	$5,870.76	$753.92
1993	1,390	169	5,054	109	157	7.8	71,811	13,445	704,854	676	430	$45,825	$6,205.52	$799.73
1994	1,371	164	4,979	104	154	7.6	73,828	13,012	662,774	672	438	$48,115	$6,513.39	$858.62
1995	1,350	157	4,961	100	154	7.4	78,554	12,374	630,718	670	435	$49,322	$6,445.18	$877.85
1996	1,330	155	4,873	96	150	7.2	81,770	11,549	595,424	654	437	$49,420	$6,418.65	$903.41
1997	1,260	148	4,720	92	148	7.1	79,007	10,731	578,186	640	433	$49,298	$6,475.07	$913.62
1998	1,218	139	4,559	87	142	7.0	80,008	10,174	544,250	614	433	$49,123	$6,612.23	$949.36
1999	1,197	136	4,583	86	143	6.9	84,667	9,870	546,257	614	430	$52,534	$6,923.35	$1,006.91
2000	1,163	131	4,496	83	140	6.7	84,858	9,392	543,054	614	438	$54,544	$7,106.05	$1,063.75
2001	1,156	132	4,634	85	145	6.7	88,873	9,395	549,035	637	438	$59,137	$7,400.01	$1,113.79
2002	1,136	130	4,688	84	147	6.6	94,280	9,266	553,044	651	442	$63,783	$7,772.93	$1,188.12
2003	1,121	129	4,634	84	152	6.6	94,725	9,206	545,385	658	434	$68,475	$8,205.10	$1,237.64
2004	1,117	128	4,730	85	154	6.5	96,345	8,979	552,388	666	431	$72,861	$8,473.18	$1,291.06
2005	1,110	128	4,740	85	161	6.5	96,760	8,896	564,782	681	424	$77,914	$8,793.26	$1,329.64
2006	1,119	128	4,848	86	165	6.5	101,845	8,932	595,805	713	433	$83,974	$9,147.40	$1,400.09
2007	1,111	131	4,967	87	169	6.4	103,532	9,105	615,290	747	443	$90,528	$9,523.22	$1,472.26
2008	1,105	131	5,023	86	170	6.3	109,398	8,943	609,159	760	446	$96,735	$9,826.94	$1,552.32
2009	1,092	127	4,857	83	168	6.2	108,738	8,850	583,845	751	447	$98,937	$10,067.96	$1,611.31
2010	1,068	125	4,693	80	169	6.2	109,045	8,699	542,809	738	437	$100,056	$10,283.35	$1,624.93
2011	1,045	121	4,598	78	170	6.2	109,423	8,502	529,435	738	434	$103,448	$10,531.65	$1,666.96
2012	1,037	120	4,447	77	170	6.3	108,880	8,017	499,938	739	435	$113,843	$11,668.15	$1,831.00
2013	1,010	117	4,238	74	162	6.3	108,599	7,934	489,106	734	453	$115,013	$12,028.02	$1,878.21
2014	1,003	116	4,206	73	168	6.4	111,384	7,849	490,554	739	440	$120,900	$12,601.35	$1,974.41

Table
2

2014 U.S. Registered Hospitals: Utilization, Personnel, and Finances

Excludes U.S.-Associated Areas, Puerto Rico, and nonregistered hospitals.

CLASSIFICATION	HOSPITALS	BEDS	ADMISSIONS	INPATIENT DAYS	ADJUSTED INPATIENT DAYS	AVERAGE DAILY CENSUS	ADJUSTED AVERAGE DAILY CENSUS	AVERAGE STAY (days)	SURGICAL OPERATIONS	OUTPATIENT VISITS Emergency	OUTPATIENT VISITS Total	NEWBORNS Bassinets	NEWBORNS Births
UNITED STATES	5,627	902,202	34,878,887	213,272,027	—	584,311	—	—	27,104,158	140,226,005	802,679,956	56,481	3,787,573
6-24 Beds	533	8,750	213,777	1,048,948	—	2,871	—	—	372,030	2,316,695	16,087,843	463	18,420
25-49	1,267	41,148	1,127,968	6,637,689	—	18,184	—	—	1,434,587	9,263,282	55,327,775	3,108	128,382
50-99	1,118	79,663	2,279,406	16,636,407	—	45,590	—	—	2,114,897	12,520,540	79,400,975	5,103	236,901
100-199	1,198	172,791	6,397,206	38,484,576	—	105,442	—	—	5,095,118	29,395,175	157,210,442	12,173	698,195
200-299	627	153,425	6,105,295	35,761,085	—	97,978	—	—	4,474,682	24,995,971	127,189,420	9,874	665,865
300-399	368	126,693	5,343,992	30,480,675	—	83,502	—	—	3,705,203	19,795,763	97,235,263	8,234	595,162
400-499	206	91,502	3,988,634	22,968,608	—	62,931	—	—	2,880,798	13,668,739	85,089,859	6,017	461,565
500 or more	310	228,230	9,422,609	61,254,039	—	167,813	—	—	7,026,843	28,269,840	185,138,379	11,509	983,083
Psychiatric	413	70,209	822,082	21,560,636	—	59,079	—	—	5,711	133,720	11,005,043	0	0
Hospitals	407	67,707	821,957	20,658,957	—	56,609	—	—	5,711	133,720	11,005,043	0	0
Inst. for Intellectual Disabilities	6	2,502	125	901,679	—	2,470	—	—		0	0	0	0
General	4,596	783,946	33,201,423	180,127,507	—	493,504	—	—	26,496,535	139,646,974	774,983,948	55,689	3,734,415
Hospitals	4,584	782,839	33,184,292	179,863,065	—	492,777	—	—	26,494,592	139,612,230	774,385,870	55,689	3,734,415
Hospital units of institutions	12	1,107	17,131	264,442	—	727	—	—	1,943	34,744	598,078	0	0
TB and other respiratory diseases	1	40	67	12,669	—	35	—	—	0	0	882	0	0
Obstetrics and gynecology	9	1,501	76,958	342,314	—	937	—	—	56,925	92,992	913,406	628	48,121
Eye, ear, nose and throat	4	137	1,894	6,263	—	17	—	—	76,154	37,320	798,066	0	0
Rehabilitation	201	15,560	273,948	3,914,058	—	10,725	—	—	13,601	0	6,316,279	0	0
Orthopedic	27	1,189	53,102	183,896	—	504	—	—	124,155	20,520	974,653	0	0
Chronic Disease	4	270	1,146	49,822	—	136	—	—	38	4,104	64,564	0	0
Surgical	16	457	20,871	85,858	—	236	—	—	46,433	70,175	305,247	0	0
Cancer	13	2,314	95,560	676,382	—	1,852	—	—	94,424	26,485	4,710,472	0	0
Heart	9	573	23,617	95,048	—	259	—	—	15,799	14,778	111,666	0	0
Acute long-term care hospital	307	22,846	241,953	5,319,557	—	14,568	—	—	124,081	64,570	1,281,277	22	830
All other	27	3,160	66,266	898,017	—	2,459	—	—	50,302	114,367	1,214,453	142	4,207
Federal	213	38,893	936,269	9,652,643	—	26,453	—	—	684,585	3,723,499	100,262,948	657	51,979
Psychiatric	10	2,417	18,972	685,837	—	1,879	—	—	522	0	3,007,944	0	0
General and other special	203	36,476	917,297	8,966,806	—	24,574	—	—	684,063	3,723,499	97,255,004	657	51,979
Nonfederal	5,414	863,309	33,942,618	203,619,384	—	557,858	—	—	26,419,573	136,502,506	702,417,008	55,824	3,735,594
Psychiatric	403	67,792	803,110	20,874,799	—	57,200	—	—	5,189	133,720	7,997,099	0	0
Hospitals	397	65,290	802,985	19,973,120	—	54,730	—	—	5,189	133,720	7,997,099	0	0
Inst. for Intellectual Disabilities	6	2,502	125	901,679	—	2470	—	—		0	0	0	0
TB and other respiratory diseases	1	40	67	12,669	12,669	35	35	189.1	0	0	882	0	0
Long-term general and other special	74	7,535	57,538	2,016,840	2,500,436	5,524	6,849	35.1	12,856	41,313	1,091,631	0	1
Short-term general and other special	4,936	787,942	33,081,903	180,715,076	365,895,321	495,099	1,003,015	5.5	26,401,528	136,327,473	693,327,396	55,824	3,735,593
Hospital units of institutions	10	1,068	15,183	258,642	258,642	711	711	17		0	220,711	0	0
Community Hospitals	4926	786,874	33,066,720	180,456,434	365,636,679	494,388	1,002,304	5.5	26,401,528	136,327,473	693,106,685	55,824	3,735,593
6-24 Beds	486	7,985	185,102	884,847	4,437,338	2,420	12,164	4.8	351,605	1,984,350	11,313,761	392	13,997
25-49	1,168	37,559	1,046,146	5,773,691	19,719,274	15,818	54,100	5.5	1,394,703	8,742,707	47,870,968	2,950	116,655
50-99	934	66,092	1,925,489	13,194,044	34,676,262	36,154	95,117	6.9	1,974,956	11,661,152	59,360,812	4,897	221,599
100-199	1,013	147,188	5,849,312	30,924,198	69,525,877	84,721	190,799	5.3	4,959,493	28,692,743	133,742,204	12,078	685,159
200-299	536	131,526	5,759,469	29,553,689	57,788,125	80,969	158,367	5.1	4,362,274	24,481,880	105,763,781	9,747	658,373
300-399	328	112,909	5,189,544	26,586,603	49,020,903	72,833	134,306	5.1	3,635,366	19,517,349	85,585,404	8,234	595,162
400-499	188	83,285	3,899,412	20,633,887	38,143,207	56,535	104,501	5.3	2,833,322	13,464,443	77,947,158	6,017	461,565
500 or more	273	200,330	9,212,246	52,905,475	92,325,693	144,938	252,950	5.7	6,889,809	27,782,849	171,522,597	11,509	983,083
Nongovernment not-for-profit	2,870	534,554	23,742,043	125,622,017	256,899,659	344,166	704,334	5.3	19,148,088	95,564,846	525,423,532	39,497	2,707,766
Investor-owned (for profit)	1,053	135,909	5,118,575	28,092,187	47,503,304	76,957	130,165	5.5	3,842,967	21,195,512	56,298,754	8,478	537,273
State and Local Government	1,003	116,411	4,206,102	26,742,230	61,233,716	73,265	167,805	6.4	3,410,473	19,567,115	111,384,399	7,849	490,554

Table 2 (Continued)

CLASSIFICATION	FULL-TIME EQUIVALENT PERSONNEL					FULL-TIME EQUIVALENT TRAINEES			EXPENSES — LABOR			EXPENSES		TOTAL	
	Physicians and Dentists	Registered Nurses	Licensed Practical Nurses	Other Salaried Personnel	Total Personnel	Medical and Dental Residents	Other Trainees	Total Trainees	Payroll (in thousands)	Employee Benefits (in thousands)	Total (in thousands)	Percent of Total	Amount (in thousands)	Adjusted per Admission	Adjusted per Inpatient Day
UNITED STATES	156,326	1,505,806	105,825	3,545,989	5,313,946	119,405	13,641	133,046	$348,678,459	$94,143,809	$442,822,267	49.6	$892,701,370	—	—
6-24 Beds	2,122	15,410	3,452	54,915	75,899	67	66	133	$4,068,260	$1,036,647	$5,104,907	49.4	$10,326,608	—	—
25-49	7,520	60,928	10,525	186,644	265,617	437	634	1,071	$14,766,407	$3,952,676	$18,719,083	51	$36,674,855	—	—
50-99	11,200	100,741	13,498	279,810	405,249	923	415	1,338	$23,859,220	$6,236,172	$30,095,392	51	$58,991,442	—	—
100-199	23,072	249,796	19,011	611,902	903,781	9,348	2,573	11,921	$57,533,381	$15,341,463	$72,874,844	50	$145,783,011	—	—
200-299	23,702	242,780	23,379	551,567	841,428	11,476	2,079	13,555	$55,432,505	$14,576,491	$70,008,997	49.8	$140,707,705	—	—
300-399	16,797	214,208	11,612	469,975	712,592	11,056	1,365	12,421	$47,306,821	$13,070,605	$60,377,426	49	$123,248,254	—	—
400-499	15,495	170,013	7,481	366,649	559,638	17,101	970	18,071	$38,960,318	$10,629,768	$49,590,086	48.7	$101,740,935	—	—
500 or more	56,418	451,930	16,867	1,024,527	1,549,742	68,997	5,539	74,536	$106,751,546	$29,299,987	$136,051,533	49.4	$275,228,562	—	—
Psychiatric	4,212	26,316	6,348	142,560	179,436	372	425	797	$9,593,227	$3,282,229	$12,875,456	71.3	$18,059,740	—	—
Hospitals	4,192	26,115	6,022	136,773	173,102	372	336	708	$9,331,040	$3,158,583	$12,489,624	71	$17,597,612	—	—
Inst. for Intellectual Disabilities	20	201	326	5,787	6,334	0	89	89	$262,187	$123,646	$385,832	83.5	$462,128	—	—
General	146,444	1,425,599	93,498	3,246,500	4,912,041	117,574	12,083	129,657	$324,873,125	$87,188,603	$412,061,727	49.1	$839,792,790	—	—
Hospitals	146,238	1,425,331	93,304	3,244,880	4,909,753	117,568	12,080	129,648	$324,706,530	$87,152,151	$411,858,681	49.1	$839,361,058	—	—
Hospital units of institutions	206	268	194	1,620	2,288	6	3	9	$166,595	$36,452	$203,047	47	$431,732	—	—
TB and other respiratory diseases	0	23	18	108	149	0	0	0	$6,595	$1,884	$8,478	74.2	$11,429	—	—
Obstetrics and gynecology	164	3,184	36	5,148	8,532	58	0	58	$619,337	$165,175	$784,512	47.1	$1,665,314	—	—
Eye, ear, nose and throat	248	418	16	2,614	3,296	84	47	131	$187,323	$51,718	$239,041	49.9	$478,782	—	—
Rehabilitation	741	12,541	1,582	43,701	58,565	241	37	278	$3,055,924	$718,253	$3,774,177	56.2	$6,712,755	—	—
Orthopedic	477	2,316	117	7,650	10,560	61	6	67	$884,513	$255,971	$1,140,484	48.7	$2,343,595	—	—
Chronic Disease	10	129	12	826	977	0	2	2	$55,527	$21,870	$77,398	64.2	$120,511	—	—
Surgical	23	919	40	1,777	2,759	0	0	0	$156,128	$37,375	$193,503	33.7	$574,018	—	—
Cancer	3,057	10,734	214	38,332	52,337	899	932	1,831	$4,026,165	$1,163,355	$5,189,519	48.2	$10,763,924	—	—
Heart	20	1,027	51	1,714	2,812	1	3	4	$182,813	$46,319	$229,132	39.3	$583,068	—	—
Acute long-term care hospital	333	18,666	3,544	44,186	66,729	7	4	11	$3,918,574	$882,979	$4,801,553	53.4	$8,990,335	—	—
All other	597	3,934	349	10,873	15,753	108	102	210	$1,119,210	$328,078	$1,447,288	55.6	$2,605,110	—	—
Federal	29,576	78,488	26,163	235,025	369,252	9,809	4,794	14,603	$28,302,180	$7,775,050	$36,077,230	56.1	$64,269,859	—	—
Psychiatric	640	2,068	666	9,154	12,528	109	117	226	$895,566	$267,600	$1,163,166	65.6	$1,772,144	—	—
General and other special	28,936	76,420	25,497	225,871	356,724	9,700	4,677	14,377	$27,406,615	$7,507,449	$34,914,064	55.9	$62,497,715	—	—
Nonfederal	126,750	1,427,318	79,662	3,310,964	4,944,694	109,596	8,847	118,443	$320,376,279	$86,368,759	$406,745,037	49.1	$828,431,511	—	—
Psychiatric	3,572	24,248	5,682	133,406	166,908	263	308	571	$8,697,661	$3,014,629	$11,712,290	71.9	$16,287,596	$170,585	$902.14
Hospitals	3,552	24,047	5,356	127,619	160,574	263	219	482	$8,435,475	$2,890,983	$11,326,457	71.6	$15,825,468	$39,222	$1,198.30
Inst. for Intellectual Disabilities	20	201	326	5,787	6,334	0	89	89	$262,187	$123,646	$385,832	83.5	$462,128	—	—
TB and other respiratory diseases	0	23	18	108	149	0	0	0	$6,595	$1,884	$8,478	74.2	$11,429	—	—
Long-term general and other special	316	4,594	811	16,142	21,863	24	6	30	$1,379,590	$384,922	$1,764,512	58.9	$2,996,276	$12,016.68	$2,211.39
Short-term general and other special	122,862	1,398,453	73,151	3,161,308	4,755,774	109,309	8,533	117,842	$310,292,433	$82,967,325	$393,259,757	48.6	$809,136,209	$17,585.46	$1,032.31
Hospital units of institutions	115	107	107	565	894	0	0	0	$89,000	$17,800	$106,800	40	$267,000	$12,015.42	$2,212.22
Community Hospitals	122,747	1,398,346	73,044	3,160,743	4,754,880	109,309	8,533	117,842	$310,203,433	$82,949,525	$393,152,957	48.6	$808,869,209	$8,692.49	$1,895.95
6-24 Beds	1,216	13,518	2,604	42,512	59,850	5	31	36	$3,164,411	$816,922	$3,981,333	47.3	$8,412,990	$8,405.41	$1,720.80
25-49	5,965	56,938	9,440	170,100	242,443	281	620	901	$13,562,643	$3,553,210	$17,115,853	50.4	$33,932,959	$9,058.80	$1,832.41
50-99	6,532	83,982	8,560	186,176	325,250	640	239	879	$18,999,786	$4,863,951	$23,863,736	50.2	$47,538,779	$9,841.49	$2,126.43
100-199	15,992	223,794	14,738	527,348	781,872	6,104	634	6,738	$49,024,104	$12,832,023	$61,856,128	48.6	$127,400,142	$10,926.75	$2,329.10
200-299	15,679	218,595	10,442	474,173	718,889	8,452	448	8,900	$47,236,249	$12,569,897	$59,806,146	48.7	$122,882,214	$11,922.56	$2,520.39
300-399	13,115	202,536	7,961	421,858	645,470	10,821	893	11,714	$43,538,470	$11,694,690	$55,233,160	48.4	$114,174,423	$13,370.89	$2,798.70
400-499	12,947	163,535	5,849	344,280	526,611	15,779	760	16,539	$36,396,181	$9,851,074	$46,247,255	48.1	$96,135,583	$16,040.12	
500 or more	51,301	435,448	13,450	954,296	1,454,495	67,227	4,908	72,135	$98,281,589	$26,767,758	$125,049,347	48.4	$298,392,121		
Nongovernment not-for-profit	100,456	1,018,317	43,875	2,330,867	3,493,515	77,422	6,679	84,101	$231,186,876	$61,133,087	$292,319,963	48.5	$602,570,590	$12,384.99	$2,345.55
Investor-owned (for profit)	4,671	179,821	12,518	325,317	522,327	5,349	145	5,494	$31,423,394	$7,088,622	$38,512,016	45.1	$85,398,401	$9,413.69	$1,797.74
State and Local Government	17,620	200,208	16,651	504,559	739,038	26,558	1,709	28,247	$47,593,163	$14,727,816	$62,320,979	51.5	$120,900,219	$12,601.35	$1,974.41

Tables 3–6

Total U.S.

TABLE 3

TOTAL UNITED STATES

U.S. Registered Community Hospitals
(Nonfederal, short-term general and other special hospitals)

Overview 2010–2014

	2014	2013	2012	2011	2010
TOTAL U.S. Community Hospitals............	**4,926**	**4,974**	**4,999**	**4,973**	**4,985**
Bed Size Category					
6-24	486	469	462	445	424
25-49	1,168	1,186	1,192	1,177	1,167
50-99	934	959	954	955	970
100-199	1,013	995	1,012	1,005	1,029
200-299	536	571	570	582	585
300-399	328	334	348	353	352
400-499	188	183	189	184	185
500 + ...	273	277	272	272	273
Location					
Hospitals Urban.........................	3,071	3,003	3,019	2,989	2,998
Hospitals Rural	1,855	1,971	1,980	1,984	1,987
Control					
State and Local Government...............	1,003	1,010	1,037	1,045	1,068
Not for Profit	2,870	2,904	2,894	2,903	2,904
Investor owned	1,053	1,060	1,068	1,025	1,013
Physician Models					
Independent Practice Association	483	473	496	514	563
Group Practice without Walls...............	195	185	165	161	159
Open Physician-Hospital Organization	578	597	620	622	630
Closed Physician-Hospital Organization	226	230	219	210	203
Management Service Organization	395	423	441	446	454
Integrated Salary Model...................	1,889	1,886	1,844	1,795	1,728
Equity Model	93	99	84	76	80
Foundation..............................	284	299	269	263	261
Insurance Products					
Health Maintenance Organization	714	698	627	640	614
Preferred Provider Organization.............	687	676	576	744	740
Indemnity Fee for Service	271	240	210	253	260
Managed Care Contracts					
Health Maintenance Organization	2,660	2,655	2,697	2,665	2,677
Preferred Provider Organization.............	2,971	3,012	3,030	3,045	3,074
Affiliations					
Hospitals in a System.....................	3,183	3,144	3,100	3,007	2,941
Hospitals in a Network	1,619	1,582	1,508	1,535	1,508
Hospitals in a Group Purchasing Organization..	3,485	3,581	3,519	3,562	3,595

TABLE 3

TOTAL UNITED STATES

U.S. Registered Community Hospitals
(Nonfederal, short-term general and other special hospitals)

Utilization, Personnel, Revenue and Expenses, Community Health Indicators 2010–2014

	2014	2013	2012	2011	2010
TOTAL FACILITY (Includes Hospital and Nursing Home Units)					
Utilization - Inpatient					
Beds	786,874	795,603	800,566	797,403	804,943
Admissions	33,066,720	33,609,083	34,422,071	34,843,085	35,149,427
Inpatient Days	180,456,434	182,370,189	185,423,035	187,072,013	189,593,349
Average Length of Stay.	5.5	5.4	5.4	5.4	5.4
Inpatient Surgeries	9,015,467	9,147,264	9,513,598	9,638,467	9,954,821
Births.	3,735,593	3,699,411	3,715,479	3,730,342	3,818,399
Utilization - Outpatient					
Emergency Outpatient Visits	136,327,473	133,611,670	133,221,030	129,461,658	127,249,317
Other Outpatient Visits.	556,779,212	544,339,450	541,750,301	526,617,284	524,174,400
Total Outpatient Visits	693,106,685	677,951,120	674,971,331	656,078,942	651,423,717
Outpatient Surgeries	17,386,061	17,418,773	17,297,633	17,269,245	17,357,177
Personnel					
Full Time RNs	1,152,496	1,120,741	1,103,906	1,071,952	1,055,118
Full Time LPNs	62,046	66,122	69,318	72,641	76,503
Part Time RNs	493,395	491,401	494,530	483,351	477,739
Part Time LPNs	22,042	24,125	25,892	26,448	29,164
Total Full Time	4,152,678	4,126,815	4,105,295	4,034,205	3,989,587
Total Part Time	1,445,935	1,453,298	1,471,619	1,446,076	1,427,136
Revenue - Inpatient					
Gross Inpatient Revenue	$1,490,571,905,696	$1,419,185,900,000	$1,355,940,500,000	$1,275,806,700,000	$1,224,790,500,000
Revenue - Outpatient					
Gross Outpatient Revenue	$1,286,154,215,073	$1,173,050,700,000	$1,075,704,400,000	$968,928,635,990	$887,419,059,972
Revenue and Expenses - Totals					
(Includes Inpatient and Outpatient)					
Total Gross Revenue	$2,776,726,120,665	$2,592,236,500,000	$2,431,645,000,000	$2,244,735,400,000	$2,112,209,600,000
Deductions from Revenue	1,963,288,605,002	1,812,842,700,000	1,669,437,800,000	1,545,016,300,000	1,435,826,300,000
Net Patient Revenue	813,437,515,663	779,393,886,769	762,207,146,496	699,719,097,711	676,383,280,857
Other Operating Revenue	51,117,414,348	50,139,467,030	47,528,382,573	43,297,884,991	41,269,017,419
Other Nonoperating Revenue	17,720,027,270	19,765,262,658	11,599,107,141	12,267,965,061	13,251,393,842
Total Net Revenue.	882,274,957,281	849,298,616,457	821,334,636,210	755,284,947,763	730,903,692,118
Total Expenses.	808,869,209,436	782,035,349,979	756,916,756,696	702,091,033,815	677,968,038,012
HOSPITAL UNIT (Excludes Separate Nursing Home Units)					
Utilization - Inpatient					
Beds	744,273	748,824	751,490	749,181	755,091
Admissions	32,899,718	33,421,331	34,217,866	34,636,454	34,935,503
Inpatient Days	167,093,881	167,637,410	169,860,722	171,803,076	173,686,925
Average Length of Stay.	5.1	5.0	5.0	5.0	5.0
Personnel					
Total Full Time.	4,118,998	4,093,683	4,068,209	4,002,112	3,955,083
Total Part Time	1,428,488	1,435,155	1,452,480	1,428,754	1,407,838
Revenue and Expenses - Totals					
(Includes Inpatient and Outpatient)					
Total Net Revenue.	$878,421,503,993	$845,194,660,817	$817,155,645,229	$751,284,115,404	$726,685,542,179
Total Expenses.	805,597,791,488	778,422,090,039	753,064,177,148	698,572,269,130	674,188,184,839
COMMUNITY HEALTH INDICATORS PER 1000 POPULATION					
Total Population (in thousands)	318,857	316,129	313,914	311,592	309,051
Inpatient					
Beds	2.5	2.5	2.6	2.6	2.6
Admissions	103.7	106.3	109.7	111.8	113.7
Inpatient Days	565.9	576.9	590.7	600.4	613.5
Inpatient Surgeries	28.3	28.9	30.3	30.9	32.2
Births.	11.7	11.7	11.8	12.0	12.4
Outpatient					
Emergency Outpatient Visits	427.6	422.6	424.4	415.5	411.7
Other Outpatient Visits.	1,746.2	1,721.9	1,725.8	1,690.1	1,696.1
Total Outpatient Visits	2,173.7	2,144.5	2,150.2	2,105.6	2,107.8
Outpatient Surgeries	54.5	55.1	55.1	55.4	56.2
Expense per Capita (per person)	$2,536.8	$2,473.8	$2,411.2	$2,253.2	$2,193.7

Total U.S.

TABLE 4

BED SIZE CATEGORY 6-24

U.S. Registered Community Hospitals
(Nonfederal, short-term general and other special hospitals)

Overview 2010–2014

	2014	2013	2012	2011	2010
Total Community Hospitals in Bed Size Category 6-24..................	**486**	**469**	**462**	**445**	**424**
Location					
Hospitals Urban...........................	143	122	120	114	113
Hospitals Rural	343	347	342	331	311
Control					
State and Local Government...............	170	170	176	178	165
Not for Profit............................	256	245	235	216	207
Investor owned	60	54	51	51	52
Physician Models					
Independent Practice Association	39	39	46	46	51
Group Practice without Walls................	16	13	12	12	10
Open Physician-Hospital Organization	32	31	31	32	29
Closed Physician-Hospital Organization	9	7	8	8	5
Management Service Organization	14	14	18	16	17
Integrated Salary Model....................	181	163	163	149	120
Equity Model.............................	2	8	9	5	3
Foundation..............................	17	15	16	14	10
Insurance Products					
Health Maintenance Organization	47	48	42	37	40
Preferred Provider Organization..............	51	49	39	44	44
Indemnity Fee for Service	18	18	13	13	13
Managed Care Contracts					
Health Maintenance Organization	195	180	181	163	156
Preferred Provider Organization..............	255	247	244	231	218
Affiliations					
Hospitals in a System.....................	221	205	207	185	172
Hospitals in a Network....................	147	145	133	138	129
Hospitals in a Group Purchasing Organization..	329	330	317	306	291

Bed Size Categories

TABLE 4

BED SIZE CATEGORY 6-24

U.S. Registered Community Hospitals
(Nonfederal, short-term general and other special hospitals)

Utilization, Personnel, Revenue and Expenses, Community Health Indicators 2010–2014

	2014	2013	2012	2011	2010
TOTAL FACILITY (Includes Hospital and Nursing Home Units)					
Utilization - Inpatient					
Beds	7,985	7,763	7,791	7,616	7,261
Admissions	185,102	189,339	197,448	197,272	198,692
Inpatient Days	884,847	862,961	879,985	888,064	854,226
Average Length of Stay	4.8	4.6	4.5	4.5	4.3
Inpatient Surgeries	41,522	38,962	41,274	35,479	36,003
Births	13,997	15,322	18,058	14,880	13,839
Utilization - Outpatient					
Emergency Outpatient Visits	1,984,350	1,955,889	1,929,787	1,702,152	1,658,487
Other Outpatient Visits	9,329,411	8,932,227	8,697,985	8,828,732	8,275,935
Total Outpatient Visits	11,313,761	10,888,116	10,627,772	10,530,884	9,934,422
Outpatient Surgeries	310,083	283,781	285,969	271,645	271,260
Personnel					
Full Time RNs	10,431	9,648	9,066	8,052	7,587
Full Time LPNs	2,157	2,258	2,044	2,104	2,113
Part Time RNs	6,172	5,692	5,508	4,752	4,701
Part Time LPNs	891	958	903	1,012	886
Total Full Time	47,948	45,873	42,797	40,408	38,328
Total Part Time	23,877	21,820	20,824	19,087	17,746
Revenue - Inpatient					
Gross Inpatient Revenue	$3,966,579,112	$3,397,090,171	$3,344,514,225	$2,808,082,491	$2,786,370,995
Revenue - Outpatient					
Gross Outpatient Revenue	$13,215,154,469	$11,459,413,010	$10,460,225,077	$8,967,777,277	$8,039,286,106
Revenue and Expenses - Totals					
(Includes Inpatient and Outpatient)					
Total Gross Revenue	$17,181,733,581	$14,856,503,181	$13,804,739,302	$11,775,859,768	$10,825,657,101
Deductions from Revenue	9,267,998,526	7,671,633,328	6,997,808,590	6,019,723,826	5,474,162,402
Net Patient Revenue	7,913,735,055	7,184,869,853	6,806,930,712	5,756,135,942	5,351,494,699
Other Operating Revenue	871,277,026	763,864,461	611,148,966	620,276,695	540,121,094
Other Nonoperating Revenue	174,678,558	143,595,341	154,545,670	107,732,522	103,852,868
Total Net Revenue	8,959,690,639	8,092,329,655	7,572,625,348	6,484,145,159	5,995,468,661
Total Expenses	8,412,989,501	7,609,006,694	6,984,976,928	6,128,099,984	5,644,509,939
HOSPITAL UNIT (Excludes Separate Nursing Home Units)					
Utilization - Inpatient					
Beds	7,961	7,733	7,738	7,610	7,225
Admissions	184,940	189,316	197,163	197,272	198,651
Inpatient Days	859,795	853,632	854,715	885,028	841,349
Average Length of Stay	4.6	4.5	4.3	4.5	4.2
Personnel					
Total Full Time	47,820	45,498	42,674	40,404	38,313
Total Part Time	23,786	21,381	20,730	19,087	17,743
Revenue and Expenses - Totals					
(Includes Inpatient and Outpatient)					
Total Net Revenue	$8,952,854,779	$8,086,815,684	$7,561,431,638	$6,483,007,236	$5,990,190,925
Total Expenses	8,407,448,861	7,606,122,912	6,979,227,864	6,127,873,361	5,642,553,901

Bed Size Categories

TABLE 4

BED SIZE CATEGORY 25-49

U.S. Registered Community Hospitals
(Nonfederal, short-term general and other special hospitals)

Overview 2010–2014

	2014	2013	2012	2011	2010
Total Community Hospitals in					
Bed Size Category 25-49	**1,168**	**1,186**	**1,192**	**1,177**	**1,167**
Location					
Hospitals Urban............................	415	414	420	403	408
Hospitals Rural	753	772	772	774	759
Control					
State and Local Government................	364	363	367	366	381
Not for Profit	569	576	574	570	547
Investor owned	235	247	251	241	239
Physician Models					
Independent Practice Association	90	87	97	96	102
Group Practice without Walls...............	35	29	25	30	32
Open Physician-Hospital Organization	73	72	79	80	82
Closed Physician-Hospital Organization	33	33	23	25	23
Management Service Organization	52	50	55	56	54
Integrated Salary Model....................	395	382	358	353	344
Equity Model	11	10	9	13	17
Foundation...............................	43	47	44	41	39
Insurance Products					
Health Maintenance Organization	113	106	90	93	86
Preferred Provider Organization.............	111	114	94	142	134
Indemnity Fee for Service	46	40	31	47	44
Managed Care Contracts					
Health Maintenance Organization	509	499	502	477	471
Preferred Provider Organization.............	637	638	636	631	636
Affiliations					
Hospitals in a System.....................	641	642	639	620	598
Hospitals in a Network....................	331	326	309	305	302
Hospitals in a Group Purchasing Organization..	783	799	780	781	791

TABLE 4

BED SIZE CATEGORY 25-49

U.S. Registered Community Hospitals
(Nonfederal, short-term general and other special hospitals)

Utilization, Personnel, Revenue and Expenses, Community Health Indicators 2010–2014

	2014	2013	2012	2011	2010
TOTAL FACILITY (Includes Hospital and Nursing Home Units)					
Utilization - Inpatient					
Beds	37,559	38,039	38,338	37,680	37,446
Admissions	1,046,146	1,087,215	1,128,446	1,173,246	1,168,665
Inpatient Days	5,773,691	5,927,960	6,029,293	6,091,172	6,116,350
Average Length of Stay	5.5	5.5	5.3	5.2	5.2
Inpatient Surgeries	218,499	226,655	235,988	241,364	256,940
Births	116,655	118,178	115,996	112,584	107,380
Utilization - Outpatient					
Emergency Outpatient Visits	8,742,707	8,584,767	8,566,426	8,170,484	7,923,353
Other Outpatient Visits	39,128,261	38,868,368	38,126,632	36,927,369	35,175,869
Total Outpatient Visits	47,870,968	47,453,135	46,693,058	45,097,853	43,099,222
Outpatient Surgeries	1,176,204	1,151,191	1,147,708	1,084,955	1,092,740
Personnel					
Full Time RNs	43,863	43,974	42,864	39,915	37,943
Full Time LPNs	7,859	8,032	8,417	8,460	8,776
Part Time RNs	26,118	25,153	24,910	23,665	22,187
Part Time LPNs	3,153	3,071	3,356	3,365	3,605
Total Full Time	198,284	200,077	201,196	194,434	187,568
Total Part Time	90,117	88,138	88,578	86,421	81,895
Revenue - Inpatient					
Gross Inpatient Revenue	$27,689,000,672	$26,991,103,197	$26,339,586,346	$23,060,034,924	$21,382,867,485
Revenue - Outpatient					
Gross Outpatient Revenue	$54,623,143,963	$51,160,634,612	$47,719,363,855	$43,836,287,394	$39,164,706,833
Revenue and Expenses - Totals					
(Includes Inpatient and Outpatient)					
Total Gross Revenue	$82,312,144,635	$78,151,737,809	$74,058,950,201	$66,896,322,318	$60,547,574,318
Deductions from Revenue	49,503,831,252	46,095,620,354	42,336,288,207	38,545,311,880	34,313,307,874
Net Patient Revenue	32,808,313,383	32,056,117,455	31,722,661,994	28,351,010,438	26,234,266,444
Other Operating Revenue	2,886,287,487	2,820,302,433	2,679,807,646	2,558,100,321	2,209,537,503
Other Nonoperating Revenue	614,271,220	629,745,342	466,597,263	465,541,424	523,520,663
Total Net Revenue	36,308,872,090	35,506,165,230	34,869,066,903	31,374,652,183	28,967,324,610
Total Expenses	33,932,958,728	33,077,261,551	32,080,809,215	29,219,811,844	27,075,731,145
HOSPITAL UNIT (Excludes Separate Nursing Home Units)					
Utilization - Inpatient					
Beds	36,136	36,683	36,965	36,335	35,924
Admissions	1,043,548	1,085,021	1,126,060	1,171,231	1,166,430
Inpatient Days	5,353,884	5,481,761	5,586,318	5,661,438	5,638,505
Average Length of Stay	5.1	5.1	5	4.8	4.8
Personnel					
Total Full Time	197,313	199,177	200,121	193,678	186,670
Total Part Time	89,487	87,448	87,785	85,897	81,286
Revenue and Expenses - Totals					
(Includes Inpatient and Outpatient)					
Total Net Revenue	$36,204,291,881	$35,403,536,439	$34,771,427,302	$31,292,864,199	$28,881,412,934
Total Expenses	33,845,511,122	32,981,475,196	31,999,027,638	29,151,001,828	27,009,348,946

Bed Size Categories

TABLE **4**

BED SIZE CATEGORY 50-99

U.S. Registered Community Hospitals
(Nonfederal, short-term general and other special hospitals)

Overview 2010–2014

	2014	2013	2012	2011	2010
Total Community Hospitals in					
Bed Size Category 50-99	**934**	**959**	**954**	**955**	**970**
Location					
Hospitals Urban	521	500	489	484	483
Hospitals Rural	413	459	465	471	487
Control					
State and Local Government	177	184	185	190	194
Not for Profit	467	475	470	478	485
Investor owned	290	300	299	287	291
Physician Models					
Independent Practice Association	52	55	61	66	84
Group Practice without Walls	22	19	21	21	21
Open Physician-Hospital Organization	88	96	98	89	93
Closed Physician-Hospital Organization	29	30	29	32	33
Management Service Organization	47	46	49	48	54
Integrated Salary Model	296	299	296	292	288
Equity Model	9	9	9	10	12
Foundation	32	35	34	35	40
Insurance Products					
Health Maintenance Organization	107	100	94	98	89
Preferred Provider Organization	122	110	98	129	128
Indemnity Fee for Service	44	37	37	40	49
Managed Care Contracts					
Health Maintenance Organization	424	423	434	426	444
Preferred Provider Organization	484	505	512	508	533
Affiliations					
Hospitals in a System	620	621	604	588	584
Hospitals in a Network	251	260	254	256	260
Hospitals in a Group Purchasing Organization . .	597	637	628	635	649

Bed Size Categories

TABLE 4

U.S. Registered Community Hospitals
(Nonfederal, short-term general and other special hospitals)

Utilization, Personnel, Revenue and Expenses, Community Health Indicators 2010–2014

	2014	2013	2012	2011	2010
TOTAL FACILITY (Includes Hospital and Nursing Home Units)					
Utilization - Inpatient					
Beds	66,092	67,892	67,879	67,844	69,470
Admissions	1,925,489	2,021,449	2,017,239	2,104,041	2,173,195
Inpatient Days	13,194,044	13,639,948	13,678,515	13,720,587	13,960,874
Average Length of Stay	6.9	6.7	6.8	6.5	6.4
Inpatient Surgeries	436,457	464,612	477,962	498,804	543,313
Births	221,599	224,180	222,207	223,326	228,035
Utilization - Outpatient					
Emergency Outpatient Visits	11,661,152	11,796,586	11,275,005	11,503,565	11,667,902
Other Outpatient Visits	47,699,660	46,326,471	45,524,947	44,622,553	46,033,464
Total Outpatient Visits	59,360,812	58,123,057	56,799,952	56,126,118	57,701,366
Outpatient Surgeries	1,538,499	1,541,697	1,507,344	1,542,936	1,592,532
Personnel					
Full Time RNs	65,846	65,776	63,278	61,781	60,774
Full Time LPNs	7,039	7,803	8,560	8,721	9,718
Part Time RNs	36,268	36,146	34,249	33,998	33,585
Part Time LPNs	3,035	3,492	3,584	3,685	4,125
Total Full Time	264,580	268,350	261,529	260,825	260,463
Total Part Time	123,100	124,962	122,577	120,605	118,372
Revenue - Inpatient					
Gross Inpatient Revenue	$60,897,389,721	$59,688,634,837	$55,035,035,760	$53,109,381,343	$52,180,741,692
Revenue - Outpatient					
Gross Outpatient Revenue	$84,425,058,692	$78,655,991,052	$69,635,311,624	$66,009,645,599	$60,748,431,980
Revenue and Expenses - Totals					
(Includes Inpatient and Outpatient)					
Total Gross Revenue	$145,322,448,309	$138,344,625,889	$124,670,347,384	$119,119,026,942	$112,929,173,672
Deductions from Revenue	96,448,247,473	90,642,831,824	79,025,510,314	76,709,358,028	71,250,437,701
Net Patient Revenue	48,874,200,836	47,701,794,065	45,644,837,070	42,409,668,914	41,678,735,971
Other Operating Revenue	2,547,669,918	2,476,450,842	1,974,942,100	1,689,476,095	1,566,850,196
Other Nonoperating Revenue	1,357,720,719	780,849,538	927,504,094	625,595,709	677,949,955
Total Net Revenue	52,779,591,473	50,959,094,445	48,547,283,264	44,724,740,718	43,923,536,122
Total Expenses	47,538,778,511	46,328,180,009	43,488,785,543	41,141,854,495	40,509,092,623
HOSPITAL UNIT (Excludes Separate Nursing Home Units)					
Utilization - Inpatient					
Beds	58,022	59,427	59,055	58,517	60,417
Admissions	1,910,191	2,006,130	1,999,782	2,086,226	2,152,715
Inpatient Days	10,722,434	11,006,139	10,929,906	10,790,706	11,108,738
Average Length of Stay	5.6	5.5	5.5	5.2	5.2
Personnel					
Total Full Time	259,351	263,494	256,240	255,669	255,262
Total Part Time	119,115	121,202	118,696	116,620	114,674
Revenue and Expenses - Totals					
(Includes Inpatient and Outpatient)					
Total Net Revenue	$52,187,481,082	$50,396,086,960	$47,999,122,812	$44,157,904,896	$43,379,453,757
Total Expenses	47,084,233,054	45,871,570,407	43,042,562,713	40,660,522,689	40,049,446,577

Bed Size Categories

TABLE 4

BED SIZE CATEGORY 100-199

U.S. Registered Community Hospitals
(Nonfederal, short-term general and other special hospitals)

Overview 2010–2014

	2014	2013	2012	2011	2010
Total Community Hospitals in					
Bed Size Category 100-199...............	1,013	995	1,012	1,005	1,029
Location					
Hospitals Urban..........................	754	711	717	707	707
Hospitals Rural	259	284	295	298	322
Control					
State and Local Government...............	128	123	135	135	149
Not for Profit	626	621	617	623	633
Investor owned	259	251	260	247	247
Physician Models					
Independent Practice Association	102	94	97	107	120
Group Practice without Walls...............	41	39	36	35	36
Open Physician-Hospital Organization	147	140	142	144	152
Closed Physician-Hospital Organization	48	45	48	51	47
Management Service Organization	88	91	106	102	103
Integrated Salary Model....................	368	354	345	343	332
Equity Model............................	25	26	21	20	17
Foundation..............................	64	71	62	59	56
Insurance Products					
Health Maintenance Organization	147	139	125	132	124
Preferred Provider Organization.............	147	142	122	142	136
Indemnity Fee for Service	69	55	52	58	52
Managed Care Contracts					
Health Maintenance Organization	583	567	566	578	587
Preferred Provider Organization.............	625	610	606	624	641
Affiliations					
Hospitals in a System.....................	727	691	686	667	655
Hospitals in a Network....................	321	293	281	280	278
Hospitals in a Group Purchasing Organization..	714	710	688	705	724

TABLE 4

BED SIZE CATEGORY 100-199

U.S. Registered Community Hospitals
(Nonfederal, short-term general and other special hospitals)

Utilization, Personnel, Revenue and Expenses, Community Health Indicators 2010–2014

	2014	2013	2012	2011	2010
TOTAL FACILITY (Includes Hospital and Nursing Home Units)					
Utilization - Inpatient					
Beds	147,188	143,760	145,556	143,843	148,090
Admissions	5,849,312	5,754,158	5,920,309	6,022,274	6,124,987
Inpatient Days	30,924,198	30,164,685	30,892,477	31,348,118	32,616,034
Average Length of Stay	5.3	5.2	5.2	5.2	5.3
Inpatient Surgeries	1,495,432	1,472,473	1,546,794	1,520,872	1,602,340
Births	685,159	654,405	658,328	677,253	706,284
Utilization - Outpatient					
Emergency Outpatient Visits	28,692,743	27,201,787	27,668,989	26,551,709	26,433,098
Other Outpatient Visits	105,049,461	96,360,321	96,096,051	94,003,431	94,469,225
Total Outpatient Visits	133,742,204	123,562,108	123,765,040	120,555,140	120,902,323
Outpatient Surgeries	3,464,061	3,419,797	3,421,257	3,466,539	3,551,479
Personnel					
Full Time RNs	179,199	168,819	167,593	162,016	163,437
Full Time LPNs	12,384	12,856	13,807	14,534	15,414
Part Time RNs	89,200	85,350	85,380	84,492	87,526
Part Time LPNs	4,702	5,199	5,356	5,653	6,135
Total Full Time	652,976	618,661	622,757	612,257	624,072
Total Part Time	271,272	261,701	265,049	265,264	270,145
Revenue - Inpatient					
Gross Inpatient Revenue	$224,322,560,387	$206,931,061,736	$196,130,283,474	$181,129,764,497	$177,873,737,781
Revenue - Outpatient					
Gross Outpatient Revenue	$238,070,878,699	$208,345,611,345	$190,830,856,203	$172,268,570,520	$160,748,748,573
Revenue and Expenses - Totals					
(Includes Inpatient and Outpatient)					
Total Gross Revenue	$462,393,439,086	$415,276,658,664	$386,961,139,677	$353,398,335,017	$338,622,486,354
Deductions from Revenue	331,553,610,396	294,786,238,076	269,772,483,763	245,217,347,870	231,276,346,434
Net Patient Revenue	130,839,828,690	120,490,420,588	117,188,655,914	108,180,987,147	107,346,139,920
Other Operating Revenue	5,908,515,946	5,523,192,766	5,062,039,669	4,265,506,812	4,194,548,704
Other Nonoperating Revenue	2,283,016,011	2,575,090,869	1,638,797,895	1,324,614,718	1,589,574,499
Total Net Revenue	139,031,360,647	128,588,704,223	123,889,493,478	113,771,108,677	113,130,263,123
Total Expenses	127,400,142,442	117,726,795,452	112,758,082,370	105,195,692,008	104,618,604,747
HOSPITAL UNIT (Excludes Separate Nursing Home Units)					
Utilization - Inpatient					
Beds	135,469	131,892	132,541	131,102	134,182
Admissions	5,812,483	5,713,320	5,876,426	5,976,691	6,074,709
Inpatient Days	27,315,765	26,497,775	26,855,548	27,367,543	28,160,867
Average Length of Stay	4.7	4.6	4.6	4.6	4.6
Personnel					
Total Full Time	645,486	611,021	613,726	604,314	614,788
Total Part Time	266,626	256,801	259,764	260,194	264,091
Revenue and Expenses - Totals					
(Includes Inpatient and Outpatient)					
Total Net Revenue	$138,178,193,223	$127,741,585,255	$122,970,772,210	$112,746,343,253	$112,109,514,588
Total Expenses	126,683,059,991	116,987,799,038	111,908,745,686	104,375,763,548	103,732,105,185

TABLE 4

BED SIZE CATEGORY 200-299

U.S. Registered Community Hospitals
(Nonfederal, short-term general and other special hospitals)

Overview 2010–2014

	2014	2013	2012	2011	2010
Total Community Hospitals in					
Bed Size Category 200-299	**536**	**571**	**570**	**582**	**585**
Location					
Hospitals Urban.	467	486	487	498	505
Hospitals Rural	69	85	83	84	80
Control					
State and Local Government.	58	57	62	58	63
Not for Profit	365	399	393	410	422
Investor owned	113	115	115	114	100
Physician Models					
Independent Practice Association	63	65	56	60	67
Group Practice without Walls.	26	28	22	23	18
Open Physician-Hospital Organization	83	91	98	108	111
Closed Physician-Hospital Organization	26	38	30	26	28
Management Service Organization	63	73	69	81	76
Integrated Salary Model	221	247	238	225	223
Equity Model	14	20	15	13	17
Foundation.	40	46	34	38	40
Insurance Products					
Health Maintenance Organization	92	106	90	95	93
Preferred Provider Organization.	82	91	77	105	105
Indemnity Fee for Service	35	38	32	37	35
Managed Care Contracts					
Health Maintenance Organization	328	358	373	379	380
Preferred Provider Organization.	341	374	383	399	402
Affiliations					
Hospitals in a System.	392	410	390	392	386
Hospitals in a Network	190	197	185	194	192
Hospitals in a Group Purchasing Organization. .	378	418	424	443	448

TABLE 4

BED SIZE CATEGORY 200-299

U.S. Registered Community Hospitals
(Nonfederal, short-term general and other special hospitals)

Utilization, Personnel, Revenue and Expenses, Community Health Indicators 2010–2014

	2014	2013	2012	2011	2010
TOTAL FACILITY (Includes Hospital and Nursing Home Units)					
Utilization - Inpatient					
Beds	131,526	140,113	139,212	141,308	142,616
Admissions	5,759,469	6,156,487	6,297,821	6,463,753	6,569,492
Inpatient Days	29,553,689	31,466,013	32,150,843	32,799,097	33,301,779
Average Length of Stay	5.1	5.1	5.1	5.1	5.1
Inpatient Surgeries	1,523,670	1,623,431	1,728,626	1,749,337	1,896,663
Births	658,373	668,891	661,428	660,610	681,848
Utilization - Outpatient					
Emergency Outpatient Visits	24,481,880	24,975,730	24,468,359	24,513,239	24,171,792
Other Outpatient Visits	81,281,901	87,945,697	87,195,255	85,387,424	86,489,482
Total Outpatient Visits	105,763,781	112,921,427	111,663,614	109,900,663	110,661,274
Outpatient Surgeries	2,838,604	2,999,018	2,963,873	3,017,123	3,001,309
Personnel					
Full Time RNs	178,755	181,464	178,938	179,617	178,567
Full Time LPNs	8,803	10,044	10,635	11,593	12,698
Part Time RNs	80,217	87,905	89,327	86,739	84,923
Part Time LPNs	3,304	3,689	4,108	4,315	5,133
Total Full Time	613,324	647,716	654,260	655,559	657,452
Total Part Time	230,745	254,023	257,126	255,998	252,299
Revenue - Inpatient					
Gross Inpatient Revenue	$248,302,339,484	$243,975,095,899	$240,835,907,576	$222,460,322,498	$216,302,711,528
Revenue - Outpatient					
Gross Outpatient Revenue	$211,646,176,712	$200,229,741,755	$185,911,616,840	$167,530,250,112	$152,845,016,955
Revenue and Expenses - Totals					
(Includes Inpatient and Outpatient)					
Total Gross Revenue	$459,948,516,196	$444,204,837,654	$426,747,524,416	$389,990,572,610	$369,147,728,483
Deductions from Revenue	335,144,597,503	316,380,880,125	300,061,387,153	272,710,512,076	254,962,232,713
Net Patient Revenue	124,803,918,693	127,823,957,529	126,686,137,263	117,280,060,534	114,185,495,770
Other Operating Revenue	6,648,909,930	6,482,336,012	5,987,888,496	5,683,916,062	5,345,831,411
Other Nonoperating Revenue	3,014,355,360	2,877,258,321	1,814,706,798	2,168,529,841	2,413,672,808
Total Net Revenue	134,467,183,983	137,183,551,862	134,488,732,557	125,132,506,437	121,944,999,989
Total Expenses	122,882,213,725	127,003,057,863	124,808,644,131	116,575,732,582	113,049,739,427
HOSPITAL UNIT (Excludes Separate Nursing Home Units)					
Utilization - Inpatient					
Beds	124,442	132,439	130,652	133,352	133,765
Admissions	5,722,377	6,114,738	6,248,381	6,414,383	6,516,545
Inpatient Days	27,364,700	29,079,526	29,421,703	30,290,801	30,497,421
Average Length of Stay	4.8	4.8	4.7	4.7	4.7
Personnel					
Total Full Time	606,969	642,090	647,761	649,600	650,650
Total Part Time	227,587	251,422	254,363	253,312	248,794
Revenue and Expenses - Totals					
(Includes Inpatient and Outpatient)					
Total Net Revenue	$133,835,590,497	$136,494,821,942	$133,703,328,242	$124,426,000,759	$121,195,426,366
Total Expenses	122,357,952,282	126,404,652,829	124,088,653,959	115,962,048,197	112,407,841,598

TABLE 4

BED SIZE CATEGORY 300-399

U.S. Registered Community Hospitals
(Nonfederal, short-term general and other special hospitals)

Overview 2010–2014

	2014	2013	2012	2011	2010
Total Community Hospitals in					
Bed Size Category 300-399	**328**	**334**	**348**	**353**	**352**
Location					
Hospitals Urban.	315	316	331	332	329
Hospitals Rural	13	18	17	21	23
Control					
State and Local Government.	29	37	37	44	41
Not for Profit	242	241	255	258	261
Investor owned	57	56	56	51	50
Physician Models					
Independent Practice Association	50	46	47	49	52
Group Practice without Walls.	20	23	21	15	15
Open Physician-Hospital Organization	65	69	67	71	66
Closed Physician-Hospital Organization	25	25	30	28	28
Management Service Organization	38	48	49	49	57
Integrated Salary Model	156	162	168	165	161
Equity Model	14	6	6	4	5
Foundation.	36	30	30	27	27
Insurance Products					
Health Maintenance Organization	72	64	60	63	61
Preferred Provider Organization.	62	55	47	65	66
Indemnity Fee for Service	22	18	14	19	18
Managed Care Contracts					
Health Maintenance Organization	243	247	254	264	263
Preferred Provider Organization.	248	250	260	273	269
Affiliations					
Hospitals in a System.	239	237	241	237	234
Hospitals in a Network	151	133	128	146	147
Hospitals in a Group Purchasing Organization. .	276	278	278	291	296

Bed Size Categories

TABLE 4

BED SIZE CATEGORY 300-399

U.S. Registered Community Hospitals
(Nonfederal, short-term general and other special hospitals)

Utilization, Personnel, Revenue and Expenses, Community Health Indicators 2010–2014

	2014	2013	2012	2011	2010
TOTAL FACILITY (Includes Hospital and Nursing Home Units)					
Utilization - Inpatient					
Beds	112,909	115,511	120,554	122,269	121,749
Admissions	5,189,544	5,343,652	5,659,683	5,850,631	5,835,325
Inpatient Days	26,586,603	27,347,329	28,628,393	29,754,662	29,931,672
Average Length of Stay	5.1	5.1	5.1	5.1	5.1
Inpatient Surgeries	1,409,981	1,421,836	1,505,394	1,577,523	1,594,088
Births	595,162	607,340	635,069	661,840	669,356
Utilization - Outpatient					
Emergency Outpatient Visits	19,517,349	18,931,461	19,494,322	19,606,197	18,788,786
Other Outpatient Visits	66,068,055	70,815,508	74,292,746	75,676,049	71,726,267
Total Outpatient Visits	85,585,404	89,746,969	93,787,068	95,282,246	90,515,053
Outpatient Surgeries	2,225,385	2,317,170	2,419,594	2,450,334	2,401,308
Personnel					
Full Time RNs	166,905	165,887	167,220	166,975	159,878
Full Time LPNs	6,918	7,556	8,157	8,862	8,875
Part Time RNs	71,258	68,700	74,735	75,111	73,727
Part Time LPNs	2,086	2,196	2,519	2,778	3,090
Total Full Time	559,496	573,637	592,655	589,570	572,775
Total Part Time	195,367	190,809	210,937	212,248	211,094
Revenue - Inpatient					
Gross Inpatient Revenue	$250,071,810,658	$240,832,001,022	$230,446,967,570	$216,619,573,502	$209,508,102,124
Revenue - Outpatient					
Gross Outpatient Revenue	$187,976,265,233	$175,534,042,359	$164,159,129,172	$149,199,860,634	$133,493,602,189
Revenue and Expenses - Totals (Includes Inpatient and Outpatient)					
Total Gross Revenue	$438,048,075,891	$416,366,043,381	$394,606,096,742	$365,819,434,136	$343,001,704,313
Deductions from Revenue	320,458,201,969	300,900,054,698	277,863,090,524	256,798,261,828	239,740,752,936
Net Patient Revenue	117,589,873,922	115,465,988,683	116,743,006,218	109,021,172,308	103,260,951,377
Other Operating Revenue	5,996,352,921	6,912,306,120	6,414,161,778	6,181,177,363	5,624,897,632
Other Nonoperating Revenue	2,179,681,513	3,455,675,896	1,472,292,314	1,684,050,046	2,187,362,723
Total Net Revenue	125,765,908,356	125,833,970,699	124,629,460,310	116,886,399,717	111,073,211,732
Total Expenses	114,174,422,976	114,313,944,143	114,103,095,511	107,750,738,297	102,319,306,727
HOSPITAL UNIT (Excludes Separate Nursing Home Units)					
Utilization - Inpatient					
Beds	108,904	110,605	115,302	116,402	115,138
Admissions	5,161,239	5,311,319	5,626,701	5,812,423	5,794,184
Inpatient Days	25,374,527	25,900,164	27,018,257	27,951,385	27,890,368
Average Length of Stay	4.9	4.9	4.8	4.8	4.8
Personnel					
Total Full Time	555,223	569,603	588,298	585,534	567,683
Total Part Time	193,985	189,117	209,136	210,406	208,623
Revenue and Expenses - Totals (Includes Inpatient and Outpatient)					
Total Net Revenue	$125,144,792,457	$125,251,711,673	$124,094,300,216	$116,327,869,334	$110,402,770,436
Total Expenses	113,703,110,583	113,842,852,106	113,626,750,271	107,307,019,085	101,715,147,145

Bed Size Categories

TABLE 4

BED SIZE CATEGORY 400-499

U.S. Registered Community Hospitals
(Nonfederal, short-term general and other special hospitals)

Overview 2010–2014

	2014	2013	2012	2011	2010
Total Community Hospitals in Bed Size Category 400-499	**188**	**183**	**189**	**184**	**185**
Location					
Hospitals Urban..........................	185	179	186	181	182
Hospitals Rural	3	4	3	3	3
Control					
State and Local Government................	31	30	29	26	28
Not for Profit...........................	138	135	142	141	139
Investor owned	19	18	18	17	18
Physician Models					
Independent Practice Association	34	30	32	31	27
Group Practice without Walls...............	15	16	14	14	13
Open Physician-Hospital Organization	33	36	44	40	35
Closed Physician-Hospital Organization	20	20	16	12	13
Management Service Organization	34	35	33	35	30
Integrated Salary Model...................	103	98	96	90	94
Equity Model	7	7	6	4	4
Foundation..............................	24	27	24	24	24
Insurance Products					
Health Maintenance Organization	48	44	38	37	38
Preferred Provider Organization..............	42	42	37	40	41
Indemnity Fee for Service	11	8	8	13	15
Managed Care Contracts					
Health Maintenance Organization	149	140	151	148	149
Preferred Provider Organization..............	149	144	152	150	147
Affiliations					
Hospitals in a System.....................	141	135	137	127	128
Hospitals in a Network....................	85	85	88	86	78
Hospitals in a Group Purchasing Organization..	162	154	159	160	158

TABLE 4

BED SIZE CATEGORY 400-499

U.S. Registered Community Hospitals
(Nonfederal, short-term general and other special hospitals)

Utilization, Personnel, Revenue and Expenses, Community Health Indicators 2010–2014

	2014	2013	2012	2011	2010
TOTAL FACILITY (Includes Hospital and Nursing Home Units)					
Utilization - Inpatient					
Beds	83,285	81,148	84,007	81,699	82,071
Admissions	3,899,412	3,750,238	3,966,019	3,862,877	3,869,124
Inpatient Days	20,633,887	20,029,447	20,755,259	20,364,896	20,521,474
Average Length of Stay	5.3	5.3	5.2	5.3	5.3
Inpatient Surgeries	1,084,572	1,038,085	1,137,327	1,150,202	1,178,350
Births	461,565	417,270	427,993	410,117	408,256
Utilization - Outpatient					
Emergency Outpatient Visits	13,464,443	12,285,620	12,993,712	11,929,789	11,546,221
Other Outpatient Visits	64,482,715	59,073,331	59,418,937	54,498,516	53,996,342
Total Outpatient Visits	77,947,158	71,358,951	72,412,649	66,428,305	65,542,563
Outpatient Surgeries	1,748,750	1,607,610	1,669,549	1,623,929	1,665,216
Personnel					
Full Time RNs	136,099	125,451	131,578	123,351	121,762
Full Time LPNs	5,063	5,246	5,571	5,525	6,176
Part Time RNs	56,071	54,284	55,526	53,067	53,293
Part Time LPNs	1,612	1,992	2,269	1,972	2,317
Total Full Time	468,458	440,221	462,528	439,370	441,431
Total Part Time	153,436	152,826	159,252	149,644	146,459
Revenue - Inpatient					
Gross Inpatient Revenue	$178,999,206,730	$165,377,218,755	$165,404,143,916	$158,709,548,655	$150,837,747,313
Revenue - Outpatient					
Gross Outpatient Revenue	$143,088,198,726	$125,422,311,131	$119,532,259,113	$105,408,223,039	$98,160,076,960
Revenue and Expenses - Totals					
(Includes Inpatient and Outpatient)					
Total Gross Revenue	$322,087,405,456	$290,799,529,886	$284,936,403,029	$264,117,771,694	$248,997,824,273
Deductions from Revenue	227,067,664,476	204,455,874,952	197,528,264,702	184,087,484,155	172,382,284,117
Net Patient Revenue	95,019,740,980	86,343,654,934	87,408,138,327	80,030,287,539	76,615,540,156
Other Operating Revenue	6,360,621,218	5,485,613,820	5,272,639,678	4,601,079,434	4,922,929,664
Other Nonoperating Revenue	2,149,108,579	2,567,834,662	1,325,875,743	1,374,562,424	1,471,629,299
Total Net Revenue	103,529,470,777	94,397,103,416	94,006,653,748	86,005,929,397	83,010,099,119
Total Expenses	96,135,582,660	87,818,900,913	87,804,964,580	80,196,968,394	77,854,509,046
HOSPITAL UNIT (Excludes Separate Nursing Home Units)					
Utilization - Inpatient					
Beds	80,282	77,123	80,458	78,997	79,722
Admissions	3,886,098	3,734,868	3,947,024	3,848,071	3,854,485
Inpatient Days	19,618,360	18,697,496	19,600,701	19,494,041	19,770,661
Average Length of Stay	5	5	5	5.1	5.1
Personnel					
Total Full Time	466,094	436,927	459,192	437,087	439,282
Total Part Time	152,150	151,242	157,372	148,452	145,585
Revenue and Expenses - Totals					
(Includes Inpatient and Outpatient)					
Total Net Revenue	$103,193,608,338	$93,975,576,086	$93,581,430,291	$85,724,707,161	$82,724,653,206
Total Expenses	95,830,792,663	87,456,206,840	87,395,944,309	79,940,658,386	77,613,265,522

TABLE **4**

BED SIZE CATEGORY 500 +

U.S. Registered Community Hospitals
(Nonfederal, short-term general and other special hospitals)

Overview 2010–2014

	2014	2013	2012	2011	2010
Total Community Hospitals in					
Bed Size Category 500 +.................	273	277	272	272	273
Location					
Hospitals Urban...........................	271	275	269	270	271
Hospitals Rural	2	2	3	2	2
Control					
State and Local Government................	46	46	46	48	47
Not for Profit	207	212	208	207	210
Investor owned	20	19	18	17	16
Physician Models					
Independent Practice Association	53	57	60	59	60
Group Practice without Walls................	20	18	14	11	14
Open Physician-Hospital Organization	57	62	61	58	62
Closed Physician-Hospital Organization	36	32	35	28	26
Management Service Organization	59	66	62	59	63
Integrated Salary Model....................	169	181	180	178	166
Equity Model............................	11	13	9	7	5
Foundation..............................	28	28	25	25	25
Insurance Products					
Health Maintenance Organization	88	91	88	85	83
Preferred Provider Organization..............	70	73	62	77	86
Indemnity Fee for Service	26	26	23	26	34
Managed Care Contracts					
Health Maintenance Organization	229	241	236	230	227
Preferred Provider Organization..............	232	244	237	229	228
Affiliations					
Hospitals in a System.....................	202	203	196	191	184
Hospitals in a Network....................	143	143	130	130	122
Hospitals in a Group Purchasing Organization..	246	255	245	241	238

TABLE 4

BED SIZE CATEGORY 500 +

U.S. Registered Community Hospitals
(Nonfederal, short-term general and other special hospitals)

Utilization, Personnel, Revenue and Expenses, Community Health Indicators 2010–2014

	2014	2013	2012	2011	2010
TOTAL FACILITY (Includes Hospital and Nursing Home Units)					
Utilization - Inpatient					
Beds	200,330	201,377	197,229	195,144	196,240
Admissions	9,212,246	9,306,545	9,235,106	9,168,991	9,209,947
Inpatient Days	52,905,475	52,931,846	52,408,270	52,105,417	52,290,940
Average Length of Stay	5.7	5.7	5.7	5.7	5.7
Inpatient Surgeries	2,805,334	2,861,210	2,840,233	2,864,886	2,847,124
Births	983,083	993,825	976,400	969,732	1,003,401
Utilization - Outpatient					
Emergency Outpatient Visits	27,782,849	27,879,830	26,824,430	25,484,523	25,059,678
Other Outpatient Visits	143,739,748	136,017,527	132,397,748	126,673,210	128,007,816
Total Outpatient Visits	171,522,597	163,897,357	159,222,178	152,157,733	153,067,494
Outpatient Surgeries	4,084,475	4,098,509	3,882,339	3,811,784	3,781,333
Personnel					
Full Time RNs	371,398	359,722	343,369	330,245	325,170
Full Time LPNs	11,823	12,327	12,127	12,842	12,733
Part Time RNs	128,091	128,171	124,895	121,527	117,797
Part Time LPNs	3,259	3,528	3,797	3,668	3,873
Total Full Time	1,347,612	1,332,280	1,267,573	1,241,782	1,207,498
Total Part Time	358,021	359,019	347,276	336,809	329,126
Revenue - Inpatient					
Gross Inpatient Revenue	$496,323,018,932	$471,993,651,262	$438,404,095,774	$417,910,035,060	$393,918,219,709
Revenue - Outpatient					
Gross Outpatient Revenue	$353,109,338,579	$322,242,954,475	$287,455,681,774	$255,708,021,415	$234,219,190,376
Revenue and Expenses - Totals					
(Includes Inpatient and Outpatient)					
Total Gross Revenue	$849,432,357,511	$794,236,605,737	$725,859,777,548	$673,618,056,475	$628,137,410,085
Deductions from Revenue	593,844,453,407	551,909,522,075	495,852,998,550	464,928,281,586	426,426,753,565
Net Patient Revenue	255,587,904,104	242,327,083,662	230,006,778,998	208,689,774,889	201,710,656,520
Other Operating Revenue	19,897,779,902	19,675,400,576	19,525,754,240	17,698,352,209	16,864,301,215
Other Nonoperating Revenue	5,947,195,310	6,735,212,689	3,798,787,364	4,517,338,377	4,283,831,027
Total Net Revenue	281,432,879,316	268,737,696,927	253,331,320,602	230,905,465,475	222,858,788,762
Total Expenses	258,392,120,893	248,158,203,354	234,887,398,418	215,882,136,211	206,896,544,358
HOSPITAL UNIT (Excludes Separate Nursing Home Units)					
Utilization - Inpatient					
Beds	193,057	192,922	188,779	186,866	188,718
Admissions	9,178,842	9,266,619	9,196,329	9,130,157	9,177,784
Inpatient Days	50,484,416	50,120,917	49,593,574	49,362,134	49,779,016
Average Length of Stay	5.5	5.4	5.4	5.4	5.4
Personnel					
Total Full Time	1,340,742	1,325,873	1,260,197	1,235,826	1,202,435
Total Part Time	355,752	356,542	344,634	334,786	327,042
Revenue and Expenses - Totals					
(Includes Inpatient and Outpatient)					
Total Net Revenue	$280,724,691,736	$267,844,526,778	$252,473,832,518	$230,125,418,566	$222,002,119,967
Total Expenses	257,685,682,932	247,271,410,711	234,023,264,708	215,047,382,036	206,018,475,965

Bed Size Categories

Census Divisions

Census Division 1

New England
Connecticut, Maine, Massachusetts, New Hampshire, Rhode Island, Vermont

Census Division 2

Middle Atlantic
New Jersey, New York, Pennsylvania

Census Division 3

South Atlantic
Delaware, District of Columbia, Florida, Georgia, Maryland, North Carolina, South Carolina, Virginia, West Virginia

Census Division 4

East North Central
Illinois, Indiana, Michigan, Ohio, Wisconsin

Census Division 5

East South Central
Alabama, Kentucky, Mississippi, Tennessee

Census Division 6

West North Central
Iowa, Kansas, Minnesota, Missouri, Nebraska, North Dakota, South Dakota

Census Division 7

West South Central
Arkansas, Louisiana, Oklahoma, Texas

Census Division 8

Mountain
Arizona, Colorado, Idaho, Montana, Nevada, New Mexico, Utah, Wyoming

Census Division 9

Pacific
Alaska, California, Hawaii, Oregon, Washington

U.S. Census Divisions

TABLE 5

U.S. CENSUS DIVISION 1: NEW ENGLAND

U.S. Registered Community Hospitals
(Nonfederal, short-term general and other special hospitals)

Overview 2010–2014

	2014	2013	2012	2011	2010
Total Community Hospitals					
in Census Division 1, New England	199	203	207	204	203
Bed Size Category					
6-24	8	7	10	10	10
25-49	43	44	43	42	39
50-99	45	45	47	40	40
100-199	54	55	51	56	59
200-299	19	23	26	27	25
300-399	14	13	15	15	14
400-499	5	5	4	3	4
500 + ...	11	11	11	11	12
Location					
Hospitals Urban.......................	144	146	149	146	145
Hospitals Rural	55	57	58	58	58
Control					
State and Local Government...............	7	6	6	4	4
Not for Profit	167	170	176	181	182
Investor owned	25	27	25	19	17
Physician Models					
Independent Practice Association	32	34	32	36	44
Group Practice without Walls...............	6	8	7	9	11
Open Physician-Hospital Organization	44	41	43	47	52
Closed Physician-Hospital Organization	9	10	12	12	14
Management Service Organization	16	17	20	21	24
Integrated Salary Model....................	87	93	101	105	107
Equity Model	5	5	6	4	4
Foundation..............................	14	12	14	16	13
Insurance Products					
Health Maintenance Organization	16	13	15	18	19
Preferred Provider Organization.............	9	9	9	14	9
Indemnity Fee for Service	3	3	4	8	6
Managed Care Contracts					
Health Maintenance Organization	111	116	119	137	141
Preferred Provider Organization.............	115	116	119	133	136
Affiliations					
Hospitals in a System.....................	105	105	102	93	89
Hospitals in a Network....................	79	77	75	80	75
Hospitals in a Group Purchasing Organization..	141	147	148	157	166

TABLE 5

U.S. CENSUS DIVISION 1: NEW ENGLAND

U.S. Registered Community Hospitals
(Nonfederal, short-term general and other special hospitals)

Utilization, Personnel, Revenue and Expenses, Community Health Indicators 2010–2014

	2014	2013	2012	2011	2010
TOTAL FACILITY (Includes Hospital and Nursing Home Units)					
Utilization - Inpatient					
Beds	33,531	34,028	34,399	33,693	33,974
Admissions	1,540,755	1,597,809	1,608,353	1,677,325	1,668,378
Inpatient Days	8,450,523	8,611,159	8,482,806	8,650,119	8,813,799
Average Length of Stay	5.5	5.4	5.3	5.2	5.3
Inpatient Surgeries	407,432	409,361	418,336	429,342	439,721
Births	147,729	146,765	146,147	159,359	152,389
Utilization - Outpatient					
Emergency Outpatient Visits	7,027,573	7,168,129	7,131,256	7,018,233	7,120,183
Other Outpatient Visits	41,324,371	41,529,159	40,756,179	40,285,469	39,615,363
Total Outpatient Visits	48,351,944	48,697,288	47,887,435	47,303,702	46,735,546
Outpatient Surgeries	950,041	949,198	960,370	954,123	1,018,591
Personnel					
Full Time RNs	48,640	47,004	46,323	46,138	44,258
Full Time LPNs	1,773	1,800	1,816	1,794	1,811
Part Time RNs	41,290	40,843	41,454	41,003	39,689
Part Time LPNs	1,051	1,203	1,370	1,361	1,359
Total Full Time	230,443	230,028	226,202	227,567	223,298
Total Part Time	124,558	122,493	126,716	128,182	123,799
Revenue - Inpatient					
Gross Inpatient Revenue	$58,025,515,968	$55,981,458,810	$52,549,975,311	$49,993,866,945	$47,986,647,777
Revenue - Outpatient					
Gross Outpatient Revenue	$68,057,938,276	$64,787,872,297	$60,296,411,970	$55,511,810,142	$52,517,753,883
Revenue and Expenses - Totals					
(Includes Inpatient and Outpatient)					
Total Gross Revenue	$126,083,454,244	$120,769,331,107	$112,846,387,281	$105,505,677,087	$100,504,401,660
Deductions from Revenue	79,336,535,611	75,150,281,353	68,108,106,958	62,731,335,770	59,098,902,583
Net Patient Revenue	46,746,918,633	45,619,049,754	44,738,280,323	42,774,341,317	41,405,499,077
Other Operating Revenue	5,201,941,863	5,170,226,128	4,894,336,432	4,641,150,617	4,151,761,895
Other Nonoperating Revenue	594,068,158	1,095,149,728	464,999,614	187,237,842	426,472,039
Total Net Revenue	52,542,928,654	51,884,425,610	50,097,616,369	47,602,729,776	45,983,733,011
Total Expenses	49,846,135,493	48,855,355,041	47,321,636,263	45,537,927,696	44,366,268,718
HOSPITAL UNIT (Excludes Separate Nursing Home Units)					
Utilization - Inpatient					
Beds	32,632	33,135	33,332	32,627	32,710
Admissions	1,537,589	1,594,828	1,605,312	1,674,145	1,662,431
Inpatient Days	8,151,517	8,301,445	8,161,998	8,384,172	8,377,660
Average Length of Stay	5.3	5.2	5.1	5	5
Personnel					
Total Full Time	229,607	229,182	224,884	226,972	222,354
Total Part Time	123,749	121,946	125,777	127,672	123,029
Revenue and Expenses - Totals					
(Includes Inpatient and Outpatient)					
Total Net Revenue	$52,459,070,954	$51,788,888,807	$49,974,043,473	$47,525,027,006	$45,855,486,664
Total Expenses	49,758,477,399	48,773,242,820	47,206,585,210	45,467,953,143	44,254,639,824
COMMUNITY HEALTH INDICATORS PER 1000 POPULATION					
Total Population (in thousands)	14,681	14,619	14,563	14,492	14,474
Inpatient					
Beds	2.3	2.3	2.4	2.3	2.3
Admissions	105.0	109.3	110.4	115.7	115.3
Inpatient Days	575.6	589.0	582.5	596.9	608.9
Inpatient Surgeries	27.8	28.0	28.7	29.6	30.4
Births	10.1	10.0	10.0	11.0	10.5
Outpatient					
Emergency Outpatient Visits	478.7	490.3	489.7	484.3	491.9
Other Outpatient Visits	2,814.9	2,840.8	2,798.7	2,779.8	2,737.0
Total Outpatient Visits	3,293.6	3,331.1	3,288.4	3,264.0	3,228.9
Outpatient Surgeries	64.7	64.9	65.9	65.8	70.4
Expense per Capita (per person)	$3,395.3	$3,342.0	$3,249.5	$3,142.2	$3,065.2

TABLE 5

U.S. CENSUS DIVISION 2: MIDDLE ATLANTIC

U.S. Registered Community Hospitals
(Nonfederal, short-term general and other special hospitals)

Overview 2010–2014

	2014	2013	2012	2011	2010
Total Community Hospitals					
in Census Division 2, Middle Atlantic.......	434	444	447	449	454
Bed Size Category					
6-24	11	10	11	9	8
25-49	35	37	36	36	38
50-99	63	63	63	66	66
100-199	109	106	107	106	102
200-299	80	90	91	91	98
300-399	52	53	52	54	53
400-499	28	27	30	33	33
500 + ...	56	58	57	54	56
Location					
Hospitals Urban..........................	360	359	362	364	367
Hospitals Rural	74	85	85	85	87
Control					
State and Local Government................	27	31	31	30	30
Not for Profit	348	353	354	362	373
Investor owned	59	60	62	57	51
Physician Models					
Independent Practice Association	63	62	61	53	54
Group Practice without Walls................	16	16	17	12	17
Open Physician-Hospital Organization	38	40	42	39	40
Closed Physician-Hospital Organization	16	15	19	15	15
Management Service Organization	52	49	52	47	51
Integrated Salary Model	187	195	182	175	172
Equity Model	8	8	7	3	2
Foundation................................	17	17	15	18	14
Insurance Products					
Health Maintenance Organization	91	97	91	90	80
Preferred Provider Organization..............	57	74	65	69	79
Indemnity Fee for Service	29	40	37	31	42
Managed Care Contracts					
Health Maintenance Organization	269	281	295	284	286
Preferred Provider Organization..............	260	277	285	274	277
Affiliations					
Hospitals in a System......................	276	277	261	254	242
Hospitals in a Network.....................	171	166	157	163	157
Hospitals in a Group Purchasing Organization..	301	335	323	321	321

TABLE 5

U.S. CENSUS DIVISION 2: MIDDLE ATLANTIC

U.S. Registered Community Hospitals
(Nonfederal, short-term general and other special hospitals)

Utilization, Personnel, Revenue and Expenses, Community Health Indicators 2010–2014

	2014	2013	2012	2011	2010
TOTAL FACILITY (Includes Hospital and Nursing Home Units)					
Utilization - Inpatient					
Beds	113,947	116,588	117,624	118,152	120,495
Admissions	4,833,693	4,974,821	5,183,982	5,308,422	5,387,182
Inpatient Days	29,417,955	30,254,395	31,440,731	31,927,960	32,429,928
Average Length of Stay	6.1	6.1	6.1	6	6
Inpatient Surgeries	1,295,330	1,327,290	1,404,460	1,385,212	1,472,258
Births	461,201	460,691	468,787	473,951	473,143
Utilization - Outpatient					
Emergency Outpatient Visits	18,448,665	18,464,278	18,321,971	18,128,050	17,544,922
Other Outpatient Visits	92,218,023	91,471,231	92,940,002	89,610,828	90,638,433
Total Outpatient Visits	110,666,688	109,935,509	111,261,973	107,738,878	108,183,355
Outpatient Surgeries	2,609,583	2,644,536	2,604,246	2,612,230	2,662,613
Personnel					
Full Time RNs	169,247	166,205	164,025	163,685	159,336
Full Time LPNs	7,861	8,442	8,908	9,399	9,477
Part Time RNs	61,908	61,534	61,911	62,925	61,970
Part Time LPNs	2,347	2,676	2,910	3,059	3,392
Total Full Time	655,994	665,974	667,785	663,442	641,848
Total Part Time	194,911	197,905	200,851	201,876	193,048
Revenue - Inpatient					
Gross Inpatient Revenue	$245,751,731,763	$237,733,249,795	$232,928,664,012	$224,663,669,372	$214,875,701,636
Revenue - Outpatient					
Gross Outpatient Revenue	$181,102,970,514	$169,822,609,385	$159,129,515,739	$142,077,957,104	$131,067,665,392
Revenue and Expenses - Totals					
(Includes Inpatient and Outpatient)					
Total Gross Revenue	$426,854,702,277	$407,555,859,180	$392,058,179,751	$366,741,626,476	$345,943,367,028
Deductions from Revenue	304,781,462,214	290,276,723,196	276,630,776,133	258,245,571,725	241,791,805,319
Net Patient Revenue	122,073,240,063	117,279,135,984	115,427,403,618	108,496,054,751	104,151,561,709
Other Operating Revenue	8,866,772,815	8,770,801,527	7,842,143,044	7,014,856,042	6,773,917,247
Other Nonoperating Revenue	2,070,612,992	2,945,630,852	1,401,364,085	1,370,628,711	1,636,895,627
Total Net Revenue	133,010,625,870	128,995,568,363	124,670,910,747	116,881,539,504	112,562,374,583
Total Expenses	126,964,965,969	123,273,293,065	119,193,201,375	112,027,433,487	107,964,477,816
HOSPITAL UNIT (Excludes Separate Nursing Home Units)					
Utilization - Inpatient					
Beds	106,758	108,138	108,572	108,920	112,240
Admissions	4,802,392	4,936,296	5,143,373	5,266,742	5,349,564
Inpatient Days	26,989,568	27,418,799	28,351,497	28,745,893	29,691,180
Average Length of Stay	5.6	5.6	5.5	5.5	5.6
Personnel					
Total Full Time	649,963	659,374	660,600	657,123	636,513
Total Part Time	192,025	194,622	197,298	198,919	189,998
Revenue and Expenses - Totals					
(Includes Inpatient and Outpatient)					
Total Net Revenue	$132,143,884,524	$128,084,425,548	$123,724,968,154	$116,030,325,922	$111,642,685,649
Total Expenses	126,161,477,280	122,409,617,966	118,279,090,752	111,216,627,510	107,117,179,018
COMMUNITY HEALTH INDICATORS PER 1000 POPULATION					
Total Population (in thousands)	41,472	41,324	41,198	41,029	40,943
Inpatient					
Beds	2.7	2.8	2.9	2.9	2.9
Admissions	116.6	120.4	125.8	129.4	131.6
Inpatient Days	709.4	732.1	763.2	778.2	792.1
Inpatient Surgeries	31.2	32.1	34.1	33.8	36.0
Births	11.1	11.1	11.4	11.6	11.6
Outpatient					
Emergency Outpatient Visits	444.9	446.8	444.7	441.8	428.5
Other Outpatient Visits	2,223.6	2,213.5	2,255.9	2,184.1	2,213.8
Total Outpatient Visits	2,668.5	2,660.3	2,700.6	2,625.9	2,642.3
Outpatient Surgeries	62.9	64.0	63.2	63.7	65.0
Expense per Capita (per person)	$3,061.5	$2,983.1	$2,893.2	$2,730.4	$2,636.9

TABLE 5

U.S. CENSUS DIVISION 3: SOUTH ATLANTIC

U.S. Registered Community Hospitals
(Nonfederal, short-term general and other special hospitals)

Overview 2010–2014

	2014	2013	2012	2011	2010
Total Community Hospitals					
in Census Division 3, South Atlantic	754	758	766	759	758
Bed Size Category					
6-24	29	23	22	22	21
25-49	139	142	139	130	129
50-99	139	141	138	138	133
100-199	179	175	192	193	196
200-299	104	110	109	110	115
300-399	60	64	66	66	65
400-499	41	36	37	33	34
500 + ...	63	67	63	67	65
Location					
Hospitals Urban.	553	521	526	515	514
Hospitals Rural	201	237	240	244	244
Control					
State and Local Government	129	129	135	137	141
Not for Profit	399	407	403	404	398
Investor owned	226	222	228	218	219
Physician Models					
Independent Practice Association	49	48	52	49	52
Group Practice without Walls.	26	30	30	23	23
Open Physician-Hospital Organization	65	69	77	78	79
Closed Physician-Hospital Organization	46	45	42	37	38
Management Service Organization	51	70	72	66	67
Integrated Salary Model	279	292	291	287	287
Equity Model	16	17	19	20	21
Foundation.	15	15	17	19	20
Insurance Products					
Health Maintenance Organization	91	88	70	78	74
Preferred Provider Organization.	94	96	73	95	94
Indemnity Fee for Service	44	37	26	32	29
Managed Care Contracts					
Health Maintenance Organization	400	414	410	428	417
Preferred Provider Organization.	421	443	432	455	448
Affiliations					
Hospitals in a System.	572	564	554	527	504
Hospitals in a Network	234	229	220	218	215
Hospitals in a Group Purchasing Organization. .	509	525	516	522	538

TABLE 5

U.S. CENSUS DIVISION 3: SOUTH ATLANTIC

U.S. Registered Community Hospitals
(Nonfederal, short-term general and other special hospitals)

Utilization, Personnel, Revenue and Expenses, Community Health Indicators 2010–2014

	2014	2013	2012	2011	2010
TOTAL FACILITY (Includes Hospital and Nursing Home Units)					
Utilization - Inpatient					
Beds	154,927	156,366	156,937	156,421	156,678
Admissions	6,782,630	6,775,396	6,928,298	6,995,044	6,970,769
Inpatient Days	37,244,934	37,330,440	37,724,388	37,874,666	37,775,346
Average Length of Stay.	5.5	5.5	5.4	5.4	5.4
Inpatient Surgeries.	1,837,366	1,885,705	1,904,557	1,922,638	1,978,051
Births.	689,817	688,383	690,305	691,803	718,161
Utilization - Outpatient					
Emergency Outpatient Visits.	28,173,654	27,180,478	26,665,515	25,719,396	25,132,194
Other Outpatient Visits.	77,490,400	76,008,760	74,855,137	72,465,338	70,980,844
Total Outpatient Visits	105,664,054	103,189,238	101,520,652	98,184,734	96,113,038
Outpatient Surgeries	3,360,000	3,402,928	3,293,896	3,285,368	3,275,089
Personnel					
Full Time RNs	236,993	229,245	226,678	218,388	214,222
Full Time LPNs	10,766	11,445	12,717	13,119	14,299
Part Time RNs.	74,694	73,838	72,103	71,740	73,321
Part Time LPNs	2,822	3,227	3,438	3,608	4,092
Total Full Time.	789,982	777,852	782,368	764,221	753,621
Total Part Time	213,576	211,042	209,662	206,195	204,742
Revenue - Inpatient					
Gross Inpatient Revenue.	$278,261,148,984	$262,531,564,774	$247,143,243,581	$230,857,582,404	$221,881,724,341
Revenue - Outpatient					
Gross Outpatient Revenue	$233,116,826,117	$211,522,275,589	$191,354,643,518	$171,171,466,560	$156,997,699,889
Revenue and Expenses - Totals					
(Includes Inpatient and Outpatient)					
Total Gross Revenue.	$511,377,975,101	$474,053,840,363	$438,497,887,099	$402,029,048,964	$378,879,424,230
Deductions from Revenue.	364,940,729,770	334,573,003,794	301,779,297,485	278,266,927,544	257,534,395,622
Net Patient Revenue.	146,437,245,331	139,480,836,569	136,718,589,614	123,762,121,420	121,345,028,608
Other Operating Revenue	6,500,381,754	6,380,425,184	6,785,768,283	6,233,574,974	5,739,614,294
Other Nonoperating Revenue	3,174,196,022	3,307,649,993	2,215,518,159	1,983,730,368	2,153,138,363
Total Net Revenue.	156,111,823,107	149,168,911,746	145,719,876,056	131,979,426,762	129,237,781,265
Total Expenses.	140,819,951,923	135,926,142,419	132,934,775,278	122,100,282,752	118,053,521,062
HOSPITAL UNIT (Excludes Separate Nursing Home Units)					
Utilization - Inpatient					
Beds	145,997	146,568	146,488	145,614	145,304
Admissions	6,746,808	6,734,481	6,885,814	6,952,755	6,925,183
Inpatient Days	34,371,920	34,230,779	34,334,087	34,472,561	34,041,050
Average Length of Stay.	5.1	5.1	5	5	4.9
Personnel					
Total Full Time.	783,227	770,841	774,599	756,853	745,348
Total Part Time	211,393	208,582	207,045	203,449	201,603
Revenue and Expenses - Totals					
(Includes Inpatient and Outpatient)					
Total Net Revenue.	$155,327,357,125	$148,368,495,581	$144,879,731,362	$131,160,884,248	$128,322,166,959
Total Expenses.	140,110,701,843	135,196,659,731	132,134,543,784	121,286,710,334	117,214,899,415
COMMUNITY HEALTH INDICATORS PER 1000 POPULATION					
Total Population (in thousands)	62,515	61,784	61,189	60,514	59,659
Inpatient					
Beds	2.5	2.5	2.6	2.6	2.6
Admissions	108.5	109.7	113.2	115.6	116.8
Inpatient Days	595.8	604.2	616.5	625.9	633.2
Inpatient Surgeries.	29.4	30.5	31.1	31.8	33.2
Births.	11.0	11.1	11.3	11.4	12.0
Outpatient					
Emergency Outpatient Visits.	450.7	439.9	435.8	425.0	421.3
Other Outpatient Visits.	1,239.6	1,230.2	1,223.4	1,197.5	1,189.8
Total Outpatient Visits	1,690.2	1,670.2	1,659.1	1,622.5	1,611.0
Outpatient Surgeries	53.7	55.1	53.8	54.3	54.9
Expense per Capita (per person).	$2,252.6	$2,200.0	$2,172.5	$2,017.7	$1,978.8

TABLE 5

U.S. CENSUS DIVISION 4: EAST NORTH CENTRAL

U.S. Registered Community Hospitals
(Nonfederal, short-term general and other special hospitals)

Overview 2010–2014

	2014	2013	2012	2011	2010
Total Community Hospitals					
in Census Division 4, East North Central....	769	775	776	774	777
Bed Size Category					
6-24	63	59	57	45	43
25-49	197	203	204	204	198
50-99	140	148	146	155	163
100-199	171	162	161	155	151
200-299	84	90	84	93	100
300-399	45	42	55	56	56
400-499	30	30	29	27	26
500 + ...	39	41	40	39	40
Location					
Hospitals Urban..........................	499	502	503	501	503
Hospitals Rural	270	273	273	273	274
Control					
State and Local Government...............	86	87	90	89	96
Not for Profit	579	587	588	592	590
Investor owned	104	101	98	93	91
Physician Models					
Independent Practice Association	72	67	71	69	73
Group Practice without Walls...............	41	43	27	30	25
Open Physician-Hospital Organization	162	173	162	163	164
Closed Physician-Hospital Organization	59	57	46	52	51
Management Service Organization	68	74	65	82	87
Integrated Salary Model	358	353	346	321	312
Equity Model	35	39	22	21	22
Foundation...............................	47	53	40	49	59
Insurance Products					
Health Maintenance Organization	161	163	152	151	145
Preferred Provider Organization.............	156	161	141	161	165
Indemnity Fee for Service	56	54	52	54	57
Managed Care Contracts					
Health Maintenance Organization	526	519	527	514	531
Preferred Provider Organization.............	551	556	555	547	568
Affiliations					
Hospitals in a System.....................	518	503	492	486	475
Hospitals in a Network....................	292	282	277	272	277
Hospitals in a Group Purchasing Organization..	611	613	618	608	632

TABLE 5

U.S. CENSUS DIVISION 4: EAST NORTH CENTRAL

U.S. Registered Community Hospitals
(Nonfederal, short-term general and other special hospitals)

Utilization, Personnel, Revenue and Expenses, Community Health Indicators 2010–2014

	2014	2013	2012	2011	2010
TOTAL FACILITY (Includes Hospital and Nursing Home Units)					
Utilization - Inpatient					
Beds	119,389	120,050	121,997	122,555	124,528
Admissions	5,171,957	5,309,578	5,477,164	5,518,124	5,573,945
Inpatient Days	26,063,576	26,367,306	27,190,027	27,603,703	28,088,741
Average Length of Stay...........	5	5	5	5	5
Inpatient Surgeries...............	1,391,133	1,415,474	1,499,944	1,537,005	1,598,684
Births..........................	521,134	520,879	524,244	531,487	549,668
Utilization - Outpatient					
Emergency Outpatient Visits........	22,166,060	21,840,082	22,161,580	21,873,056	21,645,563
Other Outpatient Visits.............	120,541,672	115,696,131	114,778,170	110,723,087	110,255,848
Total Outpatient Visits	142,707,732	137,536,213	136,939,750	132,596,143	131,901,411
Outpatient Surgeries	3,107,718	3,116,354	3,185,907	3,152,571	3,207,896
Personnel					
Full Time RNs	183,359	178,559	176,706	171,026	166,190
Full Time LPNs	7,142	7,894	7,987	9,094	8,792
Part Time RNs...................	98,575	95,846	99,210	97,012	97,309
Part Time LPNs	3,784	4,236	4,590	4,841	5,200
Total Full Time...................	677,119	670,958	672,905	661,130	656,411
Total Part Time	302,675	295,422	302,574	301,819	305,777
Revenue - Inpatient					
Gross Inpatient Revenue..........	$204,202,256,852	$193,599,807,491	$187,228,187,292	$176,586,489,578	$169,254,285,621
Revenue - Outpatient					
Gross Outpatient Revenue	$220,428,044,679	$200,738,677,953	$185,825,760,037	$167,198,588,978	$153,605,458,204
Revenue and Expenses - Totals **(Includes Inpatient and Outpatient)**					
Total Gross Revenue.............	$424,630,301,531	$394,338,485,444	$373,053,947,329	$343,785,078,556	$322,859,743,825
Deductions from Revenue.........	286,324,202,816	263,377,222,866	243,148,787,597	224,785,581,163	206,741,773,300
Net Patient Revenue.............	138,306,098,715	130,961,262,578	129,905,159,732	118,999,497,393	116,117,970,525
Other Operating Revenue	8,812,043,264	8,342,665,932	7,734,468,170	7,235,875,567	6,838,675,527
Other Nonoperating Revenue	3,723,265,436	3,963,965,511	2,372,671,286	2,481,023,683	2,812,190,226
Total Net Revenue...............	150,841,407,415	143,267,894,021	140,012,299,188	128,716,396,643	125,768,836,278
Total Expenses..................	135,485,952,281	130,380,820,276	128,508,223,081	118,844,737,908	116,021,099,796
HOSPITAL UNIT (Excludes Separate Nursing Home Units)					
Utilization - Inpatient					
Beds	114,725	115,570	116,777	117,051	118,315
Admissions	5,143,469	5,281,193	5,443,973	5,480,695	5,532,131
Inpatient Days	24,663,750	25,031,404	25,617,733	25,917,067	26,193,965
Average Length of Stay...........	4.8	4.7	4.7	4.7	4.7
Personnel					
Total Full Time...................	674,594	668,467	669,734	657,862	652,317
Total Part Time	300,448	293,112	299,781	298,789	302,371
Revenue and Expenses - Totals **(Includes Inpatient and Outpatient)**					
Total Net Revenue...............	$150,456,619,070	$142,884,583,269	$139,565,247,628	$128,223,217,900	$125,272,982,180
Total Expenses..................	135,157,396,593	130,048,404,828	128,116,255,360	118,428,199,417	115,557,672,594
COMMUNITY HEALTH INDICATORS PER 1000 POPULATION					
Total Population (in thousands)	46,739	46,662	46,567	46,519	46,522
Inpatient					
Beds	2.6	2.6	2.6	2.6	2.7
Admissions	110.7	113.8	117.6	118.6	119.8
Inpatient Days	557.6	565.1	583.9	593.4	603.8
Inpatient Surgeries...............	29.8	30.3	32.2	33.0	34.4
Births..........................	11.1	11.2	11.3	11.4	11.8
Outpatient					
Emergency Outpatient Visits........	474.3	468.0	475.9	470.2	465.3
Other Outpatient Visits.............	2,579.0	2,479.4	2,464.8	2,380.2	2,370.0
Total Outpatient Visits	3,053.3	2,947.5	2,940.7	2,850.4	2,835.3
Outpatient Surgeries	66.5	66.8	68.4	67.8	69.0
**Expense per Capita (per person).....	$2,898.8	$2,794.1	$2,759.7	$2,554.8	$2,493.9

U.S. Census Divisions

TABLE 5

U.S. CENSUS DIVISION 5: EAST SOUTH CENTRAL

U.S. Registered Community Hospitals
(Nonfederal, short-term general and other special hospitals)

Overview 2010–2014

	2014	2013	2012	2011	2010
Total Community Hospitals					
in Census Division 5, East South Central ...	422	432	433	440	441
Bed Size Category					
6-24	17	19	21	22	16
25-49	119	123	125	125	128
50-99	96	98	95	98	100
100-199	95	97	97	99	104
200-299	41	42	41	40	35
300-399	25	24	24	25	25
400-499	8	9	8	10	14
500 + ...	21	20	22	21	19
Location					
Hospitals Urban..........................	202	200	200	207	208
Hospitals Rural	220	232	233	233	233
Control					
State and Local Government...............	109	113	111	112	112
Not for Profit	174	177	176	177	182
Investor owned	139	142	146	151	147
Physician Models					
Independent Practice Association	26	24	30	31	36
Group Practice without Walls................	8	7	7	7	7
Open Physician-Hospital Organization	47	43	45	43	43
Closed Physician-Hospital Organization	9	8	12	10	8
Management Service Organization	35	32	44	46	39
Integrated Salary Model....................	110	112	113	111	114
Equity Model	4	4	2	1	1
Foundation................................	16	20	15	21	22
Insurance Products					
Health Maintenance Organization	37	30	26	25	32
Preferred Provider Organization..............	78	78	65	80	75
Indemnity Fee for Service	23	23	19	18	21
Managed Care Contracts					
Health Maintenance Organization	146	152	159	165	165
Preferred Provider Organization..............	186	184	194	204	215
Affiliations					
Hospitals in a System......................	297	300	295	294	289
Hospitals in a Network.....................	97	97	89	91	101
Hospitals in a Group Purchasing Organization..	167	175	192	194	205

TABLE 5

U.S. CENSUS DIVISION 5: EAST SOUTH CENTRAL

U.S. Registered Community Hospitals
(Nonfederal, short-term general and other special hospitals)

Utilization, Personnel, Revenue and Expenses, Community Health Indicators 2010–2014

	2014	2013	2012	2011	2010
TOTAL FACILITY (Includes Hospital and Nursing Home Units)					
Utilization - Inpatient					
Beds	61,455	62,235	62,199	62,478	63,079
Admissions	2,382,356	2,419,265	2,430,269	2,424,397	2,486,454
Inpatient Days	13,251,868	13,421,013	13,150,314	13,300,397	13,614,893
Average Length of Stay	5.6	5.5	5.4	5.5	5.5
Inpatient Surgeries	668,236	676,161	728,421	732,580	728,125
Births	215,205	215,234	209,932	207,943	221,646
Utilization - Outpatient					
Emergency Outpatient Visits	9,880,646	9,732,264	9,782,661	9,526,218	9,527,974
Other Outpatient Visits	26,326,661	25,969,056	25,794,437	25,425,473	25,726,751
Total Outpatient Visits	36,207,307	35,701,320	35,577,098	34,951,691	35,254,725
Outpatient Surgeries	1,333,554	1,351,037	1,405,286	1,386,491	1,344,976
Personnel					
Full Time RNs	79,234	77,713	75,991	75,308	73,350
Full Time LPNs	5,437	6,016	6,263	6,748	7,457
Part Time RNs	23,554	24,713	25,437	24,560	25,319
Part Time LPNs	1,357	1,534	1,640	1,692	2,052
Total Full Time	269,802	267,164	266,388	265,560	262,113
Total Part Time	65,471	68,124	71,714	68,968	72,591
Revenue - Inpatient					
Gross Inpatient Revenue	$89,841,024,641	$85,886,311,001	$80,646,954,304	$75,686,751,272	$73,345,815,567
Revenue - Outpatient					
Gross Outpatient Revenue	$85,434,786,619	$76,616,972,839	$71,015,770,262	$61,846,614,466	$56,798,252,271
Revenue and Expenses - Totals					
(Includes Inpatient and Outpatient)					
Total Gross Revenue	$175,275,811,260	$162,503,283,840	$151,662,724,566	$137,533,365,738	$130,144,067,838
Deductions from Revenue	130,101,544,284	118,611,464,301	109,016,339,180	99,633,059,934	92,627,817,898
Net Patient Revenue	45,174,266,976	43,891,819,539	42,646,385,386	37,900,305,804	37,516,249,940
Other Operating Revenue	2,043,790,399	1,929,535,883	1,820,681,077	1,532,546,010	1,479,335,426
Other Nonoperating Revenue	714,113,663	758,473,581	407,005,231	481,348,514	696,071,058
Total Net Revenue	47,932,171,038	46,579,829,003	44,874,071,694	39,914,200,328	39,691,656,424
Total Expenses	44,391,934,950	42,687,366,112	41,101,364,805	36,909,370,915	36,471,494,399
HOSPITAL UNIT (Excludes Separate Nursing Home Units)					
Utilization - Inpatient					
Beds	58,048	58,109	58,411	58,770	58,946
Admissions	2,370,834	2,403,639	2,413,202	2,407,693	2,471,184
Inpatient Days	12,184,169	12,117,469	11,963,248	12,159,845	12,327,182
Average Length of Stay	5.1	5	5	5.1	5
Personnel					
Total Full Time	266,798	263,499	263,124	262,518	258,805
Total Part Time	64,643	66,771	70,861	68,301	71,637
Revenue and Expenses - Totals					
(Includes Inpatient and Outpatient)					
Total Net Revenue	$47,734,520,006	$46,303,139,122	$44,641,587,474	$39,631,141,073	$39,425,199,072
Total Expenses	44,227,387,246	42,457,268,955	40,885,625,657	36,701,651,997	36,231,662,045
COMMUNITY HEALTH INDICATORS PER 1000 POPULATION					
Total Population (in thousands)	18,806	18,716	18,644	18,554	18,368
Inpatient					
Beds	3.3	3.3	3.3	3.4	3.4
Admissions	126.7	129.3	130.4	130.7	135.4
Inpatient Days	704.7	717.1	705.4	716.8	741.2
Inpatient Surgeries	35.5	36.1	39.1	39.5	39.6
Births	11.4	11.5	11.3	11.2	12.1
Outpatient					
Emergency Outpatient Visits	525.4	520.0	524.7	513.4	518.7
Other Outpatient Visits	1,399.9	1,387.5	1,383.6	1,370.4	1,400.7
Total Outpatient Visits	1,925.3	1,907.5	1,908.3	1,883.8	1,919.4
Outpatient Surgeries	70.9	72.2	75.4	74.7	73.2
Expense per Capita (per person)	$2,360.5	$2,280.8	$2,204.6	$1,989.3	$1,985.6

TABLE 5

U.S. CENSUS DIVISION 6: WEST NORTH CENTRAL

U.S. Registered Community Hospitals
(Nonfederal, short-term general and other special hospitals)

Overview 2010–2014

	2014	2013	2012	2011	2010
Total Community Hospitals					
in Census Division 6, West North Central . . .	**686**	**683**	**692**	**682**	**685**
Bed Size Category					
6-24	135	134	128	126	113
25-49	219	212	217	218	220
50-99	149	156	160	154	164
100-199	95	90	97	91	97
200-299	35	37	35	38	35
300-399	22	24	25	25	28
400-499	13	14	14	14	12
500 + ...	18	16	16	16	16
Location					
Hospitals Urban.	241	224	226	220	223
Hospitals Rural	445	459	466	462	462
Control					
State and Local Government.	227	228	233	236	235
Not for Profit	403	401	405	396	398
Investor owned	56	54	54	50	52
Physician Models					
Independent Practice Association	55	55	63	62	70
Group Practice without Walls.	10	12	16	12	11
Open Physician-Hospital Organization	63	68	70	68	70
Closed Physician-Hospital Organization	21	23	26	26	23
Management Service Organization	12	12	16	20	17
Integrated Salary Model	361	341	336	330	317
Equity Model	6	6	7	6	2
Foundation.	15	18	17	22	17
Insurance Products					
Health Maintenance Organization	73	68	59	56	59
Preferred Provider Organization.	76	67	69	89	88
Indemnity Fee for Service	23	19	20	29	27
Managed Care Contracts					
Health Maintenance Organization	334	312	318	311	310
Preferred Provider Organization.	445	433	445	442	446
Affiliations					
Hospitals in a System.	375	367	372	352	348
Hospitals in a Network	296	291	288	287	277
Hospitals in a Group Purchasing Organization. .	553	551	562	557	552

TABLE 5

U.S. CENSUS DIVISION 6: WEST NORTH CENTRAL

U.S. Registered Community Hospitals
(Nonfederal, short-term general and other special hospitals)

Utilization, Personnel, Revenue and Expenses, Community Health Indicators 2010–2014

	2014	2013	2012	2011	2010
TOTAL FACILITY (Includes Hospital and Nursing Home Units)					
Utilization - Inpatient					
Beds	66,847	67,386	68,455	67,559	68,830
Admissions	2,331,707	2,355,948	2,421,698	2,453,988	2,464,267
Inpatient Days	14,150,091	14,286,092	14,638,214	14,718,938	14,928,227
Average Length of Stay	6.1	6.1	6	6	6.1
Inpatient Surgeries	639,400	649,575	667,171	674,685	683,170
Births	270,276	267,407	268,618	264,259	264,621
Utilization - Outpatient					
Emergency Outpatient Visits	8,750,133	8,653,473	8,725,139	8,573,615	8,260,672
Other Outpatient Visits	53,611,188	51,914,260	52,156,664	49,766,340	50,003,264
Total Outpatient Visits	62,361,321	60,567,733	60,881,803	58,339,955	58,263,936
Outpatient Surgeries	1,366,852	1,356,009	1,381,534	1,352,232	1,322,974
Personnel					
Full Time RNs	82,331	81,791	78,654	75,384	73,425
Full Time LPNs	7,106	7,140	7,145	7,158	7,282
Part Time RNs	54,685	53,163	54,342	51,864	52,648
Part Time LPNs	3,947	3,944	4,109	4,132	4,485
Total Full Time	330,504	336,351	311,613	301,105	297,067
Total Part Time	161,716	161,075	164,991	160,171	164,985
Revenue - Inpatient					
Gross Inpatient Revenue	$85,253,852,745	$80,759,847,710	$77,970,550,986	$74,583,373,377	$71,077,555,297
Revenue - Outpatient					
Gross Outpatient Revenue	$89,991,409,306	$81,195,833,655	$76,310,450,463	$68,953,101,651	$62,710,234,207
Revenue and Expenses - Totals					
(Includes Inpatient and Outpatient)					
Total Gross Revenue	$175,245,262,051	$161,955,681,365	$154,281,001,449	$143,536,475,028	$133,787,789,504
Deductions from Revenue	113,156,490,271	102,735,424,002	96,278,090,518	89,596,077,363	82,115,750,561
Net Patient Revenue	62,088,771,780	59,220,257,363	58,002,910,931	53,940,397,665	51,672,038,943
Other Operating Revenue	3,689,823,992	3,513,084,143	3,444,366,586	2,870,841,462	2,830,841,723
Other Nonoperating Revenue	1,393,096,932	1,693,175,535	1,330,357,727	1,096,847,381	1,318,194,215
Total Net Revenue	67,171,692,704	64,426,517,041	62,777,635,244	57,908,086,508	55,821,074,881
Total Expenses	62,380,858,073	59,579,626,804	56,450,154,448	54,026,689,854	51,771,367,599
HOSPITAL UNIT (Excludes Separate Nursing Home Units)					
Utilization - Inpatient					
Beds	58,020	58,424	59,408	58,568	59,661
Admissions	2,311,150	2,336,928	2,400,701	2,432,961	2,443,671
Inpatient Days	11,395,728	11,484,252	11,768,543	11,849,105	12,018,243
Average Length of Stay	4.9	4.9	4.9	4.9	4.9
Personnel					
Total Full Time	325,019	330,962	305,819	295,954	291,819
Total Part Time	156,942	156,709	160,210	155,670	160,316
Revenue and Expenses - Totals					
(Includes Inpatient and Outpatient)					
Total Net Revenue	$66,561,154,086	$63,856,543,055	$62,194,053,711	$57,296,078,737	$55,268,629,929
Total Expenses	61,856,005,299	59,040,011,689	55,903,031,384	53,536,656,669	51,251,683,260
COMMUNITY HEALTH INDICATORS PER 1000 POPULATION					
Total Population (in thousands)	21,006	20,886	20,750	20,640	20,451
Inpatient					
Beds	3.2	3.2	3.3	3.3	3.4
Admissions	111.0	112.8	116.7	118.9	120.5
Inpatient Days	673.6	684.0	705.5	713.1	729.9
Inpatient Surgeries	30.4	31.1	32.2	32.7	33.4
Births	12.9	12.8	12.9	12.8	12.9
Outpatient					
Emergency Outpatient Visits	416.6	414.3	420.5	415.4	403.9
Other Outpatient Visits	2,552.2	2,485.6	2,513.6	2,411.2	2,445.0
Total Outpatient Visits	2,968.7	2,900.0	2,934.1	2,826.6	2,848.9
Outpatient Surgeries	65.1	64.9	66.6	65.5	64.7
Expense per Capita (per person)	$2,969.7	$2,852.7	$2,720.5	$2,617.6	$2,531.4

TABLE 5

U.S. CENSUS DIVISION 7: WEST SOUTH CENTRAL

U.S. Registered Community Hospitals
(Nonfederal, short-term general and other special hospitals)

Overview 2010–2014

	2014	2013	2012	2011	2010
Total Community Hospitals					
in Census Division 7, West South Central...	734	746	749	746	750
Bed Size Category					
6-24	118	118	117	114	119
25-49	220	223	224	226	220
50-99	140	149	149	144	146
100-199	105	101	104	109	115
200-299	59	62	62	62	61
300-399	37	39	40	37	35
400-499	20	19	19	20	20
500 + ...	35	35	34	34	34
Location					
Hospitals Urban.........................	444	438	439	431	436
Hospitals Rural	290	308	310	315	314
Control					
State and Local Government...............	195	195	206	210	221
Not for Profit	278	282	275	276	267
Investor owned	261	269	268	260	262
Physician Models					
Independent Practice Association	82	80	82	94	109
Group Practice without Walls................	50	34	28	31	33
Open Physician-Hospital Organization	109	117	128	126	128
Closed Physician-Hospital Organization	38	40	38	32	30
Management Service Organization	81	83	88	93	94
Integrated Salary Model....................	224	228	215	211	181
Equity Model	6	10	11	10	16
Foundation..............................	44	52	48	47	43
Insurance Products					
Health Maintenance Organization	112	104	93	101	96
Preferred Provider Organization..............	101	88	76	116	118
Indemnity Fee for Service	45	25	22	34	36
Managed Care Contracts					
Health Maintenance Organization	478	481	468	457	449
Preferred Provider Organization..............	540	559	542	554	540
Affiliations					
Hospitals in a System.....................	449	452	451	436	434
Hospitals in a Network	206	204	193	193	184
Hospitals in a Group Purchasing Organization..	617	637	625	629	623

TABLE 5

U.S. CENSUS DIVISION 7: WEST SOUTH CENTRAL

U.S. Registered Community Hospitals
(Nonfederal, short-term general and other special hospitals)

Utilization, Personnel, Revenue and Expenses, Community Health Indicators 2010–2014

	2014	2013	2012	2011	2010
TOTAL FACILITY (Includes Hospital and Nursing Home Units)					
Utilization - Inpatient					
Beds	96,935	97,967	97,260	96,825	97,399
Admissions	3,815,555	3,852,821	3,908,065	3,929,807	4,005,387
Inpatient Days	20,297,127	20,284,467	20,396,936	20,460,393	20,922,699
Average Length of Stay	5.3	5.3	5.2	5.2	5.2
Inpatient Surgeries	1,052,155	1,055,227	1,080,738	1,118,349	1,150,547
Births	548,587	530,165	516,124	503,256	528,045
Utilization - Outpatient					
Emergency Outpatient Visits	16,436,178	16,301,738	16,269,062	15,575,261	15,392,542
Other Outpatient Visits	46,546,602	45,227,309	45,892,246	44,066,578	45,924,148
Total Outpatient Visits	62,982,780	61,529,047	62,161,308	59,641,839	61,316,690
Outpatient Surgeries	1,760,763	1,719,039	1,675,034	1,683,472	1,707,264
Personnel					
Full Time RNs	134,254	131,052	126,908	121,426	123,112
Full Time LPNs	12,312	13,147	13,783	14,606	15,573
Part Time RNs	36,642	37,846	36,330	35,553	33,058
Part Time LPNs	2,982	3,153	3,352	3,347	3,961
Total Full Time	446,541	440,358	435,758	428,649	434,296
Total Part Time	105,097	110,628	106,477	103,538	99,628
Revenue - Inpatient					
Gross Inpatient Revenue	$176,549,411,040	$165,441,811,098	$157,197,100,160	$146,271,380,775	$139,926,153,510
Revenue - Outpatient					
Gross Outpatient Revenue	$142,960,299,246	$129,896,699,181	$118,343,524,306	$104,883,587,404	$95,633,086,065
Revenue and Expenses - Totals					
(Includes Inpatient and Outpatient)					
Total Gross Revenue	$319,509,710,182	$295,338,510,279	$275,540,624,466	$251,154,968,179	$235,559,239,575
Deductions from Revenue	237,893,364,240	218,013,431,324	199,811,182,037	184,194,250,743	169,768,881,745
Net Patient Revenue	81,616,345,942	77,325,078,955	75,729,442,429	66,960,717,436	65,790,357,830
Other Operating Revenue	6,555,581,679	6,605,401,355	6,473,296,689	5,893,843,564	5,622,273,906
Other Nonoperating Revenue	2,101,925,461	1,436,996,905	1,074,127,947	1,909,520,980	1,791,442,768
Total Net Revenue	90,273,853,082	85,367,477,215	83,276,867,065	74,764,081,980	73,204,074,504
Total Expenses	80,310,161,311	77,562,496,193	74,523,034,451	67,280,680,393	65,549,933,822
HOSPITAL UNIT (Excludes Separate Nursing Home Units)					
Utilization - Inpatient					
Beds	95,357	95,923	95,188	94,783	95,427
Admissions	3,806,387	3,841,094	3,894,508	3,916,503	3,991,294
Inpatient Days	19,863,060	19,723,627	19,839,649	19,861,338	20,336,517
Average Length of Stay	5.2	5.1	5.1	5.1	5.1
Personnel					
Total Full Time	443,560	438,804	433,602	427,100	432,842
Total Part Time	103,992	110,195	106,091	103,146	99,156
Revenue and Expenses - Totals					
(Includes Inpatient and Outpatient)					
Total Net Revenue	$90,157,740,671	$85,208,123,466	$83,105,764,389	$74,607,353,353	$73,043,779,992
Total Expenses	80,211,596,887	77,432,447,297	74,387,874,023	67,137,888,126	65,399,265,396
COMMUNITY HEALTH INDICATORS PER 1000 POPULATION					
Total Population (in thousands)	38,451	37,884	37,425	36,979	36,378
Inpatient					
Beds	2.5	2.6	2.6	2.6	2.7
Admissions	99.2	101.7	104.4	106.3	110.1
Inpatient Days	527.9	535.4	545.0	553.3	575.2
Inpatient Surgeries	27.4	27.9	28.9	30.2	31.6
Births	14.3	14.0	13.8	13.6	14.5
Outpatient					
Emergency Outpatient Visits	427.5	430.3	434.7	421.2	423.1
Other Outpatient Visits	1,210.5	1,193.8	1,226.2	1,191.7	1,262.4
Total Outpatient Visits	1,638.0	1,624.2	1,661.0	1,612.9	1,685.6
Outpatient Surgeries	45.8	45.4	44.8	45.5	46.9
Expense per Capita (per person)	$2,088.6	$2,047.4	$1,991.3	$1,819.4	$1,801.9

U.S. Census Divisions

TABLE 5

U.S. CENSUS DIVISION 8: MOUNTAIN

U.S. Registered Community Hospitals
(Nonfederal, short-term general and other special hospitals)

Overview 2010–2014

	2014	2013	2012	2011	2010
Total Community Hospitals					
in Census Division 8, Mountain............	388	390	388	384	382
Bed Size Category					
6-24.....................................	62	57	57	55	53
25-49...................................	97	103	102	99	98
50-99...................................	90	87	84	87	88
100-199.................................	61	65	65	63	66
200-299.................................	33	33	34	35	32
300-399.................................	19	20	20	20	21
400-499.................................	14	13	14	13	11
500 +...................................	12	12	12	12	13
Location					
Hospitals Urban.........................	199	193	193	191	189
Hospitals Rural	189	197	195	193	193
Control					
State and Local Government................	90	90	93	94	94
Not for Profit	201	202	196	197	195
Investor owned	97	98	99	93	93
Physician Models					
Independent Practice Association	28	32	40	41	42
Group Practice without Walls...............	11	13	12	13	8
Open Physician-Hospital Organization	36	34	37	36	34
Closed Physician-Hospital Organization	15	14	13	15	14
Management Service Organization	20	22	21	24	27
Integrated Salary Model....................	154	150	148	140	125
Equity Model............................	4	4	4	5	5
Foundation..............................	14	13	12	12	13
Insurance Products					
Health Maintenance Organization	51	57	55	57	54
Preferred Provider Organization..............	58	53	40	58	56
Indemnity Fee for Service	27	24	20	26	27
Managed Care Contracts					
Health Maintenance Organization	139	142	143	141	147
Preferred Provider Organization..............	185	193	190	184	185
Affiliations					
Hospitals in a System.....................	236	234	234	229	230
Hospitals in a Network	106	107	99	110	112
Hospitals in a Group Purchasing Organization..	254	268	240	259	248

TABLE 5

U.S. CENSUS DIVISION 8: MOUNTAIN

U.S. Registered Community Hospitals
(Nonfederal, short-term general and other special hospitals)

Utilization, Personnel, Revenue and Expenses, Community Health Indicators 2010–2014

	2014	2013	2012	2011	2010
TOTAL FACILITY (Includes Hospital and Nursing Home Units)					
Utilization - Inpatient					
Beds	47,180	47,322	47,501	47,119	46,872
Admissions	1,953,896	1,962,391	2,060,596	2,064,195	2,091,454
Inpatient Days	9,968,995	9,977,101	10,231,226	10,303,057	10,379,491
Average Length of Stay	5.1	5.1	5	5	5
Inpatient Surgeries	545,379	559,564	614,124	646,125	662,412
Births	266,986	266,237	269,841	268,969	278,694
Utilization - Outpatient					
Emergency Outpatient Visits	8,133,174	7,787,157	7,821,770	7,567,323	7,497,043
Other Outpatient Visits	34,775,370	32,829,124	32,436,477	31,476,244	29,432,803
Total Outpatient Visits	42,908,544	40,616,281	40,258,247	39,043,567	36,929,846
Outpatient Surgeries	1,028,103	1,024,797	982,976	996,441	982,327
Personnel					
Full Time RNs	73,010	69,945	66,845	64,271	66,717
Full Time LPNs	2,978	3,039	3,085	3,129	3,511
Part Time RNs	24,993	26,487	26,537	25,828	23,141
Part Time LPNs	986	1,109	1,204	1,197	1,170
Total Full Time	247,663	241,359	234,035	228,851	233,880
Total Part Time	74,968	80,434	78,088	76,297	68,863
Revenue - Inpatient					
Gross Inpatient Revenue	$94,555,922,887	$87,638,841,277	$83,441,071,276	$77,570,487,787	$74,568,371,912
Revenue - Outpatient					
Gross Outpatient Revenue	$82,354,172,215	$73,378,356,271	$65,655,835,782	$59,010,644,319	$53,530,101,037
Revenue and Expenses - Totals					
(Includes Inpatient and Outpatient)					
Total Gross Revenue	$176,910,095,102	$161,017,197,548	$149,096,907,058	$136,581,132,106	$128,098,472,949
Deductions from Revenue	126,585,492,260	113,683,233,185	102,954,441,992	94,240,727,395	86,894,343,376
Net Patient Revenue	50,324,602,842	47,333,964,363	46,142,465,066	42,340,404,711	41,204,129,573
Other Operating Revenue	2,073,527,886	2,195,077,380	1,890,523,158	1,885,009,958	1,804,886,179
Other Nonoperating Revenue	900,910,913	686,369,507	353,858,460	497,930,676	550,761,263
Total Net Revenue	53,299,041,641	50,215,411,250	48,386,846,684	44,723,345,345	43,559,777,015
Total Expenses	47,158,491,064	45,094,874,475	43,346,401,522	40,362,478,873	38,771,182,258
HOSPITAL UNIT (Excludes Separate Nursing Home Units)					
Utilization - Inpatient					
Beds	44,210	44,166	44,388	43,922	43,563
Admissions	1,946,984	1,954,560	2,052,402	2,054,557	2,081,194
Inpatient Days	9,128,451	9,030,424	9,282,591	9,320,023	9,356,938
Average Length of Stay	4.7	4.6	4.5	4.5	4.5
Personnel					
Total Full Time	245,906	239,029	232,008	226,920	231,537
Total Part Time	73,885	78,848	76,862	75,224	67,617
Revenue and Expenses - Totals					
(Includes Inpatient and Outpatient)					
Total Net Revenue	$53,094,299,493	$49,982,879,096	$48,172,247,901	$44,490,329,013	$43,323,260,876
Total Expenses	46,989,068,835	44,908,887,608	43,160,567,568	40,156,890,139	38,565,221,584
COMMUNITY HEALTH INDICATORS PER 1000 POPULATION					
Total Population (in thousands)	23,197	22,881	22,618	22,373	22,379
Inpatient					
Beds	2.0	2.1	2.1	2.1	2.1
Admissions	84.2	85.8	91.1	92.3	93.5
Inpatient Days	429.8	436.0	452.4	460.5	463.8
Inpatient Surgeries	23.5	24.5	27.2	28.9	29.6
Births	11.5	11.6	11.9	12.0	12.5
Outpatient					
Emergency Outpatient Visits	350.6	340.3	345.8	338.2	335.0
Other Outpatient Visits	1,499.1	1,434.8	1,434.1	1,406.9	1,315.2
Total Outpatient Visits	1,849.7	1,775.1	1,779.9	1,745.1	1,650.2
Outpatient Surgeries	44.3	44.8	43.5	44.5	43.9
Expense per Capita (per person)	$2,032.9	$1,970.8	$1,916.5	$1,804.0	$1,732.5

U.S. Census Divisions

TABLE 5

U.S. CENSUS DIVISION 9: PACIFIC

U.S. Registered Community Hospitals
(Nonfederal, short-term general and other special hospitals)

Overview 2010–2014

	2014	2013	2012	2011	2010
Total Community Hospitals					
in Census Division 9, Pacific	540	543	541	535	535
Bed Size Category					
6-24	43	42	39	42	41
25-49	99	99	102	97	97
50-99	72	72	72	73	70
100-199	144	144	138	133	139
200-299	81	84	88	86	84
300-399	54	55	51	55	55
400-499	29	30	34	31	31
500 + ...	18	17	17	18	18
Location					
Hospitals Urban.	429	420	421	414	413
Hospitals Rural	111	123	120	121	122
Control					
State and Local Government.	133	131	132	133	135
Not for Profit	321	325	321	318	319
Investor owned	86	87	88	84	81
Physician Models					
Independent Practice Association	76	71	65	79	83
Group Practice without Walls.	27	22	21	24	24
Open Physician-Hospital Organization	14	12	16	22	20
Closed Physician-Hospital Organization	13	18	11	11	10
Management Service Organization	60	64	63	47	48
Integrated Salary Model.	129	122	112	115	113
Equity Model	9	6	6	6	7
Foundation.	102	99	91	59	60
Insurance Products					
Health Maintenance Organization	82	78	66	64	55
Preferred Provider Organization.	58	50	38	62	56
Indemnity Fee for Service	21	15	10	21	15
Managed Care Contracts					
Health Maintenance Organization	257	238	258	228	231
Preferred Provider Organization.	268	251	268	252	259
Affiliations					
Hospitals in a System.	355	342	339	336	330
Hospitals in a Network	138	129	110	121	110
Hospitals in a Group Purchasing Organization. .	332	330	295	315	310

TABLE 5

U.S. CENSUS DIVISION 9: PACIFIC

U.S. Registered Community Hospitals
(Nonfederal, short-term general and other special hospitals)

Utilization, Personnel, Revenue and Expenses, Community Health Indicators 2010–2014

	2014	2013	2012	2011	2010
TOTAL FACILITY (Includes Hospital and Nursing Home Units)					
Utilization - Inpatient					
Beds	92,663	93,661	94,194	92,601	93,088
Admissions	4,254,171	4,361,054	4,403,646	4,471,783	4,501,591
Inpatient Days	21,611,365	21,838,216	22,168,393	22,232,780	22,640,225
Average Length of Stay	5.1	5	5	5	5
Inpatient Surgeries	1,179,036	1,168,907	1,195,847	1,192,531	1,241,853
Births	614,658	603,650	621,481	629,315	632,032
Utilization - Outpatient					
Emergency Outpatient Visits	17,311,390	16,484,071	16,342,076	15,480,506	15,128,224
Other Outpatient Visits	63,944,925	63,694,420	62,140,989	62,797,927	61,596,946
Total Outpatient Visits	81,256,315	80,178,491	78,483,065	78,278,433	76,725,170
Outpatient Surgeries	1,869,447	1,854,875	1,808,384	1,846,317	1,835,447
Personnel					
Full Time RNs	145,428	139,227	141,776	136,326	134,508
Full Time LPNs	6,671	7,199	7,614	7,594	8,301
Part Time RNs	77,054	77,131	77,206	72,866	71,284
Part Time LPNs	2,766	3,043	3,279	3,211	3,453
Total Full Time	504,630	496,771	508,241	493,680	487,053
Total Part Time	202,963	206,175	210,546	199,030	193,703
Revenue - Inpatient					
Gross Inpatient Revenue	$258,131,040,816	$249,612,964,923	$236,834,787,719	$219,593,141,460	$211,874,242,966
Revenue - Outpatient					
Gross Outpatient Revenue	$182,707,768,101	$165,091,402,569	$147,772,531,581	$138,274,865,366	$124,558,809,024
Revenue and Expenses - Totals					
(Includes Inpatient and Outpatient)					
Total Gross Revenue	$440,838,808,917	$414,704,353,075	$384,607,319,300	$357,868,006,826	$336,433,051,990
Deductions from Revenue	320,168,783,536	296,421,871,411	271,710,809,903	253,322,749,612	239,252,607,338
Net Patient Revenue	120,670,025,381	118,282,481,664	112,896,509,397	104,545,257,214	97,180,444,652
Other Operating Revenue	7,373,550,696	7,232,249,498	6,642,799,134	5,990,186,797	6,027,711,222
Other Nonoperating Revenue	3,047,837,693	3,877,851,046	1,979,204,632	2,259,696,906	1,866,228,283
Total Net Revenue	131,091,413,770	129,392,582,208	121,518,513,163	112,795,140,917	105,074,384,157
Total Expenses	121,510,758,372	118,675,375,594	113,537,965,473	105,001,431,937	98,998,692,542
HOSPITAL UNIT (Excludes Separate Nursing Home Units)					
Utilization - Inpatient					
Beds	88,526	88,791	88,926	88,926	88,925
Admissions	4,234,105	4,338,312	4,378,581	4,450,403	4,478,851
Inpatient Days	20,345,718	20,299,211	20,541,376	21,093,072	21,344,190
Average Length of Stay	4.8	4.7	4.7	4.7	4.8
Personnel					
Total Full Time	500,324	493,525	503,839	490,810	483,548
Total Part Time	201,411	204,370	208,555	197,584	192,111
Revenue and Expenses - Totals					
(Includes Inpatient and Outpatient)					
Total Net Revenue	$130,486,858,064	$128,717,582,873	$120,898,001,137	$112,319,758,152	$104,531,350,858
Total Expenses	121,125,680,106	118,155,549,145	112,990,603,410	104,639,691,795	98,595,961,703
COMMUNITY HEALTH INDICATORS PER 1000 POPULATION					
Total Population (in thousands)	51,991	51,373	50,962	50,491	49,877
Inpatient					
Beds	1.8	1.8	1.8	1.8	1.9
Admissions	81.8	84.9	86.4	88.6	90.3
Inpatient Days	415.7	425.1	435.0	440.3	453.9
Inpatient Surgeries	22.7	22.8	23.5	23.6	24.9
Births	11.8	11.8	12.2	12.5	12.7
Outpatient					
Emergency Outpatient Visits	333.0	320.9	320.7	306.6	303.3
Other Outpatient Visits	1,229.9	1,239.8	1,219.4	1,243.7	1,235.0
Total Outpatient Visits	1,562.9	1,560.7	1,540.0	1,550.3	1,538.3
Outpatient Surgeries	36.0	36.1	35.5	36.6	36.8
Expense per Capita (per person)	$2,337.2	$2,310.1	$2,227.9	$2,079.6	$1,984.8

TABLE 6

ALABAMA

U.S. Registered Community Hospitals
(Nonfederal, short-term general and other special hospitals)

Overview 2010–2014

	2014	2013	2012	2011	2010
Total Community Hospitals in Alabama	96	97	97	102	105
Bed Size Category					
6-24	5	5	7	9	7
25-49	22	24	23	23	27
50-99	22	21	21	21	22
100-199	26	25	23	24	28
200-299	8	9	10	12	9
300-399	6	6	6	6	6
400-499	2	2	2	3	3
500 + ...	5	5	5	4	3
Location					
Hospitals Urban.	56	53	52	57	58
Hospitals Rural	40	44	45	45	47
Control					
State and Local Government.	40	39	38	39	40
Not for Profit	23	24	24	24	24
Investor owned	33	34	35	39	41
Physician Models					
Independent Practice Association	2	2	3	4	7
Group Practice without Walls.	0	0	0	0	1
Open Physician-Hospital Organization	6	6	6	7	7
Closed Physician-Hospital Organization	0	0	4	4	0
Management Service Organization	3	3	11	10	7
Integrated Salary Model.	8	9	13	13	18
Equity Model	0	0	0	0	0
Foundation.	4	4	4	5	7
Insurance Products					
Health Maintenance Organization	4	4	2	3	7
Preferred Provider Organization.	7	7	9	12	8
Indemnity Fee for Service	1	1	0	1	1
Managed Care Contracts					
Health Maintenance Organization	28	29	34	35	37
Preferred Provider Organization.	32	33	43	44	51
Affiliations					
Hospitals in a System.	61	62	61	61	64
Hospitals in a Network.	8	6	8	8	9
Hospitals in a Group Purchasing Organization. .	36	37	50	53	56

TABLE 6

ALABAMA

U.S. Registered Community Hospitals
(Nonfederal, short-term general and other special hospitals)

Utilization, Personnel, Revenue and Expenses, Community Health Indicators 2010–2014

	2014	2013	2012	2011	2010
TOTAL FACILITY (Includes Hospital and Nursing Home Units)					
Utilization - Inpatient					
Beds	14,959	15,129	14,983	15,387	15,086
Admissions	632,358	641,249	650,116	625,425	642,309
Inpatient Days	3,335,338	3,369,852	3,235,410	3,259,740	3,336,285
Average Length of Stay	5.3	5.3	5	5.2	5.2
Inpatient Surgeries	179,858	188,370	216,437	225,340	197,605
Births	57,863	57,811	54,169	56,038	58,287
Utilization - Outpatient					
Emergency Outpatient Visits	2,347,239	2,279,572	2,349,349	2,301,480	2,304,682
Other Outpatient Visits	6,169,200	6,032,550	5,787,211	6,428,214	6,496,039
Total Outpatient Visits	8,516,439	8,312,122	8,136,560	8,729,694	8,800,721
Outpatient Surgeries	358,555	377,910	416,822	410,937	372,359
Personnel					
Full Time RNs	21,330	20,357	18,971	19,179	19,033
Full Time LPNs	1,112	1,207	1,284	1,334	1,533
Part Time RNs	5,856	6,329	6,450	6,030	6,521
Part Time LPNs	284	376	423	407	544
Total Full Time	68,620	67,282	63,711	63,640	63,565
Total Part Time	15,991	16,854	17,393	16,258	17,485
Revenue - Inpatient					
Gross Inpatient Revenue	$22,806,578,952	$22,037,388,309	$21,905,302,437	$20,721,285,712	$20,382,077,101
Revenue - Outpatient					
Gross Outpatient Revenue	$20,942,673,592	$19,204,120,871	$18,451,159,730	$16,116,899,016	$15,107,168,189
Revenue and Expenses - Totals					
(Includes Inpatient and Outpatient)					
Total Gross Revenue	$43,749,252,544	$41,241,509,180	$40,356,462,167	$36,838,184,728	$35,489,245,290
Deductions from Revenue	33,567,813,199	31,119,196,377	30,849,527,537	28,275,034,462	26,885,327,851
Net Patient Revenue	10,181,439,345	10,122,312,803	9,506,934,630	8,563,150,266	8,603,917,439
Other Operating Revenue	613,765,569	574,099,002	530,660,281	419,270,245	398,593,891
Other Nonoperating Revenue	219,428,307	239,417,197	117,222,122	124,960,404	180,032,402
Total Net Revenue	11,014,633,221	10,935,829,002	10,154,817,033	9,107,380,915	9,182,543,732
Total Expenses	9,892,819,354	9,699,338,172	9,009,790,217	8,285,877,588	8,334,444,846
HOSPITAL UNIT (Excludes Separate Nursing Home Units)					
Utilization - Inpatient					
Beds	14,593	14,695	14,684	14,953	14,569
Admissions	631,419	640,039	649,138	624,134	641,118
Inpatient Days	3,218,620	3,231,272	3,135,159	3,142,919	3,188,617
Average Length of Stay	5.1	5	4.8	5	5
Personnel					
Total Full Time	68,149	66,636	63,419	63,302	63,159
Total Part Time	15,913	16,433	17,324	16,224	17,373
Revenue and Expenses - Totals					
(Includes Inpatient and Outpatient)					
Total Net Revenue	$10,995,481,060	$10,910,655,198	$10,139,471,861	$9,085,772,314	$9,160,325,136
Total Expenses	9,877,795,683	9,676,090,169	8,994,674,312	8,272,890,643	8,308,793,595
COMMUNITY HEALTH INDICATORS PER 1000 POPULATION					
Total Population (in thousands)	4,849	4,834	4,822	4,803	4,730
Inpatient					
Beds	3.1	3.1	3.1	3.2	3.2
Admissions	130.4	132.7	134.8	130.2	135.8
Inpatient Days	687.8	697.2	671.0	678.7	705.4
Inpatient Surgeries	37.1	39.0	44.9	46.9	41.8
Births	11.9	12.0	11.2	11.7	12.3
Outpatient					
Emergency Outpatient Visits	484.0	471.6	487.2	479.2	487.3
Other Outpatient Visits	1,272.2	1,248.0	1,200.2	1,338.4	1,373.5
Total Outpatient Visits	1,756.2	1,719.6	1,687.4	1,817.6	1,860.8
Outpatient Surgeries	73.9	78.2	86.4	85.6	78.7
Expense per Capita (per person)	$2,040.0	$2,006.6	$1,868.5	$1,725.2	$1,762.2

States

TABLE 6

ALASKA

U.S. Registered Community Hospitals
(Nonfederal, short-term general and other special hospitals)

Overview 2010–2014

	2014	2013	2012	2011	2010
Total Community Hospitals in Alaska.........	22	22	23	23	22
Bed Size Category					
6-24.....................................	5	5	7	7	6
25-49....................................	7	9	8	7	7
50-99....................................	5	3	3	4	4
100-199..................................	3	3	3	3	3
200-299..................................	1	1	1	1	1
300-399..................................	0	1	1	1	1
400-499..................................	1	0	0	0	0
500 +....................................	0	0	0	0	0
Location					
Hospitals Urban..........................	6	6	6	6	5
Hospitals Rural..........................	16	16	17	17	17
Control					
State and Local Government...............	7	7	7	7	7
Not for Profit...........................	13	13	14	14	13
Investor owned..........................	2	2	2	2	2
Physician Models					
Independent Practice Association...........	1	1	1	1	1
Group Practice without Walls..............	0	0	0	0	0
Open Physician-Hospital Organization........	1	1	2	2	2
Closed Physician-Hospital Organization.......	0	1	1	1	1
Management Service Organization...........	0	0	0	0	0
Integrated Salary Model....................	5	4	3	4	4
Equity Model.............................	0	0	0	0	0
Foundation...............................	2	1	0	0	0
Insurance Products					
Health Maintenance Organization...........	0	0	0	0	0
Preferred Provider Organization.............	3	2	1	4	1
Indemnity Fee for Service	1	0	0	1	0
Managed Care Contracts					
Health Maintenance Organization...........	1	0	0	1	0
Preferred Provider Organization.............	8	4	5	7	5
Affiliations					
Hospitals in a System.....................	8	8	8	9	9
Hospitals in a Network....................	2	1	2	1	3
Hospitals in a Group Purchasing Organization..	8	9	6	8	8

TABLE 6

ALASKA

U.S. Registered Community Hospitals
(Nonfederal, short-term general and other special hospitals)

Utilization, Personnel, Revenue and Expenses, Community Health Indicators 2010–2014

	2014	2013	2012	2011	2010
TOTAL FACILITY (Includes Hospital and Nursing Home Units)					
Utilization - Inpatient					
Beds	1,633	1,560	1,549	1,556	1,543
Admissions	53,386	57,621	56,131	54,715	57,005
Inpatient Days	376,135	376,393	341,987	340,060	342,960
Average Length of Stay	7	6.5	6.1	6.2	6
Inpatient Surgeries	14,712	13,001	15,613	16,420	17,999
Births	8,985	7,372	8,522	9,196	8,919
Utilization - Outpatient					
Emergency Outpatient Visits	303,956	257,285	290,711	315,181	296,573
Other Outpatient Visits	1,474,745	1,110,025	1,161,515	1,450,455	1,486,369
Total Outpatient Visits	1,778,701	1,367,310	1,452,226	1,765,636	1,782,942
Outpatient Surgeries	37,675	39,216	40,892	43,714	47,417
Personnel					
Full Time RNs	2,492	2,095	2,209	2,456	2,238
Full Time LPNs	129	150	145	177	178
Part Time RNs	862	823	893	820	906
Part Time LPNs	34	45	37	35	28
Total Full Time	9,228	8,364	8,723	10,064	9,608
Total Part Time	2,357	2,726	2,467	2,177	2,584
Revenue - Inpatient					
Gross Inpatient Revenue	$3,131,261,783	$2,857,156,569	$2,628,751,616	$2,510,713,374	$2,340,223,028
Revenue - Outpatient					
Gross Outpatient Revenue	$3,067,062,814	$2,965,846,524	$2,524,384,455	$2,540,116,099	$2,263,620,240
Revenue and Expenses - Totals					
(Includes Inpatient and Outpatient)					
Total Gross Revenue	$6,198,324,597	$5,823,003,093	$5,153,136,071	$5,050,829,473	$4,603,843,268
Deductions from Revenue	3,994,064,697	3,746,662,160	3,134,854,935	3,205,558,785	2,836,623,088
Net Patient Revenue	2,204,259,900	2,076,340,933	2,018,281,136	1,845,270,688	1,767,220,180
Other Operating Revenue	170,454,937	100,248,551	100,656,142	216,227,533	146,570,128
Other Nonoperating Revenue	31,062,392	42,606,280	33,745,177	19,647,439	21,027,327
Total Net Revenue	2,405,777,229	2,219,195,764	2,152,682,455	2,081,145,660	1,934,817,635
Total Expenses	1,932,865,572	1,824,096,637	1,765,708,752	1,747,385,857	1,590,214,704
HOSPITAL UNIT (Excludes Separate Nursing Home Units)					
Utilization - Inpatient					
Beds	1,387	1,273	1,293	1,346	1,334
Admissions	53,166	57,215	55,667	54,498	56,797
Inpatient Days	298,489	282,965	257,797	270,835	275,518
Average Length of Stay	5.6	4.9	4.6	5	4.9
Personnel					
Total Full Time	8,949	8,116	8,486	9,855	9,428
Total Part Time	2,259	2,596	2,371	2,080	2,443
Revenue and Expenses - Totals					
(Includes Inpatient and Outpatient)					
Total Net Revenue	$2,362,196,823	$2,171,602,536	$2,105,900,495	$2,048,187,683	$1,900,578,038
Total Expenses	1,898,027,765	1,783,712,793	1,730,733,295	1,720,343,546	1,564,596,210
COMMUNITY HEALTH INDICATORS PER 1000 POPULATION					
Total Population (in thousands)	737	735	731	723	709
Inpatient					
Beds	2.2	2.1	2.1	2.2	2.2
Admissions	72.5	78.4	76.7	75.7	80.4
Inpatient Days	510.5	512.0	467.5	470.5	483.8
Inpatient Surgeries	20.0	17.7	21.3	22.7	25.4
Births	12.2	10.0	11.7	12.7	12.6
Outpatient					
Emergency Outpatient Visits	412.6	350.0	397.4	436.1	418.4
Other Outpatient Visits	2,001.7	1,510.0	1,588.0	2,006.9	2,096.8
Total Outpatient Visits	2,414.3	1,860.0	1,985.4	2,443.0	2,515.2
Outpatient Surgeries	51.1	53.3	55.9	60.5	66.9
Expense per Capita (per person)	$2,623.6	$2,481.3	$2,414.0	$2,417.8	$2,243.3

States

TABLE 6

ARIZONA

U.S. Registered Community Hospitals
(Nonfederal, short-term general and other special hospitals)

Overview 2010–2014

	2014	2013	2012	2011	2010
Total Community Hospitals in Arizona	72	72	72	70	73
Bed Size Category					
6-24	5	5	5	5	5
25-49	12	13	12	12	10
50-99	16	14	15	14	18
100-199	12	13	13	12	13
200-299	11	11	10	11	11
300-399	6	5	6	4	5
400-499	5	6	5	7	6
500 + ...	5	5	6	5	5
Location					
Hospitals Urban..........................	63	58	58	56	58
Hospitals Rural	9	14	14	14	15
Control					
State and Local Government................	4	4	4	4	5
Not for Profit	46	47	46	47	46
Investor owned	22	21	22	19	22
Physician Models					
Independent Practice Association	8	6	9	7	8
Group Practice without Walls...............	3	2	3	3	1
Open Physician-Hospital Organization	5	4	5	5	6
Closed Physician-Hospital Organization	6	4	3	2	3
Management Service Organization	5	5	7	9	8
Integrated Salary Model....................	18	16	16	19	15
Equity Model	0	0	0	0	0
Foundation...............................	1	1	1	2	2
Insurance Products					
Health Maintenance Organization	12	14	12	10	9
Preferred Provider Organization..............	12	8	4	8	7
Indemnity Fee for Service	4	2	0	5	5
Managed Care Contracts					
Health Maintenance Organization	24	23	26	30	32
Preferred Provider Organization..............	24	24	27	31	31
Affiliations					
Hospitals in a System.....................	53	49	49	46	48
Hospitals in a Network....................	21	19	17	17	19
Hospitals in a Group Purchasing Organization..	40	42	37	40	45

States

TABLE 6

ARIZONA

U.S. Registered Community Hospitals
(Nonfederal, short-term general and other special hospitals)

Utilization, Personnel, Revenue and Expenses, Community Health Indicators 2010–2014

	2014	2013	2012	2011	2010
TOTAL FACILITY (Includes Hospital and Nursing Home Units)					
Utilization - Inpatient					
Beds	13,301	13,347	13,527	13,352	13,385
Admissions	624,898	639,279	674,808	700,855	711,901
Inpatient Days	2,864,588	2,890,733	2,977,605	3,106,331	3,160,244
Average Length of Stay...........	4.6	4.5	4.4	4.4	4.4
Inpatient Surgeries..............	177,574	187,369	216,991	239,277	247,886
Births..........................	74,217	75,166	73,033	74,547	80,960
Utilization - Outpatient					
Emergency Outpatient Visits	2,080,313	2,066,382	2,309,621	2,189,955	2,240,946
Other Outpatient Visits............	6,349,105	6,673,210	6,427,396	6,362,148	5,886,520
Total Outpatient Visits	8,429,418	8,739,592	8,737,017	8,552,103	8,127,466
Outpatient Surgeries	263,000	279,931	245,168	250,415	257,530
Personnel					
Full Time RNs	23,340	22,027	20,977	20,524	22,440
Full Time LPNs	487	577	590	649	807
Part Time RNs...................	4,851	5,825	6,167	5,929	5,419
Part Time LPNs	80	114	150	152	135
Total Full Time..................	70,075	67,017	66,940	67,996	71,092
Total Part Time	12,634	14,793	16,020	15,965	14,521
Revenue - Inpatient					
Gross Inpatient Revenue...........	$29,641,292,091	$28,048,084,817	$27,609,357,979	$26,796,619,071	$26,745,329,251
Revenue - Outpatient					
Gross Outpatient Revenue	$23,766,382,533	$21,244,955,845	$18,858,344,930	$16,955,905,216	$15,678,580,294
Revenue and Expenses - Totals					
(Includes Inpatient and Outpatient)					
Total Gross Revenue..............	$53,407,674,624	$49,293,040,662	$46,467,702,909	$43,752,524,287	$42,423,909,545
Deductions from Revenue..........	39,971,629,324	36,737,029,960	34,058,007,365	32,157,030,582	30,579,491,050
Net Patient Revenue	13,436,045,300	12,556,010,702	12,409,695,544	11,595,493,705	11,844,418,495
Other Operating Revenue	534,783,788	603,598,689	475,139,314	515,033,121	504,651,779
Other Nonoperating Revenue	190,853,081	139,238,418	86,412,468	82,344,006	65,552,870
Total Net Revenue...............	14,161,682,169	13,298,847,809	12,971,247,326	12,192,870,832	12,414,623,144
Total Expenses..................	12,984,716,899	12,377,784,591	12,112,683,858	11,520,903,768	11,271,574,937
HOSPITAL UNIT (Excludes Separate Nursing Home Units)					
Utilization - Inpatient					
Beds	13,199	13,252	13,401	13,226	13,265
Admissions	623,030	637,557	672,834	698,689	709,606
Inpatient Days	2,840,826	2,863,151	2,944,802	3,063,786	3,120,611
Average Length of Stay...........	4.6	4.5	4.4	4.4	4.4
Personnel					
Total Full Time..................	69,998	66,942	66,850	67,911	70,791
Total Part Time	12,618	14,777	16,010	15,936	14,477
Revenue and Expenses - Totals					
(Includes Inpatient and Outpatient)					
Total Net Revenue...............	$14,131,564,785	$13,268,304,844	$12,943,620,235	$12,154,799,416	$12,377,572,952
Total Expenses..................	12,972,257,147	12,365,050,443	12,098,532,372	11,504,061,948	11,256,388,031
COMMUNITY HEALTH INDICATORS PER 1000 POPULATION					
Total Population (in thousands)	6,731	6,627	6,553	6,483	6,677
Inpatient					
Beds	2.0	2.0	2.1	2.1	2.0
Admissions	92.8	96.5	103.0	108.1	106.6
Inpatient Days	425.6	436.2	454.4	479.2	473.3
Inpatient Surgeries..............	26.4	28.3	33.1	36.9	37.1
Births..........................	11.0	11.3	11.1	11.5	12.1
Outpatient					
Emergency Outpatient Visits	309.0	311.8	352.4	337.8	335.6
Other Outpatient Visits............	943.2	1,007.0	980.8	981.4	881.7
Total Outpatient Visits	1,252.2	1,318.9	1,333.2	1,319.3	1,217.3
Outpatient Surgeries	39.1	42.2	37.4	38.6	38.6
Expense per Capita (per person).....	$1,929.0	$1,867.9	$1,848.3	$1,777.2	$1,688.2

States

TABLE 6

ARKANSAS

U.S. Registered Community Hospitals
(Nonfederal, short-term general and other special hospitals)

Overview 2010–2014

	2014	2013	2012	2011	2010
Total Community Hospitals in Arkansas........	81	84	83	84	85
Bed Size Category					
6-24	6	6	5	5	6
25-49	28	31	32	33	32
50-99	18	16	14	14	16
100-199	13	15	16	18	18
200-299	8	7	7	5	6
300-399	5	6	6	6	4
400-499	2	2	2	2	2
500 + ...	1	1	1	1	1
Location					
Hospitals Urban..........................	34	36	35	36	37
Hospitals Rural	47	48	48	48	48
Control					
State and Local Government................	10	10	11	11	14
Not for Profit	49	50	49	50	45
Investor owned	22	24	23	23	26
Physician Models					
Independent Practice Association	5	6	6	9	16
Group Practice without Walls................	3	5	5	5	6
Open Physician-Hospital Organization	23	24	23	24	25
Closed Physician-Hospital Organization	5	6	4	5	6
Management Service Organization	12	12	9	10	10
Integrated Salary Model	27	29	20	18	21
Equity Model	1	1	1	0	1
Foundation...............................	6	6	5	6	7
Insurance Products					
Health Maintenance Organization	15	15	14	14	14
Preferred Provider Organization..............	8	6	7	10	14
Indemnity Fee for Service	3	0	1	2	4
Managed Care Contracts					
Health Maintenance Organization	47	47	40	46	46
Preferred Provider Organization..............	56	64	53	64	62
Affiliations					
Hospitals in a System......................	45	47	46	44	46
Hospitals in a Network.....................	28	28	22	26	26
Hospitals in a Group Purchasing Organization..	68	77	61	73	67

TABLE 6

ARKANSAS

U.S. Registered Community Hospitals
(Nonfederal, short-term general and other special hospitals)

Utilization, Personnel, Revenue and Expenses, Community Health Indicators 2010–2014

	2014	2013	2012	2011	2010
TOTAL FACILITY (Includes Hospital and Nursing Home Units)					
Utilization - Inpatient					
Beds	9,284	9,452	9,417	9,425	9,451
Admissions	344,635	352,362	352,752	363,516	370,401
Inpatient Days	1,768,146	1,817,099	1,845,443	1,882,912	1,908,843
Average Length of Stay	5.1	5.2	5.2	5.2	5.2
Inpatient Surgeries	92,169	95,834	101,156	102,964	104,912
Births	35,407	36,313	35,421	36,809	36,913
Utilization - Outpatient					
Emergency Outpatient Visits	1,351,198	1,438,617	1,382,183	1,391,537	1,376,649
Other Outpatient Visits	3,727,703	3,674,902	3,743,252	3,419,087	3,645,562
Total Outpatient Visits	5,078,901	5,113,519	5,125,435	4,810,624	5,022,211
Outpatient Surgeries	172,975	174,981	174,095	160,223	155,784
Personnel					
Full Time RNs	12,022	11,915	11,964	11,429	11,059
Full Time LPNs	1,534	1,579	1,587	1,897	1,890
Part Time RNs	3,492	3,353	3,576	3,700	4,068
Part Time LPNs	411	384	455	606	663
Total Full Time	39,819	39,095	40,286	39,108	38,553
Total Part Time	10,813	9,459	10,397	10,746	11,921
Revenue - Inpatient					
Gross Inpatient Revenue	$10,809,965,954	$10,391,798,234	$9,975,710,168	$9,587,181,461	$9,211,448,957
Revenue - Outpatient					
Gross Outpatient Revenue	$10,398,394,815	$9,513,953,822	$8,663,764,850	$7,800,635,792	$7,084,460,315
Revenue and Expenses - Totals					
(Includes Inpatient and Outpatient)					
Total Gross Revenue	$21,208,360,769	$19,905,752,056	$18,639,475,018	$17,387,817,253	$16,295,909,272
Deductions from Revenue	15,305,292,104	14,135,092,803	12,820,230,814	12,106,848,283	11,007,346,255
Net Patient Revenue	5,903,068,665	5,770,659,253	5,819,244,204	5,280,968,970	5,288,563,017
Other Operating Revenue	308,493,708	269,134,329	256,162,838	220,871,438	221,189,649
Other Nonoperating Revenue	98,329,834	87,213,991	85,908,563	52,395,249	69,605,801
Total Net Revenue	6,309,892,207	6,127,007,573	6,161,315,605	5,554,235,657	5,579,358,467
Total Expenses	5,976,998,987	5,917,263,241	5,759,240,612	5,236,539,234	5,246,234,974
HOSPITAL UNIT (Excludes Separate Nursing Home Units)					
Utilization - Inpatient					
Beds	8,916	9,176	9,200	9,041	9,228
Admissions	344,078	351,947	351,712	362,005	368,895
Inpatient Days	1,666,480	1,738,385	1,774,671	1,757,602	1,830,615
Average Length of Stay	4.8	4.9	5	4.9	5
Personnel					
Total Full Time	39,591	38,944	40,123	38,835	38,362
Total Part Time	10,762	9,429	10,347	10,639	11,881
Revenue and Expenses - Totals					
(Includes Inpatient and Outpatient)					
Total Net Revenue	$6,289,224,053	$6,113,021,586	$6,148,169,295	$5,526,988,517	$5,558,657,844
Total Expenses	5,963,566,360	5,907,194,626	5,749,516,565	5,219,018,613	5,234,362,445
COMMUNITY HEALTH INDICATORS PER 1000 POPULATION					
Total Population (in thousands)	2,966	2,959	2,949	2,938	2,910
Inpatient					
Beds	3.1	3.2	3.2	3.2	3.2
Admissions	116.2	119.1	119.6	123.7	127.3
Inpatient Days	596.1	614.0	625.8	640.9	655.9
Inpatient Surgeries	31.1	32.4	34.3	35.0	36.0
Births	11.9	12.3	12.0	12.5	12.7
Outpatient					
Emergency Outpatient Visits	455.5	486.1	468.7	473.6	473.0
Other Outpatient Visits	1,256.7	1,241.8	1,269.3	1,163.8	1,252.7
Total Outpatient Visits	1,712.2	1,727.9	1,737.9	1,637.4	1,725.7
Outpatient Surgeries	58.3	59.1	59.0	54.5	53.5
Expense per Capita (per person)	$2,014.9	$1,999.5	$1,952.9	$1,782.4	$1,802.7

TABLE 6

CALIFORNIA

U.S. Registered Community Hospitals
(Nonfederal, short-term general and other special hospitals)

Overview 2010–2014

	2014	2013	2012	2011	2010
Total Community Hospitals in California	344	347	349	345	343
Bed Size Category					
6-24	13	13	11	13	13
25-49	38	40	44	39	38
50-99	41	39	40	43	42
100-199	110	109	105	101	104
200-299	61	64	67	65	61
300-399	47	47	44	47	47
400-499	22	22	25	23	24
500 + ...	12	13	13	14	14
Location					
Hospitals Urban..........................	313	316	318	314	312
Hospitals Rural	31	31	31	31	31
Control					
State and Local Government...............	64	63	66	69	69
Not for Profit	205	207	206	202	202
Investor owned	75	77	77	74	72
Physician Models					
Independent Practice Association	64	58	51	64	66
Group Practice without Walls...............	18	13	10	11	11
Open Physician-Hospital Organization	6	5	4	6	5
Closed Physician-Hospital Organization	7	9	4	5	6
Management Service Organization	48	52	46	30	28
Integrated Salary Model	22	22	20	24	24
Equity Model	8	3	2	3	3
Foundation...............................	98	91	83	51	50
Insurance Products					
Health Maintenance Organization	57	54	47	40	35
Preferred Provider Organization..............	25	20	18	24	22
Indemnity Fee for Service	13	9	8	16	11
Managed Care Contracts					
Health Maintenance Organization	162	156	168	147	156
Preferred Provider Organization..............	152	149	161	146	157
Affiliations					
Hospitals in a System......................	240	231	231	230	226
Hospitals in a Network	68	70	60	70	59
Hospitals in a Group Purchasing Organization..	198	199	174	185	182

States

TABLE 6

CALIFORNIA

U.S. Registered Community Hospitals
(Nonfederal, short-term general and other special hospitals)

Utilization, Personnel, Revenue and Expenses, Community Health Indicators 2010–2014

	2014	2013	2012	2011	2010
TOTAL FACILITY (Includes Hospital and Nursing Home Units)					
Utilization - Inpatient					
Beds	69,441	70,326	71,004	70,008	70,440
Admissions	3,184,754	3,255,312	3,304,230	3,393,166	3,423,820
Inpatient Days	16,332,640	16,482,984	16,919,921	17,090,593	17,443,427
Average Length of Stay	5.1	5.1	5.1	5	5.1
Inpatient Surgeries	842,538	835,298	867,839	858,118	907,650
Births	471,877	465,752	482,313	488,863	493,712
Utilization - Outpatient					
Emergency Outpatient Visits	12,693,166	12,088,159	11,859,123	11,073,272	10,945,256
Other Outpatient Visits	41,446,336	41,724,982	40,365,732	41,601,911	40,784,007
Total Outpatient Visits	54,139,502	53,813,141	52,224,855	52,675,183	51,729,263
Outpatient Surgeries	1,268,052	1,276,491	1,249,704	1,273,633	1,261,889
Personnel					
Full Time RNs	108,875	103,849	106,195	103,753	103,010
Full Time LPNs	5,498	5,860	6,108	6,227	6,817
Part Time RNs	55,360	54,052	55,861	50,209	48,553
Part Time LPNs	2,185	2,328	2,574	2,420	2,625
Total Full Time	364,859	359,887	370,238	365,577	358,559
Total Part Time	142,568	140,888	147,910	134,162	129,897
Revenue - Inpatient					
Gross Inpatient Revenue	$211,960,077,263	$205,071,437,854	$194,710,241,465	$183,080,834,445	$176,241,777,468
Revenue - Outpatient					
Gross Outpatient Revenue	$138,248,440,989	$123,867,181,756	$110,355,399,582	$105,412,786,768	$93,211,672,697
Revenue and Expenses - Totals					
(Includes Inpatient and Outpatient)					
Total Gross Revenue	$350,208,518,252	$328,938,605,193	$305,065,641,047	$288,493,621,213	$269,453,450,165
Deductions from Revenue	262,312,721,357	242,255,300,320	222,641,523,180	211,224,646,235	198,665,132,469
Net Patient Revenue	87,895,796,895	86,683,304,873	82,424,117,867	77,268,974,978	70,788,317,696
Other Operating Revenue	5,434,043,994	5,417,248,967	4,935,487,999	4,404,016,212	4,549,376,153
Other Nonoperating Revenue	2,565,342,915	3,336,499,298	1,579,522,303	1,779,948,031	1,405,680,400
Total Net Revenue	95,895,183,804	95,437,053,138	88,939,128,169	83,452,939,221	76,743,374,249
Total Expenses	88,682,388,820	86,710,652,989	83,074,054,310	77,265,358,490	72,279,546,582
HOSPITAL UNIT (Excludes Separate Nursing Home Units)					
Utilization - Inpatient					
Beds	66,026	66,388	66,826	67,306	67,288
Admissions	3,166,923	3,235,117	3,281,803	3,374,467	3,404,159
Inpatient Days	15,283,783	15,256,633	15,596,063	16,266,645	16,480,612
Average Length of Stay	4.8	4.7	4.8	4.8	4.8
Personnel					
Total Full Time	361,224	357,289	366,919	363,402	355,707
Total Part Time	141,348	139,433	146,283	133,098	128,661
Revenue and Expenses - Totals					
(Includes Inpatient and Outpatient)					
Total Net Revenue	$95,394,711,281	$94,867,298,781	$88,462,119,698	$83,072,725,098	$76,308,938,222
Total Expenses	88,386,060,683	86,290,640,782	82,671,685,266	77,001,174,879	71,979,685,381
COMMUNITY HEALTH INDICATORS PER 1000 POPULATION					
Total Population (in thousands)	38,803	38,333	38,041	37,692	37,267
Inpatient					
Beds	1.8	1.8	1.9	1.9	1.9
Admissions	82.1	84.9	86.9	90.0	91.9
Inpatient Days	420.9	430.0	444.8	453.4	468.1
Inpatient Surgeries	21.7	21.8	22.8	22.8	24.4
Births	12.2	12.2	12.7	13.0	13.2
Outpatient					
Emergency Outpatient Visits	327.1	315.3	311.7	293.8	293.7
Other Outpatient Visits	1,068.1	1,088.5	1,061.1	1,103.7	1,094.4
Total Outpatient Visits	1,395.3	1,403.9	1,372.8	1,397.5	1,388.1
Outpatient Surgeries	32.7	33.3	32.9	33.8	33.9
Expense per Capita (per person)	$2,285.5	$2,262.1	$2,183.8	$2,049.9	$1,939.5

TABLE 6

COLORADO

U.S. Registered Community Hospitals
(Nonfederal, short-term general and other special hospitals)

Overview 2010–2014

	2014	2013	2012	2011	2010
Total Community Hospitals in Colorado.......	82	82	82	82	80
Bed Size Category					
6-24	13	12	12	11	11
25-49	19	20	22	23	21
50-99	19	19	17	17	16
100-199	12	13	12	12	14
200-299	7	6	7	7	6
300-399	5	7	6	8	8
400-499	6	4	6	3	2
500 + ...	1	1	0	1	2
Location					
Hospitals Urban..........................	44	44	44	44	43
Hospitals Rural	38	38	38	38	37
Control					
State and Local Government...............	25	25	26	27	27
Not for Profit	40	40	39	38	37
Investor owned	17	17	17	17	16
Physician Models					
Independent Practice Association	10	10	10	11	10
Group Practice without Walls................	2	3	3	3	2
Open Physician-Hospital Organization	12	11	11	13	13
Closed Physician-Hospital Organization	2	3	3	4	3
Management Service Organization	4	4	4	4	4
Integrated Salary Model....................	41	40	40	37	34
Equity Model.............................	1	1	1	2	2
Foundation...............................	2	3	3	2	4
Insurance Products					
Health Maintenance Organization	4	7	9	9	10
Preferred Provider Organization..............	3	4	3	9	10
Indemnity Fee for Service	0	0	1	1	2
Managed Care Contracts					
Health Maintenance Organization	43	46	44	40	46
Preferred Provider Organization..............	48	55	51	45	52
Affiliations					
Hospitals in a System.....................	48	48	47	46	46
Hospitals in a Network	18	20	19	27	27
Hospitals in a Group Purchasing Organization..	60	61	54	63	60

TABLE 6

COLORADO

U.S. Registered Community Hospitals
(Nonfederal, short-term general and other special hospitals)

Utilization, Personnel, Revenue and Expenses, Community Health Indicators 2010–2014

	2014	2013	2012	2011	2010
TOTAL FACILITY (Includes Hospital and Nursing Home Units)					
Utilization - Inpatient					
Beds	10,521	10,301	10,244	10,167	10,208
Admissions	413,537	407,432	444,430	432,887	449,369
Inpatient Days	2,142,076	2,147,937	2,253,793	2,170,349	2,234,925
Average Length of Stay	5.2	5.3	5.1	5	5
Inpatient Surgeries	124,426	122,685	134,849	137,218	141,751
Births	60,944	56,439	58,253	62,264	63,653
Utilization - Outpatient					
Emergency Outpatient Visits	1,909,887	1,875,842	1,818,858	1,730,788	1,677,353
Other Outpatient Visits	6,596,461	6,904,552	7,139,929	6,934,427	6,572,791
Total Outpatient Visits	8,506,348	8,780,394	8,958,787	8,665,215	8,250,144
Outpatient Surgeries	240,077	237,551	232,063	219,321	211,730
Personnel					
Full Time RNs	16,610	15,466	15,678	15,239	15,787
Full Time LPNs	557	479	479	472	551
Part Time RNs	6,491	6,711	6,456	6,449	5,235
Part Time LPNs	175	184	191	190	179
Total Full Time	56,284	54,760	54,125	53,370	55,072
Total Part Time	18,694	20,369	17,930	18,322	15,268
Revenue - Inpatient					
Gross Inpatient Revenue	$25,459,592,142	$23,145,163,295	$22,263,097,740	$19,860,096,681	$19,013,208,766
Revenue - Outpatient					
Gross Outpatient Revenue	$22,116,867,040	$20,071,791,832	$18,360,253,142	$16,603,620,063	$14,766,810,304
Revenue and Expenses - Totals					
(Includes Inpatient and Outpatient)					
Total Gross Revenue	$47,576,459,182	$43,216,955,127	$40,623,350,882	$36,463,716,744	$33,780,019,070
Deductions from Revenue	34,750,591,784	31,041,601,067	28,720,794,917	25,752,881,907	23,450,147,224
Net Patient Revenue	12,825,867,398	12,175,354,060	11,902,555,965	10,710,834,837	10,329,871,846
Other Operating Revenue	575,219,037	601,507,479	559,939,985	513,568,821	501,184,086
Other Nonoperating Revenue	316,257,846	289,329,393	156,458,722	143,185,607	196,854,806
Total Net Revenue	13,717,344,281	13,066,190,932	12,618,954,672	11,367,589,265	11,027,910,738
Total Expenses	11,972,904,688	11,468,752,081	10,941,848,898	10,054,322,089	9,590,946,802
HOSPITAL UNIT (Excludes Separate Nursing Home Units)					
Utilization - Inpatient					
Beds	9,923	9,561	9,663	9,599	9,537
Admissions	412,005	405,640	442,623	430,676	447,782
Inpatient Days	1,982,226	1,924,396	2,067,062	1,995,737	2,026,168
Average Length of Stay	4.8	4.7	4.7	4.6	4.5
Personnel					
Total Full Time	55,945	54,115	53,774	52,935	54,554
Total Part Time	18,519	19,867	17,727	18,169	14,960
Revenue and Expenses - Totals					
(Includes Inpatient and Outpatient)					
Total Net Revenue	$13,686,549,446	$13,018,522,807	$12,577,500,290	$11,330,471,189	$10,984,832,365
Total Expenses	11,943,486,056	11,416,084,053	10,898,966,203	10,014,190,366	9,546,862,102
COMMUNITY HEALTH INDICATORS PER 1000 POPULATION					
Total Population (in thousands)	5,356	5,268	5,188	5,117	5,095
Inpatient					
Beds	2.0	2.0	2.0	2.0	2.0
Admissions	77.2	77.3	85.7	84.6	88.2
Inpatient Days	399.9	407.7	434.5	424.2	438.6
Inpatient Surgeries	23.2	23.3	26.0	26.8	27.8
Births	11.4	10.7	11.2	12.2	12.5
Outpatient					
Emergency Outpatient Visits	356.6	356.1	350.6	338.3	329.2
Other Outpatient Visits	1,231.6	1,310.6	1,376.4	1,355.2	1,290.0
Total Outpatient Visits	1,588.2	1,666.6	1,727.0	1,693.5	1,619.2
Outpatient Surgeries	44.8	45.1	44.7	42.9	41.6
Expense per Capita (per person)	$2,235.5	$2,176.9	$2,109.2	$1,965.0	$1,882.3

States

TABLE 6

CONNECTICUT

U.S. Registered Community Hospitals
(Nonfederal, short-term general and other special hospitals)

Overview 2010–2014

	2014	2013	2012	2011	2010
Total Community Hospitals in Connecticut	32	33	34	35	34
Bed Size Category					
6-24	0	0	0	0	0
25-49	3	3	2	2	1
50-99	8	8	9	8	8
100-199	11	12	10	12	10
200-299	2	2	4	4	5
300-399	4	4	5	5	5
400-499	1	1	1	1	2
500 + ...	3	3	3	3	3
Location					
Hospitals Urban..........................	30	28	29	30	29
Hospitals Rural	2	5	5	5	5
Control					
State and Local Government................	1	1	1	1	1
Not for Profit	30	31	32	33	32
Investor owned	1	1	1	1	1
Physician Models					
Independent Practice Association	6	8	7	6	7
Group Practice without Walls................	0	2	0	0	2
Open Physician-Hospital Organization	7	6	5	4	5
Closed Physician-Hospital Organization	1	3	4	3	2
Management Service Organization	3	3	6	4	5
Integrated Salary Model....................	13	16	17	17	17
Equity Model	4	4	4	1	1
Foundation...............................	10	8	8	9	5
Insurance Products					
Health Maintenance Organization	0	0	0	0	2
Preferred Provider Organization..............	0	0	1	0	0
Indemnity Fee for Service	0	0	0	0	0
Managed Care Contracts					
Health Maintenance Organization	18	20	24	25	23
Preferred Provider Organization..............	18	20	24	25	22
Affiliations					
Hospitals in a System.....................	16	17	18	15	14
Hospitals in a Network	17	16	12	12	11
Hospitals in a Group Purchasing Organization..	24	26	25	27	28

TABLE 6

CONNECTICUT

U.S. Registered Community Hospitals
(Nonfederal, short-term general and other special hospitals)

Utilization, Personnel, Revenue and Expenses, Community Health Indicators 2010–2014

	2014	2013	2012	2011	2010
TOTAL FACILITY (Includes Hospital and Nursing Home Units)					
Utilization - Inpatient					
Beds	7,806	7,811	8,120	7,745	8,091
Admissions	376,644	391,394	378,130	402,838	406,718
Inpatient Days	2,091,854	2,144,945	2,053,559	2,110,564	2,290,323
Average Length of Stay	5.6	5.5	5.4	5.2	5.6
Inpatient Surgeries	103,981	105,579	99,309	103,828	108,070
Births	36,730	36,851	35,891	37,565	37,483
Utilization - Outpatient					
Emergency Outpatient Visits	1,587,150	1,626,044	1,643,476	1,643,282	1,661,088
Other Outpatient Visits	6,900,412	7,648,981	7,342,754	6,884,506	6,605,714
Total Outpatient Visits	8,487,562	9,275,025	8,986,230	8,527,788	8,266,802
Outpatient Surgeries	214,675	217,602	216,262	204,949	201,480
Personnel					
Full Time RNs	10,250	10,664	10,989	11,075	10,483
Full Time LPNs	239	240	261	258	264
Part Time RNs	7,420	6,924	7,221	7,107	6,609
Part Time LPNs	166	190	221	229	194
Total Full Time	43,917	44,827	44,994	44,784	43,689
Total Part Time	22,315	20,843	22,084	22,538	21,507
Revenue - Inpatient					
Gross Inpatient Revenue	$16,003,371,951	$15,912,651,412	$14,329,380,117	$14,148,582,803	$13,295,787,334
Revenue - Outpatient					
Gross Outpatient Revenue	$16,409,353,871	$15,494,331,680	$13,501,775,551	$11,773,260,720	$10,537,030,956
Revenue and Expenses - Totals					
(Includes Inpatient and Outpatient)					
Total Gross Revenue	$32,412,725,822	$31,406,983,092	$27,831,155,668	$25,921,843,523	$23,832,818,290
Deductions from Revenue	21,993,137,480	21,131,372,170	18,019,019,740	16,507,379,096	15,121,712,588
Net Patient Revenue	10,419,588,342	10,275,610,922	9,812,135,928	9,414,464,427	8,711,105,702
Other Operating Revenue	485,957,179	567,209,554	562,656,610	462,365,876	455,355,109
Other Nonoperating Revenue	168,117,622	234,905,027	123,095,744	57,595,778	115,215,987
Total Net Revenue	11,073,663,143	11,077,725,503	10,497,888,282	9,934,426,081	9,281,676,798
Total Expenses	10,341,323,608	10,399,557,016	9,795,239,002	9,561,576,935	8,928,296,028
HOSPITAL UNIT (Excludes Separate Nursing Home Units)					
Utilization - Inpatient					
Beds	7,588	7,599	7,777	7,468	7,676
Admissions	375,481	390,412	377,468	402,394	405,842
Inpatient Days	2,017,478	2,069,739	1,973,687	2,109,561	2,146,637
Average Length of Stay	5.4	5.3	5.2	5.2	5.3
Personnel					
Total Full Time	43,765	44,665	44,726	44,768	43,306
Total Part Time	22,239	20,672	21,876	22,521	21,256
Revenue and Expenses - Totals					
(Includes Inpatient and Outpatient)					
Total Net Revenue	$11,049,447,956	$11,043,626,112	$10,439,662,013	$9,928,376,462	$9,235,623,435
Total Expenses	10,314,425,719	10,376,600,813	9,741,183,887	9,556,797,059	8,888,242,578
COMMUNITY HEALTH INDICATORS PER 1000 POPULATION					
Total Population (in thousands)	3,597	3,596	3,590	3,581	3,527
Inpatient					
Beds	2.2	2.2	2.3	2.2	2.3
Admissions	104.7	108.8	105.3	112.5	115.3
Inpatient Days	581.6	596.5	572.0	589.4	649.4
Inpatient Surgeries	28.9	29.4	27.7	29.0	30.6
Births	10.2	10.2	10.0	10.5	10.6
Outpatient					
Emergency Outpatient Visits	441.3	452.2	457.7	458.9	471.0
Other Outpatient Visits	1,918.6	2,127.0	2,045.1	1,922.7	1,872.9
Total Outpatient Visits	2,359.8	2,579.2	2,502.9	2,381.6	2,343.9
Outpatient Surgeries	59.7	60.5	60.2	57.2	57.1
Expense per Capita (per person)	$2,875.2	$2,891.9	$2,728.2	$2,670.3	$2,531.5

TABLE 6

DELAWARE

U.S. Registered Community Hospitals
(Nonfederal, short-term general and other special hospitals)

Overview 2010–2014

	2014	2013	2012	2011	2010
Total Community Hospitals in Delaware.......	7	7	7	7	7
Bed Size Category					
6-24....................................	0	0	0	0	0
25-49..................................	1	1	1	1	1
50-99..................................	1	1	1	0	0
100-199................................	2	2	2	2	2
200-299................................	1	1	1	2	2
300-399................................	1	1	1	1	1
400-499................................	0	0	0	0	0
500 +..................................	1	1	1	1	1
Location					
Hospitals Urban...........................	7	5	5	5	5
Hospitals Rural	0	2	2	2	2
Control					
State and Local Government................	0	0	0	0	0
Not for Profit	6	6	6	6	6
Investor owned	1	1	1	1	1
Physician Models					
Independent Practice Association	1	0	0	0	0
Group Practice without Walls................	1	1	0	0	0
Open Physician-Hospital Organization	0	0	0	0	0
Closed Physician-Hospital Organization	0	0	0	0	0
Management Service Organization	0	0	0	0	0
Integrated Salary Model....................	2	1	1	2	3
Equity Model.............................	0	0	0	0	0
Foundation...............................	1	1	1	1	1
Insurance Products					
Health Maintenance Organization	0	0	0	0	1
Preferred Provider Organization..............	0	0	0	0	1
Indemnity Fee for Service	0	0	0	0	1
Managed Care Contracts					
Health Maintenance Organization	4	3	3	3	4
Preferred Provider Organization..............	4	3	3	3	4
Affiliations					
Hospitals in a System......................	4	4	4	3	3
Hospitals in a Network.....................	0	0	0	0	0
Hospitals in a Group Purchasing Organization..	6	5	5	5	6

States

TABLE 6

DELAWARE

U.S. Registered Community Hospitals
(Nonfederal, short-term general and other special hospitals)

Utilization, Personnel, Revenue and Expenses, Community Health Indicators 2010–2014

	2014	2013	2012	2011	2010
TOTAL FACILITY (Includes Hospital and Nursing Home Units)					
Utilization - Inpatient					
Beds	2,053	2,034	1,998	2,143	2,155
Admissions	105,109	104,769	104,803	100,288	101,735
Inpatient Days	557,672	538,590	526,678	578,466	580,261
Average Length of Stay.	5.3	5.1	5	5.8	5.7
Inpatient Surgeries.	33,278	31,227	32,163	31,852	28,828
Births.	11,201	11,037	11,358	11,496	11,486
Utilization - Outpatient					
Emergency Outpatient Visits.	451,296	441,756	437,706	417,689	406,652
Other Outpatient Visits.	1,656,267	1,648,654	1,653,598	1,432,957	1,380,658
Total Outpatient Visits	2,107,563	2,090,410	2,091,304	1,850,646	1,787,310
Outpatient Surgeries	62,667	63,281	64,243	62,618	67,852
Personnel					
Full Time RNs	4,258	4,156	3,997	3,990	3,689
Full Time LPNs	131	134	142	171	126
Part Time RNs	2,076	2,082	2,166	1,927	2,195
Part Time LPNs	136	123	118	136	125
Total Full Time.	15,712	15,155	15,421	14,456	13,885
Total Part Time	5,971	5,682	5,918	5,598	5,846
Revenue - Inpatient					
Gross Inpatient Revenue.	$3,558,726,356	$3,299,554,275	$3,097,560,492	$2,830,331,928	$2,671,560,601
Revenue - Outpatient					
Gross Outpatient Revenue	$3,223,470,034	$2,900,967,707	$2,677,941,719	$2,262,497,249	$2,026,156,087
Revenue and Expenses - Totals					
(Includes Inpatient and Outpatient)					
Total Gross Revenue.	$6,782,196,390	$6,200,521,982	$5,775,502,211	$5,092,829,177	$4,697,716,688
Deductions from Revenue.	3,736,411,693	3,349,882,012	3,063,219,162	2,640,575,715	2,394,621,807
Net Patient Revenue.	3,045,784,697	2,850,639,970	2,712,283,049	2,452,253,462	2,303,094,881
Other Operating Revenue	126,674,850	110,674,336	118,067,679	178,700,023	165,608,644
Other Nonoperating Revenue	185,293,240	136,656,471	17,706,306	171,781,254	77,555,669
Total Net Revenue.	3,357,752,787	3,097,970,777	2,848,057,034	2,802,734,739	2,546,259,194
Total Expenses.	2,946,252,827	2,744,800,158	2,662,272,646	2,408,075,977	2,344,087,243
HOSPITAL UNIT (Excludes Separate Nursing Home Units)					
Utilization - Inpatient					
Beds	2,053	2,034	1,998	2,033	1,941
Admissions	105,109	104,769	104,803	99,921	101,130
Inpatient Days	557,672	538,590	526,678	540,146	509,077
Average Length of Stay.	5.3	5.1	5	5.4	5
Personnel					
Total Full Time.	15,712	15,155	15,421	14,301	13,670
Total Part Time	5,971	5,682	5,918	5,582	5,705
Revenue and Expenses - Totals					
(Includes Inpatient and Outpatient)					
Total Net Revenue.	$3,357,752,787	$3,097,970,777	$2,848,057,034	$2,791,771,225	$2,525,583,028
Total Expenses.	2,946,252,827	2,744,800,158	2,662,272,646	2,396,081,133	2,323,082,005
COMMUNITY HEALTH INDICATORS PER 1000 POPULATION					
Total Population (in thousands)	936	926	917	907	891
Inpatient					
Beds	2.2	2.2	2.2	2.4	2.4
Admissions	112.3	113.2	114.3	110.6	114.1
Inpatient Days	596.0	581.8	574.3	637.7	650.9
Inpatient Surgeries.	35.6	33.7	35.1	35.1	32.3
Births.	12.0	11.9	12.4	12.7	12.9
Outpatient					
Emergency Outpatient Visits.	482.4	477.2	477.3	460.4	456.2
Other Outpatient Visits.	1,770.2	1,780.9	1,803.1	1,579.7	1,548.8
Total Outpatient Visits	2,252.6	2,258.1	2,280.4	2,040.1	2,004.9
Outpatient Surgeries	67.0	68.4	70.1	69.0	76.1
Expense per Capita (per person).	$3,149.0	$2,965.0	$2,903.0	$2,654.6	$2,629.5

TABLE 6

DISTRICT OF COLUMBIA

U.S. Registered Community Hospitals
(Nonfederal, short-term general and other special hospitals)

Overview 2010–2014

	2014	2013	2012	2011	2010
Total Community Hospitals in District of Columbia	11	11	11	11	11
Bed Size Category					
6-24	0	0	0	0	0
25-49	0	0	0	0	0
50-99	1	1	1	1	1
100-199	2	2	2	2	2
200-299	2	2	2	3	4
300-399	4	4	4	2	1
400-499	1	0	0	1	1
500 +	1	2	2	2	2
Location					
Hospitals Urban	11	11	11	11	11
Hospitals Rural	0	0	0	0	0
Control					
State and Local Government	0	1	1	1	1
Not for Profit	8	7	7	7	7
Investor owned	3	3	3	3	3
Physician Models					
Independent Practice Association	0	1	3	0	1
Group Practice without Walls	1	2	4	1	0
Open Physician-Hospital Organization	0	0	0	0	0
Closed Physician-Hospital Organization	2	2	3	1	1
Management Service Organization	0	1	3	1	1
Integrated Salary Model	4	4	5	4	5
Equity Model	0	0	0	0	0
Foundation	0	1	1	1	1
Insurance Products					
Health Maintenance Organization	4	4	5	4	2
Preferred Provider Organization	1	1	4	1	0
Indemnity Fee for Service	1	1	0	1	0
Managed Care Contracts					
Health Maintenance Organization	7	7	8	6	7
Preferred Provider Organization	6	7	7	6	6
Affiliations					
Hospitals in a System	8	8	8	8	9
Hospitals in a Network	1	2	1	4	5
Hospitals in a Group Purchasing Organization	7	9	9	7	8

States

TABLE 6

DISTRICT OF COLUMBIA

U.S. Registered Community Hospitals
(Nonfederal, short-term general and other special hospitals)

Utilization, Personnel, Revenue and Expenses, Community Health Indicators 2010–2014

	2014	2013	2012	2011	2010
TOTAL FACILITY (Includes Hospital and Nursing Home Units)					
Utilization - Inpatient					
Beds	3,542	3,609	3,617	3,635	3,458
Admissions	127,293	132,633	132,539	131,577	131,976
Inpatient Days	924,407	946,679	933,177	954,752	926,254
Average Length of Stay	7.3	7.1	7	7.3	7
Inpatient Surgeries	40,866	43,045	39,163	40,477	41,736
Births	13,689	13,718	13,783	13,792	13,814
Utilization - Outpatient					
Emergency Outpatient Visits	497,658	482,319	499,154	455,553	430,637
Other Outpatient Visits	2,155,117	2,095,979	1,961,067	1,994,547	1,888,245
Total Outpatient Visits	2,652,775	2,578,298	2,460,221	2,450,100	2,318,882
Outpatient Surgeries	66,333	72,560	66,622	62,767	58,907
Personnel					
Full Time RNs	6,097	5,930	5,647	5,435	5,458
Full Time LPNs	236	190	249	216	267
Part Time RNs	1,416	1,544	1,318	1,643	1,966
Part Time LPNs	57	27	38	32	46
Total Full Time	22,603	23,125	22,972	22,815	22,654
Total Part Time	4,350	3,984	3,313	4,525	5,259
Revenue - Inpatient					
Gross Inpatient Revenue	$7,521,916,741	$7,091,366,429	$6,515,832,670	$6,334,158,623	$6,016,677,081
Revenue - Outpatient					
Gross Outpatient Revenue	$4,731,589,184	$4,311,322,460	$3,968,228,093	$3,932,470,181	$3,476,432,807
Revenue and Expenses - Totals					
(Includes Inpatient and Outpatient)					
Total Gross Revenue	$12,253,505,925	$11,402,688,889	$10,484,060,763	$10,266,628,804	$9,493,109,888
Deductions from Revenue	8,288,747,229	7,509,944,561	6,640,686,593	6,617,584,769	5,971,324,649
Net Patient Revenue	3,964,758,696	3,892,744,328	3,843,374,170	3,649,044,035	3,521,785,239
Other Operating Revenue	267,439,583	300,528,852	299,523,683	277,637,308	205,891,415
Other Nonoperating Revenue	124,213,686	118,719,257	-15,527,022	95,995,539	33,913,566
Total Net Revenue	4,356,411,965	4,311,992,437	4,127,370,831	4,022,676,882	3,761,590,220
Total Expenses	4,112,356,988	3,946,217,682	3,937,620,808	3,766,313,652	3,582,285,072
HOSPITAL UNIT (Excludes Separate Nursing Home Units)					
Utilization - Inpatient					
Beds	3,125	3,192	3,200	3,470	3,161
Admissions	125,602	130,885	130,696	130,232	130,125
Inpatient Days	782,484	802,846	791,242	909,564	822,314
Average Length of Stay	6.2	6.1	6.1	7	6.3
Personnel					
Total Full Time	22,285	23,026	22,602	22,710	22,327
Total Part Time	4,205	3,968	3,241	4,500	5,181
Revenue and Expenses - Totals					
(Includes Inpatient and Outpatient)					
Total Net Revenue	$4,306,684,083	$4,286,006,742	$4,074,614,436	$4,007,011,323	$3,726,836,744
Total Expenses	4,072,559,344	3,922,587,203	3,890,891,777	3,750,371,864	3,552,676,361
COMMUNITY HEALTH INDICATORS PER 1000 POPULATION					
Total Population (in thousands)	659	646	632	618	611
Inpatient					
Beds	5.4	5.6	5.7	5.9	5.7
Admissions	193.2	205.2	209.6	212.9	216.1
Inpatient Days	1,403.0	1,464.4	1,475.8	1,544.9	1,517.0
Inpatient Surgeries	62.0	66.6	61.9	65.5	68.4
Births	20.8	21.2	21.8	22.3	22.6
Outpatient					
Emergency Outpatient Visits	755.3	746.1	789.4	737.1	705.3
Other Outpatient Visits	3,270.8	3,242.3	3,101.4	3,227.4	3,092.5
Total Outpatient Visits	4,026.1	3,988.4	3,890.8	3,964.6	3,797.8
Outpatient Surgeries	100.7	112.2	105.4	101.6	96.5
Expense per Capita (per person)	$6,241.3	$6,104.5	$6,227.2	$6,094.4	$5,866.9

States

TABLE 6

FLORIDA

U.S. Registered Community Hospitals
(Nonfederal, short-term general and other special hospitals)

Overview 2010–2014

	2014	2013	2012	2011	2010
Total Community Hospitals in Florida.........	211	212	216	213	210
Bed Size Category					
6-24	4	3	4	3	2
25-49	22	24	23	21	21
50-99	40	40	39	38	39
100-199	50	50	55	55	50
200-299	36	37	37	37	38
300-399	24	24	25	27	27
400-499	13	11	10	9	9
500 + ...	22	23	23	23	24
Location					
Hospitals Urban..........................	189	182	186	184	181
Hospitals Rural	22	30	30	29	29
Control					
State and Local Government................	23	24	24	26	27
Not for Profit	79	79	80	81	79
Investor owned	109	109	112	106	104
Physician Models					
Independent Practice Association	3	3	3	5	5
Group Practice without Walls...............	5	7	6	9	7
Open Physician-Hospital Organization	15	15	19	24	19
Closed Physician-Hospital Organization	4	4	2	5	7
Management Service Organization	10	22	15	14	14
Integrated Salary Model....................	61	71	66	64	59
Equity Model	0	0	0	1	1
Foundation...............................	1	1	2	3	4
Insurance Products					
Health Maintenance Organization	15	19	14	15	11
Preferred Provider Organization..............	13	15	7	18	16
Indemnity Fee for Service	8	8	4	7	5
Managed Care Contracts					
Health Maintenance Organization	104	107	100	111	98
Preferred Provider Organization..............	101	104	100	113	101
Affiliations					
Hospitals in a System.....................	174	175	176	167	160
Hospitals in a Network....................	52	51	48	37	35
Hospitals in a Group Purchasing Organization..	116	112	113	101	106

TABLE 6

FLORIDA

U.S. Registered Community Hospitals
(Nonfederal, short-term general and other special hospitals)

Utilization, Personnel, Revenue and Expenses, Community Health Indicators 2010–2014

	2014	2013	2012	2011	2010
TOTAL FACILITY (Includes Hospital and Nursing Home Units)					
Utilization - Inpatient					
Beds	53,489	53,198	53,785	52,923	53,318
Admissions	2,473,183	2,407,117	2,472,181	2,508,311	2,452,089
Inpatient Days	12,310,835	12,063,283	12,372,261	12,365,513	12,191,209
Average Length of Stay	5	5	5	4.9	5
Inpatient Surgeries	591,885	602,806	610,533	614,726	650,557
Births	196,237	198,157	196,681	186,919	202,862
Utilization - Outpatient					
Emergency Outpatient Visits	9,063,174	8,436,473	8,126,914	7,580,718	7,559,853
Other Outpatient Visits	16,532,903	15,558,477	15,367,371	16,827,980	16,683,248
Total Outpatient Visits	25,596,077	23,994,950	23,494,285	24,408,698	24,243,101
Outpatient Surgeries	836,401	837,962	800,782	782,871	798,189
Personnel					
Full Time RNs	75,406	72,327	74,829	72,090	69,840
Full Time LPNs	2,785	3,041	3,495	3,595	4,111
Part Time RNs	19,981	20,562	18,183	16,461	16,844
Part Time LPNs	736	836	885	789	901
Total Full Time	234,719	229,333	239,356	234,893	232,349
Total Part Time	57,735	58,340	55,168	49,243	47,580
Revenue - Inpatient					
Gross Inpatient Revenue	$120,899,048,988	$113,515,265,844	$106,765,072,734	$100,263,145,301	$98,439,589,940
Revenue - Outpatient					
Gross Outpatient Revenue	$85,284,740,554	$77,113,649,369	$70,527,318,626	$63,221,928,643	$58,858,434,042
Revenue and Expenses - Totals					
(Includes Inpatient and Outpatient)					
Total Gross Revenue	$206,183,789,542	$190,628,915,213	$177,292,391,360	$163,485,073,944	$157,298,023,982
Deductions from Revenue	160,812,813,895	148,060,768,748	135,271,195,802	126,350,152,571	119,355,324,858
Net Patient Revenue	45,370,975,647	42,568,146,465	42,021,195,558	37,134,921,373	37,942,699,124
Other Operating Revenue	2,263,801,087	2,224,603,404	2,402,722,300	2,293,290,171	2,190,285,623
Other Nonoperating Revenue	714,150,459	681,074,241	498,972,173	613,632,452	562,284,781
Total Net Revenue	48,348,927,193	45,473,824,110	44,922,890,031	40,041,843,996	40,695,269,528
Total Expenses	42,851,681,447	41,035,030,196	40,816,430,398	36,908,772,722	36,318,160,204
HOSPITAL UNIT (Excludes Separate Nursing Home Units)					
Utilization - Inpatient					
Beds	52,496	52,204	52,723	52,055	52,415
Admissions	2,467,786	2,401,783	2,465,633	2,504,407	2,448,276
Inpatient Days	11,981,943	11,737,932	12,021,523	12,096,907	11,888,876
Average Length of Stay	4.9	4.9	4.9	4.8	4.9
Personnel					
Total Full Time	233,358	228,398	238,286	234,104	231,450
Total Part Time	57,444	58,061	54,951	49,111	47,423
Revenue and Expenses - Totals					
(Includes Inpatient and Outpatient)					
Total Net Revenue	$48,243,102,108	$45,368,763,076	$44,817,002,142	$39,961,735,021	$40,594,960,399
Total Expenses	42,734,599,088	40,928,021,253	40,697,886,032	36,803,286,544	36,197,864,998
COMMUNITY HEALTH INDICATORS PER 1000 POPULATION					
Total Population (in thousands)	19,893	19,553	19,318	19,058	18,678
Inpatient					
Beds	2.7	2.7	2.8	2.8	2.9
Admissions	124.3	123.1	128.0	131.6	131.3
Inpatient Days	618.8	617.0	640.5	648.9	652.7
Inpatient Surgeries	29.8	30.8	31.6	32.3	34.8
Births	9.9	10.1	10.2	9.8	10.9
Outpatient					
Emergency Outpatient Visits	455.6	431.5	420.7	397.8	404.7
Other Outpatient Visits	831.1	795.7	795.5	883.0	893.2
Total Outpatient Visits	1,286.7	1,227.2	1,216.2	1,280.8	1,297.9
Outpatient Surgeries	42.0	42.9	41.5	41.1	42.7
Expense per Capita (per person)	$2,154.1	$2,098.7	$2,112.9	$1,936.7	$1,944.4

TABLE 6

GEORGIA

U.S. Registered Community Hospitals
(Nonfederal, short-term general and other special hospitals)

Overview 2010–2014

	2014	2013	2012	2011	2010
Total Community Hospitals in Georgia	142	144	148	153	154
Bed Size Category					
6-24	3	4	4	6	6
25-49	41	40	38	38	39
50-99	22	25	25	26	24
100-199	35	33	39	41	42
200-299	14	15	18	17	17
300-399	9	8	6	6	7
400-499	7	9	10	8	10
500 + ...	11	10	8	11	9
Location					
Hospitals Urban	85	84	86	88	89
Hospitals Rural	57	60	62	65	65
Control					
State and Local Government	47	46	49	49	52
Not for Profit	64	67	66	68	66
Investor owned	31	31	33	36	36
Physician Models					
Independent Practice Association	10	8	5	6	8
Group Practice without Walls	3	0	0	0	0
Open Physician-Hospital Organization	9	12	12	14	18
Closed Physician-Hospital Organization	18	18	18	16	17
Management Service Organization	3	5	7	9	8
Integrated Salary Model	34	34	35	39	41
Equity Model	2	2	2	4	5
Foundation	3	5	3	4	4
Insurance Products					
Health Maintenance Organization	11	7	6	8	9
Preferred Provider Organization	11	10	8	15	20
Indemnity Fee for Service	2	2	2	4	5
Managed Care Contracts					
Health Maintenance Organization	64	67	67	77	81
Preferred Provider Organization	69	74	72	83	94
Affiliations					
Hospitals in a System	84	81	78	80	81
Hospitals in a Network	38	38	36	41	40
Hospitals in a Group Purchasing Organization . .	78	83	76	95	104

Table 6

GEORGIA

U.S. Registered Community Hospitals
(Nonfederal, short-term general and other special hospitals)

Utilization, Personnel, Revenue and Expenses, Community Health Indicators 2010–2014

	2014	2013	2012	2011	2010
TOTAL FACILITY (Includes Hospital and Nursing Home Units)					
Utilization - Inpatient					
Beds	24,479	24,729	24,657	25,282	25,513
Admissions	941,742	947,299	953,817	956,503	961,391
Inpatient Days	6,140,718	6,034,948	5,970,497	6,094,960	6,138,828
Average Length of Stay	6.5	6.4	6.3	6.4	6.4
Inpatient Surgeries	255,921	259,747	257,747	265,074	265,789
Births	121,828	119,564	119,564	123,546	128,531
Utilization - Outpatient					
Emergency Outpatient Visits	4,114,916	4,221,105	4,153,101	4,035,426	4,095,951
Other Outpatient Visits	11,345,271	11,801,504	10,881,116	10,740,295	10,195,629
Total Outpatient Visits	15,460,187	16,022,609	15,034,217	14,775,721	14,291,580
Outpatient Surgeries	458,180	467,792	474,453	494,889	497,929
Personnel					
Full Time RNs	34,129	32,648	31,786	30,458	30,393
Full Time LPNs	2,317	2,359	2,866	3,119	3,276
Part Time RNs	10,269	9,376	9,066	10,000	10,469
Part Time LPNs	561	628	591	740	857
Total Full Time	117,568	114,844	111,769	110,421	112,040
Total Part Time	29,727	27,612	26,565	29,260	29,110
Revenue - Inpatient					
Gross Inpatient Revenue	$38,624,004,575	$36,086,097,252	$32,638,245,514	$30,470,684,745	$28,768,523,466
Revenue - Outpatient					
Gross Outpatient Revenue	$34,584,791,447	$31,192,879,578	$26,952,133,432	$24,110,026,415	$22,700,713,568
Revenue and Expenses - Totals					
(Includes Inpatient and Outpatient)					
Total Gross Revenue	$73,208,796,022	$67,278,976,830	$59,590,378,946	$54,580,711,160	$51,469,237,034
Deductions from Revenue	52,515,635,482	47,570,657,745	41,286,051,494	38,089,080,759	35,169,736,402
Net Patient Revenue	20,693,160,540	19,708,319,085	18,304,327,452	16,491,630,401	16,299,500,632
Other Operating Revenue	933,337,513	938,355,641	896,928,314	811,702,301	773,260,104
Other Nonoperating Revenue	492,130,104	591,589,397	313,593,866	228,081,442	324,122,628
Total Net Revenue	22,118,628,157	21,238,264,123	19,514,849,632	17,531,414,144	17,396,883,364
Total Expenses	19,975,006,680	19,519,696,158	17,663,914,623	16,450,926,776	16,079,597,038
HOSPITAL UNIT (Excludes Separate Nursing Home Units)					
Utilization - Inpatient					
Beds	21,623	21,808	21,695	21,581	21,605
Admissions	936,020	939,876	947,058	949,217	953,677
Inpatient Days	5,203,686	5,145,091	4,988,750	4,924,671	4,826,637
Average Length of Stay	5.6	5.5	5.3	5.2	5.1
Personnel					
Total Full Time	115,697	113,000	109,799	107,993	109,514
Total Part Time	29,400	27,296	26,140	28,663	28,416
Revenue and Expenses - Totals					
(Includes Inpatient and Outpatient)					
Total Net Revenue	$21,950,548,763	$21,061,224,646	$19,343,288,346	$17,334,774,424	$17,166,588,760
Total Expenses	19,831,945,852	19,365,889,564	17,517,267,271	16,266,797,779	15,896,591,116
COMMUNITY HEALTH INDICATORS PER 1000 POPULATION					
Total Population (in thousands)	10,097	9,992	9,920	9,815	9,908
Inpatient					
Beds	2.4	2.5	2.5	2.6	2.6
Admissions	93.3	94.8	96.2	97.5	97.0
Inpatient Days	608.2	604.0	601.9	621.0	619.6
Inpatient Surgeries	25.3	26.0	26.0	27.0	26.8
Births	12.1	12.0	12.1	12.6	13.0
Outpatient					
Emergency Outpatient Visits	407.5	422.4	418.7	411.1	413.4
Other Outpatient Visits	1,123.6	1,181.1	1,096.9	1,094.3	1,029.0
Total Outpatient Visits	1,531.1	1,603.5	1,515.6	1,505.4	1,442.4
Outpatient Surgeries	45.4	46.8	47.8	50.4	50.3
Expense per Capita (per person)	$1,978.2	$1,953.5	$1,780.6	$1,676.1	$1,622.8

States

TABLE 6

HAWAII

U.S. Registered Community Hospitals
(Nonfederal, short-term general and other special hospitals)

Overview 2010–2014

	2014	2013	2012	2011	2010
Total Community Hospitals in Hawaii	25	25	24	23	26
Bed Size Category					
6-24	6	6	5	5	6
25-49	3	3	3	4	3
50-99	6	6	6	5	4
100-199	5	5	5	4	7
200-299	4	4	4	4	5
300-399	0	0	0	0	0
400-499	0	1	1	1	1
500 + ...	1	0	0	0	0
Location					
Hospitals Urban...........................	16	12	12	11	14
Hospitals Rural	9	13	12	12	12
Control					
State and Local Government................	10	9	10	7	8
Not for Profit	15	16	14	16	18
Investor owned	0	0	0	0	0
Physician Models					
Independent Practice Association	1	2	2	2	2
Group Practice without Walls...............	0	0	0	0	0
Open Physician-Hospital Organization	3	2	2	2	2
Closed Physician-Hospital Organization	2	2	3	2	1
Management Service Organization	0	0	0	0	0
Integrated Salary Model	7	6	9	7	7
Equity Model	0	0	0	0	0
Foundation...............................	0	0	0	0	0
Insurance Products					
Health Maintenance Organization	1	1	1	1	1
Preferred Provider Organization..............	0	0	0	3	3
Indemnity Fee for Service	0	0	0	0	1
Managed Care Contracts					
Health Maintenance Organization	13	12	14	10	7
Preferred Provider Organization..............	12	12	14	10	8
Affiliations					
Hospitals in a System......................	21	20	19	18	21
Hospitals in a Network	8	4	3	2	2
Hospitals in a Group Purchasing Organization..	14	13	15	13	15

TABLE 6

HAWAII

U.S. Registered Community Hospitals
(Nonfederal, short-term general and other special hospitals)

Utilization, Personnel, Revenue and Expenses, Community Health Indicators 2010–2014

	2014	2013	2012	2011	2010
TOTAL FACILITY (Includes Hospital and Nursing Home Units)					
Utilization - Inpatient					
Beds	2,861	2,817	2,803	2,562	3,148
Admissions	109,311	110,374	109,270	105,039	110,577
Inpatient Days	749,201	760,960	745,956	720,633	827,977
Average Length of Stay	6.9	6.9	6.8	6.9	7.5
Inpatient Surgeries	26,095	26,137	27,141	27,447	30,626
Births	10,626	10,229	11,085	10,756	9,271
Utilization - Outpatient					
Emergency Outpatient Visits	432,641	401,191	399,437	366,276	365,903
Other Outpatient Visits	1,858,155	1,752,696	1,635,223	1,639,876	1,828,179
Total Outpatient Visits	2,290,796	2,153,887	2,034,660	2,006,152	2,194,082
Outpatient Surgeries	51,497	47,416	48,246	55,968	58,602
Personnel					
Full Time RNs	4,331	4,045	3,863	3,637	3,858
Full Time LPNs	196	221	253	231	292
Part Time RNs	1,362	963	867	722	974
Part Time LPNs	47	37	46	42	53
Total Full Time	15,011	14,561	15,008	13,674	14,755
Total Part Time	3,762	2,660	3,143	2,369	3,083
Revenue - Inpatient					
Gross Inpatient Revenue	$4,181,164,838	$4,009,282,994	$4,003,578,286	$3,138,945,148	$3,433,349,265
Revenue - Outpatient					
Gross Outpatient Revenue	$3,730,384,969	$3,536,452,224	$3,523,042,969	$2,692,147,508	$2,820,300,482
Revenue and Expenses - Totals					
(Includes Inpatient and Outpatient)					
Total Gross Revenue	$7,911,549,807	$7,545,735,218	$7,526,621,255	$5,831,092,656	$6,253,649,747
Deductions from Revenue	5,025,528,223	4,709,531,039	4,871,561,656	3,693,272,779	3,827,427,740
Net Patient Revenue	2,886,021,584	2,836,204,179	2,655,059,599	2,137,819,877	2,426,222,007
Other Operating Revenue	208,715,461	208,314,941	202,568,356	170,282,864	171,665,631
Other Nonoperating Revenue	63,534,103	132,431,586	35,719,144	43,411,366	48,234,523
Total Net Revenue	3,158,271,148	3,176,950,706	2,893,347,099	2,351,514,107	2,646,122,161
Total Expenses	3,148,443,424	2,917,345,070	2,855,849,784	2,391,952,134	2,611,062,195
HOSPITAL UNIT (Excludes Separate Nursing Home Units)					
Utilization - Inpatient					
Beds	2,630	2,523	2,355	2,203	2,688
Admissions	108,182	108,687	107,534	103,143	108,956
Inpatient Days	680,962	660,686	644,358	598,213	660,450
Average Length of Stay	6.3	6.1	6	5.8	6.1
Personnel					
Total Full Time	14,838	14,355	14,408	13,399	14,428
Total Part Time	3,729	2,623	3,077	2,318	3,047
Revenue and Expenses - Totals					
(Includes Inpatient and Outpatient)					
Total Net Revenue	$3,125,503,974	$3,149,956,310	$2,828,961,559	$2,318,674,997	$2,601,754,091
Total Expenses	3,120,902,400	2,886,933,350	2,775,697,478	2,347,459,882	2,561,364,433
COMMUNITY HEALTH INDICATORS PER 1000 POPULATION					
Total Population (in thousands)	1,420	1,404	1,392	1,375	1,300
Inpatient					
Beds	2.0	2.0	2.0	1.9	2.4
Admissions	77.0	78.6	78.5	76.4	85.1
Inpatient Days	527.8	542.0	535.8	524.2	636.9
Inpatient Surgeries	18.4	18.6	19.5	20.0	23.6
Births	7.5	7.3	8.0	7.8	7.1
Outpatient					
Emergency Outpatient Visits	304.8	285.7	286.9	266.4	281.4
Other Outpatient Visits	1,309.0	1,248.3	1,174.5	1,192.8	1,406.2
Total Outpatient Visits	1,613.7	1,534.0	1,461.4	1,459.2	1,687.6
Outpatient Surgeries	36.3	33.8	34.7	40.7	45.1
Expense per Capita (per person)	$2,217.9	$2,077.8	$2,051.2	$1,739.8	$2,008.4

States

TABLE 6

IDAHO

U.S. Registered Community Hospitals
(Nonfederal, short-term general and other special hospitals)

Overview 2010–2014

	2014	2013	2012	2011	2010
Total Community Hospitals in Idaho	40	40	40	40	41
Bed Size Category					
6-24	12	12	11	12	11
25-49	11	10	13	11	12
50-99	9	9	7	8	9
100-199	3	4	5	4	5
200-299	2	2	1	2	1
300-399	2	2	2	2	2
400-499	0	0	0	0	0
500 + ...	1	1	1	1	1
Location					
Hospitals Urban..........................	14	14	14	14	15
Hospitals Rural	26	26	26	26	26
Control					
State and Local Government................	19	18	19	19	20
Not for Profit	16	17	16	17	16
Investor owned	5	5	5	4	5
Physician Models					
Independent Practice Association	1	1	4	5	5
Group Practice without Walls................	0	0	0	1	1
Open Physician-Hospital Organization	6	6	10	7	4
Closed Physician-Hospital Organization	3	1	1	2	2
Management Service Organization	0	0	0	1	3
Integrated Salary Model	14	14	15	12	13
Equity Model	1	1	1	0	0
Foundation...............................	2	1	1	1	1
Insurance Products					
Health Maintenance Organization	1	1	0	1	2
Preferred Provider Organization..............	3	2	2	2	2
Indemnity Fee for Service	2	1	1	1	0
Managed Care Contracts					
Health Maintenance Organization	12	12	14	13	14
Preferred Provider Organization..............	19	17	17	17	19
Affiliations					
Hospitals in a System.....................	21	20	21	20	23
Hospitals in a Network	10	9	10	11	13
Hospitals in a Group Purchasing Organization..	23	24	26	25	25

TABLE 6

IDAHO

U.S. Registered Community Hospitals
(Nonfederal, short-term general and other special hospitals)

Utilization, Personnel, Revenue and Expenses, Community Health Indicators 2010–2014

	2014	2013	2012	2011	2010
TOTAL FACILITY (Includes Hospital and Nursing Home Units)					
Utilization - Inpatient					
Beds	3,311	3,355	3,305	3,306	3,376
Admissions	121,728	126,164	123,794	128,742	131,375
Inpatient Days	593,788	609,999	611,785	605,718	628,840
Average Length of Stay	4.9	4.8	4.9	4.7	4.8
Inpatient Surgeries	35,856	36,416	40,313	39,858	39,614
Births	19,845	19,285	20,117	19,487	18,941
Utilization - Outpatient					
Emergency Outpatient Visits	627,163	590,382	543,272	517,995	489,718
Other Outpatient Visits	4,577,820	4,187,775	3,807,298	3,516,106	2,672,240
Total Outpatient Visits	5,204,983	4,778,157	4,350,570	4,034,101	3,161,958
Outpatient Surgeries	86,554	76,661	81,915	84,221	73,409
Personnel					
Full Time RNs	5,076	4,878	4,651	4,334	4,103
Full Time LPNs	438	448	443	458	403
Part Time RNs	2,583	2,688	2,418	2,341	2,245
Part Time LPNs	189	201	193	209	166
Total Full Time	23,357	22,143	20,340	19,181	18,010
Total Part Time	8,861	8,840	8,192	8,019	7,175
Revenue - Inpatient					
Gross Inpatient Revenue	$4,648,452,893	$4,216,564,570	$3,543,382,140	$3,108,970,857	$2,899,758,710
Revenue - Outpatient					
Gross Outpatient Revenue	$5,438,016,219	$4,739,814,434	$4,029,848,296	$3,623,818,467	$3,113,164,805
Revenue and Expenses - Totals					
(Includes Inpatient and Outpatient)					
Total Gross Revenue	$10,086,469,112	$8,956,379,004	$7,573,230,436	$6,732,789,324	$6,012,923,515
Deductions from Revenue	6,053,377,363	5,257,575,535	4,057,678,208	3,621,413,551	3,190,452,073
Net Patient Revenue	4,033,091,749	3,698,803,469	3,515,552,228	3,111,375,773	2,822,471,442
Other Operating Revenue	125,368,316	149,063,415	116,996,412	103,709,342	96,182,670
Other Nonoperating Revenue	56,565,814	38,229,484	17,730,950	49,967,037	47,366,046
Total Net Revenue	4,215,025,879	3,886,096,368	3,650,279,590	3,265,052,152	2,966,020,158
Total Expenses	3,792,866,699	3,549,202,960	3,127,967,915	2,791,035,799	2,546,624,205
HOSPITAL UNIT (Excludes Separate Nursing Home Units)					
Utilization - Inpatient					
Beds	3,136	3,087	3,041	2,950	3,027
Admissions	121,467	125,217	122,840	127,750	129,900
Inpatient Days	543,992	536,798	536,537	503,243	525,428
Average Length of Stay	4.5	4.3	4.4	3.9	4
Personnel					
Total Full Time	23,228	21,912	20,159	18,937	17,803
Total Part Time	8,761	8,716	8,074	7,878	7,040
Revenue and Expenses - Totals					
(Includes Inpatient and Outpatient)					
Total Net Revenue	$4,202,706,609	$3,858,606,336	$3,630,538,385	$3,240,672,233	$2,934,932,796
Total Expenses	3,779,790,525	3,530,094,122	3,117,054,550	2,775,730,301	2,524,919,767
COMMUNITY HEALTH INDICATORS PER 1000 POPULATION					
Total Population (in thousands)	1,634	1,612	1,596	1,585	1,560
Inpatient					
Beds	2.0	2.1	2.1	2.1	2.2
Admissions	74.5	78.3	77.6	81.2	84.2
Inpatient Days	363.3	378.4	383.4	382.2	403.2
Inpatient Surgeries	21.9	22.6	25.3	25.1	25.4
Births	12.1	12.0	12.6	12.3	12.1
Outpatient					
Emergency Outpatient Visits	383.7	366.2	340.5	326.8	314.0
Other Outpatient Visits	2,800.8	2,597.7	2,385.9	2,218.4	1,713.2
Total Outpatient Visits	3,184.5	2,963.9	2,726.4	2,545.2	2,027.2
Outpatient Surgeries	53.0	47.6	51.3	53.1	47.1
Expense per Capita (per person)	$2,320.6	$2,201.6	$1,960.2	$1,760.9	$1,632.7

States

TABLE 6

ILLINOIS

U.S. Registered Community Hospitals
(Nonfederal, short-term general and other special hospitals)

Overview 2010–2014

	2014	2013	2012	2011	2010
Total Community Hospitals in Illinois.........	189	189	188	188	189
Bed Size Category					
6-24.....................................	14	13	12	11	10
25-49....................................	36	37	38	36	32
50-99....................................	29	29	27	31	36
100-199..................................	55	54	53	51	50
200-299..................................	25	25	22	24	25
300-399..................................	16	17	20	18	19
400-499..................................	6	6	9	9	9
500 +....................................	8	8	7	8	8
Location					
Hospitals Urban.........................	130	125	124	124	125
Hospitals Rural	59	64	64	64	64
Control					
State and Local Government...............	24	23	24	24	26
Not for Profit............................	144	146	144	145	143
Investor owned	21	20	20	19	20
Physician Models					
Independent Practice Association	26	24	26	22	28
Group Practice without Walls...............	10	12	8	8	4
Open Physician-Hospital Organization	53	56	46	43	43
Closed Physician-Hospital Organization	10	11	9	11	13
Management Service Organization	19	19	21	21	22
Integrated Salary Model....................	74	71	63	59	62
Equity Model	4	5	3	3	2
Foundation...............................	9	10	8	8	13
Insurance Products					
Health Maintenance Organization	23	25	21	16	19
Preferred Provider Organization..............	15	17	13	17	17
Indemnity Fee for Service	7	6	4	7	7
Managed Care Contracts					
Health Maintenance Organization	123	120	122	114	123
Preferred Provider Organization..............	135	136	137	127	134
Affiliations					
Hospitals in a System.....................	120	118	114	113	108
Hospitals in a Network	67	58	52	43	47
Hospitals in a Group Purchasing Organization..	151	149	145	142	157

TABLE 6

ILLINOIS

U.S. Registered Community Hospitals
(Nonfederal, short-term general and other special hospitals)

Utilization, Personnel, Revenue and Expenses, Community Health Indicators 2010–2014

	2014	2013	2012	2011	2010
TOTAL FACILITY (Includes Hospital and Nursing Home Units)					
Utilization - Inpatient					
Beds	31,573	31,745	32,662	32,775	33,310
Admissions	1,380,085	1,426,848	1,484,155	1,511,770	1,542,958
Inpatient Days	6,841,826	6,865,573	7,190,230	7,398,797	7,552,956
Average Length of Stay.	5	4.8	4.8	4.9	4.9
Inpatient Surgeries.	360,213	368,428	376,684	386,166	403,226
Births.	147,464	146,392	150,234	152,929	159,563
Utilization - Outpatient					
Emergency Outpatient Visits	5,273,213	5,252,340	5,422,193	5,414,964	5,366,010
Other Outpatient Visits.	28,160,509	27,556,186	27,694,668	26,277,834	27,192,086
Total Outpatient Visits	33,433,722	32,808,526	33,116,861	31,692,798	32,558,096
Outpatient Surgeries	736,891	743,687	728,808	731,909	738,783
Personnel					
Full Time RNs	47,039	46,160	44,894	42,707	41,948
Full Time LPNs	1,468	1,679	1,684	1,730	1,769
Part Time RNs.	23,887	21,818	23,656	23,563	23,493
Part Time LPNs	558	633	690	769	808
Total Full Time.	170,080	168,524	168,745	163,470	163,519
Total Part Time	75,417	70,370	72,684	74,154	74,448
Revenue - Inpatient					
Gross Inpatient Revenue.	$59,479,867,913	$55,496,665,893	$54,040,034,827	$51,831,662,656	$50,630,716,983
Revenue - Outpatient					
Gross Outpatient Revenue	$62,657,072,479	$55,220,592,255	$51,085,072,799	$45,237,976,561	$41,884,636,238
Revenue and Expenses - Totals					
(Includes Inpatient and Outpatient)					
Total Gross Revenue.	$122,136,940,392	$110,717,258,148	$105,125,107,626	$97,069,639,217	$92,515,353,221
Deductions from Revenue.	86,861,936,578	78,196,471,517	73,249,630,932	67,477,849,736	63,248,692,053
Net Patient Revenue	35,275,003,814	32,520,786,631	31,875,476,694	29,591,789,481	29,266,661,168
Other Operating Revenue	2,092,681,737	2,131,938,656	1,930,010,171	1,900,816,882	1,918,358,653
Other Nonoperating Revenue	1,406,842,660	1,098,662,582	597,357,110	1,093,755,704	712,723,108
Total Net Revenue.	38,774,528,211	35,751,387,869	34,402,843,975	32,586,362,067	31,897,742,929
Total Expenses.	35,123,918,794	32,752,851,815	31,914,764,033	29,831,858,047	29,193,599,201
HOSPITAL UNIT (Excludes Separate Nursing Home Units)					
Utilization - Inpatient					
Beds	30,374	30,716	31,431	31,305	31,615
Admissions	1,369,430	1,417,171	1,471,741	1,497,436	1,526,371
Inpatient Days	6,547,258	6,623,180	6,891,159	7,012,553	7,117,426
Average Length of Stay.	4.8	4.7	4.7	4.7	4.7
Personnel					
Total Full Time.	169,603	167,903	168,056	162,704	162,567
Total Part Time	75,033	69,892	72,171	73,555	73,868
Revenue and Expenses - Totals					
(Includes Inpatient and Outpatient)					
Total Net Revenue.	$38,682,715,068	$35,673,229,824	$34,307,140,177	$32,474,980,131	$31,785,482,525
Total Expenses.	35,048,528,192	32,686,336,226	31,835,376,910	29,734,524,075	29,102,876,687
COMMUNITY HEALTH INDICATORS PER 1000 POPULATION					
Total Population (in thousands)	12,881	12,882	12,875	12,869	12,944
Inpatient					
Beds	2.5	2.5	2.5	2.5	2.6
Admissions	107.1	110.8	115.3	117.5	119.2
Inpatient Days	531.2	533.0	558.5	574.9	583.5
Inpatient Surgeries.	28.0	28.6	29.3	30.0	31.2
Births.	11.4	11.4	11.7	11.9	12.3
Outpatient					
Emergency Outpatient Visits	409.4	407.7	421.1	420.8	414.5
Other Outpatient Visits.	2,186.3	2,139.1	2,151.0	2,041.9	2,100.7
Total Outpatient Visits	2,595.7	2,546.8	2,572.1	2,462.7	2,515.2
Outpatient Surgeries	57.2	57.7	56.6	56.9	57.1
Expense per Capita (per person).	$2,726.9	$2,542.5	$2,478.8	$2,318.1	$2,255.3

States

TABLE 6

INDIANA

U.S. Registered Community Hospitals
(Nonfederal, short-term general and other special hospitals)

Overview 2010–2014

	2014	2013	2012	2011	2010
Total Community Hospitals in Indiana	121	123	124	125	125
Bed Size Category					
6-24	8	6	6	5	5
25-49	40	42	40	40	41
50-99	23	26	28	30	28
100-199	26	23	24	23	21
200-299	9	12	11	13	16
300-399	4	3	5	5	5
400-499	6	6	4	3	3
500 + ...	5	5	6	6	6
Location					
Hospitals Urban..........................	79	83	84	85	85
Hospitals Rural	42	40	40	40	40
Control					
State and Local Government................	30	30	30	30	33
Not for Profit	67	68	69	71	67
Investor owned	24	25	25	24	25
Physician Models					
Independent Practice Association	7	5	7	3	6
Group Practice without Walls...............	4	4	5	4	2
Open Physician-Hospital Organization	19	23	21	21	26
Closed Physician-Hospital Organization	5	5	8	7	8
Management Service Organization	8	9	7	8	9
Integrated Salary Model....................	62	61	58	53	55
Equity Model	4	4	3	3	2
Foundation...............................	6	6	4	2	5
Insurance Products					
Health Maintenance Organization	34	31	28	27	29
Preferred Provider Organization..............	28	35	29	30	33
Indemnity Fee for Service	7	9	9	4	6
Managed Care Contracts					
Health Maintenance Organization	72	64	64	62	65
Preferred Provider Organization..............	82	78	76	71	77
Affiliations					
Hospitals in a System......................	87	86	85	87	85
Hospitals in a Network	48	45	42	45	46
Hospitals in a Group Purchasing Organization..	95	96	92	87	97

TABLE 6

INDIANA

U.S. Registered Community Hospitals
(Nonfederal, short-term general and other special hospitals)

Utilization, Personnel, Revenue and Expenses, Community Health Indicators 2010–2014

	2014	2013	2012	2011	2010
TOTAL FACILITY (Includes Hospital and Nursing Home Units)					
Utilization - Inpatient					
Beds	17,193	17,264	17,556	17,467	17,759
Admissions	681,537	701,743	731,046	737,438	718,348
Inpatient Days	3,567,957	3,653,922	3,739,056	3,724,041	3,756,021
Average Length of Stay	5.2	5.2	5.1	5	5.2
Inpatient Surgeries	180,347	186,776	200,708	200,907	206,124
Births	72,348	71,984	73,460	76,049	77,124
Utilization - Outpatient					
Emergency Outpatient Visits	3,261,594	3,129,456	3,207,214	3,144,973	3,185,166
Other Outpatient Visits	15,922,420	15,270,100	14,711,090	15,367,982	15,543,606
Total Outpatient Visits	19,184,014	18,399,556	17,918,304	18,512,955	18,728,772
Outpatient Surgeries	402,487	420,844	441,917	429,164	423,827
Personnel					
Full Time RNs	22,750	23,370	23,611	23,243	22,345
Full Time LPNs	1,283	1,468	1,536	1,697	1,664
Part Time RNs	13,871	14,311	14,379	13,697	14,136
Part Time LPNs	619	711	722	768	874
Total Full Time	86,732	87,286	88,265	87,241	86,266
Total Part Time	41,307	41,032	41,617	39,619	41,019
Revenue - Inpatient					
Gross Inpatient Revenue	$28,291,483,706	$26,593,801,942	$26,099,729,709	$23,724,867,721	$21,889,172,836
Revenue - Outpatient					
Gross Outpatient Revenue	$30,389,753,127	$28,186,114,204	$26,487,465,316	$23,279,155,929	$20,791,179,952
Revenue and Expenses - Totals (Includes Inpatient and Outpatient)					
Total Gross Revenue	$58,681,236,833	$54,779,916,146	$52,587,195,025	$47,004,023,650	$42,680,352,788
Deductions from Revenue	38,981,153,394	36,132,735,438	33,296,640,742	30,555,814,094	26,936,969,969
Net Patient Revenue	19,700,083,439	18,647,180,708	19,290,554,283	16,448,209,556	15,743,382,819
Other Operating Revenue	1,263,877,365	1,042,257,524	1,104,200,980	1,117,137,691	881,745,072
Other Nonoperating Revenue	475,251,971	607,370,565	439,930,085	405,284,123	434,805,381
Total Net Revenue	21,439,212,775	20,296,808,797	20,834,685,348	17,970,631,370	17,059,933,272
Total Expenses	18,019,558,162	17,893,508,316	17,926,526,564	16,082,098,784	15,349,922,777
HOSPITAL UNIT (Excludes Separate Nursing Home Units)					
Utilization - Inpatient					
Beds	16,445	16,552	16,911	16,942	17,208
Admissions	678,617	698,347	726,693	732,496	713,224
Inpatient Days	3,351,720	3,442,577	3,569,377	3,562,156	3,584,106
Average Length of Stay	4.9	4.9	4.9	4.9	5
Personnel					
Total Full Time	86,234	86,819	87,873	86,943	85,948
Total Part Time	40,871	40,642	41,296	39,255	40,630
Revenue and Expenses - Totals (Includes Inpatient and Outpatient)					
Total Net Revenue	$21,372,452,682	$20,233,420,523	$20,781,574,841	$17,906,999,370	$17,017,380,655
Total Expenses	17,965,282,386	17,841,711,211	17,894,880,475	16,032,853,104	15,311,258,669
COMMUNITY HEALTH INDICATORS PER 1000 POPULATION					
Total Population (in thousands)	6,597	6,571	6,537	6,517	6,445
Inpatient					
Beds	2.6	2.6	2.7	2.7	2.8
Admissions	103.3	106.8	111.8	113.2	111.5
Inpatient Days	540.9	556.1	572.0	571.4	582.8
Inpatient Surgeries	27.3	28.4	30.7	30.8	32.0
Births	11.0	11.0	11.2	11.7	12.0
Outpatient					
Emergency Outpatient Visits	494.4	476.3	490.6	482.6	494.2
Other Outpatient Visits	2,413.6	2,323.9	2,250.3	2,358.2	2,411.6
Total Outpatient Visits	2,908.1	2,800.2	2,740.9	2,840.8	2,905.8
Outpatient Surgeries	61.0	64.0	67.6	65.9	65.8
Expense per Capita (per person)	$2,731.5	$2,723.1	$2,742.2	$2,467.7	$2,381.6

States

TABLE 6

IOWA

U.S. Registered Community Hospitals
(Nonfederal, short-term general and other special hospitals)

Overview 2010–2014

	2014	2013	2012	2011	2010
Total Community Hospitals in Iowa...........	118	118	118	118	118
Bed Size Category					
6-24.....................................	21	20	19	19	18
25-49....................................	50	49	48	48	49
50-99....................................	23	26	26	27	27
100-199..................................	10	9	11	10	10
200-299..................................	7	6	6	6	6
300-399..................................	4	5	5	5	5
400-499..................................	0	1	1	1	1
500 +....................................	3	2	2	2	2
Location					
Hospitals Urban...........................	35	34	34	34	34
Hospitals Rural...........................	83	84	84	84	84
Control					
State and Local Government................	59	59	59	59	59
Not for Profit.............................	57	57	57	57	57
Investor owned...........................	2	2	2	2	2
Physician Models					
Independent Practice Association............	13	13	14	12	13
Group Practice without Walls...............	3	5	5	5	4
Open Physician-Hospital Organization........	18	20	19	18	20
Closed Physician-Hospital Organization.......	10	11	11	11	10
Management Service Organization...........	7	8	8	9	8
Integrated Salary Model....................	76	77	76	74	72
Equity Model.............................	1	1	1	1	0
Foundation...............................	3	4	3	5	4
Insurance Products					
Health Maintenance Organization............	19	14	10	8	8
Preferred Provider Organization..............	17	15	12	20	23
Indemnity Fee for Service..................	5	3	4	5	5
Managed Care Contracts					
Health Maintenance Organization............	77	75	75	74	73
Preferred Provider Organization..............	95	95	95	94	99
Affiliations					
Hospitals in a System......................	73	70	69	64	66
Hospitals in a Network.....................	78	79	79	77	73
Hospitals in a Group Purchasing Organization..	117	117	116	115	115

States

TABLE 6

IOWA

U.S. Registered Community Hospitals
(Nonfederal, short-term general and other special hospitals)

Utilization, Personnel, Revenue and Expenses, Community Health Indicators 2010–2014

	2014	2013	2012	2011	2010
TOTAL FACILITY (Includes Hospital and Nursing Home Units)					
Utilization - Inpatient					
Beds	9,740	9,839	9,962	9,981	10,075
Admissions	318,999	326,593	336,765	340,412	341,744
Inpatient Days	1,958,693	2,001,590	2,022,552	2,058,730	2,058,304
Average Length of Stay	6.1	6.1	6	6	6
Inpatient Surgeries	79,279	80,936	84,008	83,333	87,343
Births	39,101	38,344	37,967	37,284	38,193
Utilization - Outpatient					
Emergency Outpatient Visits	1,290,755	1,292,810	1,297,129	1,273,985	1,223,271
Other Outpatient Visits	9,501,854	9,316,036	9,318,536	9,053,438	9,805,308
Total Outpatient Visits	10,792,609	10,608,846	10,615,665	10,327,423	11,028,579
Outpatient Surgeries	250,088	247,077	253,460	256,117	253,148
Personnel					
Full Time RNs	11,977	11,653	11,208	11,084	10,516
Full Time LPNs	738	702	761	788	775
Part Time RNs	6,502	6,734	6,913	6,843	6,988
Part Time LPNs	505	497	563	412	548
Total Full Time	45,734	45,507	44,797	44,535	43,589
Total Part Time	22,084	22,560	23,460	23,019	23,392
Revenue - Inpatient					
Gross Inpatient Revenue	$9,132,937,528	$8,806,484,946	$8,408,565,148	$7,955,026,036	$7,478,207,382
Revenue - Outpatient					
Gross Outpatient Revenue	$11,904,002,918	$10,917,710,660	$10,161,337,605	$9,276,348,064	$8,615,345,555
Revenue and Expenses - Totals					
(Includes Inpatient and Outpatient)					
Total Gross Revenue	$21,036,940,446	$19,724,195,606	$18,569,902,753	$17,231,374,100	$16,093,552,937
Deductions from Revenue	13,223,158,549	12,194,888,808	11,074,628,171	10,246,167,955	9,374,915,563
Net Patient Revenue	7,813,781,897	7,529,306,798	7,495,274,582	6,985,206,145	6,718,637,374
Other Operating Revenue	642,979,756	620,140,454	591,931,420	502,660,629	483,246,348
Other Nonoperating Revenue	306,092,900	292,293,006	149,767,795	223,831,009	236,093,511
Total Net Revenue	8,762,854,553	8,441,740,258	8,236,973,797	7,711,697,783	7,437,977,233
Total Expenses	8,129,893,480	7,832,928,280	7,709,621,525	7,174,090,504	6,934,527,799
HOSPITAL UNIT (Excludes Separate Nursing Home Units)					
Utilization - Inpatient					
Beds	8,123	8,153	8,275	8,287	8,341
Admissions	315,816	323,713	332,949	336,335	337,483
Inpatient Days	1,445,672	1,482,642	1,501,406	1,533,884	1,521,829
Average Length of Stay	4.6	4.6	4.5	4.6	4.5
Personnel					
Total Full Time	44,921	44,714	44,073	43,792	42,836
Total Part Time	21,305	21,781	22,722	22,278	22,670
Revenue and Expenses - Totals					
(Includes Inpatient and Outpatient)					
Total Net Revenue	$8,673,877,088	$8,349,001,790	$8,147,277,912	$7,624,566,231	$7,354,382,506
Total Expenses	8,055,771,463	7,756,011,550	7,631,417,462	7,096,506,924	6,860,708,589
COMMUNITY HEALTH INDICATORS PER 1000 POPULATION					
Total Population (in thousands)	3,107	3,090	3,074	3,062	3,023
Inpatient					
Beds	3.1	3.2	3.2	3.3	3.3
Admissions	102.7	105.7	109.5	111.2	113.0
Inpatient Days	630.4	647.7	657.9	672.3	680.9
Inpatient Surgeries	25.5	26.2	27.3	27.2	28.9
Births	12.6	12.4	12.4	12.2	12.6
Outpatient					
Emergency Outpatient Visits	415.4	418.3	421.9	416.0	404.6
Other Outpatient Visits	3,058.1	3,014.5	3,031.2	2,956.4	3,243.5
Total Outpatient Visits	3,473.5	3,432.8	3,453.2	3,372.4	3,648.1
Outpatient Surgeries	80.5	79.9	82.4	83.6	83.7
Expense per Capita (per person)	$2,616.5	$2,534.6	$2,507.9	$2,342.7	$2,293.9

States

TABLE 6

KANSAS

U.S. Registered Community Hospitals
(Nonfederal, short-term general and other special hospitals)

Overview 2010–2014

	2014	2013	2012	2011	2010
Total Community Hospitals in Kansas	133	130	131	132	130
Bed Size Category					
6-24	21	21	20	20	19
25-49	54	49	49	50	49
50-99	32	35	37	38	37
100-199	16	16	16	14	16
200-299	5	4	4	5	4
300-399	1	2	2	2	2
400-499	1	0	0	0	0
500 + ...	3	3	3	3	3
Location					
Hospitals Urban.........................	37	34	34	33	33
Hospitals Rural	96	96	97	99	97
Control					
State and Local Government...............	64	61	61	63	62
Not for Profit	51	51	53	53	51
Investor owned	18	18	17	16	17
Physician Models					
Independent Practice Association	9	10	13	15	13
Group Practice without Walls..............	3	3	4	3	2
Open Physician-Hospital Organization	8	11	12	12	11
Closed Physician-Hospital Organization	0	1	2	1	0
Management Service Organization	0	1	2	5	3
Integrated Salary Model...................	85	79	79	77	69
Equity Model	1	1	2	1	0
Foundation..............................	3	4	5	8	5
Insurance Products					
Health Maintenance Organization	1	2	2	1	1
Preferred Provider Organization.............	5	5	7	9	9
Indemnity Fee for Service	0	1	3	0	1
Managed Care Contracts					
Health Maintenance Organization	59	57	56	55	56
Preferred Provider Organization.............	110	109	112	110	109
Affiliations					
Hospitals in a System.....................	52	53	56	55	53
Hospitals in a Network....................	80	80	79	82	83
Hospitals in a Group Purchasing Organization..	129	129	128	129	128

TABLE 6

KANSAS

U.S. Registered Community Hospitals
(Nonfederal, short-term general and other special hospitals)

Utilization, Personnel, Revenue and Expenses, Community Health Indicators 2010–2014

	2014	2013	2012	2011	2010
TOTAL FACILITY (Includes Hospital and Nursing Home Units)					
Utilization - Inpatient					
Beds	10,028	9,998	10,127	10,023	9,965
Admissions	296,085	289,696	296,267	302,351	304,769
Inpatient Days	1,891,620	1,899,716	1,915,826	1,923,661	1,960,261
Average Length of Stay	6.4	6.6	6.5	6.4	6.4
Inpatient Surgeries	69,380	71,156	73,240	76,828	79,305
Births	38,189	37,311	38,623	38,707	39,777
Utilization - Outpatient					
Emergency Outpatient Visits	1,174,104	1,127,551	1,114,026	1,041,234	1,019,521
Other Outpatient Visits	5,982,336	5,962,793	6,179,011	5,955,302	5,660,293
Total Outpatient Visits	7,156,440	7,090,344	7,293,037	6,996,536	6,679,814
Outpatient Surgeries	160,208	156,088	166,253	161,889	157,746
Personnel					
Full Time RNs	11,919	12,146	11,619	10,968	10,852
Full Time LPNs	1,005	1,036	1,009	1,014	1,056
Part Time RNs	4,743	4,861	4,917	4,533	4,535
Part Time LPNs	356	389	405	409	441
Total Full Time	40,854	40,892	40,129	39,286	38,881
Total Part Time	14,165	14,722	14,838	14,111	14,183
Revenue - Inpatient					
Gross Inpatient Revenue	$11,791,354,318	$10,790,044,124	$10,396,751,854	$9,707,362,014	$9,158,840,266
Revenue - Outpatient					
Gross Outpatient Revenue	$11,935,261,119	$10,497,568,428	$10,046,165,626	$8,606,191,704	$7,804,133,580
Revenue and Expenses - Totals					
(Includes Inpatient and Outpatient)					
Total Gross Revenue	$23,726,615,437	$21,287,612,552	$20,442,917,480	$18,313,553,718	$16,962,973,846
Deductions from Revenue	16,686,914,957	14,616,689,279	13,766,315,018	12,295,093,634	11,147,817,611
Net Patient Revenue	7,039,700,480	6,670,923,273	6,676,602,462	6,018,460,084	5,815,156,235
Other Operating Revenue	345,399,844	288,774,222	284,943,541	215,888,633	203,257,460
Other Nonoperating Revenue	161,037,772	171,234,302	160,005,906	66,106,732	128,773,371
Total Net Revenue	7,546,138,096	7,130,931,797	7,121,551,909	6,300,455,449	6,147,187,066
Total Expenses	6,954,230,448	6,616,602,126	6,513,729,367	5,963,380,431	5,759,373,331
HOSPITAL UNIT (Excludes Separate Nursing Home Units)					
Utilization - Inpatient					
Beds	8,505	8,440	8,568	8,495	8,338
Admissions	293,840	287,249	293,835	299,829	302,003
Inpatient Days	1,435,936	1,426,105	1,440,628	1,449,789	1,447,040
Average Length of Stay	4.9	5	4.9	4.8	4.8
Personnel					
Total Full Time	39,789	39,877	39,007	38,237	37,806
Total Part Time	13,677	14,237	14,268	13,543	13,660
Revenue and Expenses - Totals					
(Includes Inpatient and Outpatient)					
Total Net Revenue	$7,464,308,710	$7,047,938,513	$7,040,162,578	$6,224,061,786	$6,068,771,082
Total Expenses	6,881,820,540	6,548,127,097	6,440,417,821	5,897,756,162	5,694,269,627
COMMUNITY HEALTH INDICATORS PER 1000 POPULATION					
Total Population (in thousands)	2,904	2,894	2,886	2,871	2,841
Inpatient					
Beds	3.5	3.5	3.5	3.5	3.5
Admissions	102.0	100.1	102.7	105.3	107.3
Inpatient Days	651.4	656.4	663.9	670.0	690.0
Inpatient Surgeries	23.9	24.6	25.4	26.8	27.9
Births	13.2	12.9	13.4	13.5	14.0
Outpatient					
Emergency Outpatient Visits	404.3	389.6	386.0	362.6	358.8
Other Outpatient Visits	2,060.0	2,060.4	2,141.1	2,074.1	1,992.3
Total Outpatient Visits	2,464.3	2,450.1	2,527.1	2,436.8	2,351.1
Outpatient Surgeries	55.2	53.9	57.6	56.4	55.5
Expense per Capita (per person)	$2,394.7	$2,286.4	$2,257.1	$2,076.9	$2,027.1

States

TABLE 6

KENTUCKY

U.S. Registered Community Hospitals
(Nonfederal, short-term general and other special hospitals)

Overview 2010–2014

	2014	2013	2012	2011	2010
Total Community Hospitals in Kentucky.......	104	106	106	106	106
Bed Size Category					
6-24	2	3	3	3	1
25-49	34	35	36	34	34
50-99	21	19	19	22	24
100-199	23	26	25	25	24
200-299	11	10	10	7	8
300-399	9	9	9	10	10
400-499	3	2	0	1	3
500 + ...	1	2	4	4	2
Location					
Hospitals Urban..........................	41	43	43	43	43
Hospitals Rural	63	63	63	63	63
Control					
State and Local Government................	11	11	12	12	11
Not for Profit	72	75	74	74	75
Investor owned	21	20	20	20	20
Physician Models					
Independent Practice Association	4	3	6	5	5
Group Practice without Walls...............	1	1	1	0	0
Open Physician-Hospital Organization	5	5	6	7	9
Closed Physician-Hospital Organization	0	1	1	2	3
Management Service Organization	9	9	10	8	8
Integrated Salary Model....................	41	40	44	42	43
Equity Model	0	0	0	0	0
Foundation...............................	1	2	2	3	4
Insurance Products					
Health Maintenance Organization	10	6	7	7	10
Preferred Provider Organization..............	13	10	7	14	15
Indemnity Fee for Service	2	4	3	5	8
Managed Care Contracts					
Health Maintenance Organization	44	41	43	44	48
Preferred Provider Organization..............	55	42	44	53	59
Affiliations					
Hospitals in a System......................	81	80	80	80	79
Hospitals in a Network.....................	30	28	24	17	22
Hospitals in a Group Purchasing Organization..	71	70	74	71	80

TABLE 6

KENTUCKY

U.S. Registered Community Hospitals
(Nonfederal, short-term general and other special hospitals)

Utilization, Personnel, Revenue and Expenses, Community Health Indicators 2010–2014

	2014	2013	2012	2011	2010
TOTAL FACILITY (Includes Hospital and Nursing Home Units)					
Utilization - Inpatient					
Beds	13,994	14,021	14,180	14,182	14,238
Admissions	558,430	578,841	572,294	599,601	608,644
Inpatient Days	2,975,806	3,026,582	2,908,461	3,061,415	3,141,502
Average Length of Stay	5.3	5.2	5.1	5.1	5.2
Inpatient Surgeries	159,471	159,628	166,885	170,702	173,656
Births	52,786	54,263	53,538	49,657	53,630
Utilization - Outpatient					
Emergency Outpatient Visits	2,332,013	2,279,740	2,404,826	2,350,367	2,386,673
Other Outpatient Visits	8,443,852	8,241,623	8,166,103	8,182,293	8,050,866
Total Outpatient Visits	10,775,865	10,521,363	10,570,929	10,532,660	10,437,539
Outpatient Surgeries	361,098	368,971	371,089	400,593	385,960
Personnel					
Full Time RNs	18,505	18,551	18,672	17,989	17,666
Full Time LPNs	1,116	1,243	1,290	1,436	1,648
Part Time RNs	6,825	6,624	6,093	6,060	6,087
Part Time LPNs	247	261	268	343	397
Total Full Time	61,865	62,625	64,131	64,035	63,493
Total Part Time	18,717	19,000	17,391	18,453	18,309
Revenue - Inpatient					
Gross Inpatient Revenue	$19,807,874,013	$18,199,474,364	$16,779,961,324	$16,313,648,119	$15,503,184,961
Revenue - Outpatient					
Gross Outpatient Revenue	$22,184,632,530	$18,314,577,975	$16,724,256,215	$15,995,475,627	$14,305,855,765
Revenue and Expenses - Totals					
(Includes Inpatient and Outpatient)					
Total Gross Revenue	$41,992,506,543	$36,514,052,339	$33,504,217,539	$32,309,123,746	$29,809,040,726
Deductions from Revenue	30,206,766,007	25,507,901,441	22,702,995,327	22,051,533,008	19,784,508,926
Net Patient Revenue	11,785,740,536	11,006,150,898	10,801,222,212	10,257,590,738	10,024,531,800
Other Operating Revenue	534,897,827	407,398,136	406,456,390	383,110,150	338,831,936
Other Nonoperating Revenue	168,148,966	237,296,737	56,938,657	135,433,381	145,526,221
Total Net Revenue	12,488,787,329	11,650,845,771	11,264,617,259	10,776,134,269	10,508,889,957
Total Expenses	11,788,394,914	10,884,059,289	10,400,750,170	10,049,280,333	9,801,870,954
HOSPITAL UNIT (Excludes Separate Nursing Home Units)					
Utilization - Inpatient					
Beds	13,542	13,319	13,573	13,595	13,367
Admissions	553,728	572,724	564,937	592,962	602,635
Inpatient Days	2,856,932	2,818,046	2,743,755	2,886,190	2,889,658
Average Length of Stay	5.2	4.9	4.9	4.9	4.8
Personnel					
Total Full Time	61,414	61,903	63,588	63,514	62,730
Total Part Time	18,576	18,769	17,221	18,315	17,998
Revenue and Expenses - Totals					
(Includes Inpatient and Outpatient)					
Total Net Revenue	$12,437,772,106	$11,593,715,843	$11,207,210,342	$10,690,507,752	$10,416,730,891
Total Expenses	11,746,322,153	10,817,318,399	10,337,675,256	9,975,988,671	9,715,872,866
COMMUNITY HEALTH INDICATORS PER 1000 POPULATION					
Total Population (in thousands)	4,413	4,395	4,380	4,369	4,339
Inpatient					
Beds	3.2	3.2	3.2	3.2	3.3
Admissions	126.5	131.7	130.6	137.2	140.3
Inpatient Days	674.3	688.6	664.0	700.7	723.9
Inpatient Surgeries	36.1	36.3	38.1	39.1	40.0
Births	12.0	12.3	12.2	11.4	12.4
Outpatient					
Emergency Outpatient Visits	528.4	518.7	549.0	537.9	550.0
Other Outpatient Visits	1,913.2	1,875.1	1,864.2	1,872.7	1,855.3
Total Outpatient Visits	2,441.6	2,393.8	2,413.2	2,410.6	2,405.3
Outpatient Surgeries	81.8	83.9	84.7	91.7	88.9
Expense per Capita (per person)	$2,671.0	$2,476.3	$2,374.4	$2,299.9	$2,258.8

TABLE 6

LOUISIANA

U.S. Registered Community Hospitals
(Nonfederal, short-term general and other special hospitals)

Overview 2010–2014

	2014	2013	2012	2011	2010
Total Community Hospitals in Louisiana	122	122	124	127	126
Bed Size Category					
6-24	16	17	17	18	18
25-49	41	38	38	40	40
50-99	20	24	25	24	22
100-199	21	19	20	19	21
200-299	12	10	10	12	12
300-399	6	7	7	8	6
400-499	3	4	4	2	3
500 + ...	3	3	3	4	4
Location					
Hospitals Urban..........................	84	74	77	77	76
Hospitals Rural	38	48	47	50	50
Control					
State and Local Government................	45	44	49	48	50
Not for Profit	41	41	38	39	38
Investor owned	36	37	37	40	38
Physician Models					
Independent Practice Association	8	6	5	7	7
Group Practice without Walls................	5	4	3	7	6
Open Physician-Hospital Organization	8	8	10	12	12
Closed Physician-Hospital Organization	3	5	5	6	5
Management Service Organization	7	7	8	5	4
Integrated Salary Model	31	25	28	30	29
Equity Model	0	1	1	0	2
Foundation...............................	2	5	4	3	1
Insurance Products					
Health Maintenance Organization	6	8	6	9	8
Preferred Provider Organization..............	9	7	7	11	10
Indemnity Fee for Service	4	2	3	2	2
Managed Care Contracts					
Health Maintenance Organization	40	44	45	45	47
Preferred Provider Organization..............	43	48	51	57	57
Affiliations					
Hospitals in a System.....................	63	59	57	60	57
Hospitals in a Network....................	22	20	22	22	22
Hospitals in a Group Purchasing Organization..	58	59	62	66	71

TABLE 6

LOUISIANA

U.S. Registered Community Hospitals
(Nonfederal, short-term general and other special hospitals)

Utilization, Personnel, Revenue and Expenses, Community Health Indicators 2010–2014

	2014	2013	2012	2011	2010
TOTAL FACILITY (Includes Hospital and Nursing Home Units)					
Utilization - Inpatient					
Beds	15,076	15,550	15,204	15,342	15,421
Admissions	561,930	565,779	582,425	607,413	625,489
Inpatient Days	3,077,460	3,073,041	3,138,473	3,257,484	3,341,419
Average Length of Stay	5.5	5.4	5.4	5.4	5.3
Inpatient Surgeries	145,240	138,430	142,744	171,534	174,853
Births	70,969	64,083	60,736	54,963	61,525
Utilization - Outpatient					
Emergency Outpatient Visits	2,739,120	2,587,672	2,539,449	2,446,704	2,514,006
Other Outpatient Visits	7,994,071	7,076,596	7,011,868	7,096,563	9,840,934
Total Outpatient Visits	10,733,191	9,664,268	9,551,317	9,543,267	12,354,940
Outpatient Surgeries	265,642	263,440	253,503	277,370	283,987
Personnel					
Full Time RNs	20,041	18,917	18,885	18,529	18,458
Full Time LPNs	2,644	2,668	2,829	2,819	2,884
Part Time RNs	7,212	6,792	5,624	5,250	4,899
Part Time LPNs	909	905	728	594	628
Total Full Time	72,928	71,050	70,723	70,360	71,458
Total Part Time	21,384	21,073	17,577	15,769	15,447
Revenue - Inpatient					
Gross Inpatient Revenue	$20,532,002,034	$19,263,175,093	$18,651,353,386	$17,640,121,981	$17,480,238,475
Revenue - Outpatient					
Gross Outpatient Revenue	$19,353,422,874	$17,447,605,153	$15,579,961,189	$14,296,885,978	$13,195,535,770
Revenue and Expenses - Totals					
(Includes Inpatient and Outpatient)					
Total Gross Revenue	$39,885,424,908	$36,710,780,246	$34,231,314,575	$31,937,007,959	$30,675,774,245
Deductions from Revenue	28,916,804,408	26,304,382,131	24,308,385,152	22,487,315,530	21,158,064,386
Net Patient Revenue	10,968,620,500	10,406,398,115	9,922,929,423	9,449,692,429	9,517,709,859
Other Operating Revenue	694,606,495	683,792,470	650,768,859	727,155,809	672,891,456
Other Nonoperating Revenue	260,144,885	167,277,594	118,810,348	297,471,661	498,721,170
Total Net Revenue	11,923,371,880	11,257,468,179	10,692,508,630	10,474,319,899	10,689,322,485
Total Expenses	11,224,972,279	10,689,977,269	10,146,975,702	9,705,109,556	9,593,366,678
HOSPITAL UNIT (Excludes Separate Nursing Home Units)					
Utilization - Inpatient					
Beds	14,530	14,850	14,552	14,874	14,721
Admissions	560,304	563,829	580,792	606,108	623,661
Inpatient Days	2,920,175	2,895,780	3,001,522	3,126,298	3,134,514
Average Length of Stay	5.2	5.1	5.2	5.2	5
Personnel					
Total Full Time	71,239	70,604	69,836	69,994	70,950
Total Part Time	20,585	20,881	17,416	15,644	15,241
Revenue and Expenses - Totals					
(Includes Inpatient and Outpatient)					
Total Net Revenue	$11,897,431,139	$11,211,808,807	$10,660,949,288	$10,452,759,116	$10,655,165,063
Total Expenses	11,203,169,688	10,646,734,797	10,112,917,995	9,680,765,455	9,556,204,131
COMMUNITY HEALTH INDICATORS PER 1000 POPULATION					
Total Population (in thousands)	4,650	4,625	4,602	4,575	4,529
Inpatient					
Beds	3.2	3.4	3.3	3.4	3.4
Admissions	120.9	122.3	126.6	132.8	138.1
Inpatient Days	661.9	664.4	682.0	712.0	737.7
Inpatient Surgeries	31.2	29.9	31.0	37.5	38.6
Births	15.3	13.9	13.2	12.0	13.6
Outpatient					
Emergency Outpatient Visits	589.1	559.4	551.8	534.8	555.0
Other Outpatient Visits	1,719.3	1,529.9	1,523.7	1,551.2	2,172.7
Total Outpatient Visits	2,308.4	2,089.4	2,075.5	2,086.0	2,727.7
Outpatient Surgeries	57.1	57.0	55.1	60.6	62.7
Expense per Capita (per person)	$2,414.1	$2,311.1	$2,205.0	$2,121.4	$2,118.0

TABLE 6

MAINE

U.S. Registered Community Hospitals
(Nonfederal, short-term general and other special hospitals)

Overview 2010–2014

	2014	2013	2012	2011	2010
Total Community Hospitals in Maine..........	35	35	37	37	37
Bed Size Category					
6-24	2	1	2	2	2
25-49	16	17	17	16	15
50-99	8	7	8	9	10
100-199	6	6	7	7	7
200-299	1	2	1	1	1
300-399	1	1	1	1	1
400-499	0	0	0	0	0
500 + ...	1	1	1	1	1
Location					
Hospitals Urban..........................	14	14	15	15	15
Hospitals Rural	21	21	22	22	22
Control					
State and Local Government................	2	2	2	2	2
Not for Profit	32	32	34	34	34
Investor owned	1	1	1	1	1
Physician Models					
Independent Practice Association	0	0	2	3	4
Group Practice without Walls................	0	1	2	4	4
Open Physician-Hospital Organization	9	8	9	10	10
Closed Physician-Hospital Organization	3	2	3	3	4
Management Service Organization	2	2	3	4	5
Integrated Salary Model	13	17	22	24	24
Equity Model	0	0	1	1	1
Foundation...............................	0	0	1	1	1
Insurance Products					
Health Maintenance Organization	4	4	3	4	5
Preferred Provider Organization..............	4	4	3	4	4
Indemnity Fee for Service	1	1	0	2	3
Managed Care Contracts					
Health Maintenance Organization	15	19	21	25	23
Preferred Provider Organization..............	18	21	23	26	26
Affiliations					
Hospitals in a System.....................	18	18	20	20	20
Hospitals in a Network....................	16	17	18	19	18
Hospitals in a Group Purchasing Organization..	26	28	32	33	33

TABLE 6

MAINE

U.S. Registered Community Hospitals
(Nonfederal, short-term general and other special hospitals)

Utilization, Personnel, Revenue and Expenses, Community Health Indicators 2010–2014

	2014	2013	2012	2011	2010
TOTAL FACILITY (Includes Hospital and Nursing Home Units)					
Utilization - Inpatient					
Beds	3,379	3,474	3,523	3,557	3,571
Admissions	135,001	139,976	142,159	144,718	145,806
Inpatient Days	772,923	782,150	783,992	814,216	808,166
Average Length of Stay	5.7	5.6	5.5	5.6	5.5
Inpatient Surgeries	39,374	40,786	42,816	39,585	42,190
Births	11,495	11,687	11,224	12,434	12,874
Utilization - Outpatient					
Emergency Outpatient Visits	771,696	795,374	790,258	765,481	790,243
Other Outpatient Visits	7,063,404	6,358,880	5,387,237	5,388,213	5,174,906
Total Outpatient Visits	7,835,100	7,154,254	6,177,495	6,153,694	5,965,149
Outpatient Surgeries	112,626	103,239	117,491	123,494	137,762
Personnel					
Full Time RNs	5,779	5,509	5,229	4,999	4,813
Full Time LPNs	255	242	190	204	248
Part Time RNs	3,944	3,503	3,884	3,429	3,658
Part Time LPNs	121	118	149	132	116
Total Full Time	25,520	24,591	23,343	23,480	22,775
Total Part Time	12,346	11,034	12,446	12,998	12,597
Revenue - Inpatient					
Gross Inpatient Revenue	$4,059,334,894	$3,801,387,888	$3,743,957,102	$3,332,670,956	$3,184,130,431
Revenue - Outpatient					
Gross Outpatient Revenue	$5,658,735,515	$5,272,970,618	$5,068,158,029	$4,713,427,286	$4,265,543,968
Revenue and Expenses - Totals (Includes Inpatient and Outpatient)					
Total Gross Revenue	$9,718,070,409	$9,074,358,506	$8,812,115,131	$8,046,098,242	$7,449,674,399
Deductions from Revenue	5,323,172,816	4,805,408,453	4,477,604,537	3,940,954,482	3,559,422,414
Net Patient Revenue	4,394,897,593	4,268,950,053	4,334,510,594	4,105,143,760	3,890,251,985
Other Operating Revenue	322,528,528	307,982,903	257,362,641	195,118,835	106,225,360
Other Nonoperating Revenue	107,159,154	85,107,098	52,339,735	40,642,341	36,578,921
Total Net Revenue	4,824,585,275	4,662,040,054	4,644,212,970	4,340,904,936	4,033,056,266
Total Expenses	4,635,468,221	4,501,336,652	4,421,717,517	4,160,648,639	4,238,756,324
HOSPITAL UNIT (Excludes Separate Nursing Home Units)					
Utilization - Inpatient					
Beds	2,983	3,078	3,109	3,135	3,185
Admissions	134,085	139,093	141,049	143,500	144,564
Inpatient Days	638,945	646,155	645,365	669,361	673,425
Average Length of Stay	4.8	4.6	4.6	4.7	4.7
Personnel					
Total Full Time	24,953	24,087	22,538	23,121	22,465
Total Part Time	11,679	10,755	11,898	12,682	12,310
Revenue and Expenses - Totals (Includes Inpatient and Outpatient)					
Total Net Revenue	$4,791,979,724	$4,629,095,790	$4,608,434,715	$4,305,024,694	$4,000,528,653
Total Expenses	4,601,902,809	4,470,359,564	4,389,756,790	4,127,705,413	4,208,922,953
COMMUNITY HEALTH INDICATORS PER 1000 POPULATION					
Total Population (in thousands)	1,330	1,328	1,329	1,328	1,313
Inpatient					
Beds	2.5	2.6	2.7	2.7	2.7
Admissions	101.5	105.4	107.0	109.0	111.1
Inpatient Days	581.1	588.8	589.8	613.0	615.5
Inpatient Surgeries	29.6	30.7	32.2	29.8	32.1
Births	8.6	8.8	8.4	9.4	9.8
Outpatient					
Emergency Outpatient Visits	580.2	598.8	594.5	576.3	601.9
Other Outpatient Visits	5,310.5	4,787.2	4,053.0	4,056.8	3,941.5
Total Outpatient Visits	5,890.7	5,386.0	4,647.6	4,633.1	4,543.4
Outpatient Surgeries	84.7	77.7	88.4	93.0	104.9
Expense per Capita (per person)	$3,485.1	$3,388.8	$3,326.6	$3,132.6	$3,228.4

TABLE 6

MARYLAND

U.S. Registered Community Hospitals
(Nonfederal, short-term general and other special hospitals)

Overview 2010–2014

	2014	2013	2012	2011	2010
Total Community Hospitals in Maryland.......	50	50	50	48	47
Bed Size Category					
6-24	0	0	0	0	0
25-49	3	3	3	3	2
50-99	9	9	8	6	6
100-199	12	9	11	14	13
200-299	12	14	11	9	11
300-399	6	8	9	8	9
400-499	6	4	6	5	4
500 + ...	2	3	2	3	2
Location					
Hospitals Urban...........................	46	44	44	42	41
Hospitals Rural	4	6	6	6	6
Control					
State and Local Government...............	0	0	0	0	0
Not for Profit	49	49	48	46	45
Investor owned	1	1	2	2	2
Physician Models					
Independent Practice Association	6	9	12	8	7
Group Practice without Walls...............	3	6	8	2	3
Open Physician-Hospital Organization	6	5	6	5	6
Closed Physician-Hospital Organization	9	9	9	4	1
Management Service Organization	5	10	14	11	10
Integrated Salary Model....................	30	31	32	29	30
Equity Model	2	3	4	4	3
Foundation...............................	6	5	6	6	6
Insurance Products					
Health Maintenance Organization	18	18	16	16	16
Preferred Provider Organization..............	8	10	13	6	5
Indemnity Fee for Service	4	5	5	2	2
Managed Care Contracts					
Health Maintenance Organization	27	29	31	30	32
Preferred Provider Organization..............	27	29	30	29	29
Affiliations					
Hospitals in a System.....................	35	35	35	32	30
Hospitals in a Network....................	14	16	16	16	17
Hospitals in a Group Purchasing Organization..	36	41	42	43	42

TABLE 6

MARYLAND

U.S. Registered Community Hospitals
(Nonfederal, short-term general and other special hospitals)

Utilization, Personnel, Revenue and Expenses, Community Health Indicators 2010–2014

	2014	2013	2012	2011	2010
TOTAL FACILITY (Includes Hospital and Nursing Home Units)					
Utilization - Inpatient					
Beds	12,027	12,392	12,271	11,887	11,682
Admissions	609,185	628,485	659,128	683,678	707,549
Inpatient Days	3,067,846	3,165,089	3,230,567	3,147,613	3,160,045
Average Length of Stay	5	5	4.9	4.6	4.5
Inpatient Surgeries	176,580	182,075	193,816	195,892	195,577
Births	65,730	66,699	67,554	68,727	69,042
Utilization - Outpatient					
Emergency Outpatient Visits	2,341,061	2,542,407	2,552,154	2,469,637	2,460,678
Other Outpatient Visits	6,671,728	6,879,374	7,244,174	6,301,934	5,912,927
Total Outpatient Visits	9,012,789	9,421,781	9,796,328	8,771,571	8,373,605
Outpatient Surgeries	352,010	355,688	348,264	363,469	352,770
Personnel					
Full Time RNs	21,205	19,966	19,382	18,228	17,338
Full Time LPNs	420	434	502	453	429
Part Time RNs	8,779	8,383	8,776	8,618	8,448
Part Time LPNs	160	212	241	188	185
Total Full Time	78,634	75,810	75,558	72,370	68,011
Total Part Time	27,551	25,681	28,069	27,470	26,604
Revenue - Inpatient					
Gross Inpatient Revenue	$11,825,919,787	$10,661,965,230	$11,340,693,112	$10,026,767,506	$9,444,745,728
Revenue - Outpatient					
Gross Outpatient Revenue	$9,739,331,110	$8,799,199,791	$8,221,461,005	$6,952,785,584	$5,942,458,212
Revenue and Expenses - Totals					
(Includes Inpatient and Outpatient)					
Total Gross Revenue	$21,565,250,897	$19,461,165,021	$19,562,154,117	$16,979,553,090	$15,387,203,940
Deductions from Revenue	7,462,716,486	5,848,369,205	5,814,859,991	4,223,063,054	3,358,927,214
Net Patient Revenue	14,102,534,411	13,612,795,816	13,747,294,126	12,756,490,036	12,028,276,726
Other Operating Revenue	745,533,295	720,549,006	587,505,820	520,917,847	481,101,758
Other Nonoperating Revenue	432,996,623	258,822,436	16,735,289	289,518,580	134,850,598
Total Net Revenue	15,281,064,329	14,592,167,258	14,351,535,235	13,566,926,463	12,644,229,082
Total Expenses	14,187,741,189	13,836,110,822	13,808,394,036	12,730,746,066	12,132,497,694
HOSPITAL UNIT (Excludes Separate Nursing Home Units)					
Utilization - Inpatient					
Beds	11,725	11,614	11,503	11,310	11,113
Admissions	605,304	621,936	653,062	677,236	700,707
Inpatient Days	2,976,468	2,926,235	3,003,853	2,995,832	2,998,068
Average Length of Stay	4.9	4.7	4.6	4.4	4.3
Personnel					
Total Full Time	78,206	75,010	74,873	71,903	67,425
Total Part Time	27,297	25,282	27,724	27,194	26,242
Revenue and Expenses - Totals					
(Includes Inpatient and Outpatient)					
Total Net Revenue	$15,213,654,834	$14,477,831,557	$14,246,938,190	$13,476,477,632	$12,543,530,248
Total Expenses	14,129,417,337	13,728,619,619	13,710,327,354	12,629,434,037	12,026,632,893
COMMUNITY HEALTH INDICATORS PER 1000 POPULATION					
Total Population (in thousands)	5,976	5,929	5,885	5,828	5,737
Inpatient					
Beds	2.0	2.1	2.1	2.0	2.0
Admissions	101.9	106.0	112.0	117.3	123.3
Inpatient Days	513.3	533.8	549.0	540.1	550.8
Inpatient Surgeries	29.5	30.7	32.9	33.6	34.1
Births	11.0	11.2	11.5	11.8	12.0
Outpatient					
Emergency Outpatient Visits	391.7	428.8	433.7	423.7	428.9
Other Outpatient Visits	1,116.3	1,160.3	1,231.0	1,081.3	1,030.6
Total Outpatient Visits	1,508.1	1,589.2	1,664.8	1,505.0	1,459.5
Outpatient Surgeries	58.9	60.0	59.2	62.4	61.5
Expense per Capita (per person)	$2,374.0	$2,333.7	$2,346.5	$2,184.3	$2,114.7

States

TABLE 6

MASSACHUSETTS

U.S. Registered Community Hospitals
(Nonfederal, short-term general and other special hospitals)

Overview 2010–2014

	2014	2013	2012	2011	2010
Total Community Hospitals in Massachusetts	79	82	83	79	79
Bed Size Category					
6-24	4	4	5	5	6
25-49	7	7	8	8	8
50-99	17	18	19	13	10
100-199	25	25	22	24	29
200-299	10	13	14	15	12
300-399	8	6	7	7	6
400-499	2	3	2	1	1
500 +	6	6	6	6	7
Location					
Hospitals Urban	76	80	81	77	77
Hospitals Rural	3	2	2	2	2
Control					
State and Local Government	4	3	3	1	1
Not for Profit	57	59	61	65	67
Investor owned	18	20	19	13	11
Physician Models					
Independent Practice Association	19	19	17	20	26
Group Practice without Walls	2	1	2	2	3
Open Physician-Hospital Organization	17	17	18	20	19
Closed Physician-Hospital Organization	5	5	5	5	7
Management Service Organization	9	9	9	11	12
Integrated Salary Model	32	30	31	32	35
Equity Model	1	1	1	2	2
Foundation	2	2	3	4	5
Insurance Products					
Health Maintenance Organization	9	7	9	11	9
Preferred Provider Organization	5	4	4	8	5
Indemnity Fee for Service	2	1	2	5	3
Managed Care Contracts					
Health Maintenance Organization	50	48	47	56	59
Preferred Provider Organization	49	47	45	51	55
Affiliations					
Hospitals in a System	53	52	51	46	43
Hospitals in a Network	26	24	24	27	25
Hospitals in a Group Purchasing Organization	52	50	50	55	62

TABLE 6

MASSACHUSETTS

U.S. Registered Community Hospitals
(Nonfederal, short-term general and other special hospitals)

Utilization, Personnel, Revenue and Expenses, Community Health Indicators 2010–2014

	2014	2013	2012	2011	2010
TOTAL FACILITY (Includes Hospital and Nursing Home Units)					
Utilization - Inpatient					
Beds	16,060	16,483	16,233	15,865	15,694
Admissions	754,971	787,003	802,312	838,080	823,246
Inpatient Days	4,116,984	4,181,114	4,130,110	4,168,038	4,164,008
Average Length of Stay	5.5	5.3	5.1	5	5.1
Inpatient Surgeries	190,086	188,191	197,450	205,653	209,277
Births	69,068	68,965	70,702	72,707	72,306
Utilization - Outpatient					
Emergency Outpatient Visits	3,186,679	3,221,445	3,164,871	3,092,821	3,153,290
Other Outpatient Visits	18,768,118	18,876,709	19,349,547	19,206,984	18,597,755
Total Outpatient Visits	21,954,797	22,098,154	22,514,418	22,299,805	21,751,045
Outpatient Surgeries	425,225	426,553	421,694	418,519	471,811
Personnel					
Full Time RNs	22,686	21,855	21,137	21,636	20,665
Full Time LPNs	798	835	868	827	797
Part Time RNs	22,458	23,005	22,948	23,007	22,332
Part Time LPNs	526	641	708	686	707
Total Full Time	114,832	115,714	113,291	114,923	112,453
Total Part Time	67,176	67,465	69,520	69,916	67,465
Revenue - Inpatient					
Gross Inpatient Revenue	$27,543,954,703	$26,147,419,070	$25,212,735,967	$23,543,488,752	$22,838,917,130
Revenue - Outpatient					
Gross Outpatient Revenue	$30,741,997,367	$29,745,996,654	$28,198,949,623	$26,601,731,821	$26,120,785,816
Revenue and Expenses - Totals					
(Includes Inpatient and Outpatient)					
Total Gross Revenue	$58,285,952,070	$55,893,415,724	$53,411,685,590	$50,145,220,573	$48,959,702,946
Deductions from Revenue	35,818,774,175	34,008,609,464	31,738,657,662	29,585,822,724	28,469,292,992
Net Patient Revenue	22,467,177,895	21,884,806,260	21,673,027,928	20,559,397,849	20,490,409,954
Other Operating Revenue	3,805,293,934	3,772,351,494	3,570,796,587	3,539,011,217	3,161,300,000
Other Nonoperating Revenue	157,175,096	600,472,377	158,781,349	59,227,576	180,218,312
Total Net Revenue	26,429,646,925	26,257,630,131	25,402,605,864	24,157,636,642	23,831,928,266
Total Expenses	25,349,887,484	24,670,533,446	24,080,576,139	23,068,835,920	22,819,002,547
HOSPITAL UNIT (Excludes Separate Nursing Home Units)					
Utilization - Inpatient					
Beds	16,031	16,454	16,204	15,836	15,569
Admissions	754,338	786,315	801,583	837,325	820,368
Inpatient Days	4,108,438	4,172,412	4,121,270	4,158,948	4,125,806
Average Length of Stay	5.4	5.3	5.1	5	5
Personnel					
Total Full Time	114,826	115,708	113,273	114,916	112,401
Total Part Time	67,161	67,446	69,452	69,898	67,389
Revenue and Expenses - Totals					
(Includes Inpatient and Outpatient)					
Total Net Revenue	$26,425,067,104	$26,252,955,720	$25,397,992,218	$24,152,583,333	$23,814,188,986
Total Expenses	25,344,892,287	24,665,183,716	24,075,430,900	23,064,002,066	22,805,667,399
COMMUNITY HEALTH INDICATORS PER 1000 POPULATION					
Total Population (in thousands)	6,745	6,693	6,646	6,588	6,631
Inpatient					
Beds	2.4	2.5	2.4	2.4	2.4
Admissions	111.9	117.6	120.7	127.2	124.1
Inpatient Days	610.3	624.7	621.4	632.7	627.9
Inpatient Surgeries	28.2	28.1	29.7	31.2	31.6
Births	10.2	10.3	10.6	11.0	10.9
Outpatient					
Emergency Outpatient Visits	472.4	481.3	476.2	469.5	475.5
Other Outpatient Visits	2,782.4	2,820.4	2,911.4	2,915.7	2,804.5
Total Outpatient Visits	3,254.8	3,301.8	3,387.6	3,385.2	3,280.1
Outpatient Surgeries	63.0	63.7	63.4	63.5	71.1
Expense per Capita (per person)	$3,758.1	$3,686.1	$3,623.2	$3,501.9	$3,441.1

States

TABLE 6

MICHIGAN

U.S. Registered Community Hospitals
(Nonfederal, short-term general and other special hospitals)

Overview 2010–2014

	2014	2013	2012	2011	2010
Total Community Hospitals in Michigan	148	151	151	153	156
Bed Size Category					
6-24	12	13	12	12	12
25-49	42	44	46	45	44
50-99	32	32	29	30	35
100-199	21	19	20	19	18
200-299	12	15	15	18	18
300-399	11	10	11	14	15
400-499	8	6	7	5	3
500 + ...	10	12	11	10	11
Location					
Hospitals Urban..........................	93	93	93	95	97
Hospitals Rural	55	58	58	58	59
Control					
State and Local Government................	12	14	15	14	14
Not for Profit	111	114	114	119	125
Investor owned	25	23	22	20	17
Physician Models					
Independent Practice Association	11	12	14	18	15
Group Practice without Walls................	8	8	8	9	9
Open Physician-Hospital Organization	42	40	45	45	39
Closed Physician-Hospital Organization	15	16	11	15	17
Management Service Organization	9	13	16	18	19
Integrated Salary Model	89	88	85	83	86
Equity Model	1	1	1	1	0
Foundation...............................	6	6	6	8	8
Insurance Products					
Health Maintenance Organization	42	40	38	39	41
Preferred Provider Organization..............	32	28	27	39	41
Indemnity Fee for Service	12	8	10	14	13
Managed Care Contracts					
Health Maintenance Organization	101	100	102	106	114
Preferred Provider Organization..............	103	102	104	110	119
Affiliations					
Hospitals in a System......................	106	100	96	96	96
Hospitals in a Network.....................	63	58	62	65	70
Hospitals in a Group Purchasing Organization..	116	116	119	121	127

TABLE 6

MICHIGAN

U.S. Registered Community Hospitals
(Nonfederal, short-term general and other special hospitals)

Utilization, Personnel, Revenue and Expenses, Community Health Indicators 2010–2014

	2014	2013	2012	2011	2010
TOTAL FACILITY (Includes Hospital and Nursing Home Units)					
Utilization - Inpatient					
Beds	24,398	25,059	25,100	25,351	25,623
Admissions	1,125,043	1,158,802	1,182,541	1,191,236	1,207,546
Inpatient Days	5,730,883	5,912,166	6,037,474	6,173,528	6,214,588
Average Length of Stay	5.1	5.1	5.1	5.2	5.1
Inpatient Surgeries	310,581	315,259	325,219	342,090	355,358
Births	106,127	107,429	106,525	107,031	111,192
Utilization - Outpatient					
Emergency Outpatient Visits	4,814,596	4,875,899	4,781,685	4,675,863	4,550,617
Other Outpatient Visits	29,132,989	27,692,597	28,037,761	26,307,833	25,699,720
Total Outpatient Visits	33,947,585	32,568,496	32,819,446	30,983,696	30,250,337
Outpatient Surgeries	680,084	674,583	678,329	656,318	704,866
Personnel					
Full Time RNs	41,409	38,800	38,759	37,356	36,166
Full Time LPNs	1,264	1,341	1,270	1,255	1,377
Part Time RNs	19,049	18,723	19,313	18,736	18,803
Part Time LPNs	709	796	748	810	916
Total Full Time	149,877	144,269	146,597	143,186	144,577
Total Part Time	61,585	61,716	63,422	63,510	64,909
Revenue - Inpatient					
Gross Inpatient Revenue	$36,289,771,030	$35,163,188,185	$34,248,317,962	$33,127,653,060	$32,307,141,469
Revenue - Outpatient					
Gross Outpatient Revenue	$38,763,168,547	$36,798,222,853	$34,632,987,398	$31,983,063,304	$30,177,541,390
Revenue and Expenses - Totals					
(Includes Inpatient and Outpatient)					
Total Gross Revenue	$75,052,939,577	$71,961,411,038	$68,881,305,360	$65,110,716,364	$62,484,682,859
Deductions from Revenue	47,734,916,913	45,245,940,980	41,938,126,634	40,060,740,730	38,000,334,594
Net Patient Revenue	27,318,022,664	26,715,470,058	26,943,178,726	25,049,975,634	24,484,348,265
Other Operating Revenue	1,388,381,837	1,525,618,772	1,306,714,292	1,133,933,341	1,105,518,315
Other Nonoperating Revenue	715,274,398	551,058,172	242,121,301	626,908,309	555,064,648
Total Net Revenue	29,421,678,899	28,792,147,002	28,492,014,319	26,810,817,284	26,144,931,228
Total Expenses	27,710,262,310	27,272,388,730	27,293,081,777	25,328,136,970	24,872,817,460
HOSPITAL UNIT (Excludes Separate Nursing Home Units)					
Utilization - Inpatient					
Beds	23,451	24,121	23,759	24,256	24,243
Admissions	1,120,926	1,154,598	1,177,789	1,187,933	1,203,343
Inpatient Days	5,411,436	5,605,462	5,600,603	5,802,388	5,761,918
Average Length of Stay	4.8	4.9	4.8	4.9	4.8
Personnel					
Total Full Time	149,252	143,689	145,517	142,322	143,514
Total Part Time	60,932	61,162	62,504	62,695	64,019
Revenue and Expenses - Totals					
(Includes Inpatient and Outpatient)					
Total Net Revenue	$29,323,229,916	$28,697,947,450	$28,374,005,103	$26,702,789,590	$26,022,486,264
Total Expenses	27,628,458,974	27,200,999,172	27,190,001,432	25,261,120,163	24,753,757,439
COMMUNITY HEALTH INDICATORS PER 1000 POPULATION					
Total Population (in thousands)	9,910	9,896	9,883	9,876	9,931
Inpatient					
Beds	2.5	2.5	2.5	2.6	2.6
Admissions	113.5	117.1	119.6	120.6	121.6
Inpatient Days	578.3	597.5	610.9	625.1	625.8
Inpatient Surgeries	31.3	31.9	32.9	34.6	35.8
Births	10.7	10.9	10.8	10.8	11.2
Outpatient					
Emergency Outpatient Visits	485.8	492.7	483.8	473.4	458.2
Other Outpatient Visits	2,939.8	2,798.5	2,836.9	2,663.8	2,587.8
Total Outpatient Visits	3,425.6	3,291.2	3,320.7	3,137.2	3,046.0
Outpatient Surgeries	68.6	68.2	68.6	66.5	71.0
Expense per Capita (per person)	$2,796.2	$2,756.0	$2,761.5	$2,564.6	$2,504.5

States

TABLE 6

MINNESOTA

U.S. Registered Community Hospitals
(Nonfederal, short-term general and other special hospitals)

Overview 2010–2014

	2014	2013	2012	2011	2010
Total Community Hospitals in Minnesota......	131	131	133	132	133
Bed Size Category					
6-24	21	21	21	23	19
25-49	35	34	32	29	29
50-99	34	35	37	34	38
100-199	26	25	26	29	30
200-299	3	4	4	4	5
300-399	5	6	7	6	5
400-499	4	3	3	4	4
500 + ...	3	3	3	3	3
Location					
Hospitals Urban............................	55	49	51	51	51
Hospitals Rural	76	82	82	81	82
Control					
State and Local Government................	33	36	37	38	36
Not for Profit	98	95	95	93	96
Investor owned	0	0	1	1	1
Physician Models					
Independent Practice Association	10	11	10	10	18
Group Practice without Walls................	1	2	2	2	3
Open Physician-Hospital Organization	7	9	8	8	9
Closed Physician-Hospital Organization	2	2	2	3	3
Management Service Organization	2	1	2	1	1
Integrated Salary Model.....................	62	61	56	52	49
Equity Model	1	1	0	1	0
Foundation...............................	1	1	1	2	1
Insurance Products					
Health Maintenance Organization	22	19	19	15	14
Preferred Provider Organization..............	23	19	19	16	15
Indemnity Fee for Service	7	6	5	6	6
Managed Care Contracts					
Health Maintenance Organization	56	47	44	47	46
Preferred Provider Organization..............	61	55	49	53	52
Affiliations					
Hospitals in a System......................	85	81	82	78	77
Hospitals in a Network.....................	29	31	30	29	27
Hospitals in a Group Purchasing Organization..	94	92	90	90	90

TABLE 6

MINNESOTA

U.S. Registered Community Hospitals
(Nonfederal, short-term general and other special hospitals)

Utilization, Personnel, Revenue and Expenses, Community Health Indicators 2010–2014

	2014	2013	2012	2011	2010
TOTAL FACILITY (Includes Hospital and Nursing Home Units)					
Utilization - Inpatient					
Beds	14,562	14,781	14,895	14,985	15,346
Admissions	548,360	562,035	583,142	596,199	591,919
Inpatient Days	3,346,653	3,395,406	3,479,304	3,592,914	3,596,879
Average Length of Stay	6.1	6	6	6	6.1
Inpatient Surgeries	175,793	181,758	166,285	178,802	177,600
Births	66,960	67,898	64,001	64,004	62,885
Utilization - Outpatient					
Emergency Outpatient Visits	1,946,061	1,933,651	1,898,093	1,928,364	1,832,257
Other Outpatient Visits	10,023,292	9,732,473	9,532,070	8,863,642	9,232,626
Total Outpatient Visits	11,969,353	11,666,124	11,430,163	10,792,006	11,064,883
Outpatient Surgeries	322,191	322,895	302,985	315,819	303,839
Personnel					
Full Time RNs	12,942	12,220	11,693	11,275	11,163
Full Time LPNs	1,492	1,559	1,538	1,491	1,467
Part Time RNs	23,902	22,010	20,586	20,434	21,198
Part Time LPNs	1,681	1,666	1,524	1,716	1,767
Total Full Time	80,627	83,940	62,967	58,426	56,863
Total Part Time	64,045	61,875	57,938	58,167	62,186
Revenue - Inpatient					
Gross Inpatient Revenue	$21,280,123,954	$20,263,141,343	$19,494,970,283	$19,485,000,173	$18,410,175,974
Revenue - Outpatient					
Gross Outpatient Revenue	$20,107,877,258	$18,010,747,799	$17,426,213,830	$16,843,850,432	$15,401,043,442
Revenue and Expenses - Totals					
(Includes Inpatient and Outpatient)					
Total Gross Revenue	$41,388,001,212	$38,273,889,142	$36,921,184,113	$36,328,850,605	$33,811,219,416
Deductions from Revenue	24,738,287,806	22,240,528,284	21,566,323,331	21,780,756,415	20,208,906,364
Net Patient Revenue	16,649,713,406	16,033,360,858	15,354,860,782	14,548,094,190	13,602,313,052
Other Operating Revenue	857,887,159	797,395,199	736,968,011	673,017,078	627,863,165
Other Nonoperating Revenue	285,082,518	285,377,987	105,178,701	265,096,109	222,331,201
Total Net Revenue	17,792,683,083	17,116,134,044	16,197,007,494	15,486,207,377	14,452,507,418
Total Expenses	16,528,924,367	15,886,275,897	15,069,347,845	14,474,689,902	13,507,569,053
HOSPITAL UNIT (Excludes Separate Nursing Home Units)					
Utilization - Inpatient					
Beds	12,428	12,773	12,798	12,651	13,128
Admissions	544,181	558,324	579,267	592,372	588,566
Inpatient Days	2,631,904	2,749,985	2,790,444	2,813,323	2,835,161
Average Length of Stay	4.8	4.9	4.8	4.7	4.8
Personnel					
Total Full Time	79,565	82,892	61,780	57,414	55,794
Total Part Time	62,199	60,139	56,197	56,546	60,461
Revenue and Expenses - Totals					
(Includes Inpatient and Outpatient)					
Total Net Revenue	$17,618,940,851	$16,969,593,334	$16,055,142,778	$15,260,507,840	$14,309,968,863
Total Expenses	16,384,436,397	15,749,642,682	14,927,729,599	14,318,110,391	13,362,374,519
COMMUNITY HEALTH INDICATORS PER 1000 POPULATION					
Total Population (in thousands)	5,457	5,420	5,379	5,345	5,290
Inpatient					
Beds	2.7	2.7	2.8	2.8	2.9
Admissions	100.5	103.7	108.4	111.5	111.9
Inpatient Days	613.3	626.4	646.8	672.2	679.9
Inpatient Surgeries	32.2	33.5	30.9	33.5	33.6
Births	12.3	12.5	11.9	12.0	11.9
Outpatient					
Emergency Outpatient Visits	356.6	356.7	352.9	360.8	346.3
Other Outpatient Visits	1,836.7	1,795.5	1,772.0	1,658.3	1,745.2
Total Outpatient Visits	2,193.3	2,152.3	2,124.9	2,019.1	2,091.5
Outpatient Surgeries	59.0	59.6	56.3	59.1	57.4
Expense per Capita (per person)	$3,028.8	$2,930.8	$2,801.4	$2,708.2	$2,553.2

States

TABLE 6

MISSISSIPPI

U.S. Registered Community Hospitals
(Nonfederal, short-term general and other special hospitals)

Overview 2010–2014

	2014	2013	2012	2011	2010
Total Community Hospitals in Mississippi	97	99	98	99	96
Bed Size Category					
6-24	2	2	2	3	2
25-49	33	32	32	32	32
50-99	22	25	24	23	22
100-199	21	22	23	24	23
200-299	10	10	8	8	6
300-399	2	1	2	2	3
400-499	2	3	3	3	3
500 + ...	5	4	4	4	5
Location					
Hospitals Urban	27	28	28	29	29
Hospitals Rural	70	71	70	70	67
Control					
State and Local Government	39	41	40	40	41
Not for Profit	29	29	29	29	27
Investor owned	29	29	29	30	28
Physician Models					
Independent Practice Association	6	5	5	5	5
Group Practice without Walls	2	2	2	2	2
Open Physician-Hospital Organization	20	15	16	18	16
Closed Physician-Hospital Organization	4	4	3	1	2
Management Service Organization	8	8	9	11	8
Integrated Salary Model	25	29	26	27	22
Equity Model	2	1	2	1	1
Foundation	7	8	7	10	7
Insurance Products					
Health Maintenance Organization	9	8	8	7	7
Preferred Provider Organization	35	37	36	37	35
Indemnity Fee for Service	10	8	9	9	9
Managed Care Contracts					
Health Maintenance Organization	23	26	26	18	14
Preferred Provider Organization	42	46	45	38	33
Affiliations					
Hospitals in a System	53	51	47	48	45
Hospitals in a Network	25	26	26	28	29
Hospitals in a Group Purchasing Organization . .	1	2	0	0	0

TABLE 6

MISSISSIPPI

U.S. Registered Community Hospitals
(Nonfederal, short-term general and other special hospitals)

Utilization, Personnel, Revenue and Expenses, Community Health Indicators 2010–2014

	2014	2013	2012	2011	2010
TOTAL FACILITY (Includes Hospital and Nursing Home Units)					
Utilization - Inpatient					
Beds	12,471	12,826	12,882	12,867	12,925
Admissions	373,189	380,059	384,078	393,566	402,947
Inpatient Days	2,511,963	2,499,123	2,505,846	2,513,957	2,557,704
Average Length of Stay	6.7	6.6	6.5	6.4	6.3
Inpatient Surgeries	97,278	100,878	104,043	102,170	107,497
Births	37,543	36,911	37,565	38,046	39,044
Utilization - Outpatient					
Emergency Outpatient Visits	1,796,073	1,794,793	1,767,684	1,761,207	1,705,959
Other Outpatient Visits	3,205,427	3,160,783	3,321,143	3,015,093	2,880,177
Total Outpatient Visits	5,001,500	4,955,576	5,088,827	4,776,300	4,586,136
Outpatient Surgeries	180,721	173,872	169,096	169,856	174,969
Personnel					
Full Time RNs	12,307	12,265	12,179	12,842	12,176
Full Time LPNs	1,236	1,427	1,437	1,475	1,570
Part Time RNs	4,113	4,134	3,784	3,346	3,489
Part Time LPNs	375	379	339	290	344
Total Full Time	46,299	46,669	46,695	48,461	46,910
Total Part Time	12,124	11,989	11,755	10,875	11,258
Revenue - Inpatient					
Gross Inpatient Revenue	$14,133,584,691	$13,886,931,276	$12,982,460,621	$10,947,704,087	$10,614,195,531
Revenue - Outpatient					
Gross Outpatient Revenue	$12,952,432,101	$12,199,680,887	$11,618,451,746	$9,159,843,292	$8,108,639,171
Revenue and Expenses - Totals					
(Includes Inpatient and Outpatient)					
Total Gross Revenue	$27,086,016,792	$26,086,612,163	$24,600,912,367	$20,107,547,379	$18,722,834,702
Deductions from Revenue	19,927,771,753	18,961,333,700	17,485,118,401	14,441,074,648	13,026,769,588
Net Patient Revenue	7,158,245,039	7,125,278,463	7,115,793,966	5,666,472,731	5,696,065,114
Other Operating Revenue	322,055,646	316,465,170	336,578,667	284,527,695	332,166,296
Other Nonoperating Revenue	109,916,744	122,250,060	124,396,684	62,903,487	101,837,598
Total Net Revenue	7,590,217,429	7,563,993,693	7,576,769,317	6,013,903,913	6,130,069,008
Total Expenses	7,188,316,628	7,101,439,812	6,982,689,683	5,804,948,349	5,635,912,981
HOSPITAL UNIT (Excludes Separate Nursing Home Units)					
Utilization - Inpatient					
Beds	10,858	11,037	11,102	11,142	11,260
Admissions	372,154	378,968	383,020	392,650	402,148
Inpatient Days	1,966,719	1,896,950	1,906,203	1,948,010	2,004,002
Average Length of Stay	5.3	5	5	5	5
Personnel					
Total Full Time	45,036	45,233	45,222	47,168	45,658
Total Part Time	11,661	11,496	11,330	10,502	10,899
Revenue and Expenses - Totals					
(Includes Inpatient and Outpatient)					
Total Net Revenue	$7,527,130,297	$7,460,470,583	$7,501,877,310	$5,924,570,004	$6,056,564,286
Total Expenses	7,140,037,508	7,040,309,114	6,920,499,818	5,744,275,169	5,576,805,214
COMMUNITY HEALTH INDICATORS PER 1000 POPULATION					
Total Population (in thousands)	2,994	2,991	2,985	2,979	2,960
Inpatient					
Beds	4.2	4.3	4.3	4.3	4.4
Admissions	124.6	127.1	128.7	132.1	136.1
Inpatient Days	839.0	835.5	839.5	844.0	864.0
Inpatient Surgeries	32.5	33.7	34.9	34.3	36.3
Births	12.5	12.3	12.6	12.8	13.2
Outpatient					
Emergency Outpatient Visits	599.9	600.0	592.2	591.3	576.2
Other Outpatient Visits	1,070.6	1,056.7	1,112.6	1,012.3	972.9
Total Outpatient Visits	1,670.5	1,656.7	1,704.8	1,603.6	1,549.1
Outpatient Surgeries	60.4	58.1	56.6	57.0	59.1
Expense per Capita (per person)	$2,400.8	$2,374.1	$2,339.3	$1,948.9	$1,903.7

States

TABLE **6**

MISSOURI

U.S. Registered Community Hospitals
(Nonfederal, short-term general and other special hospitals)

Overview 2010–2014

	2014	2013	2012	2011	2010
Total Community Hospitals in Missouri	122	123	123	120	122
Bed Size Category					
6-24	10	11	9	8	7
25-49	38	38	39	40	41
50-99	19	19	20	19	21
100-199	26	25	25	21	22
200-299	10	11	11	12	11
300-399	7	7	7	9	11
400-499	6	6	6	5	3
500 + ...	6	6	6	6	6
Location					
Hospitals Urban..........................	71	70	70	67	69
Hospitals Rural	51	53	53	53	53
Control					
State and Local Government................	31	32	34	35	35
Not for Profit	65	65	64	63	64
Investor owned	26	26	25	22	23
Physician Models					
Independent Practice Association	11	8	8	6	8
Group Practice without Walls...............	0	0	0	0	0
Open Physician-Hospital Organization	14	15	15	15	14
Closed Physician-Hospital Organization	5	6	6	7	8
Management Service Organization	0	0	0	0	1
Integrated Salary Model	75	70	66	66	67
Equity Model	1	1	1	1	1
Foundation..............................	3	4	2	2	4
Insurance Products					
Health Maintenance Organization	12	11	11	16	16
Preferred Provider Organization..............	10	10	10	14	14
Indemnity Fee for Service	5	3	2	5	4
Managed Care Contracts					
Health Maintenance Organization	97	97	99	93	95
Preferred Provider Organization..............	105	107	105	101	103
Affiliations					
Hospitals in a System.....................	77	77	77	70	72
Hospitals in a Network....................	47	39	38	36	37
Hospitals in a Group Purchasing Organization..	120	122	121	116	114

States

TABLE 6

MISSOURI

U.S. Registered Community Hospitals
(Nonfederal, short-term general and other special hospitals)

Utilization, Personnel, Revenue and Expenses, Community Health Indicators 2010–2014

	2014	2013	2012	2011	2010
TOTAL FACILITY (Includes Hospital and Nursing Home Units)					
Utilization - Inpatient					
Beds	18,613	18,899	19,032	18,749	18,745
Admissions	779,774	781,070	799,256	815,640	821,322
Inpatient Days	4,057,997	4,060,151	4,120,318	4,172,415	4,196,865
Average Length of Stay	5.2	5.2	5.2	5.1	5.1
Inpatient Surgeries	196,360	199,770	206,215	210,625	213,685
Births	74,548	74,688	75,301	73,779	74,903
Utilization - Outpatient					
Emergency Outpatient Visits	2,975,892	2,987,268	3,042,008	2,952,675	2,871,884
Other Outpatient Visits	19,055,501	18,856,989	18,024,433	17,251,450	16,929,041
Total Outpatient Visits	22,031,393	21,844,257	21,066,441	20,204,125	19,800,925
Outpatient Surgeries	380,551	385,614	382,699	370,574	374,120
Personnel					
Full Time RNs	29,757	28,943	27,597	27,023	26,334
Full Time LPNs	2,429	2,377	2,375	2,407	2,398
Part Time RNs	10,962	11,212	12,913	11,436	11,453
Part Time LPNs	528	555	664	654	719
Total Full Time	104,705	104,194	102,089	101,030	100,265
Total Part Time	32,984	33,507	38,730	35,841	36,219
Revenue - Inpatient					
Gross Inpatient Revenue	$29,539,049,363	$27,966,288,581	$27,122,625,962	$25,816,258,642	$24,578,843,364
Revenue - Outpatient					
Gross Outpatient Revenue	$30,066,527,678	$27,913,913,149	$26,031,861,914	$23,228,488,113	$20,597,557,308
Revenue and Expenses - Totals					
(Includes Inpatient and Outpatient)					
Total Gross Revenue	$59,605,577,041	$55,880,201,730	$53,154,487,876	$49,044,746,755	$45,176,400,672
Deductions from Revenue	40,798,547,659	37,726,886,672	35,362,416,605	32,241,337,674	28,944,744,487
Net Patient Revenue	18,807,029,382	18,153,315,058	17,792,071,271	16,803,409,081	16,231,656,185
Other Operating Revenue	1,104,602,991	1,154,601,122	1,281,736,177	999,246,088	1,085,534,981
Other Nonoperating Revenue	382,421,126	665,919,682	794,602,472	214,485,919	529,984,875
Total Net Revenue	20,294,053,499	19,973,835,862	19,868,409,920	18,017,141,088	17,847,176,041
Total Expenses	19,367,868,494	18,734,464,777	17,024,103,374	17,172,219,045	16,521,828,978
HOSPITAL UNIT (Excludes Separate Nursing Home Units)					
Utilization - Inpatient					
Beds	17,650	17,904	18,035	17,772	17,754
Admissions	772,501	775,368	793,155	809,450	816,764
Inpatient Days	3,769,911	3,767,287	3,822,166	3,892,314	3,946,461
Average Length of Stay	4.9	4.9	4.8	4.8	4.8
Personnel					
Total Full Time	103,901	103,345	101,135	100,248	99,631
Total Part Time	32,534	33,091	38,172	35,394	35,866
Revenue and Expenses - Totals					
(Includes Inpatient and Outpatient)					
Total Net Revenue	$20,205,003,962	$19,902,552,926	$19,777,379,107	$17,938,622,213	$17,771,368,041
Total Expenses	19,304,920,800	18,659,708,181	16,948,096,420	17,109,487,583	16,444,776,729
COMMUNITY HEALTH INDICATORS PER 1000 POPULATION					
Total Population (in thousands)	6,064	6,044	6,022	6,011	6,012
Inpatient					
Beds	3.1	3.1	3.2	3.1	3.1
Admissions	128.6	129.2	132.7	135.7	136.6
Inpatient Days	669.2	671.7	684.2	694.2	698.1
Inpatient Surgeries	32.4	33.1	34.2	35.0	35.5
Births	12.3	12.4	12.5	12.3	12.5
Outpatient					
Emergency Outpatient Visits	490.8	494.2	505.2	491.2	477.7
Other Outpatient Visits	3,142.6	3,119.9	2,993.1	2,870.1	2,816.0
Total Outpatient Visits	3,633.4	3,614.1	3,498.3	3,361.4	3,293.7
Outpatient Surgeries	62.8	63.8	63.6	61.7	62.2
Expense per Capita (per person)	$3,194.1	$3,099.6	$2,827.0	$2,856.9	$2,748.3

States

TABLE 6

MONTANA

U.S. Registered Community Hospitals
(Nonfederal, short-term general and other special hospitals)

Overview 2010–2014

	2014	2013	2012	2011	2010
Total Community Hospitals in Montana	50	50	48	48	48
Bed Size Category					
6-24	11	9	10	11	10
25-49	14	16	13	12	15
50-99	16	16	15	14	12
100-199	6	6	7	8	8
200-299	1	1	1	1	1
300-399	1	1	1	1	1
400-499	1	1	1	1	1
500 + ...	0	0	0	0	0
Location					
Hospitals Urban...........................	6	6	6	6	6
Hospitals Rural	44	44	42	42	42
Control					
State and Local Government	8	9	10	10	8
Not for Profit	41	40	37	37	39
Investor owned	1	1	1	1	1
Physician Models					
Independent Practice Association	2	5	4	5	7
Group Practice without Walls...............	2	5	4	4	3
Open Physician-Hospital Organization	4	4	4	4	5
Closed Physician-Hospital Organization	0	1	1	1	1
Management Service Organization	4	6	5	5	6
Integrated Salary Model	32	30	28	29	27
Equity Model	1	1	1	1	2
Foundation...............................	6	6	6	6	4
Insurance Products					
Health Maintenance Organization	3	2	2	4	4
Preferred Provider Organization..............	13	9	9	7	8
Indemnity Fee for Service	5	3	4	5	6
Managed Care Contracts					
Health Maintenance Organization	11	7	8	9	11
Preferred Provider Organization..............	31	26	27	25	22
Affiliations					
Hospitals in a System......................	11	11	11	12	12
Hospitals in a Network.....................	23	23	23	23	22
Hospitals in a Group Purchasing Organization..	42	45	40	41	39

TABLE 6

MONTANA

U.S. Registered Community Hospitals
(Nonfederal, short-term general and other special hospitals)

Utilization, Personnel, Revenue and Expenses, Community Health Indicators 2010–2014

	2014	2013	2012	2011	2010
TOTAL FACILITY (Includes Hospital and Nursing Home Units)					
Utilization - Inpatient					
Beds	3,685	3,722	3,710	3,626	3,692
Admissions	92,687	95,321	93,423	94,966	97,453
Inpatient Days	800,383	820,251	809,199	828,778	848,356
Average Length of Stay	8.6	8.6	8.7	8.7	8.7
Inpatient Surgeries	27,976	28,116	27,627	28,395	29,136
Births	10,613	10,245	10,191	10,254	10,217
Utilization - Outpatient					
Emergency Outpatient Visits	373,953	376,845	366,756	369,610	357,543
Other Outpatient Visits	3,108,414	3,386,696	3,218,282	3,173,110	3,146,841
Total Outpatient Visits	3,482,367	3,763,541	3,585,038	3,542,720	3,504,384
Outpatient Surgeries	55,309	52,787	48,788	47,582	48,043
Personnel					
Full Time RNs	3,374	3,304	3,191	2,860	2,946
Full Time LPNs	519	491	486	454	478
Part Time RNs	1,961	2,052	2,047	2,088	1,930
Part Time LPNs	219	238	280	256	257
Total Full Time	16,486	15,919	15,720	14,304	14,816
Total Part Time	7,698	8,209	7,743	7,502	7,138
Revenue - Inpatient					
Gross Inpatient Revenue	$2,513,809,538	$2,454,369,080	$2,279,133,191	$2,102,143,134	$2,049,917,318
Revenue - Outpatient					
Gross Outpatient Revenue	$3,520,042,567	$3,397,775,194	$2,990,024,968	$2,622,907,633	$2,452,151,901
Revenue and Expenses - Totals					
(Includes Inpatient and Outpatient)					
Total Gross Revenue	$6,033,852,105	$5,852,144,274	$5,269,158,159	$4,725,050,767	$4,502,069,219
Deductions from Revenue	3,096,468,098	3,015,777,016	2,595,587,712	2,261,961,105	2,145,913,313
Net Patient Revenue	2,937,384,007	2,836,367,258	2,673,570,447	2,463,089,662	2,356,155,906
Other Operating Revenue	143,190,912	155,924,250	110,280,462	98,796,127	93,578,995
Other Nonoperating Revenue	110,042,762	71,944,698	22,151,981	56,310,483	64,235,515
Total Net Revenue	3,190,617,681	3,064,236,206	2,806,002,890	2,618,196,272	2,513,970,416
Total Expenses	2,855,454,234	2,874,246,551	2,660,995,740	2,485,931,042	2,379,151,295
HOSPITAL UNIT (Excludes Separate Nursing Home Units)					
Utilization - Inpatient					
Beds	2,418	2,424	2,403	2,347	2,398
Admissions	90,949	93,268	91,325	92,852	95,238
Inpatient Days	435,698	426,085	410,312	430,418	442,106
Average Length of Stay	4.8	4.6	4.5	4.6	4.6
Personnel					
Total Full Time	15,739	15,182	14,970	13,628	14,038
Total Part Time	7,115	7,616	7,213	7,007	6,602
Revenue and Expenses - Totals					
(Includes Inpatient and Outpatient)					
Total Net Revenue	$3,114,852,318	$2,986,335,907	$2,733,592,548	$2,538,770,978	$2,441,209,709
Total Expenses	2,787,516,329	2,812,268,630	2,591,928,424	2,403,184,670	2,306,425,879
COMMUNITY HEALTH INDICATORS PER 1000 POPULATION					
Total Population (in thousands)	1,024	1,015	1,005	998	980
Inpatient					
Beds	3.6	3.7	3.7	3.6	3.8
Admissions	90.6	93.9	92.9	95.1	99.4
Inpatient Days	781.9	808.0	805.1	830.3	865.5
Inpatient Surgeries	27.3	27.7	27.5	28.4	29.7
Births	10.4	10.1	10.1	10.3	10.4
Outpatient					
Emergency Outpatient Visits	365.3	371.2	364.9	370.3	364.8
Other Outpatient Visits	3,036.8	3,336.1	3,201.8	3,178.8	3,210.6
Total Outpatient Visits	3,402.1	3,707.3	3,566.7	3,549.1	3,575.3
Outpatient Surgeries	54.0	52.0	48.5	47.7	49.0
Expense per Capita (per person)	$2,789.7	$2,831.3	$2,647.4	$2,490.4	$2,427.3

States

TABLE 6

NEBRASKA

U.S. Registered Community Hospitals
(Nonfederal, short-term general and other special hospitals)

Overview 2010–2014

	2014	2013	2012	2011	2010
Total Community Hospitals in Nebraska.......	89	87	89	86	88
Bed Size Category					
6-24	27	26	26	24	23
25-49	23	21	21	25	23
50-99	20	21	22	19	23
100-199	9	7	10	8	9
200-299	5	7	5	6	4
300-399	4	4	3	2	4
400-499	0	0	2	1	1
500 + ...	1	1	0	1	1
Location					
Hospitals Urban..........................	23	18	18	16	17
Hospitals Rural	66	69	71	70	71
Control					
State and Local Government...............	36	36	38	37	39
Not for Profit	49	49	49	46	46
Investor owned	4	2	2	3	3
Physician Models					
Independent Practice Association	5	4	6	6	6
Group Practice without Walls...............	1	1	2	0	1
Open Physician-Hospital Organization	12	11	11	10	12
Closed Physician-Hospital Organization	2	2	2	1	0
Management Service Organization	2	2	2	2	3
Integrated Salary Model....................	25	20	24	26	27
Equity Model	0	0	0	0	0
Foundation................................	2	2	2	1	0
Insurance Products					
Health Maintenance Organization	2	4	2	3	3
Preferred Provider Organization..............	6	4	7	12	11
Indemnity Fee for Service	0	0	1	4	3
Managed Care Contracts					
Health Maintenance Organization	15	14	16	15	16
Preferred Provider Organization..............	35	32	43	43	43
Affiliations					
Hospitals in a System.....................	30	28	29	29	26
Hospitals in a Network.....................	31	30	30	32	28
Hospitals in a Group Purchasing Organization..	37	36	42	44	47

TABLE 6

NEBRASKA

U.S. Registered Community Hospitals
(Nonfederal, short-term general and other special hospitals)

Utilization, Personnel, Revenue and Expenses, Community Health Indicators 2010–2014

	2014	2013	2012	2011	2010
TOTAL FACILITY (Includes Hospital and Nursing Home Units)					
Utilization - Inpatient					
Beds	6,674	6,784	6,997	6,592	7,246
Admissions	195,869	199,933	205,065	203,394	208,949
Inpatient Days	1,331,045	1,335,733	1,411,707	1,313,451	1,461,558
Average Length of Stay	6.8	6.7	6.9	6.5	7
Inpatient Surgeries	67,043	60,205	81,170	65,592	65,316
Births	26,037	25,323	25,859	25,778	24,575
Utilization - Outpatient					
Emergency Outpatient Visits	706,923	692,717	671,332	716,718	700,818
Other Outpatient Visits	3,867,470	4,066,743	4,556,326	4,239,738	3,870,823
Total Outpatient Visits	4,574,393	4,759,460	5,227,658	4,956,456	4,571,641
Outpatient Surgeries	124,786	119,958	130,932	118,596	112,213
Personnel					
Full Time RNs	7,861	8,332	8,429	7,863	8,038
Full Time LPNs	571	617	681	687	856
Part Time RNs	3,950	3,878	4,274	4,182	4,286
Part Time LPNs	275	296	388	393	489
Total Full Time	27,336	28,467	29,039	27,779	29,024
Total Part Time	12,701	12,462	13,789	13,543	14,502
Revenue - Inpatient					
Gross Inpatient Revenue	$7,188,591,726	$6,714,985,216	$6,600,070,735	$6,329,607,253	$6,579,976,131
Revenue - Outpatient					
Gross Outpatient Revenue	$7,542,831,120	$6,650,376,967	$6,127,521,502	$5,571,277,484	$5,335,861,059
Revenue and Expenses - Totals					
(Includes Inpatient and Outpatient)					
Total Gross Revenue	$14,731,422,846	$13,365,362,183	$12,727,592,237	$11,900,884,737	$11,915,837,190
Deductions from Revenue	9,077,024,900	8,104,547,928	7,443,134,120	7,094,550,376	7,060,882,109
Net Patient Revenue	5,654,397,946	5,260,814,255	5,284,458,117	4,806,334,361	4,854,955,081
Other Operating Revenue	319,076,285	314,198,761	276,960,199	243,522,454	211,231,348
Other Nonoperating Revenue	135,583,028	175,886,117	61,823,105	203,146,705	132,518,504
Total Net Revenue	6,109,057,259	5,750,899,133	5,623,241,421	5,253,003,520	5,198,704,933
Total Expenses	5,246,493,342	4,870,429,742	4,972,245,644	4,659,397,050	4,710,906,183
HOSPITAL UNIT (Excludes Separate Nursing Home Units)					
Utilization - Inpatient					
Beds	5,782	5,921	5,979	5,817	6,168
Admissions	194,041	197,813	202,588	201,622	206,235
Inpatient Days	1,094,583	1,074,406	1,097,274	1,082,517	1,128,398
Average Length of Stay	5.6	5.4	5.4	5.4	5.5
Personnel					
Total Full Time	26,847	27,928	28,349	27,230	28,177
Total Part Time	12,315	12,190	13,362	13,178	13,927
Revenue and Expenses - Totals					
(Includes Inpatient and Outpatient)					
Total Net Revenue	$6,053,452,583	$5,689,097,400	$5,554,405,718	$5,207,994,214	$5,123,202,118
Total Expenses	5,187,610,294	4,798,846,323	4,897,073,033	4,613,479,154	4,634,581,746
COMMUNITY HEALTH INDICATORS PER 1000 POPULATION					
Total Population (in thousands)	1,882	1,869	1,856	1,843	1,811
Inpatient					
Beds	3.5	3.6	3.8	3.6	4.0
Admissions	104.1	107.0	110.5	110.4	115.4
Inpatient Days	707.4	714.9	760.8	712.8	807.0
Inpatient Surgeries	35.6	32.2	43.7	35.6	36.1
Births	13.8	13.6	13.9	14.0	13.6
Outpatient					
Emergency Outpatient Visits	375.7	370.7	361.8	389.0	387.0
Other Outpatient Visits	2,055.5	2,176.5	2,455.5	2,300.9	2,137.3
Total Outpatient Visits	2,431.2	2,547.2	2,817.3	2,689.9	2,524.3
Outpatient Surgeries	66.3	64.2	70.6	64.4	62.0
Expense per Capita (per person)	$2,788.5	$2,606.6	$2,679.7	$2,528.7	$2,601.2

TABLE 6

NEVADA

U.S. Registered Community Hospitals
(Nonfederal, short-term general and other special hospitals)

Overview 2010–2014

	2014	2013	2012	2011	2010
Total Community Hospitals in Nevada	37	38	38	38	36
Bed Size Category					
6-24	6	5	5	4	4
25-49	6	7	6	6	6
50-99	9	10	11	12	12
100-199	7	7	7	7	6
200-299	3	3	4	4	3
300-399	3	3	2	2	2
400-499	0	0	0	0	0
500 + ...	3	3	3	3	3
Location					
Hospitals Urban..........................	27	27	27	27	25
Hospitals Rural	10	11	11	11	11
Control					
State and Local Government...............	6	6	6	6	6
Not for Profit	12	12	12	13	13
Investor owned	19	20	20	19	17
Physician Models					
Independent Practice Association	0	1	4	4	2
Group Practice without Walls................	1	1	0	0	0
Open Physician-Hospital Organization	2	3	1	1	1
Closed Physician-Hospital Organization	1	2	2	2	2
Management Service Organization	2	2	1	2	2
Integrated Salary Model	9	8	9	7	2
Equity Model	0	0	0	1	0
Foundation...............................	1	1	0	0	0
Insurance Products					
Health Maintenance Organization	6	7	6	7	7
Preferred Provider Organization..............	6	7	6	7	7
Indemnity Fee for Service	6	6	6	3	4
Managed Care Contracts					
Health Maintenance Organization	15	16	17	20	13
Preferred Provider Organization..............	15	16	17	21	15
Affiliations					
Hospitals in a System......................	27	27	27	27	25
Hospitals in a Network.....................	4	6	6	6	5
Hospitals in a Group Purchasing Organization..	17	21	18	22	16

TABLE 6

NEVADA

U.S. Registered Community Hospitals
(Nonfederal, short-term general and other special hospitals)

Utilization, Personnel, Revenue and Expenses, Community Health Indicators 2010–2014

	2014	2013	2012	2011	2010
TOTAL FACILITY (Includes Hospital and Nursing Home Units)					
Utilization - Inpatient					
Beds..........................	5,549	5,655	5,504	5,507	5,192
Admissions.....................	256,223	253,822	260,781	249,805	241,296
Inpatient Days.................	1,398,303	1,384,938	1,361,402	1,359,447	1,296,929
Average Length of Stay...........	5.5	5.5	5.2	5.4	5.4
Inpatient Surgeries..............	56,353	62,098	63,184	63,902	69,928
Births.........................	23,860	28,592	26,384	21,822	24,844
Utilization - Outpatient					
Emergency Outpatient Visits........	909,831	928,562	865,371	820,812	820,675
Other Outpatient Visits............	2,067,141	1,697,472	2,045,456	1,859,971	1,849,263
Total Outpatient Visits	2,976,972	2,626,034	2,910,827	2,680,783	2,669,938
Outpatient Surgeries	91,475	88,318	88,694	98,155	103,406
Personnel					
Full Time RNs	7,662	7,796	6,951	6,582	6,436
Full Time LPNs	276	312	322	351	406
Part Time RNs..................	1,860	1,900	1,816	2,011	1,439
Part Time LPNs	57	72	69	85	68
Total Full Time.................	22,654	22,786	21,297	20,545	20,948
Total Part Time	5,296	5,264	4,899	5,339	3,779
Revenue - Inpatient					
Gross Inpatient Revenue...........	$14,249,565,398	$13,752,019,901	$12,294,975,694	$11,616,603,674	$10,608,864,288
Revenue - Outpatient					
Gross Outpatient Revenue	$9,280,344,629	$8,132,111,085	$6,990,158,850	$6,466,989,068	$5,826,489,194
Revenue and Expenses - Totals					
(Includes Inpatient and Outpatient)					
Total Gross Revenue..............	$23,529,910,027	$21,884,130,986	$19,285,134,544	$18,083,592,742	$16,435,353,482
Deductions from Revenue..........	18,729,674,504	17,304,616,909	15,017,726,173	14,019,540,936	12,559,876,799
Net Patient Revenue	4,800,235,523	4,579,514,077	4,267,408,371	4,064,051,806	3,875,476,683
Other Operating Revenue	154,396,930	151,926,188	102,905,260	107,770,969	97,417,940
Other Nonoperating Revenue	52,723,747	28,598,769	35,498,438	75,853,300	93,314,155
Total Net Revenue...............	5,007,356,200	4,760,039,034	4,405,812,069	4,247,676,075	4,066,208,778
Total Expenses..................	4,538,309,153	4,407,998,320	4,199,882,893	4,070,512,098	3,940,182,337
HOSPITAL UNIT (Excludes Separate Nursing Home Units)					
Utilization - Inpatient					
Beds..........................	5,549	5,655	5,479	5,443	5,174
Admissions.....................	256,223	253,822	260,768	249,708	241,287
Inpatient Days.................	1,398,303	1,384,938	1,354,258	1,341,532	1,291,351
Average Length of Stay...........	5.5	5.5	5.2	5.4	5.4
Personnel					
Total Full Time..................	22,654	22,786	21,284	20,517	20,939
Total Part Time	5,296	5,264	4,899	5,312	3,779
Revenue and Expenses - Totals					
(Includes Inpatient and Outpatient)					
Total Net Revenue................	$5,007,356,200	$4,760,039,034	$4,403,869,456	$4,243,197,676	$4,065,636,650
Total Expenses..................	4,538,309,153	4,407,998,320	4,198,988,696	4,067,942,062	3,939,711,041
COMMUNITY HEALTH INDICATORS PER 1000 POPULATION					
Total Population (in thousands)	2,839	2,790	2,759	2,723	2,655
Inpatient					
Beds..........................	2.0	2.0	2.0	2.0	2.0
Admissions.....................	90.2	91.0	94.5	91.7	90.9
Inpatient Days	492.5	496.4	493.5	499.2	488.5
Inpatient Surgeries...............	19.8	22.3	22.9	23.5	26.3
Births.........................	8.4	10.2	9.6	8.0	9.4
Outpatient					
Emergency Outpatient Visits........	320.5	332.8	313.7	301.4	309.1
Other Outpatient Visits............	728.1	608.4	741.4	683.0	696.6
Total Outpatient Visits	1,048.6	941.2	1,055.1	984.4	1,005.7
Outpatient Surgeries	32.2	31.7	32.1	36.0	39.0
Expense per Capita (per person).....	$1,598.5	$1,579.9	$1,522.3	$1,494.7	$1,484.2

TABLE 6

NEW HAMPSHIRE

U.S. Registered Community Hospitals
(Nonfederal, short-term general and other special hospitals)

Overview 2010–2014

	2014	2013	2012	2011	2010
Total Community Hospitals in New Hampshire ..	28	28	28	28	28
Bed Size Category					
6-24	1	1	1	1	1
25-49	10	10	10	10	9
50-99	7	7	7	6	7
100-199	6	6	6	7	7
200-299	3	3	3	3	3
300-399	0	1	1	1	1
400-499	1	0	0	0	0
500 + ...	0	0	0	0	0
Location					
Hospitals Urban...........................	11	11	11	11	11
Hospitals Rural	17	17	17	17	17
Control					
State and Local Government................	0	0	0	0	0
Not for Profit	24	24	24	24	24
Investor owned	4	4	4	4	4
Physician Models					
Independent Practice Association	2	2	2	2	2
Group Practice without Walls................	2	2	2	2	2
Open Physician-Hospital Organization	4	4	4	5	9
Closed Physician-Hospital Organization	0	0	0	0	0
Management Service Organization	0	0	0	0	0
Integrated Salary Model....................	18	19	19	20	17
Equity Model	0	0	0	0	0
Foundation...............................	0	0	0	0	0
Insurance Products					
Health Maintenance Organization	2	0	0	0	0
Preferred Provider Organization..............	0	0	0	0	0
Indemnity Fee for Service	0	0	0	0	0
Managed Care Contracts					
Health Maintenance Organization	18	19	19	20	23
Preferred Provider Organization..............	17	18	18	19	21
Affiliations					
Hospitals in a System......................	7	7	6	6	6
Hospitals in a Network.....................	13	11	12	11	10
Hospitals in a Group Purchasing Organization..	22	24	25	25	26

States

TABLE 6

NEW HAMPSHIRE

U.S. Registered Community Hospitals
(Nonfederal, short-term general and other special hospitals)

Utilization, Personnel, Revenue and Expenses, Community Health Indicators 2010–2014

	2014	2013	2012	2011	2010
TOTAL FACILITY (Includes Hospital and Nursing Home Units)					
Utilization - Inpatient					
Beds	2,839	2,809	2,831	2,840	2,851
Admissions	117,327	119,566	119,814	122,341	119,971
Inpatient Days	630,685	628,043	627,784	634,954	624,399
Average Length of Stay	5.4	5.3	5.2	5.2	5.2
Inpatient Surgeries	34,546	32,881	33,606	34,281	33,622
Births	13,516	12,664	12,035	12,649	12,630
Utilization - Outpatient					
Emergency Outpatient Visits	644,075	700,141	652,190	677,358	667,605
Other Outpatient Visits	4,265,408	4,346,816	4,330,937	4,318,549	4,109,910
Total Outpatient Visits	4,909,483	5,046,957	4,983,127	4,995,907	4,777,515
Outpatient Surgeries	85,589	89,108	90,715	91,348	92,450
Personnel					
Full Time RNs	4,982	4,648	4,460	4,282	4,298
Full Time LPNs	254	283	278	276	278
Part Time RNs	2,926	2,889	3,068	3,128	3,008
Part Time LPNs	96	111	128	126	139
Total Full Time	22,877	21,980	21,736	21,846	22,066
Total Part Time	9,680	10,181	10,229	10,000	10,151
Revenue - Inpatient					
Gross Inpatient Revenue	$4,989,417,217	$4,696,146,268	$4,263,267,285	$4,150,081,268	$3,890,334,236
Revenue - Outpatient					
Gross Outpatient Revenue	$7,220,073,530	$6,733,412,770	$6,315,255,279	$5,916,747,273	$5,494,839,267
Revenue and Expenses - Totals					
(Includes Inpatient and Outpatient)					
Total Gross Revenue	$12,209,490,747	$11,429,559,038	$10,578,522,564	$10,066,828,541	$9,385,173,503
Deductions from Revenue	7,808,011,257	7,139,588,921	6,389,949,615	5,928,255,856	5,410,431,600
Net Patient Revenue	4,401,479,490	4,289,970,117	4,188,572,949	4,138,572,685	3,974,741,903
Other Operating Revenue	197,582,231	165,027,209	172,037,917	129,629,985	106,982,372
Other Nonoperating Revenue	123,495,316	87,925,169	65,319,726	296,520	52,157,491
Total Net Revenue	4,722,557,037	4,542,922,495	4,425,930,592	4,268,499,190	4,133,881,766
Total Expenses	4,250,644,036	4,089,847,120	4,024,997,567	3,948,270,249	3,781,620,257
HOSPITAL UNIT (Excludes Separate Nursing Home Units)					
Utilization - Inpatient					
Beds	2,736	2,706	2,728	2,710	2,721
Admissions	117,253	119,473	119,684	121,996	119,391
Inpatient Days	595,536	592,762	592,483	593,304	577,175
Average Length of Stay	5.1	5	5	4.9	4.8
Personnel					
Total Full Time	22,817	21,933	21,685	21,766	22,003
Total Part Time	9,646	10,159	10,202	9,960	10,110
Revenue and Expenses - Totals					
(Includes Inpatient and Outpatient)					
Total Net Revenue	$4,715,825,712	$4,535,848,627	$4,417,200,764	$4,256,119,678	$4,120,469,030
Total Expenses	4,244,135,217	4,083,503,383	4,017,253,998	3,938,257,684	3,770,403,066
COMMUNITY HEALTH INDICATORS PER 1000 POPULATION					
Total Population (in thousands)	1,327	1,323	1,321	1,318	1,324
Inpatient					
Beds	2.1	2.1	2.1	2.2	2.2
Admissions	88.4	90.3	90.7	92.8	90.6
Inpatient Days	475.3	474.5	475.3	481.7	471.8
Inpatient Surgeries	26.0	24.8	25.4	26.0	25.4
Births	10.2	9.6	9.1	9.6	9.5
Outpatient					
Emergency Outpatient Visits	485.4	529.0	493.8	513.9	504.4
Other Outpatient Visits	3,214.8	3,284.4	3,279.2	3,276.1	3,105.3
Total Outpatient Visits	3,700.2	3,813.5	3,773.0	3,790.0	3,609.7
Outpatient Surgeries	64.5	67.3	68.7	69.3	69.9
Expense per Capita (per person)	$3,203.6	$3,090.3	$3,047.6	$2,995.2	$2,857.2

States

TABLE 6

NEW JERSEY

U.S. Registered Community Hospitals
(Nonfederal, short-term general and other special hospitals)

Overview 2010–2014

	2014	2013	2012	2011	2010
Total Community Hospitals in New Jersey.....	75	77	77	73	73
Bed Size Category					
6-24	0	0	0	0	0
25-49	2	2	2	1	2
50-99	8	9	9	7	6
100-199	23	19	20	18	16
200-299	11	16	17	21	20
300-399	16	15	12	10	11
400-499	6	7	9	9	9
500 + ...	9	9	8	7	9
Location					
Hospitals Urban..........................	75	77	77	73	73
Hospitals Rural	0	0	0	0	0
Control					
State and Local Government................	2	4	3	2	3
Not for Profit	59	60	60	61	62
Investor owned	14	13	14	10	8
Physician Models					
Independent Practice Association	11	12	11	10	12
Group Practice without Walls................	4	4	5	1	3
Open Physician-Hospital Organization	5	5	5	3	4
Closed Physician-Hospital Organization	6	5	3	2	2
Management Service Organization	18	15	13	13	12
Integrated Salary Model....................	39	38	27	25	23
Equity Model	3	3	3	0	0
Foundation...............................	10	8	8	7	4
Insurance Products					
Health Maintenance Organization	12	17	12	7	6
Preferred Provider Organization..............	8	19	14	7	7
Indemnity Fee for Service	5	11	5	2	3
Managed Care Contracts					
Health Maintenance Organization	47	47	49	48	53
Preferred Provider Organization..............	47	48	49	47	53
Affiliations					
Hospitals in a System......................	53	54	47	42	42
Hospitals in a Network.....................	32	32	30	29	26
Hospitals in a Group Purchasing Organization..	57	59	54	53	54

TABLE 6

NEW JERSEY

U.S. Registered Community Hospitals
(Nonfederal, short-term general and other special hospitals)

Utilization, Personnel, Revenue and Expenses, Community Health Indicators 2010–2014

	2014	2013	2012	2011	2010
TOTAL FACILITY (Includes Hospital and Nursing Home Units)					
Utilization - Inpatient					
Beds............................	20,517	21,348	21,162	20,396	21,096
Admissions.....................	970,436	1,005,271	1,047,545	1,050,828	1,067,267
Inpatient Days.................	5,015,867	5,173,783	5,370,619	5,344,077	5,433,359
Average Length of Stay...........	5.2	5.1	5.1	5.1	5.1
Inpatient Surgeries...............	231,329	237,735	243,512	243,218	254,003
Births..........................	99,550	99,416	101,599	101,362	100,677
Utilization - Outpatient					
Emergency Outpatient Visits........	3,613,702	3,584,950	3,703,899	3,474,457	3,360,970
Other Outpatient Visits............	11,875,594	12,009,026	11,883,599	12,350,842	12,619,644
Total Outpatient Visits.............	15,489,296	15,593,976	15,587,498	15,825,299	15,980,614
Outpatient Surgeries	356,709	361,755	381,289	381,281	378,695
Personnel					
Full Time RNs...................	27,204	27,680	27,979	27,286	26,849
Full Time LPNs	597	692	763	881	976
Part Time RNs..................	13,504	13,141	13,111	14,084	12,933
Part Time LPNs	236	240	294	321	342
Total Full Time..................	99,374	100,545	101,341	100,956	101,574
Total Part Time	42,432	40,840	42,586	43,164	39,829
Revenue - Inpatient					
Gross Inpatient Revenue...........	$59,549,833,885	$59,880,957,599	$58,452,281,514	$56,915,377,319	$53,676,558,488
Revenue - Outpatient					
Gross Outpatient Revenue	$36,553,897,644	$34,166,641,289	$31,284,903,340	$27,132,937,292	$25,954,408,517
Revenue and Expenses - Totals					
(Includes Inpatient and Outpatient)					
Total Gross Revenue..............	$96,103,731,529	$94,047,598,888	$89,737,184,854	$84,048,314,611	$79,630,967,005
Deductions from Revenue..........	75,732,520,919	74,483,147,229	70,204,451,132	66,316,458,143	62,268,213,291
Net Patient Revenue	20,371,210,610	19,564,451,659	19,532,733,722	17,731,856,468	17,362,753,714
Other Operating Revenue	1,390,647,332	1,399,525,038	1,217,574,869	1,039,183,060	991,173,520
Other Nonoperating Revenue	230,925,324	561,510,820	398,816,960	157,790,540	355,140,452
Total Net Revenue...............	21,992,783,266	21,525,487,517	21,149,125,551	18,928,830,068	18,709,067,686
Total Expenses..................	20,672,554,704	20,199,975,055	19,790,864,680	18,237,577,704	17,953,893,599
HOSPITAL UNIT (Excludes Separate Nursing Home Units)					
Utilization - Inpatient					
Beds............................	20,133	20,929	20,632	19,853	20,533
Admissions.....................	967,029	1,001,500	1,043,187	1,046,456	1,061,552
Inpatient Days.................	4,892,006	5,037,093	5,189,878	5,168,493	5,258,495
Average Length of Stay...........	5.1	5	5	4.9	5
Personnel					
Total Full Time...................	99,061	100,231	100,839	100,398	100,902
Total Part Time	42,211	40,689	42,335	42,916	39,482
Revenue and Expenses - Totals					
(Includes Inpatient and Outpatient)					
Total Net Revenue...............	$21,947,697,784	$21,472,958,854	$21,088,046,402	$18,869,785,791	$18,584,183,240
Total Expenses..................	20,638,686,308	20,160,424,322	19,740,490,336	18,187,967,013	17,859,249,404
COMMUNITY HEALTH INDICATORS PER 1000 POPULATION					
Total Population (in thousands)	8,938	8,899	8,865	8,821	8,733
Inpatient					
Beds............................	2.3	2.4	2.4	2.3	2.4
Admissions.....................	108.6	113.0	118.2	119.1	122.2
Inpatient Days	561.2	581.4	605.9	605.8	622.2
Inpatient Surgeries...............	25.9	26.7	27.5	27.6	29.1
Births..........................	11.1	11.2	11.5	11.5	11.5
Outpatient					
Emergency Outpatient Visits........	404.3	402.8	417.8	393.9	384.9
Other Outpatient Visits............	1,328.6	1,349.4	1,340.6	1,400.1	1,445.1
Total Outpatient Visits.............	1,732.9	1,752.3	1,758.4	1,794.0	1,830.0
Outpatient Surgeries	39.9	40.6	43.0	43.2	43.4
Expense per Capita (per person).....	$2,312.8	$2,269.8	$2,232.6	$2,067.5	$2,055.9

States

TABLE 6

NEW MEXICO

U.S. Registered Community Hospitals
(Nonfederal, short-term general and other special hospitals)

Overview 2010–2014

	2014	2013	2012	2011	2010
Total Community Hospitals in New Mexico	37	37	37	36	36
Bed Size Category					
6-24	4	4	5	4	4
25-49	11	11	9	8	8
50-99	12	10	10	12	12
100-199	5	6	6	7	8
200-299	3	4	5	3	2
300-399	0	0	0	0	0
400-499	1	1	1	0	0
500 + ...	1	1	1	2	2
Location					
Hospitals Urban..........................	14	14	14	14	14
Hospitals Rural	23	23	23	22	22
Control					
State and Local Government................	6	6	6	6	6
Not for Profit	15	15	15	15	16
Investor owned	16	16	16	15	14
Physician Models					
Independent Practice Association	3	3	3	3	4
Group Practice without Walls...............	0	0	0	0	0
Open Physician-Hospital Organization	3	2	4	4	3
Closed Physician-Hospital Organization	0	0	0	0	0
Management Service Organization	1	1	0	0	0
Integrated Salary Model	12	15	11	9	11
Equity Model	0	0	0	0	0
Foundation...............................	0	0	0	0	1
Insurance Products					
Health Maintenance Organization	8	8	8	7	6
Preferred Provider Organization..............	8	8	6	7	6
Indemnity Fee for Service	8	8	4	4	5
Managed Care Contracts					
Health Maintenance Organization	16	18	16	13	14
Preferred Provider Organization..............	18	18	16	13	15
Affiliations					
Hospitals in a System.....................	27	29	29	28	28
Hospitals in a Network	12	11	11	11	11
Hospitals in a Group Purchasing Organization..	24	24	22	22	20

TABLE 6

NEW MEXICO

U.S. Registered Community Hospitals
(Nonfederal, short-term general and other special hospitals)

Utilization, Personnel, Revenue and Expenses, Community Health Indicators 2010–2014

	2014	2013	2012	2011	2010
TOTAL FACILITY (Includes Hospital and Nursing Home Units)					
Utilization - Inpatient					
Beds	3,771	3,806	4,076	4,068	3,975
Admissions	174,429	166,307	177,744	175,112	186,092
Inpatient Days	819,119	771,150	850,391	861,109	831,384
Average Length of Stay	4.7	4.6	4.8	4.9	4.5
Inpatient Surgeries	40,142	43,384	47,292	53,331	49,435
Births	22,664	22,252	23,924	21,537	23,767
Utilization - Outpatient					
Emergency Outpatient Visits	953,949	826,885	793,582	854,871	844,650
Other Outpatient Visits	4,698,796	3,657,027	3,361,978	3,740,262	3,795,337
Total Outpatient Visits	5,652,745	4,483,912	4,155,560	4,595,133	4,639,987
Outpatient Surgeries	79,654	89,154	92,264	93,352	92,079
Personnel					
Full Time RNs	6,441	6,330	6,326	5,549	6,022
Full Time LPNs	309	327	353	292	391
Part Time RNs	2,418	2,221	2,254	2,092	2,065
Part Time LPNs	104	109	100	72	124
Total Full Time	21,683	21,883	21,672	19,318	20,493
Total Part Time	6,745	6,755	6,526	5,387	5,559
Revenue - Inpatient					
Gross Inpatient Revenue	$6,839,112,627	$6,186,832,999	$6,068,430,416	$5,955,197,886	$5,597,578,195
Revenue - Outpatient					
Gross Outpatient Revenue	$7,317,852,735	$6,581,129,820	$6,116,116,964	$5,493,320,827	$5,288,644,232
Revenue and Expenses - Totals					
(Includes Inpatient and Outpatient)					
Total Gross Revenue	$14,156,965,362	$12,767,962,819	$12,184,547,380	$11,448,518,713	$10,886,222,427
Deductions from Revenue	9,903,703,375	8,697,316,188	8,059,915,659	7,609,704,329	6,965,889,535
Net Patient Revenue	4,253,261,987	4,070,646,631	4,124,631,721	3,838,814,384	3,920,332,892
Other Operating Revenue	246,751,305	220,599,613	229,495,765	211,597,602	193,738,359
Other Nonoperating Revenue	84,752,165	55,758,352	21,327,949	53,311,105	32,566,260
Total Net Revenue	4,584,765,457	4,347,004,596	4,375,455,435	4,103,723,091	4,146,637,511
Total Expenses	4,087,540,556	3,818,356,732	4,003,331,871	3,713,540,269	3,540,766,412
HOSPITAL UNIT (Excludes Separate Nursing Home Units)					
Utilization - Inpatient					
Beds	3,719	3,806	4,076	4,068	3,928
Admissions	174,406	166,307	177,744	175,112	186,058
Inpatient Days	809,549	771,150	850,391	861,109	818,802
Average Length of Stay	4.6	4.6	4.8	4.9	4.4
Personnel					
Total Full Time	21,656	21,695	21,499	19,318	20,450
Total Part Time	6,744	6,644	6,433	5,387	5,554
Revenue and Expenses - Totals					
(Includes Inpatient and Outpatient)					
Total Net Revenue	$4,579,619,544	$4,347,004,596	$4,375,455,435	$4,103,723,091	$4,145,724,111
Total Expenses	4,084,228,633	3,818,356,732	4,003,331,871	3,713,540,269	3,537,873,415
COMMUNITY HEALTH INDICATORS PER 1000 POPULATION					
Total Population (in thousands)	2,086	2,085	2,086	2,082	2,034
Inpatient					
Beds	1.8	1.8	2.0	2.0	2.0
Admissions	83.6	79.8	85.2	84.1	91.5
Inpatient Days	392.8	369.8	407.8	413.6	408.8
Inpatient Surgeries	19.2	20.8	22.7	25.6	24.3
Births	10.9	10.7	11.5	10.3	11.7
Outpatient					
Emergency Outpatient Visits	457.4	396.5	380.5	410.6	415.3
Other Outpatient Visits	2,253.0	1,753.7	1,612.0	1,796.3	1,866.1
Total Outpatient Visits	2,710.4	2,150.3	1,992.6	2,206.8	2,281.4
Outpatient Surgeries	38.2	42.8	44.2	44.8	45.3
Expense per Capita (per person)	$1,959.9	$1,831.1	$1,919.6	$1,783.4	$1,740.9

TABLE 6

NEW YORK

U.S. Registered Community Hospitals
(Nonfederal, short-term general and other special hospitals)

Overview 2010–2014

	2014	2013	2012	2011	2010
Total Community Hospitals in New York	174	177	178	182	185
Bed Size Category					
6-24	7	7	7	6	5
25-49	8	7	7	7	7
50-99	19	17	16	19	18
100-199	40	40	40	41	40
200-299	36	40	39	36	44
300-399	18	20	22	26	25
400-499	13	12	12	14	13
500 + ...	33	34	35	33	33
Location					
Hospitals Urban.	138	139	140	145	147
Hospitals Rural	36	38	38	37	38
Control					
State and Local Government.	24	25	26	26	25
Not for Profit	150	152	152	156	160
Investor owned	0	0	0	0	0
Physician Models					
Independent Practice Association	42	39	38	35	35
Group Practice without Walls.	7	6	7	5	6
Open Physician-Hospital Organization	12	12	15	14	12
Closed Physician-Hospital Organization	5	7	13	10	10
Management Service Organization	18	13	16	15	18
Integrated Salary Model.	77	83	77	77	74
Equity Model	1	1	1	2	0
Foundation.	4	5	3	3	2
Insurance Products					
Health Maintenance Organization	49	48	42	48	45
Preferred Provider Organization.	20	25	13	21	30
Indemnity Fee for Service	6	10	9	10	22
Managed Care Contracts					
Health Maintenance Organization	106	109	114	116	116
Preferred Provider Organization.	99	105	108	111	109
Affiliations					
Hospitals in a System.	95	94	87	84	82
Hospitals in a Network.	80	78	75	83	82
Hospitals in a Group Purchasing Organization. .	127	129	128	134	128

TABLE 6

NEW YORK

U.S. Registered Community Hospitals
(Nonfederal, short-term general and other special hospitals)

Utilization, Personnel, Revenue and Expenses, Community Health Indicators 2010–2014

	2014	2013	2012	2011	2010
TOTAL FACILITY (Includes Hospital and Nursing Home Units)					
Utilization - Inpatient					
Beds	55,306	56,270	57,148	58,080	59,510
Admissions	2,278,459	2,331,678	2,444,350	2,491,403	2,509,980
Inpatient Days	15,678,478	15,933,416	16,783,079	16,924,697	17,226,868
Average Length of Stay...........	6.9	6.8	6.9	6.8	6.9
Inpatient Surgeries..............	594,891	599,625	615,646	615,656	683,336
Births........................	231,715	232,325	232,967	239,622	238,062
Utilization - Outpatient					
Emergency Outpatient Visits........	8,589,335	8,616,225	8,379,030	8,432,260	8,063,821
Other Outpatient Visits............	48,413,762	47,693,175	48,264,808	45,578,620	45,586,391
Total Outpatient Visits	57,003,097	56,309,400	56,643,838	54,010,880	53,650,212
Outpatient Surgeries	1,369,867	1,374,086	1,309,661	1,335,088	1,369,360
Personnel					
Full Time RNs	85,835	82,755	80,336	81,500	79,270
Full Time LPNs	5,000	5,133	5,110	5,403	5,095
Part Time RNs..................	23,457	23,281	23,613	23,368	24,090
Part Time LPNs	1,176	1,358	1,389	1,427	1,492
Total Full Time.................	349,101	358,347	354,362	350,923	333,121
Total Part Time	81,095	84,342	84,860	85,040	80,711
Revenue - Inpatient					
Gross Inpatient Revenue...........	$102,292,546,309	$93,765,207,434	$91,398,462,566	$86,312,444,902	$83,446,219,992
Revenue - Outpatient					
Gross Outpatient Revenue	$73,697,207,463	$68,815,204,133	$62,547,461,326	$56,035,192,523	$52,554,490,709
Revenue and Expenses - Totals					
(Includes Inpatient and Outpatient)					
Total Gross Revenue..............	$175,989,753,772	$162,580,411,567	$153,945,923,892	$142,347,637,425	$136,000,710,701
Deductions from Revenue..........	113,311,427,323	103,028,887,067	95,942,060,347	87,498,353,474	83,151,232,467
Net Patient Revenue	62,678,326,449	59,551,524,500	58,003,863,545	54,849,283,951	52,849,478,234
Other Operating Revenue	5,421,095,659	5,362,994,107	4,732,632,403	4,212,820,400	4,222,330,075
Other Nonoperating Revenue	963,360,033	1,788,296,692	758,391,592	541,024,602	925,916,282
Total Net Revenue...............	69,062,782,141	66,702,815,299	63,494,887,540	59,603,128,953	57,997,724,591
Total Expenses..................	67,346,714,902	64,889,138,257	62,122,860,564	58,543,388,525	56,081,000,844
HOSPITAL UNIT (Excludes Separate Nursing Home Units)					
Utilization - Inpatient					
Beds	49,734	50,184	50,458	51,072	53,436
Admissions	2,263,824	2,314,517	2,426,083	2,471,603	2,494,952
Inpatient Days	13,756,529	13,831,403	14,420,693	14,460,605	15,107,729
Average Length of Stay...........	6.1	6	5.9	5.9	6.1
Personnel					
Total Full Time..................	344,290	353,126	348,723	346,182	329,655
Total Part Time	78,942	81,870	82,206	82,889	78,770
Revenue and Expenses - Totals					
(Includes Inpatient and Outpatient)					
Total Net Revenue...............	$68,375,734,988	$66,062,124,750	$62,830,487,679	$58,992,643,837	$57,401,240,974
Total Expenses..................	66,689,194,014	64,249,125,162	61,440,662,596	57,946,106,911	55,490,108,946
COMMUNITY HEALTH INDICATORS PER 1000 POPULATION					
Total Population (in thousands)	19,746	19,651	19,570	19,465	19,578
Inpatient					
Beds	2.8	2.9	2.9	3.0	3.0
Admissions	115.4	118.7	124.9	128.0	128.2
Inpatient Days	794.0	810.8	857.6	869.5	879.9
Inpatient Surgeries...............	30.1	30.5	31.5	31.6	34.9
Births........................	11.7	11.8	11.9	12.3	12.2
Outpatient					
Emergency Outpatient Visits........	435.0	438.5	428.2	433.2	411.9
Other Outpatient Visits............	2,451.8	2,427.0	2,466.2	2,341.5	2,328.5
Total Outpatient Visits	2,886.8	2,865.5	2,894.4	2,774.7	2,740.4
Outpatient Surgeries	69.4	69.9	66.9	68.6	69.9
Expense per Capita (per person).....	$3,410.6	$3,302.1	$3,174.4	$3,007.6	$2,864.5

States

TABLE 6

NORTH CAROLINA

U.S. Registered Community Hospitals
(Nonfederal, short-term general and other special hospitals)

Overview 2010–2014

	2014	2013	2012	2011	2010
Total Community Hospitals in North Carolina..	116	117	118	117	117
Bed Size Category					
6-24	7	5	5	3	4
25-49	24	25	26	20	19
50-99	24	23	22	28	25
100-199	30	30	31	31	35
200-299	11	12	12	13	13
300-399	5	7	8	8	6
400-499	3	2	1	1	2
500 + ...	12	13	13	13	13
Location					
Hospitals Urban..........................	67	60	61	59	59
Hospitals Rural	49	57	57	58	58
Control					
State and Local Government................	28	28	30	30	32
Not for Profit	68	72	72	75	73
Investor owned	20	17	16	12	12
Physician Models					
Independent Practice Association	7	8	8	10	10
Group Practice without Walls...............	3	3	2	1	2
Open Physician-Hospital Organization	7	9	9	9	10
Closed Physician-Hospital Organization	5	5	5	6	6
Management Service Organization	16	15	14	12	12
Integrated Salary Model....................	61	61	60	57	54
Equity Model	0	1	2	2	4
Foundation...............................	1	1	2	2	3
Insurance Products					
Health Maintenance Organization	3	4	5	6	7
Preferred Provider Organization..............	17	19	14	16	14
Indemnity Fee for Service	2	2	2	6	5
Managed Care Contracts					
Health Maintenance Organization	72	70	75	71	70
Preferred Provider Organization..............	80	81	83	77	75
Affiliations					
Hospitals in a System.....................	100	99	95	90	78
Hospitals in a Network	47	45	46	43	41
Hospitals in a Group Purchasing Organization..	95	96	99	94	90

TABLE 6

NORTH CAROLINA

U.S. Registered Community Hospitals
(Nonfederal, short-term general and other special hospitals)

Utilization, Personnel, Revenue and Expenses, Community Health Indicators 2010–2014

	2014	2013	2012	2011	2010
TOTAL FACILITY (Includes Hospital and Nursing Home Units)					
Utilization - Inpatient					
Beds	22,034	22,617	22,708	23,136	23,012
Admissions	995,842	1,011,304	1,027,640	1,035,400	1,038,337
Inpatient Days	5,496,740	5,730,722	5,726,216	5,830,425	5,852,967
Average Length of Stay	5.5	5.7	5.6	5.6	5.6
Inpatient Surgeries	277,123	278,068	281,357	287,065	293,323
Births	114,799	112,844	114,140	115,013	117,422
Utilization - Outpatient					
Emergency Outpatient Visits	4,661,360	4,689,431	4,636,192	4,448,191	4,259,853
Other Outpatient Visits	15,004,635	14,969,949	15,094,661	14,180,481	14,026,042
Total Outpatient Visits	19,665,995	19,659,380	19,730,853	18,628,672	18,285,895
Outpatient Surgeries	548,249	555,407	549,918	551,009	558,068
Personnel					
Full Time RNs	40,257	40,181	39,539	37,691	37,461
Full Time LPNs	1,373	1,532	1,454	1,457	1,585
Part Time RNs	13,863	13,150	13,727	13,740	13,790
Part Time LPNs	325	381	395	433	509
Total Full Time	138,906	138,355	138,663	134,652	130,456
Total Part Time	37,571	36,141	36,991	36,793	35,766
Revenue - Inpatient					
Gross Inpatient Revenue	$35,672,703,965	$34,091,849,676	$32,277,023,087	$30,029,780,874	$28,197,730,702
Revenue - Outpatient					
Gross Outpatient Revenue	$38,064,010,629	$34,470,700,452	$31,543,420,298	$27,738,748,951	$24,683,456,547
Revenue and Expenses - Totals					
(Includes Inpatient and Outpatient)					
Total Gross Revenue	$73,736,714,594	$68,562,550,128	$63,820,443,385	$57,768,529,825	$52,881,187,249
Deductions from Revenue	50,072,141,483	45,661,471,693	40,976,435,538	37,629,541,786	33,708,237,290
Net Patient Revenue	23,664,573,111	22,901,078,435	22,844,007,847	20,138,988,039	19,172,949,959
Other Operating Revenue	843,853,426	855,996,247	1,376,765,805	1,235,529,371	1,122,729,376
Other Nonoperating Revenue	493,237,081	551,411,198	664,882,512	273,053,042	492,730,856
Total Net Revenue	25,001,663,618	24,308,485,880	24,885,656,164	21,647,570,452	20,788,410,191
Total Expenses	23,206,884,777	22,436,224,717	22,659,692,061	20,062,914,117	18,847,920,294
HOSPITAL UNIT (Excludes Separate Nursing Home Units)					
Utilization - Inpatient					
Beds	20,591	21,092	20,823	21,041	20,841
Admissions	989,690	1,004,965	1,020,541	1,027,691	1,030,472
Inpatient Days	5,043,706	5,244,404	5,135,293	5,171,227	5,150,233
Average Length of Stay	5.1	5.2	5	5	5
Personnel					
Total Full Time	137,996	137,327	137,311	133,321	128,958
Total Part Time	37,156	35,653	36,455	36,217	35,100
Revenue and Expenses - Totals					
(Includes Inpatient and Outpatient)					
Total Net Revenue	$24,899,363,204	$24,201,100,219	$24,752,345,760	$21,508,952,533	$20,648,909,546
Total Expenses	23,109,433,313	22,329,567,069	22,524,391,595	19,925,373,321	18,715,167,064
COMMUNITY HEALTH INDICATORS PER 1000 POPULATION					
Total Population (in thousands)	9,944	9,848	9,752	9,656	9,459
Inpatient					
Beds	2.2	2.3	2.3	2.4	2.4
Admissions	100.1	102.7	105.4	107.2	109.8
Inpatient Days	552.8	581.9	587.2	603.8	618.8
Inpatient Surgeries	27.9	28.2	28.9	29.7	31.0
Births	11.5	11.5	11.7	11.9	12.4
Outpatient					
Emergency Outpatient Visits	468.8	476.2	475.4	460.6	450.4
Other Outpatient Visits	1,508.9	1,520.1	1,547.8	1,468.5	1,482.8
Total Outpatient Visits	1,977.7	1,996.3	2,023.2	1,929.2	1,933.2
Outpatient Surgeries	55.1	56.4	56.4	57.1	59.0
Expense per Capita (per person)	$2,333.8	$2,278.2	$2,323.6	$2,077.7	$1,992.6

TABLE 6

NORTH DAKOTA

U.S. Registered Community Hospitals
(Nonfederal, short-term general and other special hospitals)

Overview 2010–2014

	2014	2013	2012	2011	2010
Total Community Hospitals in North Dakota . . .	40	40	44	41	41
Bed Size Category					
6-24	16	15	14	13	10
25-49	9	10	15	14	15
50-99	8	9	8	7	8
100-199	2	1	2	2	3
200-299	3	3	3	3	3
300-399	0	0	0	0	0
400-499	1	2	1	1	1
500 + ...	1	0	1	1	1
Location					
Hospitals Urban	8	8	8	8	8
Hospitals Rural	32	32	36	33	33
Control					
State and Local Government	0	0	0	0	0
Not for Profit	38	38	41	39	39
Investor owned	2	2	3	2	2
Physician Models					
Independent Practice Association	1	2	3	3	4
Group Practice without Walls	0	0	1	0	0
Open Physician-Hospital Organization	2	1	2	1	1
Closed Physician-Hospital Organization	0	0	0	0	0
Management Service Organization	0	0	0	0	0
Integrated Salary Model	11	10	10	8	10
Equity Model	0	0	0	0	0
Foundation	1	1	1	1	1
Insurance Products					
Health Maintenance Organization	4	4	2	0	1
Preferred Provider Organization	4	4	2	5	5
Indemnity Fee for Service	0	0	0	1	2
Managed Care Contracts					
Health Maintenance Organization	5	0	1	2	1
Preferred Provider Organization	12	10	10	11	13
Affiliations					
Hospitals in a System	19	19	20	19	17
Hospitals in a Network	9	9	9	7	8
Hospitals in a Group Purchasing Organization . .	21	19	22	17	19

States

TABLE 6

NORTH DAKOTA

U.S. Registered Community Hospitals
(Nonfederal, short-term general and other special hospitals)

Utilization, Personnel, Revenue and Expenses, Community Health Indicators 2010–2014

	2014	2013	2012	2011	2010
TOTAL FACILITY (Includes Hospital and Nursing Home Units)					
Utilization - Inpatient					
Beds	3,144	2,924	3,254	3,145	3,345
Admissions	92,692	94,743	92,940	94,125	94,436
Inpatient Days	644,992	658,748	727,855	701,723	718,950
Average Length of Stay	7	7	7.8	7.5	7.6
Inpatient Surgeries	27,107	27,930	26,617	28,285	29,558
Births	12,561	11,061	14,625	12,731	12,851
Utilization - Outpatient					
Emergency Outpatient Visits	360,374	328,299	419,652	408,870	353,557
Other Outpatient Visits	2,159,913	2,007,191	2,566,926	2,540,152	2,722,180
Total Outpatient Visits	2,520,287	2,335,490	2,986,578	2,949,022	3,075,737
Outpatient Surgeries	76,723	73,072	68,599	59,702	54,165
Personnel					
Full Time RNs	3,320	3,701	3,651	3,103	2,889
Full Time LPNs	558	509	514	501	514
Part Time RNs	2,562	2,579	2,791	2,485	2,452
Part Time LPNs	462	413	441	404	392
Total Full Time	15,290	16,391	16,049	14,606	13,962
Total Part Time	8,980	8,850	9,429	8,536	8,187
Revenue - Inpatient					
Gross Inpatient Revenue	$2,706,066,510	$2,807,963,590	$2,688,456,061	$2,320,300,120	$2,092,135,268
Revenue - Outpatient					
Gross Outpatient Revenue	$4,252,502,194	$3,905,959,216	$3,413,782,975	$2,783,603,262	$2,551,094,052
Revenue and Expenses - Totals					
(Includes Inpatient and Outpatient)					
Total Gross Revenue	$6,958,568,704	$6,713,922,806	$6,102,239,036	$5,103,903,382	$4,643,229,320
Deductions from Revenue	3,822,990,720	3,821,510,799	3,415,592,851	2,807,521,605	2,493,872,027
Net Patient Revenue	3,135,577,984	2,892,412,007	2,686,646,185	2,296,381,777	2,149,357,293
Other Operating Revenue	231,190,503	161,549,912	125,508,307	107,145,231	96,921,743
Other Nonoperating Revenue	26,912,185	28,978,906	24,882,062	22,983,677	33,585,013
Total Net Revenue	3,393,680,672	3,082,940,825	2,837,036,554	2,426,510,685	2,279,864,049
Total Expenses	3,186,530,035	2,966,838,008	2,666,135,816	2,229,494,218	2,142,846,297
HOSPITAL UNIT (Excludes Separate Nursing Home Units)					
Utilization - Inpatient					
Beds	2,674	2,422	2,906	2,944	3,063
Admissions	91,882	93,845	91,966	92,902	92,796
Inpatient Days	494,750	495,592	613,301	633,852	634,164
Average Length of Stay	5.4	5.3	6.7	6.8	6.8
Personnel					
Total Full Time	14,779	16,134	15,785	14,472	13,822
Total Part Time	8,693	8,700	9,268	8,439	8,048
Revenue and Expenses - Totals					
(Includes Inpatient and Outpatient)					
Total Net Revenue	$3,355,550,091	$3,051,733,992	$2,813,596,727	$2,414,246,674	$2,258,523,169
Total Expenses	3,147,793,319	2,925,639,027	2,647,960,716	2,223,176,123	2,126,714,369
COMMUNITY HEALTH INDICATORS PER 1000 POPULATION					
Total Population (in thousands)	739	723	700	684	654
Inpatient					
Beds	4.3	4.0	4.7	4.6	5.1
Admissions	125.3	131.0	132.8	137.6	144.4
Inpatient Days	872.2	910.6	1,040.3	1,026.0	1,099.7
Inpatient Surgeries	36.7	38.6	38.0	41.4	45.2
Births	17.0	15.3	20.9	18.6	19.7
Outpatient					
Emergency Outpatient Visits	487.3	453.8	599.8	597.8	540.8
Other Outpatient Visits	2,920.8	2,774.7	3,669.0	3,714.0	4,163.8
Total Outpatient Visits	3,408.2	3,228.5	4,268.8	4,311.9	4,704.6
Outpatient Surgeries	103.8	101.0	98.1	87.3	82.8
Expense per Capita (per person)	$4,309.1	$4,101.3	$3,810.8	$3,259.8	$3,277.6

States

TABLE 6

OHIO

U.S. Registered Community Hospitals
(Nonfederal, short-term general and other special hospitals)

Overview 2010–2014

	2014	2013	2012	2011	2010
Total Community Hospitals in Ohio...........	182	183	185	183	183
Bed Size Category					
6-24	7	4	6	2	3
25-49	45	48	47	47	44
50-99	25	29	29	33	33
100-199	45	44	44	40	41
200-299	28	26	25	27	28
300-399	10	8	12	12	12
400-499	9	11	9	9	9
500 + ...	13	13	13	13	13
Location					
Hospitals Urban..........................	125	128	130	128	128
Hospitals Rural	57	55	55	55	55
Control					
State and Local Government................	18	18	19	19	21
Not for Profit	136	138	140	138	138
Investor owned	28	27	26	26	24
Physician Models					
Independent Practice Association	21	18	13	15	15
Group Practice without Walls...............	18	18	6	6	7
Open Physician-Hospital Organization	42	46	44	50	52
Closed Physician-Hospital Organization	24	21	15	15	9
Management Service Organization	30	32	19	33	35
Integrated Salary Model....................	82	79	78	70	71
Equity Model	17	18	8	8	9
Foundation...............................	24	29	20	29	31
Insurance Products					
Health Maintenance Organization	28	24	24	33	36
Preferred Provider Organization..............	37	36	31	39	43
Indemnity Fee for Service	12	13	10	14	16
Managed Care Contracts					
Health Maintenance Organization	112	115	121	114	113
Preferred Provider Organization..............	112	118	117	119	120
Affiliations					
Hospitals in a System......................	125	123	122	118	114
Hospitals in a Network.....................	72	76	77	76	77
Hospitals in a Group Purchasing Organization..	124	128	136	135	133

States

TABLE 6

OHIO

U.S. Registered Community Hospitals
(Nonfederal, short-term general and other special hospitals)

Utilization, Personnel, Revenue and Expenses, Community Health Indicators 2010–2014

	2014	2013	2012	2011	2010
TOTAL FACILITY (Includes Hospital and Nursing Home Units)					
Utilization - Inpatient					
Beds	33,566	33,222	33,659	33,828	34,316
Admissions	1,433,894	1,455,817	1,501,183	1,504,603	1,516,501
Inpatient Days	7,168,533	7,126,702	7,367,870	7,434,042	7,598,267
Average Length of Stay	5	4.9	4.9	4.9	5
Inpatient Surgeries	370,741	372,371	383,187	393,731	405,507
Births	130,762	130,476	128,393	128,695	133,946
Utilization - Outpatient					
Emergency Outpatient Visits	6,616,818	6,484,063	6,578,749	6,506,331	6,383,429
Other Outpatient Visits	32,244,279	30,776,656	30,377,613	29,390,397	29,375,819
Total Outpatient Visits	38,861,097	37,260,719	36,956,362	35,896,728	35,759,248
Outpatient Surgeries	830,099	822,722	810,268	803,825	817,556
Personnel					
Full Time RNs	56,208	54,669	54,347	52,672	51,255
Full Time LPNs	2,586	2,789	2,960	3,790	3,309
Part Time RNs	25,888	25,029	25,890	26,034	25,325
Part Time LPNs	1,311	1,407	1,785	1,788	1,808
Total Full Time	206,879	206,245	205,576	203,689	198,795
Total Part Time	76,520	72,993	76,463	78,003	76,929
Revenue - Inpatient					
Gross Inpatient Revenue	$61,289,688,782	$58,384,380,015	$55,828,522,139	$51,716,805,929	$49,069,396,749
Revenue - Outpatient					
Gross Outpatient Revenue	$63,819,780,250	$58,206,812,939	$52,981,694,494	$47,899,777,396	$44,283,440,488
Revenue and Expenses - Totals					
(Includes Inpatient and Outpatient)					
Total Gross Revenue	$125,109,469,032	$116,591,192,954	$108,810,216,633	$99,616,583,325	$93,352,837,237
Deductions from Revenue	86,231,176,288	79,710,922,376	73,204,925,076	67,235,879,337	61,559,545,620
Net Patient Revenue	38,878,292,744	36,880,270,578	35,605,291,557	32,380,703,988	31,793,291,617
Other Operating Revenue	3,104,508,063	2,927,044,680	2,642,307,155	2,439,029,875	2,302,711,954
Other Nonoperating Revenue	680,756,807	1,250,816,674	770,720,233	66,768,231	824,057,575
Total Net Revenue	42,663,557,614	41,058,131,932	39,018,318,945	34,886,502,094	34,920,061,146
Total Expenses	38,332,807,975	37,050,070,738	35,772,141,755	32,605,625,518	32,374,139,783
HOSPITAL UNIT (Excludes Separate Nursing Home Units)					
Utilization - Inpatient					
Beds	32,896	32,570	32,901	32,734	33,157
Admissions	1,425,516	1,447,101	1,491,784	1,492,180	1,503,171
Inpatient Days	6,948,319	6,909,524	7,117,086	7,086,115	7,219,041
Average Length of Stay	4.9	4.8	4.8	4.7	4.8
Personnel					
Total Full Time	206,404	205,768	205,033	202,974	197,828
Total Part Time	76,205	72,650	76,040	77,530	76,311
Revenue and Expenses - Totals					
(Includes Inpatient and Outpatient)					
Total Net Revenue	$42,603,477,149	$40,990,936,895	$38,920,461,713	$34,777,592,693	$34,807,563,235
Total Expenses	38,277,821,356	36,986,993,669	35,672,905,913	32,496,965,573	32,265,651,508
COMMUNITY HEALTH INDICATORS PER 1000 POPULATION					
Total Population (in thousands)	11,594	11,571	11,544	11,545	11,532
Inpatient					
Beds	2.9	2.9	2.9	2.9	3.0
Admissions	123.7	125.8	130.0	130.3	131.5
Inpatient Days	618.3	615.9	638.2	643.9	658.9
Inpatient Surgeries	32.0	32.2	33.2	34.1	35.2
Births	11.3	11.3	11.1	11.1	11.6
Outpatient					
Emergency Outpatient Visits	570.7	560.4	569.9	563.6	553.5
Other Outpatient Visits	2,781.1	2,659.9	2,631.4	2,545.7	2,547.3
Total Outpatient Visits	3,351.8	3,220.2	3,201.3	3,109.3	3,100.8
Outpatient Surgeries	71.6	71.1	70.2	69.6	70.9
Expense per Capita (per person)	$3,306.2	$3,202.0	$3,098.7	$2,824.2	$2,807.3

TABLE 6

OKLAHOMA

U.S. Registered Community Hospitals
(Nonfederal, short-term general and other special hospitals)

Overview 2010–2014

	2014	2013	2012	2011	2010
Total Community Hospitals in Oklahoma......	114	116	117	115	113
Bed Size Category					
6-24	23	21	21	21	22
25-49	43	46	47	44	41
50-99	23	23	23	24	22
100-199	11	12	13	14	15
200-299	4	4	3	2	2
300-399	4	4	4	4	5
400-499	0	0	0	1	1
500 + ...	6	6	6	5	5
Location					
Hospitals Urban..........................	49	51	51	49	48
Hospitals Rural	65	65	66	66	65
Control					
State and Local Government................	38	38	40	41	44
Not for Profit	36	37	37	38	36
Investor owned	40	41	40	36	33
Physician Models					
Independent Practice Association	14	14	13	16	14
Group Practice without Walls...............	8	6	5	4	6
Open Physician-Hospital Organization	9	10	12	11	9
Closed Physician-Hospital Organization	5	3	3	1	0
Management Service Organization	9	9	9	7	7
Integrated Salary Model....................	54	52	52	49	34
Equity Model	0	1	1	1	0
Foundation...............................	1	1	2	1	0
Insurance Products					
Health Maintenance Organization	13	13	13	13	8
Preferred Provider Organization..............	12	14	12	16	10
Indemnity Fee for Service	6	5	5	8	4
Managed Care Contracts					
Health Maintenance Organization	55	53	52	48	38
Preferred Provider Organization..............	78	77	76	76	63
Affiliations					
Hospitals in a System.....................	63	63	65	60	53
Hospitals in a Network....................	40	39	33	30	22
Hospitals in a Group Purchasing Organization..	88	93	95	91	87

TABLE 6

OKLAHOMA

U.S. Registered Community Hospitals
(Nonfederal, short-term general and other special hospitals)

Utilization, Personnel, Revenue and Expenses, Community Health Indicators 2010–2014

	2014	2013	2012	2011	2010
TOTAL FACILITY (Includes Hospital and Nursing Home Units)					
Utilization - Inpatient					
Beds	11,240	11,365	11,349	11,303	11,170
Admissions	393,816	412,225	424,024	424,190	429,096
Inpatient Days	2,172,592	2,221,235	2,242,204	2,257,353	2,340,946
Average Length of Stay	5.5	5.4	5.3	5.3	5.5
Inpatient Surgeries	99,213	102,141	107,089	107,010	109,345
Births	51,509	52,910	50,107	46,583	48,569
Utilization - Outpatient					
Emergency Outpatient Visits	1,856,987	1,871,330	1,908,047	1,847,389	1,762,821
Other Outpatient Visits	4,508,176	4,741,807	4,866,096	4,175,877	3,895,891
Total Outpatient Visits	6,365,163	6,613,137	6,774,143	6,023,266	5,658,712
Outpatient Surgeries	225,422	221,650	223,225	211,753	206,440
Personnel					
Full Time RNs	12,937	13,018	12,313	11,500	11,105
Full Time LPNs	1,524	1,642	1,688	1,612	1,686
Part Time RNs	4,228	3,531	4,277	4,046	3,984
Part Time LPNs	357	383	495	464	567
Total Full Time	45,097	46,292	46,426	44,647	43,629
Total Part Time	12,602	11,446	13,623	13,085	13,056
Revenue - Inpatient					
Gross Inpatient Revenue	$15,334,379,316	$14,505,192,200	$14,248,526,243	$13,445,502,051	$12,758,064,725
Revenue - Outpatient					
Gross Outpatient Revenue	$14,429,955,582	$13,122,142,376	$11,878,040,440	$10,390,808,413	$9,221,121,763
Revenue and Expenses - Totals					
(Includes Inpatient and Outpatient)					
Total Gross Revenue	$29,764,334,898	$27,627,334,576	$26,126,566,683	$23,836,310,464	$21,979,186,488
Deductions from Revenue	21,514,817,782	19,789,608,584	18,251,141,886	16,779,981,602	15,258,319,649
Net Patient Revenue	8,249,517,116	7,837,725,992	7,875,424,797	7,056,328,862	6,720,866,839
Other Operating Revenue	322,344,777	288,772,295	264,973,762	269,741,536	235,730,490
Other Nonoperating Revenue	199,331,969	244,751,865	27,381,522	185,667,771	102,371,200
Total Net Revenue	8,771,193,862	8,371,250,152	8,167,780,081	7,511,738,169	7,058,968,529
Total Expenses	7,888,228,952	7,684,078,335	7,462,798,181	6,782,884,227	6,484,581,837
HOSPITAL UNIT (Excludes Separate Nursing Home Units)					
Utilization - Inpatient					
Beds	10,997	11,095	11,086	11,033	10,981
Admissions	393,467	411,403	422,856	423,362	427,982
Inpatient Days	2,100,133	2,143,080	2,164,883	2,183,306	2,280,666
Average Length of Stay	5.3	5.2	5.1	5.2	5.3
Personnel					
Total Full Time	44,868	46,006	46,159	44,486	43,532
Total Part Time	12,524	11,382	13,555	13,026	12,983
Revenue and Expenses - Totals					
(Includes Inpatient and Outpatient)					
Total Net Revenue	$8,760,512,983	$8,358,970,765	$8,133,239,746	$7,501,813,546	$7,049,646,928
Total Expenses	7,880,119,990	7,672,845,200	7,451,915,559	6,772,484,570	6,475,775,258
COMMUNITY HEALTH INDICATORS PER 1000 POPULATION					
Total Population (in thousands)	3,878	3,851	3,815	3,792	3,724
Inpatient					
Beds	2.9	3.0	3.0	3.0	3.0
Admissions	101.5	107.1	111.2	111.9	115.2
Inpatient Days	560.2	576.9	587.8	595.4	628.5
Inpatient Surgeries	25.6	26.5	28.1	28.2	29.4
Births	13.3	13.7	13.1	12.3	13.0
Outpatient					
Emergency Outpatient Visits	478.8	486.0	500.2	487.2	473.3
Other Outpatient Visits	1,162.5	1,231.5	1,275.6	1,101.4	1,046.0
Total Outpatient Visits	1,641.3	1,717.4	1,775.7	1,588.6	1,519.3
Outpatient Surgeries	58.1	57.6	58.5	55.8	55.4
Expense per Capita (per person)	$2,034.1	$1,995.6	$1,956.3	$1,789.0	$1,741.1

TABLE 6

OREGON

U.S. Registered Community Hospitals
(Nonfederal, short-term general and other special hospitals)

Overview 2010–2014

	2014	2013	2012	2011	2010
Total Community Hospitals in Oregon	59	59	58	59	58
Bed Size Category					
6-24	9	9	8	9	9
25-49	23	20	20	20	20
50-99	5	8	9	10	10
100-199	11	11	10	9	9
200-299	4	4	4	4	4
300-399	2	2	2	2	1
400-499	3	3	3	3	3
500 + ...	2	2	2	2	2
Location					
Hospitals Urban.	33	30	30	30	29
Hospitals Rural	26	29	28	29	29
Control					
State and Local Government.	12	12	11	12	12
Not for Profit	45	45	45	45	44
Investor owned	2	2	2	2	2
Physician Models					
Independent Practice Association	9	9	10	11	12
Group Practice without Walls.	6	7	8	9	9
Open Physician-Hospital Organization	2	2	5	6	6
Closed Physician-Hospital Organization	3	6	2	2	2
Management Service Organization	11	10	14	13	14
Integrated Salary Model	54	54	41	40	39
Equity Model	0	0	1	0	0
Foundation.	2	1	4	4	5
Insurance Products					
Health Maintenance Organization	18	19	14	16	15
Preferred Provider Organization.	20	19	10	17	19
Indemnity Fee for Service	5	5	0	3	3
Managed Care Contracts					
Health Maintenance Organization	40	39	38	35	34
Preferred Provider Organization.	55	52	49	52	51
Affiliations					
Hospitals in a System.	41	41	41	40	39
Hospitals in a Network	31	30	28	28	27
Hospitals in a Group Purchasing Organization. .	58	58	56	58	57

States

TABLE 6

OREGON

U.S. Registered Community Hospitals
(Nonfederal, short-term general and other special hospitals)

Utilization, Personnel, Revenue and Expenses, Community Health Indicators 2010–2014

	2014	2013	2012	2011	2010
TOTAL FACILITY (Includes Hospital and Nursing Home Units)					
Utilization - Inpatient					
Beds	6,740	6,778	6,706	6,805	6,420
Admissions	330,065	337,228	336,677	342,649	321,334
Inpatient Days	1,441,975	1,454,053	1,429,092	1,468,277	1,387,082
Average Length of Stay	4.4	4.3	4.2	4.3	4.3
Inpatient Surgeries	120,327	123,905	119,276	123,292	114,683
Births	42,741	42,393	43,472	43,262	41,914
Utilization - Outpatient					
Emergency Outpatient Visits	1,440,808	1,399,434	1,402,280	1,404,165	1,229,539
Other Outpatient Visits	9,364,637	8,986,321	8,402,499	7,969,367	7,982,714
Total Outpatient Visits	10,805,445	10,385,755	9,804,779	9,373,532	9,212,253
Outpatient Surgeries	190,460	192,524	203,622	211,379	205,542
Personnel					
Full Time RNs	11,213	10,997	10,528	10,359	9,293
Full Time LPNs	143	142	162	185	189
Part Time RNs	7,567	7,165	7,366	7,692	7,003
Part Time LPNs	81	88	113	154	131
Total Full Time	41,277	39,732	38,512	39,278	35,968
Total Part Time	19,498	18,834	19,732	20,655	18,954
Revenue - Inpatient					
Gross Inpatient Revenue	$10,984,589,849	$10,304,742,501	$9,763,893,851	$9,510,397,093	$8,342,718,826
Revenue - Outpatient					
Gross Outpatient Revenue	$10,661,166,352	$9,695,486,581	$9,057,121,305	$8,564,788,044	$7,669,159,468
Revenue and Expenses - Totals					
(Includes Inpatient and Outpatient)					
Total Gross Revenue	$21,645,756,201	$20,000,229,082	$18,821,015,156	$18,075,185,137	$16,011,878,294
Deductions from Revenue	11,907,313,288	10,889,922,069	9,946,369,291	9,586,390,414	8,389,072,711
Net Patient Revenue	9,738,442,913	9,110,307,013	8,874,645,865	8,488,794,723	7,622,805,583
Other Operating Revenue	551,197,366	486,233,283	431,506,659	357,481,939	356,073,198
Other Nonoperating Revenue	145,430,882	116,357,557	120,073,921	115,998,119	164,944,836
Total Net Revenue	10,435,071,161	9,712,897,853	9,426,226,445	8,962,274,781	8,143,823,617
Total Expenses	9,956,534,588	9,358,601,796	9,102,609,637	8,726,772,182	7,875,937,042
HOSPITAL UNIT (Excludes Separate Nursing Home Units)					
Utilization - Inpatient					
Beds	6,659	6,610	6,538	6,618	6,233
Admissions	329,951	337,095	336,526	342,499	321,153
Inpatient Days	1,418,598	1,412,321	1,387,370	1,426,510	1,338,597
Average Length of Stay	4.3	4.2	4.1	4.2	4.2
Personnel					
Total Full Time	41,232	39,667	38,416	39,186	35,872
Total Part Time	19,458	18,780	19,687	20,579	18,863
Revenue and Expenses - Totals					
(Includes Inpatient and Outpatient)					
Total Net Revenue	$10,429,237,256	$9,702,942,089	$9,416,990,860	$8,952,622,279	$8,133,821,379
Total Expenses	9,951,469,324	9,350,034,260	9,094,089,019	8,718,381,099	7,866,577,239
COMMUNITY HEALTH INDICATORS PER 1000 POPULATION					
Total Population (in thousands)	3,970	3,930	3,899	3,872	3,856
Inpatient					
Beds	1.7	1.7	1.7	1.8	1.7
Admissions	83.1	85.8	86.3	88.5	83.3
Inpatient Days	363.2	370.0	366.5	379.2	359.8
Inpatient Surgeries	30.3	31.5	30.6	31.8	29.7
Births	10.8	10.8	11.1	11.2	10.9
Outpatient					
Emergency Outpatient Visits	362.9	356.1	359.6	362.7	318.9
Other Outpatient Visits	2,358.7	2,286.6	2,154.8	2,058.3	2,070.5
Total Outpatient Visits	2,721.6	2,642.6	2,514.5	2,420.9	2,389.4
Outpatient Surgeries	48.0	49.0	52.2	54.6	53.3
Expense per Capita (per person)	$2,507.8	$2,381.3	$2,334.4	$2,253.9	$2,042.8

States

TABLE 6

PENNSYLVANIA

U.S. Registered Community Hospitals
(Nonfederal, short-term general and other special hospitals)

Overview 2010–2014

	2014	2013	2012	2011	2010
Total Community Hospitals in Pennsylvania ...	185	190	192	194	196
Bed Size Category					
6-24	4	3	4	3	3
25-49	25	28	27	28	29
50-99	36	37	38	40	42
100-199	46	47	47	47	46
200-299	33	34	35	34	34
300-399	18	18	18	18	17
400-499	9	8	9	10	11
500 + ...	14	15	14	14	14
Location					
Hospitals Urban..........................	147	143	145	146	147
Hospitals Rural	38	47	47	48	49
Control					
State and Local Government	1	2	2	2	2
Not for Profit	139	141	142	145	151
Investor owned	45	47	48	47	43
Physician Models					
Independent Practice Association	10	11	12	8	7
Group Practice without Walls...............	5	6	5	6	8
Open Physician-Hospital Organization	21	23	22	22	24
Closed Physician-Hospital Organization	5	3	3	3	3
Management Service Organization	16	21	23	19	21
Integrated Salary Model....................	71	74	78	73	75
Equity Model	4	4	3	1	2
Foundation................................	3	4	4	8	8
Insurance Products					
Health Maintenance Organization	30	32	37	35	29
Preferred Provider Organization..............	29	30	38	41	42
Indemnity Fee for Service	18	19	23	19	17
Managed Care Contracts					
Health Maintenance Organization	116	125	132	120	117
Preferred Provider Organization..............	114	124	128	116	115
Affiliations					
Hospitals in a System.....................	128	129	127	128	118
Hospitals in a Network	59	56	52	51	49
Hospitals in a Group Purchasing Organization..	117	147	141	134	139

TABLE 6

PENNSYLVANIA

U.S. Registered Community Hospitals
(Nonfederal, short-term general and other special hospitals)

Utilization, Personnel, Revenue and Expenses, Community Health Indicators 2010–2014

	2014	2013	2012	2011	2010
TOTAL FACILITY (Includes Hospital and Nursing Home Units)					
Utilization - Inpatient					
Beds	38,124	38,970	39,314	39,676	39,889
Admissions	1,584,798	1,637,872	1,692,087	1,766,191	1,809,935
Inpatient Days	8,723,610	9,147,196	9,287,033	9,659,186	9,769,701
Average Length of Stay	5.5	5.6	5.5	5.5	5.4
Inpatient Surgeries	469,110	489,930	545,302	526,338	534,919
Births	129,936	128,950	134,221	132,967	134,404
Utilization - Outpatient					
Emergency Outpatient Visits	6,245,628	6,263,103	6,239,042	6,221,333	6,120,131
Other Outpatient Visits	31,928,667	31,769,030	32,791,595	31,681,366	32,432,398
Total Outpatient Visits	38,174,295	38,032,133	39,030,637	37,902,699	38,552,529
Outpatient Surgeries	883,007	908,695	913,296	895,861	914,558
Personnel					
Full Time RNs	56,208	55,770	55,710	54,899	53,217
Full Time LPNs	2,264	2,617	3,035	3,115	3,406
Part Time RNs	24,947	25,112	25,187	25,473	24,947
Part Time LPNs	935	1,078	1,227	1,311	1,558
Total Full Time	207,519	207,082	212,082	211,563	207,153
Total Part Time	71,384	72,723	73,405	73,672	72,508
Revenue - Inpatient					
Gross Inpatient Revenue	$83,909,351,569	$84,087,084,762	$83,077,919,932	$81,435,847,151	$77,752,923,156
Revenue - Outpatient					
Gross Outpatient Revenue	$70,851,865,407	$66,840,763,963	$65,297,151,073	$58,909,827,289	$52,558,766,166
Revenue and Expenses - Totals					
(Includes Inpatient and Outpatient)					
Total Gross Revenue	$154,761,216,976	$150,927,848,725	$148,375,071,005	$140,345,674,440	$130,311,689,322
Deductions from Revenue	115,737,513,972	112,764,688,900	110,484,264,654	104,430,760,108	96,372,359,561
Net Patient Revenue	39,023,703,004	38,163,159,825	37,890,806,351	35,914,914,332	33,939,329,761
Other Operating Revenue	2,055,029,824	2,008,282,382	1,891,935,772	1,762,852,582	1,560,413,652
Other Nonoperating Revenue	876,327,635	595,823,340	244,155,533	671,813,569	355,838,893
Total Net Revenue	41,955,060,463	40,767,265,547	40,026,897,656	38,349,580,483	35,855,582,306
Total Expenses	38,945,696,363	38,184,179,753	37,279,476,131	35,246,467,258	33,929,583,373
HOSPITAL UNIT (Excludes Separate Nursing Home Units)					
Utilization - Inpatient					
Beds	36,891	37,025	37,482	37,995	38,271
Admissions	1,571,539	1,620,279	1,674,103	1,748,683	1,793,060
Inpatient Days	8,341,033	8,550,303	8,740,926	9,116,795	9,324,956
Average Length of Stay	5.3	5.3	5.2	5.2	5.2
Personnel					
Total Full Time	206,612	206,017	211,038	210,543	205,956
Total Part Time	70,872	72,063	72,757	73,114	71,746
Revenue and Expenses - Totals					
(Includes Inpatient and Outpatient)					
Total Net Revenue	$41,820,451,752	$40,549,341,944	$39,806,434,073	$38,167,896,294	$35,657,261,435
Total Expenses	38,833,596,958	38,000,068,482	37,097,937,820	35,082,553,586	33,767,820,668
COMMUNITY HEALTH INDICATORS PER 1000 POPULATION					
Total Population (in thousands)	12,787	12,774	12,764	12,743	12,633
Inpatient					
Beds	3.0	3.1	3.1	3.1	3.2
Admissions	123.9	128.2	132.6	138.6	143.3
Inpatient Days	682.2	716.1	727.6	758.0	773.4
Inpatient Surgeries	36.7	38.4	42.7	41.3	42.3
Births	10.2	10.1	10.5	10.4	10.6
Outpatient					
Emergency Outpatient Visits	488.4	490.3	488.8	488.2	484.5
Other Outpatient Visits	2,496.9	2,487.0	2,569.2	2,486.2	2,567.3
Total Outpatient Visits	2,985.4	2,977.4	3,058.0	2,974.4	3,051.8
Outpatient Surgeries	69.1	71.1	71.6	70.3	72.4
Expense per Capita (per person)	$3,045.7	$2,989.3	$2,920.8	$2,766.0	$2,685.8

TABLE 6

RHODE ISLAND

U.S. Registered Community Hospitals
(Nonfederal, short-term general and other special hospitals)

Overview 2010–2014

	2014	2013	2012	2011	2010
Total Community Hospitals in Rhode Island ...	11	11	11	11	11
Bed Size Category					
6-24	0	0	0	0	0
25-49	0	0	0	0	0
50-99	2	2	1	1	1
100-199	5	5	5	5	5
200-299	2	2	3	3	3
300-399	1	1	1	1	1
400-499	0	0	0	0	0
500 + ...	1	1	1	1	1
Location					
Hospitals Urban..........................	11	11	11	11	11
Hospitals Rural	0	0	0	0	0
Control					
State and Local Government................	0	0	0	0	0
Not for Profit	10	10	11	11	11
Investor owned	1	1	0	0	0
Physician Models					
Independent Practice Association	5	5	4	5	5
Group Practice without Walls...............	1	1	1	1	0
Open Physician-Hospital Organization	5	5	4	5	6
Closed Physician-Hospital Organization	0	0	0	0	0
Management Service Organization	2	3	2	2	2
Integrated Salary Model	6	6	6	5	6
Equity Model	0	0	0	0	0
Foundation...............................	2	2	2	2	2
Insurance Products					
Health Maintenance Organization	1	1	1	1	1
Preferred Provider Organization..............	0	0	0	1	0
Indemnity Fee for Service	0	0	0	0	0
Managed Care Contracts					
Health Maintenance Organization	6	7	6	6	7
Preferred Provider Organization..............	8	7	6	7	7
Affiliations					
Hospitals in a System.....................	10	10	6	5	5
Hospitals in a Network....................	4	5	4	6	6
Hospitals in a Group Purchasing Organization..	7	8	6	7	7

TABLE 6

RHODE ISLAND

U.S. Registered Community Hospitals
(Nonfederal, short-term general and other special hospitals)

Utilization, Personnel, Revenue and Expenses, Community Health Indicators 2010–2014

	2014	2013	2012	2011	2010
TOTAL FACILITY (Includes Hospital and Nursing Home Units)					
Utilization - Inpatient					
Beds	2,247	2,250	2,461	2,468	2,479
Admissions	110,848	111,406	117,051	120,407	123,188
Inpatient Days	549,575	571,352	580,207	611,837	621,614
Average Length of Stay	5	5.1	5	5.1	5
Inpatient Surgeries	27,265	29,139	32,119	32,737	32,612
Births	11,363	11,352	11,045	11,249	11,492
Utilization - Outpatient					
Emergency Outpatient Visits	510,907	522,861	578,431	542,625	495,149
Other Outpatient Visits	1,509,583	1,518,166	1,605,322	1,699,025	2,127,266
Total Outpatient Visits	2,020,490	2,041,027	2,183,753	2,241,650	2,622,415
Outpatient Surgeries	66,310	66,445	67,537	67,432	66,930
Personnel					
Full Time RNs	2,724	2,322	2,656	2,426	2,251
Full Time LPNs	54	50	71	70	58
Part Time RNs	2,935	2,876	2,780	2,737	2,771
Part Time LPNs	45	52	60	60	54
Total Full Time	12,271	12,542	12,871	12,810	12,686
Total Part Time	8,356	8,313	7,847	7,800	8,001
Revenue - Inpatient					
Gross Inpatient Revenue	$4,054,821,275	$3,987,915,217	$3,911,358,415	$3,763,721,393	$3,623,363,473
Revenue - Outpatient					
Gross Outpatient Revenue	$4,583,059,093	$4,343,532,799	$4,210,401,437	$3,841,600,497	$3,560,931,543
Revenue and Expenses - Totals					
(Includes Inpatient and Outpatient)					
Total Gross Revenue	$8,637,880,368	$8,331,448,016	$8,121,759,852	$7,605,321,890	$7,184,295,016
Deductions from Revenue	5,682,487,354	5,499,978,376	5,309,722,108	4,867,608,639	4,555,181,118
Net Patient Revenue	2,955,393,014	2,831,469,640	2,812,037,744	2,737,713,251	2,629,113,898
Other Operating Revenue	250,712,004	255,547,838	259,567,063	257,774,487	265,788,290
Other Nonoperating Revenue	10,550,939	18,026,453	26,181,940	10,927,762	6,408,073
Total Net Revenue	3,216,655,957	3,105,043,931	3,097,786,747	3,006,415,500	2,901,310,261
Total Expenses	3,167,662,418	3,151,478,325	3,067,815,218	3,021,867,827	2,883,693,916
HOSPITAL UNIT (Excludes Separate Nursing Home Units)					
Utilization - Inpatient					
Beds	2,247	2,250	2,461	2,468	2,479
Admissions	110,848	111,406	117,051	120,407	123,188
Inpatient Days	549,575	571,352	580,207	611,837	621,614
Average Length of Stay	5	5.1	5	5.1	5
Personnel					
Total Full Time	12,271	12,542	12,871	12,810	12,686
Total Part Time	8,356	8,313	7,847	7,800	8,001
Revenue and Expenses - Totals					
(Includes Inpatient and Outpatient)					
Total Net Revenue	$3,216,655,957	$3,105,043,931	$3,097,786,747	$3,006,415,500	$2,901,310,261
Total Expenses	3,167,662,418	3,151,478,325	3,067,815,218	3,021,867,827	2,883,693,916
COMMUNITY HEALTH INDICATORS PER 1000 POPULATION					
Total Population (in thousands)	1,055	1,052	1,050	1,051	1,057
Inpatient					
Beds	2.1	2.1	2.3	2.3	2.3
Admissions	105.1	105.9	111.4	114.5	116.6
Inpatient Days	520.8	543.4	552.4	582.0	588.2
Inpatient Surgeries	25.8	27.7	30.6	31.1	30.9
Births	10.8	10.8	10.5	10.7	10.9
Outpatient					
Emergency Outpatient Visits	484.2	497.2	550.7	516.1	468.5
Other Outpatient Visits	1,430.6	1,443.8	1,528.5	1,616.1	2,012.8
Total Outpatient Visits	1,914.8	1,941.0	2,079.2	2,132.3	2,481.3
Outpatient Surgeries	62.8	63.2	64.3	64.1	63.3
Expense per Capita (per person)	$3,002.0	$2,997.1	$2,920.9	$2,874.4	$2,728.5

States

TABLE 6

SOUTH CAROLINA

U.S. Registered Community Hospitals
(Nonfederal, short-term general and other special hospitals)

Overview 2010–2014

	2014	2013	2012	2011	2010
Total Community Hospitals in South Carolina..	70	69	67	66	67
Bed Size Category					
6-24	5	2	1	2	1
25-49	15	16	16	17	19
50-99	15	13	13	11	10
100-199	13	14	14	14	13
200-299	8	9	9	8	9
300-399	4	5	6	6	7
400-499	6	5	4	3	3
500 + ...	4	5	4	5	5
Location					
Hospitals Urban..........................	54	45	43	41	42
Hospitals Rural	16	24	24	25	25
Control					
State and Local Government...............	19	18	18	19	17
Not for Profit	27	28	26	23	24
Investor owned	24	23	23	24	26
Physician Models					
Independent Practice Association	6	6	6	6	5
Group Practice without Walls...............	0	1	1	1	1
Open Physician-Hospital Organization	3	3	5	4	4
Closed Physician-Hospital Organization	3	3	2	2	1
Management Service Organization	0	1	1	0	2
Integrated Salary Model	19	19	20	20	19
Equity Model	2	2	2	1	0
Foundation..............................	1	0	0	0	0
Insurance Products					
Health Maintenance Organization	12	4	1	6	7
Preferred Provider Organization.............	11	3	6	9	10
Indemnity Fee for Service	6	0	0	1	6
Managed Care Contracts					
Health Maintenance Organization	42	42	40	43	39
Preferred Provider Organization.............	44	43	40	43	38
Affiliations					
Hospitals in a System.....................	54	51	50	44	44
Hospitals in a Network....................	20	13	12	12	12
Hospitals in a Group Purchasing Organization..	61	61	55	60	59

TABLE 6

SOUTH CAROLINA

U.S. Registered Community Hospitals
(Nonfederal, short-term general and other special hospitals)

Utilization, Personnel, Revenue and Expenses, Community Health Indicators 2010–2014

	2014	2013	2012	2011	2010
TOTAL FACILITY (Includes Hospital and Nursing Home Units)					
Utilization - Inpatient					
Beds	12,228	12,758	12,539	12,253	12,495
Admissions	498,690	498,344	506,072	508,652	522,793
Inpatient Days	2,784,918	2,864,513	2,861,439	2,878,860	3,002,541
Average Length of Stay	5.6	5.7	5.7	5.7	5.7
Inpatient Surgeries	177,731	194,834	197,921	194,171	194,895
Births	53,437	52,388	53,353	53,530	54,894
Utilization - Outpatient					
Emergency Outpatient Visits	2,217,906	1,575,728	1,435,010	1,687,578	1,453,696
Other Outpatient Visits	5,317,945	5,134,748	5,114,768	4,732,533	4,922,633
Total Outpatient Visits	7,535,851	6,710,476	6,549,778	6,420,111	6,376,329
Outpatient Surgeries	308,003	317,318	309,250	298,549	289,794
Personnel					
Full Time RNs	19,603	18,693	17,934	17,357	17,476
Full Time LPNs	650	722	775	947	1,062
Part Time RNs	4,900	4,641	4,652	4,897	5,184
Part Time LPNs	162	174	227	280	347
Total Full Time	61,512	60,317	60,411	58,183	58,567
Total Part Time	13,638	13,327	13,579	13,721	14,343
Revenue - Inpatient					
Gross Inpatient Revenue	$21,965,206,597	$21,575,477,093	$20,007,919,363	$19,216,509,155	$18,371,422,174
Revenue - Outpatient					
Gross Outpatient Revenue	$18,535,025,990	$17,600,043,070	$15,551,458,526	$14,306,685,453	$12,660,946,189
Revenue and Expenses - Totals					
(Includes Inpatient and Outpatient)					
Total Gross Revenue	$40,500,232,587	$39,175,520,163	$35,559,377,889	$33,523,194,608	$31,032,368,363
Deductions from Revenue	29,269,848,157	28,456,657,258	25,246,098,981	23,252,635,242	21,049,743,519
Net Patient Revenue	11,230,384,430	10,718,862,905	10,313,278,908	10,270,559,366	9,982,624,844
Other Operating Revenue	379,328,304	321,252,507	308,030,013	243,603,622	249,339,525
Other Nonoperating Revenue	249,266,110	293,338,530	277,725,354	141,294,623	210,607,769
Total Net Revenue	11,858,978,844	11,333,453,942	10,899,034,275	10,655,457,611	10,442,572,138
Total Expenses	10,299,166,490	10,033,330,821	9,729,644,756	9,707,103,556	9,349,824,264
HOSPITAL UNIT (Excludes Separate Nursing Home Units)					
Utilization - Inpatient					
Beds	11,696	12,027	11,656	11,479	11,611
Admissions	495,088	495,189	502,923	504,604	518,130
Inpatient Days	2,628,598	2,653,359	2,585,730	2,632,449	2,729,473
Average Length of Stay	5.3	5.4	5.1	5.2	5.3
Personnel					
Total Full Time	61,091	59,621	59,664	57,533	57,811
Total Part Time	13,495	13,133	13,328	13,382	14,118
Revenue and Expenses - Totals					
(Includes Inpatient and Outpatient)					
Total Net Revenue	$11,759,944,896	$11,269,144,355	$10,842,235,748	$10,577,543,806	$10,354,825,713
Total Expenses	10,216,436,727	9,974,428,391	9,666,217,448	9,635,628,294	9,272,925,368
COMMUNITY HEALTH INDICATORS PER 1000 POPULATION					
Total Population (in thousands)	4,832	4,775	4,724	4,679	4,597
Inpatient					
Beds	2.5	2.7	2.7	2.6	2.7
Admissions	103.2	104.4	107.1	108.7	113.7
Inpatient Days	576.3	599.9	605.8	615.2	653.2
Inpatient Surgeries	36.8	40.8	41.9	41.5	42.4
Births	11.1	11.0	11.3	11.4	11.9
Outpatient					
Emergency Outpatient Visits	459.0	330.0	303.8	360.7	316.2
Other Outpatient Visits	1,100.5	1,075.4	1,082.8	1,011.4	1,070.8
Total Outpatient Visits	1,559.4	1,405.4	1,386.6	1,372.0	1,387.1
Outpatient Surgeries	63.7	66.5	65.5	63.8	63.0
Expense per Capita (per person)	$2,131.2	$2,101.3	$2,059.7	$2,074.5	$2,033.9

TABLE 6

SOUTH DAKOTA

U.S. Registered Community Hospitals
(Nonfederal, short-term general and other special hospitals)

Overview 2010–2014

	2014	2013	2012	2011	2010
Total Community Hospitals in South Dakota...	53	54	54	53	53
Bed Size Category					
6-24	19	20	19	19	17
25-49	10	11	13	12	14
50-99	13	11	10	10	10
100-199	6	7	7	7	7
200-299	2	2	2	2	2
300-399	1	0	1	1	1
400-499	1	2	1	2	2
500 +	1	1	1	0	0
Location					
Hospitals Urban	12	11	11	11	11
Hospitals Rural	41	43	43	42	42
Control					
State and Local Government	4	4	4	4	4
Not for Profit	45	46	46	45	45
Investor owned	4	4	4	4	4
Physician Models					
Independent Practice Association	6	7	9	10	8
Group Practice without Walls	2	1	2	2	1
Open Physician-Hospital Organization	2	1	3	4	3
Closed Physician-Hospital Organization	2	1	3	3	2
Management Service Organization	1	0	2	3	1
Integrated Salary Model	27	24	25	27	23
Equity Model	2	2	3	2	1
Foundation	2	2	3	3	2
Insurance Products					
Health Maintenance Organization	13	14	13	13	16
Preferred Provider Organization	11	10	12	13	11
Indemnity Fee for Service	6	6	5	8	6
Managed Care Contracts					
Health Maintenance Organization	25	22	27	25	23
Preferred Provider Organization	27	25	31	30	27
Affiliations					
Hospitals in a System	39	39	39	37	37
Hospitals in a Network	22	23	23	24	21
Hospitals in a Group Purchasing Organization	35	36	43	46	39

States

TABLE 6

SOUTH DAKOTA

U.S. Registered Community Hospitals
(Nonfederal, short-term general and other special hospitals)

Utilization, Personnel, Revenue and Expenses, Community Health Indicators 2010–2014

	2014	2013	2012	2011	2010
TOTAL FACILITY (Includes Hospital and Nursing Home Units)					
Utilization - Inpatient					
Beds	4,086	4,161	4,188	4,084	4,108
Admissions	99,928	101,878	108,263	101,867	101,128
Inpatient Days	919,091	934,748	960,652	956,044	935,410
Average Length of Stay	9.2	9.2	8.9	9.4	9.2
Inpatient Surgeries	24,438	27,820	29,636	31,220	30,363
Births	12,880	12,782	12,242	11,976	11,437
Utilization - Outpatient					
Emergency Outpatient Visits	296,024	291,177	282,899	251,769	259,364
Other Outpatient Visits	3,020,822	1,972,035	1,979,362	1,862,618	1,782,993
Total Outpatient Visits	3,316,846	2,263,212	2,262,261	2,114,387	2,042,357
Outpatient Surgeries	52,305	51,305	76,606	69,535	67,743
Personnel					
Full Time RNs	4,555	4,796	4,457	4,068	3,633
Full Time LPNs	313	340	267	270	216
Part Time RNs	2,064	1,889	1,948	1,951	1,736
Part Time LPNs	140	128	124	144	129
Total Full Time	15,958	16,960	16,543	15,443	14,483
Total Part Time	6,757	7,099	6,807	6,954	6,316
Revenue - Inpatient					
Gross Inpatient Revenue	$3,615,729,346	$3,410,939,910	$3,259,110,943	$2,969,819,139	$2,779,376,912
Revenue - Outpatient					
Gross Outpatient Revenue	$4,182,407,019	$3,299,557,436	$3,103,567,011	$2,643,342,592	$2,405,199,211
Revenue and Expenses - Totals					
(Includes Inpatient and Outpatient)					
Total Gross Revenue	$7,798,136,365	$6,710,497,346	$6,362,677,954	$5,613,161,731	$5,184,576,123
Deductions from Revenue	4,809,565,680	4,030,372,232	3,649,680,422	3,130,649,704	2,884,612,400
Net Patient Revenue	2,988,570,685	2,680,125,114	2,712,997,532	2,482,512,027	2,299,963,723
Other Operating Revenue	188,687,454	176,424,473	146,318,931	129,361,349	122,786,678
Other Nonoperating Revenue	95,967,403	73,485,535	34,097,686	101,197,230	34,907,740
Total Net Revenue	3,273,225,542	2,930,035,122	2,893,414,149	2,713,070,606	2,457,658,141
Total Expenses	2,966,917,907	2,672,087,974	2,494,970,877	2,353,418,704	2,194,315,958
HOSPITAL UNIT (Excludes Separate Nursing Home Units)					
Utilization - Inpatient					
Beds	2,858	2,811	2,847	2,602	2,869
Admissions	98,889	100,616	106,941	100,451	99,824
Inpatient Days	522,972	488,235	503,324	443,426	505,190
Average Length of Stay	5.3	4.9	4.7	4.4	5.1
Personnel					
Total Full Time	15,217	16,072	15,690	14,561	13,753
Total Part Time	6,219	6,571	6,221	6,292	5,684
Revenue and Expenses - Totals					
(Includes Inpatient and Outpatient)					
Total Net Revenue	$3,190,020,801	$2,846,625,100	$2,806,088,891	$2,626,079,779	$2,382,414,150
Total Expenses	2,893,652,486	2,602,036,829	2,410,336,333	2,278,140,332	2,128,257,681
COMMUNITY HEALTH INDICATORS PER 1000 POPULATION					
Total Population (in thousands)	853	845	833	824	820
Inpatient					
Beds	4.8	4.9	5.0	5.0	5.0
Admissions	117.1	120.6	129.9	123.6	123.3
Inpatient Days	1,077.3	1,106.4	1,152.8	1,160.1	1,140.6
Inpatient Surgeries	28.6	32.9	35.6	37.9	37.0
Births	15.1	15.1	14.7	14.5	13.9
Outpatient					
Emergency Outpatient Visits	347.0	344.6	339.5	305.5	316.3
Other Outpatient Visits	3,540.7	2,334.1	2,375.2	2,260.2	2,174.2
Total Outpatient Visits	3,887.7	2,678.7	2,714.6	2,565.7	2,490.4
Outpatient Surgeries	61.3	60.7	91.9	84.4	82.6
Expense per Capita (per person)	$3,477.5	$3,162.7	$2,993.9	$2,855.8	$2,675.7

States

TABLE **6**

TENNESSEE

U.S. Registered Community Hospitals
(Nonfederal, short-term general and other special hospitals)

Overview 2010–2014

	2014	2013	2012	2011	2010
Total Community Hospitals in Tennessee	125	130	132	133	134
Bed Size Category					
6-24	8	9	9	7	6
25-49	30	32	34	36	35
50-99	31	33	31	32	32
100-199	25	24	26	26	29
200-299	12	13	13	13	12
300-399	8	8	7	7	6
400-499	1	2	3	3	5
500 + ...	10	9	9	9	9
Location					
Hospitals Urban	78	76	77	78	78
Hospitals Rural	47	54	55	55	56
Control					
State and Local Government	19	22	21	21	20
Not for Profit	50	49	49	50	56
Investor owned	56	59	62	62	58
Physician Models					
Independent Practice Association	14	14	16	17	19
Group Practice without Walls	5	4	4	5	4
Open Physician-Hospital Organization	16	17	17	11	11
Closed Physician-Hospital Organization	5	3	4	3	3
Management Service Organization	15	12	14	17	16
Integrated Salary Model	36	34	30	29	31
Equity Model	2	3	0	0	0
Foundation	4	6	2	3	4
Insurance Products					
Health Maintenance Organization	14	12	9	8	8
Preferred Provider Organization	23	24	13	17	17
Indemnity Fee for Service	10	10	7	3	3
Managed Care Contracts					
Health Maintenance Organization	51	56	56	68	66
Preferred Provider Organization	57	63	62	69	72
Affiliations					
Hospitals in a System	102	107	107	105	101
Hospitals in a Network	34	37	31	38	41
Hospitals in a Group Purchasing Organization . .	59	66	68	70	69

TABLE 6

TENNESSEE

U.S. Registered Community Hospitals
(Nonfederal, short-term general and other special hospitals)

Utilization, Personnel, Revenue and Expenses, Community Health Indicators 2010–2014

	2014	2013	2012	2011	2010
TOTAL FACILITY (Includes Hospital and Nursing Home Units)					
Utilization - Inpatient					
Beds..........................	20,031	20,259	20,154	20,042	20,830
Admissions......................	818,379	819,116	823,781	805,805	832,554
Inpatient Days	4,428,761	4,525,456	4,500,597	4,465,285	4,579,402
Average Length of Stay............	5.4	5.5	5.5	5.5	5.5
Inpatient Surgeries...............	231,629	227,285	241,056	234,368	249,367
Births..........................	67,013	66,249	64,660	64,202	70,685
Utilization - Outpatient					
Emergency Outpatient Visits........	3,405,321	3,378,159	3,260,802	3,113,164	3,130,660
Other Outpatient Visits............	8,508,182	8,534,100	8,519,980	7,799,873	8,299,669
Total Outpatient Visits	11,913,503	11,912,259	11,780,782	10,913,037	11,430,329
Outpatient Surgeries	433,180	430,284	448,279	405,105	411,688
Personnel					
Full Time RNs	27,092	26,540	26,169	25,298	24,475
Full Time LPNs	1,973	2,139	2,252	2,503	2,706
Part Time RNs..................	6,760	7,626	9,110	9,124	9,222
Part Time LPNs	451	518	610	652	767
Total Full Time.................	93,018	90,588	91,851	89,424	88,145
Total Part Time	18,639	20,281	25,175	23,382	25,539
Revenue - Inpatient					
Gross Inpatient Revenue..........	$33,092,986,985	$31,762,517,052	$28,979,229,922	$27,704,113,354	$26,846,357,974
Revenue - Outpatient					
Gross Outpatient Revenue	$29,355,048,396	$26,898,593,106	$24,221,902,571	$20,574,396,531	$19,276,589,146
Revenue and Expenses - Totals					
(Includes Inpatient and Outpatient)					
Total Gross Revenue..............	$62,448,035,381	$58,661,110,158	$53,201,132,493	$48,278,509,885	$46,122,947,120
Deductions from Revenue..........	46,399,193,325	43,023,032,783	37,978,697,915	34,865,417,816	32,931,211,533
Net Patient Revenue	16,048,842,056	15,638,077,375	15,222,434,578	13,413,092,069	13,191,735,587
Other Operating Revenue	573,071,357	631,573,575	546,985,739	445,637,920	409,743,303
Other Nonoperating Revenue	216,619,646	159,509,587	108,447,768	158,051,242	268,674,837
Total Net Revenue...............	16,838,533,059	16,429,160,537	15,877,868,085	14,016,781,231	13,870,153,727
Total Expenses..................	15,522,404,054	15,002,528,839	14,708,134,735	12,769,264,645	12,699,265,618
HOSPITAL UNIT (Excludes Separate Nursing Home Units)					
Utilization - Inpatient					
Beds..........................	19,055	19,058	19,052	19,080	19,750
Admissions......................	813,533	811,908	816,107	797,947	825,283
Inpatient Days	4,141,898	4,171,201	4,178,131	4,182,726	4,244,905
Average Length of Stay............	5.1	5.1	5.1	5.2	5.1
Personnel					
Total Full Time.................	92,199	89,727	90,895	88,534	87,258
Total Part Time	18,493	20,073	24,986	23,260	25,367
Revenue and Expenses - Totals					
(Includes Inpatient and Outpatient)					
Total Net Revenue................	$16,774,136,543	$16,338,297,498	$15,793,027,961	$13,930,291,003	$13,791,578,759
Total Expenses..................	15,463,231,902	14,923,551,273	14,632,776,271	12,708,497,514	12,630,190,370
COMMUNITY HEALTH INDICATORS PER 1000 POPULATION					
Total Population (in thousands)	6,549	6,496	6,456	6,403	6,338
Inpatient					
Beds..........................	3.1	3.1	3.1	3.1	3.3
Admissions......................	125.0	126.1	127.6	125.8	131.4
Inpatient Days	676.2	696.7	697.1	697.3	722.5
Inpatient Surgeries...............	35.4	35.0	37.3	36.6	39.3
Births..........................	10.2	10.2	10.0	10.0	11.2
Outpatient					
Emergency Outpatient Visits........	519.9	520.0	505.1	486.2	493.9
Other Outpatient Visits............	1,299.1	1,313.8	1,319.6	1,218.1	1,309.5
Total Outpatient Visits	1,819.0	1,833.8	1,824.7	1,704.3	1,803.4
Outpatient Surgeries	66.1	66.2	69.4	63.3	65.0
Expense per Capita (per person).....	$2,370.1	$2,309.5	$2,278.1	$1,994.2	$2,003.6

TABLE 6

TEXAS

U.S. Registered Community Hospitals
(Nonfederal, short-term general and other special hospitals)

Overview 2010–2014

	2014	2013	2012	2011	2010
Total Community Hospitals in Texas..........	**417**	**424**	**425**	**420**	**426**
Bed Size Category					
6-24	73	74	74	70	73
25-49	108	108	107	109	107
50-99	79	86	87	82	86
100-199	60	55	55	58	61
200-299	35	41	42	43	41
300-399	22	22	23	19	20
400-499	15	13	13	15	14
500 + ...	25	25	24	24	24
Location					
Hospitals Urban..........................	277	277	276	269	275
Hospitals Rural	140	147	149	151	151
Control					
State and Local Government................	102	103	106	110	113
Not for Profit	152	154	151	149	148
Investor owned	163	167	168	161	165
Physician Models					
Independent Practice Association	55	54	58	62	72
Group Practice without Walls................	34	19	15	15	15
Open Physician-Hospital Organization	69	75	83	79	82
Closed Physician-Hospital Organization	25	26	26	20	19
Management Service Organization	53	55	62	71	73
Integrated Salary Model	112	122	115	114	97
Equity Model	5	7	8	9	13
Foundation...............................	35	40	37	37	35
Insurance Products					
Health Maintenance Organization	78	68	60	65	66
Preferred Provider Organization..............	72	61	50	79	84
Indemnity Fee for Service	32	18	13	22	26
Managed Care Contracts					
Health Maintenance Organization	336	337	331	318	318
Preferred Provider Organization..............	363	370	362	357	358
Affiliations					
Hospitals in a System.....................	278	283	283	272	278
Hospitals in a Network....................	116	117	116	115	114
Hospitals in a Group Purchasing Organization..	403	408	407	399	398

TABLE 6

TEXAS

U.S. Registered Community Hospitals
(Nonfederal, short-term general and other special hospitals)

Utilization, Personnel, Revenue and Expenses, Community Health Indicators 2010–2014

	2014	2013	2012	2011	2010
TOTAL FACILITY (Includes Hospital and Nursing Home Units)					
Utilization - Inpatient					
Beds	61,335	61,600	61,290	60,755	61,357
Admissions	2,515,174	2,522,455	2,548,864	2,534,688	2,580,401
Inpatient Days	13,278,929	13,173,092	13,170,816	13,062,644	13,331,491
Average Length of Stay	5.3	5.2	5.2	5.2	5.2
Inpatient Surgeries	715,533	718,822	729,749	736,841	761,437
Births	390,702	376,859	369,860	364,901	381,038
Utilization - Outpatient					
Emergency Outpatient Visits	10,488,873	10,404,119	10,439,383	9,889,631	9,739,066
Other Outpatient Visits	30,316,652	29,734,004	30,271,030	29,375,051	28,541,761
Total Outpatient Visits	40,805,525	40,138,123	40,710,413	39,264,682	38,280,827
Outpatient Surgeries	1,096,724	1,058,968	1,024,211	1,034,126	1,061,053
Personnel					
Full Time RNs	89,254	87,202	83,746	79,968	82,490
Full Time LPNs	6,610	7,258	7,679	8,278	9,113
Part Time RNs	21,710	24,170	22,853	22,557	20,107
Part Time LPNs	1,305	1,481	1,674	1,683	2,103
Total Full Time	288,697	283,921	278,323	274,534	280,656
Total Part Time	60,298	68,650	64,880	63,938	59,204
Revenue - Inpatient					
Gross Inpatient Revenue	$129,873,063,736	$121,281,645,571	$114,321,510,363	$105,598,575,282	$100,476,401,353
Revenue - Outpatient					
Gross Outpatient Revenue	$98,778,525,975	$89,812,997,830	$82,221,757,827	$72,395,257,221	$66,131,968,217
Revenue and Expenses - Totals					
(Includes Inpatient and Outpatient)					
Total Gross Revenue	$228,651,589,607	$211,094,643,401	$196,543,268,190	$177,993,832,503	$166,608,369,570
Deductions from Revenue	172,156,449,946	157,784,347,806	144,431,424,185	132,820,105,328	122,345,151,455
Net Patient Revenue	56,495,139,661	53,310,295,595	52,111,844,005	45,173,727,175	44,263,218,115
Other Operating Revenue	5,230,136,699	5,363,702,261	5,301,391,230	4,676,074,781	4,492,462,311
Other Nonoperating Revenue	1,544,118,773	937,753,455	842,027,514	1,373,986,299	1,120,744,597
Total Net Revenue	63,269,395,133	59,611,751,311	58,255,262,749	51,223,788,255	49,876,425,023
Total Expenses	55,219,961,093	53,271,177,348	51,154,019,956	45,556,147,376	44,225,750,333
HOSPITAL UNIT (Excludes Separate Nursing Home Units)					
Utilization - Inpatient					
Beds	60,914	60,802	60,350	59,835	60,497
Admissions	2,508,538	2,513,915	2,539,148	2,525,028	2,570,756
Inpatient Days	13,176,272	12,946,382	12,898,573	12,794,132	13,090,722
Average Length of Stay	5.3	5.1	5.1	5.1	5.1
Personnel					
Total Full Time	287,862	283,250	277,484	273,785	279,998
Total Part Time	60,121	68,503	64,773	63,837	59,051
Revenue and Expenses - Totals					
(Includes Inpatient and Outpatient)					
Total Net Revenue	$63,210,572,496	$59,524,322,308	$58,163,406,060	$51,125,792,174	$49,780,310,157
Total Expenses	55,164,740,849	53,205,672,674	51,073,523,904	45,465,619,488	44,132,923,562
COMMUNITY HEALTH INDICATORS PER 1000 POPULATION					
Total Population (in thousands)	26,957	26,448	26,059	25,675	25,213
Inpatient					
Beds	2.3	2.3	2.4	2.4	2.4
Admissions	93.3	95.4	97.8	98.7	102.3
Inpatient Days	492.6	498.1	505.4	508.8	528.7
Inpatient Surgeries	26.5	27.2	28.0	28.7	30.2
Births	14.5	14.2	14.2	14.2	15.1
Outpatient					
Emergency Outpatient Visits	389.1	393.4	400.6	385.2	386.3
Other Outpatient Visits	1,124.6	1,124.2	1,161.6	1,144.1	1,132.0
Total Outpatient Visits	1,513.7	1,517.6	1,562.2	1,529.3	1,518.3
Outpatient Surgeries	40.7	40.0	39.3	40.3	42.1
Expense per Capita (per person)	$2,048.4	$2,014.2	$1,963.0	$1,774.4	$1,754.1

States

TABLE 6

UTAH

U.S. Registered Community Hospitals
(Nonfederal, short-term general and other special hospitals)

Overview 2010–2014

	2014	2013	2012	2011	2010
Total Community Hospitals in Utah...........	47	47	47	46	44
Bed Size Category					
6-24	10	10	9	8	8
25-49	15	15	16	16	15
50-99	3	3	3	4	3
100-199	10	10	10	9	8
200-299	5	5	4	4	5
300-399	2	2	3	3	3
400-499	1	1	1	2	2
500 + ...	1	1	1	0	0
Location					
Hospitals Urban..........................	29	28	28	28	26
Hospitals Rural	18	19	19	18	18
Control					
State and Local Government...............	6	6	6	6	6
Not for Profit	26	26	26	25	23
Investor owned	15	15	15	15	15
Physician Models					
Independent Practice Association	3	3	4	4	4
Group Practice without Walls...............	2	2	2	2	1
Open Physician-Hospital Organization	2	2	1	1	1
Closed Physician-Hospital Organization	2	2	2	3	2
Management Service Organization	2	2	2	2	2
Integrated Salary Model	17	16	19	18	13
Equity Model	1	1	1	1	1
Foundation..............................	1	1	1	1	1
Insurance Products					
Health Maintenance Organization	14	16	16	17	15
Preferred Provider Organization..............	11	14	9	15	13
Indemnity Fee for Service	1	4	4	7	5
Managed Care Contracts					
Health Maintenance Organization	13	15	13	12	14
Preferred Provider Organization..............	18	20	18	18	17
Affiliations					
Hospitals in a System.....................	38	38	38	38	36
Hospitals in a Network	14	15	8	11	11
Hospitals in a Group Purchasing Organization..	27	29	21	25	22

TABLE 6

UTAH

U.S. Registered Community Hospitals
(Nonfederal, short-term general and other special hospitals)

Utilization, Personnel, Revenue and Expenses, Community Health Indicators 2010–2014

	2014	2013	2012	2011	2010
TOTAL FACILITY (Includes Hospital and Nursing Home Units)					
Utilization - Inpatient					
Beds	5,207	5,216	5,212	5,135	5,086
Admissions	228,979	229,492	241,436	236,131	224,264
Inpatient Days	990,116	979,856	992,015	993,098	979,963
Average Length of Stay	4.3	4.3	4.1	4.2	4.4
Inpatient Surgeries	71,768	68,077	71,909	71,272	70,503
Births	48,337	47,854	51,575	52,695	49,392
Utilization - Outpatient					
Emergency Outpatient Visits	1,045,790	888,611	894,661	855,152	834,897
Other Outpatient Visits	6,364,654	5,292,520	5,459,212	4,999,514	4,642,827
Total Outpatient Visits	7,410,444	6,181,131	6,353,873	5,854,666	5,477,724
Outpatient Surgeries	186,640	174,163	166,063	174,376	166,870
Personnel					
Full Time RNs	8,573	8,280	7,273	7,462	7,303
Full Time LPNs	278	304	299	337	358
Part Time RNs	4,242	4,486	4,801	4,362	4,353
Part Time LPNs	121	148	171	181	187
Total Full Time	29,229	29,048	26,395	26,733	26,111
Total Part Time	13,061	13,993	14,612	13,696	13,418
Revenue - Inpatient					
Gross Inpatient Revenue	$10,068,204,660	$8,689,472,055	$8,253,048,052	$7,051,376,726	$6,581,097,114
Revenue - Outpatient					
Gross Outpatient Revenue	$9,365,225,858	$7,762,738,220	$6,983,551,734	$6,027,847,868	$5,300,499,527
Revenue and Expenses - Totals (Includes Inpatient and Outpatient)					
Total Gross Revenue	$19,433,430,518	$16,452,210,275	$15,236,599,786	$13,079,224,594	$11,881,596,641
Deductions from Revenue	12,693,106,100	10,308,471,435	9,233,540,993	7,638,050,195	6,906,546,426
Net Patient Revenue	6,740,324,418	6,143,738,840	6,003,058,793	5,441,174,399	4,975,050,215
Other Operating Revenue	204,338,018	229,460,960	221,419,572	265,484,132	243,975,154
Other Nonoperating Revenue	29,673,497	24,760,128	9,983,495	10,166,250	31,741,257
Total Net Revenue	6,974,335,933	6,397,959,928	6,234,461,860	5,716,824,781	5,250,766,626
Total Expenses	5,616,931,808	5,364,834,918	5,117,473,502	4,679,558,728	4,470,510,613
HOSPITAL UNIT (Excludes Separate Nursing Home Units)					
Utilization - Inpatient					
Beds	5,079	5,089	5,080	5,008	4,931
Admissions	228,206	228,932	240,784	235,615	223,117
Inpatient Days	956,057	946,093	951,874	954,737	935,962
Average Length of Stay	4.2	4.1	4	4.1	4.2
Personnel					
Total Full Time	29,176	28,977	26,322	26,670	26,037
Total Part Time	13,024	13,944	14,549	13,647	13,364
Revenue and Expenses - Totals (Includes Inpatient and Outpatient)					
Total Net Revenue	$6,966,500,892	$6,390,793,512	$6,225,430,738	$5,708,620,280	$5,239,992,029
Total Expenses	5,611,918,537	5,360,928,383	5,110,023,379	4,672,187,702	4,461,414,330
COMMUNITY HEALTH INDICATORS PER 1000 POPULATION					
Total Population (in thousands)	2,943	2,901	2,855	2,817	2,831
Inpatient					
Beds	1.8	1.8	1.8	1.8	1.8
Admissions	77.8	79.1	84.6	83.8	79.2
Inpatient Days	336.4	337.8	347.4	352.5	346.2
Inpatient Surgeries	24.4	23.5	25.2	25.3	24.9
Births	16.4	16.5	18.1	18.7	17.4
Outpatient					
Emergency Outpatient Visits	355.4	306.3	313.3	303.5	294.9
Other Outpatient Visits	2,162.7	1,824.5	1,912.0	1,774.6	1,640.1
Total Outpatient Visits	2,518.1	2,130.8	2,225.3	2,078.2	1,935.1
Outpatient Surgeries	63.4	60.0	58.2	61.9	58.9
Expense per Capita (per person)	$1,908.6	$1,849.4	$1,792.3	$1,661.1	$1,579.3

States

TABLE 6

VERMONT

U.S. Registered Community Hospitals
(Nonfederal, short-term general and other special hospitals)

Overview 2010–2014

	2014	2013	2012	2011	2010
Total Community Hospitals in Vermont	14	14	14	14	14
Bed Size Category					
6-24	1	1	2	2	1
25-49	7	7	6	6	6
50-99	3	3	3	3	4
100-199	1	1	1	1	1
200-299	1	1	1	1	1
300-399	0	0	0	0	0
400-499	1	1	1	1	1
500 + ...	0	0	0	0	0
Location					
Hospitals Urban............................	2	2	2	2	2
Hospitals Rural	12	12	12	12	12
Control					
State and Local Government................	0	0	0	0	0
Not for Profit	14	14	14	14	14
Investor owned	0	0	0	0	0
Physician Models					
Independent Practice Association	0	0	0	0	0
Group Practice without Walls...............	1	1	0	0	0
Open Physician-Hospital Organization	2	1	3	3	3
Closed Physician-Hospital Organization	0	0	0	1	1
Management Service Organization	0	0	0	0	0
Integrated Salary Model....................	5	5	6	7	8
Equity Model	0	0	0	0	0
Foundation...............................	0	0	0	0	0
Insurance Products					
Health Maintenance Organization	0	1	2	2	2
Preferred Provider Organization..............	0	1	1	1	0
Indemnity Fee for Service	0	1	2	1	0
Managed Care Contracts					
Health Maintenance Organization	4	3	2	5	6
Preferred Provider Organization..............	5	3	3	5	5
Affiliations					
Hospitals in a System.....................	1	1	1	1	1
Hospitals in a Network	3	4	5	5	5
Hospitals in a Group Purchasing Organization..	10	11	10	10	10

TABLE 6

VERMONT

U.S. Registered Community Hospitals
(Nonfederal, short-term general and other special hospitals)

Utilization, Personnel, Revenue and Expenses, Community Health Indicators 2010–2014

	2014	2013	2012	2011	2010
TOTAL FACILITY (Includes Hospital and Nursing Home Units)					
Utilization - Inpatient					
Beds	1,200	1,201	1,231	1,218	1,288
Admissions	45,964	48,464	48,887	48,941	49,449
Inpatient Days	288,502	303,555	307,154	310,510	305,289
Average Length of Stay	6.3	6.3	6.3	6.3	6.2
Inpatient Surgeries	12,180	12,785	13,036	13,258	13,950
Births	5,557	5,246	5,250	12,755	5,604
Utilization - Outpatient					
Emergency Outpatient Visits	327,066	302,264	302,030	296,666	352,808
Other Outpatient Visits	2,817,446	2,779,607	2,740,382	2,788,192	2,999,812
Total Outpatient Visits	3,144,512	3,081,871	3,042,412	3,084,858	3,352,620
Outpatient Surgeries	45,616	46,251	46,671	48,381	48,158
Personnel					
Full Time RNs	2,219	2,006	1,852	1,720	1,748
Full Time LPNs	173	150	148	159	166
Part Time RNs	1,607	1,646	1,553	1,595	1,311
Part Time LPNs	97	91	104	128	149
Total Full Time	11,026	10,374	9,967	9,724	9,629
Total Part Time	4,685	4,657	4,590	4,930	4,078
Revenue - Inpatient					
Gross Inpatient Revenue	$1,374,615,928	$1,435,938,955	$1,089,276,425	$1,055,321,773	$1,154,115,173
Revenue - Outpatient					
Gross Outpatient Revenue	$3,444,718,900	$3,197,627,776	$3,001,872,051	$2,665,042,545	$2,538,622,333
Revenue and Expenses - Totals					
(Includes Inpatient and Outpatient)					
Total Gross Revenue	$4,819,334,828	$4,633,566,731	$4,091,148,476	$3,720,364,318	$3,692,737,506
Deductions from Revenue	2,710,952,529	2,565,323,969	2,173,153,296	1,901,314,973	1,982,861,871
Net Patient Revenue	2,108,382,299	2,068,242,762	1,917,995,180	1,819,049,345	1,709,875,635
Other Operating Revenue	139,867,987	102,107,130	71,915,614	57,250,217	56,110,764
Other Nonoperating Revenue	27,570,031	68,713,604	39,281,120	18,547,865	35,893,255
Total Net Revenue	2,275,820,317	2,239,063,496	2,029,191,914	1,894,847,427	1,801,879,654
Total Expenses	2,101,149,726	2,042,602,482	1,931,290,820	1,776,728,126	1,714,899,646
HOSPITAL UNIT (Excludes Separate Nursing Home Units)					
Utilization - Inpatient					
Beds	1,047	1,048	1,053	1,010	1,080
Admissions	45,584	48,129	48,477	48,523	49,078
Inpatient Days	241,545	249,025	248,986	241,161	233,003
Average Length of Stay	5.3	5.2	5.1	5	4.7
Personnel					
Total Full Time	10,975	10,247	9,791	9,591	9,493
Total Part Time	4,668	4,601	4,502	4,811	3,963
Revenue and Expenses - Totals					
(Includes Inpatient and Outpatient)					
Total Net Revenue	$2,260,094,501	$2,222,318,627	$2,012,967,016	$1,876,507,339	$1,783,366,299
Total Expenses	2,085,458,949	2,026,117,019	1,915,144,417	1,759,323,094	1,697,709,912
COMMUNITY HEALTH INDICATORS PER 1000 POPULATION					
Total Population (in thousands)	627	627	626	626	622
Inpatient					
Beds	1.9	1.9	2.0	1.9	2.1
Admissions	73.4	77.3	78.1	78.1	79.4
Inpatient Days	460.5	484.4	490.7	495.7	490.5
Inpatient Surgeries	19.4	20.4	20.8	21.2	22.4
Births	8.9	8.4	8.4	20.4	9.0
Outpatient					
Emergency Outpatient Visits	522.0	482.4	482.5	473.6	566.8
Other Outpatient Visits	4,496.7	4,435.8	4,377.5	4,450.9	4,819.5
Total Outpatient Visits	5,018.7	4,918.2	4,860.0	4,924.5	5,386.3
Outpatient Surgeries	72.8	73.8	74.6	77.2	77.4
Expense per Capita (per person)	$3,353.5	$3,259.7	$3,085.1	$2,836.3	$2,755.2

TABLE 6

VIRGINIA

U.S. Registered Community Hospitals
(Nonfederal, short-term general and other special hospitals)

Overview 2010–2014

	2014	2013	2012	2011	2010
Total Community Hospitals in Virginia	93	93	94	89	89
Bed Size Category					
6-24	6	6	5	5	5
25-49	17	16	16	15	14
50-99	17	18	17	15	15
100-199	22	23	26	23	25
200-299	13	12	12	13	12
300-399	5	5	5	6	6
400-499	5	5	5	5	5
500 + ...	8	8	8	7	7
Location					
Hospitals Urban.	66	64	64	59	59
Hospitals Rural	27	29	30	30	30
Control					
State and Local Government.	5	5	5	4	4
Not for Profit	65	65	65	65	64
Investor owned	23	23	24	20	21
Physician Models					
Independent Practice Association	14	11	13	12	13
Group Practice without Walls.	10	9	9	9	10
Open Physician-Hospital Organization	14	14	14	8	9
Closed Physician-Hospital Organization	4	3	2	2	2
Management Service Organization	15	15	16	17	18
Integrated Salary Model	41	44	45	47	51
Equity Model	10	9	9	8	8
Foundation.	2	1	2	2	1
Insurance Products					
Health Maintenance Organization	24	28	18	18	15
Preferred Provider Organization.	25	30	15	20	18
Indemnity Fee for Service	18	15	9	9	2
Managed Care Contracts					
Health Maintenance Organization	49	60	55	59	55
Preferred Provider Organization.	50	61	57	61	59
Affiliations					
Hospitals in a System.	83	81	78	73	70
Hospitals in a Network	42	44	41	44	44
Hospitals in a Group Purchasing Organization. .	58	65	64	65	70

TABLE 6

VIRGINIA

U.S. Registered Community Hospitals
(Nonfederal, short-term general and other special hospitals)

Utilization, Personnel, Revenue and Expenses, Community Health Indicators 2010–2014

	2014	2013	2012	2011	2010
TOTAL FACILITY (Includes Hospital and Nursing Home Units)					
Utilization - Inpatient					
Beds	18,234	17,975	18,150	17,797	17,747
Admissions	775,015	780,153	796,004	788,441	776,678
Inpatient Days	4,432,096	4,436,963	4,516,303	4,391,769	4,310,430
Average Length of Stay	5.7	5.7	5.7	5.6	5.5
Inpatient Surgeries	206,310	213,323	209,255	210,890	223,354
Births	92,449	93,002	93,114	98,141	99,623
Utilization - Outpatient					
Emergency Outpatient Visits	3,644,169	3,626,500	3,600,733	3,407,824	3,256,956
Other Outpatient Visits	12,877,851	12,187,544	11,952,608	10,710,596	10,524,980
Total Outpatient Visits	16,522,020	15,814,044	15,553,341	14,118,420	13,781,936
Outpatient Surgeries	500,657	501,555	451,407	446,691	439,146
Personnel					
Full Time RNs	26,746	26,044	24,712	24,546	24,035
Full Time LPNs	1,761	1,935	2,104	2,062	2,226
Part Time RNs	10,477	10,775	10,964	11,202	11,030
Part Time LPNs	459	521	611	614	703
Total Full Time	85,289	85,502	83,946	83,312	82,310
Total Part Time	27,755	29,524	29,934	29,682	30,091
Revenue - Inpatient					
Gross Inpatient Revenue	$31,343,762,241	$29,611,485,772	$28,228,430,166	$25,657,236,400	$24,373,894,322
Revenue - Outpatient					
Gross Outpatient Revenue	$31,397,192,819	$28,296,364,383	$25,551,564,541	$22,821,731,869	$21,205,056,723
Revenue and Expenses - Totals					
(Includes Inpatient and Outpatient)					
Total Gross Revenue	$62,740,955,060	$57,907,850,155	$53,779,994,707	$48,478,968,269	$45,578,951,045
Deductions from Revenue	43,932,115,916	39,950,040,314	36,089,745,615	32,415,072,411	30,139,978,214
Net Patient Revenue	18,808,839,144	17,957,809,841	17,690,249,092	16,063,895,858	15,438,972,831
Other Operating Revenue	726,060,044	685,703,799	614,154,152	538,832,905	425,128,846
Other Nonoperating Revenue	395,330,743	484,708,430	354,593,302	170,711,732	253,492,718
Total Net Revenue	19,930,229,931	19,128,222,070	18,658,996,546	16,773,440,495	16,117,594,395
Total Expenses	17,726,816,378	17,002,869,179	16,505,378,259	15,341,349,476	14,709,796,266
HOSPITAL UNIT (Excludes Separate Nursing Home Units)					
Utilization - Inpatient					
Beds	16,586	16,327	16,467	16,091	16,163
Admissions	768,904	773,930	789,746	781,788	770,195
Inpatient Days	3,902,908	3,879,122	3,951,225	3,823,198	3,775,706
Average Length of Stay	5.1	5	5	4.9	4.9
Personnel					
Total Full Time	84,380	84,464	82,960	82,422	81,441
Total Part Time	27,369	29,137	29,503	29,292	29,637
Revenue and Expenses - Totals					
(Includes Inpatient and Outpatient)					
Total Net Revenue	$19,797,897,759	$18,989,222,239	$18,515,704,755	$16,629,452,446	$15,986,427,239
Total Expenses	17,600,918,382	16,873,364,471	16,368,213,160	15,208,955,950	14,592,391,811
COMMUNITY HEALTH INDICATORS PER 1000 POPULATION					
Total Population (in thousands)	8,326	8,260	8,186	8,097	7,952
Inpatient					
Beds	2.2	2.2	2.2	2.2	2.2
Admissions	93.1	94.4	97.2	97.4	97.7
Inpatient Days	532.3	537.1	551.7	542.4	542.0
Inpatient Surgeries	24.8	25.8	25.6	26.0	28.1
Births	11.1	11.3	11.4	12.1	12.5
Outpatient					
Emergency Outpatient Visits	437.7	439.0	439.9	420.9	409.6
Other Outpatient Visits	1,546.6	1,475.4	1,460.2	1,322.9	1,323.5
Total Outpatient Visits	1,984.3	1,914.4	1,900.0	1,743.7	1,733.1
Outpatient Surgeries	60.1	60.7	55.1	55.2	55.2
Expense per Capita (per person)	$2,129.0	$2,058.4	$2,016.3	$1,894.8	$1,849.8

TABLE 6

WASHINGTON

U.S. Registered Community Hospitals
(Nonfederal, short-term general and other special hospitals)

Overview 2010–2014

	2014	2013	2012	2011	2010
Total Community Hospitals in Washington	90	90	87	85	86
Bed Size Category					
6-24	10	9	8	8	7
25-49	28	27	27	27	29
50-99	15	16	14	11	10
100-199	15	16	15	16	16
200-299	11	11	12	12	13
300-399	5	5	4	5	6
400-499	3	4	5	4	3
500 + ...	3	2	2	2	2
Location					
Hospitals Urban..........................	61	56	55	53	53
Hospitals Rural	29	34	32	32	33
Control					
State and Local Government................	40	40	38	38	39
Not for Profit	43	44	42	41	42
Investor owned	7	6	7	6	5
Physician Models					
Independent Practice Association	1	1	1	1	2
Group Practice without Walls................	3	2	3	4	4
Open Physician-Hospital Organization	2	2	3	6	5
Closed Physician-Hospital Organization	1	0	1	1	0
Management Service Organization	1	2	3	4	6
Integrated Salary Model	41	36	39	40	39
Equity Model	1	3	3	3	4
Foundation...............................	0	6	4	4	5
Insurance Products					
Health Maintenance Organization	6	4	4	7	4
Preferred Provider Organization..............	10	9	9	14	11
Indemnity Fee for Service	2	1	2	1	0
Managed Care Contracts					
Health Maintenance Organization	41	31	38	35	34
Preferred Provider Organization..............	41	34	40	37	38
Affiliations					
Hospitals in a System......................	45	42	40	39	35
Hospitals in a Network.....................	29	24	17	20	19
Hospitals in a Group Purchasing Organization..	54	51	44	51	48

TABLE 6

WASHINGTON

U.S. Registered Community Hospitals
(Nonfederal, short-term general and other special hospitals)

Utilization, Personnel, Revenue and Expenses, Community Health Indicators 2010–2014

	2014	2013	2012	2011	2010
TOTAL FACILITY (Includes Hospital and Nursing Home Units)					
Utilization - Inpatient					
Beds	11,988	12,180	12,132	11,670	11,537
Admissions	576,655	600,519	597,338	576,214	588,855
Inpatient Days	2,711,414	2,763,826	2,731,437	2,613,217	2,638,779
Average Length of Stay	4.7	4.6	4.6	4.5	4.5
Inpatient Surgeries	175,364	170,566	165,978	167,254	170,895
Births	80,429	77,904	76,089	77,238	78,216
Utilization - Outpatient					
Emergency Outpatient Visits	2,440,819	2,338,002	2,390,525	2,321,612	2,290,953
Other Outpatient Visits	9,801,052	10,120,396	10,576,020	10,136,318	9,515,677
Total Outpatient Visits	12,241,871	12,458,398	12,966,545	12,457,930	11,806,630
Outpatient Surgeries	321,763	299,228	265,920	261,623	261,997
Personnel					
Full Time RNs	18,517	18,241	18,981	16,121	16,109
Full Time LPNs	705	826	946	774	825
Part Time RNs	11,903	14,128	12,219	13,423	13,848
Part Time LPNs	419	545	509	560	616
Total Full Time	74,255	74,227	75,760	65,087	68,163
Total Part Time	34,778	41,067	37,294	39,667	39,185
Revenue - Inpatient					
Gross Inpatient Revenue	$27,873,947,083	$27,370,345,005	$25,728,322,501	$21,352,251,400	$21,516,174,379
Revenue - Outpatient					
Gross Outpatient Revenue	$27,000,712,977	$25,026,435,484	$22,312,583,270	$19,065,026,947	$18,594,056,137
Revenue and Expenses - Totals					
(Includes Inpatient and Outpatient)					
Total Gross Revenue	$54,874,660,060	$52,396,780,489	$48,040,905,771	$40,417,278,347	$40,110,230,516
Deductions from Revenue	36,929,155,971	34,820,455,823	31,116,500,841	25,612,881,399	25,534,351,330
Net Patient Revenue	17,945,504,089	17,576,324,666	16,924,404,930	14,804,396,948	14,575,879,186
Other Operating Revenue	1,009,138,938	1,020,203,756	972,579,978	842,178,249	804,026,112
Other Nonoperating Revenue	242,467,401	249,956,325	210,144,087	300,691,951	226,341,197
Total Net Revenue	19,197,110,428	18,846,484,747	18,107,128,995	15,947,267,148	15,606,246,495
Total Expenses	17,790,525,968	17,864,679,102	16,739,742,990	14,869,963,274	14,641,932,019
HOSPITAL UNIT (Excludes Separate Nursing Home Units)					
Utilization - Inpatient					
Beds	11,824	11,997	11,914	11,453	11,382
Admissions	575,883	600,198	597,051	575,796	587,786
Inpatient Days	2,663,886	2,686,606	2,655,788	2,530,869	2,589,013
Average Length of Stay	4.6	4.5	4.4	4.4	4.4
Personnel					
Total Full Time	74,081	74,098	75,610	64,968	68,113
Total Part Time	34,617	40,938	37,137	39,509	39,097
Revenue and Expenses - Totals					
(Includes Inpatient and Outpatient)					
Total Net Revenue	$19,175,208,730	$18,825,783,157	$18,084,028,525	$15,927,548,095	$15,586,259,128
Total Expenses	17,769,219,934	17,844,227,960	16,718,398,352	14,852,332,389	14,623,738,440
COMMUNITY HEALTH INDICATORS PER 1000 POPULATION					
Total Population (in thousands)	7,062	6,971	6,897	6,830	6,746
Inpatient					
Beds	1.7	1.7	1.8	1.7	1.7
Admissions	81.7	86.1	86.6	84.4	87.3
Inpatient Days	384.0	396.5	396.0	382.6	391.2
Inpatient Surgeries	24.8	24.5	24.1	24.5	25.3
Births	11.4	11.2	11.0	11.3	11.6
Outpatient					
Emergency Outpatient Visits	345.7	335.4	346.6	339.9	339.6
Other Outpatient Visits	1,388.0	1,451.7	1,533.4	1,484.1	1,410.5
Total Outpatient Visits	1,733.6	1,787.1	1,880.0	1,824.0	1,750.1
Outpatient Surgeries	45.6	42.9	38.6	38.3	38.8
Expense per Capita (per person)	$2,519.4	$2,562.6	$2,427.1	$2,177.1	$2,170.4

States

TABLE 6

WEST VIRGINIA

U.S. Registered Community Hospitals
(Nonfederal, short-term general and other special hospitals)

Overview 2010–2014

	2014	2013	2012	2011	2010
Total Community Hospitals in West Virginia ...	54	55	55	55	56
Bed Size Category					
6-24	4	3	3	3	3
25-49	16	17	16	15	14
50-99	10	11	12	13	13
100-199	13	12	12	11	14
200-299	7	8	7	8	9
300-399	2	2	2	2	1
400-499	0	0	1	1	0
500 + ...	2	2	2	2	2
Location					
Hospitals Urban...........................	28	26	26	26	27
Hospitals Rural	26	29	29	29	29
Control					
State and Local Government................	7	7	8	8	8
Not for Profit	33	34	33	33	34
Investor owned	14	14	14	14	14
Physician Models					
Independent Practice Association	2	2	2	2	3
Group Practice without Walls................	0	1	0	0	0
Open Physician-Hospital Organization	11	11	12	14	13
Closed Physician-Hospital Organization	1	1	1	1	3
Management Service Organization	2	1	2	2	2
Integrated Salary Model....................	27	27	27	25	25
Equity Model	0	0	0	0	0
Foundation...............................	0	0	0	0	0
Insurance Products					
Health Maintenance Organization	4	4	5	5	6
Preferred Provider Organization..............	8	8	6	10	10
Indemnity Fee for Service	3	4	4	2	3
Managed Care Contracts					
Health Maintenance Organization	31	29	31	28	31
Preferred Provider Organization..............	40	41	40	40	42
Affiliations					
Hospitals in a System......................	30	30	30	30	29
Hospitals in a Network.....................	20	20	20	21	21
Hospitals in a Group Purchasing Organization..	52	53	53	52	53

TABLE 6

WEST VIRGINIA

U.S. Registered Community Hospitals
(Nonfederal, short-term general and other special hospitals)

Utilization, Personnel, Revenue and Expenses, Community Health Indicators 2010–2014

	2014	2013	2012	2011	2010
TOTAL FACILITY (Includes Hospital and Nursing Home Units)					
Utilization - Inpatient					
Beds	6,841	7,054	7,212	7,365	7,298
Admissions	256,571	265,292	276,114	282,194	278,221
Inpatient Days	1,529,702	1,549,653	1,587,250	1,632,308	1,612,811
Average Length of Stay	6	5.8	5.7	5.8	5.8
Inpatient Surgeries	77,672	80,580	82,602	82,491	83,992
Births	20,447	20,974	20,758	20,639	20,487
Utilization - Outpatient					
Emergency Outpatient Visits	1,182,114	1,164,759	1,224,551	1,216,780	1,207,918
Other Outpatient Visits	5,928,683	5,732,531	5,585,774	5,544,015	5,446,482
Total Outpatient Visits	7,110,797	6,897,290	6,810,325	6,760,795	6,654,400
Outpatient Surgeries	227,500	231,365	228,957	222,505	212,434
Personnel					
Full Time RNs	9,292	9,300	8,852	8,593	8,532
Full Time LPNs	1,093	1,098	1,130	1,099	1,217
Part Time RNs	2,933	3,325	3,251	3,252	3,395
Part Time LPNs	226	325	332	396	419
Total Full Time	35,039	35,411	34,272	33,119	33,349
Total Part Time	9,278	10,751	10,125	9,903	10,143
Revenue - Inpatient					
Gross Inpatient Revenue	$6,849,859,734	$6,598,503,203	$6,272,466,443	$6,028,967,872	$5,597,580,327
Revenue - Outpatient					
Gross Outpatient Revenue	$7,556,674,350	$6,837,148,779	$6,361,117,278	$5,824,592,215	$5,444,045,714
Revenue and Expenses - Totals					
(Includes Inpatient and Outpatient)					
Total Gross Revenue	$14,406,534,084	$13,435,651,982	$12,633,583,721	$11,853,560,087	$11,041,626,041
Deductions from Revenue	8,850,299,429	8,165,212,258	7,391,004,309	7,049,221,237	6,386,501,669
Net Patient Revenue	5,556,234,655	5,270,439,724	5,242,579,412	4,804,338,850	4,655,124,372
Other Operating Revenue	214,353,652	222,761,392	182,070,517	133,361,426	126,269,003
Other Nonoperating Revenue	87,577,976	191,330,033	86,836,379	-338,296	63,579,778
Total Net Revenue	5,858,166,283	5,684,531,149	5,511,486,308	4,937,361,980	4,844,973,153
Total Expenses	5,514,045,147	5,371,862,686	5,151,427,691	4,724,080,410	4,689,352,987
HOSPITAL UNIT (Excludes Separate Nursing Home Units)					
Utilization - Inpatient					
Beds	6,102	6,270	6,423	6,554	6,454
Admissions	253,305	261,148	271,352	277,659	272,471
Inpatient Days	1,294,455	1,303,200	1,329,793	1,378,567	1,340,666
Average Length of Stay	5.1	5	4.9	5	4.9
Personnel					
Total Full Time	34,502	34,840	33,683	32,566	32,752
Total Part Time	9,056	10,370	9,785	9,508	9,781
Revenue and Expenses - Totals					
(Includes Inpatient and Outpatient)					
Total Net Revenue	$5,798,408,691	$5,617,231,970	$5,439,544,951	$4,873,165,838	$4,774,505,282
Total Expenses	5,469,138,973	5,329,382,003	5,097,076,501	4,670,781,412	4,637,567,799
COMMUNITY HEALTH INDICATORS PER 1000 POPULATION					
Total Population (in thousands)	1,850	1,854	1,855	1,855	1,826
Inpatient					
Beds	3.7	3.8	3.9	4.0	4.0
Admissions	138.7	143.1	148.8	152.1	152.4
Inpatient Days	826.7	835.7	855.5	879.8	883.5
Inpatient Surgeries	42.0	43.5	44.5	44.5	46.0
Births	11.1	11.3	11.2	11.1	11.2
Outpatient					
Emergency Outpatient Visits	638.9	628.1	660.0	655.8	661.7
Other Outpatient Visits	3,204.1	3,091.5	3,010.5	2,988.1	2,983.5
Total Outpatient Visits	3,843.0	3,719.6	3,670.5	3,643.9	3,645.2
Outpatient Surgeries	123.0	124.8	123.4	119.9	116.4
Expense per Capita (per person)	$2,980.0	$2,897.0	$2,776.4	$2,546.2	$2,568.8

TABLE 6

WISCONSIN

U.S. Registered Community Hospitals
(Nonfederal, short-term general and other special hospitals)

Overview 2010–2014

	2014	2013	2012	2011	2010
Total Community Hospitals in Wisconsin......	129	129	128	125	124
Bed Size Category					
6-24	22	23	21	15	13
25-49	34	32	33	36	37
50-99	31	32	33	31	31
100-199	24	22	20	22	21
200-299	10	12	11	11	13
300-399	4	4	7	7	5
400-499	1	1	0	1	2
500 + ...	3	3	3	2	2
Location					
Hospitals Urban..........................	72	73	72	69	68
Hospitals Rural	57	56	56	56	56
Control					
State and Local Government................	2	2	2	2	2
Not for Profit	121	121	121	119	117
Investor owned	6	6	5	4	5
Physician Models					
Independent Practice Association	7	8	11	11	9
Group Practice without Walls...............	1	1	0	3	3
Open Physician-Hospital Organization	6	8	6	4	4
Closed Physician-Hospital Organization	5	4	3	4	4
Management Service Organization	2	1	2	2	2
Integrated Salary Model....................	51	54	62	56	38
Equity Model	9	11	7	6	9
Foundation...............................	2	2	2	2	2
Insurance Products					
Health Maintenance Organization	34	43	41	36	20
Preferred Provider Organization..............	44	45	41	36	31
Indemnity Fee for Service	18	18	19	15	15
Managed Care Contracts					
Health Maintenance Organization	118	120	118	118	116
Preferred Provider Organization..............	119	122	121	120	118
Affiliations					
Hospitals in a System.....................	80	76	75	72	72
Hospitals in a Network....................	42	45	44	43	37
Hospitals in a Group Purchasing Organization..	125	124	126	123	118

TABLE 6

WISCONSIN

U.S. Registered Community Hospitals
(Nonfederal, short-term general and other special hospitals)

Utilization, Personnel, Revenue and Expenses, Community Health Indicators 2010–2014

	2014	2013	2012	2011	2010
TOTAL FACILITY (Includes Hospital and Nursing Home Units)					
Utilization - Inpatient					
Beds	12,659	12,760	13,020	13,134	13,520
Admissions	551,398	566,368	578,239	573,077	588,592
Inpatient Days	2,754,377	2,808,943	2,855,397	2,873,295	2,966,909
Average Length of Stay	5	5	4.9	5	5
Inpatient Surgeries	169,251	172,640	214,146	214,111	228,469
Births	64,433	64,598	65,632	66,783	67,843
Utilization - Outpatient					
Emergency Outpatient Visits	2,199,839	2,098,324	2,171,739	2,130,925	2,160,341
Other Outpatient Visits	15,081,475	14,400,592	13,957,038	13,379,041	12,444,617
Total Outpatient Visits	17,281,314	16,498,916	16,128,777	15,509,966	14,604,958
Outpatient Surgeries	458,157	454,518	526,585	531,355	522,864
Personnel					
Full Time RNs	15,953	15,560	15,095	15,048	14,476
Full Time LPNs	541	617	537	622	673
Part Time RNs	15,880	15,965	15,972	14,982	15,552
Part Time LPNs	587	689	645	706	794
Total Full Time	63,551	64,634	63,722	63,544	63,254
Total Part Time	47,846	49,311	48,388	46,533	48,472
Revenue - Inpatient					
Gross Inpatient Revenue	$18,851,445,421	$17,961,771,456	$17,011,582,655	$16,185,500,212	$15,357,857,584
Revenue - Outpatient					
Gross Outpatient Revenue	$24,798,270,276	$22,326,935,702	$20,638,540,030	$18,798,615,788	$16,468,660,136
Revenue and Expenses - Totals					
(Includes Inpatient and Outpatient)					
Total Gross Revenue	$43,649,715,697	$40,288,707,158	$37,650,122,685	$34,984,116,000	$31,826,517,720
Deductions from Revenue	26,515,019,643	24,091,152,555	21,459,464,213	19,455,297,266	16,996,231,064
Net Patient Revenue	17,134,696,054	16,197,554,603	16,190,658,472	15,528,818,734	14,830,286,656
Other Operating Revenue	962,594,262	715,806,300	751,235,572	644,957,778	630,341,533
Other Nonoperating Revenue	445,139,600	456,057,518	322,542,557	288,307,316	285,539,514
Total Net Revenue	18,542,429,916	17,369,418,421	17,264,436,601	16,462,083,828	15,746,167,703
Total Expenses	16,299,405,040	15,412,000,677	15,601,708,952	14,997,018,589	14,230,620,575
HOSPITAL UNIT (Excludes Separate Nursing Home Units)					
Utilization - Inpatient					
Beds	11,559	11,611	11,775	11,814	12,092
Admissions	548,980	563,976	575,966	570,650	586,022
Inpatient Days	2,405,017	2,450,661	2,439,508	2,453,855	2,511,474
Average Length of Stay	4.4	4.3	4.2	4.3	4.3
Personnel					
Total Full Time	63,101	64,288	63,255	62,919	62,460
Total Part Time	47,407	48,766	47,770	45,754	47,543
Revenue and Expenses - Totals					
(Includes Inpatient and Outpatient)					
Total Net Revenue	$18,474,744,255	$17,289,048,577	$17,182,065,794	$16,360,856,116	$15,640,069,501
Total Expenses	16,237,305,685	15,332,364,550	15,523,090,630	14,902,736,502	14,124,128,291
COMMUNITY HEALTH INDICATORS PER 1000 POPULATION					
Total Population (in thousands)	5,758	5,743	5,726	5,712	5,669
Inpatient					
Beds	2.2	2.2	2.3	2.3	2.4
Admissions	95.8	98.6	101.0	100.3	103.8
Inpatient Days	478.4	489.1	498.6	503.0	523.4
Inpatient Surgeries	29.4	30.1	37.4	37.5	40.3
Births	11.2	11.2	11.5	11.7	12.0
Outpatient					
Emergency Outpatient Visits	382.1	365.4	379.3	373.1	381.1
Other Outpatient Visits	2,619.4	2,507.6	2,437.3	2,342.4	2,195.4
Total Outpatient Visits	3,001.5	2,873.0	2,816.6	2,715.4	2,576.5
Outpatient Surgeries	79.6	79.1	92.0	93.0	92.2
Expense per Capita (per person)	$2,831.0	$2,683.7	$2,724.5	$2,625.6	$2,510.5

States

TABLE **6**

WYOMING

U.S. Registered Community Hospitals
(Nonfederal, short-term general and other special hospitals)

Overview 2010–2014

	2014	2013	2012	2011	2010
Total Community Hospitals in Wyoming.......	23	24	24	24	24
Bed Size Category					
6-24	1	0	0	0	0
25-49	9	11	11	11	11
50-99	6	6	6	6	6
100-199	6	6	5	4	4
200-299	1	1	2	3	3
300-399	0	0	0	0	0
400-499	0	0	0	0	0
500 + ...	0	0	0	0	0
Location					
Hospitals Urban..........................	2	2	2	2	2
Hospitals Rural	21	22	22	22	22
Control					
State and Local Government................	16	16	16	16	16
Not for Profit	5	5	5	5	5
Investor owned	2	3	3	3	3
Physician Models					
Independent Practice Association	1	3	2	2	2
Group Practice without Walls...............	1	0	0	0	0
Open Physician-Hospital Organization	2	2	1	1	1
Closed Physician-Hospital Organization	1	1	1	1	1
Management Service Organization	2	2	2	1	2
Integrated Salary Model....................	11	11	10	9	10
Equity Model	0	0	0	0	0
Foundation...............................	1	0	0	0	0
Insurance Products					
Health Maintenance Organization	3	2	2	2	1
Preferred Provider Organization.............	2	1	1	3	3
Indemnity Fee for Service	1	0	0	0	0
Managed Care Contracts					
Health Maintenance Organization	5	5	5	4	3
Preferred Provider Organization.............	12	17	17	14	14
Affiliations					
Hospitals in a System.....................	11	12	12	12	12
Hospitals in a Network....................	4	4	5	4	4
Hospitals in a Group Purchasing Organization..	21	22	22	21	21

TABLE 6

WYOMING

U.S. Registered Community Hospitals
(Nonfederal, short-term general and other special hospitals)

Utilization, Personnel, Revenue and Expenses, Community Health Indicators 2010–2014

	2014	2013	2012	2011	2010
TOTAL FACILITY (Includes Hospital and Nursing Home Units)					
Utilization - Inpatient					
Beds	1,835	1,920	1,923	1,958	1,958
Admissions	41,415	44,574	44,180	45,697	49,704
Inpatient Days	360,622	372,237	375,036	378,227	398,850
Average Length of Stay.	8.7	8.4	8.5	8.3	8
Inpatient Surgeries.	11,284	11,419	11,959	12,872	14,159
Births.	6,506	6,404	6,364	6,363	6,920
Utilization - Outpatient					
Emergency Outpatient Visits	232,288	233,648	229,649	228,140	231,261
Other Outpatient Visits.	1,012,979	1,029,872	976,926	890,706	866,984
Total Outpatient Visits	1,245,267	1,263,520	1,206,575	1,118,846	1,098,245
Outpatient Surgeries	25,394	26,232	28,021	29,019	29,260
Personnel					
Full Time RNs	1,934	1,864	1,798	1,721	1,680
Full Time LPNs	114	101	113	116	117
Part Time RNs.	587	604	578	556	455
Part Time LPNs	41	43	50	52	54
Total Full Time.	7,895	7,803	7,546	7,404	7,338
Total Part Time	1,979	2,211	2,166	2,067	2,005
Revenue - Inpatient					
Gross Inpatient Revenue.	$1,135,893,538	$1,146,334,560	$1,129,646,064	$1,079,479,758	$1,072,618,270
Revenue - Outpatient					
Gross Outpatient Revenue	$1,549,440,634	$1,448,039,841	$1,327,536,898	$1,216,235,177	$1,103,760,780
Revenue and Expenses - Totals					
(Includes Inpatient and Outpatient)					
Total Gross Revenue.	$2,685,334,172	$2,594,374,401	$2,457,182,962	$2,295,714,935	$2,176,379,050
Deductions from Revenue.	1,386,941,712	1,320,845,075	1,211,190,965	1,180,144,790	1,096,026,956
Net Patient Revenue	1,298,392,460	1,273,529,326	1,245,991,997	1,115,570,145	1,080,352,094
Other Operating Revenue	89,479,580	82,996,786	74,346,388	69,049,844	74,157,196
Other Nonoperating Revenue	60,042,001	38,510,265	4,294,457	26,792,888	19,130,354
Total Net Revenue.	1,447,914,041	1,395,036,377	1,324,632,842	1,211,412,877	1,173,639,644
Total Expenses.	1,309,767,027	1,233,698,322	1,182,216,845	1,046,675,080	1,031,425,657
HOSPITAL UNIT (Excludes Separate Nursing Home Units)					
Utilization - Inpatient					
Beds	1,187	1,292	1,245	1,281	1,303
Admissions	40,698	43,817	43,484	44,155	48,206
Inpatient Days	161,800	177,813	167,355	169,461	196,510
Average Length of Stay.	4	4.1	3.8	3.8	4.1
Personnel					
Total Full Time.	7,510	7,420	7,150	7,004	6,925
Total Part Time	1,808	2,020	1,957	1,888	1,841
Revenue and Expenses - Totals					
(Includes Inpatient and Outpatient)					
Total Net Revenue.	$1,405,149,699	$1,353,272,060	$1,282,240,814	$1,170,074,150	$1,133,360,264
Total Expenses.	1,271,562,455	1,198,106,925	1,141,742,073	1,006,052,821	991,627,019
COMMUNITY HEALTH INDICATORS PER 1000 POPULATION					
Total Population (in thousands)	584	583	576	568	548
Inpatient					
Beds	3.1	3.3	3.3	3.4	3.6
Admissions	70.9	76.5	76.6	80.4	90.8
Inpatient Days	617.3	638.9	650.6	665.7	728.3
Inpatient Surgeries.	19.3	19.6	20.7	22.7	25.9
Births.	11.1	11.0	11.0	11.2	12.6
Outpatient					
Emergency Outpatient Visits	397.6	401.0	398.4	401.5	422.3
Other Outpatient Visits.	1,734.1	1,767.5	1,694.8	1,567.7	1,583.1
Total Outpatient Visits	2,131.7	2,168.5	2,093.3	1,969.3	2,005.4
Outpatient Surgeries	43.5	45.0	48.6	51.1	53.4
Expense per Capita (per person).	$2,242.2	$2,117.4	$2,051.0	$1,842.2	$1,883.4

States

Table 7

The facilities and services presented in Table 7 are listed below in alphabetical order by major heading (where applicable).

2014 Facilities and Services in the U.S. Census Divisions and States

Table 7

These data include only hospital-based facilities and services as reported by responding hospitals in Section C of the 2014 AHA Annual Survey, beginning on page 217. All hospitals are represented with Community Hospitals listed separately under United States. No estimates have been made for nonresponding hospitals. Definitions of facilities and services are listed in the Glossary, page 205.

CLASSIFICATION	HOSPITALS REPORTING	ADULT DAY CARE PROGRAM		AIRBORNE INFECTION ISOLATION ROOM		ALCOHOL/DRUG ABUSE OR DEPENDENCY INPATIENT CARE UNITS		ALCOHOL/DRUG ABUSE OR DEPENDENCY OUTPATIENT SERVICES		ALZHEIMER CENTER		AMBULANCE SERVICE		AMBULATORY SURGERY CENTER		ARTHRITIS TREATMENT CENTER		ASSISTED LIVING	
		Number	Percent	Number	Percent	Number	Percent	Number	Percent	Number	Percent	Number	Percent	Number	Percent	Number	Percent	Number	Percent
UNITED STATES	4,601	172	3.7	3,656	79.5	444	9.7	676	14.7	221	4.8	701	15.2	1,210	26.3	282	6.1	164	3.6
COMMUNITY HOSPITALS	3,921	152	3.9	3,336	85.1	311	7.9	516	13.2	206	5.3	679	17.3	1,156	29.5	266	6.8	152	3.9
CENSUS DIVISION 1, NEW ENGLAND	169	5	3.0	139	82.2	18	10.7	49	29.0	16	9.5	21	12.4	66	39.1	19	11.2	4	2.4
Connecticut	27	1	3.7	23	85.2	3	11.1	14	51.9	4	14.8	3	11.1	14	51.9	6	22.2	1	3.7
Maine	29	1	3.4	24	82.8	5	17.2	11	37.9	4	13.8	7	24.1	10	34.5	0	0.0	2	6.9
Massachusetts	68	2	2.9	51	75.0	6	8.8	19	27.9	5	7.4	6	8.8	24	35.3	8	11.8	0	0.0
New Hampshire	23	1	4.3	22	95.7	1	4.3	1	4.3	1	4.3	3	13.0	7	30.4	3	13.0	0	0.0
Rhode Island	10	0	0.0	10	100.0	0	0.0	2	20.0	1	10.0	1	10.0	7	70.0	0	0.0	0	0.0
Vermont	12	0	0.0	9	75.0	3	25.0	2	16.7	1	8.3	1	8.3	4	33.3	2	16.7	1	8.3
CENSUS DIVISION 2, MIDDLE ATLANTIC	402	34	8.5	331	82.3	62	15.4	96	23.9	36	9.0	76	18.9	176	43.8	56	13.9	9	2.2
New Jersey	68	6	8.8	55	80.9	7	10.3	20	29.4	7	10.3	21	30.9	27	39.7	10	14.7	2	2.9
New York	154	21	13.6	135	87.7	41	26.6	54	35.1	18	11.7	26	16.9	99	64.3	31	20.1	1	0.6
Pennsylvania	180	7	3.9	141	78.3	14	7.8	22	12.2	11	6.1	29	16.1	50	27.8	15	8.3	6	3.3
CENSUS DIVISION 3, SOUTH ATLANTIC	644	17	2.6	544	84.5	65	10.1	103	16.0	33	5.1	85	13.2	168	26.1	44	6.8	14	2.2
Delaware	8	2	25.0	5	62.5	0	0.0	0	0.0	1	12.5	1	12.5	4	50.0	0	0.0	0	0.0
District of Columbia	10	0	0.0	8	80.0	1	10.0	3	30.0	1	10.0	2	20.0	3	30.0	3	30.0	1	10.0
Florida	166	3	1.8	144	86.7	17	10.2	18	10.8	11	6.6	11	6.6	47	28.3	10	6.0	3	1.8
Georgia	96	3	3.1	74	77.1	8	8.3	12	12.5	3	3.1	15	15.6	21	21.9	2	2.1	3	3.1
Maryland	46	3	6.5	40	87.0	4	8.7	17	37.0	6	13.0	3	6.5	14	30.4	9	19.6	2	4.3
North Carolina	110	2	1.8	99	90.0	14	12.7	20	18.2	4	3.6	21	19.1	34	30.9	8	7.3	1	0.9
South Carolina	71	1	1.4	60	84.5	10	14.1	9	12.7	2	2.8	12	16.9	14	19.7	2	2.8	0	0.0
Virginia	76	3	3.9	67	88.2	7	9.2	17	22.4	4	5.3	13	17.1	24	31.6	6	7.9	3	3.9
West Virginia	61	0	0.0	47	77.0	4	6.6	7	11.5	1	1.6	7	11.5	7	11.5	4	6.6	1	1.6
CENSUS DIVISION 4, EAST NORTH CENTRAL	699	28	4.0	591	84.5	90	12.9	160	22.9	63	9.0	100	14.3	215	30.8	65	9.3	25	3.6
Illinois	162	12	7.4	141	87.0	15	9.3	39	24.1	8	4.9	19	11.7	39	24.1	14	8.6	4	2.5
Indiana	123	0	0.0	96	78.0	14	11.4	26	21.1	4	3.3	25	20.3	34	27.6	4	3.3	5	4.1
Michigan	130	2	1.5	113	86.9	18	13.8	28	21.5	13	10.0	18	13.8	34	26.2	14	10.8	2	1.5
Ohio	141	3	2.1	124	87.9	14	9.9	32	22.7	10	7.1	27	19.1	51	36.2	15	10.6	2	1.4
Wisconsin	143	11	7.7	117	81.8	29	20.3	35	24.5	28	19.6	11	7.7	57	39.9	18	12.6	12	8.4
CENSUS DIVISION 5, EAST SOUTH CENTRAL	377	10	2.7	268	71.1	36	9.5	34	9.0	8	2.1	53	14.1	76	20.2	8	2.1	7	1.9
Alabama	103	2	1.9	67	65.0	7	6.8	7	6.8	1	1.0	10	9.7	19	18.4	2	1.9	1	1.0
Kentucky	89	4	4.5	71	79.8	5	5.6	10	11.2	1	1.1	9	10.1	20	22.5	1	1.1	1	1.1
Mississippi	111	2	1.8	70	63.1	16	14.4	6	5.4	2	1.8	18	16.2	20	18.0	0	0.0	3	2.7
Tennessee	74	2	2.7	60	81.1	8	10.8	11	14.9	4	5.4	16	21.6	17	23.0	5	6.8	2	2.7
CENSUS DIVISION 6, WEST NORTH CENTRAL	648	31	4.8	486	75.0	67	10.3	76	11.7	29	4.5	161	24.8	123	19.0	35	5.4	60	9.3
Iowa	126	3	2.4	90	71.4	13	10.3	19	15.1	4	3.2	54	42.9	28	22.2	3	2.4	9	7.1
Kansas	151	9	6.0	108	71.5	6	4.0	4	2.6	3	2.0	21	13.9	15	9.9	4	2.6	12	7.9
Minnesota	106	10	9.4	82	77.4	11	10.4	18	17.0	8	7.5	33	31.1	27	25.5	7	6.6	17	16.0
Missouri	146	2	1.4	120	82.2	25	17.1	21	14.4	6	4.1	26	17.8	23	15.8	11	7.5	2	1.4
Nebraska	49	1	2.0	38	77.6	6	12.2	5	10.2	3	6.1	8	16.3	15	30.6	4	8.2	6	12.2
North Dakota	28	1	3.6	18	64.3	5	17.9	3	10.7	1	3.6	9	32.1	6	21.4	5	17.9	3	10.7
South Dakota	42	5	11.9	30	71.4	1	2.4	6	14.3	4	9.5	10	23.8	9	21.4	1	2.4	11	26.2
CENSUS DIVISION 7, WEST SOUTH CENTRAL	892	4	0.4	696	78.0	51	5.7	56	6.3	6	0.7	102	11.4	135	15.1	14	1.6	18	2.0
Arkansas	86	2	2.3	67	77.9	5	3.5	7	8.1	0	0.0	12	14.0	14	16.3	2	2.3	1	1.2
Louisiana	97	0	0.0	67	69.1	11	11.3	6	6.2	2	2.1	8	8.2	19	19.6	4	4.1	2	2.1
Oklahoma	127	0	0.0	96	75.6	5	3.9	9	7.1	0	0.0	14	11.0	27	21.3	1	0.8	3	2.4
Texas	582	2	0.3	466	80.1	32	5.5	34	5.8	4	0.7	68	11.7	75	12.9	7	1.2	12	2.1
CENSUS DIVISION 8, MOUNTAIN	342	22	6.4	257	75.1	23	6.7	44	12.9	16	4.7	68	19.9	96	28.1	16	4.7	19	5.6
Arizona	69	0	0.0	52	75.4	5	7.2	10	14.5	3	4.3	2	2.9	14	20.3	3	4.3	0	0.0
Colorado	74	3	4.1	60	81.1	5	6.8	8	10.8	3	4.1	16	21.6	20	27.0	4	5.4	4	5.4
Idaho	28	4	14.3	21	75.0	3	10.7	6	21.4	1	3.6	10	35.7	11	39.3	3	10.7	2	7.1
Montana	51	13	25.5	38	74.5	3	5.9	4	7.8	4	7.8	15	29.4	11	21.6	2	3.9	10	19.6
Nevada	27	0	0.0	15	55.6	2	7.4	4	14.8	0	0.0	2	7.4	8	29.6	0	0.0	1	3.7
New Mexico	33	0	0.0	26	78.8	1	3.0	3	9.1	0	0.0	7	21.2	13	39.4	2	6.1	0	0.0
Utah	34	1	2.9	26	76.5	3	8.8	4	11.8	2	5.9	6	17.6	16	47.1	2	5.9	2	6.1
Wyoming	26	1	3.8	19	73.1	1	3.8	5	19.2	3	11.5	10	38.5	3	11.5	0	0.0	2	7.7
CENSUS DIVISION 9, PACIFIC	428	21	4.9	344	80.4	32	7.5	58	13.6	14	3.3	35	8.2	155	36.2	25	5.8	8	1.9
Alaska	12	0	0.0	9	75.0	2	16.7	3	25.0	0	0.0	0	0.0	2	16.7	0	0.0	0	0.0
California	264	15	5.7	211	79.9	22	8.3	41	15.5	13	4.9	20	7.6	110	41.7	17	6.4	1	0.4
Hawaii	19	0	0.0	13	68.4	2	10.5	1	5.3	0	0.0	1	5.3	5	26.3	0	0.0	0	0.0
Oregon	61	3	4.9	54	88.5	2	3.3	6	9.8	1	1.6	8	13.1	13	21.3	4	6.6	3	4.9
Washington	72	3	4.2	57	79.2	4	5.6	7	9.7	0	0.0	6	8.3	25	34.7	4	5.6	4	5.6

Table 7 (Continued)

These data include only hospital-based facilities and services as reported by responding hospitals in Section C of the 2014 AHA Annual Survey, beginning on page 217. All hospitals are represented with Community Hospitals listed separately under United States. No estimates have been made for nonresponding hospitals. Definitions of facilities and services are listed in the Glossary, page 205.

CLASSIFICATION	HOSPITALS REPORTING	AUXILIARY Number	AUXILIARY Percent	BARIATRIC/WEIGHT CONTROL SERVICES Number	BARIATRIC/WEIGHT CONTROL SERVICES Percent	BIRTHING/LDR/LDRP ROOM Number	BIRTHING/LDR/LDRP ROOM Percent	BLOOD DONOR CENTER Number	BLOOD DONOR CENTER Percent	BREAST CANCER SCREENING Number	BREAST CANCER SCREENING Percent	BURN CARE UNITS Number	BURN CARE UNITS Percent	CASE MANAGEMENT Number	CASE MANAGEMENT Percent	CHAPLAINCY/PASTORAL CARE SERVICES Number	CHAPLAINCY/PASTORAL CARE SERVICES Percent	CHEMOTHERAPY Number	CHEMOTHERAPY Percent
UNITED STATES	4,601	2,577	56.0	1,190	25.9	2,453	53.3	291	6.3	3,205	69.7	179	3.9	4,027	87.5	3,022	65.7	2,345	51.0
COMMUNITY HOSPITALS	3,921	2,515	64.1	1,121	28.6	2,419	61.7	281	7.2	3,118	79.5	174	4.4	3,560	90.8	2,753	70.2	2,262	57.7
CENSUS DIVISION 1, NEW ENGLAND	169	97	57.4	66	39.1	113	66.9	29	17.2	134	79.3	11	6.5	163	96.4	133	78.7	121	71.6
Connecticut	27	17	63.0	18	66.7	21	77.8	5	18.5	22	81.5	1	3.7	26	96.3	25	92.6	20	74.1
Maine	29	19	65.5	8	27.6	24	82.8	0	0.0	27	93.1	2	6.9	29	100.0	21	72.4	23	79.3
Massachusetts	68	30	44.1	28	41.2	37	54.4	20	29.4	48	70.6	6	8.8	63	92.6	52	76.5	45	66.2
New Hampshire	23	15	65.2	7	30.4	16	69.6	4	17.4	19	82.6	0	0.0	23	100.0	17	73.9	16	69.6
Rhode Island	10	7	70.0	3	30.0	6	60.0	0	0.0	8	80.0	1	10.0	10	100.0	8	80.0	9	90.0
Vermont	12	9	75.0	2	16.7	9	75.0	0	0.0	10	83.3	1	8.3	12	100.0	10	83.3	8	66.7
CENSUS DIVISION 2, MIDDLE ATLANTIC	402	251	62.4	178	44.3	231	57.5	64	15.9	318	79.1	24	6.0	372	92.5	314	78.1	266	66.2
New Jersey	68	48	70.6	41	60.3	43	63.2	12	17.6	52	76.5	4	5.9	64	94.1	59	86.8	50	73.5
New York	154	106	68.8	69	44.8	104	67.5	34	22.1	136	88.3	11	7.1	149	96.8	129	83.8	113	73.4
Pennsylvania	180	97	53.9	68	37.8	84	46.7	18	10.0	130	72.2	9	5.0	159	88.3	126	70.0	103	57.2
CENSUS DIVISION 3, SOUTH ATLANTIC	644	394	61.2	185	28.7	343	53.3	48	7.5	486	75.5	24	3.7	585	90.8	503	78.1	360	55.9
Delaware	8	4	50.0	5	62.5	4	50.0	0	0.0	4	50.0	0	0.0	6	75.0	6	75.0	5	62.5
District of Columbia	10	3	30.0	6	60.0	6	60.0	2	20.0	6	60.0	1	10.0	9	90.0	9	90.0	7	70.0
Florida	166	97	58.4	55	33.1	72	43.4	9	5.4	114	68.7	9	5.4	156	94.0	126	75.9	101	60.8
Georgia	96	67	69.8	24	25.0	49	51.0	2	2.1	79	82.3	2	2.1	87	90.6	70	72.9	44	45.8
Maryland	46	38	82.6	16	34.8	30	65.2	14	30.4	33	71.7	3	6.4	41	89.1	43	93.5	38	82.6
North Carolina	110	64	58.2	33	30.0	75	68.2	7	6.4	90	81.8	3	2.7	102	92.7	93	84.5	66	60.0
South Carolina	71	40	56.3	12	16.9	40	56.3	5	7.0	53	74.6	2	2.8	63	88.7	47	66.2	27	38.0
Virginia	76	46	60.5	23	30.3	41	53.9	8	10.5	61	80.3	5	5.3	70	92.1	64	84.2	46	60.5
West Virginia	61	35	57.4	11	18.0	26	42.6	1	1.6	46	75.4	1	1.6	51	83.6	45	73.8	26	42.6
CENSUS DIVISION 4, EAST NORTH CENTRAL	699	434	62.1	194	27.8	434	62.1	38	5.4	575	82.3	32	4.6	642	91.8	522	74.7	444	63.5
Illinois	162	108	66.7	51	31.5	103	63.6	12	7.4	143	88.3	7	4.3	155	95.7	130	80.2	114	70.4
Indiana	123	59	48.0	26	21.1	75	61.0	3	2.4	94	76.4	4	3.3	112	91.1	93	75.6	65	52.8
Michigan	130	93	71.5	50	38.5	74	56.9	8	6.2	109	83.8	7	5.4	114	87.7	96	73.8	89	68.5
Ohio	141	94	66.7	39	27.7	89	63.1	12	8.5	119	84.4	8	5.7	133	94.3	116	82.3	100	70.9
Wisconsin	143	80	55.9	28	19.6	93	65.0	3	2.1	110	76.9	6	4.2	128	89.5	87	60.8	76	53.1
CENSUS DIVISION 5, EAST SOUTH CENTRAL	377	176	46.7	79	21.0	166	44.0	9	2.4	248	65.8	10	2.7	318	84.4	229	60.7	130	34.5
Alabama	103	50	48.5	25	24.3	48	46.6	4	3.9	64	62.1	4	3.9	88	85.4	58	56.3	32	31.1
Kentucky	89	53	59.6	24	27.0	40	44.9	4	4.5	71	79.8	3	3.4	83	93.3	69	77.5	42	47.2
Mississippi	111	35	31.5	15	13.5	43	38.7	0	0.0	58	52.3	1	0.9	77	69.4	40	36.0	21	18.9
Tennessee	74	38	51.4	15	20.3	35	47.3	1	1.4	55	74.3	2	2.7	70	94.6	62	83.8	35	47.3
CENSUS DIVISION 6, WEST NORTH CENTRAL	648	417	64.4	125	19.3	350	54.0	19	2.9	477	73.6	34	5.2	501	77.3	351	54.2	356	54.9
Iowa	126	107	84.9	18	14.3	77	61.1	2	1.6	113	89.7	7	5.6	106	84.1	55	43.7	84	66.7
Kansas	151	76	50.3	20	13.2	68	45.0	0	0.0	82	54.3	7	4.6	99	65.6	68	45.0	51	33.8
Minnesota	106	76	71.7	32	30.2	77	72.6	5	4.7	92	86.8	3	2.8	84	79.2	63	59.4	76	71.7
Missouri	146	98	67.1	30	20.5	68	46.6	8	5.5	103	70.5	9	6.2	129	88.4	101	69.2	74	50.7
Nebraska	49	24	49.0	13	26.5	34	69.4	0	0.0	42	85.7	5	10.2	38	77.6	30	61.2	35	71.4
North Dakota	28	15	53.6	7	25.0	10	35.7	2	7.1	17	60.7	3	10.7	22	78.6	17	60.7	12	42.9
South Dakota	42	21	50.0	5	11.9	16	38.1	2	4.8	28	66.7	0	0.0	23	54.8	17	40.5	24	57.1
CENSUS DIVISION 7, WEST SOUTH CENTRAL	892	392	43.9	176	19.7	339	38.0	27	3.0	422	47.3	16	1.8	763	85.5	452	50.7	235	26.3
Arkansas	86	56	65.1	15	17.4	33	38.4	2	2.3	47	54.7	1	1.2	73	84.9	39	45.3	26	30.2
Louisiana	97	36	37.1	23	23.7	38	39.2	5	5.2	58	59.8	3	3.1	85	87.6	54	55.7	35	36.1
Oklahoma	127	64	50.4	16	12.6	52	40.9	5	3.9	68	53.5	2	1.6	107	84.3	72	56.7	30	23.6
Texas	582	236	40.5	122	21.0	216	37.1	15	2.6	249	42.8	10	1.7	498	85.6	287	49.3	144	24.7
CENSUS DIVISION 8, MOUNTAIN	342	180	52.6	68	19.9	202	59.1	14	4.1	229	67.0	9	2.6	292	85.4	190	55.6	175	51.2
Arizona	69	29	42.0	13	18.8	34	49.3	1	1.4	39	56.5	3	4.3	67	97.1	47	68.1	35	50.7
Colorado	74	44	59.5	23	31.1	46	62.2	8	10.8	56	75.7	1	1.4	65	87.8	47	63.5	46	62.2
Idaho	28	22	78.6	7	25.0	18	64.3	2	7.1	18	64.3	1	3.6	22	78.6	16	57.1	14	50.0
Montana	51	29	56.9	4	7.8	27	52.9	0	0.0	32	62.7	0	0.0	33	64.7	19	37.3	23	45.1
Nevada	27	8	29.6	4	14.8	10	37.0	0	0.0	14	51.9	0	0.0	25	92.6	13	48.1	12	44.4
New Mexico	33	18	54.5	3	9.1	21	63.6	1	3.0	23	69.7	3	9.1	30	90.9	23	69.7	13	39.4
Utah	34	15	44.1	10	29.4	28	82.4	1	2.9	29	85.3	1	2.9	29	85.3	13	38.2	18	52.9
Wyoming	26	15	57.7	4	15.4	18	69.2	1	3.8	18	69.2	0	0.0	21	80.8	12	46.2	14	53.8
CENSUS DIVISION 9, PACIFIC	428	236	55.1	119	27.8	275	64.3	43	10.0	316	73.8	19	4.4	391	91.4	328	76.6	258	60.3
Alaska	12	3	25.0	1	8.3	8	66.7	0	0.0	8	66.7	0	0.0	9	75.0	8	66.7	7	58.3
California	264	144	54.5	81	30.7	164	62.1	41	15.5	189	71.6	14	5.3	244	92.4	204	77.3	160	60.6
Hawaii	19	6	31.6	6	31.6	8	42.1	1	5.3	13	68.4	2	10.5	16	84.2	8	42.1	11	57.9
Oregon	61	45	73.8	14	23.0	50	82.0	1	1.6	54	88.5	2	3.3	58	95.1	51	83.6	40	65.6
Washington	72	38	52.8	17	23.6	45	62.5	0	0.0	52	72.2	1	1.4	64	88.9	57	79.2	40	55.6

Table 7 (Continued)

These data include only hospital-based facilities and services as reported by responding hospitals in Section C of the 2014 AHA Annual Survey, beginning on page 217. All hospitals are represented with Community Hospitals listed separately under United States. No estimates have been made for nonresponding hospitals. Definitions of facilities and services are listed in the Glossary, page 205.

CLASSIFICATION	HOSPITALS REPORTING	CHILDREN'S WELLNESS PROGRAM Number	Percent	CHIROPRACTIC SERVICES Number	Percent	COMMUNITY OUTREACH Number	Percent	COMPLEMENTARY AND ALTERNATIVE MEDICINE SERVICES Number	Percent	COMPUTER ASSISTED ORTHOPEDIC SURGERY (CAOS) Number	Percent	CRISIS PREVENTION Number	Percent	DENTAL SERVICES Number	Percent	ENABLING SERVICES Number	Percent	ENROLLMENT ASSISTANCE SERVICES Number	Percent	EXTRACORPOREAL SHOCK WAVE LITHOTRIPTER (ESWL) Number	Percent
UNITED STATES	4,601	896	19.5	136	3.0	3,176	69.0	923	20.1	722	15.7	1,042	22.6	935	20.3	1,231	26.8	2,651	57.6	1,258	27.3
COMMUNITY HOSPITALS	3,921	865	22.1	101	2.6	2,957	75.4	862	22.0	703	17.9	901	23.0	808	20.6	1,150	29.3	2,485	63.4	1,202	30.7
CENSUS DIVISION 1, NEW ENGLAND	169	62	36.7	6	3.6	141	83.4	82	48.5	36	21.3	66	39.1	49	29.0	78	46.2	137	81.1	89	52.7
Connecticut	27	10	37.0	0	0.0	24	88.9	19	70.4	8	29.6	18	66.7	14	51.9	14	51.9	23	85.2	18	66.7
Maine	29	10	34.5	0	0.0	25	86.2	14	48.3	3	10.3	7	24.1	5	17.2	13	44.8	21	72.4	13	44.8
Massachusetts	68	25	36.8	3	4.4	53	77.9	26	38.2	13	19.1	25	36.8	14	20.6	25	36.8	56	82.4	34	50.0
New Hampshire	23	12	52.2	1	4.3	20	87.0	14	60.9	8	34.8	7	30.4	10	43.5	11	47.8	19	82.6	10	43.5
Rhode Island	10	2	20.0	1	10.0	10	100.0	3	30.0	2	20.0	6	60.0	2	20.0	8	80.0	9	90.0	7	70.0
Vermont	12	3	25.0	1	8.3	9	75.0	6	50.0	2	16.7	3	25.0	4	33.3	7	58.3	9	75.0	7	58.3
CENSUS DIVISION 2, MIDDLE ATLANTIC	402	138	34.3	22	5.5	320	79.6	124	30.8	89	22.1	167	41.5	159	39.6	167	41.5	283	70.4	151	37.6
New Jersey	68	32	47.1	3	4.4	55	80.9	28	41.2	19	27.9	40	58.8	28	41.2	35	51.5	53	77.9	23	33.8
New York	154	62	40.3	13	8.4	135	87.7	54	35.1	38	24.7	79	51.3	77	50.0	62	40.3	119	77.3	65	42.2
Pennsylvania	180	44	24.4	6	3.3	130	72.2	42	23.3	32	17.8	48	26.7	54	30.0	70	38.9	111	61.7	63	35.0
CENSUS DIVISION 3, SOUTH ATLANTIC	644	111	17.2	15	2.3	477	74.1	130	20.2	133	20.7	146	22.7	156	24.2	207	32.1	405	62.9	220	34.2
Delaware	8	5	62.5	0	0.0	5	62.5	3	37.5	3	37.5	3	37.5	3	37.5	3	37.5	5	62.5	3	37.5
District of Columbia	10	4	40.0	0	0.0	9	90.0	5	50.0	2	20.0	3	30.0	5	50.0	6	60.0	7	70.0	3	30.0
Florida	166	18	10.8	6	3.6	113	68.1	27	16.3	42	25.3	34	20.5	25	15.1	46	27.7	98	59.0	74	44.6
Georgia	96	10	10.4	3	3.1	69	71.9	17	17.7	21	21.9	18	18.8	16	16.7	26	27.1	61	63.5	31	32.3
Maryland	46	17	37.0	1	2.2	41	89.1	24	52.2	13	28.3	21	45.7	21	45.7	28	60.9	38	82.6	26	56.5
North Carolina	110	19	17.3	1	0.9	85	77.3	19	17.3	17	15.5	22	20.0	33	30.0	34	30.9	65	59.1	18	16.4
South Carolina	71	14	19.7	0	0.0	55	77.5	3	4.2	9	12.7	7	9.9	15	21.1	9	12.7	37	52.1	21	29.6
Virginia	76	11	14.5	2	2.6	56	73.7	26	34.2	22	28.9	25	32.9	24	31.6	41	53.9	59	77.6	27	35.5
West Virginia	61	13	21.3	2	3.3	44	72.1	6	9.8	4	6.6	13	21.3	14	23.0	14	23.0	35	57.4	16	26.2
CENSUS DIVISION 4, EAST NORTH CENTRAL	699	196	28.0	29	4.1	560	80.1	227	32.5	128	18.3	214	30.6	144	20.6	262	37.5	490	70.1	218	31.2
Illinois	162	50	30.9	7	4.3	134	82.7	46	28.4	41	25.3	66	40.7	44	27.2	59	36.4	112	69.1	42	25.9
Indiana	123	31	25.2	4	3.3	99	80.5	29	23.6	13	10.6	28	22.8	22	17.9	27	22.0	82	66.7	30	24.4
Michigan	130	46	35.4	4	3.1	110	84.6	46	35.4	17	13.1	41	31.5	32	24.6	62	47.7	102	78.5	46	35.4
Ohio	141	32	22.7	11	7.8	116	82.3	48	34.0	31	22.0	45	31.9	46	32.6	58	41.1	103	73.0	62	44.0
Wisconsin	143	37	25.9	3	2.1	101	70.6	58	40.6	26	18.2	34	23.8	0	0.0	56	39.2	91	63.6	38	26.6
CENSUS DIVISION 5, EAST SOUTH CENTRAL	377	46	12.2	6	1.6	238	63.1	22	5.8	41	10.9	52	13.8	66	17.5	61	16.2	161	42.7	88	23.3
Alabama	103	9	8.7	3	2.9	53	51.5	0	0.0	9	8.7	9	8.7	6	5.8	8	7.8	48	46.6	26	25.2
Kentucky	89	12	13.5	1	1.1	63	70.8	11	12.4	12	13.5	12	13.5	17	19.1	20	22.5	51	57.3	24	27.0
Mississippi	111	15	13.5	2	1.8	66	59.5	4	3.6	9	8.1	10	9.0	29	26.1	9	8.1	26	23.4	16	14.4
Tennessee	74	10	13.5	0	0.0	56	75.7	7	9.5	11	14.9	21	28.4	14	18.9	24	32.4	36	48.6	22	29.7
CENSUS DIVISION 6, WEST NORTH CENTRAL	648	109	16.8	26	4.0	419	64.7	114	17.6	54	8.3	126	19.4	106	16.4	137	21.1	332	51.2	106	16.4
Iowa	126	25	19.8	3	2.4	94	74.6	27	21.4	11	8.7	31	24.6	21	16.7	33	26.2	84	66.7	13	10.3
Kansas	151	11	7.3	11	7.3	65	43.0	7	4.6	7	4.6	8	5.3	14	9.3	12	7.9	55	36.4	20	13.2
Minnesota	106	22	20.8	11	10.4	80	75.5	31	29.2	10	9.4	25	23.6	17	16.0	20	18.9	58	54.7	19	17.9
Missouri	146	29	19.9	6	4.1	96	65.8	26	17.8	12	8.2	35	24.0	40	27.4	48	32.9	82	56.2	37	25.3
Nebraska	49	10	20.4	0	0.0	39	79.6	10	20.4	9	18.4	13	26.5	5	10.2	13	26.5	25	51.0	9	18.4
North Dakota	28	6	21.4	4	14.3	18	64.3	6	21.4	3	10.7	7	25.0	2	7.1	6	21.4	16	57.1	4	14.3
South Dakota	42	6	14.3	1	2.4	27	64.3	7	16.7	2	4.8	7	16.7	7	16.7	5	11.9	12	28.6	4	9.5
CENSUS DIVISION 7, WEST SOUTH CENTRAL	892	96	10.8	8	0.9	453	50.8	47	5.3	90	10.1	95	10.7	118	13.2	116	13.0	359	40.2	165	18.5
Arkansas	86	7	8.1	0	0.0	49	57.0	5	5.8	3	3.5	9	10.5	9	10.5	8	9.3	39	45.3	14	16.3
Louisiana	97	19	19.6	2	2.1	56	57.7	7	7.2	12	12.4	23	23.7	17	17.5	17	17.5	53	54.6	15	15.5
Oklahoma	127	12	9.4	2	1.6	67	52.8	5	3.9	9	7.1	12	9.4	18	14.2	8	6.3	44	34.6	24	18.9
Texas	582	58	10.0	4	0.7	281	48.3	30	5.2	66	11.3	51	8.8	74	12.7	83	14.3	223	38.3	112	19.2
CENSUS DIVISION 8, MOUNTAIN	342	65	19.0	11	3.2	230	67.3	76	22.2	52	15.2	79	23.1	65	19.0	78	22.8	202	59.1	80	23.4
Arizona	69	16	23.2	3	4.3	42	60.9	24	34.8	19	27.5	13	18.8	14	20.3	23	33.3	42	60.9	25	36.2
Colorado	74	10	13.5	4	5.4	57	77.0	25	33.8	12	16.2	15	20.3	12	16.2	20	27.0	47	63.5	13	17.6
Idaho	28	6	21.4	2	7.1	21	75.0	5	17.9	8	28.6	5	17.9	8	28.6	6	21.4	14	50.0	3	10.7
Montana	51	9	17.6	1	2.0	32	62.7	10	19.6	0	0.0	10	19.6	4	7.8	5	9.8	31	60.8	7	13.7
Nevada	27	6	22.2	0	0.0	15	55.6	1	3.7	4	14.8	5	18.5	3	11.1	5	18.5	13	48.1	4	14.8
New Mexico	33	6	18.2	0	0.0	22	66.7	2	6.1	0	0.0	6	18.2	9	27.3	4	12.1	21	63.6	10	30.3
Utah	34	8	23.5	1	2.9	25	73.5	6	17.6	6	17.6	17	50.0	12	35.3	11	32.4	20	58.8	13	38.2
Wyoming	26	4	15.4	0	0.0	16	61.5	3	11.5	1	3.8	8	30.8	3	11.5	4	15.4	14	53.8	5	19.2
CENSUS DIVISION 9, PACIFIC	428	73	17.1	13	3.0	338	79.0	101	23.6	99	23.1	97	22.7	72	16.8	125	29.2	282	65.9	141	32.9
Alaska	12	1	8.3	1	8.3	7	58.3	2	16.7	0	0.0	3	25.0	3	25.0	1	8.3	7	58.3	2	16.7
California	264	42	15.9	8	3.0	208	78.8	63	23.9	64	24.2	53	20.1	54	20.5	72	27.3	171	64.8	92	34.8
Hawaii	19	3	15.8	1	5.3	13	68.4	4	21.1	2	10.5	3	15.8	3	15.8	7	36.8	9	47.4	4	21.1
Oregon	61	12	19.7	1	1.6	55	90.2	17	27.9	20	32.8	12	19.7	6	9.8	23	37.7	44	72.1	21	34.4
Washington	72	15	20.8	2	2.8	55	76.4	15	20.8	13	18.1	26	36.1	6	8.3	22	30.6	51	70.8	22	30.6

Table 7 (Continued)

These data include only hospital-based facilities and services as reported by responding hospitals in Section C of the 2014 AHA Annual Survey, beginning on page 217. All hospitals are represented with Community Hospitals listed separately under United States. No estimates have been made for nonresponding hospitals. Definitions of facilities and services are listed in the Glossary, page 205.

CLASSIFICATION	HOSPITALS REPORTING	FERTILITY CLINIC No.	FERTILITY CLINIC %	FITNESS CENTER No.	FITNESS CENTER %	FREESTANDING OUTPATIENT CARE CENTER No.	%	GENETIC TESTING/COUNSELING No.	%	GERIATRIC SERVICES No.	%	HEALTH FAIR No.	%	COMMUNITY HEALTH EDUCATION No.	%	HEALTH RESEARCH No.	%	HEALTH SCREENINGS No.	%	HEMODIALYSIS No.	%	HIV/AIDS SERVICES No.	%
UNITED STATES	4,601	238	5.2	1,366	29.7	1,477	32.1	755	16.4	1,746	37.9	3,340	72.6	3,502	76.1	1,131	24.6	3,481	75.7	1,403	30.5	1,039	22.6
COMMUNITY HOSPITALS	3,921	233	5.9	1,267	32.3	1,369	34.9	723	18.4	1,589	40.5	3,155	80.5	3,261	83.2	1,043	26.6	3,275	83.5	1,316	33.6	962	24.5
CENSUS DIVISION 1, NEW ENGLAND	169	23	13.6	53	31.4	84	49.7	56	33.1	76	45.0	136	80.5	148	87.6	75	44.4	143	84.6	53	31.4	77	45.6
Connecticut	27	6	22.2	15	55.6	20	74.1	13	48.1	14	51.9	23	85.2	25	92.6	18	66.7	25	92.6	10	37.0	17	63.0
Maine	29	2	6.9	8	27.6	12	41.4	4	13.8	11	37.9	23	79.3	28	96.6	8	27.6	27	93.1	2	6.9	2	6.9
Massachusetts	68	10	14.7	14	20.6	29	42.6	26	38.2	29	42.6	52	76.5	53	77.9	30	44.1	51	75.0	29	42.6	29	42.6
New Hampshire	23	2	8.7	7	30.4	11	47.8	6	26.1	12	52.2	21	91.3	22	95.7	7	30.4	21	91.3	3	13.0	10	43.5
Rhode Island	10	1	10.0	5	50.0	8	80.0	3	30.0	7	70.0	10	100.0	9	90.0	7	70.0	9	90.0	7	70.0	6	60.0
Vermont	12	2	16.7	4	33.3	4	33.3	4	33.3	3	25.0	7	58.3	11	91.7	5	41.7	10	83.3	2	16.7	3	25.0
CENSUS DIVISION 2, MIDDLE ATLANTIC	402	48	11.9	130	32.3	221	55.0	133	33.1	223	55.5	330	82.1	338	84.1	160	39.8	336	83.6	193	48.0	168	41.8
New Jersey	68	10	14.7	22	32.4	42	61.8	31	45.6	47	69.1	53	77.9	56	82.4	39	57.4	54	79.4	46	67.6	35	51.5
New York	154	26	16.9	55	35.7	100	64.9	57	37.0	96	62.3	140	90.9	140	90.9	69	44.8	140	90.9	92	59.7	79	51.3
Pennsylvania	180	12	6.7	53	29.4	79	43.9	45	25.0	80	44.4	137	76.1	142	78.9	52	28.9	142	78.9	55	30.6	54	30.0
CENSUS DIVISION 3, SOUTH ATLANTIC	644	29	4.5	193	30.0	252	39.1	124	19.3	238	37.0	497	77.2	509	79.0	195	30.3	523	81.2	281	43.6	188	29.2
Delaware	8	0	0.0	3	37.5	5	62.5	4	50.0	3	37.5	5	62.5	6	75.0	5	62.5	6	75.0	5	62.5	4	50.0
District of Columbia	10	0	0.0	2	20.0	6	60.0	5	50.0	7	70.0	7	70.0	9	90.0	7	70.0	8	80.0	7	70.0	6	60.0
Florida	166	8	4.8	49	29.5	59	35.5	34	20.5	53	31.9	124	74.7	131	78.9	60	36.1	126	75.9	90	54.2	45	27.1
Georgia	96	2	2.1	24	25.0	39	40.6	14	14.6	29	30.2	73	76.0	71	74.0	25	26.0	81	84.4	40	41.7	23	24.0
Maryland	46	5	10.9	16	34.8	19	41.3	22	47.8	33	71.7	40	87.0	39	84.8	25	54.3	39	84.8	31	67.4	24	52.2
North Carolina	110	7	6.4	39	35.5	44	40.0	17	15.5	43	39.1	85	77.3	89	80.9	26	23.6	94	85.5	32	29.1	25	22.7
South Carolina	71	2	2.8	20	28.2	21	29.6	5	7.0	30	42.3	52	73.2	54	76.1	14	19.7	54	76.1	26	36.6	24	33.8
Virginia	76	3	3.9	18	23.7	41	53.9	18	23.7	23	30.3	60	78.9	62	81.6	24	31.6	61	80.3	32	42.1	25	32.9
West Virginia	61	2	3.3	22	36.1	18	29.5	5	8.2	19	31.1	51	83.6	48	78.7	9	14.8	54	88.5	18	29.5	12	19.7
CENSUS DIVISION 4, EAST NORTH CENTRAL	699	39	5.6	274	39.2	293	41.9	132	18.9	345	49.4	560	80.1	612	87.6	215	30.8	584	83.5	208	29.8	178	25.5
Illinois	162	12	7.4	57	35.2	67	41.4	32	19.8	83	51.2	142	87.7	143	88.3	59	36.4	145	89.5	50	30.9	48	29.6
Indiana	123	4	3.3	41	33.3	46	37.4	18	14.6	39	31.7	95	77.2	101	82.1	28	22.8	96	78.0	30	24.4	22	17.9
Michigan	130	8	6.2	48	36.9	59	45.4	25	19.2	69	53.1	107	82.3	114	87.7	53	40.8	116	89.2	43	33.1	50	38.5
Ohio	141	10	7.1	66	46.8	71	50.4	32	22.7	60	42.6	121	85.8	128	90.8	51	36.2	127	90.1	58	41.1	50	35.5
Wisconsin	143	5	3.5	62	43.4	50	35.0	25	17.5	94	65.7	95	66.4	126	88.1	24	16.8	100	69.9	27	18.9	8	5.6
CENSUS DIVISION 5, EAST SOUTH CENTRAL	377	13	3.4	97	25.7	88	23.3	37	9.8	112	29.7	261	69.2	250	66.3	63	16.7	249	66.0	96	25.5	61	16.2
Alabama	103	4	3.9	29	28.2	21	20.4	6	5.8	31	30.1	70	68.0	58	56.3	16	15.5	65	63.1	34	33.0	12	11.7
Kentucky	89	2	2.2	15	16.9	25	28.1	11	12.4	27	30.3	71	79.8	74	83.1	18	20.2	73	82.0	24	27.0	12	13.5
Mississippi	111	2	1.8	32	28.8	15	13.5	9	8.1	22	19.8	62	55.9	59	53.2	7	6.3	54	48.6	14	12.6	21	18.9
Tennessee	74	5	6.8	21	28.4	27	36.5	11	14.9	32	43.2	58	78.4	59	79.7	22	29.7	57	77.0	24	32.4	16	21.6
CENSUS DIVISION 6, WEST NORTH CENTRAL	648	27	4.2	233	36.0	118	18.2	69	10.6	255	39.4	463	71.5	502	77.5	97	15.0	523	80.7	135	20.8	105	16.2
Iowa	126	3	2.4	49	38.9	20	15.9	11	8.7	57	45.2	106	84.1	112	88.9	14	11.1	118	93.7	19	15.1	22	17.5
Kansas	151	3	2.0	41	27.2	15	9.9	11	7.3	49	32.5	84	55.6	81	53.6	10	6.6	89	58.9	18	11.9	18	11.9
Minnesota	106	7	6.6	41	38.7	22	20.8	17	16.0	49	46.2	75	70.8	91	85.8	18	17.0	90	84.9	21	19.8	21	19.8
Missouri	146	9	6.2	53	36.3	40	27.4	19	13.0	55	37.7	109	74.7	116	79.5	34	23.3	119	81.5	49	33.6	28	19.2
Nebraska	49	2	2.0	23	46.9	11	22.4	6	12.2	18	36.7	35	71.4	41	83.7	11	22.4	42	85.7	12	24.5	6	12.2
North Dakota	28	3	10.7	9	32.1	4	14.3	3	10.7	15	53.6	20	71.4	24	85.7	6	21.4	23	82.1	7	25.0	5	17.9
South Dakota	42	1	2.4	17	40.5	6	14.3	2	4.8	12	28.6	34	81.0	37	88.1	4	9.5	42	100.0	9	21.4	4	9.5
CENSUS DIVISION 7, WEST SOUTH CENTRAL	892	21	2.4	191	21.4	182	20.4	66	7.4	229	25.7	536	60.1	546	61.2	110	12.3	541	60.7	190	21.3	96	10.8
Arkansas	86	1	1.2	21	24.4	13	15.1	4	4.7	25	29.1	63	73.3	55	64.0	9	10.5	64	74.4	15	17.4	10	11.6
Louisiana	97	4	4.1	19	19.6	31	32.0	11	11.3	35	36.1	65	67.0	69	71.1	21	21.6	62	63.9	24	24.7	18	18.6
Oklahoma	127	2	1.6	23	18.1	16	12.6	8	6.3	22	17.3	73	57.5	83	65.4	15	11.8	80	63.0	24	18.9	10	7.9
Texas	582	14	2.4	128	22.0	122	21.0	43	7.4	147	25.3	335	57.6	339	58.2	65	11.2	335	57.6	127	21.8	58	10.0
CENSUS DIVISION 8, MOUNTAIN	342	13	3.8	94	27.5	96	28.1	48	14.0	116	33.9	249	72.8	261	76.3	69	20.2	261	76.3	88	25.7	62	18.1
Arizona	69	2	2.9	21	30.4	18	26.1	9	13.0	17	24.6	44	63.8	56	81.2	22	31.9	48	69.6	28	40.6	20	29.0
Colorado	74	4	5.4	27	36.5	29	39.2	22	29.7	21	28.4	52	70.3	62	83.8	22	29.7	56	75.7	21	28.4	15	20.3
Idaho	28	1	3.6	9	32.1	9	32.1	3	10.7	12	42.9	24	85.7	22	78.6	5	17.9	23	82.1	6	21.4	4	14.3
Montana	51	1	2.0	11	21.6	10	19.6	5	9.8	27	52.9	45	88.2	38	74.5	6	11.8	46	90.2	4	7.8	7	13.7
Nevada	27	0	0.0	1	3.7	6	22.2	0	0.0	7	25.9	13	48.1	15	55.6	5	18.5	14	51.9	4	14.8	3	11.1
New Mexico	33	1	3.0	8	24.2	8	24.2	1	3.0	9	27.3	24	72.7	20	60.6	3	9.1	25	75.8	7	21.2	5	15.2
Utah	34	4	11.8	13	38.2	13	38.2	8	23.5	13	38.2	27	79.4	29	85.3	8	23.5	27	79.4	12	35.3	6	17.6
Wyoming	26	0	0.0	4	15.4	3	11.5	0	0.0	10	38.5	20	76.9	19	73.1	0	0.0	22	84.6	6	23.1	2	7.7
CENSUS DIVISION 9, PACIFIC	428	25	5.8	101	23.6	143	33.4	90	21.0	152	35.5	308	72.0	336	78.5	147	34.3	321	75.0	159	37.1	104	24.3
Alaska	12	0	0.0	2	16.7	1	8.3	2	16.7	4	33.3	9	75.0	9	75.0	2	16.7	8	66.7	2	16.7	1	8.3
California	264	19	7.2	65	24.6	99	37.5	64	24.2	101	38.3	184	69.7	199	75.4	97	36.7	194	73.5	113	42.8	74	28.0
Hawaii	19	1	5.3	3	15.8	4	21.1	3	15.8	5	26.3	10	52.6	13	68.4	8	42.1	12	63.2	5	26.3	2	10.5
Oregon	61	1	1.6	20	32.8	22	36.1	6	9.8	22	36.1	50	82.0	55	90.2	15	24.6	52	85.2	16	26.2	13	21.3
Washington	72	4	5.6	11	15.3	17	23.6	15	20.8	20	27.8	55	76.4	60	83.3	25	34.7	55	76.4	23	31.9	14	19.4

Table 7 (Continued)

These data include only hospital-based facilities and services as reported by responding hospitals in Section C of the 2014 AHA Annual Survey, beginning on page 217. All hospitals are represented with Community Hospitals listed separately under United States. No estimates have been made for nonresponding hospitals. Definitions of facilities and services are listed in the Glossary, page 205.

CLASSIFICATION	HOSPITALS REPORTING	HOME HEALTH SERVICES Number	HOME HEALTH SERVICES Percent	HOSPICE Number	HOSPICE Percent	HOSPITAL-BASED OUTPATIENT CARE CENTER SERVICES Number	HOSPITAL-BASED OUTPATIENT CARE CENTER SERVICES Percent	IMMUNIZATION PROGRAM Number	IMMUNIZATION PROGRAM Percent	INDIGENT CARE CLINIC Number	INDIGENT CARE CLINIC Percent	LINGUISTIC/TRANSLATION SERVICES Number	LINGUISTIC/TRANSLATION SERVICES Percent	MEALS ON WHEELS Number	MEALS ON WHEELS Percent	MOBILE HEALTH SERVICES Number	MOBILE HEALTH SERVICES Percent	NEONATAL INTERMEDIATE CARE UNITS Number	NEONATAL INTERMEDIATE CARE UNITS Percent	NEUROLOGICAL SERVICES Number	NEUROLOGICAL SERVICES Percent	NUTRITION PROGRAMS CENTER Number	NUTRITION PROGRAMS CENTER Percent
UNITED STATES	4,601	1,143	24.8	928	20.2	3,368	73.2	1,908	41.5	776	16.9	2,544	55.3	373	8.1	520	11.3	708	15.4	2,251	48.9	3,371	73.3
COMMUNITY HOSPITALS	3,921	1,088	27.7	869	22.2	3,130	79.8	1,770	45.1	742	18.9	2,339	59.7	363	9.3	483	12.3	700	17.9	2,104	53.7	3,073	78.4
CENSUS DIVISION 1, NEW ENGLAND	169	24	14.2	40	23.7	149	88.2	102	60.4	48	28.4	120	71.0	6	3.6	23	13.6	26	15.4	119	70.4	155	91.7
Connecticut	27	2	7.4	12	44.4	25	92.6	15	55.6	14	51.9	20	74.1	1	3.7	7	25.9	5	18.5	25	92.6	25	92.6
Maine	29	3	10.3	2	6.9	25	86.2	22	75.9	9	31.0	16	55.2	1	3.4	2	6.9	3	10.3	13	44.8	29	100.0
Massachusetts	68	13	19.1	12	17.6	58	85.3	38	55.9	12	17.6	55	80.9	1	1.5	8	11.8	13	19.1	48	70.6	60	88.2
New Hampshire	23	4	17.4	7	30.4	22	95.7	13	56.5	7	30.4	14	60.9	1	4.3	3	13.0	2	8.7	17	73.9	22	95.7
Rhode Island	10	2	20.0	3	30.0	10	100.0	8	80.0	4	40.0	9	90.0	0	0.0	2	20.0	1	10.0	9	90.0	9	90.0
Vermont	12	0	0.0	4	33.3	9	75.0	6	50.0	2	16.7	6	50.0	2	16.7	1	8.3	2	16.7	7	58.3	10	83.3
CENSUS DIVISION 2, MIDDLE ATLANTIC	402	107	26.6	111	27.6	325	80.8	222	55.2	152	37.8	257	63.9	35	8.7	78	19.4	119	29.6	282	70.1	333	82.8
New Jersey	68	17	25.0	21	30.9	58	85.3	38	55.9	42	61.8	49	72.1	11	16.2	25	36.8	39	57.4	57	83.8	59	86.8
New York	154	40	26.0	45	29.2	131	85.1	96	62.3	71	46.1	119	77.3	14	9.1	38	24.7	55	35.7	113	73.4	132	85.7
Pennsylvania	180	50	27.8	45	25.0	136	75.6	88	48.9	39	21.7	89	49.4	10	5.6	15	8.3	25	13.9	112	62.2	142	78.9
CENSUS DIVISION 3, SOUTH ATLANTIC	644	140	21.7	117	18.2	479	74.4	230	35.7	110	17.1	380	59.0	23	3.6	104	16.1	136	21.1	383	59.5	496	77.0
Delaware	8	3	37.5	0	0.0	5	62.5	5	62.5	1	12.5	6	75.0	0	0.0	0	0.0	2	25.0	5	62.5	6	75.0
District of Columbia	10	2	20.0	2	20.0	9	90.0	9	90.0	5	50.0	9	90.0	1	10.0	4	40.0	3	30.0	9	90.0	10	100.0
Florida	166	33	19.9	22	13.3	114	68.7	53	31.9	29	17.5	91	54.8	2	1.2	25	15.1	27	16.3	118	71.1	118	71.1
Georgia	96	14	14.6	16	16.7	61	63.5	21	21.9	10	10.4	58	60.4	1	1.0	12	12.5	26	27.1	49	51.0	76	79.2
Maryland	46	7	15.2	7	23.9	38	82.6	29	63.0	19	41.3	36	78.3	2	4.3	10	21.7	5	10.9	37	80.4	41	89.1
North Carolina	110	28	25.5	18	16.4	91	82.7	39	35.5	18	16.4	64	58.2	3	2.7	20	18.2	33	30.0	60	54.5	85	77.3
South Carolina	71	14	19.7	11	15.5	51	71.8	17	23.9	4	5.6	38	53.5	3	4.2	9	12.7	23	32.4	30	42.3	49	69.0
Virginia	76	24	31.6	31	40.8	62	81.6	29	38.2	18	23.7	52	68.4	7	9.2	20	26.3	16	21.1	48	63.2	64	84.2
West Virginia	61	15	24.6	6	9.8	48	78.7	28	45.9	6	9.8	26	42.6	4	6.6	4	6.6	1	1.6	27	44.3	47	77.0
CENSUS DIVISION 4, EAST NORTH CENTRAL	699	201	28.8	183	26.2	570	81.5	337	48.2	160	22.9	433	61.9	111	15.9	82	11.7	87	12.4	401	57.4	593	84.8
Illinois	162	49	30.2	47	29.0	131	80.9	70	43.2	31	19.1	100	61.7	23	14.2	17	10.5	33	20.4	102	63.0	134	82.7
Indiana	123	35	28.5	30	24.4	97	78.9	49	39.8	21	17.1	68	55.3	29	23.6	11	8.9	19	15.4	62	50.4	97	78.9
Michigan	130	46	35.4	42	32.3	110	84.6	83	63.8	41	31.5	86	66.2	11	8.5	16	12.3	13	10.0	83	63.8	114	87.7
Ohio	141	45	31.9	42	29.8	119	84.4	68	48.2	45	31.9	94	66.7	14	9.9	21	14.9	22	15.6	93	66.0	123	87.2
Wisconsin	143	26	18.2	22	15.4	113	79.0	67	46.9	22	15.4	85	59.4	34	23.8	17	11.9	0	0.0	61	42.7	125	87.4
CENSUS DIVISION 5, EAST SOUTH CENTRAL	377	81	21.5	45	11.9	213	56.5	96	25.5	34	9.0	161	42.7	10	2.7	32	8.5	62	16.4	147	39.0	207	54.9
Alabama	103	25	24.3	9	8.7	60	58.3	19	18.4	7	6.8	40	38.8	4	3.9	5	4.9	8	7.8	42	40.8	50	48.5
Kentucky	89	25	28.1	8	9.0	55	61.8	16	18.0	10	11.2	48	53.9	3	3.4	11	12.4	13	14.6	47	52.8	62	69.7
Mississippi	111	11	9.9	11	9.9	51	45.9	40	36.0	12	10.8	30	27.0	2	1.8	8	7.2	32	28.8	24	21.6	40	36.0
Tennessee	74	20	27.0	17	23.0	47	63.5	21	28.4	5	6.8	43	58.1	1	1.4	8	10.8	9	12.2	34	45.9	55	74.3
CENSUS DIVISION 6, WEST NORTH CENTRAL	648	239	36.9	170	26.2	505	77.9	303	46.8	57	8.8	317	48.9	103	15.9	61	9.4	81	12.5	207	31.9	463	71.5
Iowa	126	56	44.4	50	39.7	109	86.5	68	54.0	14	11.1	68	54.0	31	24.6	11	8.7	14	11.1	37	29.4	112	88.9
Kansas	151	42	27.8	19	12.6	111	73.5	44	29.1	5	3.3	59	39.1	28	18.5	7	4.6	14	9.3	28	18.5	78	51.7
Minnesota	106	42	39.6	39	36.8	86	81.1	62	58.5	6	5.7	52	49.1	13	12.3	10	9.4	8	7.5	35	33.0	84	79.2
Missouri	146	49	33.6	26	17.8	110	75.3	68	46.6	22	15.1	82	56.2	14	9.6	17	11.6	29	19.9	74	50.7	116	79.5
Nebraska	49	26	53.1	18	36.7	40	81.6	24	49.0	4	8.2	31	63.3	9	18.4	5	10.2	7	14.3	19	38.8	37	75.5
North Dakota	28	8	28.6	7	25.0	18	64.3	14	50.0	2	7.1	10	35.7	2	7.1	3	10.7	6	21.4	6	21.4	13	46.4
South Dakota	42	16	38.1	11	26.2	31	73.8	23	54.8	4	9.5	15	35.7	6	14.3	8	19.0	3	7.1	8	19.0	23	54.8
CENSUS DIVISION 7, WEST SOUTH CENTRAL	892	153	17.2	80	9.0	549	61.5	272	30.5	78	8.7	383	42.9	39	4.4	55	6.2	91	10.2	328	36.8	550	61.7
Arkansas	86	32	37.2	7	8.1	55	64.0	15	17.4	1	1.2	35	40.7	3	3.5	8	9.3	11	12.8	26	30.2	50	58.1
Louisiana	97	14	14.4	8	8.2	57	58.8	42	43.3	15	15.5	37	38.1	2	2.1	8	8.2	9	9.3	41	42.3	61	62.9
Oklahoma	127	29	22.8	17	13.4	81	63.8	43	33.9	7	5.5	59	46.5	15	11.8	5	3.9	8	6.3	38	29.9	63	49.6
Texas	582	78	13.4	48	8.2	356	61.2	172	29.6	55	9.5	252	43.3	19	3.3	34	5.8	63	10.8	223	38.3	376	64.6
CENSUS DIVISION 8, MOUNTAIN	342	82	24.0	78	22.8	243	71.1	140	40.9	53	15.5	197	57.6	28	8.2	30	8.8	46	13.5	133	38.9	252	73.7
Arizona	69	10	14.5	8	11.6	47	68.1	21	30.4	12	17.4	42	60.9	5	7.2	7	10.1	11	15.9	39	49.3	53	76.8
Colorado	74	16	21.6	10	13.5	57	77.0	28	37.8	14	18.9	49	66.2	7	9.5	5	6.8	12	16.2	39	52.7	59	79.7
Idaho	28	8	28.6	8	28.6	20	71.4	11	39.3	3	10.7	19	67.9	3	10.7	5	17.9	1	3.6	7	25.0	20	71.4
Montana	51	16	31.4	22	43.1	41	80.4	27	52.9	9	17.6	21	41.2	10	19.6	6	11.8	3	5.9	13	25.5	38	74.5
Nevada	27	5	18.5	4	14.8	14	51.9	10	37.0	3	11.1	13	48.1	0	0.0	0	0.0	3	11.1	9	33.3	15	55.6
New Mexico	33	10	30.3	8	24.2	23	69.7	17	51.5	4	12.1	20	60.6	1	3.0	0	0.0	5	15.2	9	27.3	21	63.6
Utah	34	7	20.6	10	29.4	25	73.5	14	41.2	5	14.7	21	61.8	1	2.9	3	8.8	8	23.5	13	38.2	28	82.4
Wyoming	26	10	38.5	8	30.8	16	61.5	12	46.2	3	11.5	12	46.2	1	3.8	4	15.4	3	11.5	9	34.6	18	69.2
CENSUS DIVISION 9, PACIFIC	428	116	27.1	104	24.3	335	78.3	206	48.1	84	19.6	296	69.2	18	4.2	55	12.9	60	14.0	251	58.6	322	75.2
Alaska	12	5	41.7	3	25.0	7	58.3	6	50.0	0	0.0	5	41.7	0	0.0	0	0.0	0	0.0	4	33.3	7	58.3
California	264	65	24.6	61	23.1	203	76.9	134	50.8	62	23.5	191	72.3	12	4.5	39	14.8	32	12.1	167	63.3	191	72.3
Hawaii	19	4	21.1	2	10.5	13	68.4	4	21.1	2	10.5	13	68.4	3	15.8	1	5.3	2	10.5	10	52.6	14	73.7
Oregon	61	26	42.6	22	36.1	54	88.5	24	39.3	11	18.0	43	70.5	1	1.6	7	11.5	6	9.8	25	41.0	54	88.5
Washington	72	16	22.2	16	22.2	58	80.6	38	52.8	9	12.5	44	61.1	2	2.8	8	11.1	20	27.8	45	62.5	56	77.8

Table 7 (Continued)

These data include only hospital-based facilities and services as reported by responding hospitals in Section C of the 2014 AHA Annual Survey, beginning on page 217. All hospitals are represented with Community Hospitals listed separately under United States. No estimates have been made for nonresponding hospitals. Definitions of facilities and services are listed in the Glossary, page 205.

CLASSIFICATION	HOSPITALS REPORTING	OBSTETRICS INPATIENT CARE UNITS		OCCUPATIONAL HEALTH SERVICES		ONCOLOGY SERVICES		ORTHOPEDIC SERVICES		OTHER SPECIAL CARE UNITS		OUTPATIENT SURGERY		PAIN MANAGEMENT PROGRAM		PALLIATIVE CARE PROGRAM		PALLIATIVE CARE INPATIENT UNIT		PATIENT CONTROLLED ANALGESIA (PCA)		PATIENT EDUCATION CENTER	
		Number	Percent	Number	Percent	Number	Percent	Number	Percent	Number	Percent	Number	Percent	Number	Percent	Number	Percent	Number	Percent	Number	Percent	Number	Percent
UNITED STATES	4,601	2,499	54.3	2,897	63.0	2,348	51.0	3,171	68.9	750	16.3	3,659	79.5	2,424	52.7	1,702	37.0	475	10.3	3,180	69.1	2,481	53.9
COMMUNITY HOSPITALS	3,921	2,460	62.7	2,700	68.9	2,267	57.8	2,974	75.8	717	18.3	3,454	88.1	2,234	57.0	1,604	40.9	418	10.7	2,957	75.4	2,258	57.6
CENSUS DIVISION 1, NEW ENGLAND	169	115	68.0	136	80.5	125	74.0	145	85.8	27	16.0	143	84.6	123	72.8	94	55.6	32	18.9	137	81.1	112	66.3
Connecticut	27	21	77.8	18	66.7	21	77.8	22	81.5	9	33.3	22	81.5	21	77.8	21	77.8	7	25.9	22	81.5	17	63.0
Maine	29	24	82.8	22	75.9	22	75.9	28	96.6	8	27.6	27	93.1	20	69.0	13	44.8	5	17.2	25	86.2	17	58.6
Massachusetts	68	39	57.4	56	82.4	45	66.2	55	80.9	5	7.4	53	77.9	50	73.5	29	42.6	8	11.8	51	75.0	48	70.6
New Hampshire	23	16	69.6	20	87.0	18	78.3	21	91.3	4	17.4	21	91.3	15	65.2	16	69.6	7	30.4	20	87.0	14	60.9
Rhode Island	10	6	60.0	10	100.0	9	90.0	8	80.0	0	0.0	9	90.0	9	90.0	7	70.0	1	10.0	9	90.0	9	90.0
Vermont	12	9	75.0	10	83.3	10	83.3	11	91.7	1	8.3	11	91.7	8	66.7	8	66.7	4	33.3	10	83.3	7	58.3
CENSUS DIVISION 2, MIDDLE ATLANTIC	402	237	59.0	302	75.1	285	70.9	334	83.1	73	18.2	342	85.1	281	69.9	229	57.0	75	18.7	317	78.9	264	65.7
New Jersey	68	45	66.2	52	76.5	55	80.9	57	83.8	11	16.2	56	82.4	55	80.9	42	61.8	15	22.1	52	76.5	51	75.0
New York	154	105	68.2	126	81.8	118	76.6	135	87.7	27	17.5	144	93.5	110	71.4	108	70.1	44	28.6	132	85.7	103	66.9
Pennsylvania	180	87	48.3	124	68.9	112	62.2	142	78.9	35	19.4	142	78.9	116	64.4	79	43.9	16	8.9	133	73.9	110	61.1
CENSUS DIVISION 3, SOUTH ATLANTIC	644	351	54.5	450	69.9	365	56.7	493	76.6	133	20.7	519	80.6	353	54.8	275	42.7	69	10.7	479	74.4	395	61.3
Delaware	8	4	50.0	5	62.5	5	62.5	5	62.5	3	37.5	5	62.5	3	37.5	5	62.5	1	12.5	5	62.5	5	62.5
District of Columbia	10	6	60.0	8	80.0	8	80.0	8	80.0	3	30.0	7	70.0	7	70.0	6	60.0	3	30.0	7	70.0	9	90.0
Florida	166	76	45.8	102	61.4	102	61.4	131	78.9	45	27.1	136	81.9	89	53.6	73	44.0	21	12.7	127	76.5	94	56.6
Georgia	96	50	52.1	66	68.8	46	47.9	65	67.7	16	16.7	73	76.0	50	52.1	33	34.4	9	9.4	66	68.8	58	60.4
Maryland	46	30	65.2	38	82.6	38	82.6	39	84.8	10	21.7	40	87.0	40	87.0	34	73.9	7	15.2	40	87.0	35	76.1
North Carolina	110	75	68.2	87	79.1	66	60.0	89	80.9	26	23.6	98	89.1	75	68.2	39	35.5	11	10.0	84	76.4	66	60.0
South Carolina	71	41	57.7	49	69.0	27	38.0	56	78.9	14	19.7	54	76.1	26	36.6	21	29.6	3	4.2	53	74.6	43	60.6
Virginia	76	42	55.3	59	77.6	47	61.8	59	77.6	14	18.4	62	81.6	42	55.3	43	56.6	9	11.8	61	80.3	47	61.8
West Virginia	61	27	44.3	36	59.0	26	42.6	41	67.2	2	3.3	44	72.1	21	34.4	21	34.4	5	8.2	36	59.0	38	62.3
CENSUS DIVISION 4, EAST NORTH CENTRAL	699	438	62.7	493	70.5	450	64.4	546	78.1	206	29.5	617	88.3	469	67.1	298	42.6	91	13.0	560	80.1	487	69.7
Illinois	162	103	63.6	108	66.7	108	66.7	126	77.8	17	10.5	149	92.0	116	71.6	71	43.8	15	9.3	131	80.9	95	58.6
Indiana	123	75	61.0	81	65.9	66	53.7	94	76.4	27	22.0	101	82.1	66	53.7	38	30.9	12	9.8	98	79.7	75	61.0
Michigan	130	74	56.9	104	80.0	91	70.0	110	84.6	32	24.6	116	89.2	84	64.6	61	46.9	19	14.6	106	81.5	83	63.8
Ohio	141	91	64.5	110	78.0	101	71.6	127	90.1	22	15.6	128	90.8	107	75.9	66	46.8	29	20.6	118	83.7	105	74.5
Wisconsin	143	95	66.4	90	62.9	84	58.7	89	62.2	108	75.5	123	86.0	96	67.1	62	43.4	16	11.2	107	74.8	129	90.2
CENSUS DIVISION 5, EAST SOUTH CENTRAL	377	167	44.3	176	46.7	144	38.2	201	53.3	48	12.7	276	73.2	144	38.2	84	22.3	25	6.6	192	50.9	160	42.4
Alabama	103	48	46.6	47	45.6	36	35.0	58	56.3	10	9.7	74	71.8	40	38.8	20	19.4	7	6.8	51	49.5	41	39.8
Kentucky	89	40	44.9	46	51.7	46	51.7	60	67.4	7	7.9	74	83.1	48	53.9	27	30.3	5	5.6	56	62.9	46	51.7
Mississippi	111	43	38.7	35	31.5	26	23.4	35	31.5	15	13.5	70	63.1	30	27.0	15	13.5	4	3.6	39	35.1	40	36.0
Tennessee	74	36	48.6	48	64.9	36	48.6	48	64.9	16	21.6	58	78.4	26	35.1	22	29.7	9	12.2	46	62.2	33	44.6
CENSUS DIVISION 6, WEST NORTH CENTRAL	648	346	53.4	431	66.5	296	45.7	411	63.4	79	12.2	554	85.5	316	48.8	205	31.6	54	8.3	432	66.7	318	49.1
Iowa	126	78	61.9	89	70.6	73	57.9	90	71.4	13	10.3	118	93.7	67	53.2	38	30.2	7	5.6	97	77.0	67	53.2
Kansas	151	66	43.7	81	53.6	39	25.8	68	45.0	11	7.3	118	78.1	63	41.7	30	19.9	9	6.0	84	55.6	57	37.7
Minnesota	106	76	71.7	89	84.0	55	51.9	82	77.4	13	12.3	102	96.2	53	50.0	43	40.6	10	9.4	76	71.7	50	47.2
Missouri	146	68	46.6	100	68.5	77	52.7	103	70.5	27	18.5	112	76.7	76	52.1	55	37.7	12	8.2	108	74.0	76	52.1
Nebraska	49	30	61.2	32	65.3	29	59.2	38	77.6	7	14.3	48	98.0	29	59.2	7	14.3	7	14.3	33	67.3	27	55.1
North Dakota	28	11	39.3	13	46.4	11	39.3	12	42.9	6	21.4	23	82.1	13	46.4	6	21.4	4	14.3	14	50.0	10	35.7
South Dakota	42	17	40.5	27	64.3	12	28.6	18	42.9	2	4.8	33	78.6	15	35.7	12	28.6	5	11.9	20	47.6	19	45.2
CENSUS DIVISION 7, WEST SOUTH CENTRAL	892	345	38.7	424	47.5	255	28.6	477	53.5	86	9.6	575	64.5	321	36.0	165	18.5	33	3.7	517	58.0	356	39.9
Arkansas	86	34	39.5	41	47.7	29	33.7	43	50.0	6	7.0	59	68.6	23	26.7	12	14.0	3	3.5	47	54.7	30	34.9
Louisiana	97	42	43.3	46	47.4	35	36.1	56	57.7	7	7.2	67	69.1	30	30.9	25	25.8	2	2.1	56	57.7	41	42.3
Oklahoma	127	52	40.9	51	40.2	29	22.8	66	52.0	13	10.2	91	71.7	43	33.9	21	16.5	9	7.1	70	55.1	36	28.3
Texas	582	217	37.3	280	48.1	162	27.8	312	53.6	60	10.3	358	61.5	225	38.7	107	18.4	19	3.3	344	59.1	249	42.8
CENSUS DIVISION 8, MOUNTAIN	342	208	60.8	204	59.6	161	47.1	228	66.7	38	11.1	268	78.4	179	52.3	123	36.0	36	10.5	228	66.7	158	46.2
Arizona	69	37	53.6	45	65.2	39	56.5	49	71.0	14	20.3	52	75.4	41	59.4	26	37.7	9	13.0	49	71.0	34	49.3
Colorado	74	50	67.6	50	67.6	43	58.1	56	75.7	13	17.6	63	85.1	41	55.4	35	47.3	5	6.8	57	77.0	37	50.0
Idaho	28	21	75.0	18	64.3	11	39.3	20	71.4	3	10.7	26	92.9	14	50.0	10	35.7	4	14.3	19	67.9	16	57.1
Montana	51	26	51.0	30	58.8	18	35.3	25	49.0	1	2.0	28	54.9	21	41.2	20	39.2	5	9.8	25	49.0	19	37.3
Nevada	27	9	33.3	14	51.9	11	40.7	16	59.3	3	11.1	15	55.6	10	37.0	7	25.9	2	7.4	14	51.9	10	37.0
New Mexico	33	20	60.6	21	63.6	14	42.4	21	63.6	2	6.1	28	84.8	10	30.3	8	24.2	5	15.2	24	72.7	10	30.3
Utah	34	28	82.4	21	61.8	14	41.2	23	67.6	2	5.9	30	88.2	25	73.5	10	29.4	4	11.8	23	67.6	21	61.8
Wyoming	26	17	65.4	17	65.4	11	42.3	18	69.2	0	0.0	20	76.9	17	65.4	7	26.9	2	7.7	17	65.4	11	42.3
CENSUS DIVISION 9, PACIFIC	428	292	68.2	281	65.7	267	62.4	336	78.5	60	14.0	365	85.3	238	55.6	229	53.5	60	14.0	318	74.3	231	54.0
Alaska	12	8	66.7	7	58.3	6	50.0	7	58.3	1	8.3	9	75.0	6	50.0	4	33.3	1	8.3	9	75.0	5	41.7
California	264	179	67.8	175	66.3	168	63.6	211	79.9	29	11.0	225	85.2	149	56.4	153	58.0	40	15.2	191	72.3	140	53.0
Hawaii	19	10	52.6	14	73.7	12	63.2	14	73.7	4	21.1	13	68.4	13	68.4	9	47.4	2	10.5	10	52.6	10	52.6
Oregon	61	50	82.0	42	68.9	38	62.3	51	83.6	7	11.5	57	93.4	35	57.4	28	45.9	9	14.8	54	88.5	38	62.3
Washington	72	45	62.5	43	59.7	43	59.7	53	73.6	19	26.4	61	84.7	41	56.9	35	48.6	8	11.1	54	75.0	39	54.2

Table 7 (Continued)

These data include only hospital-based facilities and services as reported by responding hospitals in Section C of the 2014 AHA Annual Survey, beginning on page 217. All hospitals are represented with Community Hospitals listed separately under United States. No estimates have been made for nonresponding hospitals. Definitions of facilities and services are listed in the Glossary, page 205.

CLASSIFICATION	HOSPITALS REPORTING	PATIENT REPRESENTATIVE SERVICES No.	%	PHYSICAL REHAB INPATIENT CARE UNITS No.	%	PRIMARY CARE DEPARTMENT No.	%	PSYCHIATRIC INPATIENT CARE UNITS No.	%	RETIREMENT HOUSING No.	%	ROBOTIC SURGERY No.	%	RURAL HEALTH CLINIC No.	%	SLEEP CENTER No.	%	SOCIAL WORK SERVICES No.	%	SPORTS MEDICINE No.	%	SUPPORT GROUPS No.	%
UNITED STATES	4,601	3,112	67.6	1,364	29.6	1,883	40.9	1,558	33.9	131	2.8	1,267	27.5	1,016	22.1	2,140	46.5	3,878	84.3	1,889	41.1	2,868	62.3
COMMUNITY HOSPITALS	3,921	2,814	71.8	1,267	32.3	1,771	45.2	1,199	30.6	128	3.3	1,220	31.1	951	24.3	2,061	52.6	3,402	86.8	1,825	46.5	2,627	67.0
CENSUS DIVISION 1, NEW ENGLAND	169	132	78.1	42	24.9	102	60.4	89	52.7	3	1.8	57	33.7	24	14.2	90	53.3	163	96.4	107	63.3	147	87.0
Connecticut	27	24	88.9	9	33.3	17	63.0	20	74.1	1	3.7	17	63.0	1	3.7	19	70.4	26	96.3	19	70.4	26	96.3
Maine	29	23	79.3	10	34.5	25	86.2	9	31.0	1	3.4	3	10.3	12	41.4	14	48.3	28	96.6	17	58.6	28	96.6
Massachusetts	68	51	75.0	11	16.2	29	42.6	40	58.8	0	0.0	23	33.8	1	1.5	33	48.5	65	95.6	40	58.8	58	85.3
New Hampshire	23	17	73.9	5	21.7	17	73.9	8	34.8	0	0.0	6	26.1	7	30.4	14	60.9	23	100.0	17	73.9	18	78.3
Rhode Island	10	9	90.0	4	40.0	8	80.0	6	60.0	0	0.0	7	70.0	0	0.0	6	60.0	10	100.0	5	50.0	10	100.0
Vermont	12	8	66.7	3	25.0	6	50.0	6	50.0	1	8.3	1	8.3	3	25.0	4	33.3	11	91.7	9	75.0	7	58.3
CENSUS DIVISION 2, MIDDLE ATLANTIC	402	320	79.6	157	39.1	228	56.7	219	54.5	4	1.0	161	40.0	33	8.2	231	57.5	374	93.0	211	52.5	327	81.3
New Jersey	68	60	88.2	20	29.4	45	66.2	39	57.4	1	1.5	35	51.5	1	1.5	45	66.2	65	95.6	35	51.5	58	85.3
New York	154	142	92.2	63	40.9	112	72.7	89	57.8	1	0.6	64	41.6	21	13.6	80	51.9	147	95.5	92	59.7	134	87.0
Pennsylvania	180	118	65.6	74	41.1	71	39.4	91	50.6	2	1.1	62	34.4	11	6.1	106	58.9	162	90.0	84	46.7	135	75.0
CENSUS DIVISION 3, SOUTH ATLANTIC	644	463	71.9	203	31.5	240	37.3	236	36.6	7	1.1	228	35.4	88	13.7	345	53.6	551	85.6	275	42.7	436	67.7
Delaware	8	6	75.0	3	37.5	3	37.5	4	50.0	0	0.0	3	37.5	1	12.5	4	50.0	7	87.5	5	62.5	6	75.0
District of Columbia	10	8	80.0	2	20.0	6	60.0	8	80.0	0	0.0	5	50.0	0	0.0	6	60.0	10	100.0	6	60.0	8	80.0
Florida	166	115	69.3	44	26.5	54	32.5	53	31.9	3	3.1	82	49.4	18	10.8	78	47.0	132	79.5	73	44.0	113	68.1
Georgia	96	68	70.8	23	24.0	28	29.2	26	27.1	0	0.0	32	33.3	15	15.6	51	53.1	77	80.2	31	32.3	55	57.3
Maryland	46	41	89.1	12	26.1	20	43.5	30	65.2	0	0.0	21	45.7	1	2.2	33	71.7	44	95.7	24	52.2	40	87.0
North Carolina	110	77	70.0	30	27.3	47	42.7	48	43.6	3	2.7	39	35.5	15	13.6	63	57.3	100	90.9	52	47.3	76	69.1
South Carolina	71	43	60.6	52	73.2	17	23.9	19	26.8	0	0.0	11	15.5	13	18.3	42	59.2	60	84.5	24	33.8	44	62.0
Virginia	76	64	84.2	24	31.6	34	44.7	31	40.8	1	1.3	24	31.6	7	9.2	45	59.2	69	90.8	41	53.9	56	73.7
West Virginia	61	41	67.2	13	21.3	31	50.8	17	27.9	0	0.0	11	18.0	18	29.5	32	52.5	52	85.2	19	31.1	38	62.3
CENSUS DIVISION 4, EAST NORTH CENTRAL	699	557	79.7	253	36.2	364	52.1	262	37.5	23	3.3	218	31.2	138	19.7	449	64.2	646	92.4	392	56.1	558	79.8
Illinois	162	129	79.6	52	32.5	82	50.6	63	38.9	9	5.6	64	39.5	41	25.3	115	71.0	149	92.0	92	56.8	132	81.5
Indiana	123	91	74.0	40	32.5	44	35.8	46	37.4	3	2.4	27	22.0	15	12.2	76	61.8	102	82.9	52	42.3	101	82.1
Michigan	130	104	80.0	44	33.8	93	71.5	51	39.2	3	2.3	46	35.4	44	33.8	86	66.2	122	93.8	82	63.1	113	86.9
Ohio	141	120	85.1	44	31.2	75	53.2	64	45.4	0	0.0	51	36.2	11	7.8	99	70.2	139	98.6	91	64.5	115	81.6
Wisconsin	143	113	79.0	73	51.0	70	49.0	38	26.6	8	5.6	30	21.0	27	18.9	73	51.0	134	93.7	75	52.4	97	67.8
CENSUS DIVISION 5, EAST SOUTH CENTRAL	377	227	60.2	106	28.1	100	26.5	135	35.8	6	1.6	87	23.1	100	26.5	143	37.9	294	78.0	112	29.7	173	45.9
Alabama	103	47	45.6	22	21.4	16	15.5	41	39.8	3	2.9	23	22.3	18	17.5	42	40.8	65	63.1	36	35.0	41	39.8
Kentucky	89	65	73.0	18	20.2	38	42.7	29	32.6	1	1.1	19	21.3	32	36.0	49	55.1	73	82.0	28	31.5	49	55.1
Mississippi	111	63	56.8	48	43.2	23	20.7	41	36.9	1	0.9	23	20.7	45	40.5	13	11.7	95	85.6	20	18.0	39	35.1
Tennessee	74	52	70.3	18	24.3	23	31.1	24	32.4	1	1.4	22	29.7	5	6.8	39	52.7	61	82.4	28	37.8	44	59.5
CENSUS DIVISION 6, WEST NORTH CENTRAL	648	384	59.3	195	30.1	304	46.9	180	27.8	65	10.0	101	15.6	273	42.1	316	48.8	539	83.2	292	45.1	394	60.8
Iowa	126	74	58.7	28	22.2	73	57.9	38	30.2	15	11.9	20	15.9	49	38.9	66	52.4	108	85.7	62	49.2	93	73.8
Kansas	151	69	45.7	31	20.5	52	34.4	24	15.9	13	8.6	17	11.3	73	48.3	41	27.2	110	72.8	50	33.1	55	36.4
Minnesota	106	66	62.3	19	17.9	58	54.7	30	28.3	16	15.1	19	17.9	30	28.3	57	53.8	99	93.4	50	47.2	81	76.4
Missouri	146	109	74.7	88	60.3	60	41.1	62	42.5	2	1.4	27	18.5	62	42.5	88	60.3	132	90.4	69	47.3	93	63.7
Nebraska	49	29	59.2	14	28.6	23	46.9	12	24.5	2	4.1	10	20.4	27	55.1	33	67.3	39	79.6	31	63.3	31	63.3
North Dakota	28	17	60.7	9	32.1	18	64.3	9	32.1	5	17.9	4	14.3	13	46.4	13	46.4	22	78.6	15	53.6	15	53.6
South Dakota	42	20	47.6	6	14.3	20	47.6	5	11.9	12	28.6	4	9.5	19	45.2	18	42.9	29	69.0	15	35.7	26	61.9
CENSUS DIVISION 7, WEST SOUTH CENTRAL	892	497	55.7	221	24.8	208	23.3	218	24.4	9	1.0	181	20.3	180	20.2	277	31.1	666	74.7	214	24.0	364	40.8
Arkansas	86	42	48.8	21	24.4	19	22.1	29	33.7	1	1.2	15	17.4	22	25.6	39	45.3	63	73.3	24	27.9	37	43.0
Louisiana	97	51	52.6	39	40.2	37	38.1	39	40.2	3	3.1	22	22.7	23	23.7	30	30.9	77	79.4	24	24.7	41	42.3
Oklahoma	127	69	54.3	32	25.2	30	23.6	37	29.1	3	2.4	18	14.2	25	19.7	53	41.7	87	68.5	33	26.0	44	34.6
Texas	582	335	57.6	129	22.2	122	21.0	113	19.4	2	0.3	126	21.6	110	18.9	155	26.6	439	75.4	133	22.9	242	41.6
CENSUS DIVISION 8, MOUNTAIN	342	229	67.0	84	24.6	150	43.9	87	25.4	8	2.3	87	25.4	108	31.6	151	44.2	267	78.1	134	39.2	187	54.7
Arizona	69	48	69.6	20	29.0	17	24.6	19	27.5	1	1.4	22	31.9	15	21.7	18	26.1	53	76.8	20	29.0	41	59.4
Colorado	74	55	74.3	20	27.0	45	60.8	13	17.6	1	1.4	29	39.2	27	36.5	49	66.2	55	74.3	37	50.0	47	63.5
Idaho	28	21	75.0	6	21.4	14	50.0	7	25.0	0	0.0	7	25.0	16	57.1	13	46.4	22	78.6	14	50.0	14	50.0
Montana	51	31	60.8	9	17.6	29	56.9	9	17.6	4	7.8	9	17.6	29	56.9	19	37.3	44	86.3	24	47.1	24	47.1
Nevada	27	13	48.1	6	22.2	3	11.1	9	33.3	1	3.7	5	18.5	4	14.8	4	14.8	19	70.4	6	22.2	11	40.7
New Mexico	33	18	54.5	9	27.3	13	39.4	11	33.3	0	0.0	6	18.2	5	15.2	13	39.4	28	84.8	4	12.1	18	54.5
Utah	34	25	73.5	9	26.5	14	41.2	13	38.2	0	0.0	7	20.6	5	14.7	20	58.8	27	79.4	19	55.9	18	52.9
Wyoming	26	18	69.2	3	11.5	15	57.7	6	23.1	2	7.7	2	7.7	6	23.1	15	57.7	19	73.1	10	38.5	14	53.8
CENSUS DIVISION 9, PACIFIC	428	303	70.8	103	24.1	187	43.7	132	30.8	6	1.4	147	34.3	72	16.8	138	32.2	378	88.3	152	35.5	282	65.9
Alaska	12	7	58.3	2	16.7	7	58.3	5	41.7	0	0.0	3	25.0	0	0.0	5	41.7	9	75.0	4	33.3	4	33.3
California	264	183	69.3	70	26.5	95	36.0	83	31.4	3	1.1	97	36.7	34	12.9	61	23.1	242	91.7	85	32.2	168	63.6
Hawaii	19	10	52.6	2	10.5	9	47.4	6	31.6	0	0.0	4	21.1	4	21.1	5	26.3	18	94.7	8	42.1	12	63.2
Oregon	61	47	77.0	11	18.0	40	65.6	19	31.1	2	3.3	18	29.5	16	26.2	31	50.8	50	82.0	27	44.3	53	86.9
Washington	72	56	77.8	18	25.0	36	50.0	19	26.4	1	1.4	25	34.7	18	25.0	36	50.0	59	81.9	28	38.9	45	62.5

Table 7 (Continued)

These data include only hospital-based facilities and services as reported by responding hospitals in Section C of the 2014 AHA Annual Survey, beginning on page 217. All hospitals are represented with Community Hospitals listed separately under United States. No estimates have been made for nonresponding hospitals. Definitions of facilities and services are listed in the Glossary, page 205.

CLASSIFICATION	HOSPITALS REPORTING	SWING BED SERVICES Number	Percent	TEEN OUTREACH SERVICES Number	Percent	TOBACCO TREATMENT/ CESSATION PROGRAM Number	Percent	TRANSPORTATION TO HEALTH FACILITIES Number	Percent	URGENT CARE CENTER Number	Percent	VIRTUAL COLONOSCOPY Number	Percent	VOLUNTEER SERVICES DEPARTMENT Number	Percent	WOMEN'S HEALTH SERVICES Number	Percent	WOUND MANAGEMENT SERVICES Number	Percent
UNITED STATES	4,601	1,413	30.7	585	12.7	2,345	51.0	1,033	22.5	1,056	23.0	780	17.0	3,416	74.2	2,276	49.5	3,056	66.4
COMMUNITY HOSPITALS	3,921	1,370	34.9	553	14.1	2,148	54.8	885	22.6	998	25.5	756	19.3	3,181	81.1	2,181	55.6	2,815	71.8
CENSUS DIVISION 1, NEW ENGLAND	169	39	23.1	55	32.5	123	72.8	56	33.1	67	39.6	45	26.6	154	91.1	119	70.4	128	75.7
Connecticut	27	0	0.0	12	44.4	21	77.8	4	14.8	17	63.0	17	63.0	25	92.6	17	63.0	24	88.9
Maine	29	12	41.4	6	20.7	24	82.8	7	24.1	11	37.9	5	17.2	27	93.1	22	75.9	21	72.4
Massachusetts	68	5	7.4	23	33.8	42	61.8	27	39.7	23	33.8	15	22.1	60	88.2	42	61.8	49	72.1
New Hampshire	23	13	56.5	9	39.1	17	73.9	5	21.7	8	34.8	5	21.7	22	95.7	21	91.3	18	78.3
Rhode Island	10	2	20.0	3	30.0	9	90.0	8	80.0	4	40.0	2	20.0	9	90.0	9	90.0	8	80.0
Vermont	12	7	58.3	2	16.7	10	83.3	5	41.7	4	33.3	1	8.3	11	91.7	8	66.7	8	66.7
CENSUS DIVISION 2, MIDDLE ATLANTIC	402	63	15.7	104	25.9	262	65.2	131	32.6	103	25.6	98	24.4	354	88.1	274	68.2	295	73.4
New Jersey	68	7	10.3	31	45.6	40	58.8	37	54.4	19	27.9	21	30.9	60	88.2	51	75.0	56	82.4
New York	154	25	16.2	37	24.0	117	76.0	51	33.1	50	32.5	46	29.9	143	92.9	119	77.3	114	74.0
Pennsylvania	180	31	17.2	36	20.0	105	58.3	43	23.9	34	18.9	31	17.2	151	83.9	104	57.8	125	69.4
CENSUS DIVISION 3, SOUTH ATLANTIC	644	120	18.6	77	12.0	364	56.5	148	23.0	149	23.1	129	20.0	538	83.5	356	55.3	452	70.2
Delaware	8	0	0.0	3	37.5	4	50.0	4	50.0	2	25.0	1	12.5	5	62.5	4	50.0	6	75.0
District of Columbia	10	0	0.0	3	30.0	4	40.0	2	20.0	1	10.0	2	20.0	10	100.0	6	60.0	10	100.0
Florida	166	22	13.3	16	9.6	84	50.6	36	21.7	39	23.5	33	19.9	132	79.5	90	54.2	118	71.1
Georgia	96	24	25.0	9	9.4	55	57.3	22	22.9	21	21.9	15	15.6	80	83.3	51	53.1	67	69.8
Maryland	46	1	2.2	16	34.8	34	73.9	14	30.4	15	32.6	14	30.4	42	91.3	26	56.5	33	71.7
North Carolina	110	23	20.9	10	9.1	68	61.8	28	25.5	31	28.2	26	23.6	101	91.8	61	55.5	73	66.4
South Carolina	71	8	11.3	8	11.3	39	54.9	11	15.5	10	14.1	10	14.1	53	74.6	41	57.7	46	64.8
Virginia	76	17	22.4	8	10.5	43	56.6	19	25.0	16	21.1	20	26.3	67	88.2	46	60.5	62	81.6
West Virginia	61	25	41.0	4	6.6	33	54.1	12	19.7	14	23.0	8	13.1	48	78.7	31	50.8	37	60.7
CENSUS DIVISION 4, EAST NORTH CENTRAL	699	197	28.2	114	16.3	458	65.5	182	26.0	285	40.8	160	22.9	601	86.0	411	58.8	510	73.0
Illinois	162	50	30.9	28	17.3	95	58.6	52	32.1	53	32.7	45	27.8	146	90.1	101	62.3	117	72.2
Indiana	123	32	26.0	17	13.8	84	68.3	18	14.6	38	30.9	21	17.1	102	82.9	69	56.1	86	69.9
Michigan	130	23	17.7	25	19.2	92	70.8	34	26.2	57	43.8	27	20.8	119	91.5	81	62.3	98	75.4
Ohio	141	35	24.8	28	19.9	111	78.7	47	33.3	57	40.4	35	24.8	129	91.5	92	65.2	108	76.6
Wisconsin	143	57	39.9	16	11.2	76	53.1	31	21.7	80	55.9	32	22.4	105	73.4	68	47.6	101	70.6
CENSUS DIVISION 5, EAST SOUTH CENTRAL	377	135	35.8	30	8.0	154	40.8	60	15.9	54	14.3	33	8.8	252	66.8	139	36.9	159	42.2
Alabama	103	24	23.3	7	6.8	36	35.0	13	12.6	14	13.6	7	6.8	63	61.2	36	35.0	48	46.6
Kentucky	89	37	41.6	6	6.7	47	52.8	11	12.4	13	14.6	11	12.4	71	79.8	44	49.4	42	47.2
Mississippi	111	54	48.6	9	8.1	32	28.8	20	18.0	13	11.7	6	5.4	62	55.9	31	27.9	20	18.0
Tennessee	74	20	27.0	8	10.8	39	52.7	16	21.6	14	18.9	9	12.2	56	75.7	28	37.8	49	66.2
CENSUS DIVISION 6, WEST NORTH CENTRAL	648	385	59.4	61	9.4	306	47.2	157	24.2	138	21.3	92	14.2	433	66.8	256	39.5	425	65.6
Iowa	126	91	72.2	17	13.5	82	65.1	21	16.7	25	19.8	15	11.9	99	78.6	54	42.9	90	71.4
Kansas	151	99	65.6	4	2.6	44	29.1	32	21.2	19	12.6	19	12.6	74	49.0	43	28.5	89	58.9
Minnesota	106	60	56.6	11	10.4	53	50.0	20	18.9	40	37.7	19	17.9	83	78.3	42	39.6	78	73.6
Missouri	146	49	33.6	17	11.6	75	51.4	54	37.0	35	24.0	19	13.0	104	71.2	72	49.3	99	67.8
Nebraska	49	31	63.3	8	16.3	27	55.1	13	26.5	4	8.2	13	26.5	31	63.3	20	40.8	29	59.2
North Dakota	28	21	75.0	0	0.0	11	39.3	10	35.7	8	28.6	4	14.3	19	67.9	12	42.9	13	46.4
South Dakota	42	34	81.0	4	9.5	14	33.3	7	16.7	7	16.7	3	7.1	23	54.8	13	31.0	27	64.3
CENSUS DIVISION 7, WEST SOUTH CENTRAL	892	234	26.2	52	5.8	295	33.1	115	12.9	81	9.1	92	10.3	485	54.4	305	34.2	537	60.2
Arkansas	86	34	39.5	7	8.1	29	33.7	12	14.0	7	8.1	8	9.3	51	59.3	29	33.7	48	55.8
Louisiana	97	24	24.7	10	10.3	44	45.4	16	16.5	11	11.3	5	5.2	53	54.6	40	41.2	57	58.8
Oklahoma	127	55	43.3	5	3.9	56	44.1	20	15.7	12	9.4	15	11.8	87	68.5	45	35.4	71	55.9
Texas	582	121	20.8	30	5.2	166	28.5	67	11.5	51	8.8	64	11.0	294	50.5	191	32.8	361	62.0
CENSUS DIVISION 8, MOUNTAIN	342	146	42.7	34	9.9	172	50.3	75	21.9	76	22.2	54	15.8	242	70.8	183	53.5	226	66.1
Arizona	69	16	23.2	8	11.6	38	55.1	9	13.0	14	20.3	20	29.0	54	78.3	36	52.2	46	66.7
Colorado	74	29	39.2	10	13.5	36	48.6	12	16.2	9	12.2	7	9.5	57	77.0	48	64.9	58	78.4
Idaho	28	16	57.1	5	17.9	14	50.0	10	35.7	7	25.0	5	17.9	23	82.1	13	46.4	14	50.0
Montana	41	33	80.4	4	7.8	26	51.0	21	41.2	18	35.3	9	21.6	35	68.6	22	43.1	30	58.8
Nevada	27	4	14.8	0	0.0	12	44.4	4	14.8	3	11.1	0	0.0	13	48.1	8	29.6	16	59.3
New Mexico	33	10	30.3	1	3.0	15	45.5	7	21.2	8	24.2	4	12.1	18	54.5	16	48.5	23	69.7
Utah	34	12	35.3	4	11.8	15	44.1	4	11.8	8	23.5	4	11.8	24	70.6	22	64.7	21	61.8
Wyoming	26	18	69.2	2	7.7	16	61.5	8	30.8	9	34.6	3	11.5	18	69.2	18	69.2	18	69.2
CENSUS DIVISION 9, PACIFIC	428	94	22.0	58	13.6	211	49.3	109	25.5	103	24.1	77	18.0	357	83.4	233	54.4	324	75.7
Alaska	12	6	50.0	1	8.3	5	41.7	1	8.3	2	16.7	1	8.3	6	50.0	3	25.0	9	75.0
California	264	30	11.4	39	14.8	108	40.9	72	27.3	54	20.5	52	19.7	224	84.8	138	52.3	199	75.4
Hawaii	19	10	52.6	3	15.8	9	47.4	6	31.6	3	15.8	4	21.1	14	73.7	12	63.2	13	68.4
Oregon	61	30	49.2	6	9.8	47	77.0	18	29.5	19	31.1	10	16.4	54	88.5	42	68.9	54	88.5
Washington	72	18	25.0	9	12.5	42	58.3	12	16.7	25	34.7	10	13.9	59	81.9	38	52.8	49	68.1

Table 7 (Continued)

These data include only hospital-based facilities and services as reported by responding hospitals in Section C of the 2014 AHA Annual Survey, beginning on page 217. All hospitals are represented with Community Hospitals listed separately under United States. No estimates have been made for nonresponding hospitals. Definitions of facilities and services are listed in the Glossary, page 205.

CLASSIFICATION	HOSPITALS REPORTING	GENERAL MEDICAL SURGICAL CARE — ADULT UNITS #	Adult %	Pediatric #	Pediatric %	INTENSIVE CARE UNITS — CARDIAC #	Cardiac %	MEDICAL SURGICAL #	Med Surg %	NEONATAL #	Neonatal %	OTHER #	Other %	PEDIATRIC #	Pediatric %	ACUTE LONG-TERM CARE UNITS #	Acute %	LONG-TERM CARE UNITS — SKILLED NURSING #	Skilled %	INTERMEDIATE NURSING #	Interm. %	OTHER LONG-TERM CARE #	Other %
UNITED STATES	4,601	3,891	84.6	1,862	40.5	1,236	26.9	2,867	62.3	971	21.1	557	12.1	422	9.2	381	8.3	1,051	22.8	368	8.0	288	6.3
COMMUNITY HOSPITALS	3,921	3,636	92.7	1,816	46.3	1,204	30.7	2,745	70.0	954	24.3	537	13.7	413	10.5	269	6.9	977	24.9	345	8.8	242	6.2
CENSUS DIVISION 1, NEW ENGLAND	169	140	82.8	92	54.4	51	30.2	129	76.3	32	18.9	13	7.7	17	10.1	8	4.7	30	17.8	22	13.0	10	5.9
Connecticut	27	22	81.5	13	48.1	10	37.0	22	81.5	10	37.0	3	11.1	1	3.7	2	7.4	2	7.4	0	0.0	0	0.0
Maine	29	27	93.1	17	58.6	6	20.7	22	75.9	4	13.8	4	13.8	1	10.3	1	3.4	12	41.4	10	34.5	6	20.7
Massachusetts	68	50	73.5	40	58.8	24	35.3	47	69.1	13	19.1	4	5.9	8	11.8	4	5.9	8	5.9	2	2.9	3	4.4
New Hampshire	23	21	91.3	12	52.2	4	21.7	19	82.6	1	4.3	0	0.0	2	8.7	0	0.0	8	34.8	7	30.4	0	0.0
Rhode Island	10	9	90.0	5	50.0	4	40.0	8	80.0	2	10.0	0	0.0	1	10.0	0	0.0	2	20.0	2	20.0	0	0.0
Vermont	12	11	91.7	5	41.7	2	16.7	11	91.7	2	16.7	1	8.3	2	16.7	1	8.3	4	33.3	1	8.3	1	8.3
CENSUS DIVISION 2, MIDDLE ATLANTIC	402	340	84.6	189	47.0	165	41.0	304	75.6	122	30.3	52	12.9	50	12.4	23	5.7	90	22.4	16	4.0	16	4.0
New Jersey	68	56	82.4	38	55.9	27	39.7	56	82.4	23	33.8	9	13.2	14	20.6	2	2.9	10	14.7	4	5.9	2	2.9
New York	154	145	94.2	87	56.5	78	50.6	129	83.8	56	36.4	19	12.3	28	18.2	10	6.5	45	29.2	7	4.5	10	6.5
Pennsylvania	180	139	77.2	64	35.6	60	33.3	119	66.1	43	23.9	24	13.3	8	4.4	11	6.1	35	19.4	5	2.8	4	2.2
CENSUS DIVISION 3, SOUTH ATLANTIC	644	538	83.5	274	42.5	205	31.8	465	72.2	154	23.9	140	21.7	71	11.0	111	17.2	183	28.4	60	9.3	94	14.6
Delaware	8	4	50.0	3	62.5	4	50.0	6	50.0	2	37.5	0	0.0	2	25.0	0	0.0	0	0.0	0	0.0	0	0.0
District of Columbia	10	6	60.0	3	30.0	2	20.0	6	60.0	1	50.0	1	10.0	2	20.0	0	0.0	3	30.0	0	0.0	3	30.0
Florida	166	138	83.1	57	34.3	71	42.8	130	78.3	48	28.9	28	16.9	28	16.9	17	10.2	21	12.7	15	9.0	9	5.4
Georgia	96	80	83.3	27	28.1	22	22.9	60	62.5	24	25.0	7	7.3	3	3.1	7	7.3	21	21.9	5	5.2	3	3.1
Maryland	46	40	87.0	34	73.9	17	37.0	40	87.0	16	34.8	6	13.0	5	10.9	7	6.5	21	17.4	0	0.0	1	2.2
North Carolina	110	98	89.1	47	42.7	29	26.4	83	75.5	23	20.9	16	14.5	14	12.7	6	5.5	26	23.6	15	13.6	2	1.8
South Carolina	71	60	84.5	45	63.4	19	26.8	51	71.8	10	14.1	69	97.2	6	8.5	68	95.8	70	98.6	9	12.7	68	95.8
Virginia	76	62	81.6	31	40.8	21	27.6	57	75.0	20	26.3	4	5.3	6	10.5	4	5.3	15	19.7	7	9.2	4	5.3
West Virginia	61	50	82.0	25	41.0	17	27.9	34	55.7	5	8.2	4	6.6	3	4.9	5	8.2	19	31.1	8	13.1	4	6.6
CENSUS DIVISION 4, EAST NORTH CENTRAL	699	613	87.7	350	50.1	213	30.5	470	67.2	128	18.3	128	18.3	71	10.2	40	5.7	130	18.6	34	4.9	36	5.2
Illinois	162	147	90.7	91	56.2	38	23.5	116	71.6	28	17.3	18	11.1	20	12.3	9	5.6	38	23.5	8	4.9	10	6.2
Indiana	123	99	80.5	57	46.3	27	22.0	76	61.8	25	20.3	7	5.7	9	7.3	9	7.3	17	13.8	12	9.8	3	2.4
Michigan	130	117	90.0	58	44.6	39	30.0	90	69.2	23	17.7	18	13.8	10	7.7	3	2.3	28	21.5	4	3.1	7	5.4
Ohio	141	128	90.8	51	36.2	52	36.9	115	81.6	24	17.0	19	13.5	10	7.1	7	5.0	25	17.7	8	5.7	9	6.4
Wisconsin	143	122	85.3	93	65.0	57	39.9	73	51.0	28	19.6	66	46.2	22	15.4	12	8.4	22	15.4	2	1.4	7	4.9
CENSUS DIVISION 5, EAST SOUTH CENTRAL	377	327	86.7	149	39.5	108	28.6	261	69.2	60	15.9	72	19.1	28	7.4	23	6.1	74	19.6	19	5.0	23	6.1
Alabama	103	83	80.6	30	29.1	27	26.2	60	58.3	15	14.6	10	9.7	6	5.8	8	7.8	10	9.7	6	5.8	0	0.0
Kentucky	89	76	85.4	30	33.7	21	23.6	56	62.9	15	16.9	10	6.7	6	6.7	8	9.0	24	27.0	4	4.5	2	2.2
Mississippi	111	105	94.6	68	61.3	40	36.0	101	91.0	17	15.3	43	38.7	12	10.8	4	3.6	25	22.5	0	0.0	19	17.1
Tennessee	74	63	85.1	21	28.4	20	27.0	44	59.5	13	17.6	13	17.6	6	8.1	3	4.1	15	20.3	9	12.2	2	2.7
CENSUS DIVISION 6, WEST NORTH CENTRAL	648	619	95.5	282	43.5	138	21.3	315	48.6	95	14.7	52	8.0	53	8.2	40	6.2	272	42.0	127	19.6	62	9.6
Iowa	126	119	94.4	59	46.8	24	19.0	65	51.6	19	15.1	11	8.7	12	9.5	8	6.3	58	46.0	37	29.4	13	10.3
Kansas	151	135	89.4	44	29.1	19	12.6	53	35.1	17	11.3	8	5.3	10	6.6	9	6.0	66	43.7	48	31.8	15	9.9
Minnesota	106	103	97.2	47	44.3	21	19.8	56	52.8	11	10.4	6	5.7	8	7.5	3	2.8	43	40.6	3	2.8	3	2.8
Missouri	146	146	100.0	82	56.2	41	28.1	83	56.8	21	14.4	16	11.0	6	5.5	9	6.2	37	25.3	17	11.6	11	7.5
Nebraska	49	48	98.0	21	42.9	15	30.6	25	51.0	15	30.6	5	10.2	6	12.2	5	10.2	29	59.2	10	20.4	6	12.2
North Dakota	28	26	92.9	11	39.3			12	42.9	9	32.1	4	14.3	6	21.4	5	17.9	15	53.6	5	17.9	4	14.3
South Dakota	42	42	100.0	18	42.9			21	50.0	3	7.1	2	4.8	3	7.1	1	2.4	24	57.1	7	16.7	10	23.8
CENSUS DIVISION 7, WEST SOUTH CENTRAL	892	644	72.2	235	26.3	144	16.1	403	45.2	165	18.5	51	5.7	53	5.9	103	11.5	93	10.4	29	3.3	12	1.3
Arkansas	86	67	77.9	24	27.9	24	27.9	39	45.3	12	14.0	3	3.5	1	1.2	7	8.1	7	15.1	3	3.5	0	0.0
Louisiana	97	73	75.3	39	40.2	22	22.7	55	56.7	28	28.9	7	7.2	11	11.3	11	11.3	18	18.6	6	6.2	4	4.1
Oklahoma	127	105	82.7	40	31.5	19	15.0	51	40.2	13	10.2	7	5.5	6	4.7	8	6.3	26	20.5	7	5.5	4	3.1
Texas	582	399	68.6	132	22.7	79	13.6	258	44.3	112	19.2	34	5.8	35	6.0	77	13.2	36	6.2	13	2.2	4	0.7
CENSUS DIVISION 8, MOUNTAIN	342	299	87.4	124	36.3	61	17.8	198	57.9	70	20.5	18	5.3	29	8.5	15	4.4	83	24.3	33	9.6	21	6.1
Arizona	69	56	81.2	21	30.4	20	29.0	42	60.9	17	24.6	5	7.2	6	8.7	5	7.2	4	5.8	3	4.3	4	5.8
Colorado	74	67	90.5	28	37.8	14	18.9	50	67.6	25	33.8	5	6.8	9	13.0	2	2.7	13	17.6	5	6.8	3	4.1
Idaho	28	27	96.4	9	32.1	5	17.9	14	50.0	6	21.4	0	0.0	6	8.1	1	3.6	10	35.7	3	10.7	1	3.6
Montana	51	48	94.1	21	41.2	8	15.7	21	41.2	6	11.8	3	5.9	4	7.8	3	5.9	30	58.8	9	17.6	6	11.8
Nevada	27	16	59.3	6	22.2	3	11.1	13	48.1	4	12.1	3	11.0	3	11.1	3	11.1	0	0.0	0	0.0	0	0.0
New Mexico	33	30	90.9	15	45.5	4	12.1	23	69.7	4	12.1	1	3.0	3	9.1	1	3.0	4	12.1	2	6.1	1	3.0
Utah	34	31	91.2	16	47.1	7	20.6	18	52.9	9	26.5	1	2.9	1	2.9	0	0.0	10	29.4	6	17.6	0	0.0
Wyoming	26	24	92.3	8	30.8	0	0.0	17	65.4	0	0.0	1	3.8	1	3.8	0	0.0	12	46.2	5	19.2	6	23.1
CENSUS DIVISION 9, PACIFIC	428	371	86.7	167	39.0	151	35.3	322	75.2	145	33.9	31	7.2	50	11.7	18	4.2	96	22.4	28	6.5	14	3.3
Alaska	12	10	83.3	4	16.7	1	8.3	7	58.3	1	8.3	0	0.0	1	8.3	0	0.0	6	50.0	4	33.3	1	8.3
California	264	224	84.8	103	39.0	109	41.3	202	76.5	113	42.8	20	7.6	37	14.0	12	4.5	64	24.2	8	3.0	8	3.0
Hawaii	19	14	73.7	5	26.3	5	26.3	12	63.2	3	15.8	7	5.9	3	15.8	2	10.5	7	36.8	4	21.1	2	10.5
Oregon	61	60	98.4	30	49.2	18	29.5	51	83.6	10	16.4	3	4.9	4	6.6	1	1.6	9	14.8	9	14.8	1	1.6
Washington	72	63	87.5	27	37.5	18	25.0	50	69.4	18	25.0	7	9.7	5	6.9	3	4.2	10	13.9	4	4.2	2	2.8

Table 7 (Continued)

These data include only hospital-based facilities and services as reported by responding hospitals in Section C of the 2014 AHA Annual Survey, beginning on page 217. All hospitals are represented with Community Hospitals listed separately under United States. No estimates have been made for nonresponding hospitals. Definitions of facilities and services are listed in the Glossary, page 205.

CARDIOLOGY AND CARDIAC SERVICES

CLASSIFICATION	HOSPITALS REPORTING	ADULT CARDIOLOGY SERVICES Number	Percent	PEDIATRIC CARDIOLOGY SERVICES Number	Percent	ADULT DIAGNOSTIC CATHETERIZATION Number	Percent	PEDIATRIC DIAGNOSTIC CATHETERIZATION Number	Percent	ADULT INTERVENTIONAL CARDIAC CATHETERIZATION Number	Percent	PEDIATRIC INTERVENTIONAL CARDIAC CATHETERIZATION Number	Percent	ADULT CARDIAC SURGERY Number	Percent	PEDIATRIC CARDIAC SURGERY Number	Percent	ADULT CARDIAC ELECTRO-PHYSIOLOGY Number	Percent	PEDIATRIC CARDIAC ELECTRO-PHYSIOLOGY Number	Percent	CARDIAC REHABILITATION Number	Percent
UNITED STATES	4,601	2,345	51.0	413	9.0	1,778	38.6	194	4.2	1,554	33.8	173	3.8	1,119	24.3	170	3.7	1,342	29.2	205	4.5	2,431	52.8
COMMUNITY HOSPITALS	3,921	2,243	57.2	407	10.4	1,712	43.7	189	4.8	1,499	38.2	170	4.3	1,078	27.5	167	4.3	1,294	33.0	201	5.1	2,368	60.4
CENSUS DIVISION 1, NEW ENGLAND	169	111	65.7	17	10.1	70	41.4	9	5.3	52	30.8	9	5.3	38	22.5	8	4.7	60	35.5	6	3.6	117	69.2
Connecticut	27	21	77.8	3	11.1	15	55.6	1	3.7	14	51.9	1	3.7	11	40.7	1	3.7	13	48.1	1	3.7	20	74.1
Maine	29	16	55.2	4	13.8	9	31.0	1	3.4	4	13.8	1	3.4	3	10.3	1	3.4	5	17.2	1	3.4	23	79.3
Massachusetts	68	45	66.2	6	8.8	30	44.1	3	4.4	21	30.9	3	4.4	18	26.5	4	5.9	26	38.2	3	4.4	42	61.8
New Hampshire	23	14	60.9	2	8.7	8	34.8	2	8.7	7	30.4	1	4.3	3	13.0	1	4.3	7	30.4	1	4.3	17	73.9
Rhode Island	10	8	80.0	1	10.0	6	60.0	1	10.0	4	40.0	1	10.0	1	10.0	0	0.0	5	50.0	0	0.0	5	50.0
Vermont	12	7	58.3	1	8.3	2	16.7	1	8.3	2	16.7	2	16.7	2	16.7	1	8.3	4	33.3	0	0.0	10	83.3
CENSUS DIVISION 2, MIDDLE ATLANTIC	402	279	69.4	74	18.4	202	50.2	23	5.7	170	42.3	21	5.2	119	29.6	18	4.5	151	37.6	30	7.5	231	57.5
New Jersey	68	53	77.9	19	27.9	51	75.0	3	4.4	40	58.8	2	2.9	18	26.5	2	2.9	26	38.2	5	7.4	41	60.3
New York	154	117	76.0	38	24.7	67	43.5	15	9.7	54	35.1	14	9.1	39	25.3	10	6.5	60	39.0	16	10.4	86	55.8
Pennsylvania	180	109	60.6	17	9.4	84	46.7	5	2.8	76	42.2	5	2.8	62	34.4	6	3.3	65	36.1	9	5.0	104	57.8
CENSUS DIVISION 3, SOUTH ATLANTIC	644	402	62.4	60	9.3	322	50.0	28	4.3	259	40.2	25	3.9	166	25.8	26	4.0	248	38.5	30	4.7	352	54.7
Delaware	8	5	62.5	1	12.5	4	50.0	1	12.5	5	62.5	1	12.5	2	50.0	1	12.5	4	50.0	1	12.5	4	50.0
District of Columbia	10	6	60.0	1	10.0	5	50.0	1	10.0	3	30.0	1	10.0	2	20.0	1	10.0	4	40.0	1	10.0	4	40.0
Florida	166	120	72.3	24	14.5	100	60.2	12	7.2	87	52.4	9	5.4	61	36.7	11	6.6	78	47.0	10	6.0	78	47.0
Georgia	96	50	52.1	2	2.1	44	45.8	0	0.0	36	37.5	0	0.0	17	17.7	0	0.0	35	36.5	1	1.0	41	42.7
Maryland	46	35	76.1	6	13.0	33	71.7	3	6.5	25	54.3	3	6.5	10	21.7	2	4.3	31	67.4	4	8.7	31	67.4
North Carolina	110	71	64.5	12	10.9	47	42.7	5	4.5	36	32.7	5	4.5	26	23.6	5	4.5	35	31.8	6	5.5	74	67.3
South Carolina	76	36	50.7	3	4.2	29	40.8	1	1.4	16	22.5	1	1.4	17	23.9	1	1.4	18	25.4	2	2.8	37	52.1
Virginia	76	51	67.1	9	11.8	39	51.3	4	5.3	36	47.4	4	5.3	22	28.9	4	5.3	35	46.1	4	5.3	53	69.7
West Virginia	61	28	45.9	2	3.3	21	34.4	1	1.6	15	24.6	1	1.6	7	11.5	1	1.6	8	13.1	1	1.6	30	49.2
CENSUS DIVISION 4, EAST NORTH CENTRAL	699	421	60.2	69	9.9	319	45.6	26	3.7	279	39.9	24	3.4	212	30.3	25	3.6	256	36.6	31	4.4	502	71.8
Illinois	162	114	70.4	30	18.5	88	54.3	8	4.9	83	51.2	8	4.9	64	39.5	8	4.9	73	45.1	12	7.4	129	79.6
Indiana	123	59	48.0	8	6.5	47	38.2	3	2.4	43	35.0	3	2.4	31	25.2	4	3.1	35	28.5	3	2.4	78	63.4
Michigan	130	74	56.9	10	7.7	57	43.8	3	2.3	45	34.6	3	2.3	33	25.4	4	3.1	51	39.2	6	4.6	86	66.2
Ohio	141	105	74.5	14	9.9	81	57.4	8	5.7	64	45.4	6	4.3	53	37.6	6	4.3	60	42.6	6	4.3	102	72.3
Wisconsin	143	69	48.3	7	4.9	46	32.2	4	2.8	44	30.8	4	2.8	31	21.7	4	2.8	37	25.9	4	2.8	107	74.8
CENSUS DIVISION 5, EAST SOUTH CENTRAL	377	165	43.8	28	7.4	127	33.7	18	4.8	104	27.6	12	3.2	75	19.9	13	3.4	84	22.3	15	4.0	149	39.5
Alabama	103	37	35.9	5	4.9	33	32.0	6	5.8	29	28.2	3	2.9	24	23.3	3	2.9	27	26.2	3	2.9	34	33.0
Kentucky	89	47	52.8	6	6.7	39	43.8	2	2.2	28	31.5	3	2.2	20	22.5	3	2.2	18	20.2	3	3.4	53	59.6
Mississippi	111	35	31.5	6	5.4	22	19.8	2	1.8	19	17.1	1	0.9	11	9.9	2	1.8	16	14.4	2	1.8	22	19.8
Tennessee	74	46	62.2	11	14.9	33	44.6	8	10.8	28	37.8	6	8.1	20	27.0	6	8.1	23	31.1	7	9.5	40	54.1
CENSUS DIVISION 6, WEST NORTH CENTRAL	648	237	36.6	39	6.0	152	23.5	16	2.5	148	22.8	15	2.3	97	15.0	17	2.6	121	18.7	20	3.1	464	71.6
Iowa	126	42	33.3	4	3.2	27	21.4	2	1.6	27	21.4	2	1.6	13	10.3	2	1.6	21	16.7	2	1.6	109	86.5
Kansas	151	39	25.8	8	5.3	24	15.9	2	1.3	24	15.9	2	1.3	15	9.9	1	0.7	17	11.3	3	2.0	70	46.4
Minnesota	106	42	39.6	9	8.5	20	18.9	3	2.8	20	18.9	3	2.8	16	15.1	3	2.8	26	24.5	6	5.7	94	88.7
Missouri	146	76	52.1	7	4.8	55	37.7	4	2.7	52	35.6	4	2.1	36	24.7	6	4.1	38	26.0	5	3.4	93	63.7
Nebraska	49	19	38.8	5	10.2	14	28.6	1	2.0	14	28.6	1	2.0	7	14.3	3	6.1	11	22.4	2	4.1	41	83.7
North Dakota	28	9	32.1	3	10.7	6	21.4	2	7.1	6	21.4	2	7.1	6	21.4	3	10.7	5	17.9	1	3.6	22	78.6
South Dakota	42	10	23.8	3	7.1	6	14.3	2	4.8	5	11.9	2	4.8	4	9.5	1	2.4	3	7.1	1	2.4	35	83.3
CENSUS DIVISION 7, WEST SOUTH CENTRAL	892	336	37.7	41	4.6	276	30.9	24	2.7	255	28.6	22	2.5	200	22.4	20	2.2	187	21.0	23	2.6	283	31.7
Arkansas	86	34	39.5	2	2.3	24	27.9	2	2.3	24	27.9	1	1.2	21	24.4	1	1.2	15	17.4	3	3.5	32	37.2
Louisiana	97	49	50.5	10	10.3	43	44.3	5	5.2	39	40.2	3	3.1	31	32.0	3	3.1	28	28.9	3	3.1	37	38.1
Oklahoma	127	44	34.6	3	2.4	32	25.2	2	1.6	29	22.8	2	1.6	17	13.4	2	1.6	18	14.2	2	1.6	33	26.0
Texas	582	209	35.9	26	4.5	177	30.4	15	2.6	163	28.0	16	2.7	131	22.5	14	2.4	126	21.6	15	2.6	181	31.1
CENSUS DIVISION 8, MOUNTAIN	342	143	41.8	24	7.0	112	32.7	14	4.1	108	31.6	13	3.8	69	20.2	12	3.5	77	22.5	16	4.7	153	44.7
Arizona	69	43	62.3	7	10.1	33	47.8	3	4.3	34	49.3	3	4.3	21	30.4	3	4.3	24	34.8	6	8.7	29	42.0
Colorado	74	39	52.7	4	5.4	35	47.3	3	4.1	33	44.6	3	4.1	18	24.3	2	2.7	20	27.0	4	5.4	43	58.1
Idaho	28	11	39.3	3	10.7	7	25.0	1	3.6	7	25.0	1	3.6	4	14.3	1	3.6	5	17.9	1	3.6	10	35.7
Montana	51	9	17.6	2	3.9	8	15.7	0	0.0	8	15.7	0	0.0	5	9.8	0	0.0	7	13.7	1	2.0	27	52.9
Nevada	27	12	33.3	4	14.8	9	33.3	2	7.4	7	25.9	2	7.4	6	22.2	2	7.4	5	18.5	2	7.4	7	25.9
New Mexico	33	12	36.4	3	9.1	7	21.2	3	9.1	6	18.2	2	6.1	5	15.2	2	6.1	7	21.2	2	6.1	10	30.3
Utah	34	14	41.2	1	2.9	10	29.4	2	5.9	10	29.4	2	5.9	7	20.6	2	5.9	6	17.6	0	0.0	13	38.2
Wyoming	26	6	23.1	0	0.0	3	11.5	0	0.0	3	11.5	0	0.0	3	11.5	0	0.0	3	11.5	0	0.0	14	53.8
CENSUS DIVISION 9, PACIFIC	428	251	58.6	61	14.3	198	46.3	36	8.4	179	41.8	32	7.5	143	33.4	31	7.2	158	36.9	34	7.9	180	42.1
Alaska	12	4	33.3	2	16.7	3	25.0	1	8.3	3	25.0	0	0.0	1	8.3	1	8.3	2	16.7	0	0.0	6	50.0
California	264	167	63.3	43	16.3	131	49.6	20	7.6	118	44.7	20	7.6	103	39.0	20	7.6	109	41.3	21	8.0	108	40.9
Hawaii	19	9	47.4	3	15.8	7	36.8	3	15.8	7	36.8	2	10.5	6	31.6	1	5.3	7	36.8	2	10.5	5	26.3
Oregon	61	30	49.2	8	13.1	23	37.7	6	9.8	19	31.1	4	6.6	16	26.2	4	6.6	17	27.9	6	9.8	28	45.9
Washington	72	41	56.9	6	8.3	34	47.2	6	8.3	32	44.4	6	8.3	17	23.6	5	6.9	23	31.9	5	6.9	33	45.8

Table 7 (Continued)

These data include only hospital-based facilities and services as reported by responding hospitals in Section C of the 2014 AHA Annual Survey, beginning on page 217. All hospitals are represented with Community Hospitals listed separately under United States. No estimates have been made for nonresponding hospitals. Definitions of facilities and services are listed in the Glossary, page 205.

CLASSIFICATION	HOSPITALS REPORTING	EMERGENCY SERVICES — EMERGENCY DEPARTMENT Number	Percent	PEDIATRIC EMERGENCY DEPARTMENT Number	Percent	FREESTANDING/SATELLITE EMERGENCY DEPARTMENT Number	Percent	TRAUMA CENTER (CERTIFIED) Number	Percent	ENDOSCOPIC SERVICES — ENDOSCOPIC ULTRASOUND Number	Percent	ABLATION OF BARRETT'S ESOPHAGUS Number	Percent	ESOPHAGEAL IMPEDANCE STUDY Number	Percent	ENDOSCOPIC RETROGRADE CHOLANGIOPANCREATOGRAPHY Number	Percent	OPTICAL COLONOSCOPY Number	Percent
UNITED STATES	4,601	3,810	82.8	781	17.0	315	6.8	1,705	37.1	1,579	34.3	1,156	25.1	1,097	23.8	1,931	42.0	2,949	64.1
COMMUNITY HOSPITALS	3,921	3,593	91.6	751	19.2	300	7.7	1,674	42.7	1,511	38.5	1,103	28.1	1,047	26.7	1,850	47.2	2,796	71.3
CENSUS DIVISION 1, NEW ENGLAND	169	138	81.7	40	23.7	15	8.9	61	36.1	77	45.6	61	36.1	54	32.0	91	53.8	125	74.0
Connecticut	27	22	81.5	7	25.9	4	14.8	12	44.4	17	63.0	17	63.0	13	48.1	21	77.8	21	77.8
Maine	29	27	93.1	6	20.7	3	10.3	13	44.8	11	37.9	7	24.1	6	20.7	7	24.1	24	82.8
Massachusetts	68	48	70.6	17	25.0	3	4.4	17	25.0	27	39.7	20	29.4	19	27.9	37	54.4	42	61.8
New Hampshire	23	21	91.3	8	34.8	4	17.4	13	56.5	11	47.8	9	39.1	7	30.4	12	52.2	18	78.3
Rhode Island	10	9	90.0	1	10.0	1	10.0	2	20.0	8	80.0	5	50.0	6	60.0	8	80.0	9	90.0
Vermont	12	11	91.7	1	8.3	0	0.0	4	33.3	3	25.0	3	25.0	3	25.0	6	50.0	11	91.7
CENSUS DIVISION 2, MIDDLE ATLANTIC	402	327	81.3	106	26.4	29	7.2	109	27.1	204	50.7	130	32.3	126	31.3	258	64.2	284	70.6
New Jersey	68	56	82.4	36	52.9	10	14.7	18	26.5	47	69.1	34	50.0	32	47.1	51	75.0	48	70.6
New York	154	138	89.6	51	33.1	12	7.8	57	37.0	80	51.9	55	35.7	46	29.9	102	66.2	123	79.9
Pennsylvania	180	133	73.9	19	10.6	7	3.9	34	18.9	77	42.8	41	22.8	48	26.7	105	58.3	113	62.8
CENSUS DIVISION 3, SOUTH ATLANTIC	644	523	81.2	120	18.6	58	9.0	143	22.2	244	37.9	184	28.6	201	31.2	341	53.0	450	69.9
Delaware	8	5	62.5	3	37.5	2	25.0	5	62.5	2	25.0	2	25.0	3	37.5	3	37.5	5	62.5
District of Columbia	10	7	70.0	2	20.0	2	20.0	5	50.0	6	60.0	3	30.0	4	40.0	4	40.0	6	60.0
Florida	166	135	81.3	42	25.3	16	9.6	26	15.7	72	43.4	56	33.7	58	34.9	107	64.5	124	74.7
Georgia	96	78	81.3	11	11.5	2	2.1	13	13.5	38	39.6	27	28.1	31	32.3	50	52.1	66	68.8
Maryland	46	38	82.6	21	45.7	6	13.0	17	37.0	27	58.7	15	32.6	18	39.1	31	67.4	35	76.1
North Carolina	110	95	86.4	13	11.8	13	11.8	19	17.3	34	30.9	27	24.5	31	28.2	52	47.3	86	78.2
South Carolina	71	54	76.1	5	7.0	3	4.2	14	19.7	20	28.2	15	21.1	14	19.7	27	38.0	34	47.9
Virginia	76	63	82.9	18	23.7	13	17.1	13	17.1	29	38.2	26	34.2	26	34.2	44	57.9	58	76.3
West Virginia	61	48	78.7	5	8.2	1	1.6	31	50.8	16	26.2	13	21.3	16	26.2	23	37.7	36	59.0
CENSUS DIVISION 4, EAST NORTH CENTRAL	699	602	86.1	123	17.6	69	9.9	267	38.2	278	39.8	214	30.6	200	28.6	333	47.6	489	70.0
Illinois	162	150	92.6	34	21.0	13	8.0	63	38.9	72	44.4	60	37.0	48	29.6	100	61.7	123	75.9
Indiana	123	93	75.6	11	8.9	5	4.1	18	14.6	41	33.3	35	28.5	24	19.5	55	44.7	85	69.1
Michigan	130	112	86.2	26	20.0	13	10.0	46	35.4	55	42.3	29	22.3	29	22.3	55	42.3	95	73.1
Ohio	141	126	89.4	28	19.9	26	18.4	45	31.9	62	44.0	46	32.6	53	37.6	73	51.8	95	67.4
Wisconsin	143	121	84.6	24	16.8	12	8.4	95	66.4	48	33.6	44	30.8	46	32.2	50	35.0	91	63.6
CENSUS DIVISION 5, EAST SOUTH CENTRAL	377	310	82.2	43	11.4	20	5.3	146	38.7	87	23.1	73	19.4	79	21.0	120	31.8	182	48.3
Alabama	103	83	80.6	6	5.8	2	1.9	34	33.0	20	19.4	17	16.5	19	18.4	32	31.1	48	46.6
Kentucky	89	78	87.6	8	9.0	9	10.1	21	23.6	28	31.5	22	24.7	20	22.5	39	43.8	52	58.4
Mississippi	111	88	79.3	17	15.3	5	4.5	77	69.4	17	15.3	13	11.7	16	14.4	21	18.9	36	32.4
Tennessee	74	61	82.4	12	16.2	4	5.4	14	18.9	22	29.7	21	28.4	24	32.4	28	37.8	46	62.2
CENSUS DIVISION 6, WEST NORTH CENTRAL	648	581	89.7	88	13.6	22	3.4	300	46.3	142	21.9	99	15.3	101	15.6	151	23.3	428	66.0
Iowa	126	119	94.4	16	12.7	0	0.0	94	74.6	30	23.8	17	13.5	16	12.7	22	17.5	90	71.4
Kansas	151	127	84.1	14	9.3	5	3.3	27	17.9	17	11.3	19	12.6	17	11.3	26	17.2	93	61.6
Minnesota	106	100	94.3	17	16.0	4	3.8	77	72.6	32	30.2	17	16.0	16	15.1	24	22.6	76	71.7
Missouri	146	117	80.1	19	13.0	8	5.5	32	21.9	36	24.7	29	19.9	28	19.2	54	37.0	88	60.3
Nebraska	49	48	98.0	10	20.4	2	4.1	29	59.2	16	32.7	10	20.4	12	24.5	13	26.5	35	71.4
North Dakota	28	28	100.0	5	17.9	2	7.1	15	53.6	3	10.7	3	10.7	5	17.9	6	21.4	16	57.1
South Dakota	42	42	100.0	7	16.7	1	2.4	26	61.9	8	19.0	4	9.5	7	16.7	6	14.3	30	71.4
CENSUS DIVISION 7, WEST SOUTH CENTRAL	892	669	75.0	101	11.3	54	6.1	358	40.1	217	24.3	159	17.8	128	14.3	277	31.1	466	52.2
Arkansas	86	68	79.1	5	5.8	1	1.2	48	55.8	19	22.1	10	11.6	13	15.1	20	23.3	51	59.3
Louisiana	97	68	70.1	11	11.3	4	4.1	11	11.3	37	38.1	23	23.7	22	22.7	34	35.1	57	58.8
Oklahoma	127	114	89.8	21	16.5	4	3.1	55	43.3	24	18.9	22	17.3	14	11.0	35	27.6	74	58.3
Texas	582	419	72.0	64	11.0	45	7.7	244	41.9	137	23.5	104	17.9	79	13.6	188	32.3	284	48.8
CENSUS DIVISION 8, MOUNTAIN	342	291	85.1	69	20.2	30	8.8	157	45.9	109	31.9	78	22.8	81	23.7	123	36.0	219	64.0
Arizona	69	53	76.8	19	27.5	6	8.7	20	29.0	31	44.9	25	36.2	19	27.5	37	53.6	40	58.0
Colorado	74	66	89.2	10	13.5	12	16.2	55	74.3	28	37.8	22	29.7	26	35.1	37	50.0	56	75.7
Idaho	28	26	92.9	7	25.0	4	14.3	6	21.4	8	28.6	7	25.0	6	21.4	7	25.0	21	75.0
Montana	51	48	94.1	11	21.6	2	3.9	30	58.8	7	13.7	3	5.9	5	9.8	8	15.7	25	49.0
Nevada	27	16	59.3	4	14.8	1	3.7	5	18.5	7	25.9	5	18.5	1	3.7	9	33.3	14	51.9
New Mexico	33	29	87.9	5	15.2	2	6.1	9	27.3	11	33.3	8	24.2	8	24.2	10	30.3	22	66.7
Utah	34	29	85.3	8	23.5	3	8.8	18	52.9	12	35.3	7	20.6	12	35.3	13	38.2	24	70.6
Wyoming	26	24	92.3	5	19.2	0	0.0	14	53.8	5	19.2	1	3.8	4	15.4	2	7.7	17	65.4
CENSUS DIVISION 9, PACIFIC	428	369	86.2	91	21.3	18	4.2	164	38.3	221	51.6	158	36.9	127	29.7	237	55.4	306	71.5
Alaska	12	10	83.3	1	8.3	0	0.0	5	41.7	3	25.0	3	25.0	4	33.3	2	16.7	8	66.7
California	264	217	82.2	60	22.7	10	3.8	68	25.8	147	55.7	106	40.2	87	33.0	174	65.9	184	69.7
Hawaii	19	16	84.2	4	21.1	0	0.0	5	26.3	7	36.8	7	36.8	4	21.1	9	47.4	8	42.1
Oregon	61	60	98.4	10	16.4	2	3.3	40	65.6	32	52.5	21	34.4	12	19.7	20	32.8	50	82.0
Washington	72	66	91.7	16	22.2	6	8.3	46	63.9	32	44.4	21	29.2	20	27.8	32	44.4	56	77.8

Table 7 (Continued)

These data include only hospital-based facilities and services as reported by responding hospitals in Section C of the 2014 AHA Annual Survey, beginning on page 217. All hospitals are represented with Community Hospitals listed separately under United States. No estimates have been made for nonresponding hospitals. Definitions of facilities and services are listed in the Glossary, page 205.

CLASSIFICATION	HOSPITALS REPORTING	PHYSICAL REHABILITATION SERVICES												PSYCHIATRIC SERVICES									
		ASSISTIVE TECHNOLOGY CENTER		ELECTRO-DIAGNOSTIC SERVICES		PHYSICAL REHABILITATION OUTPATIENT SERVICES		PROSTHETIC ORTHOTIC SERVICES		ROBOT ASSISTED WALKING THERAPY		SIMULATED REHABILITATION ENVIRONMENT		CHILD/ADOLESCENT SERVICES		CONSULTATION/LIAISON SERVICES		EDUCATION SERVICES		EMERGENCY SERVICES		GERIATRIC SERVICES	
		Number	Percent	Number	Percent	Number	Percent	Number	Percent	Number	Percent	Number	Percent	Number	Percent	Number	Percent	Number	Percent	Number	Percent	Number	Percent
UNITED STATES	4,601	1,004	22.5	1,215	26.4	3,330	72.4	860	18.7	196	4.3	1,232	26.8	835	18.1	1,525	33.1	1,138	24.7	1,545	33.6	1,408	30.6
COMMUNITY HOSPITALS	3,921	919	23.4	1,145	29.2	3,155	80.5	775	19.8	182	4.6	1,134	28.9	618	15.8	1,296	33.1	878	22.4	1,352	34.5	1,134	28.9
CENSUS DIVISION 1, NEW ENGLAND	169	48	28.4	59	34.9	143	84.6	45	26.6	11	6.5	59	34.9	62	36.7	98	58.0	70	41.4	87	51.5	72	42.6
Connecticut	27	12	44.4	12	44.4	22	81.5	12	44.4	4	14.8	15	55.6	16	59.3	21	77.8	17	63.0	22	81.5	17	63.0
Maine	29	7	24.1	8	27.6	26	89.7	4	13.8	1	3.4	11	37.9	9	31.0	10	34.5	7	24.1	9	31.0	6	20.7
Massachusetts	68	17	25.0	26	38.2	56	82.4	14	20.6	5	7.4	21	30.9	22	32.4	42	61.8	30	44.1	32	47.1	29	42.6
New Hampshire	23	7	30.4	6	26.1	20	87.0	7	30.4	1	4.3	6	26.1	8	34.8	11	47.8	8	34.8	11	47.8	8	34.8
Rhode Island	10	2	20.0	4	40.0	8	80.0	3	30.0	0	0.0	2	20.0	4	40.0	8	80.0	4	40.0	8	80.0	7	70.0
Vermont	12	3	25.0	3	25.0	11	91.7	5	41.7	0	0.0	4	33.3	3	25.0	6	50.0	4	33.3	5	41.7	5	41.7
CENSUS DIVISION 2, MIDDLE ATLANTIC	402	126	31.3	200	49.8	317	78.9	120	29.9	34	8.5	153	38.1	129	32.1	235	58.5	157	39.1	210	52.2	196	48.8
New Jersey	68	33	48.5	40	58.8	56	82.4	30	44.1	7	10.3	33	48.5	28	41.2	49	72.1	36	52.9	47	69.1	37	54.4
New York	154	47	30.5	80	51.9	138	89.6	59	38.3	11	7.1	57	37.0	60	39.0	97	63.0	62	40.3	88	57.1	79	51.3
Pennsylvania	180	46	25.6	80	44.4	123	68.3	31	17.2	16	8.9	63	35.0	41	22.8	89	49.4	59	32.8	75	41.7	80	44.4
CENSUS DIVISION 3, SOUTH ATLANTIC	644	162	25.2	181	28.1	469	72.8	172	26.7	35	5.4	185	28.7	119	18.5	243	37.7	174	27.0	249	38.7	212	32.9
Delaware	8	2	25.0	2	25.0	5	62.5	3	37.5	0	0.0	2	25.0	4	50.0	4	50.0	4	50.0	3	37.5	4	50.0
District of Columbia	10	5	50.0	6	60.0	8	80.0	5	50.0	2	20.0	6	60.0	4	40.0	6	60.0	2	20.0	7	70.0	6	60.0
Florida	166	59	35.5	45	27.1	130	78.3	40	24.1	11	6.6	48	28.9	26	15.7	61	36.7	39	23.5	59	35.5	48	28.9
Georgia	96	8	8.3	14	14.6	69	71.9	14	14.6	1	1.0	18	18.8	8	8.3	26	27.1	15	15.6	19	19.8	23	24.0
Maryland	46	15	32.6	23	50.0	36	78.3	18	39.1	4	8.7	20	43.5	18	39.1	32	69.6	25	54.3	34	73.9	27	58.7
North Carolina	110	33	30.0	36	32.7	87	79.1	17	15.5	6	5.5	40	36.4	20	18.2	41	37.3	34	30.9	47	42.7	41	37.3
South Carolina	71	5	7.0	8	11.3	33	46.5	46	64.8	4	5.6	11	15.5	10	14.1	21	29.6	11	15.5	24	33.8	16	22.5
Virginia	76	29	38.2	30	39.5	59	77.6	20	26.3	5	6.6	30	39.5	17	22.4	35	46.1	26	34.2	39	51.3	28	36.8
West Virginia	61	6	9.8	17	27.9	42	68.9	9	14.8	2	3.3	10	16.4	12	19.7	16	26.2	18	29.5	17	27.9	19	31.1
CENSUS DIVISION 4, EAST NORTH CENTRAL	699	164	23.5	251	35.9	579	82.8	161	23.0	23	3.3	274	39.2	151	21.6	284	40.6	219	31.3	270	38.6	245	35.1
Illinois	162	34	21.0	65	40.1	140	86.4	39	24.1	6	3.7	68	42.0	45	27.8	69	42.6	62	38.3	72	44.4	65	40.1
Indiana	123	32	26.0	35	28.5	92	74.8	25	20.3	3	2.4	37	30.1	26	21.1	34	27.6	31	25.2	38	30.9	39	31.7
Michigan	130	40	30.8	55	42.3	112	86.2	24	18.5	7	5.4	52	40.0	24	18.5	63	48.5	44	33.8	59	45.4	45	34.6
Ohio	141	34	24.1	57	40.4	118	83.7	33	23.4	3	2.1	56	39.7	26	18.4	64	45.4	45	31.9	59	41.8	54	38.3
Wisconsin	143	24	16.8	39	27.3	117	81.8	40	28.0	4	2.8	61	42.7	30	21.0	54	37.8	37	25.9	42	29.4	42	29.4
CENSUS DIVISION 5, EAST SOUTH CENTRAL	377	55	14.6	71	18.8	246	65.3	45	11.9	18	4.8	66	17.5	40	10.6	79	21.0	69	18.3	91	24.1	129	34.2
Alabama	103	15	14.6	17	16.5	64	62.1	14	13.6	7	6.8	14	13.6	12	11.7	22	21.4	20	19.4	24	23.3	37	35.9
Kentucky	89	17	19.1	21	23.6	65	73.0	8	9.0	4	4.5	16	18.0	8	9.0	25	28.1	20	22.5	26	29.2	27	30.0
Mississippi	111	7	6.3	14	12.6	59	53.2	13	11.7	3	2.7	18	16.2	9	8.1	16	14.4	15	13.5	17	15.3	44	39.6
Tennessee	74	16	21.6	19	25.7	58	78.4	10	13.5	4	5.4	18	24.3	11	14.9	16	21.6	14	18.9	24	32.4	24	32.4
CENSUS DIVISION 6, WEST NORTH CENTRAL	648	108	16.7	130	20.1	522	80.6	102	15.7	17	2.6	146	22.5	114	17.6	166	25.6	139	21.5	193	29.8	169	26.1
Iowa	126	29	23.0	21	16.7	104	82.5	16	12.7	1	0.8	31	24.6	28	22.2	33	26.2	33	26.2	44	34.9	34	27.0
Kansas	151	14	9.3	15	9.9	117	77.5	12	7.9	6	4.0	21	13.9	9	6.0	14	9.3	13	8.6	29	19.2	25	16.6
Minnesota	106	23	21.7	27	25.5	97	91.5	17	16.0	3	2.8	28	26.4	26	24.5	40	37.7	28	26.4	36	34.0	53	33.0
Missouri	146	17	11.6	35	24.0	104	71.2	34	23.3	5	3.4	45	30.8	29	19.9	53	36.3	41	28.1	58	39.7	53	36.3
Nebraska	49	12	24.5	14	28.6	42	85.7	10	20.4	1	2.0	9	18.4	10	20.4	10	20.4	9	18.4	7	14.3	9	18.4
North Dakota	28	7	25.0	7	25.0	23	82.1	5	17.9	1	3.6	6	21.4	8	28.6	8	28.6	8	28.6	10	35.7	10	35.7
South Dakota	42	6	14.3	11	26.2	35	83.3	8	19.0	0	0.0	6	14.3	4	9.5	8	19.0	7	16.7	9	21.4	6	14.3
CENSUS DIVISION 7, WEST SOUTH CENTRAL	892	191	21.4	113	12.7	510	57.2	82	9.2	30	3.4	174	19.5	98	11.0	159	17.8	138	15.5	172	19.3	206	23.1
Arkansas	86	14	16.3	11	12.8	56	65.1	8	9.3	5	5.8	12	14.0	10	11.6	18	20.9	11	12.8	21	24.4	27	31.4
Louisiana	97	30	30.9	15	15.5	54	55.7	9	9.3	1	1.0	23	23.7	13	13.4	21	21.6	23	23.7	33	34.0	32	33.0
Oklahoma	127	27	21.3	20	15.7	83	65.4	16	12.6	1	0.8	19	15.0	14	11.0	30	23.6	19	15.0	27	21.3	31	24.4
Texas	582	120	20.6	67	11.5	317	54.5	49	8.4	23	4.0	120	20.6	61	10.5	90	15.5	85	14.6	91	15.6	116	19.9
CENSUS DIVISION 8, MOUNTAIN	342	86	25.1	79	23.1	241	70.5	60	17.5	15	4.4	73	21.3	48	14.0	106	31.0	74	21.6	116	33.9	90	26.3
Arizona	69	18	26.1	23	33.3	41	59.4	16	23.2	3	4.3	19	27.5	7	10.1	33	47.8	18	26.1	25	36.2	19	27.5
Colorado	74	18	24.3	21	28.4	60	81.1	17	23.0	5	6.8	20	27.0	9	12.2	20	27.0	13	17.6	21	28.4	12	16.2
Idaho	28	8	28.6	4	14.3	20	71.4	2	7.1	0	0.0	7	25.0	2	7.1	5	17.9	6	21.4	7	25.0	6	21.4
Montana	51	11	21.6	11	21.6	42	82.4	7	13.7	8	15.7	6	11.8	8	15.7	14	27.5	10	19.6	18	35.3	14	27.5
Nevada	27	6	22.2	6	22.2	13	48.1	1	3.7	3	11.1	5	18.5	6	22.2	3	11.1	4	14.8	10	37.0	8	29.6
New Mexico	33	8	24.2	8	24.2	26	78.8	3	9.1	2	6.1	6	18.2	5	15.2	10	30.3	8	24.2	10	30.3	12	36.4
Utah	34	13	38.2	8	23.5	21	61.8	9	26.5	2	5.9	7	20.6	6	17.6	14	41.2	11	32.4	16	47.1	10	29.4
Wyoming	26	4	15.4	1	3.8	18	69.2	5	19.2	0	0.0	3	11.5	5	19.2	7	26.9	4	15.4	9	34.6	9	34.6
CENSUS DIVISION 9, PACIFIC	428	94	22.0	131	30.6	303	70.8	73	17.1	13	3.0	102	23.8	74	17.3	155	36.2	98	22.9	157	36.7	89	20.8
Alaska	12	3	25.0	2	16.7	10	83.3	3	25.0	0	0.0	3	25.0	7	58.3	7	58.3	2	16.7	6	50.0	4	33.3
California	264	54	20.5	76	28.8	173	65.5	47	17.8	6	2.3	63	23.7	45	17.0	100	37.9	66	25.0	93	35.2	61	23.1
Hawaii	19	5	26.3	4	21.1	13	68.4	4	21.1	1	5.3	4	21.1	4	21.1	5	26.3	4	21.1	4	21.1	4	21.1
Oregon	61	15	24.6	20	32.8	51	83.6	8	13.1	2	3.3	8	13.1	8	13.1	20	32.8	13	21.3	25	41.0	9	14.8
Washington	72	17	23.6	29	40.3	56	77.8	11	15.3	4	5.6	24	33.3	10	13.9	23	31.9	17	23.6	29	40.3	11	15.3

Table 7 (Continued)

These data include only hospital-based facilities and services as reported by responding hospitals in Section C of the 2014 AHA Annual Survey, beginning on page 217. All hospitals are represented with Community Hospitals listed separately under United States. No estimates have been made for nonresponding hospitals. Definitions of facilities and services are listed in the Glossary, page 205.

CLASSIFICATION	HOSPITALS REPORTING	PSYCHIATRIC SERVICES — OUTPATIENT SERVICES		PARTIAL HOSPITALIZATION PROGRAM		RESIDENTIAL TREATMENT		CT SCANNER		RADIOLOGY, DIAGNOSTIC — DIAGNOSTIC RADIOISOTOPE FACILITY		ELECTRON BEAM COMPUTED TOMOGRAPHY (EBCT)		FULL-FIELD DIGITAL MAMMOGRAPHY (FFDM)		MAGNETIC RESONANCE IMAGING (MRI)		INTRAOPERATIVE MAGNETIC IMAGING		MAGNETO-ENCEPHALO-GRAPHY		MULTI-SLICE SPIRAL COMPUTED TOMOGRAPHY (<64 SLICE CT)	
		Number	Percent	Number	Percent	Number	Percent	Number	Percent	Number	Percent	Number	Percent	Number	Percent	Number	Percent	Number	Percent	Number	Percent	Number	Percent
UNITED STATES	4,601	1,268	27.6	693	15.1	293	6.4	3,831	83.3	2,580	56.1	330	7.2	2,595	56.4	3,029	65.8	223	4.8	147	3.2	2,638	57.3
COMMUNITY HOSPITALS	3,921	1,027	26.2	523	13.3	145	3.7	3,610	92.1	2,485	63.4	310	7.9	2,530	64.5	2,864	73.0	207	5.3	138	3.5	2,514	64.1
CENSUS DIVISION 1, NEW ENGLAND	169	87	51.5	56	33.1	12	7.1	142	84.0	119	70.4	9	5.3	121	71.6	115	68.0	8	4.7	7	4.1	110	65.1
Connecticut	27	19	70.4	15	55.6	4	14.8	23	85.2	21	77.8	3	11.1	19	70.4	21	77.8	2	7.4	0	0.0	19	70.4
Maine	29	10	34.5	6	20.7	0	0.0	27	93.1	23	79.3	0	0.0	24	82.8	21	72.4	0	0.0	0	0.0	19	65.5
Massachusetts	68	36	52.9	22	32.4	5	7.4	51	75.0	45	66.2	4	5.9	45	66.2	40	58.8	5	7.4	5	7.4	42	61.8
New Hampshire	23	10	43.5	5	21.7	0	0.0	21	91.3	13	56.5	0	0.0	17	73.9	13	56.5	1	4.3	2	8.7	16	69.6
Rhode Island	10	6	60.0	5	50.0	1	10.0	9	90.0	8	80.0	2	20.0	8	80.0	9	90.0	0	0.0	0	0.0	8	80.0
Vermont	12	6	50.0	3	25.0	2	16.7	11	91.7	9	75.0	0	0.0	8	66.7	11	91.7	0	0.0	0	0.0	6	50.0
CENSUS DIVISION 2, MIDDLE ATLANTIC	402	160	39.8	85	21.1	38	9.5	343	85.3	293	72.9	58	14.4	282	70.1	303	75.4	27	6.7	19	4.7	244	60.7
New Jersey	68	32	47.1	27	39.7	10	14.7	57	83.8	52	76.5	16	23.5	47	69.1	54	79.4	9	13.2	5	7.4	52	76.5
New York	154	77	50.0	31	20.1	16	10.4	145	94.2	117	76.0	22	14.3	123	79.9	123	79.9	8	5.2	7	4.5	97	63.0
Pennsylvania	180	51	28.3	27	15.0	12	6.7	141	78.3	124	68.9	20	11.1	112	62.2	126	70.0	10	5.6	7	3.9	95	52.8
CENSUS DIVISION 3, SOUTH ATLANTIC	644	164	25.5	110	17.1	45	7.0	543	84.3	426	66.1	57	8.9	405	62.9	475	73.8	28	4.3	22	3.4	422	65.5
Delaware	8	4	50.0	2	25.0	1	12.5	5	62.5	4	50.0	0	0.0	3	37.5	5	62.5	0	0.0	0	0.0	4	50.0
District of Columbia	10	5	50.0	4	40.0	1	10.0	7	70.0	6	60.0	3	30.0	5	50.0	7	70.0	3	30.0	0	0.0	6	60.0
Florida	166	38	22.9	22	13.3	11	6.6	143	86.1	115	69.3	27	16.3	111	66.9	131	78.9	11	6.6	9	5.4	121	72.9
Georgia	96	17	17.7	15	15.6	5	5.2	81	84.4	60	62.5	3	3.1	64	66.7	72	75.0	3	3.1	2	2.1	58	60.4
Maryland	46	26	56.5	24	52.2	6	13.0	40	87.0	37	80.4	4	8.7	26	56.5	35	76.1	3	6.5	3	6.5	33	71.7
North Carolina	110	28	25.5	13	11.8	6	5.5	98	89.1	70	63.6	8	7.3	69	62.7	85	77.3	5	4.5	5	4.5	79	71.8
South Carolina	71	13	18.3	9	12.7	4	5.6	56	78.9	42	59.2	2	2.8	44	62.0	47	66.2	1	1.4	1	1.3	44	62.0
Virginia	76	23	30.3	16	21.1	7	9.2	64	84.2	54	71.1	6	7.9	53	69.7	59	77.6	2	2.6	1	1.3	42	55.3
West Virginia	61	10	16.4	5	8.2	4	6.6	49	80.3	38	62.3	4	6.6	30	49.2	34	55.7	1	1.6	0	0.0	35	57.4
CENSUS DIVISION 4, EAST NORTH CENTRAL	699	229	32.8	142	20.3	49	7.0	617	88.3	476	68.1	59	8.4	475	68.0	513	73.4	48	6.9	28	4.0	411	58.8
Illinois	162	67	41.4	43	26.5	9	5.6	153	94.4	111	68.5	10	6.2	125	77.2	120	74.1	8	4.9	5	3.1	108	66.7
Indiana	123	30	24.4	22	17.9	14	11.4	98	79.7	76	61.8	12	9.8	80	65.0	93	75.6	7	5.7	7	5.7	67	54.5
Michigan	130	41	31.5	20	15.4	6	4.6	115	88.5	99	76.2	7	5.4	86	66.2	92	70.8	5	3.8	5	3.8	75	57.7
Ohio	141	48	34.0	35	24.8	8	5.7	130	92.2	108	76.6	18	12.8	99	70.2	117	83.0	12	8.5	6	4.3	107	75.9
Wisconsin	143	43	30.1	22	15.4	12	8.4	121	84.6	82	57.3	12	8.4	85	59.4	91	63.6	16	11.2	5	3.5	54	37.8
CENSUS DIVISION 5, EAST SOUTH CENTRAL	377	74	19.6	39	10.3	31	8.2	308	81.7	201	53.3	28	7.4	176	46.7	239	63.4	20	5.3	10	2.7	208	55.2
Alabama	103	23	22.3	10	9.7	4	3.4	76	80.6	53	51.5	6	5.8	39	37.9	66	64.1	2	1.9	2	1.9	56	54.4
Kentucky	89	16	18.0	11	12.4	3	3.4	76	85.4	52	58.4	5	5.6	53	59.6	67	75.3	3	3.4	3	3.4	57	64.0
Mississippi	111	14	12.6	7	6.3	18	16.2	87	78.4	52	46.8	9	8.1	39	35.1	52	46.8	9	8.1	2	1.8	48	43.2
Tennessee	74	21	28.4	11	14.9	6	8.1	62	83.8	44	59.5	8	10.8	45	60.8	54	73.0	6	8.1	3	4.1	47	63.5
CENSUS DIVISION 6, WEST NORTH CENTRAL	648	186	28.7	62	9.6	37	5.7	569	87.8	257	39.7	24	3.7	360	55.6	382	59.0	23	3.5	12	1.9	358	55.2
Iowa	126	34	27.0	10	7.9	6	4.8	116	92.1	44	34.9	6	4.8	88	69.8	76	60.3	4	3.2	2	1.6	77	61.9
Kansas	151	15	9.9	7	4.6	5	3.3	125	82.8	49	32.5	5	3.3	53	35.1	58	38.4	2	1.3	2	1.3	77	51.0
Minnesota	106	46	43.4	16	15.1	8	7.5	102	96.2	45	42.5	4	3.8	71	67.0	76	71.7	3	2.8	3	2.8	54	50.9
Missouri	146	57	39.0	15	10.3	12	8.2	118	80.8	76	52.1	6	4.1	80	54.8	111	76.0	6	4.1	3	2.1	83	56.8
Nebraska	49	16	32.7	6	12.2	3	6.1	47	95.9	21	42.9	2	4.1	35	71.4	32	65.3	3	6.1	1	2.0	29	59.2
North Dakota	28	9	32.1	6	21.4	2	7.1	23	82.1	10	35.7	1	3.6	14	50.0	13	46.4	2	7.1	1	3.6	15	53.6
South Dakota	42	9	21.4	2	4.8	1	2.4	38	90.5	12	28.6	0	0.0	19	45.2	16	38.1	1	2.4	0	0.0	22	52.4
CENSUS DIVISION 7, WEST SOUTH CENTRAL	892	155	17.4	85	9.5	40	4.5	648	72.6	354	39.7	34	3.8	336	37.7	471	52.8	31	3.5	14	1.6	433	48.5
Arkansas	86	15	17.4	7	8.1	8	9.3	68	79.1	34	39.5	4	4.7	36	41.9	51	59.3	3	3.5	2	2.3	43	50.0
Louisiana	97	29	29.9	16	16.5	3	3.1	70	72.2	47	48.5	6	6.2	56	57.7	56	57.7	3	3.1	1	1.0	47	48.5
Oklahoma	127	24	18.9	6	4.7	14	11.0	103	81.1	49	38.6	4	3.1	59	46.5	76	59.8	0	0.0	0	0.0	63	49.6
Texas	582	87	14.9	56	9.6	15	2.6	407	69.9	224	38.5	20	3.4	185	31.8	288	49.5	25	4.3	11	1.9	280	48.1
CENSUS DIVISION 8, MOUNTAIN	342	89	26.0	44	12.9	21	6.1	289	84.5	171	50.0	19	5.6	186	54.4	228	66.7	15	4.4	14	4.1	192	56.1
Arizona	69	20	29.0	9	13.0	3	4.3	54	78.3	40	58.0	2	2.9	32	46.4	48	69.6	1	1.4	7	10.1	42	60.9
Colorado	74	16	21.6	7	9.5	4	5.4	66	89.2	45	60.8	5	6.8	48	64.9	59	79.7	5	6.8	1	1.4	44	59.5
Idaho	28	9	32.1	3	10.7	2	7.1	26	92.9	13	46.4	2	7.1	14	50.0	20	71.4	2	7.1	0	0.0	19	67.9
Montana	51	12	23.5	8	15.7	3	5.9	43	84.3	17	33.3	0	0.0	14	27.5	28	54.9	2	3.9	2	3.9	28	54.9
Nevada	27	9	33.3	4	14.8	2	7.4	16	59.3	13	48.1	0	0.0	8	29.6	15	55.6	0	0.0	0	0.0	11	40.7
New Mexico	33	9	27.3	2	6.1	2	6.1	29	87.9	17	51.5	6	18.2	18	54.5	19	57.6	4	12.1	3	9.1	18	54.5
Utah	34	9	26.5	8	23.5	3	8.8	30	88.2	17	50.0	6	17.6	24	70.6	25	73.5	3	8.8	3	8.8	16	47.1
Wyoming	26	5	19.2	3	11.5	2	7.7	25	96.2	9	34.6	2	7.7	14	53.8	17	65.4	0	0.0	0	0.0	14	53.8
CENSUS DIVISION 9, PACIFIC	428	124	29.0	70	16.4	20	4.7	372	86.9	283	66.1	42	9.8	254	59.3	303	70.8	23	5.4	21	4.9	260	60.7
Alaska	12	4	33.3	3	25.0	3	25.0	10	83.3	5	41.7	0	0.0	7	58.3	7	58.3	0	0.0	0	0.0	6	50.0
California	264	84	31.8	51	19.3	8	3.0	223	84.5	177	67.0	30	11.4	149	56.4	191	72.3	17	6.4	17	6.4	154	58.3
Hawaii	19	5	26.3	3	15.8	2	10.5	14	73.7	12	63.2	2	10.5	11	57.9	11	57.9	0	0.0	0	0.0	6	31.6
Oregon	61	11	18.0	5	8.2	2	3.3	58	95.1	42	68.9	3	4.9	47	77.0	45	73.8	5	8.2	1	1.6	46	75.4
Washington	72	20	27.8	8	11.1	5	6.9	67	93.1	47	65.3	7	9.7	40	55.6	49	68.1	1	1.4	3	4.2	48	66.7

Table 7 (Continued)

These data include only hospital-based facilities and services as reported by responding hospitals in Section C of the 2014 AHA Annual Survey, beginning on page 217. All hospitals are represented with Community Hospitals listed separately under United States. No estimates have been made for nonresponding hospitals. Definitions of facilities and services are listed in the Glossary, page 205.

Columns under **RADIOLOGY, DIAGNOSTIC**: Multi-Slice Spiral Computed Tomography (64+ Slice CT), Positron Emission Tomography (PET), Positron Emission Tomography/CT (PET/CT), Single Photon Emission Computerized Tomography (SPECT), Ultrasound.
Columns under **RADIOLOGY, THERAPEUTIC**: Image-Guided Radiation Therapy (IGRT), Intensity-Modulated Radiation Therapy (IMRT), Proton Beam Therapy, Shaped Beam Radiation System, Stereotactic Radiosurgery.

CLASSIFICATION	HOSPITALS REPORTING	MS-CT No.	MS-CT %	PET No.	PET %	PET/CT No.	PET/CT %	SPECT No.	SPECT %	ULTRASOUND No.	ULTRASOUND %	IGRT No.	IGRT %	IMRT No.	IMRT %	PROTON No.	PROTON %	SHAPED BEAM No.	SHAPED BEAM %	STEREOTACTIC No.	STEREOTACTIC %
UNITED STATES	4,601	2,241	48.7	787	17.1	1,000	21.7	1,730	37.6	3,721	80.9	1,052	22.9	1,125	24.5	106	2.3	909	19.8	869	18.9
COMMUNITY HOSPITALS	3,921	2,143	54.7	752	19.2	960	24.5	1,673	42.7	3,509	89.5	1,016	25.9	1,088	27.7	97	2.5	879	22.4	849	21.7
CENSUS DIVISION 1, NEW ENGLAND	169	95	56.2	42	24.9	54	32.0	95	56.2	150	88.8	50	29.6	54	32.0	2	1.2	48	28.4	47	27.8
Connecticut	27	18	66.7	11	40.7	16	59.3	21	77.8	25	92.6	16	59.3	16	59.3	0	0.0	14	51.9	14	51.9
Maine	29	14	48.3	4	13.8	7	24.1	15	51.7	27	93.1	4	13.8	6	20.7	0	0.0	5	17.2	4	13.8
Massachusetts	68	41	60.3	17	25.0	20	29.4	34	50.0	57	83.8	23	33.8	25	36.8	2	2.9	22	32.4	21	30.9
New Hampshire	23	10	43.5	4	17.4	5	21.7	12	52.2	21	91.3	5	21.7	5	21.7	0	0.0	5	21.7	6	26.1
Rhode Island	10	5	50.0	2	20.0	2	20.0	6	60.0	9	90.0	1	10.0	1	10.0	0	0.0	1	10.0	1	10.0
Vermont	12	7	58.3	4	33.3	4	33.3	7	58.3	11	91.7	1	8.3	1	8.3	0	0.0	1	8.3	1	8.3
CENSUS DIVISION 2, MIDDLE ATLANTIC	402	250	62.2	101	25.1	123	30.6	224	55.7	346	86.1	149	37.1	167	41.5	12	3.0	136	33.8	111	27.6
New Jersey	68	41	60.3	23	33.8	29	42.6	43	63.2	59	86.8	32	47.1	37	54.4	1	1.5	36	52.9	22	32.4
New York	154	108	70.1	37	24.0	41	26.6	86	55.8	146	94.8	55	35.7	63	40.9	6	3.9	53	34.4	44	28.6
Pennsylvania	180	101	56.1	41	22.8	53	29.4	95	52.8	141	78.3	62	34.4	67	37.2	5	2.8	47	26.1	45	25.0
CENSUS DIVISION 3, SOUTH ATLANTIC	644	361	56.1	122	18.9	160	24.8	297	46.1	541	84.0	192	29.8	204	31.7	14	2.2	164	25.5	148	23.0
Delaware	8	5	62.5	2	25.0	4	50.0	4	50.0	5	62.5	4	50.0	4	50.0	0	0.0	4	50.0	3	37.5
District of Columbia	10	4	40.0	3	30.0	4	40.0	5	50.0	8	80.0	3	30.0	3	30.0	0	0.0	3	30.0	3	30.0
Florida	166	106	63.9	43	25.9	54	32.5	70	42.2	138	83.1	47	28.3	46	27.7	1	0.6	41	24.7	52	31.3
Georgia	96	50	52.1	17	17.7	27	28.1	32	33.3	83	86.5	29	30.2	29	30.2	2	2.2	24	25.0	22	22.9
Maryland	46	34	73.9	11	23.9	12	26.1	31	67.4	39	84.8	25	54.3	24	52.2	1	2.2	16	34.8	16	34.8
North Carolina	110	58	52.7	17	15.5	24	21.8	59	53.6	99	90.0	35	31.8	41	37.3	7	6.4	34	30.9	21	19.1
South Carolina	71	30	42.3	5	7.0	9	12.7	25	35.2	58	81.7	8	11.3	14	19.7	0	0.0	9	12.7	8	11.3
Virginia	76	49	64.5	14	18.4	17	22.4	47	61.8	63	82.9	32	42.1	32	42.1	2	2.6	23	30.3	15	19.7
West Virginia	61	25	41.0	10	16.4	9	14.8	24	39.3	48	78.7	9	14.8	11	18.0	0	0.0	10	16.4	8	13.1
CENSUS DIVISION 4, EAST NORTH CENTRAL	699	430	61.5	170	24.3	195	27.9	332	47.5	608	87.0	209	29.9	224	32.0	21	3.0	182	26.0	159	22.7
Illinois	162	109	67.3	32	19.8	48	29.6	77	47.5	146	90.1	52	32.1	59	36.4	5	3.1	43	26.5	41	25.3
Indiana	123	64	52.0	24	19.5	28	22.8	45	36.6	99	80.5	39	31.7	40	32.5	3	2.4	32	26.0	21	17.1
Michigan	130	92	70.8	27	20.8	36	27.7	62	47.7	120	92.3	36	27.7	40	30.8	2	1.5	37	28.5	36	27.0
Ohio	141	88	62.4	48	34.0	50	35.5	85	60.3	131	92.9	47	33.3	48	34.0	4	2.8	40	28.4	38	27.0
Wisconsin	143	77	53.8	39	27.3	33	23.1	63	44.1	112	78.3	35	24.5	37	25.9	7	4.9	30	21.0	23	16.1
CENSUS DIVISION 5, EAST SOUTH CENTRAL	377	152	40.3	60	15.9	73	19.4	139	36.9	306	81.2	67	17.8	71	18.8	8	2.1	53	14.1	56	14.9
Alabama	103	37	35.9	16	15.5	22	21.4	29	28.2	84	81.6	14	13.6	14	13.6	1	1.0	8	7.8	11	10.7
Kentucky	89	43	48.3	14	15.7	19	21.3	39	43.8	76	85.4	17	19.1	18	20.2	3	3.4	13	14.6	18	20.2
Mississippi	111	34	30.6	16	14.4	14	12.6	36	32.4	84	75.7	13	11.7	11	9.9	2	1.8	9	8.1	7	6.3
Tennessee	74	38	51.4	14	18.9	18	24.3	35	47.3	62	83.8	23	31.1	28	37.8	2	2.7	23	31.1	20	27.0
CENSUS DIVISION 6, WEST NORTH CENTRAL	648	243	37.5	66	10.2	111	17.1	183	28.2	521	80.4	100	15.4	109	16.8	13	2.0	84	13.0	79	12.2
Iowa	126	45	35.7	12	9.5	16	12.7	36	28.6	114	90.5	15	11.9	16	12.7	1	0.8	15	11.9	14	11.1
Kansas	151	35	23.2	8	5.3	12	7.9	22	14.6	102	67.5	15	9.9	17	11.3	3	2.0	15	9.9	8	5.3
Minnesota	106	60	56.6	11	10.4	19	17.9	36	34.0	92	86.8	17	16.0	20	18.9	2	1.9	11	10.4	16	15.1
Missouri	146	69	47.3	17	11.6	38	26.0	58	39.7	118	80.8	31	21.2	34	23.3	6	4.1	23	15.8	21	14.4
Nebraska	49	19	38.8	11	22.4	14	28.6	16	32.7	43	87.8	13	26.5	10	20.4	0	0.0	10	20.4	11	22.4
North Dakota	28	6	21.4	2	7.1	5	17.9	6	21.4	20	71.4	4	14.3	5	17.9	0	0.0	5	17.9	4	14.3
South Dakota	42	9	21.4	5	11.9	7	16.7	9	21.4	32	76.2	5	11.9	7	16.7	1	2.4	5	11.9	5	11.9
CENSUS DIVISION 7, WEST SOUTH CENTRAL	892	299	33.5	76	8.5	98	11.0	189	21.2	599	67.2	100	11.2	105	11.8	9	1.0	80	9.0	103	11.5
Arkansas	86	32	37.2	8	9.3	8	9.3	19	22.1	65	75.6	11	12.8	9	10.5	1	1.2	6	7.0	11	12.8
Louisiana	97	39	40.2	14	14.4	21	21.6	22	22.7	70	72.2	17	17.5	17	17.5	3	3.1	12	12.4	16	16.5
Oklahoma	127	42	33.1	14	11.0	20	15.7	24	18.9	92	72.4	19	15.0	20	15.7	1	0.8	18	14.2	13	10.2
Texas	582	186	32.0	40	6.9	48	8.2	124	21.3	372	63.9	53	9.1	59	10.1	4	0.7	44	7.6	63	10.8
CENSUS DIVISION 8, MOUNTAIN	342	172	50.3	55	16.1	65	19.0	99	28.9	281	82.2	61	17.8	64	18.7	11	3.2	57	16.7	54	15.8
Arizona	69	36	52.2	13	18.8	19	27.5	32	46.4	53	76.8	10	14.5	13	18.8	4	5.8	12	17.4	14	20.3
Colorado	74	49	66.2	14	18.9	18	24.3	22	29.7	66	89.2	18	24.3	18	24.3	4	5.4	18	24.3	15	20.3
Idaho	28	11	39.3	3	10.7	3	10.7	7	25.0	24	85.7	6	21.4	5	17.9	1	3.6	4	14.3	5	17.9
Montana	51	19	37.3	7	13.7	8	15.7	10	19.6	41	80.4	10	19.6	9	17.6	2	3.9	6	11.8	6	11.8
Nevada	27	10	37.0	3	11.1	3	11.1	4	14.8	16	59.3	4	14.8	4	14.8	0	0.0	4	14.8	4	14.8
New Mexico	33	20	60.6	5	15.2	5	15.2	9	27.3	27	81.8	7	21.2	7	21.2	0	0.0	5	15.2	5	15.2
Utah	34	19	55.9	7	20.6	8	23.5	9	26.5	30	88.2	5	14.7	7	20.6	0	0.0	7	20.6	4	11.8
Wyoming	26	8	30.8	3	11.5	1	3.8	6	23.1	24	92.3	1	3.8	1	3.8	0	0.0	1	3.8	1	3.8
CENSUS DIVISION 9, PACIFIC	428	239	55.8	95	22.2	121	28.3	172	40.2	369	86.2	124	29.0	127	29.7	16	3.7	105	24.5	112	26.2
Alaska	12	7	58.3	0	0.0	0	0.0	1	8.3	10	83.3	3	25.0	2	16.7	0	0.0	1	8.3	2	16.7
California	264	151	57.2	68	25.8	87	33.0	114	43.2	224	84.8	83	31.4	84	31.8	11	4.2	70	26.5	77	29.2
Hawaii	19	11	57.9	2	10.5	4	21.1	4	21.1	15	78.9	3	15.8	4	21.1	0	0.0	2	10.5	2	10.5
Oregon	61	31	50.8	10	16.4	11	18.0	28	45.9	58	95.1	15	24.6	15	24.6	4	6.6	13	21.3	10	16.4
Washington	72	39	54.2	15	20.8	19	26.4	25	34.7	62	86.1	20	27.8	22	30.6	1	1.4	19	26.4	21	29.2

Table 7 (Continued)

These data include only hospital-based facilities and services as reported by responding hospitals in Section C of the 2014 AHA Annual Survey, beginning on page 217. All hospitals are represented with Community Hospitals listed separately under United States. No estimates have been made for nonresponding hospitals. Definitions of facilities and services are listed in the Glossary, page 205.

CLASSIFICATION	HOSPITALS REPORTING	TRANSPLANT — BONE MARROW Number	Percent	HEART Number	Percent	KIDNEY Number	Percent	LIVER Number	Percent	LUNG Number	Percent	TISSUE Number	Percent	OTHER Number	Percent
UNITED STATES	4,601	207	4.5	133	2.9	214	4.7	129	2.8	76	1.7	375	8.2	243	5.3
COMMUNITY HOSPITALS	3,921	200	5.1	129	3.3	209	5.3	126	3.2	73	1.9	354	9.0	233	5.9
CENSUS DIVISION 1, NEW ENGLAND	169	12	7.1	6	3.6	15	8.9	7	4.1	3	1.8	19	11.2	14	8.3
Connecticut	27	1	3.7	2	7.4	2	7.4	2	7.4	0	0.0	4	14.8	3	11.1
Maine	29	0	0.0	0	0.0	1	3.4	0	0.0	0	0.0	1	3.4	0	0.0
Massachusetts	68	9	13.2	4	5.9	9	13.2	5	7.4	3	4.4	10	14.7	8	11.8
New Hampshire	23	1	4.3	0	0.0	1	4.3	0	0.0	0	0.0	1	4.3	1	4.3
Rhode Island	10	0	0.0	0	0.0	1	10.0	0	0.0	0	0.0	1	10.0	1	10.0
Vermont	12	1	8.3	0	0.0	1	8.3	0	0.0	0	0.0	2	16.7	1	8.3
CENSUS DIVISION 2, MIDDLE ATLANTIC	402	29	7.2	16	4.0	31	7.7	19	4.7	8	2.0	66	16.4	42	10.4
New Jersey	68	2	2.9	2	2.9	4	5.9	2	2.9	1	1.5	8	11.8	5	7.4
New York	154	13	8.4	5	3.2	11	7.1	6	3.9	1	0.6	30	19.5	17	11.0
Pennsylvania	180	14	7.8	9	5.0	16	8.9	11	6.1	6	3.3	28	15.6	20	11.1
CENSUS DIVISION 3, SOUTH ATLANTIC	644	37	5.7	25	3.9	31	4.8	20	3.1	13	2.0	60	9.3	42	6.5
Delaware	8	2	25.0	1	12.5	2	25.0	1	12.5	0	0.0	0	0.0	0	0.0
District of Columbia	10	2	20.0	2	20.0	3	30.0	1	10.0	0	0.0	2	20.0	3	30.0
Florida	166	12	7.2	8	4.8	8	4.8	7	4.2	5	3.0	17	10.2	7	4.2
Georgia	96	3	3.1	2	2.1	2	2.1	2	2.1	1	1.0	8	8.3	3	3.1
Maryland	46	5	10.9	2	4.3	3	6.5	2	4.3	2	4.3	7	15.2	8	17.4
North Carolina	110	4	3.6	4	3.6	5	4.5	4	3.6	2	1.8	7	6.4	10	9.1
South Carolina	71	3	4.2	1	1.4	1	1.4	1	1.4	1	1.4	4	5.6	3	4.2
Virginia	76	5	6.6	5	6.6	6	7.9	2	2.6	2	2.6	10	13.2	6	7.9
West Virginia	61	1	1.6	0	0.0	1	1.6	0	0.0	0	0.0	5	8.2	2	3.3
CENSUS DIVISION 4, EAST NORTH CENTRAL	699	34	4.9	23	3.3	33	4.7	21	3.0	19	2.7	71	10.2	32	4.6
Illinois	162	11	6.8	6	3.7	9	5.6	6	3.7	4	2.5	16	9.9	11	6.8
Indiana	123	1	0.8	2	1.6	2	1.6	1	0.8	1	0.8	9	7.3	2	1.6
Michigan	130	8	6.2	6	4.6	10	7.7	6	4.6	5	3.8	22	16.9	8	6.2
Ohio	141	9	6.4	5	3.5	8	5.7	5	3.5	5	3.5	18	12.8	6	4.3
Wisconsin	143	5	3.5	4	2.8	4	2.8	3	2.1	4	2.8	6	4.2	5	3.5
CENSUS DIVISION 5, EAST SOUTH CENTRAL	377	15	4.0	10	2.7	11	2.9	8	2.1	5	1.3	20	5.3	18	4.8
Alabama	103	2	1.9	2	1.9	2	1.9	2	1.9	1	1.0	4	3.9	4	3.9
Kentucky	89	4	4.5	3	3.4	3	3.4	2	2.2	2	2.2	4	4.5	3	3.4
Mississippi	111	1	0.9	1	0.9	2	1.8	1	0.9	0	0.0	1	0.9	1	0.9
Tennessee	74	8	10.8	4	5.4	4	5.4	3	4.1	2	2.7	11	14.9	10	13.5
CENSUS DIVISION 6, WEST NORTH CENTRAL	648	16	2.5	10	1.5	22	3.4	11	1.7	5	0.8	34	5.2	26	4.0
Iowa	126	1	0.8	1	0.8	4	3.2	1	0.8	1	0.8	2	1.6	3	2.4
Kansas	151	2	1.3	0	0.0	1	0.7	1	0.7	0	0.0	3	2.0	3	2.0
Minnesota	106	4	3.8	3	2.8	4	3.8	2	1.9	2	1.9	10	9.4	3	2.8
Missouri	146	5	3.4	4	2.7	8	5.5	6	4.1	2	1.4	10	6.8	10	6.8
Nebraska	49	3	6.1	2	4.1	1	2.0	1	2.0	0	0.0	4	8.2	3	6.1
North Dakota	28	0	0.0	0	0.0	2	7.1	0	0.0	0	0.0	2	7.1	2	7.1
South Dakota	42	1	2.4	0	0.0	2	4.8	0	0.0	0	0.0	3	7.1	2	4.8
CENSUS DIVISION 7, WEST SOUTH CENTRAL	892	22	2.5	17	1.9	33	3.7	17	1.9	10	1.1	32	3.6	23	2.6
Arkansas	86	2	2.3	2	2.3	3	3.5	1	1.2	0	0.0	2	2.3	1	1.2
Louisiana	97	2	2.1	1	1.0	3	3.1	3	3.1	1	1.0	5	5.2	3	3.1
Oklahoma	127	4	3.1	1	0.8	4	3.1	2	1.6	1	0.8	4	3.1	3	2.4
Texas	582	14	2.4	13	2.2	23	4.0	11	1.9	8	1.4	21	3.6	16	2.7
CENSUS DIVISION 8, MOUNTAIN	342	15	4.4	8	2.3	12	3.5	8	2.3	5	1.5	21	6.1	12	3.5
Arizona	69	7	10.1	2	2.9	4	5.8	3	4.3	3	4.3	9	13.0	5	7.2
Colorado	74	3	4.1	3	4.1	4	5.4	3	4.1	1	1.4	6	8.1	2	2.7
Idaho	28	1	3.6	0	0.0	0	0.0	0	0.0	0	0.0	2	7.1	1	3.6
Montana	51	0	0.0	0	0.0	0	0.0	0	0.0	0	0.0	2	3.9	0	0.0
Nevada	27	0	0.0	0	0.0	0	0.0	0	0.0	0	0.0	0	0.0	1	3.7
New Mexico	33	1	3.0	0	0.0	2	6.1	0	0.0	0	0.0	0	0.0	1	3.0
Utah	34	2	5.9	3	8.8	2	5.9	2	5.9	1	2.9	2	5.9	2	5.9
Wyoming	26	0	0.0	0	0.0	0	0.0	0	0.0	0	0.0	0	0.0	0	0.0
CENSUS DIVISION 9, PACIFIC	428	27	6.3	18	4.2	26	6.1	18	4.2	8	1.9	52	12.1	34	7.9
Alaska	12	0	0.0	0	0.0	0	0.0	0	0.0	0	0.0	0	0.0	0	0.0
California	264	19	7.2	13	4.9	18	6.8	12	4.5	7	2.7	38	14.4	24	9.1
Hawaii	19	0	0.0	0	0.0	1	5.3	1	5.3	0	0.0	0	0.0	1	5.3
Oregon	61	2	3.3	2	3.3	2	3.3	1	1.6	0	0.0	5	8.2	4	6.6
Washington	72	6	8.3	3	4.2	5	6.9	4	5.6	1	1.4	9	12.5	5	6.9

Table 8

MSAs

Metropolitan Statistical Areas

Metropolitan Statistical Areas (MSAs) definitions announced by the U.S. Office of Management and Budget (OMB) effective June 6, 2003 were added with the 2006 edition.

According to the OMB, an MSA is a geographical designation that represents an integrated social and economic unit with a large population nucleus. Under these standards, an area qualifies for recognition as an MSA if there is a city within the area of at least 50,000 with a total metropolitan population of at least 100,000. MSAs are defined as entire counties. In addition to the county containing the main city, an MSA also includes additional counties having strong economic and social ties to the central county. Such counties must have a specified level of commuting to the central counties and must meet certain standards regarding metropolitan character, such as population density.

When an MSA encompasses two or more central cities, up to three cities may be specified in the MSA title. They will be listed in order of population size. When a single central city exists, the MSA is named for that particular city. A MSA may extend beyond a single state.

An MSA containing a single core with a population of 2.5 million or more may be subdivided to form smaller groupings of counties referred to as Metropolitan Divisions. Where they exist the Metropolitan Divisions are shown in this table rather than the entire MSA.

TABLE 8

U.S. CENSUS DIVISION 1, NEW ENGLAND

U.S. Community Hospitals
(Nonfederal, short-term general and other special hospitals)

2014 Utilization, Personnel and Finances

MSAs

CLASSIFICATION	Hospitals	Beds	Admissions	Inpatient Days	Adjusted Inpatient Days	Average Daily Census	Adjusted Average Daily Census	Average Stay (days)	Surgical Operations	NEWBORNS Bassinets	NEWBORNS Births	OUTPATIENT VISITS Emergency	OUTPATIENT VISITS Total
UNITED STATES	4,926	786,874	33,066,720	180,456,434	365,636,679	494,388	1,002,304	5.5	26,401,528	55,824	3,735,593	136,327,473	693,106,685
Nonmetropolitan	1,855	116,785	3,238,473	21,307,388	64,127,906	58,370	175,723	6.6	3,512,461	9,506	383,166	21,639,508	119,516,577
Metropolitan	3,071	670,089	29,828,247	159,149,046	301,508,773	436,018	826,581	5.3	22,889,067	46,318	3,352,427	114,687,965	573,590,108
CENSUS DIVISION 1, NEW ENGLAND	199	33,531	1,540,755	8,450,523	19,610,477	23,155	53,727	5.5	1,357,473	2,430	147,729	7,027,573	48,351,944
Nonmetropolitan	55	3,486	132,876	816,976	2,601,049	2,240	7,125	6.1	157,728	376	12,930	965,541	8,636,283
Metropolitan	144	30,045	1,407,879	7,633,547	17,009,428	20,915	46,602	5.4	1,199,745	2,054	134,799	6,062,032	39,715,661
Connecticut	32	7,806	376,644	2,091,854	4,274,804	5,731	11,711	5.6	318,656	501	36,730	1,587,150	8,487,562
Nonmetropolitan	2	154	9,125	42,833	103,309	117	283	4.7	7,291	7	848	55,652	316,993
Metropolitan	30	7,652	367,519	2,049,021	4,171,495	5,614	11,428	5.6	311,365	494	35,882	1,531,498	8,170,569
Bridgeport-Stamford-Norwalk, CT .	6	1,914	85,510	460,156	970,585	1,261	2,659	5.4	61,338	165	11,390	358,081	2,346,804
Hartford-West Hartford-East Hart-ford, CT	11	2,746	131,268	738,813	1,452,249	2,024	3,978	5.6	115,140	125	12,220	539,119	2,629,455
New Haven-Milford, CT	9	2,431	120,492	700,902	1,384,841	1,921	3,794	5.8	105,591	146	9,403	428,071	2,154,262
Norwich-New London, CT.	2	440	23,609	121,318	277,337	332	760	5.1	18,954	32	1,938	133,031	748,829
Worcester, MA-CT	2	121	6,640	27,832	86,483	76	237	4.2	10,342	26	931	73,196	291,219
Maine	35	3,379	135,001	772,923	1,996,890	2,119	5,472	5.7	152,000	280	11,495	771,696	7,835,100
Nonmetropolitan	21	1,143	38,671	267,437	921,720	734	2,526	6.9	49,882	156	3,869	353,374	3,759,809
Metropolitan	14	2,236	96,330	505,486	1,075,170	1,385	2,946	5.2	102,118	124	7,626	418,322	4,075,291
Bangor, ME	4	495	26,783	129,920	276,253	356	757	4.9	29,912	20	1,783	65,063	605,947
Lewiston-Auburn, ME	2	361	16,220	71,473	182,097	196	499	4.4	12,532	35	1,283	70,883	1,055,940
Portland-South Portland, ME	8	1,380	53,327	304,093	616,820	833	1,690	5.7	59,674	69	4,560	282,376	2,413,404
Massachusetts	79	16,060	754,971	4,116,984	9,404,946	11,281	25,766	5.5	615,311	1,129	69,068	3,186,679	21,954,797
Nonmetropolitan	3	134	6,289	25,311	87,251	70	239	4.0	5,399	30	745	50,451	193,974
Metropolitan	76	15,926	748,682	4,091,673	9,317,695	11,211	25,527	5.5	609,912	1,099	68,323	3,136,228	21,760,823
Barnstable Town, MA	3	414	22,161	104,349	309,552	286	848	4.7	14,308	18	1,220	118,108	836,734
Boston, MA.	26	6,392	303,925	1,790,780	3,650,431	4,906	10,000	5.9	265,617	381	25,176	958,700	7,859,494
Cambridge-Newton-Framingham, MA.	20	4,128	193,585	1,010,248	2,644,457	2,770	7,245	5.2	147,923	364	21,561	879,320	6,298,445
Pittsfield, MA.	2	298	13,964	62,496	190,817	171	523	4.5	13,627	24	903	76,270	615,581
Providence-Warwick, RI-MA	5	1,101	58,510	276,700	623,831	758	1,709	4.7	37,559	71	4,297	394,988	1,528,663
Springfield, MA	11	1,878	75,780	441,495	937,618	1,210	2,569	5.8	59,854	94	6,584	310,106	2,244,913
Worcester, MA-CT	9	1,715	80,757	405,605	960,989	1,110	2,633	5.0	71,024	147	8,582	398,736	2,376,993
New Hampshire	28	2,839	117,327	630,685	1,716,701	1,728	4,704	5.4	120,135	276	13,516	644,075	4,909,483
Nonmetropolitan	17	1,336	53,472	312,440	892,898	856	2,445	5.8	60,207	112	4,625	264,463	2,747,682
Metropolitan	11	1,503	63,855	318,245	823,803	872	2,259	5.0	59,928	164	8,891	379,612	2,161,801
Manchester-Nashua, NH	5	815	36,897	174,732	457,736	478	1,255	4.7	30,253	102	5,141	171,597	1,160,495
Rockingham County-Strafford County, NH.	6	688	26,958	143,513	366,067	394	1,004	5.3	29,675	62	3,750	208,015	1,001,306
Rhode Island.	11	2,247	110,848	549,575	1,183,493	1,506	3,242	5.0	93,575	142	11,363	510,907	2,020,490
Metropolitan	11	2,247	110,848	549,575	1,183,493	1,506	3,242	5.0	93,575	142	11,363	510,907	2,020,490
Providence-Warwick, RI-MA	11	2,247	110,848	549,575	1,183,493	1,506	3,242	5.0	93,575	142	11,363	510,907	2,020,490
Vermont	14	1,200	45,964	288,502	1,033,643	790	2,832	6.3	57,796	102	5,557	327,066	3,144,512
Nonmetropolitan	12	719	25,319	168,955	595,871	463	1,632	6.7	34,949	71	2,843	241,601	1,617,825
Metropolitan	2	481	20,645	119,547	437,772	327	1,200	5.8	22,847	31	2,714	85,465	1,526,687
Burlington-South Burlington, VT . .	2	481	20,645	119,547	437,772	327	1,200	5.8	22,847	31	2,714	85,465	1,526,687

TABLE 8

U.S. CENSUS DIVISION 1, NEW ENGLAND

U.S. Community Hospitals
(Nonfederal, short-term general and other special hospitals)

2014 Utilization, Personnel and Finances

FULL-TIME EQUIVALENT PERSONNEL					FULL-TIME EQUIV. TRAINEES			EXPENSES						
								LABOR				TOTAL		
Physicians and Dentists	Registered Nurses	Licensed Practical Nurses	Other Salaried Personnel	Total Personnel	Medical and Dental Residents	Other Trainees	Total Trainees	Payroll (in thousands)	Employee Benefits (in thousands)	Total (in thousands)	Percent of Total	Amount (in thousands)	Adjusted per Admission	Adjusted per Inpatient Day
122,747	1,398,346	73,044	2,510,354	4,754,880	109,309	8,533	117,842	$310,203,433	$82,949,525	$393,152,940	48.6	$808,869,209	$12,015.42	$2,212.22
15,090	147,461	20,793	334,968	602,081	1,731	269	2,000	33,192,643	8,842,572	42,035,205	51.3	81,981,991	8,301.59	1,278.41
107,657	1,250,885	52,251	2,175,386	4,152,799	107,578	8,264	115,842	277,010,790	74,106,953	351,117,735	48.3	726,887,218	12,653.89	2,410.83
12,999	69,290	2,301	167,540	281,962	9,468	1,294	10,762	20,073,490	5,208,549	25,282,041	50.7	49,846,135	13,476.33	2,541.81
1,695	7,976	519	21,421	35,484	491	36	527	2,422,611	626,608	3,049,218	57.0	5,353,059	12,452.33	2,058.04
11,304	61,314	1,782	146,119	246,478	8,977	1,258	10,235	17,650,878	4,581,940	22,232,823	50.0	44,493,076	13,610.99	2,615.79
1,246	13,962	324	31,358	53,258	1,718	98	1,816	4,051,681	1,138,135	5,189,816	50.2	10,341,324	13,141.30	2,419.13
21	297	25	636	1,108	2	2	4	91,559	21,523	113,082	53.4	211,722	9,507.46	2,049.40
1,225	13,665	299	30,722	52,150	1,716	96	1,812	3,960,122	1,116,612	5,076,734	50.1	10,129,602	13,247.13	2,428.29
372	2,937	29	6,491	11,439	426	13	439	965,953	260,035	1,225,987	50.1	2,449,137	13,409.20	2,523.36
651	4,804	127	12,401	19,895	185	38	223	1,409,650	427,631	1,837,282	52.8	3,478,009	13,256.38	2,394.91
97	4,898	106	9,260	16,683	1,086	29	1,115	1,264,642	352,076	1,616,719	47.2	3,423,228	14,009.24	2,471.93
82	755	24	1,833	2,977	18	14	32	237,858	55,975	293,833	50.5	581,696	10,656.90	2,097.43
23	271	13	737	1,156	1	2	3	82,019	20,894	102,913	52.1	197,532	9,536.14	2,284.05
1,579	7,752	315	18,402	31,336	331	28	359	2,017,744	514,987	2,532,732	54.6	4,635,468	12,885.93	2,321.34
515	2,729	151	7,851	12,583	4	20	24	709,544	170,736	880,281	55.5	1,584,679	11,121.02	1,719.26
1,064	5,023	164	10,551	18,753	327	8	335	1,308,200	344,251	1,652,451	54.2	3,050,789	14,043.60	2,837.49
316	1,306	49	2,552	4,706	30	2	32	334,799	91,167	425,966	52.9	805,093	13,665.56	2,914.33
241	812	32	1,582	3,067	22	0	22	210,495	38,916	249,410	52.7	473,409	11,596.06	2,599.76
507	2,905	83	6,417	10,980	275	6	281	762,907	214,168	977,075	55.1	1,772,288	15,083.56	2,873.27
7,570	33,917	1,061	85,112	141,516	5,828	1,076	6,904	9,817,684	2,420,680	12,238,365	48.3	25,349,887	13,908.34	2,695.38
33	221	18	582	951	2	1	3	82,743	17,779	100,521	53.5	187,932	8,199.47	2,153.92
7,537	33,696	1,043	84,530	140,565	5,826	1,075	6,901	9,734,941	2,402,901	12,137,844	48.2	25,161,956	13,981.08	2,700.45
73	488	14	1,605	2,315	0	0	0	240,836	72,531	313,367	52.1	601,209	8,765.13	1,942.19
5,147	16,569	398	43,487	72,086	4,486	974	5,460	4,876,981	1,256,013	6,132,996	44.6	13,750,310	21,503.37	3,766.76
1,330	7,297	318	19,221	31,382	478	59	537	2,208,471	465,069	2,673,538	54.5	4,902,128	9,074.99	1,853.74
92	567	40	1,499	2,370	81	13	94	193,714	49,000	242,714	54.8	405,741	9,470.85	2,126.33
58	1,955	43	4,379	7,094	12	0	12	529,228	140,995	670,223	55.5	1,207,703	9,068.74	1,935.95
526	3,255	123	6,959	12,685	395	2	397	749,263	161,060	910,323	50.5	1,801,757	10,412.55	1,921.63
311	3,565	107	7,380	12,633	374	27	401	936,449	258,234	1,194,683	47.9	2,493,107	12,314.74	2,594.31
1,212	6,446	303	16,334	27,211	492	13	505	1,840,304	503,698	2,344,002	55.1	4,250,644	13,198.87	2,476.05
834	3,271	183	8,594	14,489	465	9	474	1,097,887	294,086	1,391,972	58.8	2,367,779	15,663.43	2,651.79
378	3,175	120	7,740	12,722	27	4	31	742,418	209,611	952,030	50.6	1,882,865	11,018.64	2,285.58
297	1,790	55	4,361	7,188	9	4	13	413,663	121,753	535,417	51.6	1,036,710	10,563.37	2,264.86
81	1,385	65	3,379	5,534	18	0	18	328,754	87,858	416,613	49.2	846,156	11,632.92	2,311.48
540	4,191	77	9,088	15,651	763	35	798	1,374,359	367,804	1,742,163	55.0	3,167,662	13,177.78	2,676.54
540	4,191	77	9,088	15,651	763	35	798	1,374,359	367,804	1,742,163	55.0	3,167,662	13,177.78	2,676.54
540	4,191	77	9,088	15,651	763	35	798	1,374,359	367,804	1,742,163	55.0	3,167,662	13,177.78	2,676.54
852	3,022	221	7,246	12,990	336	44	380	971,718	263,245	1,234,963	58.8	2,101,150	12,576.91	2,032.76
292	1,458	142	3,758	6,353	18	4	22	440,878	122,484	563,362	56.3	1,000,949	10,995.21	1,679.81
560	1,564	79	3,488	6,637	318	40	358	530,840	140,761	671,601	61.0	1,100,201	14,470.81	2,513.18
560	1,564	79	3,488	6,637	318	40	358	530,840	140,761	671,601	61.0	1,100,201	14,470.81	2,513.18

MSAs

TABLE 8

U.S. CENSUS DIVISION 2, MIDDLE ATLANTIC

U.S. Community Hospitals
(Nonfederal, short-term general and other special hospitals)

2014 Utilization, Personnel and Finances

CLASSIFICATION	Hospitals	Beds	Admissions	Inpatient Days	Adjusted Inpatient Days	Average Daily Census	Adjusted Average Daily Census	Average Stay (days)	Surgical Operations	NEWBORNS Bassinets	Births	OUTPATIENT VISITS Emergency	Total
UNITED STATES	4,926	786,874	33,066,720	180,456,434	365,636,679	494,388	1,002,304	5.5	26,401,528	55,824	3,735,593	136,327,473	693,106,685
Nonmetropolitan	1,855	116,785	3,238,473	21,307,388	64,127,906	58,370	175,723	6.6	3,512,461	9,506	383,166	21,639,508	119,516,577
Metropolitan	3,071	670,089	29,828,247	159,149,046	301,508,773	436,018	826,581	5.3	22,889,067	46,318	3,352,427	114,687,965	573,590,108
CENSUS DIVISION 2, MIDDLE ATLANTIC.	434	113,947	4,833,693	29,417,955	54,407,946	80,596	149,062	6.1	3,904,913	6,299	461,201	18,448,665	110,666,688
Nonmetropolitan	74	8,615	236,444	1,918,325	5,466,277	5,253	14,977	8.1	303,890	519	21,067	1,521,753	10,776,855
Metropolitan	360	105,332	4,597,249	27,499,630	48,941,669	75,343	134,085	6.0	3,601,023	5,780	440,134	16,926,912	99,889,833
New Jersey	75	20,517	970,436	5,015,867	8,328,138	13,744	22,816	5.2	588,038	1,347	99,550	3,613,702	15,489,296
Metropolitan	75	20,517	970,436	5,015,867	8,328,138	13,744	22,816	5.2	588,038	1,347	99,550	3,613,702	15,489,296
Allentown-Bethlehem-Easton, PA-NJ . .	2	251	8,730	38,406	83,910	105	230	4.4	13,957	12	692	41,373	176,689
Atlantic City-Hammonton, NJ. . . .	4	848	41,945	197,552	342,912	542	940	4.7	18,785	56	3,196	149,058	418,477
Camden, NJ	10	2,915	136,511	676,906	1,073,776	1,855	2,941	5.0	79,653	125	12,358	565,904	1,616,157
New York-Jersey City-White Plains, NY-NJ . .	31	9,177	462,862	2,254,947	3,663,041	6,177	10,035	4.9	268,010	678	51,027	1,606,014	8,427,069
Newark, NJ-PA	18	5,688	244,830	1,470,167	2,411,144	4,030	6,604	6.0	155,689	342	25,583	894,244	3,683,778
Ocean City, NJ	1	149	6,842	27,153	66,682	74	183	4.0	3,534	16	471	44,940	181,018
Trenton, NJ	5	915	42,731	225,419	447,039	618	1,226	5.3	26,505	78	3,808	184,150	539,966
Vineland-Bridgeton, NJ	2	376	19,069	99,460	182,462	272	500	5.2	15,064	32	2,077	85,903	329,971
Wilmington, DE-MD-NJ	2	198	6,916	25,857	57,172	71	157	3.7	6,841	8	338	42,116	116,171
New York	174	55,306	2,278,459	15,678,478	28,662,796	42,958	78,529	6.9	1,964,758	3,126	231,715	8,589,335	57,003,097
Nonmetropolitan	36	4,500	115,737	1,133,789	3,214,680	3,105	8,806	9.8	154,873	257	11,082	714,250	5,738,937
Metropolitan	138	50,806	2,162,722	14,544,689	25,448,116	39,853	69,723	6.7	1,809,885	2,869	220,633	7,875,085	51,264,160
Albany-Schenectady-Troy, NY . . .	9	2,386	107,383	689,426	1,233,349	1,890	3,380	6.4	91,237	110	7,386	501,996	2,732,654
Binghamton, NY.	2	619	26,742	147,645	415,217	404	1,138	5.5	34,554	46	2,626	97,903	2,462,201
Buffalo-Cheektowaga-Niagara Falls, NY . .	10	4,384	136,595	1,261,763	2,169,834	3,458	5,946	9.2	169,826	230	13,183	460,540	3,767,128
Dutchess County-Putnam County, NY. .	3	597	28,048	133,842	260,999	367	714	4.8	30,023	54	3,556	105,357	527,989
Elmira, NY	2	426	15,558	108,374	220,875	296	606	7.0	11,936	20	1,414	83,078	416,291
Glens Falls, NY	1	317	12,736	67,789	170,269	186	466	5.3	12,369	20	1,268	50,338	731,264
Ithaca, NY	1	193	6,443	30,300	103,020	83	282	4.7	6,825	21	894	28,970	230,639
Kingston, NY.	3	295	11,373	61,695	101,494	170	278	5.4	5,249	11	349	58,789	149,356
Nassau County-Suffolk County, NY. .	24	8,788	446,296	2,735,029	4,664,738	7,492	12,781	6.1	397,832	507	44,454	1,268,933	6,628,031
New York-Jersey City-White Plains, NY-NJ . .	60	26,653	1,127,600	7,628,291	12,547,623	20,903	34,378	6.8	831,868	1,433	120,593	4,314,839	24,449,487
Rochester, NY.	10	3,127	119,670	912,385	2,008,995	2,499	5,504	7.6	112,101	172	11,694	459,302	5,459,559
Syracuse, NY	6	1,934	83,570	534,567	981,401	1,464	2,688	6.4	69,727	147	8,091	258,476	2,128,863
Utica-Rome, NY.	4	813	30,895	181,777	423,784	499	1,160	5.9	26,293	60	3,051	114,762	1,143,656
Watertown-Fort Drum, NY.	3	274	9,813	51,806	146,518	142	402	5.3	10,045	38	2,074	71,802	437,042
Pennsylvania	185	38,124	1,584,798	8,723,610	17,417,012	23,894	47,717	5.5	1,352,117	1,826	129,936	6,245,628	38,174,295
Nonmetropolitan	38	4,115	120,707	784,536	2,251,597	2,148	6,171	6.5	149,017	262	9,985	807,503	5,037,918
Metropolitan	147	34,009	1,464,091	7,939,074	15,165,415	21,746	41,546	5.4	1,203,100	1,564	119,951	5,438,125	33,136,377
Allentown-Bethlehem-Easton, PA-NJ . .	8	2,212	99,165	563,864	1,085,299	1,544	2,974	5.7	65,984	88	8,829	362,950	1,825,327
Altoona, PA	4	530	22,096	116,696	257,740	319	706	5.3	20,458	30	1,429	84,018	528,983
Bloomsburg-Berwick, PA	5	1,030	31,019	223,206	385,260	611	1,055	7.2	27,099	34	917	206,305	1,188,996
Chambersburg-Waynesboro, PA. .	2	304	14,359	59,388	151,814	162	416	4.1	11,220	32	1,753	77,640	422,133
East Stroudsburg, PA	1	235	11,175	49,295	95,777	135	262	4.4	5,844	20	1,045	58,454	278,281
Erie, PA.	6	1,067	40,906	214,436	391,238	586	1,071	5.2	34,838	63	3,445	154,642	476,830
Gettysburg, PA	1	76	4,091	16,623	55,219	46	151	4.1	6,631	16	531	28,210	184,661
Harrisburg-Carlisle, PA.	8	1,850	81,110	454,295	851,285	1,245	2,334	5.6	70,022	74	7,404	301,158	2,148,036
Johnstown, PA	3	608	22,549	130,363	269,697	357	738	5.8	23,517	14	1,564	73,099	548,327
Lancaster, PA	4	1,058	44,615	203,731	421,298	559	1,155	4.6	49,254	83	6,156	174,940	1,959,706
Lebanon, PA.	1	151	7,582	37,585	104,875	103	287	5.0	9,130	19	773	50,554	267,171
Montgomery County-Bucks County-Chester County, PA . .	19	3,739	176,272	836,699	1,584,073	2,292	4,338	4.7	134,065	265	22,018	587,799	3,315,897
Philadelphia, PA.	27	8,265	375,538	2,056,560	3,501,464	5,634	9,592	5.5	287,314	274	24,145	1,265,346	6,985,135
Pittsburgh, PA	34	8,336	346,500	1,982,209	3,867,151	5,431	10,596	5.7	301,442	321	22,840	1,063,818	7,268,861
Reading, PA	3	919	35,883	171,549	334,077	469	915	4.8	23,234	56	4,422	170,369	1,383,968
Scranton-Wilkes-Barr—Hazleton, PA . .	9	1,621	66,144	349,642	727,379	957	1,993	5.3	52,836	55	4,626	308,184	1,822,401
State College, PA.	2	280	13,182	63,251	138,275	174	379	4.8	14,163	5	1,277	50,925	308,478
Williamsport, PA	3	384	13,485	107,809	263,286	295	721	8.0	18,826	15	1,206	73,602	262,247
York-Hanover, PA.	4	839	40,420	208,380	449,174	570	1,230	5.2	23,918	71	4,323	129,176	1,263,178
Youngstown-Warren-Boardman, OH-PA . .	3	505	18,000	93,493	231,034	257	633	5.2	23,305	29	1,248	216,936	697,761

TABLE 8

U.S. CENSUS DIVISION 2, MIDDLE ATLANTIC

U.S. Community Hospitals
(Nonfederal, short-term general and other special hospitals)

2014 Utilization, Personnel and Finances

FULL-TIME EQUIVALENT PERSONNEL					FULL-TIME EQUIV. TRAINEES			EXPENSES						
								LABOR				TOTAL		
Physicians and Dentists	Registered Nurses	Licensed Practical Nurses	Other Salaried Personnel	Total Personnel	Medical and Dental Residents	Other Trainees	Total Trainees	Payroll (in thousands)	Employee Benefits (in thousands)	Total (in thousands)	Percent of Total	Amount (in thousands)	Adjusted per Admission	Adjusted per Inpatient Day
122,747	1,398,346	73,044	2,510,354	4,754,880	109,309	8,533	117,842	$310,203,433	$82,949,525	$393,152,940	48.6	$808,869,209	$12,015.42	$2,212.22
15,090	147,461	20,793	334,968	602,081	1,731	269	2,000	33,192,643	8,842,572	42,035,205	51.3	81,981,991	8,301.59	1,278.41
107,657	1,250,885	52,251	2,175,386	4,152,799	107,578	8,264	115,842	277,010,790	74,106,953	351,117,735	48.3	726,887,218	12,653.89	2,410.83
25,735	200,192	9,027	391,724	722,691	29,537	1,229	30,766	51,734,404	14,480,697	66,215,097	52.2	126,964,966	14,168.47	2,333.57
1,080	9,774	1,416	24,121	42,093	257	6	263	2,298,159	615,048	2,913,204	53.7	5,426,539	7,909.13	992.73
24,655	190,418	7,611	367,603	680,598	29,280	1,223	30,503	49,436,245	13,865,650	63,301,893	52.1	121,538,427	14,687.46	2,483.33
2,814	33,954	713	65,311	117,275	3,263	54	3,317	8,506,748	1,992,687	10,499,435	50.8	20,672,555	12,739.50	2,482.25
2,814	33,954	713	65,311	117,275	3,263	54	3,317	8,506,748	1,992,687	10,499,435	50.8	20,672,555	12,739.50	2,482.25
22	335	16	723	1,240	22	1	23	85,200	20,735	105,935	50.5	209,636	11,009.13	2,498.34
78	1,443	43	2,444	4,694	50	0	50	381,678	102,958	484,637	51.8	936,228	12,883.99	2,730.23
610	4,116	115	8,864	15,325	459	9	468	1,018,460	257,933	1,276,394	46.1	2,769,664	12,750.09	2,579.37
1,113	16,103	292	30,565	54,879	1,176	20	1,196	3,976,947	875,108	4,852,054	50.8	9,543,756	12,625.52	2,605.42
869	9,523	203	18,362	33,085	1,371	18	1,389	2,474,091	573,572	3,047,664	52.8	5,768,996	14,253.37	2,392.64
0	186	0	453	765	0	6	6	48,279	16,368	64,647	58.7	110,047	6,549.66	1,650.33
106	1,584	32	2,706	5,148	66	0	66	333,104	86,529	419,633	48.2	870,862	10,301.19	1,948.07
4	483	3	834	1,511	119	0	119	144,410	46,524	190,934	55.2	346,036	9,484.32	1,896.48
12	181	9	360	628	0	0	0	44,578	12,959	57,537	49.0	117,329	7,671.08	2,052.21
15,182	97,557	5,588	205,169	371,787	17,400	459	17,859	28,970,441	8,740,580	37,711,021	56.0	67,346,715	16,269.18	2,349.62
724	4,944	824	12,848	22,299	117	4	121	1,293,112	332,508	1,625,619	56.2	2,892,893	8,684.08	899.90
14,458	92,613	4,764	192,321	349,488	17,283	455	17,738	27,677,329	8,408,073	36,085,402	56.6	64,453,822	16,933.00	2,532.75
252	4,737	189	8,192	15,707	601	12	613	870,268	198,406	1,068,674	45.2	2,365,222	12,341.62	1,917.72
269	1,143	149	3,252	5,326	87	0	87	315,087	92,798	407,884	50.8	803,397	10,254.73	1,934.88
444	6,302	476	11,099	21,333	145	98	243	1,430,431	559,899	1,990,329	56.1	3,548,305	15,182.32	1,635.29
22	915	17	1,293	2,631	5	4	9	196,421	61,842	258,263	40.5	637,998	11,523.28	2,444.45
57	720	40	1,384	2,563	21	1	22	196,407	60,145	256,552	63.2	405,885	12,535.84	1,837.63
79	455	54	1,407	2,169	0	0	0	141,847	30,560	172,407	56.5	304,923	9,531.82	1,790.83
5	283	3	607	1,046	0	0	0	63,342	26,212	89,554	51.6	173,621	7,925.74	1,685.32
5	424	18	847	1,498	0	1	1	71,376	21,510	92,887	49.9	186,054	9,572.63	1,833.15
3,989	18,532	357	35,549	66,950	4,201	12	4,213	5,950,512	1,567,800	7,518,313	58.5	12,844,899	16,762.04	2,753.62
8,083	47,762	2,293	105,591	188,712	10,935	318	11,253	15,787,670	5,035,264	20,822,935	56.3	36,979,083	19,755.84	2,947.10
991	6,364	616	13,181	24,021	668	9	677	1,445,847	392,651	1,838,497	55.8	3,295,552	12,511.64	1,640.40
119	3,439	370	6,564	11,511	572	0	572	810,641	260,926	1,071,567	52.6	2,038,929	14,142.43	2,077.57
88	1,091	97	2,291	4,130	35	0	35	281,596	69,565	351,160	57.3	612,762	8,916.53	1,445.93
55	446	85	1,064	1,891	13	0	13	115,885	30,495	146,380	56.9	257,194	9,449.74	1,755.37
7,739	68,681	2,726	121,244	233,629	8,874	716	9,590	14,257,216	3,747,430	18,004,641	46.2	38,945,696	12,174.91	2,236.07
356	4,830	592	11,273	19,794	140	2	142	1,005,047	282,540	1,287,585	50.8	2,533,647	7,177.77	1,125.27
7,383	63,851	2,134	109,971	213,835	8,734	714	9,448	13,252,169	3,464,890	16,717,056	45.9	36,412,050	12,794.73	2,400.99
660	4,285	82	7,918	15,079	508	24	532	834,580	194,249	1,028,829	45.0	2,287,883	12,251.38	2,108.07
39	873	58	1,414	2,689	35	1	36	167,988	55,101	223,088	51.7	431,357	8,586.27	1,673.61
220	1,896	78	3,314	6,400	246	15	261	400,180	104,950	505,131	47.8	1,056,511	19,173.39	2,742.33
6	455	9	1,192	1,895	0	23	23	125,846	49,144	174,990	59.6	293,831	7,907.83	1,935.47
37	473	21	847	1,589	19	1	20	91,149	24,646	115,795	49.2	235,508	10,846.91	2,458.92
133	1,693	55	2,036	4,773	49	1	50	231,615	57,774	289,389	40.1	722,369	9,628.51	1,846.37
17	211	4	418	798	0	0	0	41,689	15,056	56,745	45.0	126,131	9,281.19	2,284.20
1,020	3,738	322	8,926	15,663	912	85	997	827,047	218,391	1,045,438	45.7	2,286,051	14,809.77	2,685.41
17	851	71	2,042	3,377	75	0	75	165,949	49,347	215,296	50.7	424,795	8,770.22	1,575.08
188	1,837	127	4,172	7,391	66	0	66	469,535	153,551	623,087	53.6	1,162,672	12,491.24	2,759.74
37	221	25	704	1,192	0	0	0	57,528	19,325	76,854	45.3	169,743	8,023.41	1,618.53
516	6,248	118	11,038	20,732	316	2	318	1,398,024	316,343	1,714,367	49.4	3,468,465	10,240.31	2,189.59
3,133	18,968	329	31,462	61,945	4,823	275	5,098	4,435,554	1,171,167	5,606,719	49.1	11,417,227	17,732.83	3,260.70
1,072	14,767	351	21,265	45,120	1,356	282	1,638	2,427,036	615,516	3,042,550	38.3	7,949,919	11,227.11	2,055.76
119	1,524	85	3,528	6,144	110	2	112	375,144	76,444	451,588	47.0	961,499	13,755.16	2,878.08
85	2,204	162	3,975	7,460	33	2	35	468,311	124,158	592,469	45.3	1,307,304	9,597.71	1,797.28
15	404	10	874	1,540	0	0	0	149,778	36,617	186,395	52.8	352,978	12,114.01	2,552.73
12	632	85	784	1,864	21	0	21	117,873	31,180	149,053	42.5	350,345	11,676.61	1,330.66
39	1,712	85	2,938	5,749	148	0	148	347,970	122,136	470,105	45.0	1,043,785	11,881.18	2,323.79
18	859	57	1,124	2,435	17	1	18	119,373	29,794	149,168	41.0	363,674	7,992.14	1,574.12

MSAs

TABLE 8   U.S. CENSUS DIVISION 3, SOUTH ATLANTIC

U.S. Community Hospitals
(Nonfederal, short-term general and other special hospitals)

2014 Utilization, Personnel and Finances

CLASSIFICATION	Hospitals	Beds	Admissions	Inpatient Days	Adjusted Inpatient Days	Average Daily Census	Adjusted Average Daily Census	Average Stay (days)	Surgical Operations	NEWBORNS Bassinets	NEWBORNS Births	OUTPATIENT VISITS Emergency	OUTPATIENT VISITS Total
UNITED STATES	4,926	786,874	33,066,720	180,456,434	365,636,679	494,388	1,002,304	5.5	26,401,528	55,824	3,735,593	136,327,473	693,106,685
Nonmetropolitan	1,855	116,785	3,238,473	21,307,388	64,127,906	58,370	175,723	6.6	3,512,461	9,506	383,166	21,639,508	119,516,577
Metropolitan	3,071	670,089	29,828,247	159,149,046	301,508,773	436,018	826,581	5.3	22,889,067	46,318	3,352,427	114,687,965	573,590,108
CENSUS DIVISION 3, SOUTH ATLANTIC	754	154,927	6,782,630	37,244,934	72,483,408	102,041	198,771	5.5	5,197,366	10,150	689,817	28,173,654	105,664,054
Nonmetropolitan	201	18,035	532,791	3,681,282	9,927,184	10,090	27,208	6.9	518,037	1,321	53,235	3,760,742	13,659,233
Metropolitan	553	136,892	6,249,839	33,563,652	62,556,224	91,951	171,563	5.4	4,679,329	8,829	636,582	24,412,912	92,004,821
Delaware	7	2,053	105,109	557,672	1,072,296	1,528	2,937	5.3	95,945	96	11,201	451,296	2,107,563
Metropolitan	7	2,053	105,109	557,672	1,072,296	1,528	2,937	5.3	95,945	96	11,201	451,296	2,107,563
Dover, DE	1	347	18,581	99,427	220,701	272	605	5.4	13,987	11	2,272	92,041	568,266
Salisbury, MD-DE	2	254	15,256	61,039	138,533	167	379	4.0	17,130	23	1,738	83,298	585,033
Wilmington, DE-MD-NJ	4	1,452	71,272	397,206	713,062	1,089	1,953	5.6	64,828	62	7,191	275,957	954,264
District of Columbia	11	3,542	127,293	924,407	1,530,898	2,533	4,195	7.3	107,199	183	13,689	497,658	2,652,775
Metropolitan	11	3,542	127,293	924,407	1,530,898	2,533	4,195	7.3	107,199	183	13,689	497,658	2,652,775
Washington-Arlington-Alexandria, DC-VA-MD-WV	11	3,542	127,293	924,407	1,530,898	2,533	4,195	7.3	107,199	183	13,689	497,658	2,652,775
Florida	211	53,489	2,473,183	12,310,835	21,231,701	33,728	58,172	5.0	1,428,286	2,840	196,237	9,063,174	25,596,077
Nonmetropolitan	22	1,001	38,688	166,317	502,216	457	1,376	4.3	37,182	43	1,652	308,548	751,916
Metropolitan	189	52,488	2,434,495	12,144,518	20,729,485	33,271	56,796	5.0	1,391,104	2,797	194,585	8,754,626	24,844,161
Cape Coral-Fort Myers, FL	4	1,563	79,671	366,279	695,798	1,004	1,906	4.6	41,533	83	5,817	206,925	518,509
Crestview-Fort Walton Beach-Destin, FL	5	540	26,114	106,934	201,470	294	552	4.1	19,017	48	2,862	140,993	386,168
Deltona-Daytona Beach-Ormond Beach, FL	6	1,447	64,812	315,712	612,008	865	1,677	4.9	37,552	64	4,015	356,701	1,059,361
Fort Lauderdale-Pompano Beach-Deerfield Beach, FL	17	5,333	237,464	1,186,696	1,992,600	3,249	5,460	5.0	131,924	263	21,955	972,403	2,331,351
Gainesville, FL	3	1,449	69,344	389,645	593,509	1,067	1,626	5.6	55,794	49	5,534	167,440	1,031,993
Homosassa Springs, FL	2	326	17,448	72,240	147,353	198	404	4.1	10,384	20	1,492	63,443	263,923
Jacksonville, FL	13	4,077	190,218	961,546	1,648,023	2,635	4,516	5.1	134,515	276	17,308	743,660	2,150,780
Lakeland-Winter Haven, FL	5	1,745	75,592	346,605	629,034	949	1,724	4.6	41,312	62	5,741	357,062	686,499
Miami-Miami Beach-Kendall, FL	25	7,467	311,210	1,774,095	2,916,550	4,863	7,991	5.7	159,133	352	26,477	1,052,713	3,518,784
Naples-Immokalee-Marco Island, FL	2	914	32,863	156,098	256,098	427	702	4.7	15,085	36	3,418	117,512	337,073
North Port-Sarasota-Bradenton, FL	8	2,047	82,943	408,020	707,290	1,117	1,937	4.9	50,823	59	4,557	265,312	938,738
Ocala, FL	3	721	43,980	154,455	254,025	423	696	3.5	17,515	26	2,015	165,515	244,636
Orlando-Kissimmee-Sanford, FL	13	5,698	325,138	1,586,411	2,609,536	4,344	7,149	4.9	181,860	428	21,484	1,045,101	2,630,906
Palm Bay-Melbourne-Titusville, FL	7	1,436	59,036	294,581	498,100	807	1,365	5.0	34,497	132	5,362	206,889	696,788
Panama City, FL	5	573	29,719	148,990	263,103	409	721	5.0	17,947	37	3,576	115,423	333,402
Pensacola-Ferry Pass-Brent, FL	7	1,387	63,035	292,697	563,470	802	1,544	4.6	39,068	70	6,661	308,316	1,042,046
Port St. Lucie, FL	3	860	52,039	232,798	414,951	638	1,137	4.5	30,921	64	4,629	167,457	274,833
Punta Gorda, FL	3	700	27,325	140,504	208,503	385	571	5.1	20,091	10	1,338	76,473	154,741
Sebastian-Vero Beach, FL	3	417	19,432	104,326	178,919	286	490	5.4	8,251	22	1,048	78,179	152,034
Sebring, FL	2	330	14,902	69,418	141,996	190	389	4.7	9,088	26	1,296	71,529	226,731
Tallahassee, FL	4	794	41,523	202,276	390,730	554	1,070	4.9	22,209	62	4,606	129,782	739,252
Tampa-St. Petersburg-Clearwater, FL	34	8,955	393,255	1,989,177	3,364,024	5,450	9,217	5.1	218,657	420	28,743	1,403,540	3,659,542
West Palm Beach-Boca Raton-Delray Beach, FL	15	3,709	177,432	845,005	1,442,395	2,315	3,952	4.8	93,928	188	14,651	542,258	1,466,071
Georgia	142	24,479	941,742	6,140,718	12,581,658	16,827	34,465	6.5	714,101	1,880	121,828	4,114,916	15,460,187
Nonmetropolitan	57	5,685	127,160	1,272,772	3,219,067	3,490	8,818	10.0	135,589	345	16,416	835,994	3,088,968
Metropolitan	85	18,794	814,582	4,867,946	9,362,591	13,337	25,647	6.0	578,512	1,535	105,412	3,278,922	12,371,219
Albany, GA	2	542	20,724	118,017	281,149	323	770	5.7	13,004	42	2,494	105,783	915,839
Athens-Clarke County, GA	2	522	26,955	122,998	242,550	337	665	4.6	22,705	47	3,887	120,677	483,357
Atlanta-Sandy Springs-Roswell, GA	42	9,711	449,442	2,602,996	4,906,464	7,132	13,439	5.8	307,020	866	66,996	1,795,522	6,243,843
Augusta-Richmond County, GA-SC	8	1,500	61,835	366,552	643,408	1,004	1,762	5.9	52,927	123	5,881	261,980	1,234,487
Brunswick, GA	1	469	11,433	136,061	293,942	373	805	11.9	9,890	8	1,291	52,183	217,560
Chattanooga, TN-GA	1	185	6,144	60,693	143,994	166	395	9.9	4,918	15	682	20,670	99,777
Columbus, GA-AL	5	1,130	40,457	260,452	496,971	713	1,361	6.4	28,305	43	3,173	103,591	408,301
Dalton, GA	2	263	10,589	48,081	101,411	132	278	4.5	4,456	40	1,824	80,735	304,825
Gainesville, GA	1	773	28,895	225,757	420,846	619	1,153	7.8	19,421	64	3,675	109,888	351,388
Hinesville, GA	1	25	1,718	6,466	26,053	18	71	3.8	1,107	6	327	5,651	30,976
Macon, GA	5	1,072	45,986	269,854	446,107	739	1,222	5.9	24,561	96	2,473	123,150	530,820
Rome, GA	3	602	25,906	141,299	275,426	387	755	5.5	17,698	30	2,203	119,490	349,046
Savannah, GA	5	1,228	50,361	335,341	676,732	918	1,854	6.7	41,877	71	5,894	205,216	586,594
Valdosta, GA	3	414	15,832	93,269	213,945	256	586	5.9	12,996	40	2,212	79,208	277,189
Warner Robins, GA	4	358	18,305	80,110	193,593	220	531	4.4	17,627	44	2,400	95,178	337,217

MSAs

TABLE 8   U.S. CENSUS DIVISION 3, SOUTH ATLANTIC

U.S. Community Hospitals
(Nonfederal, short-term general and other special hospitals)

2014 Utilization, Personnel and Finances

FULL-TIME EQUIVALENT PERSONNEL					FULL-TIME EQUIV. TRAINEES			EXPENSES						
								LABOR				TOTAL		
Physicians and Dentists	Registered Nurses	Licensed Practical Nurses	Other Salaried Personnel	Total Personnel	Medical and Dental Residents	Other Trainees	Total Trainees	Payroll (in thousands)	Employee Benefits (in thousands)	Total (in thousands)	Percent of Total	Amount (in thousands)	Adjusted per Admission	Adjusted per Inpatient Day
122,747	1,398,346	73,044	2,510,354	4,754,880	109,309	8,533	117,842	$310,203,433	$82,949,525	$393,152,940	48.6	$808,869,209	$12,015.42	$2,212.22
15,090	147,461	20,793	334,968	602,081	1,731	269	2,000	33,192,643	8,842,572	42,035,205	51.3	81,981,991	8,301.59	1,278.41
107,657	1,250,885	52,251	2,175,386	4,152,799	107,578	8,264	115,842	277,010,790	74,106,953	351,117,735	48.3	726,887,218	12,653.89	2,410.83
17,562	273,484	12,140	437,707	875,071	18,009	768	18,777	52,644,564	13,113,082	65,757,653	46.7	140,819,952	10,624.83	1,942.79
1,601	22,699	2,586	44,770	84,814	326	26	352	4,213,084	1,107,837	5,320,920	49.4	10,766,169	7,377.71	1,084.51
15,961	250,785	9,554	392,937	790,257	17,683	742	18,425	48,431,479	12,005,245	60,436,733	46.5	130,053,783	11,026.58	2,078.99
545	5,297	199	10,515	18,377	319	1	320	1,290,200	392,757	1,682,956	57.1	2,946,253	14,361.95	2,747.61
545	5,297	199	10,515	18,377	319	1	320	1,290,200	392,757	1,682,956	57.1	2,946,253	14,361.95	2,747.61
54	798	44	1,693	2,932	0	0	0	220,793	61,287	282,080	58.5	481,846	11,682.54	2,183.25
62	733	31	1,487	2,595	0	0	0	144,823	48,285	193,109	49.6	388,972	11,188.61	2,807.79
429	3,766	124	7,335	12,850	319	1	320	924,583	283,184	1,207,767	58.2	2,075,435	16,072.07	2,910.59
1,467	6,805	264	11,673	23,225	1,491	63	1,554	1,835,997	364,253	2,200,250	53.5	4,112,357	19,299.95	2,686.24
1,467	6,805	264	11,673	23,225	1,491	63	1,554	1,835,997	364,253	2,200,250	53.5	4,112,357	19,299.95	2,686.24
1,467	6,805	264	11,673	23,225	1,491	63	1,554	1,835,997	364,253	2,200,250	53.5	4,112,357	19,299.95	2,686.24
4,161	85,399	3,159	125,861	257,751	5,576	255	5,831	15,630,506	3,828,721	19,459,227	45.4	42,851,681	9,911.74	2,018.29
94	1,359	173	2,901	5,292	11	3	14	254,271	59,354	313,624	47.6	658,657	5,883.96	1,311.50
4,067	84,040	2,986	122,960	252,459	5,565	252	5,817	15,376,235	3,769,368	19,145,603	45.4	42,193,025	10,018.80	2,035.41
219	2,871	140	5,134	9,889	550	32	582	616,914	199,595	816,510	51.0	1,599,738	10,538.94	2,299.14
25	645	43	949	1,965	18	0	18	111,412	22,295	133,705	41.1	325,324	6,415.01	1,614.75
253	2,179	115	4,572	8,084	41	2	43	467,446	91,640	559,086	49.1	1,139,374	8,996.31	1,861.70
638	7,911	304	10,434	22,930	286	23	309	1,414,007	301,017	1,715,023	47.0	3,646,459	9,007.45	1,830.00
3	3,191	63	4,567	8,974	574	21	595	520,168	160,004	680,171	47.1	1,444,153	13,498.02	2,433.25
29	471	31	833	1,581	13	1	14	87,217	21,854	109,071	47.2	231,230	6,508.22	1,569.23
532	7,167	148	9,119	20,308	601	23	624	1,121,223	312,964	1,434,185	43.8	3,278,038	9,875.16	1,989.07
34	2,518	90	3,975	7,996	10	0	10	417,873	95,859	513,732	49.8	1,032,338	7,518.85	1,641.15
555	11,688	470	18,933	36,902	1,713	25	1,738	2,498,938	600,605	3,099,543	47.2	6,561,220	12,531.15	2,249.65
3	1,125	32	1,283	2,925	5	0	5	165,351	27,685	193,036	44.6	432,942	8,010.76	1,690.53
34	3,168	168	4,096	8,867	49	0	49	435,899	104,181	540,080	45.1	1,197,856	8,292.88	1,693.59
30	1,050	39	1,706	3,273	17	0	17	165,129	36,044	201,173	45.0	447,344	6,104.00	1,761.02
514	12,055	285	17,812	35,447	596	31	627	2,098,026	601,918	2,699,945	39.8	6,779,827	12,673.40	2,598.10
109	1,679	58	2,195	5,183	18	19	37	345,940	78,866	424,807	49.1	865,803	8,297.90	1,738.21
52	680	64	1,240	2,398	23	0	23	165,893	40,239	206,132	44.9	459,085	8,191.65	1,744.89
100	2,016	75	2,940	6,057	104	29	133	313,247	54,354	367,601	37.6	978,649	7,893.67	1,736.83
106	1,328	66	2,514	4,730	23	0	23	282,150	70,224	352,374	49.1	718,103	7,699.19	1,730.57
16	862	37	991	2,257	31	0	31	110,261	21,650	131,911	40.3	327,247	8,073.78	1,569.51
66	626	23	1,186	2,181	6	0	6	124,387	25,007	149,394	51.9	288,020	8,146.06	1,609.78
38	622	38	897	1,834	5	0	5	94,970	26,641	121,611	51.9	234,195	7,643.95	1,649.31
121	1,452	99	2,339	4,630	70	0	70	281,100	58,622	339,722	49.9	680,242	8,503.88	1,740.95
539	13,657	445	18,819	40,068	690	43	733	2,557,866	607,529	3,165,394	45.6	6,934,593	10,439.31	2,061.40
51	5,079	153	6,426	13,980	122	3	125	980,820	210,577	1,191,397	46.0	2,591,244	8,444.05	1,796.49
2,157	39,257	2,594	65,996	130,746	1,569	115	1,684	7,409,017	1,796,818	9,205,839	46.1	19,975,007	10,471.29	1,587.63
446	5,634	936	12,192	22,659	51	9	60	1,092,750	291,500	1,384,249	50.3	2,751,859	8,036.88	854.86
1,711	33,623	1,658	53,804	108,087	1,518	106	1,624	6,316,267	1,505,317	7,821,590	45.4	17,223,147	11,003.85	1,839.57
4	825	69	1,632	2,863	21	0	21	184,043	51,012	235,055	44.8	524,490	10,837.46	1,865.52
1	972	26	2,138	3,428	0	0	0	207,055	44,901	251,956	47.0	536,054	10,087.96	2,210.08
879	18,449	759	28,571	58,475	669	74	743	3,495,324	809,822	4,305,149	44.0	9,776,448	11,473.36	1,992.56
110	2,678	143	4,081	8,170	110	4	114	519,652	117,943	637,597	46.0	1,384,947	12,522.58	2,152.52
81	356	21	719	1,417	0	0	0	128,927	32,778	161,705	54.2	298,166	12,072.00	1,014.37
29	243	24	559	996	9	2	11	52,761	16,990	69,751	54.3	128,433	8,810.65	891.93
164	1,626	115	2,713	5,531	62	4	66	298,035	71,758	369,793	46.7	792,199	9,894.44	1,594.05
1	392	35	643	1,187	0	0	0	93,210	24,314	117,525	49.5	237,372	10,184.59	2,340.69
221	1,647	48	2,927	5,581	246	18	264	227,768	55,366	283,135	46.4	609,697	11,318.98	1,448.74
7	58	14	151	269	0	0	0	17,010	4,534	21,544	54.0	39,917	5,766.74	1,532.16
26	1,801	80	1,795	4,786	130	0	130	318,037	83,160	401,197	47.8	840,147	10,945.11	1,883.28
64	985	100	1,911	3,495	39	0	39	209,325	56,557	265,882	51.7	514,124	9,970.60	1,866.65
94	2,177	78	3,414	6,789	213	3	216	351,079	62,442	413,523	43.9	941,400	10,367.50	1,391.10
12	707	51	1,259	2,506	0	0	0	105,933	44,198	150,131	45.8	327,516	9,664.66	1,530.84
18	707	95	1,291	2,594	19	1	20	108,107	29,540	137,647	50.6	272,237	6,115.91	1,406.24

Table continues

MSAs

TABLE 8

U.S. Community Hospitals
(Nonfederal, short-term general and other special hospitals)

2014 Utilization, Personnel and Finances

CLASSIFICATION	Hospitals	Beds	Admissions	Inpatient Days	Adjusted Inpatient Days	Average Daily Census	Adjusted Average Daily Census	Average Stay (days)	Surgical Operations	NEWBORNS		OUTPATIENT VISITS	
										Bassinets	Births	Emergency	Total
Maryland.	50	12,027	609,185	3,067,846	5,666,242	8,407	15,670	5.0	528,590	906	65,730	2,341,061	9,012,789
Nonmetropolitan	4	273	14,112	58,117	130,323	159	357	4.1	16,279	30	1,389	105,878	557,875
Metropolitan	46	11,754	595,073	3,009,729	5,535,919	8,248	15,313	5.1	512,311	876	64,341	2,235,183	8,454,914
Baltimore-Columbia-Towson, MD .	24	7,649	375,147	1,991,448	3,530,882	5,457	9,819	5.3	345,120	461	33,689	1,307,630	5,080,083
California-Lexington Park, MD . . .	1	89	6,681	21,564	52,917	59	145	3.2	6,500	16	1,176	53,119	236,101
Cumberland, MD-WV.	1	321	11,879	83,740	178,413	229	489	7.0	8,315	20	1,018	52,331	538,853
Hagerstown-Martinsburg, MD-WV .	1	257	16,542	63,135	120,968	173	331	3.8	7,855	41	1,996	75,182	190,825
Salisbury, MD-DE.	4	492	24,503	120,892	272,763	332	748	4.9	24,908	28	1,905	113,208	704,107
Silver Spring-Frederick-Rockville, MD.	7	1,764	99,574	453,055	805,883	1,242	2,208	4.5	62,159	224	17,771	350,645	1,012,365
Washington-Arlington-Alexandria, DC-VA-MD-WV .	7	1,064	55,696	255,896	526,236	701	1,442	4.6	51,918	74	6,119	243,184	547,636
Wilmington, DE-MD-NJ	1	118	5,051	19,999	47,857	55	131	4.0	5,536	12	667	39,884	144,944
North Carolina	116	22,034	995,842	5,496,740	12,100,164	15,056	33,160	5.5	825,372	1,628	114,799	4,661,360	19,665,995
Nonmetropolitan	49	4,545	174,657	946,758	2,658,808	2,593	7,295	5.4	146,232	458	18,488	1,217,602	4,220,966
Metropolitan	67	17,489	821,185	4,549,982	9,441,356	12,463	25,865	5.5	679,140	1,170	96,311	3,443,758	15,445,029
Asheville, NC	6	1,254	59,703	290,722	651,357	795	1,783	4.9	55,799	58	5,060	179,688	1,589,302
Burlington, NC.	1	218	9,878	46,556	130,088	128	356	4.7	8,933	21	1,305	57,560	116,779
Charlotte-Concord-Gastonia, NC-SC .	17	4,111	217,714	1,074,605	2,186,217	2,944	5,990	4.9	160,740	359	27,694	967,230	3,334,052
Durham-Chapel Hill, NC.	6	2,120	95,447	627,306	1,267,435	1,719	3,473	6.6	84,537	63	8,978	230,443	2,170,943
Fayetteville, NC	1	592	29,954	185,438	316,688	508	868	6.2	15,957	48	4,619	131,904	621,875
Goldsboro, NC.	1	274	10,660	50,185	123,077	137	337	4.7	12,718	30	1,471	61,679	203,741
Greensboro-High Point, NC.	6	1,785	70,358	405,441	942,112	1,110	2,581	5.8	44,210	111	8,728	351,447	1,380,391
Greenville, NC.	1	909	38,685	256,423	371,731	703	1,018	6.6	21,526	42	3,552	115,908	293,659
Hickory-Lenoir-Morganton, NC . . .	4	743	32,505	157,099	371,611	430	1,018	4.8	28,583	62	3,624	179,262	578,667
Jacksonville, NC	1	125	7,220	29,394	83,863	81	230	4.1	4,792	23	1,904	60,725	139,857
Myrtle Beach-Conway-North Myrtle Beach, SC-NC. .	2	141	5,466	34,633	123,125	95	338	6.3	5,704	5	495	43,430	164,268
New Bern, NC.	1	350	12,165	58,924	124,162	161	340	4.8	12,553	22	1,190	67,825	164,659
Raleigh, NC	6	1,866	87,139	489,340	1,111,931	1,340	3,047	5.6	92,434	151	14,594	439,412	2,494,987
Rocky Mount, NC	3	403	16,489	94,685	199,417	259	545	5.7	11,081	34	1,433	93,142	248,237
Wilmington, NC	2	760	39,358	205,756	404,377	564	1,108	5.2	35,076	43	4,119	139,833	375,493
Winston-Salem, NC.	9	1,838	88,444	543,475	1,034,165	1,489	2,833	6.1	84,497	98	7,545	324,270	1,568,119
South Carolina	70	12,228	498,690	2,784,918	5,251,788	7,629	14,425	5.6	485,734	849	53,437	2,217,906	7,535,851
Nonmetropolitan	16	1,843	52,556	314,949	743,336	863	2,037	6.0	51,151	164	5,395	397,066	1,111,014
Metropolitan	54	10,385	446,134	2,469,969	4,508,452	6,766	12,388	5.5	434,583	685	48,042	1,820,840	6,424,837
Augusta-Richmond County, GA-SC	2	296	12,028	62,509	106,262	171	291	5.2	9,347	18	1,094	59,178	137,756
Charleston-North Charleston, SC .	7	1,872	85,563	455,460	820,193	1,248	2,246	5.3	85,069	116	9,749	350,444	1,750,224
Charlotte-Concord-Gastonia, NC-SC .	4	534	22,928	112,623	197,194	308	540	4.9	15,982	41	2,444	119,701	231,036
Columbia, SC	8	2,176	94,302	522,003	929,076	1,431	2,584	5.5	71,087	119	9,486	300,228	1,201,848
Florence, SC.	7	1,272	45,956	278,837	486,049	763	1,332	6.1	57,784	58	3,606	149,618	352,214
Greenville-Anderson-Mauldin, SC .	14	1,898	91,476	490,270	888,610	1,343	2,433	5.4	97,768	135	10,837	405,071	1,628,686
Hilton Head Island-Bluffton-Beaufort, SC	3	309	16,327	66,279	148,534	182	406	4.1	13,564	52	2,528	52,084	158,288
Myrtle Beach-Conway-North Myrtle Beach, SC-NC. .	4	895	38,089	219,176	444,573	600	1,218	5.8	34,213	63	3,287	169,281	404,768
Spartanburg, SC	4	895	34,896	202,580	370,934	555	1,017	5.8	39,800	59	3,736	152,912	429,446
Sumter, SC.	1	238	4,569	60,232	117,027	165	321	13.2	9,969	24	1,275	62,323	130,571
Virginia.	93	18,234	775,015	4,432,096	9,439,312	12,143	25,857	5.7	706,967	1,361	92,449	3,644,169	16,522,020
Nonmetropolitan	27	2,571	67,990	512,720	1,324,932	1,406	3,628	7.5	63,953	145	5,023	459,176	1,637,600
Metropolitan	66	15,663	707,025	3,919,376	8,114,380	10,737	22,229	5.5	643,014	1,216	87,426	3,184,993	14,884,420
Blacksburg-Christiansburg-Radford, VA	4	253	15,352	62,972	153,472	173	421	4.1	18,971	24	1,942	90,819	254,593
Charlottesville, VA	3	773	38,926	209,944	445,191	575	1,220	5.4	82,357	42	3,458	110,636	2,317,342
Harrisonburg, VA	1	244	12,786	47,807	144,700	131	396	3.7	18,880	22	1,748	73,490	413,745
Kingsport-Bristol-Bristol, TN-VA . .	2	141	7,643	29,184	77,913	80	214	3.8	6,856	16	763	39,161	145,695
Lynchburg, VA.	2	1,333	31,640	334,263	655,444	916	1,796	10.6	17,338	39	2,540	103,627	574,912
Richmond, VA.	14	3,483	154,805	848,395	1,587,603	2,324	4,349	5.5	106,340	254	14,553	626,985	1,870,758
Roanoke, VA.	3	1,185	61,018	351,628	598,975	964	1,641	5.8	45,032	67	4,493	288,805	716,212
Staunton-Waynesboro, VA	2	254	11,408	47,404	140,302	130	384	4.2	15,995	21	1,145	60,868	663,832
Virginia Beach-Norfolk-Newport News, VA-NC	16	3,661	157,156	922,780	2,077,542	2,526	5,690	5.9	155,391	282	18,506	864,988	5,015,879
Washington-Arlington-Alexandria, DC-VA-MD-WV	18	3,861	193,390	952,281	2,015,262	2,609	5,521	4.9	162,305	433	36,045	856,242	2,601,648
Winchester, VA-WV	1	475	22,901	112,718	217,976	309	597	4.9	13,549	16	2,233	69,372	309,804

TABLE 8

U.S. CENSUS DIVISION 3, SOUTH ATLANTIC CONTINUED

U.S. Community Hospitals
(Nonfederal, short-term general and other special hospitals)

2014 Utilization, Personnel and Finances

	FULL-TIME EQUIVALENT PERSONNEL				FULL-TIME EQUIV. TRAINEES			EXPENSES						
								LABOR				TOTAL		
Physicians and Dentists	Registered Nurses	Licensed Practical Nurses	Other Salaried Personnel	Total Personnel	Medical and Dental Residents	Other Trainees	Total Trainees	Payroll (in thousands)	Employee Benefits (in thousands)	Total (in thousands)	Percent of Total	Amount (in thousands)	Adjusted per Admission	Adjusted per Inpatient Day
2,924	25,591	498	49,842	90,645	1,668	98	1,766	5,530,593	1,327,479	6,858,070	48.3	14,187,741	12,300.64	2,503.91
7	611	9	1,134	2,150	0	0	0	114,254	36,872	151,125	51.0	296,262	9,334.61	2,273.29
2,917	24,980	489	48,708	88,495	1,668	98	1,766	5,416,339	1,290,607	6,706,945	48.3	13,891,479	12,384.56	2,509.34
2,509	17,480	233	32,951	61,270	1,604	81	1,685	3,769,529	892,491	4,662,019	47.8	9,743,531	14,068.05	2,759.52
7	249	3	568	993	2	4	6	59,529	10,313	69,842	53.0	131,819	8,040.21	2,491.06
29	442	20	1,026	1,701	0	0	0	104,975	34,067	139,041	49.3	282,309	11,154.49	1,582.33
7	568	24	975	1,739	0	0	0	106,981	32,236	139,217	47.6	292,347	9,223.76	2,416.73
70	993	43	1,905	3,513	2	1	3	217,744	57,464	275,208	50.5	545,259	10,001.63	1,999.02
148	3,187	80	6,797	11,370	43	4	47	677,296	162,168	839,464	48.3	1,736,317	9,958.06	2,154.55
113	1,830	81	3,951	6,952	17	4	21	414,495	88,865	503,361	49.7	1,013,262	8,833.17	1,925.49
34	231	5	535	957	0	4	4	65,791	13,002	78,793	53.7	146,636	12,131.69	3,064.04
2,236	47,188	1,537	79,163	154,494	3,111	85	3,196	8,652,040	2,256,089	10,908,130	47.0	23,206,885	10,523.66	1,917.90
403	7,675	439	14,410	26,804	62	8	70	1,301,329	327,753	1,629,082	48.5	3,361,162	6,998.41	1,264.16
1,833	39,513	1,098	64,753	127,690	3,049	77	3,126	7,350,711	1,928,336	9,279,048	46.8	19,845,722	11,505.19	2,102.00
263	2,646	37	4,907	9,158	1	0	1	463,590	122,187	585,779	43.0	1,361,873	9,950.92	2,090.82
40	286	13	955	1,345	0	0	0	83,291	22,158	105,450	43.4	242,938	8,801.79	1,867.49
428	9,200	216	16,022	30,227	340	12	352	1,509,870	401,955	1,911,826	40.5	4,720,369	10,428.51	2,159.15
60	6,732	84	9,772	20,245	1,445	16	1,461	1,313,230	342,028	1,655,258	47.8	3,460,321	18,108.14	2,730.18
125	1,369	123	2,248	4,520	0	0	0	295,976	70,727	366,703	58.4	628,207	12,280.46	1,983.68
0	538	12	715	1,556	0	0	0	81,278	26,170	107,448	53.3	201,525	7,708.57	1,637.39
402	3,217	165	6,304	11,656	50	1	51	566,219	179,754	745,973	48.0	1,554,273	9,433.73	1,649.77
0	1,930	11	2,524	5,857	394	17	411	356,178	122,248	478,426	47.8	999,890	17,829.38	2,689.82
142	1,232	26	2,305	4,590	33	0	33	280,276	73,193	353,470	47.5	744,527	9,478.75	2,003.51
0	277	9	535	922	0	0	0	50,984	16,365	67,349	50.4	133,690	6,490.13	1,594.15
4	196	21	391	742	0	0	0	37,832	9,387	47,219	40.7	115,909	7,395.47	941.39
0	512	3	807	1,666	0	0	0	87,761	22,043	109,804	47.3	232,052	9,052.52	1,868.95
361	4,881	82	6,919	14,606	5	1	6	990,940	220,074	1,211,014	54.3	2,230,054	11,152.33	2,005.57
3	770	34	995	2,180	0	0	0	126,487	37,008	163,496	52.4	311,845	8,326.75	1,563.78
1	1,344	27	2,435	4,543	73	0	73	279,230	72,358	351,588	48.4	725,850	9,999.73	1,794.98
4	4,383	235	6,919	13,877	708	30	738	827,569	190,678	1,018,245	46.7	2,182,399	12,978.65	2,110.30
1,643	22,057	732	29,653	66,903	1,421	6	1,427	3,660,679	994,301	4,654,982	45.2	10,299,166	10,702.28	1,961.08
192	2,332	178	4,223	8,434	59	1	60	422,622	119,316	541,939	47.3	1,144,963	9,105.14	1,540.30
1,451	19,725	554	25,430	58,469	1,362	5	1,367	3,238,057	874,985	4,113,043	44.9	9,154,204	10,942.35	2,030.45
13	372	10	371	1,007	0	0	0	58,202	13,895	72,097	44.8	160,990	7,684.11	1,515.03
20	4,146	97	4,756	11,479	705	0	705	706,841	191,744	898,585	42.0	2,139,927	13,470.18	2,609.05
4	800	36	927	2,423	0	0	0	114,286	26,465	140,751	41.1	342,524	8,200.43	1,736.99
124	3,964	113	5,683	12,167	243	0	243	730,200	200,326	930,525	49.1	1,893,740	11,052.14	2,038.31
70	1,975	73	2,212	5,411	43	0	43	292,950	68,002	360,951	43.9	821,621	10,042.06	1,690.41
1,059	4,452	110	6,341	14,418	283	3	286	707,058	197,814	904,873	44.3	2,044,625	11,635.83	2,300.93
33	562	31	973	1,940	11	1	12	101,186	33,393	134,580	47.6	282,653	7,717.70	1,902.95
30	1,109	43	1,133	2,993	12	1	13	190,263	51,590	241,853	44.0	549,994	7,418.81	1,237.13
98	1,899	36	2,306	5,202	65	0	65	265,879	72,508	338,386	46.1	734,187	11,043.23	1,979.29
0	446	5	728	1,429	0	0	0	71,192	19,250	90,442	49.2	183,943	20,721.26	1,571.80
1,625	31,133	1,955	44,756	93,917	2,209	123	2,332	6,603,867	1,553,308	8,157,178	46.0	17,726,816	10,552.46	1,877.98
157	2,675	369	4,595	9,304	83	5	88	526,869	129,920	656,791	49.4	1,330,882	7,370.78	1,004.49
1,468	28,458	1,586	40,161	84,613	2,126	118	2,244	6,076,998	1,423,388	7,500,387	45.7	16,395,934	10,935.63	2,020.60
10	571	36	866	1,763	2	0	2	114,676	23,619	138,295	45.8	302,121	8,100.18	1,968.57
79	2,336	143	2,637	6,842	767	3	770	535,496	136,187	671,683	46.0	1,460,553	16,592.10	3,280.73
79	592	111	914	2,074	0	0	0	146,434	34,800	181,234	52.1	348,186	8,997.05	2,406.26
1	288	26	351	789	0	12	12	35,414	7,583	42,997	35.8	120,235	5,812.38	1,543.19
148	1,029	177	3,404	5,215	19	4	23	310,583	75,252	385,835	56.1	688,134	11,151.28	1,049.88
229	6,704	406	9,139	18,782	939	67	1,006	1,263,321	340,656	1,603,977	44.9	3,573,296	12,181.04	2,250.75
511	2,676	141	3,289	7,902	285	1	286	618,291	117,405	735,696	51.1	1,439,442	13,604.03	2,403.18
68	517	90	1,120	2,063	0	0	0	126,630	31,312	157,942	53.8	293,589	8,842.77	2,092.55
26	5,837	255	8,084	17,016	1	21	22	1,352,761	318,527	1,671,289	44.0	3,797,947	10,257.35	1,828.10
301	7,008	172	8,878	19,385	113	10	123	1,418,502	304,726	1,723,228	44.2	3,898,088	9,601.65	1,934.28
16	900	29	1,479	2,782	0	0	0	154,890	33,321	188,211	39.7	474,343	10,710.91	2,176.13

Table continues

MSAs

TABLE 8

U.S. Community Hospitals
(Nonfederal, short-term general and other special hospitals)

2014 Utilization, Personnel and Finances

MSAs

CLASSIFICATION	Hospitals	Beds	Admissions	Inpatient Days	Adjusted Inpatient Days	Average Daily Census	Adjusted Average Daily Census	Average Stay (days)	Surgical Operations	NEWBORNS Bassinets	NEWBORNS Births	OUTPATIENT VISITS Emergency	OUTPATIENT VISITS Total
West Virginia	54	6,841	256,571	1,529,702	3,609,349	4,190	9,890	6.0	305,172	407	20,447	1,182,114	7,110,797
Nonmetropolitan	26	2,117	57,628	409,649	1,348,502	1,122	3,697	7.1	67,651	136	4,872	436,478	2,290,894
Metropolitan	28	4,724	198,943	1,120,053	2,260,847	3,068	6,193	5.6	237,521	271	15,575	745,636	4,819,903
Beckley, WV	4	493	19,138	107,285	252,406	294	691	5.6	19,208	29	1,237	94,441	290,751
Charleston, WV	6	1,261	50,887	280,143	535,653	766	1,467	5.5	91,382	69	4,054	157,220	985,885
Cumberland, MD-WV	1	25	726	2,911	15,252	8	42	4.0	435	0	0	13,204	46,093
Hagerstown-Martinsburg, MD-WV	1	174	7,788	36,225	85,055	99	233	4.7	9,940	21	986	55,786	239,978
Huntington-Ashland, WV-KY-OH	3	746	43,229	205,812	379,083	564	1,038	4.8	30,706	55	3,165	114,321	780,519
Morgantown, WV	4	810	36,992	219,695	358,530	602	983	5.9	37,856	10	2,603	87,045	989,870
Parkersburg-Vienna, WV	2	280	13,172	70,377	128,515	193	352	5.3	11,635	19	1,465	58,582	323,464
Washington-Arlington-Alexandria, DC-VA-MD-WV	1	25	1,343	3,943	21,068	11	58	2.9	2,741	10	278	26,819	73,793
Weirton-Steubenville, WV-OH	1	168	6,090	34,223	101,627	94	278	5.6	6,375	21	272	39,683	251,268
Wheeling, WV-OH	4	698	19,141	145,839	315,193	400	863	7.6	26,747	37	1,515	88,817	794,027
Winchester, VA-WV	1	44	437	13,600	68,465	37	188	31.1	496	0	0	9,718	44,255

TABLE 8

U.S. Community Hospitals
(Nonfederal, short-term general and other special hospitals)

2014 Utilization, Personnel and Finances

FULL-TIME EQUIVALENT PERSONNEL					FULL-TIME EQUIV. TRAINEES			EXPENSES						
								LABOR				TOTAL		
Physicians and Dentists	Registered Nurses	Licensed Practical Nurses	Other Salaried Personnel	Total Personnel	Medical and Dental Residents	Other Trainees	Total Trainees	Payroll (in thousands)	Employee Benefits (in thousands)	Total (in thousands)	Percent of Total	Amount (in thousands)	Adjusted per Admission	Adjusted per Inpatient Day
804	10,757	1,202	20,248	39,013	645	22	667	2,031,666	599,356	2,631,021	47.7	5,514,045	9,131.01	1,527.71
302	2,413	482	5,315	10,171	60	0	60	500,989	143,122	644,110	52.7	1,222,383	6,550.29	906.47
502	8,344	720	14,933	28,842	585	22	607	1,530,677	456,234	1,986,911	46.3	4,291,662	10,285.19	1,898.25
49	467	138	838	1,781	3	5	8	94,715	24,464	119,179	44.0	270,753	6,489.15	1,072.69
145	2,430	207	3,904	7,945	171	0	171	410,338	126,255	536,593	44.7	1,201,213	12,108.02	2,242.52
0	40	12	100	194	0	0	0	7,445	1,677	9,122	46.9	19,449	5,112.77	1,275.18
0	345	26	672	1,280	0	0	0	59,029	15,649	74,678	48.1	155,338	8,494.90	1,826.32
87	1,482	124	2,683	4,918	0	0	0	273,258	110,371	383,629	47.9	801,271	9,759.70	2,113.71
58	1,781	104	3,559	6,443	340	16	356	352,337	95,562	447,899	45.4	985,525	15,233.17	2,748.79
39	521	7	782	1,599	18	0	18	77,419	19,392	96,810	39.4	245,844	9,678.12	1,912.96
0	74	5	141	280	0	0	0	18,151	4,534	22,685	48.2	47,057	6,557.61	2,233.60
33	335	10	501	1,116	0	1	1	52,548	14,024	66,572	55.0	121,128	6,697.69	1,191.89
85	835	79	1,692	3,117	53	0	53	177,492	42,412	219,904	52.0	423,000	7,749.37	1,342.03
6	34	8	61	169	0	0	0	7,946	1,894	9,840	46.7	21,084	9,583.85	307.96

MSAs

TABLE 8

U.S. CENSUS DIVISION 4, EAST NORTH CENTRAL

U.S. Community Hospitals
(Nonfederal, short-term general and other special hospitals)

2014 Utilization, Personnel and Finances

CLASSIFICATION	Hospitals	Beds	Admissions	Inpatient Days	Adjusted Inpatient Days	Average Daily Census	Adjusted Average Daily Census	Average Stay (days)	Surgical Operations	NEWBORNS Bassinets	NEWBORNS Births	OUTPATIENT VISITS Emergency	OUTPATIENT VISITS Total
UNITED STATES	4,926	786,874	33,066,720	180,456,434	365,636,679	494,388	1,002,304	5.5	26,401,528	55,824	3,735,593	136,327,473	693,106,685
Nonmetropolitan	1,855	116,785	3,238,473	21,307,388	64,127,906	58,370	175,723	6.6	3,512,461	9,506	383,166	21,639,508	119,516,577
Metropolitan	3,071	670,089	29,828,247	159,149,046	301,508,773	436,018	826,581	5.3	22,889,067	46,318	3,352,427	114,687,965	573,590,108
CENSUS DIVISION 4, EAST NORTH CENTRAL	769	119,389	5,171,957	26,063,576	58,744,206	71,398	161,096	5.0	4,498,851	9,465	521,134	22,166,060	142,707,732
Nonmetropolitan	270	16,698	561,567	2,953,958	10,836,544	8,090	29,694	5.3	678,856	1,661	61,453	3,932,160	25,939,528
Metropolitan	499	102,691	4,610,390	23,109,618	47,907,662	63,308	131,402	5.0	3,819,995	7,804	459,681	18,233,900	116,768,204
Illinois	189	31,573	1,380,085	6,841,826	14,833,503	18,739	40,644	5.0	1,097,104	2,582	147,464	5,273,213	33,433,722
Nonmetropolitan	59	3,408	107,592	533,486	1,909,122	1,458	5,232	5.0	129,217	267	9,843	687,351	5,199,179
Metropolitan	130	28,165	1,272,493	6,308,340	12,924,381	17,281	35,412	5.0	967,887	2,315	137,621	4,585,862	28,234,543
Bloomington, IL	3	377	16,030	63,803	134,674	175	369	4.0	11,830	52	2,430	63,686	490,756
Carbondale-Marion, IL	4	390	22,068	82,636	245,596	226	672	3.7	16,475	43	2,410	117,696	458,307
Champaign-Urbana, IL	4	609	30,899	159,516	382,264	437	1,047	5.2	23,166	47	3,574	109,741	1,179,338
Chicago-Naperville-Arlington Heights, IL	69	18,558	852,606	4,317,302	8,498,342	11,830	23,282	5.1	611,487	1,428	91,724	2,825,835	17,692,432
Danville, IL	2	130	6,495	23,395	59,572	64	164	3.6	3,951	26	586	39,853	212,899
Davenport-Moline-Rock Island, IA-IL	5	588	20,893	100,183	278,145	273	762	4.8	18,455	73	2,188	110,837	552,865
Decatur, IL	2	432	18,236	80,024	220,544	220	605	4.4	15,350	36	1,579	84,013	445,864
Elgin, IL	7	960	45,903	209,825	420,940	575	1,155	4.6	39,126	93	5,554	205,509	1,052,765
Kankakee, IL	2	468	15,438	73,423	193,590	201	530	4.8	16,397	35	1,423	72,083	580,685
Lake County-Kenosha County, IL-WI	5	892	46,431	193,017	409,150	529	1,121	4.2	40,176	116	6,325	194,108	789,816
Peoria, IL	7	1,264	54,534	290,996	565,472	797	1,549	5.3	57,010	79	5,252	180,873	1,802,583
Rockford, IL	4	841	40,529	195,692	364,716	536	1,000	4.8	32,599	80	4,499	167,497	959,008
Springfield, IL	3	934	42,901	226,309	413,753	620	1,133	5.3	33,159	54	3,472	120,563	708,105
St. Louis, MO-IL	13	1,722	59,530	292,219	737,623	798	2,023	4.9	48,706	153	6,605	293,568	1,309,120
Indiana	121	17,193	681,537	3,567,957	8,044,656	9,770	22,040	5.2	582,834	1,503	72,348	3,261,594	19,184,014
Nonmetropolitan	42	2,371	80,810	405,721	1,535,295	1,110	4,208	5.0	105,369	279	10,669	685,569	4,670,166
Metropolitan	79	14,822	600,727	3,162,236	6,509,361	8,660	17,832	5.3	477,465	1,224	61,679	2,576,025	14,513,848
Bloomington, IN	2	338	13,227	58,112	129,834	159	356	4.4	10,074	13	2,075	58,189	271,013
Cincinnati, OH-KY-IN	1	78	4,373	15,640	41,300	43	113	3.6	5,998	11	379	18,969	136,361
Columbus, IN	1	198	8,806	33,202	79,999	91	219	3.8	11,921	20	1,194	41,227	229,747
Elkhart-Goshen, IN	2	387	16,993	67,913	135,456	186	371	4.0	11,372	54	2,525	88,698	440,177
Evansville, IN-KY	6	1,174	47,453	254,962	495,883	699	1,358	5.4	38,560	62	4,614	171,911	987,882
Fort Wayne, IN	9	1,658	69,728	368,117	718,636	1,007	1,969	5.3	79,130	119	7,181	369,214	1,194,544
Gary, IN	11	2,572	103,400	583,898	1,116,444	1,599	3,058	5.6	61,134	208	5,994	437,886	2,000,990
Indianapolis-Carmel-Anderson, IN .	26	5,151	201,552	1,065,719	2,260,455	2,919	6,192	5.3	146,225	459	23,436	863,592	6,477,513
Kokomo, IN	3	330	10,580	47,401	135,602	130	371	4.5	11,281	36	1,234	52,250	314,276
Lafayette-West Lafayette, IN . . .	1	191	8,951	39,383	117,106	108	321	4.4	9,266	14	1,366	39,853	78,775
Louisville-Jefferson County, KY-IN	6	795	31,900	220,178	489,379	603	1,340	6.9	29,887	52	3,075	113,596	902,368
Michigan City-La Porte, IN	2	300	11,587	53,170	120,301	145	330	4.6	8,392	35	1,020	52,458	261,511
Muncie, IN	1	322	16,133	80,909	144,366	222	396	5.0	5,625	24	1,509	58,246	298,510
South Bend-Mishawaka, IN-MI . . .	3	771	33,747	172,126	278,899	471	764	5.1	22,552	59	3,629	104,325	350,865
Terre Haute, IN	5	557	22,297	101,506	245,701	278	674	4.6	26,048	58	2,448	105,611	569,296
Michigan	148	24,398	1,125,043	5,730,883	12,977,564	15,701	35,711	5.1	990,665	1,674	106,127	4,814,596	33,947,585
Nonmetropolitan	55	3,665	120,105	713,246	2,756,559	1,955	7,555	5.9	160,918	311	12,425	792,866	5,744,937
Metropolitan	93	20,733	1,004,938	5,017,637	10,221,005	13,746	28,156	5.0	829,747	1,363	93,702	4,021,730	28,202,648
Ann Arbor, MI	5	1,616	85,723	456,046	928,119	1,250	2,543	5.3	83,109	61	7,989	198,815	3,525,619
Battle Creek, MI	3	301	13,254	59,433	164,272	163	450	4.5	11,011	26	1,309	85,313	976,527
Bay City, MI	2	364	15,175	80,741	142,778	221	391	5.3	9,837	14	868	43,584	304,523
Detroit-Dearborn-Livonia, MI	20	4,890	245,580	1,252,797	2,500,952	3,433	6,853	5.1	175,468	303	21,288	1,040,426	6,357,570
Flint, MI	4	1,190	59,577	301,590	530,808	826	1,454	5.1	37,486	89	5,371	222,691	1,385,953
Grand Rapids-Wyoming, MI	13	2,261	102,441	525,361	1,121,887	1,439	3,073	5.1	100,751	206	13,644	527,415	4,141,586
Jackson, MI	2	346	17,837	85,511	203,454	235	558	4.8	9,708	11	1,684	82,383	487,047
Kalamazoo-Portage, MI	4	893	38,961	197,240	395,277	540	1,083	5.1	38,365	75	4,878	193,659	1,363,154
Lansing-East Lansing, MI	6	1,082	48,489	226,241	500,200	620	1,371	4.7	42,110	41	5,492	198,833	1,025,054
Midland, MI	1	265	12,225	49,428	96,036	135	263	4.0	7,710	23	464	62,093	295,605
Monroe, MI	1	179	9,061	35,321	86,896	97	238	3.9	6,580	13	786	45,070	165,947
Muskegon, MI	3	432	17,499	77,074	205,198	211	562	4.4	20,066	26	1,977	102,588	940,882
Niles-Benton Harbor, MI	2	288	16,248	71,578	147,403	196	404	4.4	7,837	35	435	84,511	416,624
Saginaw, MI	3	800	36,076	191,338	367,219	524	1,006	5.3	19,653	31	3,018	131,712	746,553
South Bend-Mishawaka, IN-MI . . .	1	25	518	1,605	14,894	4	41	3.1	637	0	0	10,526	90,771
Warren-Troy-Farmington Hills, MI .	23	5,801	286,274	1,406,333	2,815,612	3,852	7,866	4.9	259,419	409	24,499	992,111	5,979,233

TABLE 8

U.S. CENSUS DIVISION 4, EAST NORTH CENTRAL

U.S. Community Hospitals
(Nonfederal, short-term general and other special hospitals)

2014 Utilization, Personnel and Finances

FULL-TIME EQUIVALENT PERSONNEL					FULL-TIME EQUIV. TRAINEES			EXPENSES						
								LABOR				TOTAL		
Physicians and Dentists	Registered Nurses	Licensed Practical Nurses	Other Salaried Personnel	Total Personnel	Medical and Dental Residents	Other Trainees	Total Trainees	Payroll (in thousands)	Employee Benefits (in thousands)	Total (in thousands)	Percent of Total	Amount (in thousands)	Adjusted per Admission	Adjusted per Inpatient Day
122,747	1,398,346	73,044	2,510,354	4,754,880	109,309	8,533	117,842	$310,203,433	$82,949,525	$393,152,940	48.6	$808,869,209	$12,015.42	$2,212.22
15,090	147,461	20,793	334,968	602,081	1,731	269	2,000	33,192,643	8,842,572	42,035,205	51.3	81,981,991	8,301.59	1,278.41
107,657	1,250,885	52,251	2,175,386	4,152,799	107,578	8,264	115,842	277,010,790	74,106,953	351,117,735	48.3	726,887,218	12,653.89	2,410.83
23,851	232,656	9,043	438,016	805,062	21,552	1,838	23,390	51,583,426	13,507,116	65,090,546	48.0	135,485,952	11,637.94	2,306.37
3,178	27,105	2,973	64,705	112,118	180	106	286	6,612,895	1,905,141	8,518,041	52.1	16,364,961	8,304.76	1,510.16
20,673	205,551	6,070	373,311	692,944	21,372	1,732	23,104	44,970,531	11,601,975	56,572,505	47.5	119,120,991	12,317.10	2,486.47
6,092	58,989	1,748	108,248	201,710	5,658	423	6,081	12,942,310	3,458,555	16,400,874	46.7	35,123,919	11,643.14	2,367.88
595	5,350	679	12,594	22,225	32	2	34	1,224,232	378,132	1,602,367	52.6	3,039,015	8,051.35	1,591.84
5,497	53,639	1,069	95,654	179,485	5,626	421	6,047	11,718,078	3,080,423	14,798,507	46.1	32,084,903	12,156.83	2,482.51
102	589	16	1,041	2,007	18	0	18	116,782	31,938	148,719	44.7	332,884	9,850.08	2,471.77
6	915	46	1,532	2,819	19	0	19	153,406	49,955	203,362	38.7	525,905	8,734.80	2,141.34
19	1,505	57	2,042	4,249	24	0	24	228,529	60,414	288,943	38.8	744,181	10,647.28	1,946.77
4,344	36,275	599	63,348	120,935	4,969	381	5,350	8,399,501	2,192,157	10,591,662	47.1	22,510,362	13,283.19	2,648.79
4	207	18	422	756	0	0	0	42,765	9,709	52,473	42.0	124,893	7,536.41	2,096.51
52	936	22	1,698	3,037	0	0	0	143,986	34,814	178,800	41.6	429,957	7,533.59	1,545.80
57	457	58	1,748	2,626	13	0	13	149,858	31,987	181,846	46.1	394,467	7,622.85	1,788.61
5	1,928	14	3,292	5,928	0	0	0	320,069	84,876	404,945	40.4	1,003,475	10,371.51	2,383.89
59	745	29	1,533	2,592	18	0	18	140,647	30,771	171,418	45.8	373,913	9,241.78	1,931.47
54	1,828	11	3,211	5,814	0	0	0	380,835	86,501	467,336	44.4	1,052,808	10,743.16	2,573.16
410	2,493	41	4,873	8,802	279	3	282	565,043	139,588	704,632	47.2	1,493,575	13,955.77	2,641.29
274	1,676	18	3,076	5,811	4	21	25	357,177	108,420	465,598	46.8	995,547	12,782.26	2,729.65
5	1,810	62	3,363	6,136	282	5	287	326,682	103,607	430,289	41.3	1,042,686	13,114.56	2,520.07
106	2,275	78	4,475	7,973	0	11	11	392,798	115,685	508,484	48.0	1,060,251	6,810.10	1,437.39
2,103	29,682	1,587	59,363	105,990	1,116	283	1,399	6,442,082	1,645,653	8,087,734	44.9	18,019,558	11,342.27	2,239.94
589	4,050	604	10,346	17,684	3	56	59	1,031,953	279,824	1,311,779	51.1	2,565,253	8,100.51	1,670.85
1,514	25,632	983	49,017	88,306	1,113	227	1,340	5,410,128	1,365,829	6,775,955	43.8	15,454,306	12,149.32	2,374.17
9	630	32	1,209	2,148	0	0	0	134,321	32,807	167,129	46.1	362,346	12,264.22	2,790.84
0	128	15	397	630	0	0	0	31,785	10,831	42,616	57.2	74,531	6,454.01	1,804.62
0	303	33	931	1,481	0	0	0	68,361	22,616	90,977	41.1	221,158	10,423.14	2,764.51
70	930	21	1,428	2,817	9	1	10	152,651	42,077	194,728	44.1	441,866	12,989.94	3,262.06
166	2,028	48	3,507	6,795	22	81	103	370,027	102,020	472,047	43.2	1,091,776	11,387.38	2,201.68
30	2,788	109	4,156	7,902	40	2	42	430,049	115,526	545,575	40.8	1,337,447	10,144.85	1,861.09
173	3,682	135	6,212	11,565	113	9	122	760,149	195,418	955,567	46.2	2,070,057	10,468.37	1,854.15
536	10,040	357	21,273	36,804	768	114	882	2,370,563	571,723	2,942,284	43.0	6,835,521	15,106.96	3,023.96
10	460	19	1,133	1,827	0	5	5	86,763	22,009	108,773	46.1	236,195	7,580.55	1,741.82
161	427	36	821	1,690	0	9	9	144,892	33,106	177,998	52.6	338,577	12,720.81	2,891.20
98	907	75	2,508	4,112	0	0	0	227,850	54,773	282,623	51.1	552,695	7,555.95	1,129.38
68	477	18	1,139	1,983	5	0	5	125,140	33,358	158,498	47.5	333,543	12,826.09	2,772.57
113	589	12	1,081	2,043	65	2	67	96,207	27,130	123,338	41.3	298,670	10,375.51	2,068.84
17	1,241	16	1,886	3,624	70	4	74	220,351	61,380	281,731	39.9	705,529	12,705.36	2,529.69
63	1,002	57	1,336	2,885	21	0	21	191,019	41,053	232,071	41.9	554,396	9,806.94	2,256.39
5,019	50,934	1,624	93,423	173,935	6,513	216	6,729	10,942,506	2,562,714	13,505,215	48.7	27,710,262	11,118.60	2,135.24
722	5,375	640	13,938	23,703	46	14	60	1,385,759	377,900	1,763,657	50.7	3,475,280	8,185.95	1,260.73
4,297	45,559	984	79,485	150,232	6,467	202	6,669	9,556,747	2,184,814	11,741,558	48.4	24,234,983	11,720.73	2,371.10
177	6,310	119	11,135	19,765	1,498	0	1,498	1,290,800	373,639	1,664,439	49.5	3,364,126	18,846.43	3,624.67
58	825	33	1,656	2,961	2	1	3	148,123	26,020	174,143	52.2	333,325	8,749.39	2,029.11
50	483	33	1,114	1,885	15	0	15	126,442	27,076	153,518	55.1	278,412	9,928.74	1,949.96
1,321	11,106	141	17,221	35,064	2,435	67	2,502	2,428,880	482,473	2,911,351	48.6	5,992,702	12,197.97	2,396.17
87	2,506	46	3,726	7,213	333	19	352	528,603	131,151	659,755	55.3	1,192,317	11,291.63	2,246.23
339	4,596	235	9,074	16,414	156	54	210	941,369	263,001	1,204,371	41.4	2,906,225	13,375.85	2,590.48
84	547	40	2,385	3,457	0	0	0	216,939	49,032	265,972	55.0	483,981	10,596.20	2,378.82
296	2,032	24	3,893	7,197	0	12	12	462,846	90,023	552,869	53.3	1,036,983	12,737.78	2,623.43
241	2,175	17	4,155	7,564	259	0	259	537,126	126,183	663,309	55.0	1,206,062	10,498.08	2,411.16
41	526	22	946	1,781	20	2	22	128,433	34,727	163,161	49.2	331,841	13,971.08	3,455.38
17	339	6	761	1,197	18	0	18	67,562	15,601	83,163	53.0	157,006	7,043.16	1,806.83
119	711	12	2,118	3,217	30	3	33	199,304	44,352	243,656	51.2	475,987	9,949.99	2,319.65
65	816	40	1,522	2,824	30	1	31	136,863	35,922	172,785	49.6	348,577	10,444.57	2,364.79
181	1,474	47	3,004	5,381	169	12	181	319,022	79,701	398,722	52.6	758,197	10,801.30	2,064.70
16	30	0	95	170	0	0	0	13,433	2,952	16,385	64.3	25,496	5,303.93	1,711.83
1,205	11,083	169	16,680	34,142	1,502	31	1,533	2,011,001	402,960	2,413,959	45.2	5,343,745	9,463.30	1,897.90

Table continues

MSAs

TABLE 8

U.S. CENSUS DIVISION 4, EAST NORTH CENTRAL CONTINUED

U.S. Community Hospitals
(Nonfederal, short-term general and other special hospitals)

2014 Utilization, Personnel and Finances

MSAs

CLASSIFICATION	Hospitals	Beds	Admissions	Inpatient Days	Adjusted Inpatient Days	Average Daily Census	Adjusted Average Daily Census	Average Stay (days)	Surgical Operations	NEWBORNS		OUTPATIENT VISITS	
										Bassinets	Births	Emergency	Total
Ohio	182	33,566	1,433,894	7,168,533	15,277,668	19,641	41,845	5.0	1,200,840	2,574	130,762	6,616,818	38,861,097
Nonmetropolitan	57	4,505	166,087	707,560	2,100,943	1,939	5,754	4.3	181,978	546	17,624	1,228,991	6,504,740
Metropolitan	125	29,061	1,267,807	6,460,973	13,176,725	17,702	36,091	5.1	1,018,862	2,028	113,138	5,387,827	32,356,357
Akron, OH	8	1,753	83,904	406,446	905,903	1,114	2,482	4.8	60,317	104	7,160	426,170	2,243,016
Canton-Massillon, OH	5	1,208	47,280	271,446	583,358	744	1,597	5.7	39,288	111	4,731	222,765	1,366,640
Cincinnati, OH-KY-IN.	19	4,581	201,440	1,039,966	1,916,405	2,852	5,248	5.2	159,079	320	19,172	732,550	3,966,250
Cleveland-Elyria, OH	28	7,701	329,030	1,787,666	3,860,101	4,897	10,573	5.4	320,441	387	24,777	1,162,416	11,147,341
Columbus, OH.	21	5,413	248,217	1,192,890	2,358,686	3,269	6,461	4.8	196,147	429	28,626	1,054,724	6,117,774
Dayton, OH	11	2,617	111,988	517,018	1,034,070	1,415	2,833	4.6	84,117	218	10,939	548,558	2,059,466
Lima, OH	5	686	25,252	118,041	246,254	324	674	4.7	20,740	63	2,434	109,938	781,510
Mansfield, OH	2	265	10,973	50,078	94,615	137	259	4.6	5,017	24	935	51,896	259,778
Springfield, OH	1	259	14,203	61,112	114,913	167	315	4.3	4,136	25	1,226	78,948	297,717
Toledo, OH.	12	2,485	105,021	533,380	1,123,288	1,462	3,076	5.1	84,413	164	8,491	415,356	2,345,551
Weirton-Steubenville, WV-OH . . .	2	373	11,626	83,702	186,275	230	510	7.2	5,176	18	593	48,452	272,654
Wheeling, WV-OH	3	230	5,610	38,609	107,962	105	296	6.9	8,205	19	287	40,389	235,431
Youngstown-Warren-Boardman, OH-PA	8	1,490	73,263	360,619	644,895	986	1,767	4.9	31,786	146	3,767	495,665	1,263,229
Wisconsin	129	12,659	551,398	2,754,377	7,610,815	7,547	20,856	5.0	627,408	1,132	64,433	2,199,839	17,281,314
Nonmetropolitan	57	2,749	86,973	593,945	2,534,625	1,628	6,945	6.8	101,374	258	10,892	537,383	3,820,506
Metropolitan	72	9,910	464,425	2,160,432	5,076,190	5,919	13,911	4.7	526,034	874	53,541	1,662,456	13,460,808
Appleton, WI	3	375	16,902	69,236	170,730	190	468	4.1	34,282	41	2,278	63,828	307,891
Duluth, MN-WI.	1	25	487	3,101	45,996	8	126	6.4	2,536	0	0	13,015	50,951
Eau Claire, WI.	5	562	22,799	116,996	270,783	321	743	5.1	12,953	34	2,332	59,202	433,670
Fond du Lac, WI	2	185	7,217	28,854	109,918	79	301	4.0	13,586	23	845	34,170	725,237
Green Bay, WI	5	681	31,761	129,503	348,990	355	957	4.1	43,903	95	4,201	123,586	1,378,332
Janesville-Beloit, WI	4	303	13,933	63,913	194,611	175	533	4.6	15,133	18	1,810	85,031	1,416,539
La Crosse-Onalaska, WI-MN	2	420	21,717	91,968	304,717	252	834	4.2	25,179	19	2,461	68,069	1,065,889
Lake County-Kenosha County, IL-WI.	3	523	22,942	92,607	203,856	253	558	4.0	21,731	56	2,936	189,379	980,201
Madison, WI	9	1,599	72,431	397,364	990,273	1,089	2,715	5.5	151,683	104	8,367	186,798	1,782,955
Milwaukee-Waukesha-West Allis, WI.	24	3,826	190,703	899,795	1,788,234	2,464	4,898	4.7	136,966	321	20,245	620,962	4,044,307
Minneapolis-St. Paul-Bloomington, MN-WI.	4	69	3,785	11,174	55,407	31	152	3.0	6,027	21	1,042	26,663	175,026
Oshkosh-Neenah, WI	4	374	17,300	65,508	155,712	180	427	3.8	26,745	60	2,431	52,459	301,734
Racine, WI.	2	460	17,293	96,263	232,347	264	637	5.6	11,809	31	1,596	68,709	511,304
Sheboygan, WI	2	189	8,148	28,899	81,866	79	225	3.5	10,256	25	1,065	28,364	163,962
Wausau, WI	2	319	17,007	65,251	122,750	179	337	3.8	13,245	26	1,932	42,221	122,810

TABLE 8

U.S. CENSUS DIVISION 4, EAST NORTH CENTRAL CONTINUED

U.S. Community Hospitals
(Nonfederal, short-term general and other special hospitals)

2014 Utilization, Personnel and Finances

FULL-TIME EQUIVALENT PERSONNEL					FULL-TIME EQUIV. TRAINEES			EXPENSES						
								LABOR				TOTAL		
Physicians and Dentists	Registered Nurses	Licensed Practical Nurses	Other Salaried Personnel	Total Personnel	Medical and Dental Residents	Other Trainees	Total Trainees	Payroll (in thousands)	Employee Benefits (in thousands)	Total (in thousands)	Percent of Total	Amount (in thousands)	Adjusted per Admission	Adjusted per Inpatient Day
9,306	69,164	3,249	125,298	237,241	7,420	471	7,891	15,289,241	4,077,303	19,366,545	50.5	38,332,808	12,206.52	2,509.07
820	8,424	798	16,775	31,127	97	12	109	1,712,441	504,524	2,216,968	50.9	4,356,602	8,363.49	2,073.64
8,486	60,740	2,451	108,523	206,114	7,323	459	7,782	13,576,800	3,572,778	17,149,577	50.5	33,976,206	12,970.76	2,578.50
662	3,985	287	7,427	13,591	538	55	593	872,872	218,285	1,091,155	48.2	2,264,341	11,946.51	2,499.54
161	1,725	178	4,397	7,051	78	5	83	375,087	99,764	474,851	51.4	923,542	9,307.27	1,583.15
1,834	9,493	249	22,280	37,706	1,299	145	1,444	2,426,008	626,570	3,052,579	51.5	5,927,553	15,377.51	3,093.06
3,080	17,265	870	31,695	60,933	2,931	227	3,158	4,515,705	1,155,333	5,671,038	56.5	10,033,607	14,038.12	2,599.31
2,325	12,342	196	19,161	39,482	1,387	12	1,399	2,409,172	633,346	3,042,518	46.5	6,548,551	12,780.08	2,776.36
62	5,240	99	7,864	15,861	407	8	415	1,074,713	328,100	1,402,814	49.8	2,819,432	12,389.41	2,726.54
37	1,111	76	1,746	3,280	3	3	6	164,089	50,774	214,864	41.8	513,494	9,300.07	2,085.22
2	501	55	1,160	1,869	0	0	0	129,026	34,178	163,204	49.2	331,894	16,060.66	3,507.83
0	495	21	753	1,382	0	0	0	63,897	14,125	78,022	37.3	209,377	7,839.77	1,822.05
181	5,036	177	6,940	14,383	535	1	536	948,439	257,301	1,205,740	44.8	2,688,869	12,820.99	2,393.75
42	511	42	883	1,789	0	0	0	89,421	27,101	116,522	48.2	241,787	8,461.49	1,298.01
25	268	39	498	973	1	0	1	43,133	11,358	54,491	46.3	117,714	7,333.32	1,090.33
75	2,768	162	3,719	7,814	144	3	147	465,237	116,543	581,779	42.9	1,356,044	10,152.92	2,102.74
1,331	23,887	835	51,684	86,186	845	445	1,290	5,967,287	1,762,891	7,730,178	47.4	16,299,405	11,611.48	2,141.61
452	3,906	252	11,052	17,379	2	22	24	1,258,510	364,761	1,623,270	55.4	2,928,811	8,849.15	1,155.52
879	19,981	583	40,632	68,807	843	423	1,266	4,708,777	1,398,131	6,106,908	45.7	13,370,594	12,463.72	2,633.98
23	600	57	1,265	2,172	0	3	3	161,629	44,466	206,096	53.7	383,762	9,178.72	2,247.77
7	35	8	124	191	0	0	0	16,426	4,248	20,674	68.8	30,047	4,159.30	653.25
29	1,092	17	2,171	3,638	0	10	10	210,840	65,948	276,788	55.0	502,952	10,699.51	1,857.40
37	367	39	907	1,436	0	0	0	121,123	31,156	152,280	46.8	325,271	11,834.48	2,959.21
147	1,348	103	3,348	5,294	0	19	19	375,782	95,546	471,328	47.3	996,461	11,480.10	2,855.27
320	755	36	1,855	3,174	0	0	0	236,415	72,955	309,370	48.0	644,598	15,546.72	3,312.24
20	1,078	59	2,608	4,021	0	0	0	363,378	123,306	486,684	52.2	931,517	13,135.13	3,056.99
71	1,114	43	2,019	3,693	32	15	47	226,698	62,511	289,210	47.4	610,302	11,801.25	2,993.79
201	3,464	57	8,194	13,174	609	116	725	947,678	322,695	1,270,370	52.9	2,402,433	15,579.38	2,426.03
8	7,730	69	12,796	23,255	186	233	419	1,509,203	418,577	1,927,779	38.3	5,037,029	13,030.39	2,816.76
9	208	14	633	955	0	0	0	64,268	15,848	80,116	49.7	161,340	8,809.67	2,911.91
7	568	18	1,096	1,899	0	0	0	139,299	42,303	181,602	49.1	369,681	8,786.45	2,374.13
0	696	42	1,639	2,749	0	17	17	134,014	40,412	174,426	46.9	372,172	8,750.40	1,601.79
0	276	7	483	851	0	10	10	54,335	17,162	71,497	39.0	183,142	7,935.09	2,237.09
0	650	14	1,494	2,305	16	0	16	147,690	40,998	188,688	44.9	419,888	13,298.10	3,420.67

MSAs

TABLE 8

U.S. CENSUS DIVISION 5, EAST SOUTH CENTRAL

U.S. Community Hospitals
(Nonfederal, short-term general and other special hospitals)

2014 Utilization, Personnel and Finances

CLASSIFICATION	Hospitals	Beds	Admissions	Inpatient Days	Adjusted Inpatient Days	Average Daily Census	Adjusted Average Daily Census	Average Stay (days)	Surgical Operations	NEWBORNS		OUTPATIENT VISITS	
										Bassinets	Births	Emergency	Total
UNITED STATES	4,926	786,874	33,066,720	180,456,434	365,636,679	494,388	1,002,304	5.5	26,401,528	55,824	3,735,593	136,327,473	693,106,685
Nonmetropolitan	1,855	116,785	3,238,473	21,307,388	64,127,906	58,370	175,723	6.6	3,512,461	9,506	383,166	21,639,508	119,516,577
Metropolitan	3,071	670,089	29,828,247	159,149,046	301,508,773	436,018	826,581	5.3	22,889,067	46,318	3,352,427	114,687,965	573,590,108
CENSUS DIVISION 5, EAST SOUTH CENTRAL	422	61,455	2,382,356	13,251,868	27,560,016	36,292	75,505	5.6	2,001,790	4,165	215,205	9,880,646	36,207,307
Nonmetropolitan	220	19,189	541,329	3,431,576	8,649,467	9,398	23,692	6.3	514,289	1,330	50,549	3,226,576	10,807,204
Metropolitan	202	42,266	1,841,027	9,820,292	18,910,549	26,894	51,813	5.3	1,487,501	2,835	164,656	6,654,070	25,400,103
Alabama	96	14,959	632,358	3,335,338	6,659,504	9,134	18,248	5.3	538,413	1,299	57,863	2,347,239	8,516,439
Nonmetropolitan	40	2,602	76,460	375,103	1,006,966	1,027	2,760	4.9	73,149	189	6,525	560,387	1,599,918
Metropolitan	56	12,357	555,898	2,960,235	5,652,538	8,107	15,488	5.3	465,264	1,110	51,338	1,786,852	6,916,521
Anniston-Oxford-Jacksonville, AL .	3	416	16,851	77,855	178,469	213	489	4.6	12,453	33	1,701	80,488	193,267
Auburn-Opelika, AL	1	379	13,568	97,547	184,418	267	505	7.2	19,773	38	1,652	37,913	125,799
Birmingham-Hoover, AL	15	4,672	205,816	1,113,975	2,015,744	3,052	5,522	5.4	171,437	387	16,576	516,286	2,646,154
Columbus, GA-AL	1	48	1,198	16,236	16,696	44	46	13.6	0	0	0	0	3,546
Daphne-Fairhope-Foley, AL.	3	298	16,442	69,449	155,743	191	427	4.2	21,320	37	2,044	78,167	278,065
Decatur, AL	2	190	8,563	37,652	95,990	103	263	4.4	8,142	23	729	41,333	178,472
Dothan, AL	4	775	32,240	192,660	399,225	527	1,094	6.0	30,380	57	2,769	99,361	288,480
Florence-Muscle Shoals, AL	3	560	25,286	106,852	245,823	292	674	4.2	18,478	45	2,055	96,617	237,270
Gadsden, AL.	3	487	20,999	123,508	208,254	338	571	5.9	24,598	32	1,041	52,125	140,974
Huntsville, AL	4	1,195	58,329	283,378	599,900	776	1,643	4.9	56,676	93	6,297	219,167	1,013,227
Mobile, AL	5	1,338	69,179	384,608	668,872	1,052	1,833	5.6	51,035	187	6,314	183,755	637,763
Montgomery, AL	8	1,047	46,230	243,942	461,979	670	1,266	5.3	26,790	111	5,456	199,750	589,290
Tuscaloosa, AL	4	952	41,197	212,573	421,425	582	1,155	5.2	24,182	67	4,704	181,890	584,214
Kentucky	104	13,994	558,430	2,975,806	6,616,436	8,148	18,125	5.3	520,569	904	52,786	2,332,013	10,775,865
Nonmetropolitan	63	5,733	193,873	980,788	2,620,740	2,684	7,176	5.1	197,190	451	17,836	1,044,166	4,328,541
Metropolitan	41	8,261	364,557	1,995,018	3,995,696	5,464	10,949	5.5	323,379	453	34,950	1,287,847	6,447,324
Bowling Green, KY	3	564	22,965	117,204	228,020	321	625	5.1	19,305	19	2,370	83,465	186,112
Cincinnati, OH-KY-IN	5	895	45,291	210,045	409,716	576	1,122	4.6	28,985	38	4,481	202,648	1,279,005
Clarksville, TN-KY	2	164	6,513	32,178	78,297	88	214	4.9	3,885	18	631	31,897	150,300
Elizabethtown-Fort Knox, KY	2	308	13,643	65,040	135,076	178	370	4.8	12,943	26	1,578	58,833	353,876
Evansville, IN-KY	1	152	4,407	20,036	63,090	55	173	4.5	3,284	12	691	28,225	285,414
Huntington-Ashland, WV-KY-OH. .	2	616	28,341	162,318	339,559	444	930	5.7	48,216	25	2,111	84,846	582,550
Lexington-Fayette, KY	12	2,126	87,705	536,372	945,968	1,469	2,594	6.1	67,508	123	7,866	273,558	1,503,166
Louisville-Jefferson County, KY-IN	13	3,080	139,519	775,561	1,632,752	2,124	4,474	5.6	122,531	162	13,317	460,294	1,513,879
Owensboro, KY	1	356	16,173	76,264	163,218	209	447	4.7	16,722	30	1,905	64,081	593,022
Mississippi	97	12,471	373,189	2,511,963	5,318,981	6,882	14,575	6.7	277,999	727	37,543	1,796,073	5,001,500
Nonmetropolitan	70	7,293	170,139	1,436,520	3,309,437	3,935	9,069	8.4	140,077	433	17,767	949,211	2,647,124
Metropolitan	27	5,178	203,050	1,075,443	2,009,544	2,947	5,506	5.3	137,922	294	19,776	846,862	2,354,376
Gulfport-Biloxi-Pascagoula, MS . .	6	1,312	45,594	229,634	453,254	630	1,241	5.0	38,755	91	4,675	279,445	1,051,116
Hattiesburg, MS	3	756	33,350	166,209	265,439	456	728	5.0	18,090	24	3,658	116,334	222,666
Jackson, MS	15	2,775	107,457	597,261	1,128,446	1,635	3,092	5.6	75,791	155	9,700	379,949	963,506
Memphis, TN-MS-AR.	3	335	16,649	82,339	162,335	226	445	4.9	5,286	24	1,743	71,134	117,088
Tennessee	125	20,031	818,379	4,428,761	8,965,095	12,128	24,557	5.4	664,809	1,235	67,013	3,405,321	11,913,503
Nonmetropolitan	47	3,561	100,857	639,165	1,712,324	1,752	4,687	6.3	103,873	257	8,421	672,812	2,231,621
Metropolitan	78	16,470	717,522	3,789,596	7,252,771	10,376	19,870	5.3	560,936	978	58,592	2,732,509	9,681,882
Chattanooga, TN-GA	5	1,567	71,484	388,328	689,338	1,064	1,888	5.4	60,652	90	7,478	303,614	1,032,877
Clarksville, TN-KY	1	247	12,545	50,066	79,718	137	218	4.0	8,106	30	314	71,795	166,404
Cleveland, TN	2	211	8,748	39,080	95,128	107	261	4.5	7,828	19	1,072	53,143	115,292
Jackson, TN	2	769	32,300	176,279	357,575	483	980	5.5	28,920	46	3,485	97,581	223,180
Johnson City, TN	4	953	36,908	202,601	365,473	554	1,001	5.5	23,586	40	2,503	102,105	383,143
Kingsport-Bristol-Bristol, TN-VA . .	6	999	40,936	194,056	427,825	532	1,172	4.7	27,755	73	2,738	165,547	334,006
Knoxville, TN.	13	2,480	110,191	622,096	1,192,880	1,703	3,268	5.6	93,396	133	9,938	483,789	1,679,190
Memphis, TN-MS-AR.	14	3,553	138,415	797,156	1,483,736	2,182	4,066	5.8	82,416	215	15,490	563,960	1,263,577
Morristown, TN	3	320	12,264	50,916	106,386	139	291	4.2	14,405	25	1,148	72,753	185,531
Nashville-Davidson-Murfreesboro-Franklin, TN	28	5,371	253,731	1,269,018	2,454,712	3,475	6,725	5.0	213,872	307	14,426	818,222	4,298,682

TABLE 8

U.S. CENSUS DIVISION 5, EAST SOUTH CENTRAL

U.S. Community Hospitals
(Nonfederal, short-term general and other special hospitals)

2014 Utilization, Personnel and Finances

	FULL-TIME EQUIVALENT PERSONNEL				FULL-TIME EQUIV. TRAINEES			EXPENSES						
								LABOR				TOTAL		
Physicians and Dentists	Registered Nurses	Licensed Practical Nurses	Other Salaried Personnel	Total Personnel	Medical and Dental Residents	Other Trainees	Total Trainees	Payroll (in thousands)	Employee Benefits (in thousands)	Total (in thousands)	Percent of Total	Amount (in thousands)	Adjusted per Admission	Adjusted per Inpatient Day
122,747	1,398,346	73,044	2,510,354	4,754,880	109,309	8,533	117,842	$310,203,433	$82,949,525	$393,152,940	48.6	$808,869,209	$12,015.42	$2,212.22
15,090	147,461	20,793	334,968	602,081	1,731	269	2,000	33,192,643	8,842,572	42,035,205	51.3	81,981,991	8,301.59	1,278.41
107,657	1,250,885	52,251	2,175,386	4,152,799	107,578	8,264	115,842	277,010,790	74,106,953	351,117,735	48.3	726,887,218	12,653.89	2,410.83
6,193	91,010	6,107	148,545	297,054	5,112	375	5,487	16,108,838	4,114,718	20,223,550	45.6	44,391,935	8,846.59	1,610.74
1,508	20,572	2,568	41,579	78,063	228	30	258	3,699,704	979,288	4,678,988	48.2	9,708,156	6,939.68	1,122.40
4,685	70,438	3,539	106,966	218,991	4,884	345	5,229	12,409,134	3,135,430	15,544,562	44.8	34,683,779	9,583.71	1,834.10
1,205	24,258	1,254	37,258	74,990	1,586	38	1,624	3,726,560	927,245	4,653,803	47.0	9,892,819	7,678.55	1,485.52
193	2,925	323	5,754	10,824	36	4	40	436,602	115,797	552,398	49.0	1,127,874	5,358.07	1,120.07
1,012	21,333	931	31,504	64,166	1,550	34	1,584	3,289,958	811,448	4,101,405	46.8	8,764,945	8,131.72	1,550.62
40	489	41	961	1,789	14	0	14	85,528	22,496	108,024	49.4	218,704	5,697.93	1,225.44
63	897	61	1,627	3,130	170	0	170	93,180	37,757	130,936	55.2	237,253	9,249.28	1,286.50
244	8,090	203	10,430	22,479	899	1	900	1,326,488	312,821	1,639,311	44.1	3,717,601	9,996.48	1,844.28
0	47	1	85	156	0	0	0	7,881	1,594	9,475	51.4	18,450	14,975.28	1,105.03
35	543	38	948	1,847	16	0	16	82,269	20,528	102,797	47.2	217,666	5,918.86	1,397.60
32	280	35	660	1,180	9	1	10	51,175	16,052	67,227	54.3	123,899	5,695.19	1,290.75
71	1,138	136	2,193	4,019	3	0	3	201,779	39,522	241,302	47.6	506,531	7,507.39	1,268.79
62	592	40	1,167	2,177	17	1	18	90,750	25,144	115,894	47.8	242,265	4,168.21	985.53
47	696	32	765	1,939	0	0	0	87,957	16,948	104,905	43.7	239,842	6,609.94	1,151.68
179	2,887	143	4,190	8,271	22	2	24	381,838	111,134	492,971	51.4	959,342	7,699.93	1,599.17
148	2,353	38	3,900	7,394	377	7	384	411,912	103,769	515,681	50.8	1,014,348	8,346.90	1,516.51
42	1,772	67	2,254	4,944	17	2	19	237,747	49,684	287,431	38.9	738,274	8,017.83	1,598.07
49	1,549	96	2,324	4,841	6	20	26	231,453	53,999	285,451	53.8	530,771	6,463.99	1,259.47
974	21,921	1,243	35,779	70,296	885	38	923	4,033,894	1,120,488	5,154,380	43.7	11,788,395	9,152.79	1,781.68
627	7,101	724	13,888	26,218	105	12	117	1,324,977	374,320	1,699,293	46.6	3,647,872	6,960.02	1,391.92
347	14,820	519	21,891	44,078	780	26	806	2,708,917	746,168	3,455,087	42.4	8,140,523	10,657.46	2,037.32
2	793	15	1,147	2,335	0	0	0	136,268	34,582	170,850	46.4	368,024	8,215.01	1,614.00
7	1,354	35	2,740	4,405	24	0	24	321,007	101,733	422,741	50.4	838,759	9,140.60	2,047.17
20	251	22	541	983	7	0	7	50,755	13,169	63,925	49.3	129,787	8,277.73	1,657.62
53	485	38	974	1,803	20	0	20	99,464	28,322	127,785	49.4	258,512	9,213.49	1,913.83
30	316	29	622	1,106	8	3	11	38,636	14,511	53,147	51.3	103,543	7,461.52	1,641.20
130	1,168	79	2,253	4,200	85	4	89	259,966	71,669	331,636	46.7	710,117	11,470.33	2,091.29
27	3,999	102	5,134	11,387	626	9	635	676,227	179,668	855,895	39.4	2,170,953	12,878.80	2,294.95
77	5,729	147	6,659	14,916	10	10	20	998,230	263,429	1,261,660	40.1	3,150,075	10,342.59	1,929.30
1	725	52	1,821	2,943	0	0	0	128,364	39,085	167,448	40.8	410,753	11,867.01	2,516.59
826	14,362	1,418	26,293	51,734	622	9	631	2,789,354	699,482	3,488,837	48.5	7,188,317	9,174.97	1,351.45
497	6,779	1,000	14,367	26,669	52	9	61	1,295,391	333,292	1,628,684	49.0	3,324,856	8,412.74	1,004.66
329	7,583	418	11,926	25,065	570	0	570	1,493,963	366,191	1,860,153	48.1	3,863,460	9,950.88	1,922.56
219	2,046	103	2,676	6,410	0	0	0	418,535	95,255	513,790	50.4	1,018,660	10,944.39	2,247.09
39	1,040	87	1,959	3,880	6	0	6	194,765	50,439	245,204	46.1	532,365	9,786.49	2,005.60
71	4,003	200	6,533	13,288	564	0	564	775,562	192,549	968,111	47.5	2,038,738	9,799.41	1,806.68
0	494	28	758	1,487	0	0	0	105,102	27,947	133,048	48.6	273,697	8,361.76	1,686.00
3,188	30,469	2,192	49,215	100,034	2,019	290	2,309	5,559,031	1,367,503	6,926,530	44.6	15,522,404	9,361.15	1,731.43
191	3,767	521	7,570	14,352	35	5	40	642,735	155,879	798,613	49.7	1,607,553	5,973.84	938.81
2,997	26,702	1,671	41,645	85,682	1,984	285	2,269	4,916,296	1,211,623	6,127,917	44.0	13,914,851	10,017.36	1,918.56
200	2,547	110	3,659	7,628	212	39	251	522,055	127,530	649,585	49.6	1,309,596	10,326.25	1,899.79
7	409	17	468	1,076	16	0	16	55,472	12,818	68,291	44.6	152,990	7,659.07	1,919.14
4	384	25	403	1,048	0	1	1	47,293	9,808	57,101	40.9	139,459	6,521.35	1,466.01
9	1,199	179	2,584	4,483	5	0	5	223,927	61,831	285,757	47.6	599,711	9,183.79	1,677.16
0	1,320	73	1,410	3,279	0	96	96	174,476	38,406	212,881	41.3	515,803	7,779.37	1,411.33
3	1,490	59	2,138	4,347	0	8	8	186,254	57,223	243,477	35.0	696,299	7,202.70	1,627.53
209	4,300	308	6,014	13,111	31	16	47	761,774	174,692	936,466	44.2	2,118,417	9,938.43	1,775.88
126	5,590	182	9,481	17,938	512	21	533	954,067	249,383	1,203,450	40.8	2,952,662	10,987.30	1,990.02
6	381	23	495	1,088	3	0	3	58,327	11,896	70,222	44.9	156,424	6,079.42	1,470.34
2,433	9,082	695	14,993	31,684	1,205	104	1,309	1,932,652	468,037	2,400,687	45.5	5,273,490	10,873.27	2,148.31

MSAs

TABLE 8

U.S. CENSUS DIVISION 6, WEST NORTH CENTRAL

U.S. Community Hospitals
(Nonfederal, short-term general and other special hospitals)

2014 Utilization, Personnel and Finances

CLASSIFICATION	Hospitals	Beds	Admissions	Inpatient Days	Adjusted Inpatient Days	Average Daily Census	Adjusted Average Daily Census	Average Stay (days)	Surgical Operations	NEWBORNS Bassinets	Births	OUTPATIENT VISITS Emergency	Total
UNITED STATES	4,926	786,874	33,066,720	180,456,434	365,636,679	494,388	1,002,304	5.5	26,401,528	55,824	3,735,593	136,327,473	693,106,685
Nonmetropolitan	1,855	116,785	3,238,473	21,307,388	64,127,906	58,370	175,723	6.6	3,512,461	9,506	383,166	21,639,508	119,516,577
Metropolitan	3,071	670,089	29,828,247	159,149,046	301,508,773	436,018	826,581	5.3	22,889,067	46,318	3,352,427	114,687,965	573,590,108
CENSUS DIVISION 6, WEST NORTH CENTRAL	686	66,847	2,331,707	14,150,091	34,197,336	38,758	93,778	6.1	2,006,252	4,798	270,276	8,750,133	62,361,321
Nonmetropolitan	445	22,892	462,527	4,252,114	13,705,241	11,644	37,569	9.2	531,201	1,722	61,446	2,654,776	22,212,684
Metropolitan	241	43,955	1,869,180	9,897,977	20,492,095	27,114	56,209	5.3	1,475,051	3,076	208,830	6,095,357	40,148,637
Iowa	118	9,740	318,999	1,958,693	5,625,692	5,362	15,415	6.1	329,367	718	39,101	1,290,755	10,792,609
Nonmetropolitan	83	4,093	85,161	735,078	2,809,672	2,009	7,702	8.6	125,189	317	10,466	508,641	5,068,710
Metropolitan	35	5,647	233,838	1,223,615	2,816,020	3,353	7,713	5.2	204,178	401	28,635	782,114	5,723,899
Ames, IA	2	260	8,707	61,697	156,971	169	430	7.1	9,966	17	1,143	29,316	190,660
Cedar Rapids, IA	4	751	27,945	163,076	492,560	448	1,350	5.8	25,267	54	3,285	112,192	1,054,498
Davenport-Moline-Rock Island, IA-IL	3	482	22,325	88,746	174,892	243	479	4.0	12,235	33	2,784	97,895	228,772
Des Moines-West Des Moines, IA	8	1,526	67,643	354,442	699,496	971	1,916	5.2	46,894	113	10,050	203,695	941,781
Dubuque, IA	3	364	13,510	73,047	147,717	200	405	5.4	13,818	34	1,651	48,317	137,236
Iowa City, IA	3	1,007	39,525	242,248	508,057	663	1,392	6.1	34,652	53	3,456	84,999	1,531,223
Omaha-Council Bluffs, NE-IA. . . .	3	293	13,422	49,036	113,359	135	310	3.7	12,345	22	1,029	55,873	183,216
Sioux City, IA-NE-SD	3	363	19,022	83,821	158,533	229	434	4.4	10,875	36	2,471	64,739	370,430
Waterloo-Cedar Falls, IA	6	601	21,739	107,502	364,435	295	997	4.9	38,126	39	2,766	85,088	1,086,083
Kansas.	133	10,028	296,085	1,891,620	4,597,617	5,183	12,612	6.4	229,588	694	38,189	1,174,104	7,156,440
Nonmetropolitan	96	4,521	81,290	780,831	2,448,550	2,139	6,710	9.6	85,675	314	10,124	377,847	3,273,264
Metropolitan	37	5,507	214,795	1,110,789	2,149,067	3,044	5,902	5.2	143,913	380	28,065	796,257	3,883,176
Kansas City, MO-KS.	14	2,430	101,500	520,283	1,010,474	1,426	2,782	5.1	77,439	181	13,174	330,410	2,166,332
Lawrence, KS	1	152	6,875	23,484	90,599	64	248	3.4	4,735	13	1,119	37,222	166,129
Manhattan, KS.	3	268	6,056	44,665	140,634	122	386	7.4	4,695	26	1,157	31,223	210,939
Topeka, KS	6	827	31,630	161,351	320,716	441	878	5.1	17,280	39	3,004	100,116	447,137
Wichita, KS.	13	1,830	68,734	361,006	586,644	991	1,608	5.3	39,764	121	9,611	297,286	892,639
Minnesota.	131	14,562	548,360	3,346,653	7,862,590	9,168	21,599	6.1	497,984	1,287	66,960	1,946,061	11,969,353
Nonmetropolitan	76	4,357	83,799	927,307	3,009,938	2,542	8,250	11.1	110,302	331	12,633	542,882	4,481,519
Metropolitan	55	10,205	464,561	2,419,346	4,852,652	6,626	13,349	5.2	387,682	956	54,327	1,403,179	7,487,834
Duluth, MN-WI.	10	1,193	38,713	264,189	729,480	723	1,999	6.8	39,507	86	3,065	130,782	608,733
Grand Forks, ND-MN	2	124	1,484	30,002	112,167	82	308	20.2	2,789	11	193	9,719	83,329
Mankato-North Mankato, MN. . . .	2	183	10,382	39,865	89,918	110	246	3.8	7,821	26	1,497	34,446	309,303
Minneapolis-St. Paul-Bloomington, MN-WI.	32	6,387	329,209	1,524,358	2,760,557	4,174	7,562	4.6	257,833	678	42,837	1,056,891	5,272,851
Rochester, MN	4	1,559	57,332	382,639	723,451	1,049	1,982	6.7	62,979	118	3,712	103,098	671,612
St. Cloud, MN	5	759	27,441	178,293	437,079	488	1,252	6.5	16,753	37	3,023	68,243	542,006
Missouri	122	18,613	779,774	4,057,997	8,914,851	11,110	24,428	5.2	576,911	1,239	74,548	2,975,892	22,031,393
Nonmetropolitan	51	2,994	97,410	453,400	1,528,042	1,238	4,191	4.7	83,565	308	11,635	629,395	4,910,061
Metropolitan	71	15,619	682,364	3,604,597	7,386,809	9,872	20,237	5.3	493,346	931	62,913	2,346,497	17,121,332
Cape Girardeau, MO-IL	2	498	20,933	98,538	207,458	270	569	4.7	16,082	33	2,000	74,527	725,599
Columbia, MO.	3	841	40,600	201,742	334,111	553	915	5.0	35,985	41	4,071	89,576	989,712
Jefferson City, MO	3	303	12,871	54,593	145,047	150	398	4.2	10,600	24	1,604	73,348	651,951
Joplin, MO	4	649	27,641	144,290	324,662	395	889	5.2	16,004	65	3,096	138,833	1,034,581
Kansas City, MO-KS	23	3,760	156,383	879,799	1,878,038	2,409	5,144	5.6	104,280	202	14,764	649,449	3,793,135
Springfield, MO	5	1,411	74,368	347,101	832,567	951	2,281	4.7	68,999	92	6,942	254,075	2,507,718
St. Joseph, MO-KS.	1	352	16,283	69,894	170,865	191	468	4.3	11,179	20	1,637	55,229	916,535
St. Louis, MO-IL.	30	7,805	333,285	1,808,640	3,494,061	4,953	9,573	5.4	230,217	454	28,799	1,011,460	6,502,101
Nebraska	89	6,674	195,869	1,331,045	3,064,743	3,647	8,403	6.8	191,829	504	26,037	706,923	4,574,393
Nonmetropolitan	66	2,929	61,159	546,755	1,507,470	1,498	4,137	8.9	68,525	254	7,289	294,308	2,279,824
Metropolitan	23	3,745	134,710	784,290	1,557,273	2,149	4,266	5.8	123,304	250	18,748	412,615	2,294,569
Grand Island, NE	4	345	8,788	51,341	124,511	141	341	5.8	8,416	22	1,266	32,187	144,644
Lincoln, NE.	5	973	38,116	243,434	451,794	667	1,238	6.4	25,530	65	5,116	114,146	392,932
Omaha-Council Bluffs, NE-IA. . . .	14	2,427	87,806	489,515	980,968	1,341	2,687	5.6	89,358	163	12,366	266,282	1,756,993

TABLE 8

U.S. CENSUS DIVISION 6, WEST NORTH CENTRAL

U.S. Community Hospitals
(Nonfederal, short-term general and other special hospitals)

2014 Utilization, Personnel and Finances

| | FULL-TIME EQUIVALENT PERSONNEL | | | | FULL-TIME EQUIV. TRAINEES | | | EXPENSES | | | | | | |
| | | | | | | | | LABOR | | | | TOTAL | | |
Physicians and Dentists	Registered Nurses	Licensed Practical Nurses	Other Salaried Personnel	Total Personnel	Medical and Dental Residents	Other Trainees	Total Trainees	Payroll (in thousands)	Employee Benefits (in thousands)	Total (in thousands)	Percent of Total	Amount (in thousands)	Adjusted per Admission	Adjusted per Inpatient Day
122,747	1,398,346	73,044	2,510,354	4,754,880	109,309	8,533	117,842	$310,203,433	$82,949,525	$393,152,940	48.6	$808,869,209	$12,015.42	$2,212.22
15,090	147,461	20,793	334,968	602,081	1,731	269	2,000	33,192,643	8,842,572	42,035,205	51.3	81,981,991	8,301.59	1,278.41
107,657	1,250,885	52,251	2,175,386	4,152,799	107,578	8,264	115,842	277,010,790	74,106,953	351,117,735	48.3	726,887,218	12,653.89	2,410.83
13,151	109,667	9,075	228,383	405,814	5,068	481	5,549	24,314,048	6,263,782	30,577,824	49.0	62,380,858	11,560.90	1,824.14
2,856	24,311	4,474	59,678	104,446	98	14	112	5,799,747	1,473,779	7,273,528	51.7	14,063,913	8,954.89	1,026.17
10,295	85,356	4,601	168,705	301,368	4,970	467	5,437	18,514,302	4,790,002	23,304,296	48.2	48,316,945	12,630.83	2,357.83
1,182	15,232	993	31,865	55,971	768	38	806	3,161,673	858,108	4,019,784	49.4	8,129,893	9,505.58	1,445.14
531	5,403	657	12,215	21,459	17	0	17	1,129,463	297,973	1,427,437	51.8	2,755,052	8,258.33	980.56
651	9,829	336	19,650	34,512	751	38	789	2,032,210	560,135	2,592,347	48.2	5,374,842	10,303.20	1,908.67
2	345	14	750	1,263	0	0	0	71,149	23,209	94,358	51.5	183,078	9,705.17	1,166.32
24	1,193	43	2,825	4,497	0	2	2	236,721	66,113	302,834	48.1	628,964	8,388.20	1,276.93
1	698	7	1,045	1,975	10	0	10	115,766	24,508	140,275	36.8	381,450	8,172.12	2,181.06
283	2,705	39	5,216	9,218	189	9	198	576,351	142,232	718,582	49.3	1,457,739	10,984.73	2,083.99
8	608	16	1,113	1,906	0	0	0	90,215	21,286	111,501	44.5	250,359	8,980.20	1,694.86
123	2,283	20	4,421	8,082	547	25	572	486,330	173,199	659,529	50.2	1,312,514	16,348.59	2,583.40
12	375	10	739	1,274	0	0	0	77,015	19,800	96,816	46.4	208,651	6,647.89	1,840.62
66	712	21	1,382	2,502	2	0	2	142,579	35,741	178,321	48.8	365,650	10,012.86	2,306.46
132	910	166	2,159	3,795	3	2	5	236,083	54,046	290,131	49.5	586,437	8,103.09	1,609.17
1,095	14,289	1,180	23,726	47,756	7	177	184	2,818,944	666,422	3,485,364	50.1	6,954,230	10,179.09	1,512.57
432	4,310	655	9,817	18,258	0	0	0	928,084	220,296	1,148,379	53.9	2,128,653	8,717.84	869.35
663	9,979	525	13,909	29,498	7	177	184	1,890,861	446,126	2,336,985	48.4	4,825,578	10,991.80	2,245.43
225	5,137	75	6,605	14,300	0	169	169	933,660	227,712	1,161,372	44.8	2,589,949	12,123.92	2,563.10
41	317	29	707	1,223	0	0	0	74,332	16,027	90,359	50.3	179,633	6,772.72	1,982.72
20	241	25	410	819	0	0	0	54,685	11,296	65,981	50.2	110,509	6,959.45	785.79
286	1,391	341	2,624	5,368	0	0	0	356,169	85,261	441,429	58.0	761,280	11,193.81	2,373.69
91	2,893	55	3,563	7,788	7	8	15	472,014	105,830	577,844	48.8	1,184,207	10,299.06	2,018.61
5,483	24,892	2,328	67,125	110,271	2,286	94	2,380	6,954,637	1,893,066	8,847,701	53.5	16,528,924	13,987.46	2,102.22
564	4,247	1,216	12,370	20,582	9	7	16	1,276,336	337,980	1,614,317	50.8	3,175,094	10,570.71	1,054.87
4,919	20,645	1,112	54,755	89,689	2,277	87	2,364	5,678,301	1,555,085	7,233,384	54.2	13,353,831	15,151.92	2,751.86
534	1,838	241	4,949	8,235	9	0	9	653,025	167,448	820,472	59.7	1,374,908	14,648.02	1,884.78
17	126	18	409	627	1	2	3	33,758	8,506	42,264	53.0	79,683	13,874.89	710.40
127	433	73	1,160	2,014	0	0	0	122,727	32,144	154,871	48.7	318,187	13,652.00	3,538.64
2,106	13,012	440	25,630	45,376	999	85	1,084	3,833,324	1,054,259	4,887,581	54.3	9,002,770	15,154.34	3,261.22
2,100	3,845	132	19,516	28,122	1,253	0	1,253	723,874	196,354	920,229	50.3	1,839,934	16,459.13	2,543.27
35	1,391	208	3,091	5,315	15	0	15	311,594	96,374	407,967	55.3	738,349	14,048.80	1,689.28
3,191	35,239	2,696	65,745	119,216	1,849	131	1,980	6,959,510	1,789,867	8,749,371	45.2	19,367,868	11,235.08	2,172.54
581	4,277	1,058	10,502	18,169	47	0	47	963,872	249,618	1,213,488	50.6	2,399,718	7,327.70	1,570.45
2,610	30,962	1,638	55,243	101,047	1,802	131	1,933	5,995,638	1,540,249	7,535,883	44.4	16,968,151	12,151.45	2,297.09
185	1,070	129	2,500	4,397	0	17	17	279,432	65,536	344,969	47.7	722,854	16,276.46	3,484.34
29	1,560	213	3,610	5,796	378	7	385	304,955	119,033	423,987	42.1	1,008,163	14,609.15	3,017.45
93	569	124	1,181	2,225	10	0	10	120,350	32,649	152,999	48.5	315,361	9,292.01	2,174.20
155	1,231	64	2,372	4,491	22	0	22	281,064	59,451	340,515	49.4	689,369	10,959.77	2,123.35
496	7,168	218	13,245	23,288	213	107	320	1,498,236	345,080	1,843,316	46.2	3,987,172	13,201.60	2,123.05
829	3,689	490	9,487	15,926	0	0	0	662,574	179,263	841,836	41.6	2,022,392	11,176.71	2,429.10
165	734	152	1,934	3,159	0	0	0	243,986	58,069	302,056	56.4	535,262	13,446.78	3,132.66
658	14,941	248	20,914	41,765	1,179	0	1,179	2,605,040	681,166	3,286,205	42.7	7,687,576	11,588.93	2,200.18
590	9,831	702	18,285	33,582	97	11	108	1,933,223	513,346	2,446,566	46.6	5,246,493	11,773.57	1,711.89
332	3,331	533	7,457	13,459	24	5	29	708,503	193,087	901,588	49.7	1,812,365	10,411.28	1,202.26
258	6,500	169	10,828	20,123	73	6	79	1,224,720	320,260	1,544,978	45.0	3,434,128	12,646.91	2,205.22
10	364	24	724	1,334	1	0	1	59,004	18,038	77,043	40.1	192,034	10,274.12	1,542.30
54	1,677	49	2,823	5,101	22	4	26	295,940	84,295	380,234	46.8	812,009	11,339.33	1,797.30
194	4,459	96	7,281	13,688	50	2	52	869,776	217,926	1,087,701	44.8	2,430,085	13,408.26	2,477.23

Table continues

MSAs

TABLE 8

U.S. CENSUS DIVISION 6, WEST NORTH CENTRAL CONTINUED

U.S. Community Hospitals
(Nonfederal, short-term general and other special hospitals)

2014 Utilization, Personnel and Finances

CLASSIFICATION	Hospitals	Beds	Admissions	Inpatient Days	Adjusted Inpatient Days	Average Daily Census	Adjusted Average Daily Census	Average Stay (days)	Surgical Operations	NEWBORNS		OUTPATIENT VISITS	
										Bassinets	Births	Emergency	Total
North Dakota	40	3,144	92,692	644,992	1,838,164	1,769	5,035	7.0	103,830	147	12,561	360,374	2,520,287
Nonmetropolitan	32	1,629	23,714	305,909	989,385	839	2,709	12.9	28,487	52	4,149	148,743	757,569
Metropolitan	8	1,515	68,978	339,083	848,779	930	2,326	4.9	75,343	95	8,412	211,631	1,762,718
Bismarck, ND	3	520	22,838	103,222	169,510	283	465	4.5	17,695	27	2,584	55,689	410,116
Fargo, ND-MN	3	634	32,782	156,313	422,219	429	1,157	4.8	45,263	45	4,012	84,385	572,887
Grand Forks, ND-MN	2	361	13,358	79,548	257,050	218	704	6.0	12,385	23	1,816	71,557	779,715
South Dakota	53	4,086	99,928	919,091	2,293,679	2,519	6,286	9.2	76,743	209	12,880	296,024	3,316,846
Nonmetropolitan	41	2,369	29,994	502,834	1,412,184	1,379	3,870	16.8	29,458	146	5,150	152,960	1,441,737
Metropolitan	12	1,717	69,934	416,257	881,495	1,140	2,416	6.0	47,285	63	7,730	143,064	1,875,109
Rapid City, SD	4	591	20,366	155,506	295,086	426	809	7.6	9,372	24	2,295	64,853	258,428
Sioux Falls, SD	8	1,126	49,568	260,751	586,409	714	1,607	5.3	37,913	39	5,435	78,211	1,616,681

MSAs

2014 Utilization, Personnel and Finances

FULL-TIME EQUIVALENT PERSONNEL					FULL-TIME EQUIV. TRAINEES			EXPENSES						
								LABOR				TOTAL		
Physicians and Dentists	Registered Nurses	Licensed Practical Nurses	Other Salaried Personnel	Total Personnel	Medical and Dental Residents	Other Trainees	Total Trainees	Payroll (in thousands)	Employee Benefits (in thousands)	Total (in thousands)	Percent of Total	Amount (in thousands)	Adjusted per Admission	Adjusted per Inpatient Day
893	4,601	790	11,683	19,740	32	5	37	1,269,239	259,347	1,528,587	48.0	3,186,530	11,761.06	1,733.54
232	1,214	212	3,399	5,758	0	2	2	393,260	73,956	467,216	53.3	876,959	8,942.90	886.37
661	3,387	578	8,284	13,982	32	3	35	875,980	185,391	1,061,371	46.0	2,309,571	13,359.62	2,721.05
272	1,304	156	2,977	5,234	7	0	7	265,013	47,570	312,583	45.3	690,697	18,258.88	4,074.67
168	1,523	377	2,915	5,388	0	0	0	357,474	81,602	439,076	38.9	1,129,538	12,492.54	2,675.24
221	560	45	2,392	3,360	25	3	28	253,492	56,220	309,712	63.3	489,337	10,963.81	1,903.66
717	5,583	386	9,954	19,278	29	25	54	1,216,821	283,627	1,500,451	50.6	2,966,918	12,611.39	1,293.52
184	1,529	143	3,918	6,761	1	0	1	400,229	100,870	501,103	54.7	916,074	9,876.17	648.69
533	4,054	243	6,036	12,517	28	25	53	816,592	182,757	999,348	48.7	2,050,844	14,391.79	2,326.55
74	925	47	1,484	3,018	28	0	28	194,652	25,456	220,107	48.1	457,415	13,488.71	1,550.11
459	3,129	196	4,552	9,499	0	25	25	621,941	157,301	779,241	48.9	1,593,429	14,673.81	2,717.27

MSAs

TABLE 8

U.S. CENSUS DIVISION 7, WEST SOUTH CENTRAL

U.S. Community Hospitals
(Nonfederal, short-term general and other special hospitals)

2014 Utilization, Personnel and Finances

CLASSIFICATION	Hospitals	Beds	Admissions	Inpatient Days	Adjusted Inpatient Days	Average Daily Census	Adjusted Average Daily Census	Average Stay (days)	Surgical Operations	NEWBORNS Bassinets	Births	OUTPATIENT VISITS Emergency	Total
UNITED STATES	4,926	786,874	33,066,720	180,456,434	365,636,679	494,388	1,002,304	5.5	26,401,528	55,824	3,735,593	136,327,473	693,106,685
Nonmetropolitan	1,855	116,785	3,238,473	21,307,388	64,127,906	58,370	175,723	6.6	3,512,461	9,506	383,166	21,639,508	119,516,577
Metropolitan	3,071	670,089	29,828,247	159,149,046	301,508,773	436,018	826,581	5.3	22,889,067	46,318	3,352,427	114,687,965	573,590,108
CENSUS DIVISION 7, WEST SOUTH CENTRAL	734	96,935	3,815,555	20,297,127	38,809,882	55,614	106,423	5.3	2,812,918	7,451	548,587	16,436,178	62,982,780
Nonmetropolitan	290	14,451	410,138	1,881,428	5,585,865	5,153	15,303	4.6	351,943	1,245	55,456	2,832,815	11,230,821
Metropolitan	444	82,484	3,405,417	18,415,699	33,224,017	50,461	91,120	5.4	2,460,975	6,206	493,131	13,603,363	51,751,959
Arkansas	81	9,284	344,635	1,768,146	3,648,454	4,844	9,995	5.1	265,144	654	35,407	1,351,198	5,078,901
Nonmetropolitan	47	3,092	88,318	468,630	1,271,912	1,282	3,485	5.3	66,189	223	9,242	516,522	1,932,820
Metropolitan	34	6,192	256,317	1,299,516	2,376,542	3,562	6,510	5.1	198,955	431	26,165	834,676	3,146,081
Fayetteville-Springdale-Rogers, AR-MO. .	6	909	44,893	182,985	331,265	502	907	4.1	43,396	73	6,447	182,449	534,235
Fort Smith, AR-OK	6	869	33,832	183,928	328,163	504	899	5.4	32,447	54	3,735	124,539	372,256
Hot Springs, AR.	3	501	18,515	96,217	173,846	263	476	5.2	16,252	27	1,423	65,290	217,976
Jonesboro, AR.	3	634	26,454	117,600	254,675	323	698	4.4	15,270	46	2,080	87,480	319,033
Little Rock-North Little Rock-Con-way, AR. .	14	2,921	123,268	666,882	1,175,031	1,828	3,219	5.4	86,935	195	11,662	318,164	1,500,593
Pine Bluff, AR	1	333	9,137	51,175	108,583	140	297	5.6	4,655	36	818	52,085	194,146
Texarkana, TX-AR	1	25	218	729	4,979	2	14	3.3	0	0	0	4,669	7,842
Louisiana	122	15,076	561,930	3,077,460	6,341,380	8,428	17,388	5.5	410,882	1,010	70,969	2,739,120	10,733,191
Nonmetropolitan	38	2,059	59,563	277,463	758,370	757	2,081	4.7	54,946	139	7,844	361,039	1,307,252
Metropolitan	84	13,017	502,367	2,799,997	5,583,010	7,671	15,307	5.6	355,936	871	63,125	2,378,081	9,425,939
Alexandria, LA	5	737	29,537	159,244	267,364	437	732	5.4	16,805	55	3,182	118,892	381,275
Baton Rouge, LA	12	2,433	80,507	555,128	1,298,076	1,521	3,558	6.9	57,390	150	11,261	366,768	1,498,334
Hammond, LA	3	328	12,224	64,370	132,632	176	363	5.3	12,931	26	1,391	91,271	495,092
Houma-Thibodaux, LA	5	517	23,960	106,280	232,064	291	636	4.4	19,231	44	3,408	146,057	538,196
Lafayette, LA	14	1,554	58,824	321,827	597,948	883	1,639	5.5	33,131	139	9,338	295,918	1,115,660
Lake Charles, LA	7	733	27,480	142,615	322,845	391	883	5.2	27,570	54	3,639	138,761	586,383
Monroe, LA.	8	806	36,093	192,147	318,557	526	874	5.3	19,185	38	3,646	136,975	462,411
New Orleans-Metairie, LA.	19	3,894	147,316	829,141	1,636,882	2,271	4,493	5.6	117,857	224	18,023	722,898	3,106,888
Shreveport-Bossier City, LA	11	2,015	86,426	429,245	776,642	1,175	2,129	5.0	51,836	141	9,237	360,541	1,241,700
Oklahoma	114	11,240	393,816	2,172,592	4,618,989	5,958	12,659	5.5	324,635	865	51,509	1,856,987	6,365,163
Nonmetropolitan	65	3,560	99,274	464,420	1,366,239	1,274	3,745	4.7	99,141	328	13,754	673,660	2,377,819
Metropolitan	49	7,680	294,542	1,708,172	3,252,750	4,684	8,914	5.8	225,494	537	37,755	1,183,327	3,987,344
Fort Smith, AR-OK	2	85	2,095	8,598	23,357	24	64	4.1	804	11	218	29,606	43,218
Lawton, OK	2	556	13,831	120,031	276,474	329	758	8.7	10,783	43	1,798	72,205	220,781
Oklahoma City, OK.	23	4,014	148,929	911,958	1,669,035	2,499	4,574	6.1	125,665	313	20,300	682,952	2,245,224
Tulsa, OK.	22	3,025	129,687	667,585	1,283,884	1,832	3,518	5.1	88,242	170	15,439	398,564	1,478,121
Texas	417	61,335	2,515,174	13,278,929	24,201,059	36,384	66,381	5.3	1,812,257	4,922	390,702	10,488,873	40,805,525
Nonmetropolitan	140	5,740	162,983	670,915	2,189,344	1,840	5,992	4.1	131,667	555	24,616	1,281,594	5,612,930
Metropolitan	277	55,595	2,352,191	12,608,014	22,011,715	34,544	60,389	5.4	1,680,590	4,367	366,086	9,207,279	35,192,595
Abilene, TX.	5	661	22,613	120,946	234,308	331	642	5.3	20,200	46	2,815	95,679	391,806
Amarillo, TX	5	892	40,894	218,412	348,142	599	955	5.3	20,047	54	4,779	121,775	384,772
Austin-Round Rock, TX	24	3,220	152,104	752,049	1,282,642	2,059	3,515	4.9	115,704	350	27,123	711,404	2,521,108
Beaumont-Port Arthur, TX.	7	1,132	44,276	213,331	412,224	585	1,130	4.8	32,827	81	5,079	228,928	595,999
Brownsville-Harlingen, TX.	3	892	38,280	192,257	290,781	526	797	5.0	24,895	72	7,343	132,644	254,325
College Station-Bryan, TX.	4	432	19,591	91,951	187,586	252	513	4.7	18,906	58	2,795	99,001	337,294
Corpus Christi, TX	6	1,458	61,203	336,764	521,339	923	1,429	5.5	36,744	92	7,579	259,959	561,216
Dallas-Plano-Irving, TX	51	9,079	391,994	2,131,947	3,633,825	5,842	9,957	5.4	236,309	775	60,264	1,645,004	5,264,167
El Paso, TX	6	1,773	78,768	373,217	611,530	1,022	1,675	4.7	47,805	172	15,280	293,149	1,307,099
Fort Worth-Arlington, TX.	28	4,815	217,210	1,130,385	1,896,565	3,094	5,196	5.2	151,247	366	33,752	1,060,753	2,875,067
Houston-The Woodlands-Sugar Land, TX . .	63	14,340	607,288	3,481,154	6,315,530	9,534	17,323	5.7	429,372	1,228	99,194	2,042,272	9,612,911
Killeen-Temple, TX	6	961	43,141	207,264	505,991	567	1,387	4.8	40,763	58	4,860	210,822	1,923,798
Laredo, TX	2	509	22,678	115,700	201,397	317	552	5.1	21,111	63	5,974	82,962	257,918
Longview, TX	5	699	26,431	127,995	250,791	352	687	4.8	26,328	77	4,127	153,233	360,911
Lubbock, TX	6	1,162	53,221	264,979	463,090	728	1,269	5.0	39,146	95	5,469	177,544	770,431
McAllen-Edinburg-Mission, TX . . .	7	2,172	90,548	425,489	726,051	1,166	1,990	4.7	90,709	180	17,796	257,660	608,966
Midland, TX	3	322	13,083	71,411	136,757	196	374	5.5	9,715	26	2,550	63,883	163,456
Odessa, TX	2	581	19,587	102,144	176,105	280	483	5.2	12,185	39	4,389	78,265	367,269
San Angelo, TX.	2	429	16,383	76,886	165,611	211	454	4.7	20,849	36	2,061	73,521	186,983
San Antonio-New Braunfels, TX. .	17	5,695	238,102	1,270,477	2,071,308	3,480	5,673	5.3	166,770	325	33,754	797,921	3,953,373
Sherman-Denison, TX	2	529	19,083	97,236	170,221	267	466	5.1	16,227	35	1,535	80,467	156,320
Texarkana, TX-AR	5	714	23,061	131,061	220,893	360	606	5.7	11,463	31	2,789	111,575	253,585
Tyler, TX	7	1,183	50,276	275,635	470,614	757	1,290	5.5	41,785	30	3,286	146,077	1,039,328
Victoria, TX	3	564	16,422	82,809	155,538	228	426	5.0	18,584	18	2,156	75,744	205,146
Waco, TX.	3	929	28,382	230,261	416,863	631	1,200	8.1	16,907	40	7,101	116,648	641,966
Wichita Falls, TX	5	452	17,572	86,254	146,013	237	400	4.9	13,990	20	2,236	90,390	197,381

MSAs

TABLE 8

U.S. CENSUS DIVISION 7, WEST SOUTH CENTRAL

U.S. Community Hospitals
(Nonfederal, short-term general and other special hospitals)

2014 Utilization, Personnel and Finances

| FULL-TIME EQUIVALENT PERSONNEL | | | | | FULL-TIME EQUIV. TRAINEES | | | EXPENSES | | | | | | |
| | | | | | | | | LABOR | | | | TOTAL | | |
Physicians and Dentists	Registered Nurses	Licensed Practical Nurses	Other Salaried Personnel	Total Personnel	Medical and Dental Residents	Other Trainees	Total Trainees	Payroll (in thousands)	Employee Benefits (in thousands)	Total (in thousands)	Percent of Total	Amount (in thousands)	Adjusted per Admission	Adjusted per Inpatient Day
122,747	1,398,346	73,044	2,510,354	4,754,880	109,309	8,533	117,842	$310,203,433	$82,949,525	$393,152,940	48.6	$808,869,209	$12,015.42	$2,212.22
15,090	147,461	20,793	334,968	602,081	1,731	269	2,000	33,192,643	8,842,572	42,035,205	51.3	81,981,991	8,301.59	1,278.41
107,657	1,250,885	52,251	2,175,386	4,152,799	107,578	8,264	115,842	277,010,790	74,106,953	351,117,735	48.3	726,887,218	12,653.89	2,410.83
6,349	152,591	13,830	238,982	492,693	5,170	1,207	6,377	29,694,031	6,942,583	36,636,613	45.6	80,310,161	10,597.57	2,069.32
756	15,501	4,335	32,588	63,478	86	22	108	3,087,911	748,214	3,836,121	48.2	7,960,284	6,481.21	1,425.08
5,593	137,090	9,495	206,394	429,215	5,084	1,185	6,269	26,606,120	6,194,369	32,800,492	45.3	72,349,877	11,393.76	2,177.64
600	13,773	1,742	22,463	45,190	22	12	34	2,172,923	506,720	2,679,639	44.8	5,976,999	8,098.54	1,638.23
235	3,345	864	6,397	12,847	13	1	14	585,616	136,628	722,240	50.1	1,440,579	5,783.51	1,132.61
365	10,428	878	16,066	32,343	9	11	20	1,587,308	370,092	1,957,399	43.1	4,536,420	9,277.88	1,908.83
111	1,632	159	2,260	4,970	1	0	1	218,861	46,429	265,292	43.3	612,072	7,028.76	1,847.68
93	1,106	220	1,906	3,828	0	0	0	158,725	45,397	204,122	38.5	530,222	8,177.14	1,615.73
30	632	44	644	1,692	0	0	0	93,065	23,600	116,664	46.5	250,642	7,369.44	1,441.75
27	1,019	115	1,563	3,037	3	0	3	139,901	34,389	174,290	41.6	419,244	7,296.15	1,646.19
89	5,630	291	9,090	17,529	5	10	15	898,100	205,824	1,103,923	43.4	2,545,841	11,331.01	2,166.62
15	397	44	570	1,228	0	1	1	72,666	13,904	86,569	51.7	167,398	8,634.55	1,541.66
0	12	5	33	59	0	0	0	5,990	548	6,539	59.4	11,001	7,388.48	2,209.57
2,222	23,646	3,100	41,864	82,845	719	53	772	4,118,262	928,826	5,047,089	45.0	11,224,972	9,465.01	1,770.12
152	2,320	470	4,745	9,097	23	10	33	409,813	95,892	505,706	48.7	1,038,914	6,021.01	1,369.93
2,070	21,326	2,630	37,119	73,748	696	43	739	3,708,450	832,933	4,541,383	44.6	10,186,058	10,051.41	1,824.47
35	982	71	1,418	3,078	16	1	17	158,279	39,613	197,892	43.2	458,563	9,024.52	1,715.13
282	3,503	446	6,618	13,240	86	0	86	733,420	146,545	879,964	45.1	1,949,686	10,411.76	1,501.98
99	577	72	1,693	2,684	0	0	0	161,493	42,096	203,589	62.9	323,632	12,750.47	2,440.08
63	826	112	1,959	3,411	0	8	8	174,990	39,428	214,418	44.1	486,760	9,108.02	2,097.53
99	2,241	250	3,376	7,083	13	1	14	380,242	86,673	466,915	43.6	1,070,702	9,696.28	1,790.63
102	1,240	213	2,266	4,411	1	14	15	185,850	50,036	235,887	42.5	554,909	8,630.94	1,718.81
40	1,043	196	2,036	3,812	0	0	0	205,996	50,460	256,457	46.3	553,829	8,955.84	1,738.55
991	7,775	839	11,664	24,555	368	16	384	1,267,255	256,235	1,523,490	42.1	3,614,816	12,160.00	2,208.35
359	3,139	431	6,089	11,474	212	3	215	440,925	121,846	562,771	48.0	1,173,161	7,211.82	1,510.56
811	15,058	1,715	25,920	51,145	182	64	246	2,837,626	667,777	3,505,402	44.4	7,888,229	9,002.62	1,707.78
265	3,779	804	7,637	14,825	49	4	53	772,773	181,562	954,335	49.2	1,940,535	6,669.95	1,420.35
546	11,279	911	18,283	36,320	133	60	193	2,064,853	486,215	2,551,067	42.9	5,947,694	10,162.17	1,828.51
6	60	52	286	475	0	0	0	15,805	3,908	19,713	56.5	34,918	5,932.33	1,494.96
101	383	154	1,080	1,928	1	0	1	114,408	20,775	135,183	46.4	291,358	9,260.65	1,053.84
347	6,446	434	9,152	19,230	118	58	176	1,155,841	278,569	1,434,413	42.8	3,352,811	11,666.78	2,008.83
92	4,390	271	7,765	14,687	14	2	16	778,795	182,962	961,758	42.4	2,268,607	8,707.03	1,766.99
2,716	100,114	7,273	148,735	313,513	4,247	1,078	5,325	20,565,219	4,839,261	25,404,483	46.0	55,219,961	11,557.20	2,281.72
104	6,057	2,197	13,809	26,709	1	7	8	1,319,709	334,132	1,653,840	46.7	3,540,256	6,865.75	1,617.04
2,612	94,057	5,076	134,926	286,804	4,246	1,071	5,317	19,245,510	4,505,130	23,750,643	46.0	51,679,705	12,124.75	2,347.83
3	884	156	1,062	2,694	0	36	36	145,755	30,249	176,003	42.3	416,383	9,493.88	1,777.07
1	1,355	73	1,863	3,840	0	0	0	216,614	46,775	263,389	43.4	606,398	8,794.50	1,741.81
324	7,100	180	7,984	19,055	312	31	343	1,255,121	268,077	1,523,199	45.9	3,319,268	12,170.26	2,587.84
3	1,541	134	1,638	3,887	0	0	0	248,927	56,282	305,211	42.9	711,967	7,973.47	1,727.14
1	877	100	968	2,547	0	0	0	186,757	34,187	220,943	43.7	505,653	8,730.19	1,738.95
40	740	52	1,152	2,239	0	0	0	126,458	34,538	160,996	44.6	361,181	9,073.54	1,925.42
57	1,983	121	3,352	6,605	146	3	149	369,472	94,194	463,666	43.9	1,057,079	10,963.84	2,027.62
390	16,304	385	23,590	48,640	1,133	9	1,142	3,721,124	826,735	4,547,858	48.5	9,368,356	13,375.38	2,578.10
38	2,469	77	3,782	7,687	0	0	0	442,995	103,453	546,447	38.1	1,434,923	10,928.91	2,346.45
13	8,857	535	12,557	26,087	289	6	295	1,740,603	439,392	2,179,996	47.0	4,637,860	12,223.65	2,445.40
1,303	27,670	1,015	41,925	88,212	1,008	935	1,943	6,474,984	1,627,271	8,102,257	46.7	17,351,654	15,118.30	2,747.46
5	2,120	324	3,724	7,417	619	24	643	346,019	70,671	416,691	38.6	1,080,730	9,915.87	2,135.87
0	590	31	816	1,769	0	0	0	92,097	20,761	112,858	30.5	370,196	9,356.42	1,838.14
0	992	25	1,034	2,562	0	0	0	155,823	33,015	188,838	41.7	452,994	8,275.67	1,806.26
0	2,318	160	3,077	6,582	0	0	0	355,560	93,895	449,455	41.8	1,076,147	11,317.38	2,323.84
39	2,790	147	3,752	8,271	0	3	3	439,793	92,388	532,180	51.9	1,025,298	6,495.69	1,412.16
1	503	53	1,041	1,939	21	0	21	113,105	25,433	138,537	50.6	273,848	10,128.63	2,002.44
0	703	47	1,074	2,191	0	0	0	140,457	33,559	174,016	50.1	347,139	10,281.02	1,971.20
0	606	109	977	2,075	0	0	0	109,206	21,339	130,545	42.2	309,148	8,710.35	1,866.71
183	8,208	685	10,117	23,788	550	9	559	1,533,398	309,638	1,843,036	44.8	4,111,421	10,354.63	1,984.95
49	630	45	1,071	2,012	0	0	0	101,143	24,242	125,385	42.2	297,198	8,903.20	1,745.95
0	852	130	1,157	2,609	0	0	0	129,108	31,485	160,594	43.7	367,738	8,770.91	1,664.78
66	1,747	257	3,253	6,532	83	2	85	376,754	92,850	469,603	41.5	1,129,080	12,265.95	2,399.16
20	600	90	949	1,903	0	0	0	108,356	25,780	134,137	49.6	270,646	8,422.68	1,740.06
76	978	67	1,773	3,300	85	13	98	169,648	40,892	210,539	46.1	456,320	8,445.20	1,094.65
0	640	78	1,238	2,361	0	0	0	146,235	28,030	174,264	51.1	341,060	10,864.90	2,335.82

MSAs

TABLE 8

U.S. CENSUS DIVISION 8, MOUNTAIN

U.S. Community Hospitals
(Nonfederal, short-term general and other special hospitals)

2014 Utilization, Personnel and Finances

MSAs

CLASSIFICATION	Hospitals	Beds	Admissions	Inpatient Days	Adjusted Inpatient Days	Average Daily Census	Adjusted Average Daily Census	Average Stay (days)	Surgical Operations	NEWBORNS Bassinets	NEWBORNS Births	OUTPATIENT VISITS Emergency	OUTPATIENT VISITS Total
UNITED STATES	4,926	786,874	33,066,720	180,456,434	365,636,679	494,388	1,002,304	5.5	26,401,528	55,824	3,735,593	136,327,473	693,106,685
Nonmetropolitan	1,855	116,785	3,238,473	21,307,388	64,127,906	58,370	175,723	6.6	3,512,461	9,506	383,166	21,639,508	119,516,577
Metropolitan	3,071	670,089	29,828,247	159,149,046	301,508,773	436,018	826,581	5.3	22,889,067	46,318	3,352,427	114,687,965	573,590,108
CENSUS DIVISION 8, MOUNTAIN . . .	388	47,180	1,953,896	9,968,995	20,727,010	27,326	56,788	5.1	1,573,482	4,093	266,986	8,133,174	42,908,544
Nonmetropolitan	189	8,750	209,299	1,499,829	4,696,345	4,115	12,868	7.2	260,255	859	40,307	1,592,372	9,200,033
Metropolitan	199	38,430	1,744,597	8,469,166	16,030,665	23,211	43,920	4.9	1,313,227	3,234	226,679	6,540,802	33,708,511
Arizona.	72	13,301	624,898	2,864,588	5,300,255	7,851	14,521	4.6	440,574	991	74,217	2,080,313	8,429,418
Nonmetropolitan	9	322	13,233	39,989	138,740	110	380	3.0	15,136	55	3,029	89,618	324,400
Metropolitan	63	12,979	611,665	2,824,599	5,161,515	7,741	14,141	4.6	425,438	936	71,188	1,990,695	8,105,018
Flagstaff, AZ.	3	345	17,507	72,752	150,100	200	411	4.2	13,815	33	1,861	82,501	847,142
Lake Havasu City-Kingman, AZ . .	4	571	25,941	116,170	235,553	318	646	4.5	18,280	33	1,640	127,119	594,810
Phoenix-Mesa-Scottsdale, AZ . . .	37	8,532	417,210	1,924,754	3,425,396	5,275	9,384	4.6	282,983	661	48,725	1,141,439	4,665,302
Prescott, AZ.	3	316	14,809	54,635	117,158	150	322	3.7	8,788	27	1,661	96,994	230,922
Sierra Vista-Douglas, AZ	4	167	5,872	23,787	108,426	65	297	4.1	3,831	17	1,058	38,192	160,163
Tucson, AZ.	10	2,601	112,440	555,444	970,366	1,522	2,658	4.9	87,476	146	12,895	432,881	1,424,815
Yuma, AZ.	2	447	17,886	77,057	154,516	211	423	4.3	10,265	19	3,348	71,569	181,864
Colorado.	82	10,521	413,537	2,142,076	4,510,017	5,873	12,357	5.2	364,503	960	60,944	1,909,887	8,506,348
Nonmetropolitan	38	1,576	34,925	235,180	877,971	645	2,407	6.7	47,318	154	6,653	284,129	1,705,205
Metropolitan	44	8,945	378,612	1,906,896	3,632,046	5,228	9,950	5.0	317,185	806	54,291	1,625,758	6,801,143
Boulder, CO	4	610	31,703	129,818	263,996	356	723	4.1	24,814	92	6,749	123,722	730,687
Colorado Springs, CO	5	966	43,947	191,029	397,447	524	1,088	4.3	37,794	86	7,305	235,371	759,392
Denver-Aurora-Lakewood, CO . . .	24	5,522	226,977	1,200,400	2,149,011	3,290	5,887	5.3	194,882	464	29,955	892,323	3,933,328
Fort Collins, CO.	4	565	28,038	115,163	250,898	316	688	4.1	19,799	60	4,594	128,315	587,081
Grand Junction, CO	3	494	14,744	101,966	220,745	280	605	6.9	11,177	32	2,101	65,190	331,082
Greeley, CO	2	265	12,871	58,392	119,088	160	327	4.5	8,383	38	1,503	58,034	162,559
Pueblo, CO.	2	523	20,332	110,128	230,861	302	632	5.4	20,336	34	2,084	122,803	297,014
Idaho.	40	3,311	121,728	593,788	1,452,448	1,631	3,977	4.9	122,410	283	19,845	627,163	5,204,983
Nonmetropolitan	26	1,032	26,755	164,198	519,348	454	1,420	6.1	38,139	107	6,262	182,598	1,597,280
Metropolitan	14	2,279	94,973	429,590	933,100	1,177	2,557	4.5	84,271	176	13,583	444,565	3,607,703
Boise City, ID	8	1,317	55,602	237,082	527,621	650	1,445	4.3	54,192	114	8,724	231,958	2,629,190
Coeur d'Alene, ID.	1	251	12,996	62,097	147,829	170	405	4.8	10,857	18	1,693	48,555	281,101
Idaho Falls, ID.	2	352	12,548	73,585	133,918	202	367	5.9	7,419	13	860	99,521	235,510
Lewiston, ID-WA	1	119	4,745	20,844	44,387	57	122	4.4	3,764	12	692	25,692	130,322
Logan, UT-ID	1	65	469	1,535	4,981	4	14	3.3	539	5	72	2,671	6,514
Pocatello, ID.	1	175	8,613	34,447	74,364	94	204	4.0	7,500	14	1,542	36,168	325,066
Montana.	50	3,685	92,687	800,383	2,129,016	2,192	5,837	8.6	83,285	209	10,613	373,953	3,482,367
Nonmetropolitan	44	2,292	39,128	466,078	1,352,234	1,277	3,709	11.9	35,959	124	4,665	212,719	1,475,436
Metropolitan	6	1,393	53,559	334,305	776,782	915	2,128	6.2	47,326	85	5,948	161,234	2,006,931
Billings, MT.	3	624	26,571	162,414	415,623	444	1,139	6.1	21,426	40	2,909	80,766	1,163,070
Great Falls, MT	1	441	13,490	107,167	223,870	294	613	7.9	7,914	24	1,542	33,876	438,873
Missoula, MT	2	328	13,498	64,724	137,289	177	376	4.8	17,986	21	1,497	46,592	404,988
Nevada	37	5,549	256,223	1,398,303	2,397,085	3,832	6,568	5.5	147,828	292	23,860	909,831	2,976,972
Nonmetropolitan	10	275	9,076	41,308	137,218	114	376	4.6	13,896	32	1,652	94,066	493,967
Metropolitan	27	5,274	247,147	1,356,995	2,259,867	3,718	6,192	5.5	133,932	260	22,208	815,765	2,483,005
Carson City, NV.	1	190	10,860	48,799	91,001	134	249	4.5	5,410	12	910	34,832	219,066
Las Vegas-Henderson-Paradise, NV.	19	3,848	185,717	1,055,779	1,740,702	2,893	4,771	5.7	89,693	171	16,072	581,494	1,519,298
Reno, NV.	7	1,236	50,570	252,417	428,164	691	1,172	5.0	38,829	77	5,226	199,439	744,641
New Mexico.	37	3,771	174,429	819,119	1,907,932	2,243	5,225	4.7	119,796	506	22,664	953,949	5,652,745
Nonmetropolitan	23	1,242	46,989	178,716	535,780	488	1,466	3.8	47,789	160	8,433	449,404	1,845,895
Metropolitan	14	2,529	127,440	640,403	1,372,152	1,755	3,759	5.0	72,007	346	14,231	504,545	3,806,850
Albuquerque, NM.	9	1,657	86,511	466,871	1,045,786	1,280	2,864	5.4	47,288	254	10,123	301,025	2,617,117
Farmington, NM.	1	198	9,815	44,305	88,182	121	242	4.5	5,627	22	1,293	51,559	698,186
Las Cruces, NM.	3	406	18,874	78,307	139,250	214	382	4.1	12,182	46	1,753	106,914	277,093
Santa Fe, NM	1	268	12,240	50,920	98,934	140	271	4.2	6,910	24	1,062	45,047	214,454

2014 Utilization, Personnel and Finances

	FULL-TIME EQUIVALENT PERSONNEL					FULL-TIME EQUIV. TRAINEES			EXPENSES						
									LABOR				TOTAL		
Physicians and Dentists	Registered Nurses	Licensed Practical Nurses	Other Salaried Personnel	Total Personnel	Medical and Dental Residents	Other Trainees	Total Trainees	Payroll (in thousands)	Employee Benefits (in thousands)	Total (in thousands)	Percent of Total	Amount (in thousands)	Adjusted per Admission	Adjusted per Inpatient Day
122,747	1,398,346	73,044	2,510,354	4,754,880	109,309	8,533	117,842	$310,203,433	$82,949,525	$393,152,940	48.6	$808,869,209	$12,015.42	$2,212.22
15,090	147,461	20,793	334,968	602,081	1,731	269	2,000	33,192,643	8,842,572	42,035,205	51.3	81,981,991	8,301.59	1,278.41
107,657	1,250,885	52,251	2,175,386	4,152,799	107,578	8,264	115,842	277,010,790	74,106,953	351,117,735	48.3	726,887,218	12,653.89	2,410.83
6,536	85,510	3,473	146,051	281,593	3,184	364	3,548	17,970,109	4,340,749	22,310,856	47.3	47,158,491	11,823.61	2,275.22
1,577	11,478	1,217	27,461	48,947	39	16	55	2,784,000	675,124	3,459,121	51.4	6,729,136	9,993.04	1,432.85
4,959	74,032	2,256	118,590	232,646	3,145	348	3,493	15,186,109	3,665,626	18,851,735	46.6	40,429,355	12,195.44	2,522.00
1,596	25,765	527	36,574	74,977	1,333	78	1,411	4,930,840	1,151,035	6,081,878	46.8	12,984,717	11,138.00	2,449.83
62	667	51	1,475	2,702	4	4	8	153,691	38,115	191,808	49.4	388,627	8,565.73	2,801.12
1,534	25,098	476	35,099	72,275	1,329	74	1,403	4,777,149	1,112,920	5,890,070	46.8	12,596,090	11,242.16	2,440.39
133	850	4	1,576	2,966	2	0	2	207,593	50,445	258,037	51.8	498,402	13,888.09	3,320.47
82	1,027	55	1,932	3,623	21	0	21	201,568	52,629	254,198	50.0	508,578	9,699.59	2,159.08
1,156	17,233	308	23,254	48,297	1,261	35	1,296	3,258,844	773,424	4,032,270	47.2	8,550,483	11,432.95	2,496.20
100	646	0	1,147	2,189	0	0	0	133,969	40,492	174,460	48.6	358,716	11,166.62	3,061.82
21	177	10	597	959	1	1	2	63,692	15,449	79,141	53.1	149,060	6,451.68	1,374.76
31	4,539	89	5,611	12,319	34	1	35	783,827	151,628	935,455	43.0	2,176,452	11,240.09	2,242.92
11	626	10	982	1,922	10	37	47	127,656	28,853	156,509	44.2	354,399	10,019.47	2,293.61
1,298	19,855	644	35,035	65,042	467	126	593	4,506,037	1,062,529	5,568,562	46.5	11,972,905	14,223.61	2,654.74
362	2,277	240	5,727	9,909	6	1	7	594,840	154,243	749,081	51.3	1,460,638	12,261.08	1,663.65
936	17,578	404	29,308	55,133	461	125	586	3,911,197	908,286	4,819,481	45.8	10,512,267	14,547.13	2,894.31
95	1,130	27	2,734	4,345	2	0	2	314,536	72,430	386,966	47.4	816,300	12,599.35	3,092.09
87	1,561	22	2,863	5,323	0	22	22	395,013	92,573	487,586	46.4	1,049,908	11,306.23	2,641.63
627	11,584	236	17,516	34,470	351	95	446	2,514,108	570,119	3,084,225	46.5	6,628,617	16,179.91	3,084.50
9	1,254	35	2,153	3,843	21	0	21	277,776	77,480	355,256	42.7	832,224	14,198.37	3,316.98
79	553	12	1,388	2,308	25	2	27	146,031	38,432	184,463	42.0	439,157	15,661.82	1,989.43
2	595	7	1,018	1,835	33	1	34	102,678	23,699	126,377	37.2	340,176	13,437.71	2,856.51
37	901	65	1,636	3,009	29	5	34	161,055	33,553	194,608	47.9	405,886	9,366.46	1,758.14
917	6,364	529	15,933	27,736	35	17	52	1,524,347	342,579	1,866,925	49.2	3,792,867	13,047.04	2,611.36
179	1,687	252	4,513	7,938	2	3	5	371,682	92,237	463,918	50.1	925,510	11,144.81	1,782.06
738	4,677	277	11,420	19,798	33	14	47	1,152,665	250,342	1,403,007	48.9	2,867,357	13,807.74	3,072.94
567	3,050	163	8,339	14,035	3	13	16	762,229	161,250	923,479	48.7	1,897,925	15,181.58	3,597.14
94	466	10	1,318	2,077	6	0	6	168,343	40,097	208,440	55.4	376,348	12,164.58	2,545.83
13	541	32	695	1,516	19	0	19	84,342	19,831	104,172	45.6	228,658	10,640.22	1,707.45
17	217	12	427	770	5	1	6	53,648	14,018	67,667	48.4	139,717	13,827.86	3,147.69
6	64	9	155	275	0	0	0	7,434	2,200	9,635	53.4	18,050	11,859.23	3,623.72
41	339	51	486	1,125	0	0	0	76,668	12,946	89,614	43.4	206,659	11,114.28	2,779.02
952	4,358	629	11,991	20,322	14	0	14	1,217,007	266,738	1,483,744	52.0	2,855,454	11,822.16	1,341.21
383	2,249	283	6,277	10,584	1	0	1	582,939	133,975	716,913	54.5	1,314,788	10,999.65	972.31
569	2,109	346	5,714	9,738	13	0	13	634,068	132,763	766,831	49.8	1,540,666	12,628.00	1,983.40
359	934	179	3,119	5,096	13	0	13	356,382	80,603	436,985	52.2	837,842	12,858.22	2,015.87
85	560	76	1,361	2,352	0	0	0	152,248	31,684	183,932	51.8	354,921	12,594.79	1,585.39
125	615	91	1,234	2,290	0	0	0	125,438	20,476	145,914	41.9	347,903	12,137.29	2,534.09
206	8,593	304	11,526	24,968	314	19	333	1,719,022	420,540	2,139,559	47.1	4,538,309	10,092.91	1,893.26
35	441	29	858	1,664	0	0	0	103,489	24,659	128,147	49.6	258,508	9,076.20	1,883.92
171	8,152	275	10,668	23,304	314	19	333	1,615,533	395,881	2,011,412	47.0	4,279,801	10,161.67	1,893.83
0	336	6	441	988	0	0	0	66,895	16,467	83,362	41.6	200,240	9,887.42	2,200.42
156	5,828	218	7,533	16,522	291	19	310	1,226,955	307,879	1,534,833	48.7	3,152,400	10,107.51	1,810.99
15	1,988	51	2,694	5,794	23	0	23	321,684	71,535	393,217	42.4	927,161	10,413.80	2,165.43
963	7,650	364	12,087	24,923	78	52	130	1,630,599	361,736	1,992,336	48.7	4,087,541	9,886.83	2,142.39
260	1,883	152	3,644	7,049	20	3	23	427,647	90,262	517,910	47.3	1,093,820	7,466.30	2,041.55
703	5,767	212	8,443	17,874	58	49	107	1,202,952	271,474	1,474,426	49.3	2,993,721	11,215.29	2,181.77
574	4,196	147	5,995	12,782	17	48	65	880,752	185,479	1,066,231	48.6	2,192,093	11,511.58	2,096.12
74	452	6	766	1,661	0	0	0	116,696	34,633	151,329	60.4	250,389	12,817.45	2,839.46
16	637	38	819	1,797	21	0	21	105,652	24,362	130,015	44.3	293,245	8,835.35	2,105.89
39	482	21	863	1,634	20	1	21	99,852	26,999	126,851	49.2	257,994	10,848.27	2,607.73

Table continues

MSAs

TABLE 8

U.S. CENSUS DIVISION 8, MOUNTAIN CONTINUED

U.S. Community Hospitals
(Nonfederal, short-term general and other special hospitals)

2014 Utilization, Personnel and Finances

MSAs

CLASSIFICATION	Hospitals	Beds	Admissions	Inpatient Days	Adjusted Inpatient Days	Average Daily Census	Adjusted Average Daily Census	Average Stay (days)	Surgical Operations	NEWBORNS		OUTPATIENT VISITS	
										Bassinets	Births	Emergency	Total
Utah	47	5,207	228,979	990,116	2,046,353	2,714	5,606	4.3	258,408	689	48,337	1,045,790	7,410,444
Nonmetropolitan	18	605	16,143	92,769	295,242	254	808	5.7	35,507	104	5,505	124,283	766,076
Metropolitan	29	4,602	212,836	897,347	1,751,111	2,460	4,798	4.2	222,901	585	42,832	921,507	6,644,368
Logan, UT-ID	2	161	7,366	21,255	55,493	58	152	2.9	11,694	34	2,565	28,003	373,010
Ogden-Clearfield, UT.	6	851	36,748	137,643	265,063	378	726	3.7	35,273	114	7,997	164,472	621,281
Provo-Orem, UT.	6	729	35,385	137,101	259,894	375	711	3.9	37,071	133	10,282	130,008	1,169,571
Salt Lake City, UT	14	2,600	118,011	545,284	1,063,283	1,495	2,915	4.6	125,826	288	19,610	553,308	3,979,186
St. George, UT	1	261	15,326	56,064	107,378	154	294	3.7	13,037	16	2,378	45,716	501,320
Wyoming	23	1,835	41,415	360,622	983,904	990	2,697	8.7	36,678	163	6,506	232,288	1,245,267
Nonmetropolitan	21	1,406	23,050	281,591	839,812	773	2,302	12.2	26,511	123	4,108	155,555	991,774
Metropolitan	2	429	18,365	79,031	144,092	217	395	4.3	10,167	40	2,398	76,733	253,493
Casper, WY	1	191	8,807	33,033	51,882	91	142	3.8	5,137	24	1,205	37,287	84,961
Cheyenne, WY	1	238	9,558	45,998	92,210	126	253	4.8	5,030	16	1,193	39,446	168,532

TABLE 8

U.S. CENSUS DIVISION 8, MOUNTAIN CONTINUED

U.S. Community Hospitals
(Nonfederal, short-term general and other special hospitals)

2014 Utilization, Personnel and Finances

FULL-TIME EQUIVALENT PERSONNEL					FULL-TIME EQUIV. TRAINEES			EXPENSES						
								LABOR				TOTAL		
Physicians and Dentists	Registered Nurses	Licensed Practical Nurses	Other Salaried Personnel	Total Personnel	Medical and Dental Residents	Other Trainees	Total Trainees	Payroll (in thousands)	Employee Benefits (in thousands)	Total (in thousands)	Percent of Total	Amount (in thousands)	Adjusted per Admission	Adjusted per inpatient Day
280	10,698	341	18,089	34,745	942	69	1,011	1,883,193	583,918	2,467,113	43.9	5,616,932	11,714.51	2,744.85
70	810	98	1,727	3,119	5	5	10	163,732	43,849	207,581	48.9	424,249	7,290.25	1,436.95
210	9,888	243	16,362	31,626	937	64	1,001	1,719,461	540,069	2,259,532	43.5	5,192,683	12,325.64	2,965.36
3	281	10	792	1,222	0	0	0	54,370	18,266	72,636	43.2	168,177	8,729.19	3,030.59
21	1,474	49	2,347	4,476	30	0	30	244,230	68,770	313,000	43.7	716,905	10,268.34	2,704.66
20	1,445	36	2,442	4,604	52	8	60	232,764	75,231	307,996	43.8	703,057	10,065.82	2,705.17
165	6,171	148	9,986	19,710	855	56	911	1,087,671	344,241	1,431,912	44.2	3,243,169	13,918.64	3,050.15
1	517	0	795	1,614	0	0	0	100,427	33,561	133,988	37.1	361,375	12,311.36	3,365.45
324	2,227	135	4,816	8,880	1	3	4	559,064	151,676	710,739	54.3	1,309,767	12,341.74	1,331.19
226	1,464	112	3,240	5,982	1	0	1	385,979	97,784	483,763	56.1	862,996	11,800.36	1,027.61
98	763	23	1,576	2,898	0	3	3	173,085	53,892	226,976	50.8	446,771	13,541.80	3,100.60
17	311	7	528	1,046	0	3	3	67,589	25,362	92,952	48.7	190,911	13,802.16	3,679.72
81	452	16	1,048	1,852	0	0	0	105,495	28,529	134,024	52.4	255,860	13,353.84	2,774.75

MSAs

TABLE 8

U.S. CENSUS DIVISION 9, PACIFIC

U.S. Community Hospitals
(Nonfederal, short-term general and other special hospitals)

2014 Utilization, Personnel and Finances

MSAs

CLASSIFICATION	Hospitals	Beds	Admissions	Inpatient Days	Adjusted Inpatient Days	Average Daily Census	Adjusted Average Daily Census	Average Stay (days)	Surgical Operations	NEWBORNS Bassinets	NEWBORNS Births	OUTPATIENT VISITS Emergency	OUTPATIENT VISITS Total
UNITED STATES	4,926	786,874	33,066,720	180,456,434	365,636,679	494,388	1,002,304	5.5	26,401,528	55,824	3,735,593	136,327,473	693,106,685
Nonmetropolitan	1,855	116,785	3,238,473	21,307,388	64,127,906	58,370	175,723	6.6	3,512,461	9,506	383,166	21,639,508	119,516,577
Metropolitan.................	3,071	670,089	29,828,247	159,149,046	301,508,773	436,018	826,581	5.3	22,889,067	46,318	3,352,427	114,687,965	573,590,108
CENSUS DIVISION 9, PACIFIC	540	92,663	4,254,171	21,611,365	39,096,398	59,208	107,154	5.1	3,048,483	6,973	614,658	17,311,390	81,256,315
Nonmetropolitan	111	4,669	151,502	871,900	2,659,934	2,387	7,287	5.8	196,262	473	26,723	1,152,773	7,053,936
Metropolitan.................	429	87,994	4,102,669	20,739,465	36,436,464	56,821	99,867	5.1	2,852,221	6,500	587,935	16,158,617	74,202,379
Alaska	22	1,633	53,386	376,135	889,538	1,033	2,436	7.0	52,387	180	8,985	303,956	1,778,701
Nonmetropolitan	16	612	12,649	130,211	441,648	358	1,209	10.3	19,210	51	2,718	92,608	609,145
Metropolitan.................	6	1,021	40,737	245,924	447,890	675	1,227	6.0	33,177	129	6,267	211,348	1,169,556
Anchorage, AK	5	804	35,917	198,635	341,496	545	936	5.5	28,123	113	5,200	175,753	843,986
Fairbanks, AK	1	217	4,820	47,289	106,394	130	291	9.8	5,054	16	1,067	35,595	325,570
California	344	69,441	3,184,754	16,332,640	28,191,587	44,742	77,250	5.1	2,110,590	4,878	471,877	12,693,166	54,139,502
Nonmetropolitan	31	1,319	48,993	250,881	711,589	684	1,951	5.1	59,392	126	8,299	436,490	2,356,737
Metropolitan.................	313	68,122	3,135,761	16,081,759	27,479,998	44,058	75,299	5.1	2,051,198	4,752	463,578	12,256,676	51,782,765
Anaheim-Santa Ana-Irvine, CA...	24	5,364	249,399	1,177,826	2,065,632	3,224	5,657	4.7	172,636	403	39,709	831,772	3,491,428
Bakersfield, CA	10	1,663	65,467	320,291	630,793	877	1,728	4.9	40,943	95	12,301	256,521	880,529
Chico, CA	4	495	29,400	130,705	272,659	357	747	4.4	16,270	43	3,220	121,621	779,320
El Centro, CA	2	268	13,665	37,565	92,710	103	254	2.7	7,941	31	2,976	92,528	302,675
Fresno, CA.............	8	1,772	77,644	433,721	802,005	1,189	2,197	5.6	40,669	101	12,714	212,729	1,744,291
Hanford-Corcoran, CA	2	248	11,625	43,697	110,446	120	303	3.8	13,025	30	2,429	112,701	625,696
Los Angeles-Long Beach-Glendale, CA	87	20,326	943,328	4,803,752	7,822,921	13,160	21,431	5.1	545,894	1,336	127,120	2,994,009	12,314,403
Madera, CA	2	462	16,996	95,915	149,209	263	409	5.6	16,329	10	1,604	138,730	394,689
Merced, CA	2	222	12,197	45,645	86,492	125	237	3.7	7,197	28	1,480	95,705	253,159
Modesto, CA............	4	1,044	52,529	318,197	505,873	872	1,386	6.1	32,803	87	8,461	235,636	458,037
Napa, CA..............	2	290	12,220	54,652	97,691	149	268	4.5	12,057	10	1,051	37,733	281,915
Oakland-Hayward-Berkeley, CA..	19	4,071	185,379	965,395	1,645,270	2,645	4,524	5.2	102,587	302	27,172	1,011,702	4,430,638
Oxnard-Thousand Oaks-Ventura, CA	6	1,221	59,674	302,207	576,592	827	1,579	5.1	36,594	112	10,709	244,726	1,196,303
Redding, CA	3	484	20,325	112,468	233,693	308	640	5.5	12,705	12	2,058	75,416	215,572
Riverside-San Bernardino-Ontario, CA	34	7,182	343,573	1,654,575	2,687,308	4,535	7,362	4.8	211,683	534	50,963	1,457,072	4,037,840
Sacramento-Roseville-Arden-Arcade, CA.............	17	3,934	190,986	941,521	1,566,431	2,578	4,294	4.9	149,067	253	22,856	784,687	3,039,433
Salinas, CA	4	689	31,089	147,958	225,946	405	619	4.8	18,513	79	6,621	152,144	571,549
San Diego-Carlsbad, CA	20	5,274	285,661	1,445,010	2,567,436	3,958	7,033	5.1	205,346	308	41,205	981,907	3,131,196
San Francisco-Redwood City-South San Francisco, CA	16	4,710	143,680	1,138,942	1,822,225	3,122	4,990	7.9	121,199	188	18,029	656,798	4,640,288
San Jose-Sunnyvale-Santa Clara, CA	11	3,031	151,734	786,687	1,373,860	2,156	3,764	5.2	122,161	312	28,855	554,298	4,414,625
San Luis Obispo-Paso Robles-Arroyo Grande, CA	4	432	16,413	67,493	115,194	186	315	4.1	11,794	41	2,470	93,415	209,125
San Rafael, CA	3	329	15,094	63,374	119,744	174	328	4.2	12,082	15	1,416	56,540	287,801
Santa Cruz-Watsonville, CA	3	359	16,669	68,330	112,077	187	307	4.1	17,469	50	3,201	71,788	277,465
Santa Maria-Santa Barbara, CA..	5	898	33,578	211,273	380,045	579	1,042	6.3	24,529	52	6,748	152,645	479,015
Santa Rosa, CA	6	616	31,238	135,728	261,512	372	718	4.3	24,351	44	5,079	107,890	473,561
Stockton-Lodi, CA.........	7	1,165	55,761	232,780	480,234	639	1,315	4.2	35,452	122	9,666	312,233	1,366,587
Vallejo-Fairfield, CA	4	660	26,241	111,124	216,070	304	592	4.2	18,098	65	4,409	131,788	475,961
Visalia-Porterville, CA	3	680	32,269	182,427	357,924	500	981	5.7	15,855	53	7,021	226,958	845,750
Yuba City, CA............	1	233	11,927	52,501	102,006	144	279	4.4	5,949	36	2,035	54,984	163,914
Hawaii	25	2,861	109,311	749,201	1,459,618	2,052	3,999	6.9	77,592	201	10,626	432,641	2,290,796
Nonmetropolitan	9	696	19,320	170,784	410,840	467	1,125	8.8	20,269	45	3,413	96,218	331,196
Metropolitan.................	16	2,165	89,991	578,417	1,048,778	1,585	2,874	6.4	57,323	156	7,213	336,423	1,959,600
Kahului-Wailuku-Lahaina, HI	4	258	10,990	58,669	134,568	161	369	5.3	2,983	26	1,202	22,578	109,074
Urban Honolulu, HI	12	1,907	79,001	519,748	914,210	1,424	2,505	6.6	54,340	130	6,011	313,845	1,850,526
Oregon....................	59	6,740	330,065	1,441,975	2,977,329	3,951	8,158	4.4	310,787	640	42,741	1,440,808	10,805,445
Nonmetropolitan	26	1,041	40,405	166,216	555,607	456	1,522	4.1	42,538	142	6,221	296,143	2,319,169
Metropolitan.................	33	5,699	289,660	1,275,759	2,421,722	3,495	6,636	4.4	268,249	498	36,520	1,144,665	8,486,276
Albany, OR.............	2	95	4,112	14,904	57,171	40	157	3.6	9,025	14	858	45,372	494,459
Bend-Redmond, OR	2	298	17,585	67,296	113,205	184	310	3.8	18,962	33	2,131	57,803	166,198
Corvallis, OR.	1	165	8,743	41,888	74,745	115	205	4.8	9,612	20	1,021	25,459	367,597
Eugene, OR	5	631	33,842	150,362	252,142	413	691	4.4	20,984	52	3,692	142,872	416,231
Grants Pass, OR	1	111	7,000	22,351	44,527	61	122	3.2	4,021	12	753	38,518	227,634
Medford, OR.	3	498	23,152	104,524	184,245	286	505	4.5	21,539	34	2,359	85,612	781,297
Portland-Vancouver-Hillsboro, OR-WA	15	3,379	167,854	758,413	1,452,642	2,078	3,980	4.5	165,510	284	20,835	603,550	5,401,710
Salem, OR.	4	522	27,372	116,021	243,045	318	666	4.2	18,596	49	4,871	145,479	631,150

TABLE 8

U.S. CENSUS DIVISION 9, PACIFIC

U.S. Community Hospitals
(Nonfederal, short-term general and other special hospitals)

2014 Utilization, Personnel and Finances

FULL-TIME EQUIVALENT PERSONNEL					FULL-TIME EQUIV. TRAINEES			EXPENSES						
								LABOR				TOTAL		
Physicians and Dentists	Registered Nurses	Licensed Practical Nurses	Other Salaried Personnel	Total Personnel	Medical and Dental Residents	Other Trainees	Total Trainees	Payroll (in thousands)	Employee Benefits (in thousands)	Total (in thousands)	Percent of Total	Amount (in thousands)	Adjusted per Admission	Adjusted per Inpatient Day
122,747	1,398,346	73,044	2,510,354	4,754,880	109,309	8,533	117,842	$310,203,433	$82,949,525	$393,152,940	48.6	$808,869,209	$12,015.42	$2,212.22
15,090	147,461	20,793	334,968	602,081	1,731	269	2,000	33,192,643	8,842,572	42,035,205	51.3	81,981,991	8,301.59	1,278.41
107,657	1,250,885	52,251	2,175,386	4,152,799	107,578	8,264	115,842	277,010,790	74,106,953	351,117,735	48.3	726,887,218	12,653.89	2,410.83
10,371	183,946	8,048	313,406	592,940	12,209	977	13,186	46,080,522	14,978,248	61,058,760	50.2	121,510,758	15,611.74	3,107.98
839	8,045	705	18,645	32,638	26	13	39	2,274,532	711,533	2,986,064	53.2	5,609,775	12,233.11	2,108.99
9,532	175,901	7,343	294,761	560,302	12,183	964	13,147	43,805,991	14,266,715	58,072,696	50.1	115,900,984	15,823.27	3,180.91
194	2,918	144	5,405	10,278	121	10	131	744,142	226,847	970,989	50.2	1,932,866	16,152.57	2,172.89
115	849	82	2,281	3,942	5	4	9	297,869	98,925	396,794	53.9	736,594	16,633.80	1,667.83
79	2,069	62	3,124	6,336	116	6	122	446,273	127,923	574,195	48.0	1,196,271	15,869.87	2,670.90
72	1,769	62	2,458	5,275	116	6	122	361,961	102,861	464,821	47.2	985,797	15,275.16	2,886.70
7	300	0	666	1,061	0	0	0	84,312	25,062	109,374	52.0	210,474	19,409.23	1,978.25
5,376	136,545	6,581	221,253	426,130	9,219	810	10,029	33,219,033	11,530,459	44,749,485	50.5	88,682,389	15,906.02	3,145.70
96	2,526	251	5,331	9,428	6	5	11	659,742	245,578	905,320	50.3	1,801,077	13,201.66	2,531.06
5,280	134,019	6,330	215,922	416,702	9,213	805	10,018	32,559,291	11,284,881	43,844,165	50.5	86,881,312	15,973.85	3,161.62
145	10,501	272	16,337	31,449	127	2	129	2,124,873	744,081	2,868,955	47.4	6,054,333	13,681.46	2,930.98
171	2,450	169	4,333	8,580	35	4	39	586,694	169,789	756,481	49.9	1,517,191	12,416.86	2,405.21
63	1,088	67	2,001	3,696	22	5	27	305,737	87,790	393,527	50.1	785,212	13,554.96	2,879.83
24	390	32	817	1,514	7	2	9	86,062	22,836	108,898	50.7	214,701	6,385.55	2,315.84
208	2,529	120	5,083	9,180	192	12	204	607,720	169,916	777,637	48.1	1,616,797	11,068.80	2,015.94
0	345	40	1,502	2,066	12	0	12	112,465	37,714	150,179	47.5	316,274	10,456.02	2,863.60
2,017	41,262	2,277	64,212	128,317	3,715	333	4,048	9,116,927	2,973,031	12,089,958	49.3	24,534,915	15,787.75	3,136.29
1	703	39	1,332	2,639	0	4	4	209,827	88,700	298,528	59.8	498,835	18,493.18	3,343.20
0	415	25	664	1,277	24	0	24	107,761	34,357	142,118	49.2	289,100	11,961.61	3,342.51
23	2,530	43	2,494	5,858	19	4	23	455,491	159,067	614,559	52.7	1,166,726	14,648.16	2,306.36
0	526	6	1,074	1,871	0	0	0	145,002	67,162	212,164	47.5	446,528	20,485.76	4,570.82
401	7,478	440	13,682	24,709	346	8	354	2,284,871	891,023	3,175,894	52.8	6,015,418	18,734.72	3,656.19
97	2,003	116	3,371	6,450	67	4	71	589,847	181,026	770,872	50.1	1,538,730	13,311.27	2,668.66
19	889	29	1,221	2,423	26	0	26	191,993	70,222	262,215	50.1	523,127	14,838.37	2,238.52
918	13,838	1,009	19,214	40,788	951	71	1,022	2,643,425	793,582	3,437,006	49.9	6,890,317	12,124.86	2,564.02
261	8,787	236	13,997	25,995	906	6	912	2,441,471	856,469	3,297,941	51.8	6,371,783	19,913.13	4,067.71
39	1,228	35	2,216	4,001	30	0	30	383,961	208,180	592,140	59.5	995,017	20,991.93	4,403.78
23	12,460	409	17,472	34,682	761	302	1,063	2,606,739	741,763	3,348,500	49.3	6,790,674	13,063.43	2,644.92
310	7,078	344	13,985	24,608	191	8	199	2,503,950	1,057,055	3,561,006	52.1	6,831,104	26,775.20	3,748.77
183	6,997	200	13,183	23,457	1,512	20	1,532	2,630,542	1,192,132	3,822,674	53.4	7,162,390	27,176.90	5,213.33
5	694	11	733	1,688	1	0	1	156,317	35,386	191,703	50.9	376,357	13,346.93	3,267.15
22	717	18	1,467	2,474	7	0	7	207,252	66,411	273,663	53.3	512,982	17,829.83	4,283.99
8	690	18	1,116	2,027	8	0	8	216,827	77,508	294,335	58.7	501,114	17,652.92	4,471.15
20	1,478	66	2,144	4,259	59	0	59	360,847	99,798	460,646	43.3	1,063,451	18,756.40	2,798.22
34	1,513	46	2,119	4,181	44	1	45	301,817	124,398	426,213	48.6	877,262	15,022.90	3,354.58
179	2,463	114	4,472	8,338	79	7	86	492,946	136,597	629,542	51.0	1,233,513	10,690.04	2,568.57
56	1,397	47	2,565	4,479	22	5	27	333,698	90,707	424,404	52.8	804,531	15,767.38	3,723.47
25	1,211	87	2,469	4,482	36	5	41	265,434	79,472	344,905	52.4	658,613	10,350.84	1,840.09
28	359	15	647	1,214	14	2	16	88,794	28,709	117,502	39.9	294,318	12,700.90	2,885.30
455	5,011	219	8,522	16,811	46	35	81	1,294,117	349,298	1,643,416	52.2	3,148,443	15,143.23	2,157.03
68	843	60	1,576	2,936	11	1	12	210,833	67,519	278,352	53.8	517,094	11,991.70	1,258.63
387	4,168	159	6,946	13,875	35	34	69	1,083,284	281,779	1,365,064	51.9	2,631,349	15,967.89	2,508.97
43	370	30	785	1,435	15	0	15	105,169	29,907	135,077	49.7	272,044	11,513.64	2,021.61
344	3,798	129	6,161	12,440	20	34	54	978,115	251,871	1,229,987	52.1	2,359,305	16,713.46	2,580.70
1,681	15,002	186	26,524	49,785	1,201	39	1,240	3,747,791	1,167,761	4,915,549	49.4	9,956,535	14,358.14	3,344.12
368	2,071	66	5,205	8,945	0	0	0	624,034	175,829	799,862	54.7	1,461,982	11,131.53	2,631.32
1,313	12,931	120	21,319	40,840	1,201	39	1,240	3,123,757	991,932	4,115,687	48.5	8,494,552	15,112.04	3,507.65
89	276	8	714	1,264	0	2	2	107,561	32,828	140,389	55.2	254,352	15,978.86	4,448.96
72	649	4	1,844	2,769	0	0	0	187,275	57,657	244,932	50.0	489,928	16,288.05	4,327.80
91	351	7	824	1,477	87	15	102	134,646	40,607	175,253	53.1	330,159	21,162.68	4,417.14
85	1,148	13	1,990	3,559	0	0	0	288,060	82,446	370,505	46.8	791,699	13,758.38	3,139.89
12	193	8	486	828	0	0	0	43,383	21,206	64,589	51.9	124,381	8,919.41	2,793.39
32	1,044	13	1,505	3,058	0	1	1	192,721	84,461	277,182	45.8	605,731	14,610.01	3,287.64
822	7,913	57	11,603	23,541	1,114	21	1,135	1,843,287	587,095	2,430,381	47.2	5,147,495	15,704.16	3,543.54
110	1,357	10	2,353	4,344	0	0	0	326,823	85,633	412,456	54.9	750,808	12,559.52	3,089.17

Table continues

MSAs

TABLE 8

U.S. CENSUS DIVISION 9, PACIFIC CONTINUED

U.S. Community Hospitals
(Nonfederal, short-term general and other special hospitals)

2014 Utilization, Personnel and Finances

MSAs

CLASSIFICATION	Hospitals	Beds	Admissions	Inpatient Days	Adjusted Inpatient Days	Average Daily Census	Adjusted Average Daily Census	Average Stay (days)	Surgical Operations	NEWBORNS Bassinets	NEWBORNS Births	OUTPATIENT VISITS Emergency	OUTPATIENT VISITS Total
Washington	90	11,988	576,655	2,711,414	5,578,326	7,430	15,311	4.7	497,127	1,074	80,429	2,440,819	12,241,871
Nonmetropolitan	29	1,001	30,135	153,808	540,250	422	1,480	5.1	54,853	109	6,072	231,314	1,437,689
Metropolitan	61	10,987	546,520	2,557,606	5,038,076	7,008	13,831	4.7	442,274	965	74,357	2,209,505	10,804,182
Bellingham, WA	1	253	14,845	60,072	116,716	165	320	4.0	7,026	20	1,705	18,785	89,430
Bremerton-Silverdale, WA	1	260	13,760	56,173	111,594	154	306	4.1	10,336	22	1,765	67,965	194,693
Kennewick-Richland, WA	4	443	22,196	88,613	204,431	243	560	4.0	18,522	37	4,658	186,575	781,184
Lewiston, ID-WA	1	25	1,182	4,156	16,992	11	47	3.5	2,393	0	0	16,116	85,583
Longview, WA	1	200	7,729	31,667	86,675	87	237	4.1	4,364	14	882	51,768	180,302
Mount Vernon-Anacortes, WA	3	205	10,124	38,850	120,250	107	355	3.8	29,424	27	1,559	49,786	704,082
Olympia-Tumwater, WA	2	432	22,989	99,607	155,110	273	425	4.3	18,344	49	2,811	83,370	353,685
Portland-Vancouver-Hillsboro, OR-WA	2	664	33,656	138,843	250,293	381	686	4.1	12,403	82	4,884	84,153	369,654
Seattle-Bellevue-Everett, WA	21	4,760	255,515	1,222,132	2,378,826	3,347	6,519	4.8	194,289	409	33,541	919,202	5,566,909
Spokane-Spokane Valley, WA	9	1,596	59,032	330,357	601,740	905	1,649	5.6	57,837	104	7,089	219,749	683,197
Tacoma-Lakewood, WA	6	1,289	69,184	322,496	628,045	884	1,720	4.7	50,331	95	9,474	302,803	850,000
Walla Walla, WA	3	162	5,654	34,898	75,574	95	208	6.2	6,962	22	812	28,347	204,024
Wenatchee, WA	3	232	11,588	53,116	97,679	146	267	4.6	9,243	25	1,475	43,763	207,104
Yakima, WA	4	466	19,066	76,626	194,151	210	532	4.0	20,800	59	3,702	137,123	534,335

TABLE 8

U.S. Community Hospitals
(Nonfederal, short-term general and other special hospitals)

2014 Utilization, Personnel and Finances

FULL-TIME EQUIVALENT PERSONNEL					FULL-TIME EQUIV. TRAINEES			EXPENSES						
								LABOR				TOTAL		
Physicians and Dentists	Registered Nurses	Licensed Practical Nurses	Other Salaried Personnel	Total Personnel	Medical and Dental Residents	Other Trainees	Total Trainees	Payroll (in thousands)	Employee Benefits (in thousands)	Total (in thousands)	Percent of Total	Amount (in thousands)	Adjusted per Admission	Adjusted per Inpatient Day
2,665	24,470	918	51,702	89,936	1,622	83	1,705	7,075,440	1,703,883	8,779,321	49.3	17,790,526	14,989.36	3,189.22
192	1,756	246	4,252	7,387	4	3	7	482,054	123,682	605,736	55.4	1,093,027	10,570.45	2,023.19
2,473	22,714	672	47,450	82,549	1,618	80	1,698	6,593,386	1,580,201	8,173,585	49.0	16,697,499	15,411.09	3,314.26
60	747	32	1,339	2,548	32	1	33	165,541	48,145	213,686	51.1	418,206	14,499.40	3,583.11
0	0	0	2,018	2,018	0	0	0	161,799	43,158	204,957	53.3	384,370	14,060.95	3,444.36
168	973	51	2,177	4,057	10	1	11	297,341	72,373	369,714	53.1	696,058	13,657.03	3,404.85
12	90	11	221	383	1	2	3	23,111	6,242	29,353	50.3	58,386	12,080.70	3,436.09
63	332	4	739	1,299	0	0	0	102,534	30,169	132,703	52.9	250,735	11,852.26	2,892.81
96	513	15	1,363	2,303	21	2	23	152,377	32,469	184,846	50.8	364,163	11,569.92	3,028.38
11	831	28	1,241	2,424	1	24	25	177,051	22,038	199,089	53.2	373,994	10,242.75	2,411.15
129	1,358	31	2,368	4,399	69	4	73	308,399	84,704	393,102	51.4	764,462	12,650.38	3,054.27
1,373	11,537	244	23,530	41,174	1,398	25	1,423	3,528,314	865,439	4,393,751	48.4	9,077,845	18,212.48	3,816.10
57	2,229	41	3,971	6,994	6	13	19	527,078	82,647	609,725	40.0	1,525,842	14,811.26	2,535.72
373	2,404	142	5,260	8,950	78	4	82	761,886	197,553	959,439	55.4	1,730,350	12,823.20	2,755.14
77	356	26	722	1,418	1	2	3	99,210	12,979	112,189	55.3	202,796	12,496.67	2,683.41
14	520	13	677	1,538	0	0	0	101,517	26,300	127,818	43.8	291,793	14,418.80	2,987.27
40	824	34	1,824	3,044	1	2	3	187,228	55,985	243,213	43.5	558,498	11,384.68	2,876.62

MSAs

Statistics for Health Care Systems and their Hospitals

The following tables describing health care systems refers to information in section B of the 2016 *AHA Guide*. Table 1 shows the number of health care systems by type of control. Table 2 provides a breakdown of the number of systems that own, lease, sponsor or contract manage hospitals within each control category. Table 3 gives the number of hospitals and beds in each control category as well as total hospitals and beds. Finally, shows the percentage of hospitals and beds in each control category.

For more information on health care systems, please write to the Section for Health Care Systems, 155 N. Wacker Drive, Chicago, Illinois 60606 or call 312/422–3000.

Table 1. Multihospital Health Care Systems, by Type of Organizaton Control

Type of Control	Code	Number of Systems
Catholic (Roman) church–related	CC	31
Other church–related	CO	7
Subtotal, church–related		38
Other not–for–profit	NP	307
Subtotal, not–for–profit		345
Investor Owned	IO	82
Federal Government	FG	5
Total		432

Table 2. Multihospital Health Care Systems, by Type of Ownership and Control

Type of Ownership	Catholic Church–Related (CC)	Other Church–Related (CO)	Total Church–Related (CC + CO)	Other Not–for–Profit (NP)	Total Not–for–Profit (CC, CO, + NP)	Investor–Owned (IO)	Federal Govern–ment (FG)	All Systems
Systems that only own, lease or sponsor	23	5	28	268	296	71	5	372
Systems that only contract–manage	0	0	0	3	3	3	0	6
Systems that manage, own, lease, or sponsor	8	2	10	34	44	8	0	52
Total	31	7	38	305	343	82	5	430

Table 3. Hospitals and Beds in Multihospital Health Care Systems, by Type of Ownership and Control

Type of Ownership	Catholic Church–Related (CC) H	B	Other Church–Related (CO) H	B	Total Church–Related (CC + CO) H	B	Other Not–for–Profit (NP) H	B	Total Not–for–Profit (CC, CO, + NP) H	B	Investor–Owned (IO) H	B	Federal Govern–ment (FG) H	B	All Systems H	B
Owned, leased or sponsored	579	105,147	74	16,564	653	121,711	1,536	327,830	2,189	449,541	1,369	162,067	212	40,484	3,770	652,092
Contract–managed	44	2,016	3	497	47	2,513	104	9,315	151	11,828	108	6,185	0	0	259	18,013
Total	623	107,163	77	17,061	700	124,224	1,640	337,145	2,340	461,369	1,477	168,252	212	40,484	4,029	670,105

H = hospitals; **B** = beds.

Table 4. Hospitals and Beds in Multihospital Health Care Systems, by Type of Ownership and Control as a Percentage of All Systems

Type of Ownership	Catholic Church–Related (CC) H	B	Other Church–Related (CO) H	B	Total Church–Related (CC + CO) H	B	Other Not–for–Profit (NP) H	B	Total Not–for–Profit (CC, CO, + NP) H	B	Investor–Owned (IO) H	B	Federal Govern–ment (FG) H	B	All Systems H	B
Owned, leased or sponsored	15.4	16.1	2.0	2.5	17.3	18.7	40.7	50.3	58.1	68.9	36.3	24.9	5.6	6.2	100.0	100.0
Contract–managed	17.0	11.2	1.2	2.8	18.1	14.0	40.2	51.7	58.3	65.7	41.7	34.3	0.0	0.0	100.0	100.0
Total	15.5	16.0	1.9	2.5	17.4	18.5	40.7	50.3	58.1	68.9	36.7	25.1	5.3	6.0	100.0	100.0

H = hospitals; **B** = beds.
*Please note that figures may not always equal the provided subtotal or total percentages due to rounding.

Glossary

This glossary explains specific terms as they are used in the tables and text of AHA Hospital Statistics

Ablation of Barrett's esophagus: Premalignant condition that can lead to adenocarcinoma of the esophagus. The non surgical ablation of the premalignant tissue in Barrett's esophagus by the application of thermal energy or light through an endoscope passed from the mouth into the esophagus.

Acute long term care: Providers specialized acute hospital care to medically complex patients who are critically ill, have multisystem complications and/or failure, and require hospitalization averaging 25 days, in a facility offering specialized treatment programs and therapeutic intervention on a 24 hour/7day a week basis.

Adjusted admission: An aggregate measure of workload reflecting the sum of admissions and equivalent admissions attributed to outpatient services. The number of equivalent admissions attributed to outpatient services is derived by multiplying admissions by the ratio of outpatient revenue to inpatient revenue.

$$\text{Adjusted admissions} = \text{admissions} + \left[\text{admissions} * \left(\frac{\text{outpatient revenue}}{\text{inpatient revenue}} \right) \right]$$

Adjusted average daily census: An estimate of the average number of patients (both inpatients and outpatients) receiving care each day during the reporting period, which is usually 12 months. The figure is derived by dividing the number of inpatient day equivalents (also called adjusted inpatient days) by the number of days in the reporting period.

Adjusted inpatient days: An aggregate measure of workload reflecting the sum of inpatient days and equivalent patient days attributed to outpatient services. The number of equivalent patient days attributed to outpatient services is derived by multiplying inpatient days by the ratio of outpatient revenue to inpatient revenue.

$$\text{Adjusted inpatient days} = \text{inpatient days} + \left[\text{inpatient days} * \left(\frac{\text{outpatient revenue}}{\text{inpatient revenue}} \right) \right]$$

Admissions: The number of patients, excluding newborns, accepted for inpatient service during the reporting period; the number includes patients who visit the emergency room and are later admitted for inpatient service.

Adult Cardiac Surgery: Includes minimally invasive procedures that include surgery done with only a small incision or no incision at all, such as through a laparoscope or an endoscope and more invasive major surgical procedures that include open chest and open heart surgery.

Adult Cardiology Services: An organized clinical service offering diagnostic and interventional procedures to manage the full range of adult heart conditions.

Adult day care program: Program providing supervision, medical and psychological care, and social activities for older adults who live at home or in another family setting, but cannot be alone or prefer to be with others during the day. May include intake assessment, health monitoring, occupational therapy, personal care, noon meal, and transportation services.

Adult Diagnostic/invasive catheterization: (also called coronary angiography or coronary arteriography) is used to assist in diagnosing complex heart conditions. Cardiac angiography involves the insertion of a tiny catheter into the artery in the groin then carefully threading the catheter up into the aorta where the coronary arteries originate. Once the catheter is in place, a dye is injected which allows the cardiologist to see the size, shape, and distribution of the coronary arteries. These images are used to diagnose heart disease and to determine, among other things, whether or not surgery is indicated.

Adult Interventional cardiac catheterization: Non surgical procedure that utilizes the same basic principles as diagnostic catheterization and then uses advanced techniques to improve the heart's function. It can be a less-invasive alternative to heart surgery.

Airborne infection isolation room: A single-occupancy room for patient care where environmental factors are controlled in an effort to minimize the transmission of those infectious agents, usually spread person to person by droplet nuclei associated with coughing and inhalation. Such rooms typically have specific ventilation requirements for controlled ventilation, air pressure and filtration.

Alcoholism-drug abuse or dependency inpatient care: Provides diagnosis and therapeutic services to patients with alcoholism or other drug dependencies. Includes care for inpatient/residential treatment for patients whose course of treatment involves more intensive care than provided in an outpatient setting or where patient requires supervised withdrawal.

Alcoholism-drug abuse or dependency outpatient services: Organized hospital services that provide medical care and/or rehabilitative treatment services to outpatients for whom the primary diagnosis is alcoholism or other chemical dependency.

Alzheimer Center: Facility that offers care to persons with Alzheimer's disease and their families through an integrated program of clinical services, research, and education.

Ambulance services: Provision of ambulance services to the ill and injured who require medical attention on a scheduled or unscheduled basis.

Ambulatory Surgery Center: Facility that provides care to patients requiring surgery who are admitted and discharged on the same day. Ambulatory surgery centers are distinct from same day surgical units within the hospital outpatient departments for purposes of Medicare payments.

Arthritis treatment center: Specifically equipped and staffed center for the diagnosis and treatment of arthritis and other joint disorders.

Assisted living: A special combination of housing, supportive services, personalized assistance and health care designed to respond to the individual needs of those who need help in activities of daily living and instrumental activities of daily living. Supportive services are available, 24 hours a day, to meet scheduled and unscheduled needs, in a way that promotes maximum independence and dignity for each resident and encourages the involvement of a resident's family, neighbor and friends.

Assistive Technology Center: A program providing access to specialized hardware and software with adaptations allowing individuals greater independence with mobility, dexterity, or increased communication options.

Auxiliary: A volunteer community organization formed to assist the hospital in carrying out its purpose and to serve as a link between the institution and the community.

Average daily census: The average number of people served on an inpatient basis on a single day during the reporting period; the figure is calculated by dividing the number of inpatient days by the number of days in the reporting period.

Bariatric/weight control services: Bariatrics is the medical practice of weight reduction.

Beds: Number of beds regularly maintained (set up and staffed for use) for inpatients as of the close of the reporting period. Excludes newborn bassinets.

Bed-size category: Hospitals are categorized by the number of beds set up and staffed for use at the end of the reporting period. The eight categories in Hospital Statistics are: 6 to 24 beds; 25 to 49; 50 to 99; 100 to 199; 200 to 299; 300 to 399; 400 to 499; and 500 or more.

Birthing room-LDR room-LDRP room: A single-room type of maternity care with a more homelike setting for families than the traditional three-room unit (labor/delivery/recovery) with a separate postpartum area. A birthing room combines labor and delivery in one room. An LDR room accommodates three stages in the birthing process—labor, delivery, and recovery. An LDRP room accommodates all four stages of the birth process—labor, delivery, recovery, and postpartum.

Births: Total number of infants born in the hospital during the reporting period. Births do not include infants transferred from other institutions, and are excluded from admission and discharge figures.

Blood Donor Center: A facility that performs, or is responsible for the collection, processing, testing or distribution of blood and components.

Bone marrow transplant: See definition for Transplant service on page 216.

Breast cancer screening/mammograms: Mammography screening – The use of breast x-ray to detect unsuspected breast cancer in asymptomatic women. Diagnostic mammography – The x-ray imaging of breast tissue in symptomatic women who are considered to have a substantial likelihood of having breast cancer already.

Burn care: Provides care to severely burned patients. Severely burned patients are those with any of the following: (1) second-degree burns of more than 25% total body surface area for adults or 20% total body surface area for children: (2) third-degree burns of more than 10% total body surface area; (3) any severe burns of the hands, face, eyes, ears, or feet; or (4) all inhalation injuries, electrical burns, complicated burn injuries involving fractures and other major traumas, and all other poor risk factors.

Cardiac electrophysiology: Evaluation and management of patients with complex rhythm or conduction abnormalities, including diagnostic testing, treatment of arrhythmias by catheter ablation or drug therapy, and pacemaker/defibrillator implantation and follow-up.

Cardiac intensive care: Provides patient care of a more specialized nature than the usual medical and surgical care, on the basis of physicians' orders and approved nursing care plans. The unit is staffed with specially trained nursing personnel and contains monitoring and specialized support or treatment equipment for patients who, because of heart seizure, open-heart surgery, or other life-threatening conditions, require intensified, comprehensive observation and care. May include myocardial infarction, pulmonary care, and heart transplant units.

Cardiac Rehabilitation: A medically supervised program to help heart patients recover quickly and improve their overall physical and mental functioning. The goal is to reduce risk of another cardiac event or to keep an already present heart condition from getting worse. Cardiac rehabilitation programs include: counseling to patients, an exercise program, helping patients modify risk factors such as smoking and high blood pressure, providing vocational guidance to enable the patient to return to work, supplying information on physical limitations and lending emotional support.

Case management: A system of assessment, treatment planning, referral and follow-up that ensures the provision of comprehensive and continuous services and the coordination of payment and reimbursement for care.

Chaplaincy/pastoral care services: A service ministering religious activities and providing pastoral counseling to patients, their families, and staff of a health care organization.

Chemotherapy: An organized program for the treatment of cancer by the use of drugs or chemicals.

Children's wellness program: A program that encourages improved health status and a healthful lifestyle of children through health education, exercise, nutrition and health promotion.

Chiropractic services: An organized clinical service including spinal manipulation or adjustment and related diagnostic and therapeutic services.

Closed physician-hospital organization (Closed PHO): A joint venture between the hospital and physicians who have been selected on the basis of cost-effectiveness and/or high quality. The PHO can act as a unified agent in managed care contracting, own a managed care plan, own and operate ambulatory care centers or ancillary services projects, or provide administrative services to physician members.

Community health education: Education that provides health information to individuals and populations, as well as support for personal, family and community health decisions with the objective of improving health status.

Community hospitals: All nonfederal, short-term general, and special hospitals whose facilities and services are available to the public. (Special hospitals include obstetrics and gynecology; eye, ear, nose, and throat; rehabilitation; orthopedic; and other individually described specialty services.) Short-term general and special childrens hospitals are also considered to be community hospitals.

A hospital may include a nursing-home-type unit and still be classified as short-term, provided that the majority of its patients are admitted to units where the average length of stay is less than 30 days. Therefore, statistics for community hospitals often include some data about such nursing-home-type units. An example

is furnished by Montana, where in 1995 63.6 percent of all hospitals classified as community hospitals include nursing-home-type units. Expense, revenue, utilization, and personnel data for these hospitals include data about their nursing-home-type units. Thus, total admissions to Montana community hospitals in 1995 were 96,154; total inpatient days, 997,759; total expenses, $791,806,393; and total payroll expenses, $352,583,331. If nursing-home-type unit data were excluded, these same items would be 94,034; 457,340; 752,567,865; and $328,911841, respectively.

Note that before 1972, hospital units of institutions such as prison and college infirmaries were included in the category of community hospitals. Including these units made this category equivalent to the short-term general and other special hospitals category. Although these hospital units are few in number and small in size, this change in definition should be taken into consideration when comparing data.

Community outreach: A program that systematically interacts with the community to identify those in need of services, alerting persons and their families to the availability of services, locating needed services, and enabling persons to enter the service delivery system.

Complementary and alternative medicine services: Organized hospital services or formal arrangements to providers that provide care or treatment not based solely on traditional western allopathic medical teachings as instructed in most U.S. medical schools. Includes any of the following: acupuncture, chiropractic, homeopathy, osteopathy, diet and lifestyle changes, herbal medicine, message therapy, etc.

Computer assisted orthopedic surgery (CAOS): Orthopedic surgery using computer technology, enabling three-dimensional graphic models to visualize a patient's anatomy.

Control: The type of organization responsible for establishing policy concerning the overall operation of hospitals. The three major categories are government (including federal, state, and local); nongovernment (nonprofit); and investor-owned (for-profit).

Crisis prevention: Services provided in order to promote physical and mental well being and the early identification of disease and ill health prior to the onset and recognition of symptoms so as to permit early treatment.

CT scanner: Computed tomographic scanner for head or whole body scans.

Deduction from revenue: The difference between revenue at full established rates (gross) and the payment actually received from payers (net).

Dental Services: An organized dental service or dentists on staff, not necessarily involving special facilities, providing dental or oral services to inpatients or outpatients.

Diagnostic radioisotope facility: The use of radioactive isotopes (Radiopharmaceuticals) as tracers or indicators to detect an abnormal condition or disease.

Electrodiagnostic Services: Diagnostic testing services for nerve and muscle function including services such as nerve conduction studies and needle electromyography.

Electron beam computed tomography (EBCT): A high tech computed tomography scan used to detect coronary artery disease by measuring coronary calcifications. This imaging procedure uses electron beams which are magnetically steered to produce a visual of the coronary artery and the images are produced faster than conventional CT scans.

Emergency department: Hospital facilities for the provision of unscheduled outpatient services to patients whose conditions require immediate care.

Emergency room visits: The number of visits to the emergency unit. When emergency outpatients are admitted to the inpatient areas of the hospital, they are counted as emergency room visits and subsequently, as inpatient admissions.

Emergency services: Health services that are provided after the onset of a medical condition that manifests itself by symptoms of sufficient severity, including severe pain, that the absence of immediate medical attention could reasonably be expected by a prudent layperson, who possesses an average knowledge of health and medicine, to result in placing the patient's health in serious jeopardy.

Enabling services: A program that is designed to help the patient access health care services by offering any of the following: transportation services and/or referrals to local social services agencies.

End of Life: Services offered to patients suffering from chronic, severe, and life-threatening diseases including comprehensive services that give patients and caregivers the resources and the confidence to manage symptoms, avoid emergency room admissions and frequent hospitalization, and remain in familiar and comfortable settings.

Endoscopic retrograde cholangiopancreatography (ERCP): A procedure in which a catheter is introduced through an endoscope into the bile ducts and pancreatic ducts. Injection of contrast materials permits detailed x-ray of these structures. The procedure is used diagnostically as well as therapeutically to relieve obstruction or remove stones.

Endoscopic ultrasound: Specially designed endoscope that incorporates an ultrasound transductor used to obtain detailed images of organs in the chest and abdomen. The endoscope can be passed through the mouth or the anus. When combined with needle biopsy the procedure can assist in diagnosis and staging of cancer.

Enrollment (insurance) assistance services: A program that provides enrollment assistance for patients who are potentially eligible for public health insurance programs such as Medicaid, State Children's Health Insurance, or local/state indigent care programs. The specific services offered could include explanation of benefits, assist applicants in completing the application and locating all relevant documents, conduct eligibility interviews, and/or forward applications and documentation to state/local social service or health agency.

Equity model: An arrangement that allows established practitioners to become shareholders in a professional corporation in exchange for tangible and intangible assets of their existing practices.

Esophageal impedance study: A test in which a catheter is placed through the nose into the esophagus to measure whether gas or liquids are passing from the stomach into the esophagus and causing symptoms.

Expenses: Includes all expenses for the reporting period including payroll, non-payroll, and all operating expenses. *Payroll expenses* include all salaries and wages. *Non-payroll expenses* are all professional fees and those salary expenditures excluded from payroll. *Labor related expenses* are defined as payroll expenses plus employee benefits. *Non-labor related expenses* are all other non-payroll expenses. Bad debt has been reclassified from an expense to a deduction from revenue in accordance with the revised AICPA Audit Guide. Note: Financial data may not add due to rounding.

Expenses per adjusted admission stay: Total expenses divided by adjusted admissions (see *adjusted admission*).

Expenses per adjusted inpatient days: Expenses divided by adjusted inpatient days (see *adjusted inpatient days*).

Extracorporeal shock wave lithotripter (ESWL): A medical device used for treating stones in the kidney or urethra. The device disintegrates kidney stones noninvasively through the transmission of acoustic shock waves directed at the stones.

Fertility Clinic: A specialized program set in an infertility center that provides counseling and education as well as advanced reproductive techniques such as: injectable therapy, reproductive surgeries, treatment for endometriosis, male factor infertility, tubal reversals, in vitro fertilization (IVF), donor eggs, and other such services to help patients achieve successful pregnancies.

Fitness center: Provides exercise, testing, or evaluation programs and fitness activities to the community and hospital employees.

Foundation: A corporation, organized as a hospital affiliate or subsidiary, that purchases both tangible and intangible assets of one or more medical group practices. Physicians remain in a separate corporate entity but sign a professional services agreement with the foundation.

Freestanding outpatient care center: A facility owned and operated by the hospital, that is physically separate from the hospital and provides various medical treatments and diagnostic services on an outpatient basis only. Laboratory and radiology services are usually available.

Full-field digital mammography (FFDM): Combines the x-ray generators and tubes used in analog screen-film mammography (SFM) with a detector plate that converts the x-rays into a digital signal.

Full time equivalent employees (FTE): Full time personnel on payroll plus one half of the part time personnel on payroll. For purposes of *AHA Hospital Statistics*, full time and part time medical and dental residents/interns and other trainees are excluded from the calculation.

General medical-surgical care: Provides acute care to patients in medical and surgical units on the basis of physicians' orders and approved nursing care plans.

Genetic testing/counseling: A service equipped with adequate laboratory facilities and directed by a qualified physician to advise parents and prospective parents on potential problems in cases of genetic defects. A genetic test is the analysis of human DNA, RNA, chromosomes, proteins, and certain metabolites in order to detect heritable disease-related genotypes, mutations, phenotypes, or karyotypes for clinical purposes. Genetic tests can have diverse purposes, including the diagnosis of genetic diseases in newborns, children, and adults; the identification of future health risks; the prediction of drug responses; and the assessment of risks to future children.

Geriatric services: The branch of medicine dealing with the physiology of aging and the diagnosis and treatment of disease affecting the aged. Services could include: Adult day care; Alzheimer's diagnostic-assessment services; Comprehensive geriatric assessment; Emergency response system; Geriatric acute care unit; and/or Geriatric clinics.

Government, nonfederal, state, local: Controlled by an agency of state, county, or city government.

Gross inpatient revenue: Revenue from services rendered to inpatients at full established rates (also known as "charges").

Gross outpatient revenue: Revenue from services rendered to outpatients at full established rates.

Group practice without walls: In this organization, the hospital sponsors the formation of a physician group or provides capital to physicians to establish one. The group shares administrative expenses,

although the physicians remain independent practitioners.

Group Purchasing Organization: An organization whose primary function is to negotiate contracts for the purpose of purchasing for members of the group or has a central supply site for its members.

Health fair: Community health education events that focus on the prevention of disease and promotion of health through such activities as audiovisual exhibits and free diagnostic services.

Health maintenance organization (HMO): A health care organization that acts as both insurer and provider of comprehensive but specified medical services in return for prospective per capita (capitation) payments.

Health Research: Organized hospital research program in any of the following areas: basic research, clinical research, community health research, and/or research on innovative health care delivery.

Health screening: A preliminary procedure such as a test or examination to detect the most characteristic sign or signs of a disorder that may require further investigation.

Heart transplant: See definition for Transplant services on page 216.

Hemodialysis: Provision of equipment and personnel for the treatment of renal insufficiency on an inpatient or outpatient basis.

HIV-AIDS services: (could include). *HIV-AIDS unit* – Special unit or team designated and equipped specifically for diagnosis, treatment, continuing care planning, and counseling services for HIV-AIDS patients and their families. *General inpatient care for HIV-AIDS* – Inpatient diagnosis and treatment for human immunodeficiency virus and acquired immunodeficiency syndrome patients, but dedicated unit is not available. *Specialized outpatient program for HIV-AIDS* – Special outpatient program providing diagnostic, treatment, continuing care planning, and counseling for HIV-AIDS patients and their families.

Home health services: Service providing nursing, therapy, and health-related homemaker or social services in the patient's home.

Hospice: A program providing palliative care, chiefly medical relief of pain and supportive services, addressing the emotional, social, financial, and legal needs of terminally ill patients and their families. Care can be provided in a variety of settings, both inpatient and at home.

Hospital unit: The hospital operation, excluding activity pertaining to nursing-home-type unit (as described below), for the following items: Admissions, Beds, FTEs (full-time, part-time, and total), Inpatient Days, Length of Stay, Net Revenue, and Total Expense.

Hospital unit of institutions: A hospital unit that is not open to the public and is contained within a nonhospital unit. An example is an infirmary that is contained within a college.

Hospitals in a network: Hospitals participating in a group that may include other hospitals, physicians, other providers, insurers, and/or community agencies that work together to coordinate and deliver a broad spectrum of services to the community.

Hospitals in a system: Hospitals belonging to a corporate body that owns and/or manages health provider facilities or health-related subsidiaries; the system may also own non-health-related facilities.

Image-guided radiation therapy (IGRT): Automated system for image-guided radiation therapy that enables clinicians to obtain high-resolution x-ray images to pinpoint tumor sites, adjust patient positioning when necessary, and complete a treatment, all within the standard treatment time slot, allowing for more effective cancer treatments.

Immunization program: Program that plans, coordinates and conducts immunization services in the community.

Indemnity fee for service: The traditional type of health insurance, in which the insured is reimbursed for covered expenses without regard to choice of provider. Payment up to a stated limit may be made either to the individual incurring and claiming the expense, or directly to providers.

Independent practice association (IPA): An IPA is a legal entity that holds managed care contracts and contracts with physicians, usually in solo practice, to provide care either on a fee-for-services or capitated basis. The purpose of an IPA is to assist solo physicians in obtaining managed care contracts.

Indigent care clinic: Health care services for uninsured and underinsured persons where care is free of charge or charged on a sliding scale. This would include "free clinics" staffed by volunteer practitioners, but could also be staffed by employees with sponsoring health care organizations subsidizing the cost of service.

Inpatient days: The number of adult and pediatric days of care, excluding newborn days of care, rendered during the entire reporting period.

Inpatient palliative care unit: An inpatient palliative care ward is a physically discreet, inpatient nursing unit where the focus is palliative care. The patient care focus is on symptom relief for complex patients who may be continuing to undergo primary treatment. Care is delivered by palliative medicine specialists.

Inpatient surgeries: Surgical services provided to patients who remain in the hospital overnight.

Insurance product: In tables 3 through 6, the insurance product can be owned by the hospital, the hospital's system or network, or co-owned with an insurer.

Integrated salary model: In this arrangement, physicians are salaried by the hospital or other entity of a health system to provide medical services for primary care and specialty care.

Intensity-Modulated Radiation Therapy (IMRT): A type of three-dimensional radiation therapy, which improves the targeting of treatment delivery in a way that is likely to decrease damage to normal tissues and allows varying intensities.

Intermediate nursing care: Provides health-related services (skilled nursing care and social services) to residents with a variety of physical conditions or functional disabilities. These residents do not require the care provided by a hospital or skilled nursing facility, but do need supervision and support services.

Intraoperative magnetic resonance imaging: An integrated surgery system which provides an MRI system in an operating room. The system allows for immediate evaluation of the degree to tumor resection while the patient is undergoing a surgical resection. Intraoperative MRI exists when a MRI (low-field or high-field) is placed in the operating theater and is used during surgical resection without moving the patient from the operating room to the diagnostic imaging suite.

Investor-owned, for-profit: Investor-owned, for-profit hospitals are those controlled on a for-profit basis by an individual, partnership, or profit-making corporation.

Kidney transplant: See definition for Transplant sevices on page 216.

Labor-related expenses: Payroll expenses plus employee benefits. *Non-labor-related expenses refers* to all other nonpayroll expenses, such as interest depreciation, supplies, purchased services, professional fees, and others.

Length of stay (LOS): LOS refers to the average number of days a patient stays at the facility. Short-term hospitals are those where the average LOS is less than 30 days. Long-term hospitals are those where the average LOS is 30 days or more. The figure is derived by dividing the number of inpatient days by the number of admissions.

Note that this publication carries two LOS variables: *total facility length of stay and hospital unit length of stay. Total facility* includes admissions and inpatient days from nursing-home-type units under control of the hospital. In *hospital unit length of stay*, nursing home utilization is subtracted.

Licensed practical nurse (LPN): A nurse who has graduated from an approved school of practical (vocational) nursing and works under the supervision of registered nurses and/or physicians.

Linguistic/Translation services: Services provided by the hospital designed to make health care more accessible to non-English speaking patients and their physicians.

Liver transplant: See definition for Transplant on page 216.

Long-term: Hospitals are classified either short-term or long-term according to the average length of stay (LOS). A long-term hospital is one in which the average LOS is 30 days or more.

Lung transplant: See definition for Transplant services on page 216.

Magnetic resonance imaging (MRI): The use of a uniform magnetic field and radio frequencies to study tissue and structure of the body. This procedure enables the visualization of biochemical activity of the cell in vivo without the use of ionizing radiation, radio-isotopic substances, or high-frequency sound.

Magnetoencephalography: a noninvasive neurophysiological measurement tool used to study magnetic fields generated by neuronal activity of the brain. The primary uses of MEG include assisting surgeons in localizing the source of epilepsy, sensory mapping, and the study of brain function. When it is combined with structural imaging, it is known as magnetic source imaging (MSI).

Managed care: A term covering a broad spectrum of arrangements for health care delivery and financing, including managed indemnity plans (MIP), health maintenance organizations (HMO), preferred provider organizations (PPO), point-of-service plans (POS), and direct contracting arrangements between employers and providers.

Managed care contract: A contract between the hospital and a managed care organization.

Management services organization (MSO): A corporation owned by the hospital or a physician/hospital joint venture that provides management services to one or more medical group practices. As part of a full-service management agreement, the MSO purchases the tangible assets of the practices and leases them back, employs all non-physician staff, and provides all supplies/administrative systems for a fee.

Meals on wheels: A hospital sponsored program which delivers meals to people, usually the elderly, who are unable to prepare their own meals. Low cost, nutritional meals are delivered to individuals' homes on a regular basis.

Medical surgical intensive care: Provides patient care of a more intensive nature than the usual medical and surgical care, on the basis of physicians' orders and approved nursing care plans. These units are staffed with specially trained nursing personnel and contain monitoring and specialized support equipment for patients who, because of shock, trauma, or other life-threatening conditions, require

intensified, comprehensive observation and care. Includes mixed intensive care units.

Mobile health services: Vans and other vehicles used to deliver primary care services.

Multi-slice spiral computed tomography (<64 slice CT): A specialized computed tomography procedure that provides three-dimensional processing and allows narrower and multiple slices with increased spatial resolution and faster scanning times as compared to a regular computed tomography scan.

Multi-slice spiral computed tomography (64+ slice CT): Involves the acquisition of volumetric tomographic x-ray absorption data expressed in Hounsfield units using multiple rows of detectors. 64+ systems reconstruct the equivalent of 64 or greater slices to cover the imaged volume.

Neonatal intensive care: A unit that must be separate from the newborn nursery providing intensive care to all sick infants including those with the very lowest birth weights (less than 1500 grams). NICU has potential for providing mechanical ventilation, neonatal surgery, and special care for the sickest infants born in the hospital or transferred from another institution. A full-time neonatologist serves as director of the NICU.

Neonatal intermediate care: A unit that must be separate from the normal newborn nursery and that provides intermediate and/or recovery care and some specialized services, including immediate resuscitation, intravenous therapy, and capacity for prolonged oxygen therapy and monitoring.

Net patient revenue: The estimated net realizable amounts from patients, third-party payers, and others for services rendered. The number includes estimated retroactive adjustments called for by agreements with third-party payers; retroactive adjustments are accrued on an estimated basis in the period the related services are rendered and then adjusted later as final settlements are determined.

Net total revenue: Net patient revenue plus all other revenue, including contributions, endowment revenue, governmental grants, and all other payments not made on behalf of individual patients.

Neurological services: Services provided by the hospital dealing with the operative and nonoperative management of disorders of the central, peripheral, and autonomic nervous system.

Nongovernment, nonprofit: Hospitals that are nongovernment, nonprofit are controlled by not-for-profit organizations, including religious organizations (Catholic hospitals, for example), fraternal societies, and others.

Nursing-home-type unit/facility: A unit/ facility that primarily offers the following type of services to a majority of all admissions:

- *Skilled nursing:* The provision of medical and nursing care services, health-related services, and social services under the supervision of a registered nurse on a 24-hour basis.

- *Intermediate care:* The provision, on a regular basis, of health-related care and services to individuals who do not require the degree of care or treatment that a skilled nursing unit is designed to provide.

- *Personal care:* The provision of general supervision and direct personal care services for residents who require assistance in activities of daily living but who do not need nursing services or inpatient care. Medical and nursing services are available as needed.

- *Sheltered/residential care:* The provision of general supervision and protective services for residents who do not need nursing services or continuous personal care services in the conduct of daily life. Medical and nursing services are available as needed.

Nutrition programs: Those services within a health care facility which are designed to provide inexpensive, nutritionally sound meals to patients.

Obstetrics: Levels should be designated: (1) unit provides services for uncomplicated maternity and newborn cases; (2) unit provides services for uncomplicated cases, the majority of complicated problems, and special neonatal services; and (3) unit provides services for all serious illnesses and abnormalities and is supervised by a full-time maternal/fetal specialist.

Occupational health services: Includes services designed to protect the safety of employees from hazards in the work environment.

Oncology services: Inpatient and outpatient services for patients with cancer, including comprehensive care, support and guidance in addition to patient education and prevention, chemotherapy, counseling and other treatment methods.

Open physician hospital organization (Open PHO): A joint venture between the hospital and all members of the medical staff who wish to participate. The open PHO can act as a unified agent in managed care contracting, own a managed care plan, own and operate ambulatory care centers or ancillary services projects, or provide administrative services to physician members.

Optical colonoscopy: An examination of the interior of the colon using a long, flexible, lighted tube with a small built-in camera.

Orthopedic services: Services provided for the prevention or correction of injuries or disorders of the skeletal system and associated muscles, joints and ligaments.

Osteopathic hospitals: Osteopathic medicine is a medical practice based on a theory that diseases are due chiefly to a loss of structural integrity, which can be restored by manipulation of the neuro-muscular and skeletal systems, supplemented by therapeutic measures (such as medicine or surgery).

Other Intensive Care: A specially staffed, specialty equipped, separate section of a hospital dedicated to the observation, care, and treatment of patients with life threatening illnesses, injuries, or complications from which recovery is possible. It provides special expertise and facilities for the support of vital function and utilizes the skill of medical nursing and other staff experienced in the management of these problems.

Other long-term care: Provision of long-term care other than skilled nursing care or intermediate care for those who do not require daily medical or nursing services, but may require some assistance in the activities of daily living. This can include residential care, elderly care, or sheltered care facilities for developmentally disabled.

Other special care: Provides care to patients requiring care more intensive than that provided in the acute area, yet not sufficiently intensive to require admission to an intensive care unit. Patients admitted to this area are usually transferred here from an intensive care unit once their condition has improved. These units are sometimes referred to as definitive observation, step-down, or progressive care units.

Other transplant: See definition for Transplant services on page 216.

Outpatient care: Treatment provided to patients who do not remain in the hospital for overnight care. Hospitals may deliver outpatient care on site or through a facility owned and operated by the hospital, but physically separate from the hospital. In addition to treating minor illnesses or injuries, a free-standing center will stabilize seriously ill or injured patients before transporting them to a hospital. Laboratory and radiology services are usually available.

Outpatient care center (Freestanding): A facility owned and operated by the hospital, but physically separate from the hospital, that provides various medical treatments on an outpatient basis only. In addition to treating minor illnesses or injuries, the center will stabilize seriously ill or injured patients before transporting them to a hospital. Laboratory and radiology services are usually available.

Outpatient care center-services (Hospital-based): Organized hospital health care services offered by appointment on an ambulatory basis. Services may include outpatient surgery, examination, diagnosis, and treatment of a variety of medical conditions on a nonemergency basis, and laboratory and other diagnostic testing as ordered by staff or outside physician referral.

Outpatient surgery: Scheduled surgical services provided to patients who do not remain in the hospital overnight. The surgery may be performed in operating suites also used for inpatient surgery, specially designated surgical suites for outpatient surgery, or procedure rooms within an outpatient care facility.

Outpatient visit: A visit by a patient who is not lodged in the hospital while receiving medical, dental, or other services. Each visit an outpatient makes to a discrete unit constitutes one visit regardless of the number of diagnostic and/or therapeutic treatments that the patient receives. Total outpatient visits should include all clinic visits, referred visits, observation services, outpatient surgeries, and emergency room visits.

Pain Management Program: A recognized clinical service or program providing specialized medical care, drugs or therapies for the management of acute or chronic pain or other distressing symptom, administered by specially trained physicians and other clinicians, to patients suffering from acute illness of diverse causes.

Palliative Care Inpatient Unit: An inpatient palliative care ward is a physically discreet, inpatient nursing unit where the focus is palliative care. The patient care focus is on symptom relief for complex patients who may be continuing to undergo primary treatment. Care is delivered by palliative medicine specialists.

Palliative care program: An organized program providing specialized medical care, drugs or therapies for the management of acute or chronic pain and/or the control of symptoms administered by specially trained physicians and other clinicians; and supportive care services, such as counseling on advanced directives, spiritual care, and social services, to patients with advanced disease and their families.

Patient Controlled Analgesia (PCA). Patient-controlled Analgesia (PCA) is intravenously administered pain medicine under the patient's control. The patient has a button on the end of a cord than can be pushed at will, whenever more pain medicine is desired. This button will only deliver more pain medicine at pre-determined intervals, as programmed by the doctor's order.

Patient education center: Written goals and objectives for the patient and/or family related to therapeutic regimens, medical procedures, and self care.

Patient representative services: Organized hospital services providing personnel through whom patients and staff can seek solutions to institutional problems affecting the delivery of high-quality care and services.

Payroll expenses: Includes all salaries and wages. All professional fees and salary expenditures excluded from payroll, such as employee benefits, are defined as nonpayroll expenses and are included in total expenses.

Pediatric Cardiac Surgery: Includes minimally invasive procedures that include surgery done with only a small incision or no incision at all, such as through a laparoscope or an endoscope and more invasive major surgical procedures that include open chest and open heart surgery.

Pediatric Cardiology Services: An organized clinical service offering diagnostic and interventional procedures to manage the full range of pediatric heart conditions.

Pediatric Diagnostic/invasive catheterization: (also called coronary angiography or coronary arteriography) is used to assist in diagnosing complex heart conditions. Cardiac angiography involves the insertion of a tiny catheter into the artery in the groin then carefully threading the catheter up into the aorta where the coronary arteries originate. Once the catheter is in place, a dye is injected which allows the cardiologist to see the size, shape, and distribution of the coronary arteries. These images are used to diagnose heart disease and to determine, among other things, whether or not surgery is indicated.

Pediatric intensive care: Provides care to pediatric patients that is of a more intensive nature than that usually provided to pediatric patients. The unit is staffed with specially trained personnel and contains monitoring and specialized support equipment for treatment of patients who, because of shock, trauma, or other life-threatening conditions, require intensified, comprehensive observation and care.

Pediatric Interventional cardiac catheterization: Non surgical procedure that utilizes the same basic principles as diagnostic catheterization and then uses advanced techniques to improve the heart's function. It can be a less-invasive alternative to heart surgery.

Pediatric medical-surgical care: Provides acute care to pediatric patients on the basis of physicians' orders and approved nursing care plans.

Personnel: Number of persons on the hospital payroll at the end of the reporting period. Personnel are recorded in *Hospital Statistics* as full-time equivalents (FTEs), which are calculated by adding the number of full-time personnel to one-half the number of part-time personnel, excluding medical and dental residents, interns, and other trainees. *Per 100 adjusted census* indicates the ratio of personnel to adjusted average daily census, calculated on a per-100 basis.

Physical rehabilitation inpatient care: Provides care encompassing a comprehensive array of restoration services for the disabled and all support services necessary to help patients attain their maximum functional capacity.

Physical rehabilitation outpatient services: Outpatient program providing medical, health-related, therapy, social, and/or vocational services to help disabled persons attain or retain their maximum functional capacity.

Population: Population refers to the residential population of the United States. This includes both civilian and military personnel. Note that population is being used to calculate the values *for community health indicators per 1000 population.*

Positron emission tomography/CT (PET/CT): Provides metabolic functional information for the monitoring of chemotherapy, radiotherapy and surgical planning.

Positron emission tomography scanner (PET): A nuclear medicine imaging technology which uses radioactive (positron emitting) isotopes created in a cyclotron or generator and computers to produce composite pictures of the brain and heart at work. PET scanning produces sectional images depicting metabolic activity or blood flow rather than anatomy.

Preferred provider organization (PPO): A pre-set arrangement in which purchasers and providers agree to furnish specified health services to a group of employees/patients.

Primary care department: A unit or clinic within the hospital that provides primary care services (e.g. general pediatric care, general internal medicine, family practice, gynecology) through hospital-salaried medical and/or nursing staff, focusing on evaluating and diagnosing medical problems and providing medical treatment on an outpatient basis.

Prosthetic and Orthotic Services: Services providing comprehensive prosthetic and orthotic evaluation, fitting, and training.

Proton beam therapy: A form of radiation therapy which administers proton beams. While producing the same biologic effects as x-ray beams, the energy distribution of protons differs from conventional x-ray beams in that they can be more precisely focused in tissue volumes in a three-dimensional pattern resulting in less surrounding tissue damage than conventional radiation therapy permitting administration of higher doses.

Psychiatric child-adolescent services: Provides care to emotionally disturbed children and adolescents, including those admitted for diagnosis and those admitted for treatment.

Psychiatric consultation-liaison services: Provides organized psychiatric consultation/liaison services to nonpsychiatric hospital staff and/or departments on psychological aspects of medical care that may be generic or specific to individual patients.

Psychiatric education services: Provides psychiatric educational services to community agencies and workers such as schools, police, courts, public health nurses, welfare agencies, clergy, and so forth. The purpose is to expand the mental health knowledge and competence of personnel not working in the mental health field and to promote good mental health through improved understanding, attitudes, and behavioral patterns.

Psychiatric emergency services: Services of facilities available on a 24-hour basis to provide immediate unscheduled out-patient care, diagnosis, evaluation, crisis intervention, and assistance to persons suffering acute emotional or mental distress.

Psychiatric geriatric services: Provides care to emotionally disturbed elderly patients, including those admitted for diagnosis and those admitted for treatment.

Psychiatric inpatient care: Provides acute or long-term care to emotionally disturbed patients, including patients admitted for diagnosis and those admitted for treatment of psychiatric problems, on the basis of physicians' orders and approved nursing care plans. Long-term care may include intensive supervision to the chronically mentally ill, mentally disordered, or other mentally incompetent persons.

Psychiatric outpatient services: Provides medical care, including diagnosis and treatment, of psychiatric outpatients.

Psychiatric partial hospitalization program: Organized hospital services of intensive day/evening outpatient services of three hours of more duration, distinguished from other outpatient visits of one hour.

Psychiatric residential treatment: Overnight psychiatric care in conjunction with an intensive treatment program in a setting other than a hospital.

Radiology, diagnostic: The branch of radiology that deals with the utilization of all modalities of radiant energy in medical diagnoses and therapeutic procedures using radiologic guidance. This includes, but is not restricted to, imaging techniques and methodologies utilizing radiation emitted by x-ray tubes, radionnuclides, and ultrasonographic devices and the radiofrequency electromagnetic radiation emitted by atoms.

Radiology, therapeutic: The branch of medicine concerned with radioactive substances and using various techniques of visualization, with the diagnosis and treatment of disease using any of the various sources of radiant energy. Services could include: megavoltage radiation therapy; radioactive implants; stereotactic radiosurgery; therapeutic radioisotope facility; X-ray radiation therapy.

Registered nurse (RN): A nurse who has graduated from an approved school of nursing and who is currently registered by the state. RNs are responsible for the nature and quality of all nursing care that patients receive. In these tables, the number of RNs does not include those registered nurses more appropriately reported in other occupational categories, such as facility administrators, which are listed under *all other personnel* (Tables 1 and 2).

Rehabilitation services: A wide array of restoration services for disabled and recuperating patients, including all support services necessary to help them attain their maximum functional capacity.

Retirement housing: A facility which provides social activities to senior citizens, usually retired persons, who do not require health care but some short-term skilled nursing care may be provided. A retirement center may furnish housing and may also have acute hospital and long-term care facilities, or it may arrange for acute and long term care through affiliated institutions.

Robot-assisted walking therapy: A form of physical therapy that uses a robotic device to assist patients who are relearning how to walk.

Robotic surgery: The use of mechanical guidance devices to remotely manipulate surgical instrumentation.

Rural: A rural hospital is located outside a Metropolitan Statistical Area (MSA), as designated by the U.S. Office of Management and Budget (OMB) effective June 6, 2003. An urban area is a geographically defined, integrated social and economic unit with a large population nucleus. Micropolitan areas, which are new to the OMB June 6, 2003 definitions, continue to be classified as rural for purposes of this publication.

Rural Health Clinic: A clinic located in a rural, medically under-served area in the United States that has a separate reimbursement structure from the standard medical office under the Medicare and Medicaid programs.

Satellite Emergency Department: A facility owned and operated by the hospital but physically separate from the hospital for the provision of unscheduled outpatient services to patients whose conditions require immediate care. A freestanding ED is not physically connected to a hospital, but has all necessary emergency staffing and equipment on-site.

Shaped beam radiation system: A precise, non-invasive treatment that involves targeting beams of radiation that mirrors the exact size and shape of a tumor at a specific area of a tumor to shrink or destroy cancerous cells. This procedure delivers a therapeutic dose of radiation that conforms precisely to the shape of the tumor, thus minimizing the risk to nearby tissues.

Simulated rehabilitation environment: Rehabilitation focused on retraining functional skills in a contextually appropriate environment (simulated home and community settings) or in a traditional setting (gymnasium) using motor learning principles.

Single photon emission computerized tomography (SPECT): A nuclear medicine imaging technology that combines existing technology of gamma camera imaging with computed tomographic imaging technology to provide a more precise and clear image.

Skilled nursing care: Provides non-acute medical and skilled nursing care services, therapy, and social services under the supervision of a licensed registered nurse on a 24-hour basis.

Sleep Center: Specially equipped and staffed center for the diagnosis and treatment of sleep disorders.

Social work services (could include): Organized services that are properly directed and sufficiently staffed by qualified individuals who provide assistance and counseling to patients and their families in dealing with social, emotional, and environmental problems associated with illness or disability, often in the context of financial or discharge planning coordination.

Sports medicine: Provision of diagnostic screening and assessment and clinical and rehabilitation services for the prevention and treatment of sports-related injuries.

Stereotactic radiosurgery: Stereotactic radiosurgery (SRS) is a radiotherapy modality that delivers a high dosage of radiation to a discrete treatment area in as few as one treatment session. Includes gamma knife, cyberknife, etc.

Support groups: A hospital sponsored program that allows a group of individuals with the same or similar problems who meet periodically to share experiences, problems, and solutions in order to support each other.

Surgical operations: Those surgical operations, whether major or minor, performed in the operating room(s). A surgical operation involving more than one surgical procedure is still considered only one surgical operation.

Swing bed services: A hospital bed that can be used to provide either acute or long-term care depending on community or patient needs. To be eligible a hospital must have a Medicare provider agreement in place, have fewer than 100 beds, be located in a rural area, do not have a 24 hour nursing service waiver in effect, have not been terminated from the program in the prior two years, and meet various service conditions.

Teen outreach services: A program focusing on the teenager which encourages an improved health status and a healthful lifestyle including physical, emotional, mental, social, spiritual and economic health through education, exercise, nutrition and health promotion.

Tissue transplant: See definition for Transplant sevices on page 216.

Tobacco treatment/cessation program: Organized hospital services with the purpose of ending tobacco-use habits of patients addicted to tobacco/nicotine.

Transplant services: The branch of medicine that transfers an organ or tissue from one person to another or from one body part to another to replace a diseased structure or to restore function or to change appearance. Services could include: bone marrow transplant program; heart, lung, kidney, intestine, or tissue transplant. The other transplant services include transplant services other than bone marrow, heart, kidney, liver, lung, tissue and heart/lung or other multi-transplant surgeries.

Transportation to health facilities: A long-term care support service designed to assist the mobility of the elderly. Some programs offer improved financial access by offering reduced rates and barrier-free buses or vans with ramps and lifts to assist the elderly or handicapped; others offer subsidies for public transport systems or operate mini-bus services exclusively for use by senior citizens.

Trauma center (certified): A facility to provide emergency and specialized intensive care to critically ill and injured patients. **Level 1:** A regional resource trauma center, which is capable of providing total care for every aspect of injury and plays a leadership role in trauma research and education. **Level 2:** A community trauma center, which is capable of providing trauma care to all but the most severely injured patients who require highly specialized care. **Level 3:** A rural trauma hospital, which is capable of providing care to a large number of injury victims and can resuscitate and stabilize more severely injured patients so that they can be transported to Level 1 or 2 facilities.

Ultrasound: The use of acoustic waves above the range of 20,000 cycles per second to visualize internal body structures.

Urban: An urban hospital is located inside a Metropolitan Statistical Area (MSA), designated by the U.S. Office of Management and Budget effective June 6, 2003. An urban areas is a geographically defined, integrated social and economic unit with a large population base. Micropolitan areas, which are new to the OMB June 6, 2003 definitions, are not considered to be urban for purposes of this publication.

Urgent care center: A facility that provides care and treatment for problems that are not life-threatening but require attention over the short term.

Virtual colonoscopy: Noninvasive screening procedure used to visualize, analyze and detect cancerous or potentially cancerous polyps in the colon.

Volunteer services department: An organized hospital department responsible for coordinating the services of volunteers working within the institution.

Women's health center/services: An area set aside for coordinated education and treatment services specifically for and promoted to women as provided by this special unit. Services may or may not include obstetrics but include a range of services other than OB.

Wound Management Services: Services for patients with chronic wounds and nonhealing wounds often resulting from diabetes, poor circulation, improper seating and immunocompromising conditions. The goals are to progress chronic wounds through stages of healing, reduce and eliminate infections, increase physical function to minimize complications from current wounds and prevent future chronic wounds. Wound management services are provided on an inpatient or outpatient basis, depending on the intensity of service needed.

2014 AHA Annual Survey
Health Forum, L.L.C.

A. REPORTING PERIOD (please refer to the instructions and definitions at the end of this questionnaire)

Report data for a full 12-month period, preferably your last completed fiscal year (365 days). Be consistent in using the same reporting period for responses throughout various sections of this survey.

1. Reporting Period used (beginning and ending date) ...... __ __ / __ __ / __ __ __ __   to __ __ / __ __ / __ __ __ __
                                                           Month   Day   Year   Month Day   Year

2. a. Were you in operation 12 full months
    at the end of your reporting period? .... YES ☐ NO ☐
   b. Number of days open
      during reporting period .... _____

3. Indicate the beginning of your current fiscal year .... __ __ / __ __ / __ __ __ __
                                                      Month   Day   Year

B. ORGANIZATIONAL STRUCTURE

1. CONTROL

Indicate the type of organization that is responsible for establishing policy for overall operation of your hospital. CHECK ONLY ONE:

Government, nonfederal
- ☐ 12 State
- ☐ 13 County
- ☐ 14 City
- ☐ 15 City-County
- ☐ 16 Hospital district or authority

Nongovernment, not-for profit (NFP)
- ☐ 21 Church-operated
- ☐ 23 Other not-for-profit (including NFP Corporation)

Investor-owned, for-profit
- ☐ 31 Individual
- ☐ 32 Partnership
- ☐ 33 Corporation

Government, federal
- ☐ 41 Air Force
- ☐ 42 Army
- ☐ 43 Navy
- ☐ 44 Public Health Service
- ☐ 45 Veterans' Affairs
- ☐ 46 Federal other than 41-45 or 47-48
- ☐ 47 PHS Indian Service
- ☐ 48 Department of Justice

2. SERVICE

Indicate the ONE category that BEST describes your hospital or the type of service it provides to the MAJORITY of patients:

- ☐ 10 General medical and surgical
- ☐ 11 Hospital unit of an institution (prison hospital, college infirmary)
- ☐ 12 Hospital unit within a facility for persons with intellectual disabilities
- ☐ 13 Surgical
- ☐ 22 Psychiatric
- ☐ 33 Tuberculosis and other respiratory diseases
- ☐ 41 Cancer
- ☐ 42 Heart
- ☐ 44 Obstetrics and gynecology
- ☐ 45 Eye, ear, nose, and throat

- ☐ 46 Rehabilitation
- ☐ 47 Orthopedic
- ☐ 48 Chronic disease
- ☐ 62 Intellectual disabilities
- ☐ 80 Acute long-term care hospital
- ☐ 82 Alcoholism and other chemical dependency
- ☐ 49 Other - specify treatment area: _____

B. ORGANIZATIONAL STRUCTURE (continued)

3. OTHER

    a.   Does your hospital restrict admissions primarily to children? .... YES ☐   NO ☐

    b.   Does the hospital itself operate subsidiary corporations? .... YES ☐   NO ☐

    c.   Is the hospital contract managed? If yes, please provide the name, city, and state of the organization.... YES ☐   NO ☐

            Name: _____ City: _____ State: _____

    d.   Is the hospital a participant in a network? ....YES ☐   NO ☐
            If yes, please provide the name, city, state and telephone number of the network(s).

            Name: _____ City: _____ State: _____ Telephone_____

            Name: _____ City: _____ State: _____ Telephone_____

            Name: _____ City: _____ State: _____ Telephone_____

    e.   Is your hospital owned in whole or in part by physicians or a physician group?...YES ☐   NO ☐

    f.   If you checked 80 Acute long-term care hospital (LTCH) in Section B2 (Service), please indicate if you are a freestanding LTCH or a LTCH arranged within a general acute care hospital.
           ☐ Free standing LTCH   ☐ LTCH arranged in a general acute care hospital

           If you are arranged in a general acute care hospital, what is your host hospital's name?

           Name_____ City_____ State_____

C. FACILITIES AND SERVICES

For each service or facility listed below, please check all the categories that describe how each item is provided **as of the last day of the reporting period**. Check all categories that apply for an item. If you check column (1) C1-19, please include the number of **staffed beds**. *The sum of the beds reported in 1-19 should equal Section D(1b), beds set up and staffed on page 9.*

	(1) Owned or provided by my hospital or its subsidiary	(2) Provided by my Health System (in my local community)	(3) Provided through a formal contractual arrangement or joint venture with another provider that is not in my system (in my local community)	(4) Do Not Provide
1. General medical-surgical care ....(#Beds_____)	☐	☐	☐	☐
2. Pediatric medical-surgical care ....(#Beds_____)	☐	☐	☐	☐
3. Obstetrics............[Hospital level of unit (1-3):(_____)] (#Beds_____)	☐	☐	☐	☐
4. Medical-surgical intensive care ....(#Beds_____)	☐	☐	☐	☐
5. Cardiac intensive care ....(#Beds_____)	☐	☐	☐	☐
6. Neonatal intensive care ....(#Beds_____)	☐	☐	☐	☐
7. Neonatal intermediate care ....(#Beds_____)	☐	☐	☐	☐
8. Pediatric intensive care..(#Beds_____)	☐	☐	☐	☐
9. Burn care..(#Beds_____)	☐	☐	☐	☐
10. Other special care _____...........(#Beds_____)	☐	☐	☐	☐
11. Other intensive care_____...........(#Beds_____)	☐	☐	☐	☐
12. Physical rehabilitation ....(#Beds_____)	☐	☐	☐	☐
13. Alcoholism-drug abuse or dependency care ....(#Beds_____)	☐	☐	☐	☐
14. Psychiatric care ....(#Beds_____)	☐	☐	☐	☐
15. Skilled nursing care ....(#Beds_____)	☐	☐	☐	☐
16. Intermediate nursing care ....(#Beds_____)	☐	☐	☐	☐
17. Acute long-term care..(#Beds_____)	☐	☐	☐	☐
18. Other long-term care..(#Beds_____)	☐	☐	☐	☐
19. Other care _____ ....(#Beds_____)	☐	☐	☐	☐
20. Adult day care program..	☐	☐	☐	☐
21. Airborne infection isolation room...................... (#rooms _____)	☐	☐	☐	☐
22. Alcoholism-drug abuse or dependency outpatient services.............	☐	☐	☐	☐
23. Alzheimer Center...	☐	☐	☐	☐
24. Ambulance services..	☐	☐	☐	☐
25. Ambulatory surgery center	☐	☐	☐	☐
26. Arthritis treatment center..	☐	☐	☐	☐
27. ....A ssisted living	☐	☐	☐	☐
28. ....A uxiliary	☐	☐	☐	☐
29. ....B ariatric/weight control services	☐	☐	☐	☐
30. ....B irthing room/LDR room/LDRP room	☐	☐	☐	☐
31. ....B lood Donor Center...	☐	☐	☐	☐
32. ....B reast cancer screening/mammograms	☐	☐	☐	☐

C. FACILITIES AND SERVICES (continued)

	(1) Owned or provided by my hospital or its subsidiary	(2) Provided by my Health System (in my local community)	(3) Provided through a formal contractual arrangement or joint venture with another provider that is not in my system (in my local community)	(4) Do Not Provide
33. Cardiology and cardiac surgery services				
a. Adult cardiology services	☐	☐	☐	☐
b. Pediatric cardiology services	☐	☐	☐	☐
c. Adult diagnostic catheterization	☐	☐	☐	☐
d. Pediatric diagnostic catheterization	☐	☐	☐	☐
e. Adult interventional cardiac catheterization	☐	☐	☐	☐
f. Pediatric interventional cardiac catheterization	☐	☐	☐	☐
g. Adult cardiac surgery	☐	☐	☐	☐
h. Pediatric cardiac surgery	☐	☐	☐	☐
i. Adult cardiac electrophysiology	☐	☐	☐	☐
j. Pediatric cardiac electrophysiology	☐	☐	☐	☐
k. Cardiac rehabilitation	☐	☐	☐	☐
34. Case management	☐	☐	☐	☐
35. Chaplaincy/pastoral care services	☐	☐	☐	☐
36. Chemotherapy	☐	☐	☐	☐
37. Children's wellness program	☐	☐	☐	☐
38. Chiropractic services	☐	☐	☐	☐
39. Community outreach	☐	☐	☐	☐
40. Complementary and alternative medicine services	☐	☐	☐	☐
41. Computer assisted orthopedic surgery (CAOS)	☐	☐	☐	☐
42. Crisis prevention	☐	☐	☐	☐
43. Dental services	☐	☐	☐	☐
44. Emergency services				
a. Emergency department	☐	☐	☐	☐
b. Pediatric emergency department	☐	☐	☐	☐
c. Satellite emergency department	☐	☐	☐	☐
d. If you checked column 1 for Satellite ED (44c), is the department open 24 hours a day, 7 days a week?	Yes ☐		No ☐	
e. Trauma center (certified) ….[Hospital level of unit (1-3) _____]	☐	☐	☐	☐
45. Enabling services	☐	☐	☐	☐
46. Endoscopic services				
a. Optical colonoscopy	☐	☐	☐	☐
b. Endoscopic ultrasound	☐	☐	☐	☐
c. Ablation of Barrett's esophagus	☐	☐	☐	☐
d. Esophageal impedance study	☐	☐	☐	☐
e. Endoscopic retrograde cholangiopancreatography (ERCP)	☐	☐	☐	☐
47. Enrollment (insurance) assistance services	☐	☐	☐	☐
48. Extracorporeal shock wave lithotripter (ESWL)	☐	☐	☐	☐
49. Fertility clinic	☐	☐	☐	☐
50. Fitness center	☐	☐	☐	☐
51. Freestanding outpatient care center	☐	☐	☐	☐
52. Geriatric services	☐	☐	☐	☐
53. Health fair	☐	☐	☐	☐

C. FACILITIES AND SERVICES (continued)

	(1) Owned or provided by my hospital or its subsidiary	(2) Provided by my Health System (in my local community)	(3) Provided through a formal contractual arrangement or joint venture with another provider that is not in my system (in my local community)	(4) Do Not Provide
54. Community health education	☐	☐	☐	☐
55. Genetic testing/counseling	☐	☐	☐	☐
56. Health screenings	☐	☐	☐	☐
57. Health research	☐	☐	☐	☐
58. Hemodialysis	☐	☐	☐	☐
59. HIV/AIDS services	☐	☐	☐	☐
60. Home health services	☐	☐	☐	☐
61. Hospice program	☐	☐	☐	☐
62. Hospital-based outpatient care center services	☐	☐	☐	☐
63. Immunization program	☐	☐	☐	☐
64. Indigent care clinic	☐	☐	☐	☐
65. Linguistic/translation services	☐	☐	☐	☐
66. Meals on wheels	☐	☐	☐	☐
67. Mobile health services	☐	☐	☐	☐
68. Neurological services	☐	☐	☐	☐
69. Nutrition program	☐	☐	☐	☐
70. Occupational health services	☐	☐	☐	☐
71. Oncology services	☐	☐	☐	☐
72. Orthopedic services	☐	☐	☐	☐
73. Outpatient surgery	☐	☐	☐	☐
74. Pain management program	☐	☐	☐	☐
75. Palliative care program	☐	☐	☐	☐
76. Palliative care inpatient unit	☐	☐	☐	☐
77. Patient controlled analgesia (PCA)	☐	☐	☐	☐
78. Patient education center	☐	☐	☐	☐
79. Patient representative services	☐	☐	☐	☐
80. Physical rehabilitation services				
a. Assistive technology center	☐	☐	☐	☐
b. Electrodiagnostic services	☐	☐	☐	☐
c. Physical rehabilitation outpatient services	☐	☐	☐	☐
d. Prosthetic and orthotic services	☐	☐	☐	☐
e. Robot-assisted walking therapy	☐	☐	☐	☐
f. Simulated rehabilitation environment	☐	☐	☐	☐
81. Primary care department	☐	☐	☐	☐
82. Psychiatric services				
a. Psychiatric child-adolescent services	☐	☐	☐	☐
b. Psychiatric consultation-liaison services	☐	☐	☐	☐
c. Psychiatric education services	☐	☐	☐	☐
d. Psychiatric emergency services	☐	☐	☐	☐
e. Psychiatric geriatric services	☐	☐	☐	☐
f. Psychiatric outpatient services	☐	☐	☐	☐
g. Psychiatric partial hospitalization services	☐	☐	☐	☐
h. Psychiatric residential treatment	☐	☐	☐	☐

	(1) Owned or provided by my hospital or its subsidiary	(2) Provided by my Health System (in my local community)	(3) Provided through a formal contractual arrangement or joint venture with another provider that is not in my system (in my local community)	(4) Do Not Provide
83. Radiology, diagnostic				
a. CT Scanner	☐	☐	☐	☐
b. Diagnostic radioisotope facility	☐	☐	☐	☐
c. Electron beam computed tomography (EBCT)	☐	☐	☐	☐
d. Full-field digital mammography (FFDM)	☐	☐	☐	☐
e. Magnetic resonance imaging (MRI)	☐	☐	☐	☐
f. Intraoperative magnetic resonance imaging	☐	☐	☐	☐
g. Magnetoencephalography (MEG)	☐	☐	☐	☐
h. Multi-slice spiral computed tomography (<64+ slice CT)	☐	☐	☐	☐
i. Multi-slice spiral computed tomography (64+ slice CT)	☐	☐	☐	☐
j. Positron emission tomography (PET)	☐	☐	☐	☐
k. Positron emission tomography/CT (PET/CT)	☐	☐	☐	☐
l. Single photon emission computerized tomography (SPECT)	☐	☐	☐	☐
m. Utrasound	☐	☐	☐	☐
84. Radiology, therapeutic				
a. Image-guided radiation therapy (IGRT)	☐	☐	☐	☐
b. Intensity-modulated radiation therapy (IMRT)	☐	☐	☐	☐
a. Proton beam therapy	☐	☐	☐	☐
b. Shaped beam radiation system	☐	☐	☐	☐
c. Stereotactic radiosurgery	☐	☐	☐	☐
85. Retirement housing	☐	☐	☐	☐
86. Robotic surgery	☐	☐	☐	☐
87. Rural health clinic	☐	☐	☐	☐
88. Sleep center	☐	☐	☐	☐
89. Social work services	☐	☐	☐	☐
90. Sports medicine	☐	☐	☐	☐
91. Support groups	☐	☐	☐	☐
92. Swing bed services	☐	☐	☐	☐
93. Teen outreach services	☐	☐	☐	☐
94. Tobacco treatment/cessation program	☐	☐	☐	☐
95. Transplant services				
a. Bone marrow	☐	☐	☐	☐
b. Heart	☐	☐	☐	☐
c. Kidney	☐	☐	☐	☐
d. Liver	☐	☐	☐	☐
e. Lung	☐	☐	☐	☐
f. Tissue	☐	☐	☐	☐
g. Other	☐	☐	☐	☐
96. Transportation to health services	☐	☐	☐	☐
97. Urgent care center	☐	☐	☐	☐
98. Virtual colonoscopy	☐	☐	☐	☐
99. Volunteer services department	☐	☐	☐	☐
100. Women's health center/services	☐	☐	☐	☐
101. Wound management services	☐	☐	☐	☐

C. FACILITIES AND SERVICES (continued)

102a. In which of the following physician arrangements does your hospital or system/network participate? Column 3 refers to the networks that were identified in section B, question 3d. For hospital level physician arrangements that are reported in column 1, please report the number of physicians involved.

		(1) My Hospital	(2) My Health System	(3) My Health Network	(4) Do Not Provide
a. Independent Practice Association (IPA)	(# of physicians _____)	☐	☐	☐	☐
b. Group practice without walls	(# of physicians _____)	☐	☐	☐	☐
c. Open Physician-Hospital Organization (PHO)	(# of physicians _____)	☐	☐	☐	☐
d. Closed Physician-Hospital Organization (PHO)	(# of physicians _____)	☐	☐	☐	☐
e. Management Service Organization (MSO)	(# of physicians _____)	☐	☐	☐	☐
f. Integrated Salary Model	(# of physicians _____)	☐	☐	☐	☐
g. Equity Model	(# of physicians _____)	☐	☐	☐	☐
h. Foundation	(# of physicians _____)	☐	☐	☐	☐
i. Other, please specify _____	(# of physicians _____)	☐	☐	☐	☐

102b. Looking across all the relationships identified in question 102a, what is the total number of physicians (count each physician only once) that are engaged in an arrangement with your hospital that allows for joint contracting with payors or shared responsibility for financial risk or clinical performance between the hospital and physician? (arrangement may be at the hospital, system or network level) # of physicians _____

103a. Does your hospital participate in any joint venture arrangements with physicians or physician groups?   YES ☐   NO ☐

103b. If your hospital participates in any joint ventures with physicians or physician groups, please indicate which types of services are involved in those joint ventures. (Check all that apply)

    a. ☐ Limited service hospital

    b. ☐ Ambulatory surgical centers

    c. ☐ Imaging centers

    d. ☐ Other _____

103c. If you selected 'a. Limited Service Hospital', please tell us what type(s) of services are provided. (Check all that apply)

    a. ☐ Cardiac

    b. ☐ Orthopedic

    c. ☐ Surgical

    d. ☐ Other _____

103d. Does your hospital participate in joint venture arrangements with organizations other than physician groups?   YES ☐   NO ☐

104a. Has your hospital or health care system established an accountable care organization (ACO)?   YES ☐   NO ☐

104b. If yes, please indicate the patient population that participates in the ACO. (Check all that apply)

    a. ☐ Medicaid

    b. ☐ Medicare

    c. ☐ Privately insured

    d. ☐ Other, please specify_____

105. Does your hospital have an established medical home program?   YES ☐   NO ☐

106. Does your hospital participate in a bundled payment program involving inpatient, physician, and/or post acute care services where the hospital receives a single payment from a payor for a package of services and then distributes payments to participating providers of care (such as a single fee for hospital and physician services for a specific procedure, e.g., hip replacement, CABG)?   YES ☐   NO ☐

C. FACILITIES AND SERVICES (continued)

107. Does your hospital, health system or health network have an equity interest in any of the following insurance products? (Check all that apply) Contractual relationships with HMOs and PPOs should not be reported here but in Question 108. Column 3 refers to the networks that were identified in section B, question 3d.

	(1) My Hospital	(2) My Health System	(3) My Health Network	(4) Joint Venture with Insurer	(5) Do Not Provide
a. .... ealth Maintenance Organization..................	☐	☐	☐	☐	☐
b. .... referred Provider Organization.	☐	☐	☐	☐	☐
c. .... ndemnity Fee for Service Plan	☐	☐	☐	☐	☐

108. Does your hospital have a formal written contract that specifies the obligations of each party with:

    a. Health maintenance organization (HMO) .... YES ☐   NO ☐   **b.** If YES, how many contracts? _____

    c. Preferred provider organization (PPO) .... YES ☐   NO ☐   **d.** If YES, how many contracts? _____

109. What percentage of the hospital's net patient revenue is paid on a capitated basis? If the hospital does not participate in capitated arrangements, please enter "0"   _____ %

110. What percentage of the hospital's net patient revenue is paid on a shared risk basis?   _____ %

111. Does your hospital contract directly with employers or a coalition of employers to provide care on a capitated, predetermined, or shared risk basis? ....YES ☐   NO ☐

112. If your hospital has arrangements to care for a specific group of enrollees in exchange for a capitated payment, how many lives are covered?   _____

113. Does your hospital have contracts with commercial payors where payment is tied to performance on quality/safety metrics?   YES ☐   NO ☐

114a. Does your hospital conduct an internal survey of the hospital's quality/safety culture at least every 18 months?   YES ☐   NO ☐

114b. If yes, please indicate the response rate for the most recent survey.   _____ %

114c. If yes, are valid results available at the level of individual units (e.g., medical ICUs, cardiothoracic surgery)?   YES ☐   NO ☐

D. TOTAL FACILITY BEDS, UTILIZATION, FINANCES, AND STAFFING

Please report beds, utilization, financial, and staffing data for the 12-month period that is consistent with the period reported on page 1. Report financial data for reporting period only. Include within your operations all activities that are wholly owned by the hospital, including subsidiary corporations regardless of where the activity is physically located. Please do not include within your operations distinct and separate divisions that may be owned by your hospital's parent corporation. If final figures are not available, please estimate. Round to the nearest dollar. Report all personnel who were on the payroll and whose payroll expenses are reported in D3f. (Please refer to specific definitions on pages 21-23.)

	(1) Total Facility	(2) Nursing Home Unit/Facility
Fill out column (2) if hospital owns and operates a nursing home type unit/facility. Column (1) should be the combined total of hospital plus nursing home unit/facility.		

1. BEDS AND UTILIZATION

	(1) Total Facility	(2) Nursing Home Unit/Facility
a. Total licensed beds	_____	_____
b. Beds set up and staffed for use at the end of the reporting period	_____	_____
c. Bassinets set up and staffed for use at the end of the reporting period	_____	
d. Births (exclude fetal deaths)	_____	
e. Admissions (exclude newborns; include neonatal & swing admissions)	_____	_____
f. Inpatient days (exclude newborns; include neonatal & swing days)	_____	_____
g. Emergency department visits	_____	
h. Total outpatient visits (include emergency department visits & outpatient surgeries)	_____	
i. Inpatient surgical operations	_____	
j. Number of operating rooms	_____	
k. Outpatient surgical operations	_____	

2. MEDICARE/MEDICAID UTILIZATION (exclude newborns; include neonatal & swing days and deaths)

	(1) Total Facility	(2) Nursing Home Unit/Facility
a1. Total Medicare (Title XVIII) inpatient discharges (including Medicare Managed Care)	_____	_____
a2. How many Medicare inpatient discharges were Medicare Managed Care?	_____	_____
b1. Total Medicare (Title XVIII) inpatient days (including Medicare Managed Care)	_____	_____
b2. How many Medicare inpatient days were Medicare Managed Care?	_____	_____
c1. Total Medicaid (Title XIX) inpatient discharges (including Medicaid Managed Care)	_____	_____
c2. How many Medicaid inpatient discharges were Medicaid Managed Care?	_____	_____
d1. Total Medicaid (Title XIX) inpatient days (including Medicaid Managed Care)	_____	_____
d2. How many Medicaid inpatient days were Medicaid Managed Care?	_____	_____

3. FINANCIAL

	(1) Total Facility	(2) Nursing Home Unit/Facility
*a. Net patient revenue (treat bad debt as a deduction from gross revenue)	_____.00	_____.00
*b. Tax appropriations	_____.00	
*c. Other operating revenue	_____.00	
*d. Nonoperating revenue	_____.00	
*e. TOTAL REVENUE (add 3a thru 3d)	_____.00	_____.00
f. Payroll expenses (only)	_____.00	_____.00
g. Employee benefits	_____.00	_____.00
h. Depreciation expense (for reporting period only)	_____.00	
i. Interest expense	_____.00	
j. Supply expense	_____.00	
k. All other expenses	_____.00	
l. TOTAL EXPENSES (add 3f thru 3k. Exclude bad debt)	_____.00	_____.00

4. REVENUE BY TYPE

	(1) Total Facility
*a. Total gross inpatient revenue	_____.00
*b. Total gross outpatient revenue	_____.00
*c. Total gross patient revenue	_____.00

D. TOTAL FACILITY BEDS, UTILIZATION, FINANCES, AND STAFFING (continued)

*5. UNCOMPENSATED CARE & PROVIDER TAXES

a. Bad debt (Revenue forgone at full established rates. Include in gross revenue) .... _____ .00

b. Financial Assistance (includes Charity Care) (Revenue forgone at full-established rates. Include in gross revenue.)........ _____ .00

c. Is your bad debt (5a) reported on the basis of full charges?　　　　YES ☐　　　　NO ☐

d.　Does your state have a provider Medicaid tax/assessment program?　　YES ☐　　　　NO ☐

e.　If yes, please report the total gross amount paid into the program.. _____ .00

f.　Due to differing accounting standards, please indicate whether the provider tax/assessment amount is included in:
　　　1. Total expenses　　　　　　　　　　　　　　　　　　　　YES ☐　　　　NO ☐
　　　2. Deductions from net patient revenue　　　　　　　　　　YES ☐　　　　NO ☐

*6. REVENUE BY PAYOR (report total facility gross and net figures)

	(1) Gross	(2) Net
*a. GOVERNMENT　(1) Medicare:		
a) Fee for service patient revenue	_____ .00	_____ .00
b) Managed care revenue	_____ .00	_____ .00
c) Total (a + b)	_____ **.00**	_____ **.00**
(2) Medicaid:		
a)　Fee for service patient revenue...............................	_____ .00	_____ .00
b)　Managed care revenue	_____ .00	_____ .00
c) Medicaid Disproportionate Share Hospital Payments (DSH)		_____ .00
d) Medicaid supplemental payments: not including Medicaid Disproportionate Share Hospital Payments (DSH)		_____ .00
e) Total (a + b + c + d)	_____ **.00**	_____ **.00**
(3) Other government	_____ .00	_____ .00
*b. NONGOVERNMENT　(1)　Self-pay..	_____ .00	_____ .00
(2)　Third-party payors:		
a)　Managed care (includes HMO and PPO)	_____ .00	_____ .00
b)　Other third-party payors	_____ .00	_____ .00
c)　Total third-party payors (a + b)	_____ **.00**	_____ **.00**
(3)　All Other nongovernment...............................	_____ .00	_____ .00
*c. TOTAL	_____ **.00**	_____ **.00**

(Total gross should equal 4c on page 9. Total net should equal 3a on page 9.)

Are the financial data on pages 9 and 10 from your audited financial statement? .... YES ☐　NO ☐

---

7. FIXED ASSETS
a.　Property, plant and equipment at <u>cost</u> .... _____ .00
b.　Accumulated <u>depreciation</u> .... _____ .00
c.　Net property, plant and equipment (a-b) .... _____ .00
d.　Total gross square feet of your physical plant used for or in support of your
　　healthcare activities.. _____

8. TOTAL CAPITAL EXPENSES
Include all expenses used to acquire assets, including buildings, remodeling projects, equipment, or property.　_____ .00

D. TOTAL FACILITY BEDS, UTILIZATION, FINANCES, AND STAFFING (continued)

9. INFORMATION TECHNOLOGY

  *a. IT operating expense.._____.00

  *b. IT capital expense... ...._____.00

  *c. Number of employed IT staff (in FTEs) ...._____

  *d. Number of outsourced IT staff (in FTEs)... _____

  e. Does your hospital have an electronic health record? (see definition)

    ☐ Yes, fully implemented   ☐ Yes, partially implemented   ☐ No

10. STAFFING

Report full-time (35 hours or more) and part-time (less than 35 hours) personnel who were on the hospital/facility **payroll at the end of your reporting period.** Include members of religious orders for whom dollar equivalents were reported. Exclude private-duty nurses, volunteers, and all personnel whose salary is financed entirely by outside research grants. Exclude physicians and dentists who are paid on a fee basis. FTE is the total number of hours worked by all employees over the full (12 month) reporting period divided by the normal number of hours worked by a full-time employee for that same time period. For example, if your hospital considers a normal workweek for a full-time employee to be 40 hours, a total of 2,080 would be worked over a full year (52 weeks). If the total number of hours worked by all employees on the payroll is 208,000, then the number of Full-Time Equivalents (FTE) is 100 (employees). The FTE calculation for a specific occupational category such as registered nurses is exactly the same. The calculation for each occupational category should be based on the number of hours worked by staff employed in that specific category.

For each occupational category, please report the number of staff vacancies as of the last day of your reporting period. A vacancy is defined as a budgeted staff position which is unfilled as of the last day of the reporting period and for which the hospital is actively seeking either a full-time or part-time permanent replacement. Personnel who work in more than one area should be included only in the category of their primary responsibility and should be counted only once.

	(1) Full-Time (35 hr/wk or more) On Payroll	(2) Part-Time (Less than 35hr/wk) On Payroll	(3) FTE	(4) Vacancies
a. Physicians	_____	_____	_____	_____
b. Dentists	_____	_____	_____	_____
c. Medical and dental residents/interns	_____	_____	_____	_____
d. Other trainees	_____	_____	_____	_____
e. Registered nurses	_____	_____	_____	_____
f. Licensed practical (vocational) nurses	_____	_____	_____	_____
g. Nursing assistive personnel	_____	_____	_____	_____
h. Radiology technicians	_____	_____	_____	_____
i. Laboratory technicians	_____	_____	_____	_____
j. Pharmacists, licensed	_____	_____	_____	_____
k. Pharmacy technicians	_____	_____	_____	_____
l. Respiratory therapists	_____	_____	_____	_____
m. All other personnel	_____	_____	_____	_____
n. Total facility personnel (add 10a through 10m)	_____	_____	_____	_____

(Total facility personnel (a-n) should include hospital plus nursing home type unit/facility personnel also reported separately in 10o and 10p.)

o. Nursing home type unit/facility registered nurses	_____	_____	_____	_____
p. Total nursing home type unit/facility personnel	_____	_____	_____	_____

q. For your employed RNs reported above (D.10.e), please report the number of full time equivalents who are involved in direct patient care.

    _____ Number of direct patient care FTEs

*These data will be treated as confidential and not released without written permission. AHA will however, share these data with your respective state hospital association and, if requested, with your appropriate metropolitan/regional association.

For members of the Catholic Health Association of the United States (CHA), AHA will also share these data with CHA unless there are objections expressed by checking this box☐. The state/metropolitan/regional association and CHA may not release these data without written permission from the hospital.

D. TOTAL FACILITY BEDS, UTILIZATION, FINANCES, AND STAFFING (continued)

11. PRIVILEGED PHYSICIANS

Report the total number of physicians with privileges at your hospital by type of relationship with the hospital. The sum of the physicians reported in 11a-11f should equal the total number of privileged physicians (11g) in the hospital.

	(1) Total Employed	(2) Total Individual Contract	(3) Total Group Contract	(4) Not Employed or Under Contract	(5) Total Privileged (add columns 1-4)
a. Primary care (general practitioner, general internal medicine, family practice, general pediatrics, obstetrics/gynecology, geriatrics)	_____	_____	_____	_____	_____
b. Emergency medicine	_____	_____	_____	_____	_____
c. Hospitalist	_____	_____	_____	_____	_____
d. Intensivist	_____	_____	_____	_____	_____
e. Radiologist/pathologist/anesthesiologist	_____	_____	_____	_____	_____
f. Other specialist	_____	_____	_____	_____	_____
g. Total (add 11a-11f)	_____	_____	_____	_____	_____

12. HOSPITALISTS

a. Do hospitalists provide care for patients in your hospital? (if no, please skip to 13).............. YES ☐   NO ☐ (if yes, please report in D.11c.)

b. If yes, please report the total number of full-time equivalents (FTE) hospitalists......................FTE _____

13. INTENSIVISTS

a. Do intensivists provide care for patients in your hospital? (If no, please skip to 14) YES ☐   NO ☐ (if yes, please report in D.11d.)

b. If yes, please report the total number of FTE intensivists and assign them to the following areas. Please indicate whether the intensive care area is closed to intensivists. (Meaning that only intensivists are authorized to care for ICU patients.)

		FTE	Closed to Intensivists
1.	Medical-surgical intensive care	_____	☐
2.	Cardiac intensive care	_____	☐
3.	Neonatal intensive care	_____	☐
4.	Pediatric intensive care	_____	☐
5.	Other intensive care	_____	☐
6.	Total	_____	

14. ADVANCED PRACTICE REGISTERED NURSES

a. Do advanced practice nurses/physician assistants provide care for patients in your hospital? .... YES ☐   NO ☐
(if no, please skip to 15)

b. If yes, please report the number of full time, part time and FTE advanced practice nurses/physician assistants who provide care for patients in your hospital.
_____ Full-time   _____ Part-time   _____ FTE

c. If yes, please indicate the type of service provided. (check all that apply)
☐ Primary care   ☐ Anesthesia services (Certified registered nurse anesthetist)   ☐ Emergency department care

☐ Other specialty care   ☐ Patient education   ☐ Case management   ☐ Other

15. FOREIGN EDUCATED NURSES

a. Did your facility hire more foreign-educated nurses (including contract or agency nurses) to help fill RN vacancies in 2014 vs. 2013?
More ☐   Less ☐   Same ☐   Did not hire foreign nurses ☐

b. From which countries/continents are you recruiting foreign-educated nurses? (check all that apply)
Africa ☐   South Korea ☐   Canada ☐   Philippines ☐   China ☐   India ☐   Other ☐

E. SUPPLEMENTAL INFORMATION

1. Does your hospital provide services through one or more satellite facilities?　　　　YES ☐　　　NO ☐

2. Does the hospital participate in a group purchasing arrangement?　　　　YES ☐　　　NO ☐

   If yes, please provide the name, city, and state of the group purchasing organization(s).

   Name: _____ City: _____ State: _____

   Name: _____ City: _____ State: _____

   Name: _____ City: _____ State: _____

3. Does the hospital purchase medical/surgical supplies directly through a distributor?　　　　YES ☐　　　NO ☐
   If yes, please provide the name of the distributor(s).

   Name: _____

   Name: _____

   Name: _____

4. If your hospital hired RNs during the reporting period, how many were new graduates from nursing schools? _____

5. Use this space for comments or to elaborate on any information supplied on this survey. Refer to the response by page, section and item name.

_____

_____

_____

_____

_____

_____

_____

_____

_____

_____

_____

_____

_____

_____

_____

_____

_____

_____

_____

_____

As declared previously, hospital specific revenue data are treated as confidential. AHA's policy is not to release these data without written permission from your institution. The AHA will however, share these data with your respective state hospital association and if requested with your appropriate metropolitan/regional association.

On occasion, the AHA is asked to provide these data to external organizations, both public and private, for their use in analyzing crucial health care policy or research issues. The AHA is requesting your permission to allow us to release your confidential data to those requests that we consider legitimate and worthwhile. In every instance of disclosure, the receiving organization will be prohibited from releasing hospital specific information.

Please indicate below whether or not you agree to these types of disclosure:

[ ] I hereby grant AHA permission to release my hospital's revenue data to external users that the AHA determines have a legitimate and worthwhile need to gain access to these data subject to the user's agreement with the AHA not to release hospital specific information.

_____

Chief Executive Officer   Date

[ ] I do not grant AHA permission to release my confidential data.

_____

Chief Executive Officer   Date

Does your hospital or health system have an Internet or Homepage address?   Yes ☐   No ☐

If yes, please provide the address: http:// _____

Thank you for your cooperation in completing this survey. If there are any questions about your responses to this survey, who should be contacted?

_____   (____)_____
Name (please print)   Title   (Area Code) Telephone Number

____/____/____   _____   (____)_____
Date of Completion   Chief Executive Officer   Hospital's Main Fax Number

Contact Email address: _____

NOTE: PLEASE PHOTOCOPY THE INFORMATION FOR YOUR HOSPITAL FILE BEFORE RETURNING THE ORIGINAL FORM TO THE AMERICAN HOSPITAL ASSOCIATION. ALSO, PLEASE FORWARD A PHOTOCOPY OF THE COMPLETED QUESTIONNAIRE TO YOUR STATE HOSPITAL ASSOCIATION.

THANK YOU

REPORTING PERIOD
Instructions

INSTRUCTIONS AND DEFINITIONS FOR THE 2014 ANNUAL SURVEY OF HOSPITALS.
For purposes of this survey, a hospital is defined as the organization or corporate entity licensed or registered as a hospital by a state to provide diagnostic and therapeutic patient services for a variety of medical conditions, both surgical and nonsurgical.

1. **Reporting period used (beginning and ending date):** Record the beginning and ending dates of the reporting period in an eight-digit number: for example, January 1, 2014 should be shown as 01/01/2014. Number of days should equal the time span between the two dates that the hospital was open. If you are reporting for less than 365 days, utilization and finances should be presented for days reported only.
2. **Were you in operation 12 full months at the end of your reporting period?** If you are reporting for less than 365 days, utilization and finances should be presented for days reported only.
3. **Number of days open during reporting period:** Number of days should equal the time span between the two dates that the hospital was open.

SECTION B
ORGANIZATIONAL STRUCTURE
Instructions and Definitions

1. **CONTROL**
   Check the box to the left of the type of organization that is responsible for establishing policy for overall operation of the hospital.
   Government, nonfederal.
   State. Controlled by an agency of state government.
   County. Controlled by an agency of county government.
   City. Controlled by an agency of municipal government.
   City-County. Controlled jointly by agencies of municipal and county governments.
   Hospital district or authority. Controlled by a political subdivision of a state, county, or city created solely for the purpose of establishing and maintaining medical care or health-related care institutions.
   Nongovernment, not for profit. Controlled by not-for-profit organizations, including religious organizations (Catholic hospitals, for example), community hospitals, cooperative hospitals, hospitals operated by fraternal societies, and so forth.
   Investor owned, for profit. Controlled on a for profit basis by an individual, partnership, or a profit making corporation.
   Government, federal. Controlled by an agency or department of the federal government.

2. **SERVICE**
   Indicate the ONE category that best describes the type of service that your hospital provides to the majority of patients.
   General medical and surgical. Provides diagnostic and therapeutic services to patients for a variety of medical conditions, both surgical and nonsurgical.
   Hospital unit of an institution. Provides diagnostic and therapeutic services to patients in an institution.
   Hospital unit within a facility for persons with intellectual disabilities. Provides diagnostic and therapeutic services to persons with intellectual disabilities.
   Surgical. An acute care specialty hospital where 2/3 or more of its inpatient claims are for surgical/diagnosis related groups.
   Psychiatric. Provides diagnostic and therapeutic services to patients with mental or emotional disorders.
   Tuberculosis and other respiratory diseases. Provides medical care and rehabilitative services to patients for whom the primary diagnosis is tuberculosis or other respiratory diseases.
   Cancer. Provides medical care to patients for whom the primary diagnosis is cancer.
   Heart. Provides diagnosis and treatment of heart disease.
   Obstetrics and gynecology. Provides medical and surgical treatment to pregnant women and to mothers following delivery. Also provides diagnostic and therapeutic services to women with diseases or disorders of the reproductive organs.
   Eye, ear, nose, and throat. Provides diagnosis and treatment of diseases and injuries of the eyes, ears, nose, and throat.
   Rehabilitation. Provides a comprehensive array of restoration services for people with disabilities and all support services necessary to help them attain their maximum functional capacity.
   Orthopedic. Provides corrective treatment of deformities, diseases, and ailments of the locomotive apparatus, especially affecting the limbs, bones, muscles, and joints.
   Chronic disease. Provides medical and skilled nursing services to patients with long-term illnesses who are not in an acute phase, but who require an intensity of services not available in nursing homes.
   Intellectual Disabilities Provides health-related care on a regular basis to patients with developmental or intellectual disabilities who cannot be treated in a skilled nursing unit.
   Acute long term care hospital. Provides high acuity interdisciplinary services to medically complex patients that require more intensive recuperation and care than can be provided in a typical nursing facility.
   Alcoholism and other chemical dependency. Provides diagnostic and therapeutic services to patients with alcoholism or other drug dependencies.

3. **OTHER**
   a. **Children admissions.** A hospital whose primary focus is the health and treatment of children and adolescents.
   b. **Subsidiary.** A company that is wholly controlled by another or one that is more than 50% owned by another organization.
   c. **Contract managed.** General day-to-day management of an entire organization by another organization under a formal contract. Managing organization reports directly to the board of trustees or owners of the managed organization; managed organization retains total legal responsibility and ownership of the facility's assets and liabilities.
   d. **Network.** A group of hospitals, physicians, other providers, insurers and/or community agencies that voluntarily work together to coordinate and deliver health services.

Owned/provided by the hospital or its subsidiary. All patient revenues, expenses and utilization related to the provision of the service are reflected in the hospital's statistics reported elsewhere in this survey.

Provided by my Health System (in my local community). Another health care provider in the same system as your hospital provides the service and patient revenue, expenses, and utilization related to the provision of the service are recorded at the point where the service was provided and would not be reflected in your hospital's statistics reported elsewhere in this survey. (A system is a corporate body that owns, leases, religiously sponsors and/or manages health providers)

Provided through a formal contractual arrangement or joint venture with another provider that is not in my system. All patient revenues and utilization related to the provision of the service are recorded at the site where the service was provided and would not be reflected in your hospital statistics reported elsewhere in this survey. (A joint venture is a contractual arrangement between two or more parties forming an unincorporated business. The participants in the arrangement remain independent and separate outside of the venture's purpose.)

1. **General medical-surgical care.** Provides acute care to patients in medical and surgical units on the basis of physicians' orders and approved nursing care plans.
2. **Pediatric medical-surgical care.** Provides acute care to pediatric patients on the basis of physicians' orders and approved nursing care plans.
3. **Obstetrics.** For service owned or provided by the hospital, level should be designated: (1) unit provides services for uncomplicated maternity and newborn cases; (2) unit provides services for uncomplicated cases, the majority of complicated problems, and special neonatal services; and (3) unit provides services for all serious illnesses and abnormalities and is supervised by a full-time maternal/fetal specialist.
4. **Medical surgical intensive care.** Provides patient care of a more intensive nature than the usual medical and surgical care, on the basis of physicians' orders and approved nursing care plans. These units are staffed with specially trained nursing personnel and contain monitoring and specialized support equipment for patients who because of shock, trauma or other life-threatening conditions require intensified comprehensive observation and care. Includes mixed intensive care units.
5. **Cardiac intensive care.** Provides patient care of a more specialized nature than the usual medical and surgical care, on the basis of physicians' orders and approved nursing care plans. The unit is staffed with specially trained nursing personnel and contains monitoring and specialized support or treatment equipment for patients who, because of heart seizure, open-heart surgery, or other life-threatening conditions, require intensified, comprehensive observation and care. May include myocardial infarction, pulmonary care, and heart transplant units.
6. **Neonatal intensive care.** A unit that must be separate from the newborn nursery providing intensive care to all sick infants including those with the very lowest birth weights (less than 1500 grams). NICU has potential for providing mechanical ventilation, neonatal surgery, and special care for the sickest infants born in the hospital or transferred from another institution. A full-time neonatologist serves as director of the NICU.
7. **Neonatal intermediate care.** A unit that must be separate from the normal newborn nursery and that provides intermediate and/or recovery care and some specialized services, including immediate resuscitation, intravenous therapy, and capacity for prolonged oxygen therapy and monitoring.
8. **Pediatric intensive care.** Provides care to pediatric patients that is of a more intensive nature than that usually provided to pediatric patients. The unit is staffed with specially trained personnel and contains monitoring and specialized support equipment for treatment of patients who, because of shock, trauma, or other life-threatening conditions, require intensified, comprehensive observation and care.
9. **Burn care.** Provides care to severely burned patients. Severely burned patients are those with any of the following: (1) second-degree burns of more than 25% total body surface area for adults or 20% total body surface area for children: (2) third-degree burns of more than 10% total body surface area; (3) any severe burns of the hands, face, eyes, ears, or feet; or (4) all inhalation injuries, electrical burns, complicated burn injuries involving fractures and other major traumas, and all other poor risk factors.
10. **Other special care.** Provides care to patients requiring care more intensive than that provided in the acute area, yet not sufficiently intensive to require admission to an intensive care unit. Patients admitted to this area are usually transferred here from an intensive care unit once their condition has improved. These units are sometimes referred to as definitive observation, step-down or progressive care units.
11. **Other intensive care.** A specially staffed, specialty equipped, separate section of a hospital dedicated to the observation, care, and treatment of patients with life threatening illnesses, injuries, or complications from which recovery is possible. It provides special expertise and facilities for the support of vital function and utilizes the skill of medical nursing and other staff experienced in the management of these problems.
12. **Physical rehabilitation.** Provides care encompassing a comprehensive array of restoration services for people with disabilities and all support services necessary to help patients attain their maximum functional capacity.
13. **Alcoholism-drug abuse or dependency care.** Provides diagnosis and therapeutic services to patients with alcoholism or other drug dependencies. Includes care for inpatient/residential treatment for patients whose course of treatment involves more intensive care than provided in an outpatient setting or where patient requires supervised withdrawal.
14. **Psychiatric care.** Provides acute or long-term care to patients with mental or emotional disorders, including patients admitted for diagnosis and those admitted for treatment of psychiatric disorders, on the basis of physicians' orders and approved nursing care plans. Long-term care may include intensive supervision to persons with chronic/severe mental illness.
15. **Skilled nursing care.** Provides non-acute medical and skilled nursing care services, therapy, and social services under the supervision of a licensed registered nurse on a 24-hour basis.
16. **Intermediate nursing care.** Provides health-related services (skilled nursing care and social services) to residents with a variety of physical conditions or functional disabilities. These residents do not require the care provided by a hospital or skilled nursing facility, but do need supervision and support services.
17. **Acute long-term care.** Provides specialized acute hospital care to medically complex patients who are critically ill, have multisystem complications and/or failure, and require hospitalization averaging 25 days, in a facility offering specialized treatment programs and therapeutic intervention on a 24-hour/7 day a week basis.
18. **Other long-term care.** Provision of long-term care other than skilled nursing care or intermediate care for those who do not require daily medical or nursing services, but may requires some assistance in the activities of daily living. This can include residential care, elderly care, or care facilities for those with developmental or intellectual disabilities.
19. **Other care.** (specify) Any type of care other than those listed above.
    The sum of the beds reported in Section C 1-19 should equal what you have reported in Section D(1b) for beds set up and staffed.
20. **Adult day care program.** Program providing supervision, medical and psychological care, and social activities for older adults who live at home or in another family setting, but cannot be alone or prefer to be with others during the day. May include intake assessment, health monitoring, occupational therapy, personal care, noon meal, and transportation services.
21. **Airborne infection isolation room.** A single-occupancy room for patient care where environmental factors are controlled in an effort to minimize the transmission of those infectious agents, usually spread person to person by droplet nuclei associated with coughing and inhalation. Such rooms typically have specific ventilation requirements for controlled ventilation, air pressure and filtration.
22. **Alcoholism-drug abuse or dependency outpatient services.** Organized hospital services that provide medical care and/or rehabilitative

treatment services to outpatients for whom the primary diagnosis is alcoholism or other chemical dependency.

23. **Alzheimer center.** Facility that offers care to persons with Alzheimer's disease and their families through an integrated program of clinical services, research, and education.
24. **Ambulance services.** Provision of ambulance service to the ill and injured who require medical attention on a scheduled and unscheduled basis.
25. **Ambulatory surgery center.** Facility that provides care to patients requiring surgery that are admitted and discharged on the same day. Ambulatory surgery centers are distinct from same day surgical units within the hospital outpatient departments for purposes of Medicare payment.
26. **Arthritis treatment center.** Specifically equipped and staffed center for the diagnosis and treatment of arthritis and other joint disorders.
27. **Assisted living.** A special combination of housing, supportive services, personalized assistance and health care designed to respond to the individual needs of those who need help in activities of daily living and instrumental activities of daily living. Supportive services are available, 24 hours a day, to meet scheduled and unscheduled needs, in a way that promotes maximum independence and dignity for each resident and encourages the involvement of a resident's family, neighbor and friends.
28. **Auxiliary.** A volunteer community organization formed to assist the hospital in carrying out its purpose and to serve as a link between the institution and the community.
29. **Bariatric/weight control services.** The medical practice of weight reduction.
30. **Birthing room/LDR room/LDRP room.** A single-room type of maternity care with a more homelike setting for families than the traditional three-room unit (labor/delivery/recovery) with a separate postpartum area. A birthing room combines labor and delivery in one room. An LDR room accommodates three stages in the birthing process--labor, delivery, and recovery. An LDRP room accommodates all four stages of the birth process--labor, delivery, recovery, and postpartum.
31. **Blood donor center.** A facility that performs, or is responsible for the collection, processing, testing or distribution of blood and components.
32. **Breast cancer screening/mammograms.** Mammography screening - The use of breast x-ray to detect unsuspected breast cancer in asymptomatic women. Diagnostic mammography - The x-ray imaging of breast tissue in symptomatic women who are considered to have a substantial likelihood of having breast cancer already.
33. **Cardiology and cardiac surgery services.** Services which include the diagnosis and treatment of diseases and disorders involving the heart and circulatory system.
    a-b. Cardiology services. An organized clinical service offering diagnostic and interventional procedures to manage the full range of heart conditions.
    c-d. Diagnostic catheterization. (also called coronary angiography or coronary arteriography) is used to assist in diagnosing complex heart conditions. Cardiac angiography involves the insertion of a tiny catheter into the artery in the groin then carefully threading the catheter up into the aorta where the coronary arteries originate. Once the catheter is in place, a dye is injected which allows the cardiologist to see the size, shape, and distribution of the coronary arteries. These images are used to diagnose heart disease and to determine, among other things, whether or not surgery is indicated.
    e-f. Interventional cardiac catheterization. Nonsurgical procedure that utilizes the same basic principles as diagnostic catheterization and then uses advanced techniques to improve the heart's function. It can be a less invasive alternative to heart surgery.
    g-h. Cardiac surgery. Includes minimally invasive procedures that include surgery done with only a small incision or no incision at all, such as through a laparoscope or an endoscope and more invasive major surgical procedures that include open chest and open heart surgery.
    i-j. Cardiac electrophysiology. Evaluation and management of patients with complex rhythm or conduction abnormalities, including diagnostic testing, treatment of arrhythmias by catheter ablation or drug therapy, and pacemaker/defibrillator implantation and follow-up.
    k. Cardiac rehabilitation. A medically supervised program to help heart patients recover quickly and improve their overall physical and mental functioning. The goal is to reduce risk of another cardiac event or to keep an already present heart condition from getting worse. Cardiac rehabilitation programs include: counseling to patients, an exercise program, helping patients modify risk factors such as smoking and high blood pressure, providing vocational guidance to enable the patient to return to work, supplying information on physical limitations and lending emotional support.
34. **Case management.** A system of assessment, treatment planning, referral and follow-up that ensures the provision of comprehensive and continuous services and the coordination of payment and reimbursement for care.
35. **Chaplaincy/pastoral care services.** A service ministering religious activities and providing pastoral counseling to patients, their families, and staff of a health care organization.
36. **Chemotherapy.** An organized program for the treatment of cancer by the use of drugs or chemicals.
37. **Children's wellness program.** A program that encourages improved health status and a healthful lifestyle of children through health education, exercise, nutrition and health promotion.
38. **Chiropractic services.** An organized clinical service including spinal manipulation or adjustment and related diagnostic and therapeutic services.
39. **Community outreach.** A program that systematically interacts with the community to identify those in need of services, alerting persons and their families to the availability of services, locating needed services, and enabling persons to enter the service delivery system.
40. **Complementary and alternative medicine services.** Organized hospital services or formal arrangements to providers that provide care or treatment not based solely on traditional western allopathic medical teachings as instructed in most U.S. medical schools. Includes any of the following: acupuncture, chiropractic, homeopathy, osteopathy, diet and lifestyle changes, herbal medicine, massage therapy, etc.
41. **Computer assisted orthopedic surgery (CAOS).** Orthopedic surgery using computer technology, enabling three-dimensional graphic models to visualize a patient's anatomy.
42. **Crisis prevention.** Services provided in order to promote physical and mental wellbeing and the early identification of disease and ill health prior to the onset and recognition of symptoms so as to permit early treatment.
43. **Dental Services.** An organized dental service or dentists on staff, not necessarily involving special facilities, providing dental or oral services to inpatients or outpatients.
44. **Emergency services.** Health services that are provided after the onset of a medical condition that manifests itself by symptoms of sufficient severity, including severe pain, that the absence of immediate medical attention could reasonably be expected by a prudent layperson, who possesses an average knowledge of health and medicine, to result in placing the patient's health in serious jeopardy.
    a-b. Emergency department. Hospital facilities for the provision of unscheduled outpatient services to patients whose conditions require immediate care.
    c.   Satellite Emergency Department. A facility owned and operated by the hospital but physically separate from the hospital for the provision of unscheduled outpatient services to patients whose conditions require immediate care. A freestanding ED is not physically connected to a hospital, but has all necessary emergency staffing and equipment on-site.
    e. Trauma center (certified). A facility to provide emergency and specialized intensive care to critically ill and injured patients. For service owned or provided by the hospital, please specify trauma level. Level 1: A regional resource trauma center, which is capable of providing total care for every aspect of injury and plays a leadership role in trauma research and education. Level 2: A community trauma center, which is capable of providing trauma care to all but the most severely injured patients who require highly specialized care. Level 3: A rural trauma hospital, which is capable of providing care to a large number of injury victims and can resuscitate and stabilize more severely injured patients so that they can be transported to level 1 or 2 facilities. Please provide explanation on page 13 if necessary.

45. **Enabling services.** A program that is designed to help the patient access health care services by offering any of the following: transportation services and/or referrals to local social services agencies.

46. **Endoscopic services.**
   a. **Optical colonoscopy.** An examination of the interior of the colon using a long, flexible, lighted tube with a small built-in camera.
   b. **Endoscopic ultrasound.** Specially designed endoscope that incorporates an ultrasound transducer used to obtain detailed images of organs in the chest and abdomen. The endoscope can be passed through the mouth or the anus. When combined with needle biopsy the procedure can assist in diagnosis of disease and staging of cancer.
   c. **Ablation of Barrett's esophagus.** Premalignant condition that can lead to adenocarcinoma of the esophagus. The nonsurgical ablation of premalignant tissue in Barrett's esophagus by the application of thermal energy or light through an endoscope passed from the mouth into the esophagus.
   d. **Esophageal impedance study.** A test in which a catheter is placed through the nose into the esophagus to measure whether gas or liquids are passing from the stomach into the esophagus and causing symptoms.
   e. **Endoscopic retrograde cholangiopancreatography (ERCP).** A procedure in which a catheter is introduced through an endoscope into the bile ducts and pancreatic ducts. Injection of contrast material permits detailed x-ray of these structures. The procedure is used diagnostically as well as therapeutically to relieve obstruction or remove stones.

47. **Enrollment (insurance) assistance services.** A program that provides enrollment assistance for patients who are potentially eligible for public health insurance programs such as Medicaid, State Children's Health Insurance, or local/state indigent care programs. The specific services offered could include explanation of benefits, assist applicants in completing the application and locating all relevant documents, conduct eligibility interviews, and/or forward applications and documentation to state/local social service or health agency.

48. **Extracorporeal shock wave lithotripter (ESWL).** A medical device used for treating stones in the kidney or urethra. The device disintegrates kidney stones noninvasively through the transmission of acoustic shock waves directed at the stones.

49. **Fertility clinic.** A specialized program set in an infertility center that provides counseling and education as well as advanced reproductive techniques such as: injectable therapy, reproductive surgeries, treatment for endometriosis, male factor infertility, tubal reversals, in vitro fertilization (IVF), donor eggs, and other such services to help patients achieve successful pregnancies.

50. **Fitness center.** Provides exercise, testing, or evaluation programs and fitness activities to the community and hospital employees.

51. **Freestanding outpatient care center.** A facility owned and operated by the hospital, that is physically separate from the hospital and provides various medical treatments and diagnostic services on an outpatient basis only. Laboratory and radiology services are usually available.

52. **Geriatric services.** The branch of medicine dealing with the physiology of aging and the diagnosis and treatment of disease affecting the aged. Services could include: Adult day care; Alzheimer's diagnostic-assessment services; Comprehensive geriatric assessment; Emergency response system; Geriatric acute care unit; and/or Geriatric clinics.

53. **Health fair.** Community health education events that focus on the prevention of disease and promotion of health through such activities as audiovisual exhibits and free diagnostic services.

54. **Community health education.** Education that provides health information to individuals and populations as well as support for personal, family and community health decisions with the objective of improving health status.

55. **Genetic testing/counseling.** A service equipped with adequate laboratory facilities and directed by a qualified physician to advise patients on potential genetic diagnosis of vulnerabilities to inherited diseases. A genetic test is the analysis of human DNA, RNA, chromosomes, proteins, and certain metabolites in order to detect heritable disease-related genotypes, mutations, phenotypes, or karyotypes for clinical purposes. Genetic tests can have diverse purposes, including the diagnosis of genetic diseases in newborns, children, and adults; the identification of future health risks; the prediction of drug responses; and the assessment of risks to future children.

56. **Health screening.** A preliminary procedure such as a test or examination to detect the most characteristic sign or signs of a disorder that may require further investigation.

57. **Health research.** Organized hospital research program in any of the following areas: basic research, clinical research, community health research, and/or research on innovative health care delivery.

58. **Hemodialysis.** Provision of equipment and personnel for the treatment of renal insufficiency on an inpatient or outpatient basis.

59. **HIV/AIDS services.** Diagnosis, treatment, continuing care planning, and counseling services for HIV/AIDS patients and their families. Could include: HIV/AIDS unit, special unit or designated team, general inpatient care, or specialized outpatient program.

60. **Home health services.** Service providing nursing, therapy, and health-related homemaker or social services in the patient's home.

61. **Hospice.** A program providing palliative care, chiefly medical relief of pain and supportive services, addressing the emotional, social, financial, and legal needs of terminally ill patients and their families. Care can be provided in a variety of settings, both inpatient and at home.

62. **Hospital-based outpatient care center-services.** Organized hospital health care services offered by appointment on an ambulatory basis. Services may include outpatient surgery, examination, diagnosis, and treatment of a variety of medical conditions on a nonemergency basis, and laboratory and other diagnostic testing as ordered by staff or outside physician referral.

63. **Immunization program.** Program that plans, coordinates and conducts immunization services in the community.

64. **Indigent care clinic.** Health care services for uninsured and underinsured persons where care is free of charge or charged on a sliding scale. This would include "free clinics" staffed by volunteer practitioners, but could also be staffed by employees with the sponsoring health care organization subsidizing the cost of service.

65. **Linguistic/translation services.** Services provided by the hospital designed to make health care more accessible to non-English speaking patients and their physicians.

66. **Meals on wheels.** A hospital sponsored program which delivers meals to people, usually the elderly, who are unable to prepare their own meals. Low cost, nutritional meals are delivered to individuals' homes on a regular basis.

67. **Mobile health services.** Vans and other vehicles used for delivery to primary care services.

68. **Neurological services.** Services provided by the hospital dealing with the operative and nonoperative management of disorders of the central, peripheral, and autonomic nervous systems.

69. **Nutrition programs.** Services within a health care facility which are designed to provide inexpensive, nutritionally sound meals to patients.

70. **Occupational health services.** Includes services designed to protect the safety of employees from hazards in the work environment.

71. **Oncology services.** Inpatient and outpatient services for patients with cancer, including comprehensive care, support and guidance in addition to patient education and prevention, chemotherapy, counseling and other treatment methods.

72. **Orthopedic services.** Services provided for the prevention or correction of injuries or disorders of the skeletal system and associated muscles, joints and ligaments.

73. **Outpatient surgery.** Scheduled surgical services provided to patients who do not remain in the hospital overnight. The surgery may be performed in operating suites also used for inpatient surgery, specially designated surgical suites for outpatient surgery, or procedure rooms within an outpatient care facility.

74. **Pain management program.** A recognized clinical service or program providing specialized medical care, drugs or therapies for the management of acute or chronic pain and other distressing symptoms, administered by specially trained physicians and other clinicians, to patients suffering from acute illnesses of diverse causes.

75. **Palliative care program.** An organized program providing specialized medical care, drugs or therapies for the management of acute or chronic pain and/or the control of symptoms administered by specially trained physicians and other clinicians; and supportive care services, such as counseling on advanced directives, spiritual care, and social services, to patients with advanced diseases and their families.

76. **Palliative care inpatient unit.** An inpatient palliative care ward is a physically discreet, inpatient nursing unit where the focus is palliative care. The patient care focus is on symptom relief for complex patients who may be continuing to undergo primary treatment. Care is delivered by palliative medicine specialists.

77. **Patient controlled analgesia (PCA).** Intravenously administered pain medicine under the patient's control. The patient has a button on the end of a cord than can be pushed at will, whenever more pain medicine is desired. This button will only deliver more pain medicine at predetermined intervals, as programmed by the doctor's order.

78. **Patient education center.** Written goals and objectives for the patient and/or family related to therapeutic regimens, medical procedures, and self-care.

79. **Patient representative services.** Organized hospital services providing personnel through whom patients and staff can seek solutions to institutional problems affecting the delivery of high quality care and services.

80. **Physical rehabilitation services.** Program providing medical, health-related, therapy, social, and/or vocational services to help people with disabilities attain or retain their maximum functional capacity.
   a. **Assistive technology center.** A program providing access to specialized hardware and software with adaptations allowing individuals greater independence with mobility, dexterity, or increased communication options.
   b. **Electrodiagnostic services.** Diagnostic testing services for nerve and muscle function such as nerve conduction studies and needle electromyography.
   c. **Physical rehabilitation outpatient services.** Outpatient program providing medical, health-related, therapy, social, and/or vocational services to help people with disabilities attain or retain their maximum functional capacity.
   d. **Prosthetic and orthotic services.** Services providing comprehensive prosthetic and orthotic evaluation, fitting, and training.
   e. **Robot-assisted walking therapy.** A form of physical therapy that uses a robotic device to assist patients who are relearning how to walk.
   f. **Simulated rehabilitation environment.** Rehabilitation focused on retraining functional skills in a contextually appropriate environment (simulated home and community settings) or in a traditional setting (gymnasium) using motor learning principles.

81. **Primary care department.** A unit or clinic within the hospital that provides primary care services (e.g., general pediatric care, general internal medicine, family practice, gynecology) through hospital-salaried medical and/or nursing staff, focusing on evaluating and diagnosing medical problems and providing medical treatment on an outpatient basis.

82. **Psychiatric services.** Services provided by the hospital that offer immediate initial evaluation and treatment to patients with mental or emotional disorders.
   a. **Psychiatric child-adolescent services.** Provides care to children and adolescents with mental or emotional disorders, including those admitted for diagnosis and those admitted for treatment.
   b. **Psychiatric consultation-liaison services.** Provides organized psychiatric consultation/liaison services to nonpsychiatric hospital staff and/or departments on psychological aspects of medical care that may be generic or specific to individual patients.
   c. **Psychiatric education services.** Provides psychiatric educational services to community agencies and workers such as schools, police, courts, public health nurses, welfare agencies, clergy, and so forth. The purpose is to expand the mental health knowledge and competence of personnel not working in the mental health field and to promote good mental health through improved understanding, attitudes, and behavioral patterns.
   d. **Psychiatric emergency services.** Services of facilities available on a 24-hour basis to provide immediate unscheduled outpatient care, diagnosis, evaluation, crisis intervention, and assistance to persons suffering acute emotional or mental distress.
   e. **Psychiatric geriatric services.** Provides care to elderly patients with mental or emotional disorders, including those admitted for diagnosis and those admitted for treatment.
   f. **Psychiatric outpatient services.** Provides medical care, including diagnosis and treatment, of psychiatric outpatients.
   g. **Psychiatric partial hospitalization program.** Organized hospital services providing intensive day/evening outpatient services of three hours or more duration, distinguished from other outpatient visits of one hour.
   h. **Psychiatric residential treatment.** Overnight psychiatric care in conjunction with an intensive treatment program in a setting other than a hospital.

83. **Radiology, diagnostic.** The branch of radiology that deals with the utilization of all modalities of radiant energy in medical diagnoses and therapeutic procedures using radiologic guidance. This includes, but is not restricted to, imaging techniques and methodologies utilizing radiation emitted by x-ray tubes, radionuclides, and ultrasonographic devices and the radiofrequency electromagnetic radiation emitted by atoms.
   a. **CT Scanner.** Computed tomographic scanner for head or whole body scans.
   b. **Diagnostic radioisotope facility.** The use of radioactive isotopes (Radiopharmaceuticals) as tracers or indicators to detect an abnormal condition or disease.
   c. **Electron beam computed tomography (EBCT).** A high tech computed tomography scan used to detect coronary artery disease by measuring coronary calcifications. This imaging procedure uses electron beams which are magnetically steered to produce a visual of the coronary artery and the images are produced faster than conventional CT scans.
   d. **Full-field digital mammography (FFDM).** Combines the x-ray generators and tubes used in analog screen-film mammography (SFM) with a detector plate that converts the x-rays into a digital signal.
   e. **Magnetic resonance imaging (MRI).** The use of a uniform magnetic field and radio frequencies to study tissue and structure of the body. This procedure enables the visualization of biochemical activity of the cell in vivo without the use of ionizing radiation, radioisotopic substances or high-frequency sound.
   f. **Intraoperative magnetic resonance imaging.** An integrated surgery system which provides an MRI system in an operating room. The system allows for immediate evaluation of the degree to tumor resection while the patient is undergoing a surgical resection. Intraoperative MRI exists when a MRI (low-field or high-field) is placed in the operating theater and is used during surgical resection without moving the patient from the operating room to the diagnostic imaging suite.
   g. **Magnetoencephalography (MEG).** A noninvasive neurophysiological measurement tool used to study magnetic fields generated by neuronal activity of the brain. MEG provides direct information about the dynamics of evoked and spontaneous neural activity and its location in the brain. The primary uses of MEG include assisting surgeons in localizing the source of epilepsy, sensory mapping, and the study of brain function. When it is combined with structural imaging, it is known as *magnetic source imaging* (MSI).
   h. **Multi-slice spiral computed tomography (<64+slice CT).** A specialized computed tomography procedure that provides three-dimensional processing and allows narrower and multiple slices with increased spatial resolution and faster scanning times as compared to a regular computed tomography scan.
   i. **Multi-slice spiral computed tomography (64+ slice CT).** Involves the acquisition of volumetric tomographic x-ray absorption data expressed in Hounsfield units using multiple rows of detectors. 64+ systems reconstruct the equivalent of 64 or more slices to cover the imaged volume.
   j. **Positron emission tomography (PET).** A nuclear medicine imaging technology which uses radioactive (positron emitting) isotopes created in a cyclotron or generator and computers to produce composite pictures of the brain and heart at work. PET scanning produces sectional images depicting metabolic activity or blood flow rather than anatomy.

k. Positron emission tomography/CT (PET/CT). Provides metabolic functional information for the monitoring of chemotherapy, radiotherapy and surgical planning.

l. Single photon emission computerized tomography (SPECT). A nuclear medicine imaging technology that combines existing technology of gamma camera imaging with computed tomographic imaging technology to provide a clearer and more precise image.

m. Ultrasound. The use of acoustic waves above the range of 20,000 cycles per second to visualize internal body structures.

84. **Radiology, therapeutic.** The branch of medicine concerned with radioactive substances and using various techniques of visualization, with the diagnosis and treatment of disease using any of the various sources of radiant energy. Services could include: megavoltage radiation therapy; radioactive implants; stereotactic radiosurgery; therapeutic radioisotope facility; X-ray radiation therapy.

   a. **Image-guided radiation therapy (IGRT).** Automated system for image-guided radiation therapy that enables clinicians to obtain high-resolution x-ray images to pinpoint tumor sites, adjust patient positioning when necessary, and complete a treatment, all within the standard treatment time slot, allowing for more effective cancer treatments.

   b. **Intensity-Modulated Radiation Therapy (IMRT).** A type of three-dimensional radiation therapy which improves treatment delivery by targeting a tumor in a way that is likely to decrease damage to normal tissues and allows for varying intensities.

   c. **Proton beam therapy.** A form of radiation therapy which administers proton beams. While producing the same biologic effects as x-ray beams, the energy distribution of protons differs from conventional x-ray beams: proton beams can be more precisely focused in tissue volumes in a three-dimensional pattern, resulting in less surrounding tissue damage than conventional radiation therapy, permitting administration of higher doses.

   d. **Shaped beam radiation system.** A precise, noninvasive treatment that involves targeted beams of radiation that mirror the exact size and shape of a tumor at a specific area to shrink or destroy cancerous cells. This procedure delivers a therapeutic dose of radiation that conforms precisely to the shape of the tumor, thus minimizing the risk to nearby tissues.

   e. **Stereotactic radiosurgery.** A radiotherapy modality that delivers a high dosage of radiation to a discrete treatment area in as few as one treatment session. Includes Gamma Knife, Cyberknife, etc.

85. **Retirement housing.** A facility that provides social activities to senior citizens, usually retired persons, who do not require health care but some short-term skilled nursing care may be provided. A retirement center may furnish housing and may also have acute hospital and long-term care facilities, or it may arrange for acute and long-term care through affiliated institutions.

86. **Robotic surgery.** The use of mechanical guidance devices to remotely manipulate surgical instrumentation.

87. **Rural health clinic.** A clinic located in a rural, medically under-served area in the United States that has a separate reimbursement structure from the standard medical office under the Medicare and Medicaid programs.

88. **Sleep center.** Specially equipped and staffed center for the diagnosis and treatment of sleep disorders.

89. **Social work services.** Could include: organized services that are properly directed and sufficiently staffed by qualified individuals who provide assistance and counseling to patients and their families in dealing with social, emotional, and environmental problems associated with illness or disability, often in the context of financial or discharge planning coordination.

90. **Sports medicine.** Provision of diagnostic screening, assessment, clinical and rehabilitation services for the prevention and treatment of sports-related injuries.

91. **Support groups.** A hospital sponsored program that allows a group of individuals with common experiences or issues who meet periodically to share experiences, problems, and solutions in order to support each other.

92. **Swing bed services.** A hospital bed that can be used to provide either acute or long-term care depending on community or patient needs. To be eligible a hospital must have a Medicare provider agreement in place, have fewer than 100 beds, be located in a rural area, not have a 24-hour nursing service waiver in effect, have not been terminated from the program in the prior two years, and meet various service conditions.

93. **Teen outreach services.** A program focusing on the teenager which encourages an improved health status and a healthful lifestyle including physical, emotional, mental, social, spiritual and economic health through education, exercise, nutrition and health promotion.

94. **Tobacco treatment/cessation program.** Organized hospital services with the purpose of ending tobacco-use habits of patients addicted to tobacco/nicotine.

95. **Transplant services.** The branch of medicine that transfers an organ or tissue from one person to another or from one body part to another, to replace a diseased structure or to restore function or to change appearance. Services could include: Bone marrow transplant; heart, lung, kidney, intestine, or tissue transplant. Please include heart/lung or other multi-transplant surgeries in 'other'.

96. **Transportation to health facilities.** A long-term care support service designed to assist the mobility of the elderly. Some programs offer improved financial access by offering reduced rates and barrier-free buses or vans with ramps and lifts to assist the elderly or people with disabilities; others offer subsidies for public transport systems or operate mini-bus services exclusively for use by senior citizens.

97. **Urgent care center.** A facility that provides care and treatment for problems that are not life threatening but require attention over the short term.

98. **Virtual colonoscopy.** Noninvasive screening procedure used to visualize, analyze and detect cancerous or potentially cancerous polyps in the colon.

99. **Volunteer services department.** An organized hospital department responsible for coordinating the services of volunteers working within the institution.

100. **Women's health center/services.** An area set aside for coordinated education and treatment services specifically for and promoted to women as provided by this special unit. Services may or may not include obstetrics but include a range of services other than OB.

101. **Wound management services.** Services for patients with chronic wounds and nonhealing wounds often resulting from diabetes, poor circulation, improper seating and immunocompromising conditions. The goals are to progress chronic wounds through stages of healing, reduce and eliminate infections, increase physical function to minimize complications from current wounds and prevent future chronic wounds. Wound management services are provided on an inpatient or outpatient basis, depending on the intensity of service needed.

102a. **Physician arrangements.** An integrated healthcare delivery program implementing physician compensation and incentive systems for managed care services.

   a. **Independent practice association (IPA).** A legal entity that holds managed care contracts. The IPA then contracts with physicians, usually in solo practice, to provide care either on a fee-for-service or capitated basis. The purpose of an IPA is to assist solo physicians in obtaining managed care contracts.

   b. **Group practice without walls.** Hospital sponsors the formation of, or provides capital to physicians to establish, a "quasi" group to share administrative expenses while remaining independent practitioners.

   c. **Open physician-hospital organization (PHO).** A joint venture between the hospital and all members of the medical staff who wish to participate. The PHO can act as a unified agent in managed care contracting, own a managed care plan, own and operate ambulatory care centers or ancillary services projects, or provide administrative services to physician members.

   d. **Closed physician-hospital organization (PHO).** A PHO that restricts physician membership to those practitioners who meet criteria for cost effectiveness and/or high quality.

   e. **Management services organization (MSO).** A corporation, owned by the hospital or a physician/hospital joint venture, that provides management services to one or more medical group practices. The MSO purchases the tangible assets of the practices and leases them back as part of a full-service management agreement, under which the MSO employs all non-physician staff and provides all supplies/administrative systems for a fee.

   f. **Integrated salary model.** Physicians are salaried by the hospital or another entity of a health system to provide medical services for primary care and specialty care.

g. **Equity model.** Allows established practitioners to become shareholders in a professional corporation in exchange for tangible and intangible assets of their existing practices.

h. **Foundation.** A corporation, organized either as a hospital affiliate or subsidiary, which purchases both the tangible and intangible assets of one or more medical group practices. Physicians remain in a separate corporate entity but sign a professional services agreement with the foundation.

102b. Of all physician arrangements listed in question 102a (a-i), indicate the total number of physicians (count each physician only once) that are engaged in an arrangement with your hospital that allows for joint contracting with payors or shared responsibility for financial risk or clinical performance between the hospital and physician (arrangement may be at the hospital, system or network level). *Joint contracting* does not include contracting between physicians participating in an independent practice.

103. **Joint venture.** A contractual arrangement between two or more parties forming an unincorporated business. The participants in the arrangement remain independent and separate outside of the venture's purpose.

104a. **Accountable Care Organization (ACO) Contract.** An ACO contract has two essential elements: (1) accountability for the total costs of care for the population of patients attributed to the primary care physicians in the organization; (2) financial incentives that link the magnitude of bonus payments to performance on quality measures (which could include technical quality, patient experience and/or health outcome measures) This will generally involve a contract where the payor establishes a target budget for one or more years for the total costs of care for the agreed-upon patient population, the payor tracks actual spending and performance on quality; and the provider receives bonus payments that could include a share of savings that are (or are not) contingent on meeting quality targets, with (or without) additional bonuses related to performance on those quality measures.

105. **Patient-Centered Medical Home.** The medical home concept refers to the provision of comprehensive primary care services that facilitates communication and shared decision-making between the patient, his/her primary care providers, other providers, and the patient's family.

106. **Bundling.** Bundling is a payment mechanism whereby a provider entity receives a single payment for services provided across one or parts of the care continuum. For example, an entity might receive a single payment for the hospital and physician services provided as part of an inpatient stay or might receive a single payment for the post-acute care services involved in a single episode of care. The entity then has responsibility for compensating each of the individual providers involved in the episode of care.

109. **Capitation.** An at-risk payment arrangement in which an organization receives a fixed prearranged payment and in turn guarantees to deliver or arrange all medically necessary care required by enrollees in the capitated plan. The fixed amount is specified within contractual agreements between the payor and the involved organization. The fixed payment amount is based on an actuarial assessment of the services required by enrollees and the costs of providing these services, recognizing enrollees' adjustment factors such as age, sex, and family size.

110. **Shared risk payments.** A payment arrangement in which a hospital and a managed care organization share the risk of adverse claims experience. Methods for sharing risk could include: capitation with partial refunds or supplements if billed hospital charges or costs differ from capitated payments, and service or discharge-based payments with withholds and bonus payouts that depend on expenditure targets.

114. **Quality/Safety Survey.** Examples of a patient safety culture survey are the Safety Attitudes Questionnaire and the AHRQ Hospital Survey on Patient Safety Culture. Impromptu surveys of only certain staff or units, and other narrowly based initiatives do not qualify as quality/safety surveys for the purpose of this question.

SECTION D
TOTAL FACILITY BEDS, UTILIZATION, FINANCES, AND STAFFING
Instructions and Definitions

For the purposes of this survey, a nursing home type unit/facility provides **long-term care for the elderly or other patients requiring chronic care** in a non-acute setting in any of the following categories: *Skilled nursing care *Intermediate care *Other long-term care (*see page 16) The nursing home type unit/facility is to be owned and operated by the hospital. Only one legal entity may be vested with title to the physical property or operate under the authority of a duly executed lease of the physical property.

1 a. **Total licensed beds.** Report the total number of beds authorized by the state licensing (certifying) agency.

b. **Beds set up and staffed.** Report the number of beds regularly available (those set up and staffed for use) at the end of the reporting period. Report only operating beds, not constructed bed capacity. Include all bed facilities that are set up and staffed for use by inpatients that have no other bed facilities, such as pediatric bassinets, isolation units and quiet rooms. Exclude newborn bassinets and bed facilities for patients receiving special procedures for a portion of their stay and who have other bed facilities assigned to or reserved for them. Exclude, for example, labor room, post anesthesia, or postoperative recovery room beds, psychiatric holding beds, observation beds, and beds that are used only as holding facilities for patients prior to their transfer to another hospital.

c. **Bassinets set up and staffed.** Report the number of normal newborn bassinets. Do not include neonatal intensive care or intermediate care bassinets. These should be reported on page 3, C6 and C7.

d. **Births.** Total births should exclude fetal deaths.

e. **Admissions.** Include the number of adult and pediatric admissions (exclude births). This figure should include all patients admitted during the reporting period, including neonatal and swing admissions.

f. **Inpatient days.** Report the number of adult and pediatric days of care rendered during the entire reporting period. Do not include days of care rendered for normal infants born in the hospital, but do include those for their mothers. Include days of care for infants born in the hospital and transferred into a neonatal care unit. Also include swing bed inpatient days. An inpatient day of care (also commonly referred to as a patient day or a census day, or by some federal hospitals as an occupied bed day) is a period of service between the census-taking hours on two successive calendar days, the day of discharge being counted only when the patient was admitted the same day.

g. **Emergency department visits.** Should reflect the number of visits to the emergency unit. Emergency outpatients can be admitted to the inpatient areas of the hospital, but they are still counted as emergency visits and subsequently as inpatient admissions.

h. **Total outpatient visits.** A visit by a patient who is not lodged in the hospital while receiving medical, dental, or other services. Each appearance of an outpatient in each unit constitutes one visit regardless of the number of diagnostic and/or therapeutic treatments that the patient receives. Total outpatient visits should include all clinic visits, referred visits, observation services, outpatient surgeries (also reported on line D1k), home health service visits, and emergency department visits (also reported on line D1g).

Clinic visits should reflect total number of visits to each specialized medical unit that is responsible for the diagnosis and treatment of patients on an outpatient, nonemergency basis. (e.g., alcoholism, dental, gynecology.) Visits to the satellite clinics and primary group practices should be included if revenue is received by the hospital.

Referred visits should reflect total number of outpatient ancillary visits to each specialty unit of the hospital established for providing technical aid used in the diagnosis and treatment of patients. Examples of such units are diagnostic radiology, EKG, pharmacy, etc.

Observation services are those services furnished on a hospital's premises, including use of a bed and periodic monitoring by a hospital's nursing or other staff, which are reasonable and necessary to evaluate an outpatient's condition or determine the need for a possible admission to the hospital as an inpatient. Observation services usually do not exceed 24 hours; however, there is no hourly limit on the extent to which they may be used.

Home health service visits are visits by home health personnel to a patient's residence.

i. **Inpatient surgical operations.** Count each patient undergoing surgery as one surgical operation regardless of the number of surgical procedures that were performed while the patient was in the operating or procedure room.

j. **Operating room.** A unit/room of a hospital or other health care facility in which surgical procedures requiring anesthesia are performed.

k. **Outpatient surgical operations.** For outpatient surgical operations, please record operations performed on patients who do not remain in the hospital overnight. Include all operations whether performed in the inpatient operating rooms or in procedure rooms located in an outpatient facility. Include an endoscopy only when used as an operative tool and not when used for diagnosis alone. Count each patient undergoing surgery as one surgical operation regardless of the number of surgical procedures that were performed while the patient was in the operating or procedure room.

2a2. Managed Care Medicare Discharges. A discharge day where a Medicare Managed Care Plan is the source of payment.

2b2. Managed Care Medicare Inpatient Days. An inpatient day where a Medicare Managed Care Plan is the source of payment.

2c2. Managed Care Medicaid Discharges. A discharge day where a Medicaid Managed Care Plan is the source of payment.

2d2. Managed Care Medicaid Inpatient Days. An inpatient day where a Medicaid Managed Care Plan is the source of payment.

3a. Net patient revenue. Reported at the estimated net realizable amounts from patients, third-party payors, and others for services rendered, including estimated retroactive adjustments under reimbursement agreements with third-party payors. Retroactive adjustments are accrued on an estimated basis in the period the related services are rendered and adjusted in future periods, as final settlements are determined.

3b. Tax appropriations. A predetermined amount set aside by the government from its taxing authority to support the operation of the hospital.

3c. Other operating revenue. Revenue that arises from the normal day-to-day operations from services other than health care provided to patients. Includes sales and services to nonpatients, and revenue from miscellaneous sources (rental of hospital space, sale of cafeteria meals, gift shop sales). Also include operating gains in this category.

3d. Nonoperating revenue. Includes investment income, extraordinary gains and other nonoperating gains.

3e. Total revenue. Add net patient revenue, tax appropriations, other operating revenue and nonoperating revenue.

3f. Payroll expenses. Include payroll for all personnel including medical and dental residents/interns and trainees.

3g. Employee benefits. Includes social security, group insurance, retirement benefits, workman's compensation, unemployment insurance, etc.

3h. Depreciation expense (for reporting period only). Report only the depreciation expense applicable to the reporting period. The amount should also be included in accumulated depreciation (D7b).

3i. Interest expense. Report interest expense for the reporting period only.

3j. Supply expense. The net cost of all tangible items that are expensed including freight, standard distribution cost, and sales and use tax minus rebates. This would exclude labor, labor-related expenses and services as well as some tangible items that are frequently provided as part of labor costs.

3k. All other expenses. Any total facility expenses not included in 3f-3j.

3l. Total expenses. Add 3f-3k. Includes all payroll and non-payroll expenses as well as any nonoperating losses (including extraordinary losses). **Treat bad debt as a deduction from gross patient revenue and not as an expense.**

4a. Total gross inpatient revenue. The hospital's full-established rates(charges) for all services rendered to inpatients.

4b. Total gross outpatient revenue. The hospital's full-established rates(charges) for all services rendered to outpatients.

4c. Total gross patient revenue. Add total gross inpatient revenue and total gross outpatient revenue.

5. **Uncompensated care.** Care for which no payment is expected or no charge is made. It is the sum of bad debt and charity care absorbed by a hospital or other health care organization in providing medical care for patients who are uninsured or are unable to pay.

5a. Bad debt. The provision for actual or expected uncollectibles resulting from the extension of credit. Report as a deduction from gross revenue. <u>**For Question 6 (Revenue by payor), if you cannot break out your bad debt by payor, deduct the amount from self-pay.**</u>

5b. Financial Assistance (Includes Charity care). Financial assistance and charity care refer to health services provided free of charge or at reduced rates to individuals who meet certain financial criteria. <u>For purposes of this survey, charity care is measured on the basis of revenue forgone, at full-established rates.</u>

5d. Medicaid Provider Tax, Fee or Assessment. Dollars paid as a result of a state law that authorizes collecting revenue from specified categories of providers. Federal matching funds may be received for the revenue collected from providers and some or all of the revenues may be returned directly or indirectly back to providers in the form of a Medicaid payment.

6. **REVENUE BY PAYOR**

6a1 Medicare. Should agree with the Medicare utilization reported in questions D2a1-D2b2.

6a1a Fee for service patient revenue. Include traditional Medicare fee-for-service.

6a1c. Total. Medicare revenue (add Medicare fee for service patient revenue and Medicare managed care revenue).

6a2. Medicaid. Should agree with Medicaid utilization reported in questions D2c1-D2d2.

6a2a. Fee for service patient revenue. Do not include Medicaid disproportionate share payments (DSH) or other Medicaid supplemental payments.

6a2c. Medicaid disproportionate share payment (DSH). DSH minus associated provider taxes or assessments. <u>Report in 'Net' column only.</u>

6a2d. Medicaid supplemental payments. Supplemental payments the Medicaid program pays the hospital that are NOT Medicaid DSH, minus associated provider taxes or assessments. <u>Report in 'Net' column only.</u>

7a-c. Fixed Assets. Represent land and physical properties that are consumed or used in the creation of economic activity by the health care entity. The historical or acquisition costs are used in recording fixed assets. Net plant, property, and equipment represent the original costs of these items less accumulated depreciation and amortization.

7d. Gross Square Footage. Include all inpatient, outpatient, office, and support space used for or in support of your health care activities. Exclude exterior, roof, and garage space in the figure.

8. **Capital Expenses.** Expenses used to acquire assets, including buildings, remodeling projects, equipment, or property.

9. **Information Technology.**

a. **IT Operating expense.** Exclude department depreciation and operating dollars paid against capital leases.

b. **IT Capital expense.** Include IT capital expense for the current year only. Any capital expense that is carried forward from the previous year should be excluded from this figure. Include IT related capital included in the budget of other departments. (e.g., lab, radiology) if known or can be reasonably estimated. Include the total value of capital leases to be signed in the current year.

c. **Number of Employed IT staff (in FTEs).** Number of full-time equivalent (FTE) staff employed in the IT department/organization and on the hospital payroll.

d. **Total number of outsourced IT staff (in FTEs).** i.e., contracted staff.

e. **Electronic Health Record.** An electronic health record (EHR) integrates electronically originated and maintained patient-level clinical health information, derived from multiple sources, into one point of access. An EHR replaces the paper medical record as the primary source of patient information.

10. Full-Time Equivalent (FTE) is the total number of hours worked by all employees over the full 12-month reporting period, divided by the normal number of hours worked by a full-time employee for that same time period. For example, if your hospital considers a normal workweek for a full-time employee to be 40 hours, a total of 2,080 would be worked over a full year (52 weeks). If the total number of hours worked by all employees on the payroll is 208,000, then the number of full-time equivalents (FTE) is 100 (employees). The FTE calculation for a specific occupational category such as registered nurses is exactly the same. The calculation for each occupational category should be based on the number of hours worked by staff employed in that specific category.

  a-b. Physicians and dentists. Include only those physicians and dentists engaged in clinical practice and on the payroll. Those who hold administrative positions should be reported in all other personnel. (10m)

  d. Other trainees. A trainee is a person who has not completed the necessary requirements for certification or met the qualifications required for full salary under a related occupational category. Exclude medical and dental residents/interns who should be reported on line 10c.

  e. Registered nurses. Nurses who have graduated from approved schools of nursing and who are currently registered by the state. They are responsible for the nature and quality of all nursing care that patients receive. Do not include any registered nurses more appropriately reported in other occupational categories, such as facility administrators, and therefore listed under all other personnel. (10m)

  f. Licensed practical (vocational) nurses. Nurses who have graduated from an approved school of practical (vocational) nursing who work under the supervision of registered nurses and/or physicians.

  g. Nursing assistive personnel. Certified nursing assistant or equivalent unlicensed staff assigned to patient care units and reporting to nursing.

  h. Radiology technicians. Technical positions in imaging fields, including, but not limited to, radiology, sonography, nuclear medicine, radiation therapy, CT, MRI.

  i. Laboratory technicians. Professional and technical positions in all areas of the laboratory, including, but not limited to, histology, phlebotomy, microbiology, pathology, chemistry, etc.

  j. Pharmacists, licensed. Persons licensed within the state who are concerned with the preparation and distribution of medicinal products.

  k. Pharmacy technicians. Persons who assist the pharmacist with selected activities, including medication profile reviews for drug incompatibilities, typing labels and prescription packaging, handling of purchase records and inventory control.

  l. Respiratory Therapists. An allied health professional who specializes in scientific knowledge and theory of clinical problems of respiratory care. Duties include the collection and evaluation of patient data to determine an appropriate care plan, selection and assembly of equipment, conduction of therapeutic procedures, and modification of prescribed plans to achieve one or more specific objectives.

  m. All other personnel. This should include all other personnel not already accounted for in other categories.

  n. Total facility personnel. Add 10a-10m. Includes the total facility personnel - hospital plus nursing home type unit/facility personnel (for those hospitals that own and operate a nursing home type unit/facility.)

  o-p. Nursing home type unit/facility personnel. These lines should be filled out only by hospitals that own and operate a nursing home type unit/facility, where only one legal entity is vested with title to the physical property or operates under the authority of a duly executed lease of the physical property. If nursing home type unit/facility personnel are reported on the total facility personnel lines (10a-m), but cannot be broken out, please write "cannot break out" on this line.

  q. Direct patient care RN. Registered nurses providing care directly to patients. Direct patient care responsibilities are patient-centered nursing activities carried out in the presence of the patient (such as admission, transfer/discharge, patient teaching, patient communication, treatments, counseling, and administration of medication.)

11. Privileged Physicians. Report the total number of physicians (by type) on the medical staff with privileges except those with courtesy, honorary and provisional privileges. Do not include residents or interns. Physicians that provide only non-clinical services (administrative services, medical director services, etc.) should be excluded.

  Employed by your hospital. Physicians that are either direct hospital employees or employees of a hospital subsidiary corporation.

  Individual contract. An independent physician under a formal contract to provide services at your hospital including at outpatient facilities, clinics and offices

  Group contract. A physician that is part of a group (group practice, faculty practice plan or medical foundation) under a formal contract to provide services at your hospital including at inpatient and outpatient facilities, clinics and offices.

  Not employed or under contract. Other physicians with privileges that have no employment or contractual relationship with the hospital to provide services.

  The sum of the physicians reported in 11a-11f should equal the total number of privileged physicians in the hospital.

  a. Primary care. A physician that provides primary care services including general practice, general internal medicine, family practice, general pediatrics, obstetrics/gynecology and geriatrics.

  b. Emergency medicine. Physicians who provide care in the emergency department.

  c. Hospitalist. Physicians whose primary professional focus is the care of hospitalized medical patients (through clinical, education, administrative and research activity).

  d. Intensivist. A physician with special training to work with critically ill patients. Intensivists generally provided medical-surgical, cardiac, neonatal, pediatric and other types of intensive care.

  e. Radiologist/pathologist/anesthesiologist. Radiologist. A physician who has specialized training in imaging, including but not limited to radiology, sonography, nuclear medicine, radiation therapy, CT, MRI. **Pathologist.** A physician who examines samples of body tissues for diagnostic purposes. **Anesthesiologist.** A physician who specializes in administering medications or other agents that prevent or relieve pain, especially during surgery.

  f. Other specialist. Other physicians not included in the above categories that specialize in a specific type of medical care.

14. Advanced Practice Registered Nurses. Registered nurses with advanced didactic and clinical education, knowledge, skills, and scope of practice. Includes: **Physician assistant.** A healthcare professional licensed to practice medicine with supervision of a licensed physician. **Nurse practitioner.** A registered nurse with at least a master's degree in nursing and advanced education in primary care, capable of independent practice in a variety of settings. **Clinical nurse specialist (CNS).** A registered nurse who, through a formal graduate degree (masters or doctorate) CNS education program, has expertise in a specialty area of nursing practice. CNSs are clinical experts in the diagnosis and treatment of illness, and the delivery of evidence-based nursing interventions.

14c. Primary care. Medical services including general practice, general internal medicine, family practice, general pediatrics, obstetrics/gynecology. **Emergency department care.** The provision of unscheduled outpatient services to patients whose conditions require immediate care in the emergency department setting. **Other specialty care.** A clinic that provides specialized medical care beyond the scope of primary care. **Patient education.** Goals and objectives for the patient and/or family related to therapeutic regimens, medical procedures and self-care. **Case management.** A system of assessment, treatment planning, referral and follow-up that ensures the provision of comprehensive and continuous services and the coordination of payment and reimbursement for care. **Other.** Any type of care other than those listed above.

15. Foreign-educated nurses. Individuals who are foreign born and received basic nursing education in a foreign country. In general many of these nurses come to the US on employment-based visas which allow them to obtain a green card.

SECTION E. SUPPLEMENTAL INFORMATION
DEFINITIONS

1. **Satellite facility.** Services are available at a facility geographically remote from the hospital campus.
2. **Group Purchasing Organization.** An organization whose primary function is to negotiate contracts for the purpose of purchasing for members of the group or has a central supply site for its members.
3. **Distributor.** An entity that typically does not manufacture most of its own products but purchases and re-sells these products. Such a business usually maintains an inventory of products for sales to hospitals and physician offices and others.